$\mathcal{H}$OSPITALITY

AN INTRODUCTION

SIXTEENTH EDITION

ROBERT A. BRYMER
FLORIDA STATE UNIVERSITY

RHETT A. BRYMER
MIAMI UNIVERSITY

LISA N. CAIN
FLORIDA INTERNATIONAL UNIVERSITY

40th *Edition*
ANNIVERSARY

Kendall Hunt
publishing company

Book Team
Chairman and Chief Executive Officer Mark C. Falb
President and Chief Operating Officer Chad M. Chandlee
Vice President, Higher Education David L. Tart
Director of Publishing Partnerships Paul B. Carty
Senior Developmental Coordinator Angela Willenbring
Vice President, Operations Timothy J. Beitzel
Senior Permissions Editor Caroline Kieler
Cover Designer Suzanne Millius

Cover image © Shutterstock.com

www.kendallhunt.com
Send all inquiries to:
4050 Westmark Drive
Dubuque, IA 52004-1840
Copyright © 1977 by Robert A. Brymer
Copyright © 1979, 1981, 1984, 1988, 1991, 1995, 1998, 2000, 2002, 2004, 2007,
2009, 2011, 2014, 2017 by Kendall Hunt Publishing Company

ISBN 978-1-4652-9924-6

DEDICATIONS

To God and the tremendous blessing he's been to my family and me. To my wife, best friend, and love of my life, Becky, who has enriched my life more than I ever dreamed it could be. To my awesome grandson Luke Andrew Brymer, who means the world to me.

—*Robert A. Brymer*

For Luke, the next in line.

—*Rhett A. Brymer*

To my husband, my best friend, and the original Dr. Cain, Christopher, your unending patience, your persistent encouragement, and your boundless love have helped me to achieve so much. I wouldn't want to do it without you. To Henry, my amazing son, you have shown me love I never knew existed. I love you both.

—*Lisa N. Cain*

BRIEF CONTENTS

CONTENTS

PART TWO HOSPITALITY COMPANIES 65

6 Independent and Entrepreneurial Operations 67

Julene Boger, Northern Arizona University

7 Chain Operations 77

Radesh Palakurthi, The University of Memphis

8 Franchising and Referral Organizations 95

Tierney Orfgen McCleary, Eastern Michigan University

PART FOUR HOSPITALITY CAREER MENU   217

LODGING, FOOD AND BEVERAGE

LODGING

BEVERAGE

CLUBS, SPORTS AND RECREATION

MORE EXCITING CAREER OPTIONS

PREFACE

We believe that it is important to give students a well-rounded background in hospitality to pique their curiosity. But from there, it is equally important to highlight as many career paths as possible, so that students can identify areas about which they want to learn. Many students come from other disciplines and say, "Oh, if I had known all these choices, I would have switched majors." It is up to us to show them how vast the industry is, and how many choices and options they can have. We believe this book provides this focus.

There are many introduction to hospitality textbooks available. While this book similarly explores many of the general themes common to traditional business and hospitality topics in the first three sections, this book is unique in that it also highlights many different career paths that may otherwise go unnoticed in other texts. We know that it is important to discuss the common areas so that students may understand the context in which the industry is housed. However, we also find it pivotal to explore the topics that make hospitality distinctive. These topics are revealed in the wide variety of options available in each grouping in the text.

Hospitality: An *Introduction* is systematically organized for the introductory student. The book begins with a broad overview exploring how and why the industry developed into its different components and the emerging trends of our industry, and defines hospitality service excellence. From there, we wanted to get students involved in the industry and offered Chapter 5 to learn the associations and rating programs of which everyone should be aware, and to inspire them to join so that they can begin their valuable networking and learn the applications of the theory from our classes. The second section, *Hospitality Companies*, gradually narrows the focus to include an introduction to different forms of organizations and management that are available. These topics discuss the different business structures that are available in hospitality. While other industries also use these formats, hospitality abounds with them and has honed them to a fine science. Additionally, we included Chapter 10 to inform the students about the similarities and differences that businesses in this industry have on an international scale. These first two sections give students the overall knowledge they need to learn more about this exciting industry and understand the general scope.

The third section, *Hospitality Operations*, explores seven of the general areas of business: leadership and ethics; marketing; managing revenue and expenses; human resources management; facilities, safety, and security; technology; and law. Except for facilities, safety and security, these topics can be found in a business curriculum. However, in this book, we explore the subjects that are similar yet different in the service industry. In the final section, *Hospitality Career Menu*, we review many specific industry segments and career options available to prospective managers. The goal is to provide a survey approach to hospitality, while offering the information needed to help students proceed into more advanced courses and readings.

As you can see, this book has a vast amount of information for students that both excites them and allows them to go deeper into the subjects that most interest them. Because we have a chapter on each topic, it allows students to have enough basic knowledge to know whether the world of hospitality is for them, and most importantly, what their niche might be.

ABOUT THE AUTHORS

ROBERT A. BRYMER

Robert A. Brymer, CHA, is the Cecil B. Day Professor of Hotel Management in the Dedman School of Hospitality, at Florida State University. He has been recognized in the following ways:

- Appointed to the *White House Conference on Travel and Tourism*
- Stevenson Fletcher CHRIE Achievement Award
- Van Nostrand Reinhold CHRIE Research Award
- Florida State University Teaching Award
- Certified Hotel Administrator by the American Hotel & Lodging Association

Dr. Brymer has held management and supervisory positions with Hyatt Hotels, Westin Hotels, and Hospitality Management Corporation. In 2000, while on sabbatical from Florida State University, he worked for several months in daily operations at The Ritz-Carlton Hotel, in Sydney, Australia. His management workshops have been presented for more than 7000 leaders in the hotel industry, across North America, Asia, Europe, and the Middle East.

Dr. Brymer earned his doctorate in Psychology from The University of Denver, an M.B.A. in Hotel, Restaurant, & Institutional Management from Michigan State University, and a B.S./B.A. in Hotel & Restaurant Management from The University of Denver. He also served active duty in the United States Marine Corps.

RHETT A. BRYMER

Rhett Brymer is the John Mee Endowed Assistant Professor of Management at the Farmer School of Business at Miami University in Oxford, Ohio. He completed his Ph.D. from Texas A&M University in the field of business strategy, his M.S. in instructional systems design and M.B.A. from Florida State University, and B.A. in chemistry from Kenyon College. His general research interest is in strategic human capital, specifically how firms manage their recruiting pipelines, their turnover, and their incentives for performance. Dr. Brymer has industry interests in beverage operations and teaches a course on the craft brewing industry. Prior to academia, he worked in hospitality operations in full and quick service restaurants and in catering/ special events. Dr. Brymer also worked as a chemist in biotechnology, and as a human capital consultant. He has published in the *Journal of Management, Strategic Organization, Academy of Management Education and Learning*, and in *MIT Sloan Sports Analytics*, among other outlets.

LISA N. CAIN

Lisa Cain, Ph.D., CHE, is an Assistant Professor at Florida International University's Chaplin School of Hospitality and Tourism Management in Miami, Florida. Dr. Cain earned her Ph.D. from the University of Nevada, Las Vegas in Hospitality Administration, her M.S. from Florida International University in Hospitality Management, and her B.A. from Smith College in English Language and Literature. She also spent a year of study at Oxford University in Oxford, England. Dr. Cain's main research interests involve understanding restaurant workers' behaviors, specifically work life balance among salaried employees in the hospitality industry and substance use and overuse among all restaurant employees. Dr. Cain worked in fine-dining restaurants for several years prior to her entry into academia. Her main interests outside of the classroom include spending time with her family, traveling, and running.

ACKNOWLEDGMENTS

This is the sixteenth edition and 40th anniversary of the book, as the first edition was released in 1977. Our book is a collection of readings written by numerous authors representing colleges and universities across the United States. These authors have written chapters specifically for this book, and without their generous contributions the publication of this edition would not have been possible. They have truly created an outstanding edition, and we are very grateful for the special role each and every author played.

Elizabeth Aube-VanPatten, Johnson & Wales University

Diana S. Barber, Georgia State University

Bart Bartlett, The Pennsylvania State University

Julene Boger, Northern Arizona University

Cydna Bougae, New York University

Sherie Brezina, Florida Gulf Coast University

Chris Brown, Kennesaw State University

Eric A. Brown, Iowa State University

Shatina Chen, University of Alabama

Michael D. Collins, University of San Francisco

Wanda M. Costen, Northern Arizona University

Molly J. Dahm, Lamar University

Chris DeSessa, Johnson & Wales University

Christina K. Dimitriou, State University New York at Plattsburgh

Brad J. Engeldinger, Sierra College

Thorir Erlingsson, Kennesaw State University

Don Farr, Florida State University

Reginald Foucar-Szocki, James Madison University

Bernard N. Fried, Hotelschool, The Hague, The Netherlands

James E. Griffin, Johnson & Wales University

Christian E. Hardigree, Kennesaw State University

Bradford Hudson, Boston College

Kathleen E. King, Northern Arizona University

Seung Hyun (Jenna) Lee, East Carolina University

Neil Marrin, James Madison University

Tierney Orfgen McCleary, Eastern Michigan University

Robert A. McMullin, East Stroudsburg University

© Lukasz Janyst/Shutterstock.com

PART 1

HOSPITALITY INDUSTRY

CHAPTER *1*

WELCOME TO HOSPITALITY

AUTHORS

Robert A. Brymer, Florida State University
Rhett A. Brymer, Miami University
Lisa N. Cain, Florida International University

LEARNING OBJECTIVES

- Provide an overview of the industry.
- Provide an overview of this book so that you will know what to expect.

CHAPTER OUTLINE

The Service-Hospitality Connection
Key Content
Hospitality
   Lodging
   Foodservice
Summary

KEY TERMS

Ambience or servicescape	Service experience
Moment of truth	Service product

Welcome to the EXCITING world of HOSPITAL-ITY! This book introduces you to one of the fastest-growing industries globally. It comes to you at a time when the wonderful world of hospitality has never been more dynamic! On a broad scale, hospitality enterprises are part of the service industry and possess unique characteristics that differentiate them from manufacturing firms. Most important for you to understand is that the hospitality product is intangible. This means that, unlike a pair of jeans that you can take back and exchange, a service once offered or experienced cannot be taken back. Once a guest meets and interacts with the employee—which is known as the moment of truth—the **service experience** is created, for better or worse. Overall, hospitality encompasses those service organizations that offer food, drink, lodging, and entertainment. In the modern industry, you will find that many of these fields are interrelated. You may not realize, for instance, that sculptors are needed in food organizations to create ice and edible displays for banquets and restaurants. Interior designers are needed to help create the exotic fantasy of a casino's pirate world or a themed Chinese restaurant. Meeting and event planners can organize weddings at Disneyland or a meeting of the local bar association or perhaps even a convention of 10,000 attendees. Hospitality enterprises need quality employees and leaders with many different types of skills, from artists to public

relations to accountants. They need special individuals who like people and truly want to help make the guests' experience the best possible. The authors in this book will introduce you to an industry that is consumer oriented. Chapter after chapter will reaffirm that, in the world of hospitality, taking good care of the guest is the single most critical element for success.

THE SERVICE– HOSPITALITY CONNECTION

For a better understanding of where the industry fits in the economy, please refer to Figure 1.1. Starting at the top of that chart—The Economy—you will see that the economy is made up of agriculture, manufacturing, and service. They are three separate parts of the economy, yet each plays a role in the service part of the economy. In the past, agriculture and manufacturing contributed the most to the economy. Agriculture focuses on growing the food that is necessary for survival. Once that production process is stable and people have enough to eat, the economy moves on to manufacturing. Manufacturing helps build products that make life easier. We can evaluate these products with our five senses like touch or smell. As other countries have developed cheaper

THE ECONOMY

Agriculture • Manufacturing • Service

THE SERVICE SECTOR

Financial Firms • Healthcare • Realty Firms • Telecommunications •
Tourism (Hospitality, Entertainment, Recreation, Transportation)

THE HOSPITALITY INDUSTRY

Hospitality • Entertainment • Transportation • **Restaurants:** Fine Dining, Full Service/Bistro, Cafeteria, Buffet, Quick Service, Carryout • **Foodservice in Lodging:** Full Dining Room, Informal Dining Room, Banquets, Room Service, Snack Bars • **On-Site/Noncommercial:** Airlines, Business and Industry, College and School, Healthcare, Concessions, Correctional, Military • **Catering:** On Premises, Off Premises • **Clubs:** Country Club, City Club, Health Club • **Lodging:** Luxury Hotel, Convention Hotel, Midmarket Hotel, Limited Service Motel, Extended Stay Hotel, Bed and Breakfast, Resort Hotel, Vacation Ownership Hotel, Noncommercial Housing

FIGURE 1.1 The Service-Hospitality Connection

A guest spends more money for the ambience and the service of a hotel.

labor, the role of American manufacturing in our global economy has changed. Now the service sector is the United States' most dominant contributor to the global economy.

This shift of dominance from agriculture and manufacturing to service has required people to acquire different skills. In an agricultural economy, people were engaged in growing crops and getting them prepared for consumer consumption. Service played a very small role because most of the focus was on climates and crops. In a manufacturing economy, people were occupied with the process of creating a product and what machinery could be used to speed up the process. Service played a more important role because more people were involved in the process. In today's service economy, there is no tangible product—the product is mostly service—and the quality of that product rests in the mind of the guest.

In a hotel, the room is the tangible product. However, in picking the hotel, the guest spends more money for the ambience and the service. By the same token, people go to a restaurant to eat, but the way they are treated is just as important. Think about your best experience in a restaurant. You enjoyed the food, of course. However, what if the server was rude? What would happen to your feeling about the restaurant experience? Herein lies the difficult and exciting part of this industry: forecasting the guests' service expectations. The skills necessary to survive in an agricultural economy and manufacturing economy are physical and mental. In the service economy, they are more interpersonal and intellectual. For many people, this is quite a change and a difficult transition. Figure 1.1 illustrates the relationship between the economy, service, and the hospitality industry.

KEY CONTENT

Hospitality: An Introduction is systematically organized for the introductory student. The book begins with a broad overview exploring how and why the industry developed into the different components and what the current trends are that are shaping the future of the industry. Further, it is important to understand the realities and career opportunities that you may not be aware of in hospitality; therefore, we present you with Chapter 4. This first section gives you the overall knowledge you need to learn more about this exciting industry, where it's been, where it's going, and how you can fit in!

The second section, *Hospitality Companies*, gradually narrows the focus to include an introduction to different forms of industry expansion, organizations, and management that are current in the industry. Next, *Hospitality Operations* explores six of the general areas of business that are key to success in the industry, including a specific focus on service excellence. In the final section, *Hospitality Career Menu*, we review many industry-specific fields and career options available to prospective managers. Please see Figure 1.2 for a graphic view of how the book is organized. The goal is to provide a survey approach to hospitality, while offering the information needed to help students proceed into more advanced courses and readings.

HOSPITALITY

The hospitality industry includes many different segments, as can be seen in Figures 1.1 and 1.2, including recreation, entertainment, travel, foodservice, lodging, and many others. We will devote a little more time in this chapter to lodging and foodservice, the two largest sectors. Although they are the largest, they are closely related and work hand in hand with many other vital segments of this vast industry.

LODGING

If you were to ask 10 people to give you an example of the lodging industry, you might get answers like: a resort in the Bahamas or Hawaii; a small inn in Vermont; a bed and breakfast in Cape May, New Jersey; a small exclusive converted castle in France; a roadside motel in Akron, Ohio; a 1,200-room luxury hotel in New York; a 100-room budget motel in Fresno, California; an all-suite hotel in Memphis; a mega hotel in Las Vegas; and an apartment hotel in London. All these answers, although different in some ways, represent examples of the lodging industry. The common bond is that they all have sleeping rooms.

However, the amenities and quality of service will vary from concept to concept. A Motel 6 will give you a clean room with bed and bath, while a Marriott might provide you with additional amenities like a fitness center and a swimming pool. A resort will allow you to walk around the grounds and play golf or go to the spa and have a clean room with bed and bath. Some will have extensive foodservice with two or three restaurants with different cuisines and 24-hour room service. Some will have one restaurant that serves breakfast, lunch, and dinner. An apartment or residential hotel may provide the guests with a fully equipped kitchen. A bed and breakfast will serve only breakfast. Some will have no foodservice except for a vending machine with snacks and soft drinks. The profitability percentage of a sold guest room is usually higher than selling a meal. Therefore,

many owners make the decision not to have foodservice in their properties because of the profitability picture and the difficulty of operating a foodservice facility. In some cases, lodging owners want to provide foodservice for their guests and will lease the foodservice facility.

Some lodging facilities will have five employees to service each room, while others will have two or more employees per room. The Peninsula Hotel in Hong Kong changes your linens and towels several times a day to provide the ultimate in service, while other hotels will ask you to throw the towels on the floor only when you want them changed to protect the environment. If you think about how much water and soap it takes to wash all those sheets and towels, you can see that even using towels one more day before washing them can make a big difference in water usage. In places that regularly have droughts, like California, this is an important factor. It is amazing that there are over 50,000 lodging operations in the United States. What incredible opportunity.

The lodging industry is very broad and varied, with each segment requiring a different skill set. Can you imagine the amount of experience you would need

HOSPITALITY INDUSTRY

Welcome to Hospitality • Hospitality History • Emerging Trends • Hospitality Service Excellence •
Industry Trade Associations and Rating Services

HOSPITALITY COMPANIES

Independent and Entrepreneurial Operations • Chain Operations • Franchising and Referral Organizations •
Contract and Asset Management • International Hospitality Companies

HOSPITALITY OPERATIONS

Leadership and Ethics • Marketing • Managing Revenue and Expenses • Human Resource Management •
Facilities, Safety, and Security • Technology • Law

HOSPITALITY CAREER MENU

Career Expectations and Realities • Lodging Industries • Hotel Operations • Food Service Industry • Restaurant Operations •
Culinary Arts • Beverage Industry • Bar and Beverage Operations • Private Club Operations • Sports and Recreation Management • Spas
and Fitness Centers • Sports and Entertainment Centers • Golf Management • Sports, Medicine, and Tourism Specialty Areas • Event
Management • Meetings and Conventions Management • Casinos • Attractions Management • Cruise Ships • Senior Services Management • Healthcare Service Excellence • Management Consulting • Hospitality Real Estate • Hospitality and Tourism Education

FIGURE 1.2 Organization of the Book

to run one of those mega properties in Las Vegas with 4,000 to 5,000 rooms? You would actually be running a medium-sized corporation. You would need to have experience in all facets of hotel operations, excellent interpersonal and leadership skills, extensive food and beverage experience to run 12 to 24 different venues, plus excellent knowledge of the gaming industry. Obviously, to run a 100-room or less property without food and beverage would require much less experience than the Vegas property. Some managers of these properties have less than 5 years of experience in the lodging business.

The basic strategy in the lodging business is to sell rooms; that is pretty obvious. The challenge for marketing is to bring people in to buy rooms. Once the guest is at the property, a challenge might be to sell them the kind of room they desire at a price that represents value to the guest. Like quality, the guest, not the management of the property, determines value. A guest room is a perishable product. If it is not sold on any one night, that revenue is lost, so the challenge is to know how to sell that room based on the guests' expectations and their perception of value.

FOODSERVICE

This part of the hospitality industry is growing at a dramatic rate. The reason for this growth is that consumers are changing their eating habits. In the 1950s, the woman stayed at home and cooked for her husband and two children. The measure of her success as a wife and mother was her cooking abilities and how much time she labored in the kitchen. Going out to eat was only for special occasions. Now, there are varieties of households, ranging from singles to one-parent families to couples with no kids to the two-parent family. To meet their economic needs, the adults in the family are working longer hours. Therefore, there is less time to spend buying groceries and preparing meals. As a result, more people are consuming meals away from their homes or are bringing prepared food home to eat. The increase in second-income families and the inadequate time to prepare meals is a significant factor in this trend.

However, this industry is far more than just food and service. For example, how many different reasons can you think of for going out to eat? Hunger, of course. However, what else? How about getting together with friends to socialize or impressing a special someone,

The atmosphere is an important aspect of the restaurant experience.

or creating a romantic mood. Because there are so many different reasons for eating out, it makes sense that restaurants come in all types of price ranges and service qualities to meet the needs of their guests. For example, quick-service restaurants cater to our frantic on-the-go lifestyle. Family restaurants attempt to keep kids occupied with activities like placemats that they can draw on while they wait for their food. At the upper end of the spectrum are restaurants that serve great food and deliver exceptional service. In each of these different venues, understanding the guests' needs and providing the kind of good food and service they want is important.

However, there is another aspect of any service environment: **ambience or servicescape**. Ambience is made up of the décor, the sound level, the lighting, the furniture, and the symphony of dining sounds created by both the diners themselves—their conversation and laughter—and the clanking of dishes and silverware. What type of ambience do you like when going out to eat? When Windows on the World reopened in 1996, the president of Windows, Joe Baum, announced at the employee orientation, "We are not in the restaurant business; we are in the entertainment business because we are creating a unique experience." He took the notion of a dining experience to the next level. Windows on the World went on to become the highest-volume restaurant in the United States. Unfortunately, that ended on September 11, 2001, when the industry and the world lost many good people.

The restaurant segment of the foodservice industry can be a trip around the world. In any major city, you can experience food from almost any country in the world. New taste sensations are created as chefs blend different cuisines to produce what is called "fusion" cuisine. For example, the blending of the flavors from Chinese and French cuisine produces a new, unique taste. Creative themes and décor can enhance the eating experience by transporting the guest to any country in the world or make them feel like they are in the 18th or the 23rd century. The diversity of the restaurant segment is immense. As a customer, you can spend 5 dollars for dinner or you can spend 100 dollars for dinner. You can select from an assortment of 5 beverages or a selection of 1,000 varieties of wine. You can also experience an operation that is owned by an individual who has one restaurant and works at it all the time or a restaurant that is one of a thousand restaurants owned by a corporation, where the owners are never around. For the employee, both entreprencurial properties and franchises have advantages and disadvantages.

In addition, the foodservice industry is made up of more than just restaurants. The noncommercial foodservice industry feeds students—elementary, secondary, and college—as well as patients and corporate employees. The challenge is to offer food they will eat and that is nutritious. In some college dining programs, a cafeteria is set aside just for vegetarians. That goes a long way to meet and exceed the expectations of the customer. There will be many students who will choose that university because they have a vegetarian cafeteria. Hospital foodservice is challenging in that meals must be suitable for all kinds of diets that are required by patients. Many institutional dining facilities (hospitals, schools, companies) have gone to branding. Branding is taking a known brand like McDonald's and opening that facility in a hospital or a school. This trend brings to the operation the name recognition and appeal that goes with it, as well as the standards of operation for that brand.

An often-overlooked segment of the foodservice industry is the private club segment. Private clubs are owned and run by their members. Therefore, the focus is on satisfying the needs of a small group of people. You know these people because they come in regularly, and they expect that you will know their names and their preferences for drinks and food. These operations can provide an exciting, interesting place to work, especially if the club has a large foodservice facility that serves à la carte and has catering for special events. In addition to the foodservice

operation, a manager could end up managing the challenges of other activities like a golf course or tennis courts.

Probably the largest segment of this industry is the quick-service or fast-food restaurants. As we mentioned earlier, quick-service meets our needs for food when we are on the run. As you know, you can eat in or drive through, which affords a variety of eating options like eating at your desk or in the car on the way to classes. Quick-service restaurants are continually trying to reinvent themselves, but the eating public continues to go for that hamburger, fried chicken, and pizza.

Another subdivision of the foodservice business is found in special events and catering. Special events include foodservice at outdoor concerts, golf tournaments, tennis tournaments, and huge events like the Olympics. These events are intense and many times more difficult to operate because the dining tents and kitchens are often temporary. During the Winter 2002 Olympics, the foodservice people were providing 100,000 meals per day. The dining tent in the Olympic Village housed 1,300 seats, a huge kitchen, and a full-service McDonald's. Working in stadiums and arenas is a unique challenge because they contain almost every segment of the foodservice industry: concession stands, private clubs, luxury skyboxes, à la carte restaurants, and catering for special events. As a free bonus, you get the excitement of watching a major sporting event. As you can see, foodservice has a broad variety of venues that will be explored in this book. Knowing about all these different types will allow you to decide whether this is the career path for you.

SUMMARY

The bottom line in the hospitality business is managing the **moments of truth**. A moment of truth is any time the guest comes in contact with anything that represents the operation. The perception of that contact could be positive or negative. Those contacts could be the condition of the parking lot, the friendliness of the voice on the phone when the reservation was made, the cleanliness of the entranceway, the greeting by the front desk person or a hostess, the speediness of the elevator, and so on. In a one-night stay or the time it takes to enjoy a meal, the guest could experience 100 moments of truth. The greatest challenge in the industry is to manage those moments of truth so that they are positive for the guest who then wants to return and tell their friends how wonderful their encounter was. These happy memories create the desire in our guests and everyone who hears their stories to come and experience the adventure. Hospitality and service are interwoven in this exciting worldwide industry. Enjoy your exploration into the industry, companies, operations, and careers. It is *our* pleasure to welcome you!

RESOURCES

Internet Sites

Career Builder: www.careerbuilder.com

Hospitality Net: www.hospitalitynet.org

HCareers: www.hcareers.com

Hospitality Online: www.hospitalityonline.com

REVIEW QUESTIONS

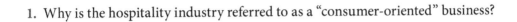

1. Why is the hospitality industry referred to as a "consumer-oriented" business?

2. What are the three separate parts of the economy described by the authors? Define each.

3. Describe the major shift in the economy concerning manufacturing industries and service industries.

4. What is the product in a service economy?

5. Who judges the quality level of service?

6. What are the skills necessary to survive in the service economy?

7. Describe the various segments of the hospitality industry.

8. Describe the current trends in the foodservice industry. How and why are they changing?

9. List three to five factors that influence decisions concerning a meal away from home.

10. What is fusion cuisine?

11. What is a challenge of the noncommercial food industry?

12. Describe the different attributes of the private club segment of the hospitality industry.

13. What are the common menu choices of fast-food restaurants?

14. What types of venues are likely to cater to or hold special events?

15. What makes working in stadiums and arenas a unique challenge?

16. Give six examples of different types of lodging.

17. What is the range of employees per guest room ratio? How does that vary within the lodging industry?

18. What are the different types of foodservices you will find in many hotels?

19. What type of lodging management skills would be needed to run a mega-property in Las Vegas?

20. What is meant by the concept that a guest room is perishable?

21. List five examples of "moments of truth" in a hospitality setting.

22. What is one of the greatest challenges related to managing moments of truth?

Hotel Astor, New York

© Susan Law Cain/Shutterstock.com

CHAPTER 2

HISTORY

AUTHORS	*Bradford T. Hudson, Boston College* *Mark E. Young, University of Houston*
LEARNING OBJECTIVES	• Acquire introductory knowledge about the history of hospitality as a business. • Understand the ancient origins of the modern hospitality industry. • Understand the role of economic, technological, and social context in the evolution of the hospitality industry in the past. • Understand how the organization and structure of the hospitality industry have changed over time. • Understand the concepts of brand heritage and heritage tourism in the modern hospitality industry.

CHAPTER OUTLINE	The Ancient and Medieval World
	The Nineteenth Century
	The Modern Era
	Recent Developments
	    Restaurants
	    Cruise Lines and Airlines
	    Theme Parks
	Perspective
	Summary

KEY TERMS	AccorHotels Bakken Auguste Escoffier Best Western Astor House Brand heritage

Brown Palace Hotel
Carnival Cruise Line
César Ritz
Chain
Code of Hammurabi
Conrad Hilton
Cunard Line
Darden Restaurants
Delmonico's
Disneyland
Ellsworth Statler
Environmental tourism
Ernest Henderson
Food tourism
Franchising
Fred Harvey
Grand Hotel
Grand tour
Heritage tourism
Hilton Hotels
Holiday Inn
Hospitia
Hotel del Coronado
Howard Johnson
J. Willard Marriott
J. W. (Bill) Marriott, Jr.
Kemmons Wilson
Knott's Berry Farm
M.K. Guertin

Management contract
Marriott Hotels
McDonald's
P&O Line
Palace Hotel
Palmer House
Parker House Hotel
Portfolio
Property
Ray Kroc
REIT
Ritz-Carlton Hotels
Samuel Cunard
Savoy Hotel
Segment
Sheraton Hotels
Silk Road
Starwood Hotels
Statler Hotels
Ted Arison
Theme park
Tivoli Gardens
Tremont House
Union Oyster House
Waldorf-Astoria Hotel
Walt Disney
White Castle
Wyndham Hotel Group

THE ANCIENT AND MEDIEVAL WORLD

The history of the hospitality industry begins in the early days of human civilization. Throughout the ancient world, the business of hospitality followed the concentration of populations into towns, the development of road systems and transoceanic travel, the growth of interregional trade, and the adoption of exchangeable currency.

Among the evidence of early hospitality that exists today is a stela (or stone marker) displayed at the Louvre Museum in Paris, which contains laws established around 1750 BC by Hammurabi, the ruler of Babylonia. The **Code of Hammurabi** includes regulations for innkeepers and tavern keepers on issues related to pricing and licensing.[1]

During the classical period, the Roman Empire had a burgeoning hospitality sector. The Romans built an extensive network of roads throughout the Mediterranean region, which required the establishment of lodging venues for travelers. Modern tourists can visit the ruins of several *hospitia* (or guest places) in the town of Pompeii, near the modern city of Naples in Italy, which was buried by a volcanic eruption in 79 AD.[2]

The **Silk Road**, which dates to 1229 AD, encompassed a variety of ancient routes between Europe and points in Asia. Merchants and traders used this system to transport goods, including silk, spices, and gemstones. *Caravanserai* (or caravan houses) subsequently appeared throughout the region. Modern travelers can visit several such sites in Turkey, including the Sultan Han near Aksaray.[3]

In Japan, modern travelers can stay at the Houshi Ryokan in Ishikawa, which traces its origins to 718 AD. A system of rest houses for travelers was first established during the Nara period circa 750 AD.[4] These evolved into inns during the later medieval period, many of which survive to the present era.

THE NINETEENTH CENTURY

Inns and taverns, small simple operations providing lodging, food, and drink, date back to the twelfth century in Europe and to the sixteenth century in America. These small establishments not only served the local lodging and dining needs, they also served as informal meeting places for the local communities. As cities grew, the taverns gave way to much-larger establishments, eventually ushering in the more modern hotels.

Although many global civilizations have influenced the traditions and practices of hospitality, the modern business of hospitality developed predominantly in Europe and America during the nineteenth century. This period is characterized by a significant acceleration in the pace of technological and economic development, especially in manufacturing and transportation powered by steam. The Industrial Revolution created vast new wealth among investors and business owners, resulting in the development of a new managerial class to operate the new huge companies, and contributed to the widespread emergence of an economic middle class.[5] These factors, in turn, resulted in a dramatic increase in leisure and business travel.

In Europe, during the nineteenth century, a new style of hotel appeared with luxurious amenities and opulent décor reminiscent of royal residences.[6] These palace hotels were built to accommodate wealthy industrialists and European nobility, who were taking extended international vacations. The route from Britain to Italy was known as the **Grand Tour**, a term that eventually became associated with visits by Americans to a variety of European destinations.

Famous city hotels of this period included the Hotel des Bergues in Geneva (1834), the Grand Hôtel de Louvre in Paris (1855), and the Hotel Imperial in Vienna (1873). This era also included the first resort hotels, which were built in locations that would offer either health benefits (such as near mineral spas) or cooler temperatures (such as near mountains or oceans). These included the Hotel Minerva in Baden-Baden (1872), the Hotel Victoria-Jungfrau in Interlaken (1865), and the Hôtel de Paris in Monte Carlo (1864).

The most famous hotel of the late nineteenth century was the **Savoy Hotel** in London (1889), which still operates today. The Savoy was one of the first major buildings powered entirely by electricity and one of the first hotels to offer private *en suite* bathrooms. Shortly after its construction, the owner hired Swiss hotelier **César Ritz** as Managing Director and French cook **Auguste Escoffier** as *Chef de Cuisine*

The famous Savoy Hotel in London as it stands today.

(chief of the kitchen).[7] The pair would subsequently become the most famous hospitality professionals in history. Ritz eventually built his own luxury hotel empire, which has evolved into the modern **Ritz-Carlton** brand.

In the United States, the first lodging property that we would recognize as a modern hotel was the **Tremont House** in Boston (1829). It included innovative features such as private guest rooms and indoor plumbing, albeit with shared bathrooms.[8] Other famous early hotels included the **Astor House** in New York (1836) and the **Parker House** in Boston (1855).

Palace hotels also appeared in the United States during the second half of the nineteenth century. Famous city hotels included the **Waldorf-Astoria** Hotel in New York (1893–1897), the **Palmer House** in Chicago (1875), the **Brown Palace Hotel** in Denver (1892), and the **Palace Hotel** in San Francisco (1875). Celebrated resort hotels included the **Grand Hotel** on Mackinac Island in Michigan (1887), and the **Hotel del Coronado** in San Diego (1888).

THE MODERN ERA

The palace hotels of the nineteenth century defined standards that remain in effect today within luxury hotels. At the same time, there was a growing need to provide rooms for the burgeoning middle class traveller. The concepts introduced in these new mid-level class hotels also continue in the vast majority of hotels today.

The most famous American hotelier of the first half of the twentieth century was **Ellsworth Statler**.[9] After an early career as a hotel employee and restaurant

entrepreneur, he built the Statler Hotel in Buffalo (1908). The hotel was so popular that he quickly expanded his business, eventually operating hotels in several major cities.

Statler Hotels featured comfortable accommodations and a full range of services previously offered only in luxury hotels, but they were moderately priced and targeted toward the economic middle class. Statler was also famous for his innovations in amenities and technology. His hotels were designed for efficiency and guest comfort. Statler hotels offered a litany of industry firsts, including bathrooms in every guest room, telephones, ice (cool) water, a light switch by the door, a lock for the door, and free morning newspapers for everyone.

The seeming contradiction between high quality and moderate price was made possible by an innovative approach to building and managing hotels. Statler properties were unusually large and therefore offered economies of scale, meaning that fixed costs could be distributed across a large number of customers. They were also differentiated by the efficient design of operating systems and architectural elements, such as centralized plumbing risers.

Statler created the modern hotel for business travelers and the burgeoning middle class travelers, but other pioneers using the same formula soon followed him. **Conrad Hilton** of **Hilton Hotels**, **Ernest Henderson** of **Sheraton Hotels**, and a host of others followed Statler in hotel management.

Conrad Hilton bought his first hotel in 1919 and built an international chain during the next five decades. Started in Texas, Hilton developed into a southwestern regional hotel chain and, finally, in 1943, became the first coast-to-coast hotel chain. Along the way Hilton acquired several historic properties, including the Waldorf-Astoria Hotel in New York and the Palmer House in Chicago. Hilton Hotels' acquisition of the Statler chain in 1954 made the combined company the largest hotel operator in the world at the time.[10]

J. Willard Marriott started his career as a restaurateur in Washington, DC, during the late 1920s. At the urging of his son, **J. W. (Bill) Marriott, Jr.**, he opened his first hotel in 1957, and eventually decided to focus exclusively on lodging. In 1983 **Marriott Hotels** created the Courtyard brand and began to build and purchase other hotels with the goal of serving different market needs and creating segmentation within the industry. In 1987 Marriott acquired Residence Inn and bought the Ritz-Carlton Hotels in 1995, thereby acquiring a historical legacy that can be traced back to César Ritz.[11]

At the same time that chains for business travelers were being built, other pioneers were reinventing the economy hotel. Inexpensive lodging was common throughout the United States, but quality levels were inconsistent and often poor. **Howard Johnson** in the east and **M.K. Guertin**, founder of **Best Western**, in the west met these needs. As highway construction grew, in particular construction of the interstate highway system from the mid 1950s, highway maintenance crews and other people began to travel more by automobile. Urban hotels were unable to meet the needs of the automobile travelling public. After encountering disappointing accommodations on a family vacation, **Kemmons Wilson** envisioned a chain of inexpensive roadside hotels oriented toward families traveling by automobile with a limited budget.[12] He founded **Holiday Inn** in 1952, and within two decades it was the largest hotel chain in the United States. Soon a host of other brands, including Ramada Inns, Travel Lodge, and La Quinta Inns, were appearing along the highway landscape.

RECENT DEVELOPMENTS

The basic elements of the modern hotel were firmly established by the middle of the twentieth century, especially from the viewpoint of the guest. However, several important developments have occurred in recent years related to the structure and operations of the industry.

First, ownership of individual properties has shifted away from hotel companies. A century ago, the real estate (building and land) associated with most hotels was owned by the company that operated the hotel, although in some cases they leased the property to an individual who managed the hotel. Over the past three decades, however, ownership and management functions have been separated for financial reasons, so that independent investors now own most hotels. For modern hotel investors the most popular arrangement is the **REIT** (Real Estate Investment Trust), where investors own the property and earn a share of the profits from the hotel lessee or management company. The hotel companies still control their brand names, but they merely operate hotels on behalf of owners, based on **management contracts**.

Second, the hotel industry has been divided into parts. A century ago, there was no standardized system for understanding what to expect at a specific hotel **property** (or individual location). Now the industry is organized according to price and quality levels known as **segments**, which progress upward from the economy segment to the luxury segment.

Third, the industry has become consolidated through acquisition. A generation ago, almost every hotel brand was owned and operated separately. However, over the past three decades, the major hotel companies have assembled **portfolios** (or collections) of hotel brands. These have been created to fulfill the growth ambitions of parent companies, to diversify investment and risk, and in response to the increasing segmentation of the industry. Hilton was the first to acquire a major competitor (the now defunct Statler brand) and has subsequently acquired or created twelve other brands, including Waldorf-Astoria, Doubletree, Embassy Suites, Curio, Home2 Suites, and Hampton. **Wyndham Hotel Group** was created by the merger of a separate hotel company with a REIT and then acquisition of several other brands (now totaling 15 including Super 8, Wingate, and Days Inn). A REIT named **Starwood Hotels** purchased Sheraton Hotels and then acquired or created ten other brands, including St. Regis, Westin, and W Hotels. Marriott Hotels has acquired or created more than 17 different hotel brands, including Ritz-Carlton, Renaissance, Courtyard, and Residence Inn. In what may usher in a new round of hotel mergers, starting in 2015 French-owned **AccorHotels** announced it would buy FRHI Holdings, the owner of Fairmont, Raffles, and Swissôtel, and Marriott Corporation successfully acquired Starwood Hotels and their eleven brands in creating the largest international hotel company with over 5400 hotels and 1.1 million rooms.[13]

RESTAURANTS

The hotel and restaurant industries were connected throughout much of history, as inns or taverns that also offered lodging upstairs typically provided meals downstairs. This tradition continues to the present day, as a portion of revenues in full-service hotels continues to derive from restaurants on premise or from banquet operations.

Independent restaurants (separate from hotels) emerged in Europe and America during the eighteenth and nineteenth centuries.[14] The social and economic factors that contributed to the rise of the hotel industry also helped create the burgeoning restaurant business. The first American establishments that we would recognize as modern restaurants were the **Union Oyster House** in Boston (1826) and **Delmonico's** in New York (1837), both of which are still operating.

The earliest chain restaurant operator was probably **Fred Harvey**, who opened a restaurant in the railroad station at Topeka, Kansas, in 1876. The company succeeded based on his formula for excellent food, good service, and reasonable prices. By the turn of the century, the Fred Harvey Company operated an extensive network of restaurants and hotels along the route of the Atchison, Topeka, and Santa Fe Railway Company.[15]

The most important early pioneer in the quick-service segment is White Castle, which opened its first hamburger restaurant in Wichita, Kansas in 1921. **White Castle** established a system involving counter service, mass production of a limited menu, strict sanitation procedures, and a chain of identical units.[16]

The White Castle formula was adopted by the McDonald brothers, who opened the first **McDonald's** restaurant in California two decades later (1948). Shortly thereafter, an enterprising milkshake machine salesman named **Ray Kroc** convinced the McDonalds to sell the franchise rights to their concept. Kroc subsequently created the largest restaurant brand in the world.[17]

Several important developments have occurred in recent years related to the structure and operations of the restaurant industry. First, **franchising** has become a widespread method of growing restaurant brands. This is a technique in which an independent entrepreneur pays for the rights to use the brand, recipes, and operating system of a leading restaurant company. Second, the restaurant industry has been organized into **segments** based on price and quality, which progress upward from the quick-service (or fast-food) segment to the fine dining segment. Third, the industry has become consolidated

McDonald's golden arches represent the largest restaurant brand in the world.

through acquisition. For example, **Darden Restaurants** owns several major brands, including Capital Grille, Longhorn Steakhouse, and Olive Garden. Lastly, the chain restaurant paradigm has matured to encompass concepts in every segment, including fine dining restaurants operated by celebrity chefs such as Wolfgang Puck.

CRUISE LINES AND AIRLINES

Ships have been an established mode of transportation for thousands of years, but a new style of passenger ship was introduced during the nineteenth century. Steamships were larger and faster than their predecessors. They also had features and interior décor that resembled luxury hotels, intended to cater to wealthy industrialists and their families, who were traveling from America to Europe (and within Europe) on the Grand Tour.

The **Cunard Line** was founded in 1839 by **Samuel Cunard** to operate transatlantic vessels between Britain and the United States. By the early twentieth century, it had become one of the most prestigious shipping companies in the world. A leading competitor was the White Star Line, which owned the ill-fated ship *Titanic*. The two companies eventually merged (1934), and shortly thereafter Cunard built the famous ships *Queen Mary* and *Queen Elizabeth*.[18]

The original purpose of ocean liners was to transport people and cargo from point to point, in a manner similar to modern airlines. The Peninsular and Oriental Steam Navigation Company (or **P&O**) advertised a new type of service in 1843, offering voyages with a series of stops in the Mediterranean for tourists interested in visiting historical sites.[19] This was the start of leisure cruising.

A century later in 1958, the jet engine was introduced to commercial passenger aircraft, making intercontinental air travel fast and safe. Ships could no longer compete, and the oceanic passenger industry effectively disappeared within a decade. Many of the ships were scrapped, but some were adapted for leisure cruising. However, the passenger profile remained essentially the same, predominated by older and wealthier customers.

In 1972, **Ted Arison** purchased a former ocean liner from the Canadian Pacific Line and offered cruises from Miami to the Caribbean. Arison believed that a market existed for moderately priced voyages aimed at a younger audience, with extensive onboard activities and without the formality of the transatlantic ocean liners. He called his company **Carnival Cruise Line**, renamed his first ship *Mardi Gras*, and adopted the slogan "The Fun Ships." This was the start of the modern cruise industry.[20] Within two decades, Carnival had become the largest cruise line in the world and had acquired the historic Cunard and P&O brands.

THEME PARKS

The Industrial Revolution not only generated phenomenal wealth for capitalist barons, but it also created a new economic middle class with increasing amounts of disposable income and leisure time. Entrepreneurs naturally created new products and services to meet the growing demand for entertainment.

Dyrehavsbakken or **Bakken** is an amusement park in Copenhagen, Denmark, that traces its origins to the sixteenth century. The park was opened to the public on a seasonal basis for festivals in 1756. By the late nineteenth century, Bakken had evolved into a permanent venue, offering rides and other amenities found in modern amusement parks.[21] Meanwhile across town, the famous Tivoli Gardens opened in 1843. Both are still operating.

Theme parks emerged as a special type of amusement park, in which every aspect of the park had a story or design with a shared theme. The first operations that we would recognize as modern theme parks were Sea Lion Park (1895) and Steeplechase Park (1897) at Coney Island in New York, the former with an ocean theme and the latter with a horseracing theme.[22]

Another pioneer in the theme park industry was **Knott's Berry Farm**, which started as a farm stand and restaurant in Buena Park, California (1928). A few years later, to give restaurant customers something to do while waiting for a table, the Knott family built a western "ghost town" attraction, which has evolved into a full-scale theme park.[23]

Perhaps the most important moment in the history of theme parks occurred when **Disneyland** opened in Anaheim, California (1955). **Walt Disney**, originally a commercial artist, founded a cartoon movie production company in Hollywood in 1923. Three decades later, he was a major producer of both live action and animated films. Disney envisioned an amusement park that would allow guests to immerse themselves in the imaginary worlds depicted in Disney cartoons and movies, where both adults and children could enjoy the entertainment together. The company subsequently opened Walt Disney World in Orlando, Florida (1971). The latter has grown into a vast entertainment complex encompassing four subsidiary theme parks and numerous hospitality operations, constituting the largest single-site employer of any type in the United States.[24]

Walt Disney's vision has grown into a vast entertainment complex for adults and children to enjoy.

PERSPECTIVE

You may be wondering, if we are preparing hospitality students for the future, why are we focusing here on the past? Although seemingly arcane, business history is actually quite relevant to contemporary issues in hospitality management. Faculty members at Harvard Business School have argued persuasively that the historical approach can be applied to modern business education in important ways.[25] The historical perspective contributes to an appreciation of the economic, technological, and social factors that influence business. An understanding of the evolution of industries and the history of specific firms also contributes to our analysis of the strategic dynamics of modern companies. Those who understand the history of our industry will be better prepared to anticipate its future, especially in identifying the next generation of opportunities that may emerge.

History is also embedded within the identities of older companies, products, and places. **Brand heritage** is an emerging topic within the marketing discipline, which suggests that the consumer appeal of products and services offered by older companies may be enhanced by the historical characters of their brands.[26] Many of the hospitality companies and properties discussed in this chapter continue to operate today, and their historical status is one reason that customers choose such offerings over competitors. Historic Hotels of America is an organization devoted exclusively to marketing for older hotels. It represents more than 200 famous hotels throughout the United States, which are currently managed by a variety of hotel companies.

Heritage tourism is a related topic that considers travel to historic cities, ancient ruins, museums, and other locations that reference our past.[27] This explains the interest in sites from classical antiquity for travelers on the Grand Tour of Europe during the nineteenth century. It also explains the attraction of historical sites throughout the United States today, such as Colonial Williamsburg in Virginia.

Growing in popularity are two other subcategories of tourism, **food tourism** and **environmental tourism**. Both of these niche forms of tourism have grown rapidly, catering to travellers who want to experience the unconventional or travellers looking for uncommon experiences. The destinations for food tourism and especially environmental tourism cater to more exotic locations not found within the United States. For its part, the hospitality industry is rapidly developing products for this growing number of experiential niche tourists and guests to enjoy.

SUMMARY

The hospitality business has its origins in the ancient past. Over the centuries, the standards and practices of hospitality have evolved as civilization has progressed. The industry has developed in response to changes in social structure and cultural norms, travel and migration behavior, industrial and economic systems, and technology. Two patterns are particularly clear. First, the hospitality industry has been influenced by transportation technology and infrastructure such as roads, railroads, steamships, automobiles, and aircraft. Second, the hospitality industry has been influenced by the vast increase in the scale and distribution of wealth resulting from the Industrial Revolution.

RESOURCES

Internet Sites

Many of the companies, hotels, and restaurants described in this chapter still exist. You can find their websites by using any popular search engine, such as Google. Some of these websites have subsidiary pages that describe the history of the company or property. These are often located in sections such as "About Us" or "Company Information." The pages usually have titles such as "Our History," "Timeline," or "Company Heritage." To find these sections and pages, review the links at the bottom of the main page or use the "Site Map" feature.

Historic Hotels of America (www.historichotels.org) is a marketing organization that represents more than 250 historic hotels, which are currently managed by a variety of hotel companies. This is a good place to start if you are seeking information about specific properties.

ENDNOTES

1. King, L. W. (1898). *The Letters and Inscriptions of Hammurabi [etc.]*. London: Luzac. In C. F. Kent. (1903). The Recently Discovered Civil Code of Hammurabi. *Biblical World*, 21 (3), pp. 175–190.

2. O'Gorman, K. D., Baxter, I., and Scott, B. (2007). Exploring Pompeii: Discovering Hospitality through Research Synergy. *Tourism and Hospitality Research*, 7 (2), pp. 89–99.

3. Yavuz, A. T. (1997). The Concepts That Shape Anatolian Seljuq Caravanserais. In G. Necipoglu (ed.), *Muqarnas XIV: An Annual on the Visual Culture of the Islamic World*, pp. 80–95. Leiden: Brill.

4. Japan Ryokan Association. (2010). *Origins and History of the Japanese Ryokan*. Tokyo: Japan Ryokan Association.

5. Chandler, A. D., Jr. (1977). *The Visible Hand: The Managerial Revolution in American Business*. Cambridge: Belknap.

6. Denby, E. (1998). *Grand Hotels*. London: Reaktion. In C. Donzel, A. Gregory, and M. Walter. (1989). *Grand American Hotels*. New York: Vendome. In A. K. Sandoval-Strausz. (2007). *Hotel: An American History*. New Haven: Yale University.

7. Jackson, S. (1964). *The Savoy: The Romance of a Great Hotel*. New York: E. P. Dutton. In M. L. Ritz. (1938). *César Ritz: Host to the World*. Philadelphia: J. P. Lippincott.

8. Lee, H. (1965). Boston's Greatest Hotel. *Old-Time New England*, 55 (200), pp. 97–106.

9. Turkel, S. (2005). Ellsworth Milton Statler: Hotel Man of the Half Century. *Lodging Hospitality*, 61 (5), pp. 64–68.

10. Hilton, C. (1957). *Be My Guest*. Englewood Cliffs, NJ: Prentice Hall. In Hilton Buys Chain of Statler Hotels. (1954). *New York Times*, August 4, p. 1.

11. O'Brien, R. (1977). *Marriott: The J. Willard Marriott Story*. Salt Lake City, UT: Deseret. In Marriott to Acquire a Ritz-Carlton Stake. (1995). New York Times, March 7, p. D4.

12. Brewster, M. (2004). Kemmons Wilson: America's Innkeeper. *Business Week*, October 11.

13. (2015, November 19). The ten largest hotel companies by brand. HotelNewsNow website Retrieved from http://www.hotelnewsnow.com/Article/17129/The-10-largest-hotel-companies-by-room-count

14. Spang, R. (1999). *The Invention of the Restaurant*. Cambridge: Harvard University.

15. Fried, S. (2010). *Appetite for America: How Visionary Businessman Fred Harvey Built a Railroad Hospitality Empire that Civilized the Wild West*. New York: Bantam.

16. Hogan, D. G. (1997). *Selling 'em by the Sack: White Castle and the Creation of American Food*. New York: New York University.

17. Love, J. (1986). *McDonald's: Behind the Arches*. New York: Bantam.

18. Hyde, F. E. (1975). *Cunard and the North Atlantic, 1840–1973: A History of Shipping and Financial Management*. Atlantic Highlands, NJ: Humanities Press.

19. P&O Cruises. (2010). *History*. www.pocruises.com.au

20. Garin, K. A. (2005). *Devils on the Deep Blue Sea: The Dreams, Schemes and Showdowns That Built America's Cruise-Ship Empires*. New York: Viking.

21. A/S Dyrehavsbakken. (2010). *The History of Bakken*. www.bakken.dk

22. Sterngrass, J. (2001). *First Resorts: Pursuing Pleasure at Saratoga Springs, Newport & Coney Island*. Baltimore: Johns Hopkins University.

23. Knott's Berry Farm. (2010). *Historical Background.* www.knotts.com

24. Smith, D. (1996). *Disney A to Z: The Official Encyclopedia.* New York: Hyperion. In Walt Disney Company. (2010). *Corporate History and Walt Disney World Facts.* www.corporate.disney.go

25. Kantrow, A. M. (1986). Why History Matters to Managers. *Harvard Business Review,* 64 (1), pp. 81–88.

26. Hudson, B. T. (2011). Brand Heritage and the Renaissance of Cunard. *European Journal of Marketing,* forthcoming; M. Urde, S. A. Greyser, and J. M. T. Balmer. (2007). Corporate Brands with a Heritage. *Journal of Brand Management,* 15 (1), pp. 4–19.

27. Dallen, T. J. and Boyd, S. W. (2003). *Heritage Tourism.* London: Prentice Hall.

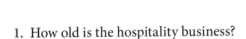

REVIEW QUESTIONS

1. How old is the hospitality business?

2. Identify a specific example of the hospitality business prior to the year 1700.

3. Identify a famous hotel that was built during the period 1800–1899.

4. Identify one pioneering company in each of the following parts of the hospitality industry: hotel, restaurant, cruise line, theme park. Briefly describe the history of each of these companies, and identify the individuals who founded these companies.

5. How did economic, technological, and social context influence the evolution of the hospitality industry in the past? Explain and provide a specific example.

6. How have the organization and structure of the hotel industry changed over time? Explain and provide a specific example.

7. What is brand heritage? What is heritage tourism? How do these concepts relate to each other? Define and explain.

CHAPTER *3*

EMERGING TRENDS

AUTHOR

Michael Oshins, Boston University

LEARNING OBJECTIVES

- Identify major trends of the hospitality industry.
- List the characteristics of the Millennial generation.
- Recognize trends in hotel brands and customizing service experiences.
- Identify the impact on travelers of the sharing economy and technology.
- Identify environmental trends affecting hospitality companies.

CHAPTER OUTLINE

Trend 1: Millennials—The New Power Segment
Trend 2: Taking Control of Health and Well-Being
Trend 3: Disruption and the Sharing Economy
    Transportation
    On-Demand Workers
    Accommodations
Trend 4: Environmental Awareness and Global Uncertainties
    Being Green
    Weather and Pollution Challenges
    Changes in Political Situations
    Ethnic, Cultural, and Religious Tensions
    Economic Instability and Shifts
Trend 5: Chinese Travel Wave
Trend 6: Brand Power

CHAPTER OUTLINE
(Continued)

Trend 7: Technology, Technology, Technology
    Technology-Driven, Self-Sufficient Travelers
    Changing Online Distribution Landscape
    Power of Social Networks
Trend 8: Customization Rules
Summary

KEY TERMS

AirBnB	Independent contractors
Alliance brand	Kimpton
Authentic experiences	LGBT
Baby boomers	Luxury collection
Booking.com	Macau
Brand conversion	Millennials
Canopy	Moxy
Centric	On-demand workers
Chinese tourists	OTAs
Edition	Priceline
Element	Sharing economy
Environmental Awareness	Social networks
EVEN	TripAdvisor
Expedia	Uber
Foodies	Virtual Reality (VR)
IHG	Word of mouth

TREND 1: MILLENNIALS— THE NEW POWER SEGMENT

Millennials, defined by a birth range of 1980–2000, are the fastest growing segment in the hospitality industry. Although **baby boomers** (1946–1964) are retiring and have both more time and money to travel, Millennials will be a driving force for future travel.[1] "Exploration, interaction, and emotional experience [are] the hallmark of Millennials and [they] are expected to represent 50% of all travelers by 2025."[2] Millennials will gravitate toward businesses that are very technically advanced. This demographic uses technology for everything...checking into a hotel and paying for it, dining, shopping. Millennials will also tell about their experiences on every avenue of social media such as Twitter and Yelp. They will voice any complaints on **Trip Advisor**.

This 18–35-year-old segment also presents a contradiction of travel spending habits. Although they may have lower income than other age segments, Millennials are willing to splurge more for experienced-based purchases, such access to luxury lounges in airports.[3] "**Foodies**" are a distinct subset of this market looking for a gourmet experience at reasonable prices. Culture buffs, **LGBT** (Lesbian, Gay, Bi-sexual and Transgender), and multi-generational travelers are looking for unique and novel experiences. "Two-thirds (66%) of Millennial high-frequency travelers rate "unique rewards" as an important factor when choosing a hotel loyalty program, compared with just 43% of their older counterparts."[4] Half of Millennials stayed at independent hotels last year, 20% more than baby boomers.[5]

There are additional opportunities to cater to this growing market segment. The larger hotel companies are designing new brands with the younger lifestyle preferences in mind, such as **Moxy** by Marriott, **Canopy** by Hilton, and **Centric** by Hyatt.[6] Marketing to this younger generation accustomed to the online gaming world, Marriott launched a 4-D virtual travel experience with a **virtual reality (VR)** booth that teleports people to three different sites (developed by the same company that produces the HBO series *Game of Thrones*).[7] Similarly, "Shangri-La hotels and New York's Ludlow hotel created virtual reality experiences of their properties that allow potential guests to see what it would be like to stay at their locations."[8] For an operational application, a virtual concierge may allow guests to not only hear and read about services, but also experience them firsthand.[9]

TREND 2: TAKING CONTROL OF HEALTH AND WELL-BEING

The drive towards healthier living continues to gain wide popularity. Internal biochemistry and personal fitness data-tracking products such as Fitbit and Apple Watch continue to grow. Healthier eating and greater attention to all-natural foods, reduced GMOs, locally sourced products, and organic produce continue to move into mainstream practices. The hospitality industry is also embracing this healthier-living lifestyle. Both urban and resort spa revenues have increased (7.7% and 4.6% respectively) in recent years.[10] InterContinental's **(IHG) EVEN** hotel brand and Starwood's **Element** brand are both designed with an explicit wellness focus.[11] "Six Sense Resorts offers a new lighting strategy that uses LED lights to help guests fall asleep and to enhance body alertness.[12]" The lights have a special technology that allows guests to sleep more soundly. The light emits less 'blue' light and therefore enhances relaxation and uses technology developed for NASA to help astronauts regulate their body rhythms naturally. Hilton now designates and outfits hypoallergenic hotel rooms that have special air filtration systems.[13]

An example of a less-expensive tactic catering to this healthier-living trend, Westin has teamed up with New Balance sneaker company to offer guests at 190 properties the availability to rent running shoes (with disposable insoles), as well as complete running outfits.[14] To reach the same cohort of customers seeking to exercise during their stay, Omni Hotels and Resorts supplies a "Get Fit Kit" with free weights and yoga mats for customers to use in the comfort of their hotel room.[15] Marriott, in Chicago, has been test-marketing a healthy vending machine, featuring handcrafted salads, sandwiches, and snacks made fresh every day using locally sourced ingredients.[16] These companies are not focusing on wellness solely with altruist intent: wellness tourism is expected to grow to a more than $675-billion market by 2017.[17]

Traditional taxi services are being disrupted by new ride choices.

TREND 3: DISRUPTION AND THE SHARING ECONOMY

The **sharing economy** has grown rapidly over the last few years and will continue to increase at an impressive pace throughout the world. Peer-to-peer networks will expand and mature as they compete with traditional travel services. Three technology-aided areas that affect the hospitality industry include:

Transportation. Disrupting taxi and car-hire services, companies such as Sidecar, Lyft, BlaBlaCar, Hailo, and **Uber** continue to challenge the status quo and raise legal issues in every locale they enter. The most successful peer-to-peer service is Uber. Now in 67 countries, Uber has clocked over one billion (1,000,000,000) rides. InterContinental Hotel Group (IHG) is co-marketing Uber's services, enabling IHG loyalty members to not only order rides through their rewards program, but also to create "Ride Reminders" through IHG reservation emails in advance of their stay.[18]

On-Demand Workers. To address fluctuating staffing needs, companies are hiring more **on-demand workers** like **independent contractors** (self-employed) who work on specific projects or for discrete periods of time. They do not get the same company benefits, such as healthcare insurance and vacation or sick time, that full-time employees enjoy. Companies hire on-demand workers for flexibility, to save money, and to limit their liability.[19] On-demand workers, such as those referred through companies including Handybook (cleaning services), Crowdflower (digital /data jobs), and TaskRabbit (errands and house jobs), blur the line between employees and independent contractors.[20] This on-demand or contract worker

model is facing legal challenges. Uber and three food delivery companies (GrubHub, DoorDash, and Caviar) are being sued for allegedly classifying workers improperly as independent contractors while treating them as employees.[21]

Accommodations. Alternatives to hotel accommodations continue to be on the rise, including using local homes or apartments with companies such as CouchSurfing, HomeExchange, Love Home Swap, VBRO, Flipkey, OneFineStay, HomeAway, and Be Mate.[22] The biggest, current challenge to hotels is **AirBnB**. As of December 2015, AirBnB has over one million rooms available for rent[23] and valuation worth over $25 billion,[24] which is more than Hyatt, Wyndham, or InterContinental Hotel Group. Expanding in over 190 countries, AirBnB now represents 10.4% of room inventory in London, 17.2% in New York City, and 11.9% in Paris, and by the end of 2016 worldwide inventory is expected to rise to 129 million.[25] Although 90% of AirBnB customers are leisure travelers, going forward the company could also more aggressively target business travelers.

TREND 4: ENVIRONMENTAL AWARENESS AND GLOBAL UNCERTAINTIES

Through technology, the world has become smaller, that is, more immediately connected. Through technology the sharing of scientific and political information is immediate. Our greater access to and deeper understanding of environmental science and world politics has significant impact in the hospitality field. Specifically, **environmental awareness**, changes in political parties, ethnic/cultural/religious tensions, weather/pollution challenges, and economic instability or shifts may impact the times, places, and ways in which people choose to travel.

Being Green. Although customers are generally not willing to pay for eco-features,[26] the hospitality industry will continue the efforts it began in the last decade to enact eco-friendly practices and focus on environmental sustainability. Common practices such as customer-approved reduction in laundry, low-energy light bulbs, water-saving shower heads, improved temperature management systems, and more energy-efficient products will continue to be developed and implemented.

The Icelandic volcano erupted in 2010, disrupting air traffic in Europe for weeks.

Weather and Pollution Challenges. As highlighted by the United Nations Conference on Climate Change in Paris (December 2015), there is a worldwide imperative for countries to work together to reduce the rise of global warming and climate change.[27] The Icelandic volcano eruption in 2010 disrupted air traffic in Europe for several weeks. The high levels of air pollution in China and recent catastrophic tsunamis in Japan and Indonesia negatively affect tourism. Closer to home, Hurricane Katrina in New Orleans, Hurricane Sandy in New York City, record-setting blizzards in the winter of 2015 in Boston, droughts in California, and record flooding in the South and Midwest are further examples of the weather-related events that have a detrimental impact in the hospitality industry.

Changes in Political Situations. Changes in political parties or leadership on national, state, and local levels will continue to affect hospitality organizations in both positive and negative ways. An unforeseen crackdown in corruption by the Chinese government resulted in billions of dollars in decreased revenues in **Macau**, the world's largest gambling destination.[28] Improved relationships with Cuba will provide tourism opportunities, as well as new competition for other Caribbean destinations. Changes in tax laws, increases in the minimum wage (e.g. $15/hour in New York for quick-service restaurant employees), immigration policies, and local ordinances, such as Massachusetts loosening restrictions on liquor license applications, are all examples of shifting political environments that will continue in the future.

Ethnic, Cultural, and Religious Tensions. The exit of millions of refugees from Syria into Europe, political unrest in Venezuela, widespread instability in the Middle East, and the conflict over rights to control the South China Sea are challenges that will not be resolved in the near future. Paris has experienced the most violence in 2015 it has seen since World War II. As ethnic, cultural, and religious tensions continue to create civil unrest around the world, the threat of terrorism and negative impact on travel and tourism will persist.[29]

Economic Instability and Shifts. Economic instability in Greece, fluctuations in energy prices, and strengthening and weakening of exchange rates are examples of economic shifts that affect tourism opportunities. For example, the decoupling of the Swiss franc at a fixed exchange rate with the euro currency may hurt the Swiss economy.[30] If the franc increases in value, it will cause a relative rise in prices for Europeans to purchase goods and services in Switzerland with a less strong euro and may cause a decline in Swiss sales—especially for border towns that draw customers from other countries.

TREND 5: CHINESE TRAVEL WAVE

For much of the last two decades, there has been a continuous push by western countries and corporations to enter the Chinese market, including a wide range of hotel and restaurant segments as well as the opening of a $5 billion, full-scale Disney theme park outside Shanghai in 2016. In addition to the influx of hospitality companies entering the Chinese market, there has also been a growing impact of **Chinese tourists** abroad. Although many countries are increasing their outbound travel, the number of Chinese tourists travelling abroad is staggering:

recruit to travel

- Close to 100 million outward-bound Chinese travelers
- Chinese spend the most of any tourists: $129 billion in 2013; the next closest country was the United States with $86 billion, $40 billion less than Chinese tourists
- They are expected to spend more on luxury goods abroad than tourists from all other countries...*combined*
- By 2020, foreign trips by Chinese tourists will double and spending will triple[31]

As indicated by the estimates above, this travel wave could be the tip of the proverbial pagoda. Even with these huge numbers, only 5% of China's population now own passports, and most Chinese trips stay closer to home with Hong Kong and Macau as their two biggest travel destinations. In 2013, Chinese travelers could visit just 44 other countries without a pre-arranged visa, whereas Americans and Britons could visit over 170. Evidence shows that merely simplifying the process for traveling to other countries can have a significant impact. When the United States simplified travel by allowing Chinese to apply for visas online with pick up in any of 900 local banks, Chinese travel to the United States increased by 22%. Even more significantly, when the Maldives waived their visa process with China, Chinese travel to that country increased by over 45%.[32]

TREND 6: BRAND POWER

Hotel brands continue to grow in size and strength, as hotels continue to consolidate through mergers and acquisitions. Larger hotel companies offer economies of scale for purchasing products and marketing, build a greater customer base with more locations, and provide better negotiating leverage for more favorable commission rates with online travel agencies (**OTAs**). Marriott Corporation, with its 17 brands, successfully acquired Starwood Hotels and their eleven brands in creating the largest international hotel company with over 5400 hotels and 1.1 million rooms.[33] IIHG purchased **Kimpton**, a collection of 62 boutique hotels located throughout the United States. The recent creation or expansion of additional brands entering the market include Marriott's **EDITION** (a joint effort with boutique designer Ian Schrager), AC and Moxy hotels, Commune's tommie and Thompson brands, Richard Branson's Virgin Hotels, Baccarat Hotels, Hilton's Canopy brand and Hyatt's new Centric properties. These new brands will continue to test the market and compete for current and new customers on a global level.

A second trend has been **brand conversion**, or the conversion of independent hotels to branded properties. "Research has long suggested that independent hotels can enjoy a number of benefits by affiliating with a brand. Apart from the marketing value of the brand name, a newly branded hotel will likely receive managerial advice and training, not to mention capital it can use to improve the property."[34] This idea has been implemented in three iterations. First, independent hotels *convert* to a branded property, such as the century-old Copley Plaza in Boston becoming the Fairmont Copley Hotel. Second, independent hotels can keep their name and *jointly* use a brand. Hilton leveraged the iconic Waldorf-Astoria name to create a luxury brand, whereby many properties combine their original name with the Hilton brand, such as Florida's *Boca Beach Club*, a *Waldorf Astoria Resort* and *Arizona Biltmore*, a *Waldorf Astoria Resort*. Third, independent hotels keep their identity but *align* themselves with a major hotel company through an **alliance brand**. Examples such as Boston's Liberty Hotel joining Starwood's *Luxury Collection* and Colorado's The Brown Palace as a member of Marriott's *Autograph Collection* illustrate the opportunity to benefit from the power of brands while still maintaining their independent appeal.

TREND 7: TECHNOLOGY, TECHNOLOGY, TECHNOLOGY

Technology continues to have a substantial impact on all businesses and the hospitality industry is no exception. As technology continues to become more mobile, processing speeds of data increase, companies develop more integrated and focused applications, and information is more accessible on a global and local scale, trends continue to emerge in a variety of areas. Some of the more influential ones include:

Technology-Driven, Self-Sufficient Travelers. "With the rise of smartphones and tablets, travelers now have remarkable connectivity that allows them to

Smart phones, tablets, and other forms of technology have made it easier to make travel arrangements and share information.

make travel arrangements and share information before, during, and after their trips."[35] "Innovative technologies on a mobile platform will be expected as more individuals rely on digital concierge services."[36] People assume that they will be able check in from any device, such as their smart phone or tablet, and with location software, that they will easily find places of interest near their chosen area.

Changing Online Distribution Landscape. The connection from customers to hospitality companies will continue to shift and change as online travel agencies (OTAs) and new players adapt to new opportunities and shifting partnerships. The merger of **Expedia** and Orbitz with their plethora of sites (Expedia, Hotels.com, Travelocity, Hotwire, Trivago, Orbitz, Cheapticket, etc.) affords them greater negotiating leverage with travel companies (hotels, airlines, car rental companies, etc.). **Priceline** (Priceline, Kayak, and Booking.com) continues to be a top distribution company, boasting three of the top ten travel websites; **Booking.com** is the travel industry's top booking website with over 40 million unique monthly visitors.[37]

TripAdvisor's original focus was a website for customers to rate hospitality companies and provide personal experiences and advice. The website added an "instant booking option" in 2015, allowing customers to book travel plans in addition to reading and writing reviews. This new feature increases TripAdvisor's ability to capture online reservation business, as well as its potential to become the most powerful booking site. Taking a different approach than the large OTAs mentioned above is Lola. Lola, a Boston-based high tech start-up by the founders of Kayak.com, blends online travel technology with live travel agents. Travel agents work with customers while the customers are using the Lola phone application or website.[38]

Power of Social Networks. Before the Internet age, one of the most powerful and elusive marketing tools was **word-of-mouth**. The rise of social network sites designed for content sharing creates a robust venue for sharing views, opinions, and experiences on an immediate and global level. **Social networks** and sites designed for content sharing such as Facebook, Instagram, YouTube, Pinterest, Twitter, Vine, and China's Weibo provide forums for anyone to voice a perspective with friends and strangers alike.

Sites designed to enable customers to rate, rank, and discuss hospitality experiences can have a significant impact on the profitability of a company. Yelp has millions of users who review restaurants. Studies have shown that an increase in a hotel's online reputation on TripAdvisor can increase a property's occupancy rate and revenue.[39] Managing an online reputation through social media will continue to play an important role in a company's overall marketing strategy. For more information on managing online reputations, refer to two articles by Leora Lanz in the *Boston Hospitality Review*: http://www.bu.edu/bhr.

TREND 8: CUSTOMIZATION RULES

Providing a positive customer experience and creating value is still at the heart of any hospitality business in its effort to satisfy customers, have them come back, and spread positive word of mouth to friends and social networks. Managing customer relationships through collecting and analyzing data has become very sophisticated; the science behind data analytics allows companies to personalize services for each individual customer.[40] Hotels, restaurants, and travel companies use niche positioning and provide focused expertise for specific interests from craft beers to star gazing. The trend towards emphasizing **authentic experiences** by highlighting local attributes, including cuisines, landscapes, and attractions, continues to foster a more engaging customer experience.

SUMMARY

As explained in the history chapter, the hospitality industry has been present since the early days of human civilization. In the past few years, multiple trends touching upon different facets of the hospitality industry have emerged. This chapter highlights eight current industry trends, including hospitality companies (hotel brands, online travel agencies, and sharing economy companies), customer segments (Millennials and Chinese travelers), global circumstances (environmental factors, greater health consciousness focus, and technological advances), and methods of satisfying customers (customization). These overarching themes provide greater insight and perspective as the reader explores the industry in greater detail throughout this text.

RESOURCES

Internet Sites

In addition to referencing the citations at the end of this chapter, there are a variety of resources available to investigate industry trends, including:

Smartbrief—industry trends aggregator: http://www.smartbrief.com

Hospitality trends and in-depth reporting: http://www.skift.com

Wall Street Journal covers a breadth of hospitality trends: http://www.wsj.com

US National Restaurant Association website: http://www.restaurant.org/Home

American Hotel & Lodging Association website: http://ahla.com

World Travel and Tourism Council global data: http://www.wttc.org

Electronic library for the World Tourism Organization: http://www.e-unwto.org

For information about specific segments, using a search engine, such as Google (or Google Scholar for academic research), is often yields worthwhile results.

ENDNOTES

1. Shillingsaw, J. (2015, January 28). Survey says: millennials now drive leisure travel in U.S. *Travelpulse*. Retrieved from http://www.travelpulse.com/news/travel-agents/survey-says-millennials-now-drive-leisure-travel-in-us.html

2. McGuire, K. (2015, January 27). Top 10 global trends that will impact hospitality in 2015 [Web log comment]. Retrieved from http://blogs.sas.com/content/hospitality/2015/01/27/top-10-global-trends-that-will-impact-hospitality-in-2015/

3. Kressman, J. (2016, January 5). *Skift*. Retrieved from: http://skift.com/2016/01/05/millennial-travel-spending-is-all-about-selective-splurging/

4. Bagel, A. (2014, July 7). Study examines why Millennials choose loyalty programs. *Hotels*. Retrieved from: www.hotelsmag.com/Industry/News/Details/51885

5. McGuire, K. (2015, January 27). Top 10 global trends that will impact hospitality in 2015 [Web log comment]. Retrieved from http://blogs.sas.com/content/hospitality/2015/01/27/top-10-global-trends-that-will-impact-hospitality-in-2015/

6. Rosenbloom, S. (2015, March 17) Hotels for the next generation. *New York Times* Retrieved from http://www.nytimes.com/2015/03/22/travel/hotels-for-the-next-generation.html

7. Trejos, N. (2014, September 22). Marriott 'teleports' guests to Hawaii, London. *USA Today*. Retrieved from http://www.usatoday.com/story/dispatches/2014/09/22/marriott-hotels-virtual-travel-transporter/15904019/

8. Mandelbaum, A. (2015, November 10). Are virtual reality concierges coming? *Hotels*. Retrieved from http://www.hotelsmag.com/Industry/News/Details/62358

9. Ibid.

10. Foster, A. and Finkelstein, J. (2015). In hotels health and spas equals wealth. *Boston Hospitality Review* 3 (1). Retrieved from http://www.bu.edu/bhr/2015/02/01/in-hotels-health-and-spas-equals-wealth/

11. Luke, M. (2014, August 4). Health and wellness hotel trends, Even & Element. Hospitalitynet.org. Retrieved from http://www.hospitalitynet.org/news/4066420.html

12. Ruggia, J. (2015, October 22). Six senses unveils new "healthy" hotel lighting strategy, Travelpulse. Retrieved from http://www.travelpulse.com/news/hotels-and-resorts/six-senses-unveils-new-healthy-hotel-lighting-strategy.html

13. (2015). Guest experience: top trends to look for in 2015. Smartbrief media services report. Retrieved from http://www2.smartbrief.com/hosted/mkt1636/wsj_trends_final_opt.pdf

14. McKinlay, R. (2013, March 8). Westin teams up with New Balance for gear lending service. Retrieved from http://www.citmagazine.com/article/1173991/westin-teams-new-balance-gear-lending-service

15. (2015). Guest experience: top trends to look for in 2015. Smartbrief media services report. Retrieved from http://www2.smartbrief.com/hosted/mkt1636/wsj_trends_final_opt.pdf

16. Marriott.com (2014, September 8). Retrieved from http://news.marriott.com/2014/09/marriott-hotels-serves-up-a-fresh-approach-healthy-vending-machine-debuts-a-traveler-inspired-innova.html

17. "The Global Wellness Tourism Economy Report." Global Wellness Institute. Prepared by SRI International. October 2013. http://www.globalspaandwellnesssummit.org/images/stories/pdf/wellness_tourism_economy_exec_sum_final_10022013.pdf

18. Julia (2015, November 30). Uber + IHG = more rewarding rides [web post]. Retrieved from https://newsroom.uber.com

19. On demand worker. Silicon Valley Dictionary (2016). Retrieved from http://svdictionary.com/words/on-demand-worker

20. Weber, L. (2015, January 27). On demand workers: we are not robots. *Wall Street Journal*. Retrieved from http://www.wsj.com/articles/on-demand-workers-we-are-not-robots-1422406524

21. O'Brien, S. (2015. September 24). Uber isn't the only on-demand firm being sued. CNN Money website. Retrieved from http://money.cnn.com/2015/09/24/technology/lawsuit-grubhub-doordash-caviar/

22. Festa, J. (2015, May 22). 8 great alternatives to hotels. USA Today travel website. Retrieved from http://roadwarriorvoices.com/2015/05/22/hotel-alternatives/

23. Weed, J. (2015, May 12). Airbnb grows to a million rooms, and hotel rivals are quiet, for now. *New York Times*. Retrieved from http://www.nytimes.com/2015/05/12/business/airbnb-grows-to-a-million-rooms-and-hotel-rivals-are-quiet-for-now.html?_r=0

24. Demos, T. (2015, June 26). Airbnb raises $1.5 billion in one of largest private placements. *Wall Street Journal*. Retrieved from http://www.wsj.com/articles/airbnb-raises-1-5-billion-in-one-of-largest-private-placements-1435363506

25. Mudallal, Z. (2015, January 20). Airbnb will soon be booking more rooms than the world's largest hotel chains. *Quartz* Retrieved from http://qz.com/329735/airbnb-will-soon-be-booking-more-rooms-than-the-worlds-largest-hotel-chains/

26. McGuire, K. (2015, January 27). Top 10 global trends that will impact hospitality in 2015 [Web log comment]. Retrieved from http://blogs.sas.com/content/hospitality/2015/01/27/top-10-global-trends-that-will-impact-hospitality-in-2015/

27. (2015) United Nations conference on climate change. [website] Retrieved from http://www.cop21.gouv.fr/en/learn/what-is-cop21/

28. O'Keefe, K. (2015, March 3). China corruption crackdown deals Macau a rough hand. *Wall Street Journal* Retrieved from http://www.wsj.com/articles/china-corruption-crackdown-deals-macau-a-rough-hand-1425364603?cb=logged0.7779393738601357

29. McGuire, K. (2015, January 27). Top 10 global trends that will impact hospitality in 2015 [Web log comment]. Retrieved from http://blogs.sas.com/content/hospitality/2015/01/27/top-10-global-trends-that-will-impact-hospitality-in-2015/

30. Coming to a Beach Near You; Chinese Tourists. *The Economist* Apr 19 2014: 53–4.

31. Ibid.

32. Ibid.

33. (2015, November 19). The ten largest hotel companies by brand. HotelNewsNow website Retrieved from http://www.hotelnewsnow.com/Article/17129/The-10-largest-hotel-companies-by-room-count

34. Dev, C. S. (2015). Hotel brand conversions: What works and what doesn't. *Cornell Hospitality Report*, 15(21), 3–11.

35. Linton, H., & Kwortnik, R. J. (2015). The mobile revolution is here: are you ready? [Electronic article]. *Cornell Hospitality Reports*, 15(6), 6–18.

36. McGuire, K. (2015, January 27). Top 10 global trends that will impact hospitality in 2015 [Web log comment]. Retrieved from http://blogs.sas.com/content/hospitality/2015/01/27/top-10-global-trends-that-will-impact-hospitality-in-2015/

37. EbizMBA (2016, January). Top 15 most visited travel websites. Retrieved from http://www.ebizmba.com/articles/travel-websites.

38. Woodward, C. (20015, December 2). Kayak vets' travel startup, now called Lola, is building software for travel agents. *BetaBoston* Retrieved from: http://www.betaboston.com/news/2015/12/02/kayak-vets-travel-startup-now-called-lola-is-building-software-for-travel-agents/

39. Anderson, C. (2012). The impact of social media on lodging performance [Electronic article]. *Cornell Hospitality Reports*, 12(15), 6–11.

40. Phillips, D. (2015, Summer). Some science behind personalization. *Hospitality Upgrade*, 152.

REVIEW QUESTIONS

1. Why are Millennials an important demographic for the hospitality industry? Identify three Millennial subsets that companies can segment.

2. How are hotel companies embracing the trend towards healthier lifestyles?

3. Identify three areas where the sharing economy can affect the hospitality industry. Highlight one company that represents each area.

4. Using examples, explain five areas where the environment impacts the hospitality industry.

5. What evidence is there to support the claim that the Chinese tourism market is appealing?

6. What are three different methods by which independent hotels are joining branded hotel companies such as Marriott or Hilton?

7. Identify and explain three areas in which technology impacts the hospitality industry.

8. How can a hotel effectively customize a service? Research two examples in your location of hospitality companies that customize an experience for a target market.

© Kzenon/Shutterstock.com

CHAPTER 4

HOSPITALITY SERVICE EXCELLENCE

AUTHOR

Chris Woodruff, Lake Michigan College

LEARNING OBJECTIVES

- Explain the importance of stellar guest service in the hospitality industry.
- Describe the Service Circle for Hospitality and how these considerations must be followed.
- Explain the history of the pineapple as the international symbol of hospitality.
- List important personality and professional traits (soft skills) needed to be an excellent guest service provider.
- Understand how guest expectations should direct your levels of guest service.
- Recognize when service recovery is needed, what service recovery is, and skills needed to successfully implement for guest service excellence.

CHAPTER OUTLINE

Hospitality Service Fundamentals

History of the Pineapple

Who Is Involved In Guest Service?

Foundations of Service Excellence

Guest Service Soft Skills

The Service Circle Seven

Service Recovery

Service Quality Starts in Hospitality

The Pineapple Tie Guy

Summary

Back of house (BOH)

Front of house (FOH)

Hard skills

Hospitality guest service

Moments of truth

Nonverbal communication

Service excellence

Service recovery

Soft skills

Spirit of the pineapple

HOSPITALITY SERVICE FUNDAMENTALS

Before you can become a great guest service provider you must first understand how to give great guest service in the hospitality industry. Service is defined as work or assistance done for others as an occupation or business. But guest service in the hospitality industry is so much more than that. When you try to define hospitality guest service, words like greeting, warm welcome, generous, cordial, polite, nice, kindness, and welcoming guests should all come to mind. Because this is truly what a guest service leader does. **Hospitality guest service** involves welcoming complete strangers and in a very short time making them feel welcome and like they are a part of the family. In fact many hospitality companies have made this part of their marketing: when you dine or stay with them "you are family."

But guest service is more than just the act of being nice. It is also all about business and profits. When you look at our industry in general the service provided is the biggest and sometimes only way to differentiate between two businesses. A cheeseburger may taste the same from two different restaurants; so many times the guest will choose the restaurant that provides better guest service. And two hotel rooms may look exactly the same, so it is the service provided while the guest is there that may be their decision factor on where to stay.

HISTORY OF THE PINEAPPLE

The **pineapple** has served as the international symbol of hospitality for much of the history of time. It is believed that Christopher Columbus and his crew enjoyed this new fruit from Guadalupe. He then brought them back to share in Europe. In Colonial America families started putting pineapples on the table when entertaining guests. If the guests spent the night there would be pineapples put in the room, or carved on the bedposts or headboards. Also, early explorers brought pineapples back from journeys to the West Indies. They would put the pineapples at their doors or on their fence posts to give the public notice that they were home and weary travelers could stop in for a nice meal, lodging, and friendship. So

The pineapple is the international symbol of hospitality.

the pineapple has become the international symbol of hospitality, and it is the symbol of grace, friendliness, and warmth.

WHO IS INVOLVED IN GUEST SERVICE?

Let's just give the answer up front. And hopefully by now you understand that all staff members are involved in delivering great guest service. But let's look specifically at some of the major service providers.

Corporate Executives. You may wonder how the CEO of a major hotel company has influence on the guest service being delivered at a hotel in Stevensville, Michigan. Or how the VP of Guest Experience for a major restaurant company has an impact on the service of a restaurant in Stillwater, Oklahoma. But they do. The service attitude starts at the top of any organization and trickles down to all the other levels. If the corporation's practices or beliefs are focused around the guest then that shows all involved that guest service is a major foundation of that company.

Hospitality Managers. Just like corporate executives, top management at an individual hospitality property has an even greater impact on the guest service offered by the employees. If the manager

BOH employees should be able to provide guest service on a daily basis.

shows little regard for guest satisfaction, and shows through his or her actions that guest service is not important, then the employees will not have a guest service mentality either.

Line Level, Front of House (FOH) Employees. **Front of house (FOH)** employees are the most important part of providing great guest service as they are the front line staff who interact with your guests more than anyone else. The FOH staff needs to be trained in great guest service and be given the tools necessary to provide the service that your guests are looking for.

Line Level, Back of House (BOH) Employees. Although housekeepers, stewards, and other **back of house (BOH)** employees are not directly involved in guest service, they should be trained like they are! While their main job duties are not guest related, more and more they are being expected to answer questions from guests, and be able to handle guest complaints like any other staff member. While they are not traditionally guest service providers, they provide guest service on a daily basis.

FOUNDATIONS OF SERVICE EXCELLENCE

While we could write a whole book (and there are many!) on the traits of delivering great guest service, or **service excellence**, here are a few founding principles.

We Have Guests, Not Customers or Clients! While this may not seem like much of a difference, it is a huge step in understanding guest service. In our industry, we invite people into our business to either enjoy a nice meal that we have prepared for them or to provide a place for them to rest. These are the definitions of guests. So, with whatever you do to reference our "customers," make sure you understand that they are truly our guests.

"The Guest Is Always Right." While this is a common phrase in our industry, to better explain quality guest service let's look at guest service from another perspective. "The guest is not always right, but they are still always our guest." While this is just a little different wording, it is hugely different in the mindset of quality guest service.

Be Guest Focused in Everything You Do. Walking a mile in your guest's shoes may be a lot of walking! But treating them like you would want to be treated is a lot easier. Anticipate guest needs and wants, and try to meet those needs. Also think about what would happen if you were offered the same guest service as you are offering to your guests. Is it what you want? Is it fair? Is it the best solution? Answering these questions, and knowing how you would feel if it happened to you, are great teaching moments for delivering quality guest service.

What You Don't Say Says a Lot. **Nonverbal communications** say so much more than what you do say. Not using eye contact, rolling your eyes, putting your hands on your hips, crossing your arms, and many other nonverbal acts show that you do not care about the guest or helping meet their needs.

You Have Two Ears and One Mouth for a Reason! Another guest service mistake is that the guest service provider thinks they have to be fully in control from the start, and getting a solution quickly is the only way to succeed. And while a speedy solution is important, if you do not listen to the guest first, you will most likely never meet his or her true needs. Seek first to understand your guest's needs. Only then should you seek to be understood by the guests. You should listen twice as much as you talk.

Moments of truth are more than just the "first impression" a guest gets about your business. Such a moment may be the first impression a guest receives, but more importantly it is any time that a guest forms an opinion about your business. That is why it is so important to make sure every guest experience and every guest interaction is as good as you can make it!

Give Guests What They Want, Not What You Want.
A key point I tell someone who is interested in opening a restaurant is that they must have a menu of foods that other people like, not just what they like. The same holds true for guest service. Give your guests what they want, not what you want to give them. A trendy technology right now is to allow a guest to order a meal from a tablet device at the table. A server would not take the order, only bring the items after they are ordered. Is this good guest service? You may say no, but if you are providing guests with what they want, then you are. While we should never allow technology to take over, remember that providing the guests with what they want is the key.

A Very Frustrating Occurrence is the Rule of 10–1. It is known that if someone has a bad experience they will tell ten people. And if they have a great experience they will tell only one person. This is true across all fields, but it is especially true in hospitality. Great guest service is, and should be, expected in our industry. So keep this in mind. We do not give great service for the praise, and we know if we have given great guest service that is a reward in itself.

It Takes No More Time to be Hospitable. It actually takes less time to make a guest happy than it does to upset them. Also it is much easier to say "yes" than it is to say "no." Always try to say yes to your guests. While many find any reason to say no, to be a great guest service provider you should find every reason to "Say Yes to Your Guest!"

Yes, You Are Acting. Remember, whenever you are serving a guest you are an "actor" on a "stage." To paraphrase William Shakespeare, "All the hospitality businesses are a stage, and the employees merely players." You may be having a bad day, but you must not let that show to your guests. Remember even if they are the 500th person you have checked in that day, they are checking in for the first time. So you must give your 500th guest the same smile and hospitable attitude you gave the first guest.

It Makes the Job Better. If you are committed to offering great guest service to every guest every time, then the whole experience YOU have becomes better! When you provide great guest service you know you are doing a great job and that makes you want to keep doing it. Remember that in our industry, you influence every guest stay, every time. You can either make the guest's experience memorable, or something he or she would rather forget! Make sure you do the former.

GUEST SERVICE SOFT SKILLS

Soft skills are so important in the hospitality industry. Skills like checking a guest in or running a daily report are known as **hard skills** or the technical skills needed to do a job. And while these skills are very important, soft skills are just as, if not more, important.

Soft skills are the skills one possesses to better interact with other employees and your guests. These are much harder to teach, and to learn. But these are also the skills that will help you and your business stand out. Many soft skills that you possess or learn have a direct impact on guest satisfaction.

THE SERVICE CIRCLE SEVEN

These are seven steps to assuring you are providing the guest service that is needed and desired.

Know what your guests truly want

Determine Standards of Performance based on those needs

Train and develop all your staff to develop and teach those Standards of Performance

Monitor the service being offered to your guests

Offer service recovery if needed

Continually evaluate your service circle

Make changes as needed to keep current with guest needs

If you offer great guest service to every guest every time, the whole experience becomes better.

THE 12 SOFT SKILLS

Listening – You have heard many sayings about listening. "Seek first to understand, only then attempt to be understood." Or "People don't care how much you know, until they know how much you care." Or "You have two ears and one mouth for a reason. Listen twice as much as you talk!" These all say basically the same thing. Many times for stellar guest service, guests just want yowvu to listen to them and truly understand their situation.

Being Attentive – Not only understanding the problem, but also being able to understand what the guest truly is requesting.

Good Communication – Being very clear on what you can and cannot do for a guest is very important to avoid confusion and offer great guest service.

Flexibility and Creativity – Realizing that every guest is unique and that great guest service is not always the same for every guest. Being able to decide how to provide great guest service to that guest at that time.

Body Language – Nonverbal communication such as nodding in agreement, a look of true concern for your guests, not cutting the guest off, and fully listening to them are all ways you can tell your guests you care about them and their needs without saying a word!

Teamwork – No one works alone in the hospitality industry. Teamwork and being able to work in teams is vitally important to offering stellar guest service. Sometimes you cannot handle every guest need and being able to communicate to others what is needed is a great skill to have.

Empathy – Having empathy towards your guests, showing that you truly understand their needs, being emotionally connected to the guest, and truly wanting what they want builds trust that can last a very long time.

Patience – Although most guest service needs and concerns are not too involved the time and effort it may take to satisfy them may be much longer. Patience is a virtue especially in the hospitality industry.

Confidence – Confidence in yourself and your ability to assist a guest go a long way towards guest trust, and also makes guests confident that you will take care of their needs.

Decision Making – "Thinking on your feet" is a skill that is so important in the hospitality industry. And it also a skill that can help with solving guest concerns.

Positive Attitude – A "can-do" attitude shows a guest that you are on their side and want to help them however you can and helps smooth out any bumps that may occur on the road to a positive guest experience.

Sense of Humor – Having a sense of humor can help resolve many guest servicev issues. Humor shows you have a positive attitude and can help lighten the interaction to put the guest at ease that you will find a solution.

SERVICE RECOVERY

No matter how hard you try to work at quality guest service, some guests will not feel they have been offered exceptional guest service. And while sometimes it is not your fault, or may not even be true, the guest still feels they have been wronged and seeks some sort of satisfaction. As mentioned above your guest may not always be right, but they are still always your guest. Having this attitude sets a positive outlook on service recovery. Service recovery is the action taken after a service failure to correct the situation and to try to save that guest for future business. It is weird to think, but you should be thanking a guest who complains about their service failure because they are giving you a chance to make up for it and keep them as a guest. This initial positive attitude in seeing a problem as an opportunity goes a long way towards guest satisfaction. Just as there are soft skills needed for exceptional guest service, there are also certain ones needed for successful service recovery.

SERVICE QUALITY STARTS IN HOSPITALITY

We are fortunate to have two (while there are many more) companies in the hospitality industry that are world-renowned for their guest service, the Ritz

THE FIVE SERVICE RECOVERY STEPS

Quick Response — The more time that a guest spends feeling wronged without a resolution the more frustrated they become. Treat every service failure as a priority. Treat every guest like they are following you around waiting for an answer. If this person was waiting and heard all the things you did, and didn't do, to help with their situation it may make them more upset. Delays in communication include not sending an e-mail and not returning a phone call, and both inactions send the same message. But if the guest only had to stand next to you for a very short time it shows them you are serious about their satisfaction and that they are a priority to you. Returning communication promptly to a guest sends the same positive message.

Take Ownership — Getting past the initial "That wasn't my fault," or "That's not my job" attitude is key to starting down the road to service recovery. If you get the complaint, take ownership of the situation. Do not get defensive or try to blame the guest or tell them they are wrong. Tell them you are truly sorry for the situation, and will do whatever it takes to resolve the situation.

Solve the Problem — As mentioned before, the ability to think on your feet and offer a solution to a guest service situation is a vital part of service recovery. Offer a solution that will make the guest feel comfortable. Employees who are empowered to make these decisions will have more control of handling the situation, which will then make the service recovery quicker and more meaningful. The same solution is not the same for every guest, so make sure the solution you offer is what the guest is truly seeking.

Follow Through — Treat the guest as if they are still following you around until you follow up with them to make sure the solution offered has truly resolved the situation. You may find out there is more follow up needed, or it may be the end of the service recovery and you have saved this guest's experience. Many times how you handle a situation determines if that guest will return. So while service failure is not something you ever hope to have, how quickly and effectively you handle the service recovery can go a long way.

Communicate and Document — Many times if one guest has a complaint, they are not the only one. They are just the only one who complained. After the service recovery is handled to the guest's satisfaction, keep an internal record of the guest service failure, how the situation was resolved, and any other notes about the situation. This can help to show patterns of service failure to correct, to avoid the same service failure down the road, and can eliminate the problem all together.

Carlton Hotel Company and the Disney Company. Guest service best practices in the hospitality industry are easily transferrable to other industries that are looking to improve their guest service. Other industries such as healthcare and retail look to the hospitality industry for their guest service training when trying to improve their customer experience.

Not everyone is "cut out" to be in the hospitality industry. It is not an easy industry to be in and you must have the right attitude for it. The hospitality industry is very competitive and employers are looking for people who can not only do the technical tasks or hard skills of checking people in or taking a food order, but also they are looking more than ever for people who know how to enhance the guest experience with their high commitment to guest service. If you want to be successful in the hospitality industry, you must first be able to provide great world class guest service.

THE PINEAPPLE TIE GUY

Chris Woodruff is the Program Chair for the Hospitality Program at Lake Michigan College in Benton Harbor, Michigan. He is known to his students and many others in the hospitality industry as "The Pineapple Tie Guy!" Every tie he wears in the classroom or to industry events and conferences has pineapples on it. Why does he do this?

"Well, it started out just for my students. I wore pineapple ties to remind the students about the importance of guest service in our industry and that it is a key component to being successful in our industry. And now I wear them to industry events and people know to look to make sure they are on the tie! It is a fun way to remind everyone in our industry that hospitality is what separates us from all other industries, and providing great exceptional world class service to every guest every time is what will make you successful in our industry!"

SUMMARY

Guest service is vital to the success of any hospitality business. Knowing how to provide outstanding guest service will make you that much more valuable to potential employers. But knowing what skills are important to guest satisfaction is something that must be learned. Understanding the Service Circle Seven can help to make sure you are providing excellent service, as well as remembering the spirit of the pineapple. Service recovery is also important as it can help "save" a guest who did not have a great experience, and it is also your chance to keep them as a future guest. Guest service is what separates your business from others and makes every day of your time in the hospitality industry more rewarding.

RESOURCES

Internet Sites

Lake Michigan College Hospitality Management: www.lakemichigancollege.edu/hospitality

The Disney Company: www.disney.com

The Ritz Carlton Hotel Company: www.ritzcarlton.com

William Shakespeare All the World's A Stage: www.artofeurope.com/shakespeare/sha9.htm

CASE STUDY

You are the general manager of the largest hotel in the area. It is a full service hotel with 250 rooms, a restaurant, and conference facilities. No other hotel in the area has more than 50 rooms, nor are any of your competitors full service. You find out that a new 150-room property is being built right down the street from you and will be open in 6 months. You are worried that the new hotel will take away your business since it will be a newer hotel.

1. What can you do in terms of guest service to make sure your guests do not go to the new hotel?

2. Why is guest service so important in this case?

Name: _____ Date: _____

1. What are front of house and back of house in the hospitality industry?

2. What are some nonverbal communications? Why are they so important?

3. What is service recovery in terms of providing great guest service?

4. Who determines if the quality of guest service you provide is good or bad?

5. What are some important traits you need to have in order to be successful in the hospitality industry?

6. What is a moment of truth?

7. List some traits that you feel make you a great provider of guest service.

8. Why is the pineapple known as the symbol of hospitality?

9. What are three soft skills needed to provide exceptional guest service?

10. Does a guest service experience have to be face to face with a guest? Why or why not?

11. What does it mean when we say you are always on stage in a hospitality business?

12. Why is your attitude so important in providing quality guest service?

© Ken Wolter/Shutterstock.com

CHAPTER 5

INDUSTRY TRADE ASSOCIATIONS AND RATING SERVICES

AUTHORS

Hsiangting Shatina Chen, University of Alabama
Kimberly S. Severt, University of Alabama

LEARNING OBJECTIVES

- Understand the functions and services provided by industry associations.
- Become familiar with major industry associations in different segments of the hospitality industry.
- Know how hotel and restaurant rating systems are constructed and why rating services matter in the hospitality industry.

CHAPTER OUTLINE

What is an Industry Association?

Types of Association Meetings

Functions and Services Provided by Industry Associations

    Industry Resources

    Education

    Research

    Networking

    Job Resources

Associations in the Hospitality Industry

Rating Systems in the Hospitality Industry

Online Reviews

Summary

© Kendall Hunt Publishing Co.

KEY TERMS

Advocacy
Annual convention
Associations
Chapter meetings
Networking
Online reviews
Rating systems
Regional meetings
Word-of-mouth

WHAT IS AN INDUSTRY ASSOCIATION?

Industry **associations**, also as known as trade associations, are professional organizations that enable their members to accomplish a common purpose, provide networking opportunities, and support the industry growth. Many industry associations are non-profit organizations and consist of active members from a particular profession. For example, the Society of Human Resource Management (SHRM) is a professional human resource association that provides education, research, and business networking for global human resource professionals. With more than 275,000 members in 160 countries around the world, SHRM attracts anyone who is interested or involved in the field of human resource management.

There are numerous types of industry associations in the United States that can be valuable for personal and career development, and most have bylaws that govern the membership, board of officers, and other staff in the organization. Typically, members pay annual dues to associations to govern internal operations and offer services. Memberships in an industry association can vary in terms of different levels; some memberships can be pricey. However, considering all the services and opportunities provided by the organization, your career could greatly benefit in the long term from such an investment. In addition, many associations provide reduced rates for student members and chapters. By joining with a student membership, you can gain valuable information, educational resources, and networking from the industry. In the following sections, we will discuss the functions and benefits provided by an industry association.

TYPES OF ASSOCIATION MEETINGS

To meet the needs of association members, there are three types of meetings: chapter, regional, and annual. Each of these meetings serves a different purpose for both the association and its members. **Chapter meetings** provide an intimate environment for members to network with one another. These meetings are smaller and foster a sense of community that offers members the opportunity to create a support structure and resource center to aid in their everyday professional careers.

Many annual association meetings allow members to earn continuing education credits.

By contrast, **regional meetings** are larger in scope and include a number of chapter groups. Regional meetings are often a shorter distance for members than the annual meeting, thus they provide an excellent alternative for members who cannot afford the additional cost to attend the annual meeting. Examples of these meetings include: educational presentations, special speakers, networking, and community service opportunities.

Annual conventions or annual association meetings provide members the ability to earn continuing education credits for industry certifications and networking on a national and international scale. According to Astroff and Abbey (2006), associations earn approximately 34% of their annual income from the association's annual conference and exhibition. Since membership in associations is voluntary, attracting new members and retaining current membership by providing their desired benefits is a primary goal for associations. A recent study reported that the most important reason for attending a chapter, regional, or annual meeting was the relevance of the program.[1] This fact highlights the importance of knowing members' needs and expectations for each type of meeting.

FUNCTIONS AND SERVICES PROVIDED BY INDUSTRY ASSOCIATIONS

Industry associations provide many functions and services that benefit their members. Essentially, these functions and services can be categorized into five aspects: industry resources, education, research, networking, and job resources.

INDUSTRY RESOURCES

Most industry associations provide the depth and breadth of industry resources and tools that professionals will need for their jobs. For instance, the National Restaurant Association (NRA) offers relevant information about restaurant operation and management, marketing and sales techniques, food and nutrition information, and workforce management. On the NRA website, you can find a variety of tools and guides that assist restaurant and foodservice professionals in gaining managerial perspectives and increasing business profitability. Some industry associations may provide information related to industry standards and regulations, code of ethics, and how-to toolkits for members who are seeking consultant services. In addition, since the industry regulations and practices may be changed periodically, many industry associations provide updates and clarification for new regulations and practices.

Industry associations also play an important role in **advocacy**—the act or process of influencing public policy in a direction favorable and supportive to the industry. These advocacy issues include labor and workforce laws, tax reform, union organizing, sustainability practices, and other legislative and lobbying subjects. A great example is the American Hotel & Lodging Association (AH&LA) Government Affairs Department. AH&LA, a national association that represents all stakeholders in the lodging industry, also provides members with national advocacy on Capitol Hill to outline legislative priorities and promote prosperity for the lodging industry (see AH&LA website).

EDUCATION

The second benefit of industry associations is that they provide enormous education opportunities and professional development for their members. These educational programs include professional certifications, workforce training, distance learning, workshops, webcasts, and seminars. For example, the American Hotel & Lodging Educational Institute (AH&LEI) offers certification workshops and examinations for the Certification in Hotel Industry Analytics (CHIA) and the Certified Hospitality Administrator (CHA). AH&LEI also has different training programs and learning materials for various positions in hotels from line employees and supervisors to executives. Association members can access the information center on its website, receive discounts on ordering learning materials, and get certifications for their particular profession. The Convention Industry Council (CIC) is an industry association for meeting professionals that provides the Certified Meeting Planner (CMP) program, which is an international standard representing knowledge, excellence, and professionalism in the meeting and event industry. Meeting professionals who seek the qualifications and designations will apply for the CMP exams through the CIC. Many meeting professionals will also join the Professional Convention Management Association (PCMA), which provides CMP study guides, exam preparation, and practice tests for their members to prepare for the CMP certification.

Aside from educational materials, many associations include an education foundation and offer a wide range of scholarship opportunities. These scholarships may be offered to students or working professionals who want to advance their skills and gain more industry knowledge. AH&LA, NRA, and some local hospitality associations consist of educational foundations and offer scholarship opportunities to students who want to advance their education and career in the hospitality industry.

RESEARCH

Being industry professionals, it is important to understand current issues and trends that will impact the hospitality industry. What direction will the hostility business take? How will economic policies and social issues reshape the business environment? How has consumer behavior been changed over time, and how can we offer better products and services? Industry professionals would like to stay informed on these issues that may affect their jobs and companies in the future. Therefore, one important function of industry associations is to consolidate updated news and trends for their members. Some associations will deliver weekly e-newsletters that provide timely information; others may release annual whitepapers and benchmark reports that address particular issues. Industry associations often publish research, statistics, and industry facts for professionals to enhance their knowledge and skills as well as to develop strategic planning for their organizations.

Members of industry associations have the opportunity to build connections through meetings and events.

NETWORKING

Most associations provide great networking opportunities for members through hosted events, conferences, tradeshows, and annual conventions. These meetings provide a tremendous opportunity to meet other people in the industry. For instance, the National Restaurant Association hosts the largest annual foodservice tradeshow in the United States. Every year, more than 2,000 foodservices companies and 42,000 attendees from different countries join this food show. Both personal connections and business relationships can be built through the association's network and gathering events. As a result, the major function of an industry association is to provide a networking platform and directory to share ideas and knowledge with others, and also to build connections in the industry.

JOB RESOURCES

As mentioned earlier, industry associations provide tremendous opportunities to help industry professionals advance their careers. The final important function of industry associations is to offer members job resources and a career portal. Both job seekers and recruiters can access associations' websites to browse and search employment opportunities. Members can post their résumés, connect to potential employers, and receive job match notifications from the associations. As a student, you should utilize these job resources from industry associations and start building your résumé to catch the attention of hospitality companies.

ASSOCIATIONS IN THE HOSPITALITY INDUSTRY

There are numerous hospitality and tourism associations that support the growth and development of the hospitality industry. This growth and development is achieved by the opportunities for industry professionals to improve their knowledge of industry related issues, update skills needed to stay competitive, and learn from other professionals with related interests. Hospitality associations have played a vital role in implementing code of conduct standards and advocating industry initiatives such as labor issues, sustainable practices, and legislative matters.

Even though the hospitality industry encompasses a wide array of professional career opportunities, there are multiple associations that support each of these professions as indicated in Table 5.1. Whether you are interested in food and beverage, lodging, exhibitions, marketing, finance, or meetings and events, there's an association that will help you maximize your full potential.

RATING SYSTEMS IN THE HOSPITALITY INDUSTRY

Industry associations often set standards, provide guidelines, and establish certifications for professionals in the hospitality industry. Similarly, some organizations set standards to evaluate hotel and restaurant facilities, products, and services. The **rating systems** are designed to identify hotel and restaurant business segments based upon the standards and guidelines. Not only are the rating systems indicators for excellence in hospitality, they also provide information for travelers on basic facilities and services that can be expected.

There are many different rating systems used by various organizations in the world. A five-star hotel in New York City may be different form a five-star hotel in New Delhi, India. In the United States, the most common rating systems used in the hospitality industry are the American Automobile Association (AAA) and the Forbes Travel Guide. The AAA and Forbes Travel Guide have professionally trained inspectors who evaluate the worldwide hospitality

Table 5.1 Hospitality and Tourism Related Associations

	Association	Acronym
Food & Beverage	National Restaurant Association	NRA
	The National Association of College University Food Services	NACUFS
	Association of Nutrition and Foodservice Professionals	ANFP
	National Association for Catering and Events	NACE
	American Beverage Association	ABA
Lodging	American Hotel and Lodging Association	AH&LA
	Hospitality Sales and Marketing Association International	HSMAI
	Hospitality Financial and Technology Professionals	HFTP
Tourism	U.S. Travel Association	USTA
	Global Business Travel Association	GBTA
	American Society of Travel Agents	ASTA
	National Tour Association	NTA
Meetings & Events	Meeting Professionals International	MPI
	Professional Convention Management Association	PCMA
	International Special Events Society	ISES
	Convention Industry Council	CIC
	International Association of Exhibitions and Events	IAEE
	Event Service Professionals Association	ESPA
	Society of Incentive Travel Executives	SITE
	Destination Marketing Association International	DMAI
	American Society of Association Executives	ASAE

facilities and services and give their recommendations and feedback. The AAA uses a diamond rating system; the five diamonds award is the highest award, which symbolizes that the property has outstanding attributes and an impeccable standard of excellence. Similarly, Forbes Travel Guide uses the five-star standard to distinguish superior quality and guest experience. Since 1958, Forbes Travel Guide has used the five-star rating system, using over 500 individual criteria, to determine a global benchmark for hotels, restaurants, spas, and travel destinations.

ONLINE REVIEWS

With the continued growth of social media platforms and usage of technology, many travelers rely on online customer reviews instead of conventional hospitality rating systems.[2] TripAdvisor, Yelp.com, and Urbanspoon.com are user-generated content websites that provide information for consumers. In addition, some online travel agencies, such as Hotels.com, Expedia, and others, integrate travelers' reviews

Customer review sites, such as Yelp.com, provide information to consumers and help them make decisions.

of hotels. Since online travel booking has increased rapidly in recent years, travelers tend to read online reviews before making a hotel or restaurant reservation. According to the research, more than 80% of travelers will read at least 6 to 12 reviews on social media sites before making a decision, and 53% of travelers will not book a hotel that does not contain reviews from other travelers.[3] Another survey by TrustYou indicated that travelers are 3.9 times more likely to choose a hotel with higher review scores when the prices are the same.[4]

In the hospitality industry, the influence of word-of-mouth (WOM) is the most important information source for consumers when they are making a purchase decision. Outstanding experiences are the most persuasive and powerful strategies to market a company's products and services. Since the development of the Internet, social media and online platforms have shared information and enabled word-of-mouth effects to reach millions of prospective customers. As a result, online reviews have been viewed as an electronic word-of-mouth (eWOM), which plays an essential part of hospitality sales and marketing.[5] eWOMs not only possess a substantial amount of information and recommendations, but also provide prompt exchanges of communication among worldwide consumers.

While the conventional rating systems have experienced inspectors who provide an objective assessment by utilizing certain standards, online reviews are constructed by consumers' subjective experiences and opinions. Also, a five-star hotel may have a three-star customer recommendation on a social media site, which may create confusion for travelers. Thus, the issue of using customers' feedback on social media platforms is controversial, and it is sometimes difficult to ensure unbiased reviews.[6] However, managing online reviews is as important as keeping the quality standard in rating systems. More and more hospitality companies have begun focusing on managing online reviews, such as providing rapid responses to handle customer complaints, generating conversations and interactions with customers on social media sites, and sharing positive customer experiences with others. Maintaining a positive online reputation has shown a significant effect on business sales; it has become a vital part of marketing to drive demand and distribution. In the service-driven industry, consumers like their voices to be heard and to be given timely responses from hospitality companies.

SUMMARY

Understanding the function and services provided by industry associations and getting involved with the associations will be very beneficial for your education and career development. There are three types of association meetings: chapter, regional, and annual convention. The basic functions and services provided by industry associations include five aspects: industry resources, education, research, networking, and job resources. There are many different associations in the hospitality industry. Depending on your profession, you should consider joining one or a few industry associations in order to build up your professional networks.

The rating systems in the hospitality industry are designed for identifying hotels and restaurants business segments based upon standards and guidelines. The traditional rating systems for U.S. lodging are the American Automobile Association (AAA) and Forbes Travel Guide. Online reviews are important because they are generated by customers in real time and spread rapidly and widely. Thus, hospitality business should carefully maintain their reviews through social media platforms.

RESOURCES

Internet Sites

National Restaurant Association:
http://www.restaurant.org/

The National Association of College University Food Services: https://www.nacufs.org/

Association of Nutrition and Foodservice Professionals: http://www.anfponline.org/

National Association for Catering and Events: http://www.nace.net/

American Beverage Association:
http://www.ameribev.org/

American Hotel and Lodging Association:
http://www.ahla.com/

Hospitality Sales and Marketing Association International: http://www.hsmai.org/

Hospitality Financial and Technology Professionals: http://www.hftp.org/

U.S. Travel Association:
https://www.ustravel.org/

Global Business Travel Association:
http://www.gbta.org/Pages/default.aspx

American Society of Travel Agents:
http://www.asta.org/

National Tour Association:
http://www.ntaonline.com/

Meeting Professionals International:
http://www.mpiweb.org/

Professional Convention Management Association: http://www.pcma.org/

International Special Events Society:
http://www.ises.com/

Convention Industry Council:
http://www.conventionindustry.org/

International Association of Exhibitions and Events: http://www.iaee.com/

Event Service Professionals Association:
http://www.espaonline.org/

Society of Incentive Travel Executives:
http://www.siteglobal.com/

Destination Marketing Association International:
http://www.destinationmarketing.org/

American Society of Association Executives:
http://www.asaecenter.org/

ENDNOTES

1. Fjelstul, J., Severt, K. & Breiter, D. (2010). Building association attendance: Difference between chapter, regional and annual meetings from the perception of the association members. *Event Management*, 14, pp183–192.

2. Hensens, W. (2015). The future of hotel rating. *Journal of Tourism Futures*, 1(1), 69–73.

3. Tnooz. (2014). Vast majority of TripAdvisor users read at least 6–12 reviews before choosing hotel. Retrieved from http://www.tnooz.com/article/ tripadvisor-online-review-insights-phocuswright-study/.

4. Siahaan, R. (2015). Online Booking Trends to watch for 2015. Retrieved from http://www.pelicansolution.com/news/online-booking-trends-to-watch-for-in-2015.aspx

5. Litvin, S. W., Goldsmith, R. E., & Pan, B. (2008). Electronic word-of-mouth in hospitality and tourism management. *Tourism Management*, 29(3), 458–468.

6. Hensens, W. (2015). The future of hotel rating. *Journal of Tourism Futures*, 1(1), 69–73.

REFERENCES

Astroff, M. & Abbey, J. (2006). *Convention Sales and Services* (7th ed.) Las Vegas, NV: Waterbury Press.

Fjelstul, J., Severt, K. & Breiter, D. (2010). Building association attendance: Difference between chapter, regional and annual meetings from the perception of the association members. *Event Management*, 14, pp183–192.

Hensens, W. (2015). The future of hotel rating. *Journal of Tourism Futures*, 1(1), 69–73.

Litvin, S. W., Goldsmith, R. E., & Pan, B. (2008). Electronic word-of-mouth in hospitality and tourism management. *Tourism Management*, 29(3), 458–468.

Siahaan, R. (2015). Online Booking Trends to watch for 2015. Retrieved from http://www.pelicansolution.com/news/online-booking-trends-to-watch-for-in-2015.aspx

Tnooz. (2014). Vast majority of TripAdvisor users read at least 6–12 reviews before choosing hotel. Retrieved from http://www.tnooz.com/article/ tripadvisor-online-review-insights-phocuswright-study/.

REVIEW QUESTIONS

1. Explain the functions and services associations provide in varied industries and give an example.

2. How has social media changed the way people seek reviews for hospitality products and services?

3. Why do people join an association, and how can they expect to benefit from being a member?

4. Explain the importance of networking with other members of an association.

5. Explain the difference between chapter, regional, and annual association meetings.

© Anna Jedynak/Shutterstock.com

PART 2

HOSPITALITY COMPANIES

© August_0802/Shutterstock.com

CHAPTER *6*

ENTREPRENEURIAL AND INDEPENDENT OPERATIONS

AUTHOR	*Julene Boger, Northern Arizona University*
LEARNING OBJECTIVES	• Enumerate the advantages of being an entrepreneur.
	• Illustrate the traits and skills represented by successful entrepreneurs.
	• Discuss the facets of independent hotel and restaurant operations.
	• Explain how an independent foodservice operation can be different.
CHAPTER OUTLINE	Entrepreneurship in Hospitality
	Entrepreneurial Traits
	Advantages of Hospitality Entrepreneurship
	Challenges of an Independent Hospitality Business
	Independent Foodservice Establishments
	Independent Lodging Properties
	Eco Hotels/Sustainability
	Summary

KEY TERMS		
	Bed and Breakfast (B&B)	Entrepreneur
	Boutique hotels	Franchise
	Bureau (CVB)	Independent operations
	Convention and Visitor	Seasonal properties
	Eco lodges/hotels	Single unit operations

© *Kendall Hunt Publishing Co.*

ENTREPRENEURSHIP IN HOSPITALITY

You like making decisions; you are flexible, resilient, persistent, and independent: you may be an entrepreneur. The hospitality industry offers many opportunities for entrepreneurs to start and own their own businesses: from restaurants, to bed and breakfasts, inns, hotels, resorts, and others. In fact, more than 7 out of 10 restaurants are independent facilities, and 93% of foodservice locations have fewer than 50 employees.[1] While the foodservice industry is often the way entrepreneurs get started, after all, many entrepreneurs start out selling lemonade as a child, the lodging industry as well as other hospitality-related fields hold many opportunities for the budding entrepreneur. Starting and owning your own hospitality business can be rewarding both personally and financially. It offers many advantages. For starters, you are your own boss. There is no corporate entity telling you how, why, and what to do. You are the decision maker with all of the joys and frustrations that entrepreneurship entails. One misconception about entrepreneurship is that if you are the boss, you can set your own hours and do only what you want to do. In the hospitality industry the customer, or as we prefer to say, the guest, is the focus of our business and therefore the boss!

ENTREPRENEURIAL TRAITS

What is an entrepreneur? This may be a new word to you, as you may be more familiar with the term owner. According to the Merriam-Webster Dictionary, an **entrepreneur** is "one who organizes, manages, and assumes the risks of a business or enterprise."[2] To be honest with you, that sounds like a generic description of any manager accompanied by the daunting word risk. While there is risk involved with any business, in the case of an entrepreneur, it means that they are ultimately responsible for all of the decision making. It is their business.

Entrepreneurs are different from managers in that they often run the business on a day-to-day basis, like a manager, but they are also the driving force and idea generator. They come up with the concept for the business and are responsible for making things work. It can be very exciting, but it requires planning, research, and hard work. One trait that sets successful entrepreneurs apart from other business people is that they have a driving passion for their business. It is sometimes said that you should own your own business when you can think of nothing else…now don't throw caution to the wind, it does take more than thinking to get a business up and running. It takes a good idea, preferably a good location, especially in the hospitality business, and a good team of people surrounding you. Not only should an entrepreneur be passionate about their business, they also need to be self-motivated and able to motivate others. There will be no one telling you what and how to structure, organize, and run your business; therefore, you need sufficient drive to make things happen. If you prefer to lead rather than follow, this may be the path for you.

Another trait of entrepreneurs is that they exude confidence and a willingness to learn from others. Business founders are flexible and confident that they can make the right decisions to make their business profitable. Entrepreneurs are not afraid of failure. Failure, it is said, is very often the best teacher. Sometimes they need to veer off the pathway intended for the business, but ultimately they are forging ahead to make a viable, successful business. For example, Sue wanted to start a bakery because she loved to bake muffins, cookies, brownies, and cupcakes, and everyone said she was a superb baker. But after some research she found out that her area would not support a bakery of this type, so she expanded her concept to include a deli, where she serves soup, salads, sandwiches, and all of the bakery treats she enjoys making. Sue is still following her dream; she just needed to be flexible and listen to the customer to find a way to be successful.

According to Eric Wagner in a *Forbes* magazine article, the "Seven Traits of Incredibly Successful Entrepreneurs,"[3] entrepreneurs:

1. Have abounding curiosity.
2. Are bursting with creativity.
3. Have clarity of vision.
4. Have a great ability to communicate.
5. Have leadership acumen.
6. Love risk and taking action.
7. Are tenacious beyond belief.

To make a business a success, the original plan for it may need to be modified along the way.

If you have many of the above traits and love serving the guest, my guess is that you would be a great entrepreneur.

Sir Richard Branson, founder of the Virgin Group, shared with Forbes magazine some advice for new entrepreneurs: "Don't be Afraid of Fear."[4] Embrace the fear of the unknown, use the adrenaline created by that fear, surround yourself with positive people, and don't be afraid to ask for advice and help.

ADVANTAGES OF HOSPITALITY ENTREPRENEURSHIP

How does being an entrepreneur translate to the world of hospitality? As you will continue to learn, hospitality is a huge umbrella with many different businesses underneath. However, for our purposes we will just focus on the Lodging and Foodservice industries. Why would you want to start a business in this field? It is often a field where people have experience. According to the *National Restaurant Association (NRA) Factbook* "one half of all adults have worked in the restaurant industry at some point in their lives."[5] Because the hospitality industry has many entry-level jobs, it is often an area in which people have experience, and when starting a business it is best that you have previously worked in that type of business, otherwise you wouldn't know where to start. There are choices to make when starting a hospitality business. Do you want to make all of the decisions yourself and open an independent business or are you interested in buying into a proven way of doing business by buying a **franchise**? Let's suppose you choose not to follow the franchise path and

prefer to start your own business and develop it from the ground up; the biggest advantage is the ability to use your creativity to make it unique.

What is an independent business? For the purposes of this chapter it means no brand affiliation. Rather than being a part of a larger organization like a McDonald's, Applebee's, or Holiday Inn, the **independent operation** would not be a part of any chain of businesses. The business would be your own ideas done your way; you would not be dependent on any corporate philosophies or mandates when running the business. The decision making would be all yours and the business could be a true reflection of your curiosity and creativity. Not all independent businesses are entrepreneurial in nature. Entrepreneurial ventures just mean that the person that owns the business runs the business, whereas you can have an independent business owned and managed by different people or different groups of people.[6]

While being the final decision maker on all levels is highly satisfying to the entrepreneur, it does provide a downside and that is the lack of brand affiliation. In our highly branded world, people look forward to knowing what they can expect. Chains spend much time determining standards and guidelines to ensure the guest experience is the same no matter which property the guest experiences. In many cases, customers have a lasting relationship with a brand. Do you have a brand of sports shoes that you always buy? What about a brand of soft drink that you cannot live without? We all have brands to which we are loyal because we know what to expect. When you go to a McDonald's or Applebee's you know the type of food and service they offer, and their menu is pretty much

When you go into any Applebee's, you have a pretty good idea what to expect of the food and the service.

the same no matter where you go. In today's world this is an advantage because brands help consumers associate the value of the product with their recognition of the brand name. The name represents the features, benefits, and quality of the product being purchased.

CHALLENGES OF AN INDEPENDENT HOSPITALITY BUSINESS

The advantages of independence are many, but in the hospitality field there are also challenges to being an independent property. The challenges are a lack of a widely recognized brand name, chain marketing, national reservation system, and national frequent guest programs. Even though your facility may not have a brand name, your name may have strong brand appeal locally, or your region may be marketed by a chamber of commerce or a **Convention and Visitor's Bureau (CVB)**, letting people know you are there. Due to improvements in technology, reservation systems, web pages, social media, and many other services found only with chain affiliation in the past are now available and can be found at a reasonable fee even for the small independent business. No longer does a hotel property need to be a part of a chain for the guests to find them on the web or find their toll free number; in fact, an independent website can be an advantage for hotels where all of the rooms are unique. These properties can have their own website with pictures of each of their distinctive rooms to help prospective guests make better choices regarding where they would like to stay. This would not be as easy to accomplish with a chain website.

INDEPENDENT FOODSERVICE ESTABLISHMENTS

Nearly one in 10 working Americans, nearly 14 million people in 2015, are employed in the restaurant industry. More than 90 percent of restaurants have fewer than 50 employees with 70 percent of restaurants being single-unit restaurants.[7] The restaurant industry employs nearly 10 percent of the entire U.S. workforce, giving you an idea of the size and scope of the industry.[8] Foodservice businesses may consist of street vendors, with only one employee, or may be large operations with multiple employees. The restaurant industry is very entrepreneurial with

a predominance of businesses being independent. Eighty percent of employees feel the restaurant business is an area, regardless of background, that would allow an individual to start their own business.[9] This speaks to the localization and the creativity characterized by the foodservice industry. Guests like to go to local establishments that cater to their specific needs, and an independent facility can be more flexible. In today's world, the public is very interested in the local food trends, obtaining ingredients from local farmers, creativity with local ingredients, and the knowledge of where their food is coming from. Independent operators seem to be leading this movement.

The advantages of owning and running your own foodservice establishment are endless, but the most important part of the equation is the creativity. Chain operations dictate the menu, décor, operational methods, and of course the name. Being an independent restaurateur can validate your need for expression and freedom by adding value to the guest experience. A culmination of hospitality experiences will ultimately provide you with a platform from which to launch your own hospitality entity.

INDEPENDENT LODGING PROPERTIES

According to InterContinental Hotels Group (IHG), 53 percent of total room supply (globally) is in the branded hotels. This number is a result of benchmarking with properties of similar size and market segment of IHG. The four companies included with IHG are Starwood, Marriott, Hilton, and Accor.[10] In the U.S., the number of independent/unbranded hotels is 30 percent of industry supply.

Defining "independent" can be very difficult. Some think of it only as having the entrepreneurial approach with an independent mindset. Others think of it as the character of the property itself (architecture) and incorporate local flair in guestroom furnishings, décor, and food. These aspects provide the guest with a memorable experience rather than the standard "one size fits all" experience of the branded property.

Independent hotels are able to operate without the costs and the constraints of a franchise or branded property. Today's independent lodging operators can compare to the artisan cheesemakers, third wave coffee experts, and artisan brewmasters in our industry. The independent owner is able to set their own standard for the property; this includes the style of customer service extended to guests.

Independent **seasonal properties** are found in tourist destinations that are seasonal in nature. They always fill during the busy season and are often closed in the off-season. Chains prefer year-round properties. An advantage of chain affiliation, besides their brand name, is their reservation system. In the case of an independent, highly seasonal location or resort, a reservation system is likely to bring more business than the hotel can handle during the busy season, and the customer must pay for reservation services at the independent property without the independent property benefitting from those booking fees. This does not describe all independent lodging properties, but it is true of many of the independent properties. Cape Cod, Massachusetts, and The Dells and Door County, Wisconsin, are examples of localities that predominately support independent seasonal properties. These hotels rely on their desirable location and strong local marketing agencies to make travelers aware of their existence. These locations are typically marketed through print channels by local chambers of commerce and CVBs.

There are also properties that have extended their seasons to include memorable events during the off-season, such as large chef events/competitions. A number of these properties are actually large, working ranches in some of the most beautiful areas of the United States. Examples include Paw's Up Resort (rated very high in the luxury segment), Triple Creek Ranch, and Rock Creek Ranch and Resort. All three of these properties are working ranches in Montana that share the ranch lifestyle with visitors. These properties are very popular with visitors from the East Coast as well as visitors from Europe. Many events revolve around family activities in which everyone gets to participate. They are most certainly not the "dude ranches" of the 70's and 80's. These properties personalize many of the elements guests want in order to create a memorable experience.

Brands have the advertising power to buy media exposure, but today independent properties can find their target market and compete with their branded cousins as effectively through the Internet and social media. Independents can also be those hotels that are historic in nature with unique rooms that would be difficult to list in standard hotel format. The uniqueness of each room lends itself better to the marketing of each room separately and offers the guest a truly memorable individualized experience. Today, many guests are looking for something different from the perceived "cookie-cutter" image of the branded hotel. They want to stay in one-of-a-kind properties such as small **boutique hotels** and other intimate properties.

Bed and Breakfasts (B&Bs) are also a type of independent lodging property. They offer the intimacy and uniqueness not usually found in chain properties. For the most part these are all independent operations with no chain affiliation; in fact, 79 percent of B&B owners live on the premises.[11] B&Bs on average have six rooms, offer breakfast with the room, and offer many common amenities prized by the traveling public such as wireless and HD televisions in the rooms.[12]

Bed and Breakfast establishments offer the intimacy and uniqueness not usually found in chain properties.

© Karin Hildebrand Lau/Shutterstock.com

Independent hotels aid in the rise of real estate prices in the neighborhoods they choose to enter. The economy often improves and food often gets better. The art obtained comes from local artists, sometimes creating a local gallery within the walls of the independent property. Often these properties will offer training opportunities for local students and often employees/managers will become mentors to challenged youth in the neighborhoods. The owner may also have local roots, becoming a philanthropist for the neighborhood. Owners of independent properties are very tied to the local culture with a strong desire to give back by investing in the community. Locally handmade confectionaries/chocolates may grace the pillows in the guest rooms, employees may have uniforms made by the local seamstress, chefs may develop relationships with the local farmer or greenhouse, and local electricians and plumbers may be called upon for repairs or updates. Independent operators can add life and vitality to smaller locales.

ECO HOTELS/SUSTAINABILITY

Eco hotels and resorts are lodging properties that provide independent opportunities. These properties are usually considered to be destination properties located in areas where conservation and environmental issues are taken very seriously. These properties provide a special niche for certain personalities of the intended guest. The Eco property strives for sustainability, leaving a smaller environmental footprint than a branded property. Often included in these properties are health and wellness programs that have a goal of assisting the guest to disconnect from the hustle and bustle of our busy world. Local foods are used to create healthy meals; recipes are shared and cooking techniques taught to the guest to incorporate into their daily lifestyle. Yoga classes, meditation, various healing modalities are incorporated into the daily activities, creating a sense of peace and calmness for the guest to enjoy while visiting, and, as with the healthy eating style, the guests may continue these activities upon returning to their daily lives. The guest is encouraged to unplug from the technology that surrounds us on a daily basis; cell phone, Internet, television are very often not available in the areas where these properties are located.

Owning a property such as this brings very different challenges; high material cost, limited materials, limited labor pool, expensive transportation costs,

PERSONAL INPUT FROM AN INDEPENDENT RESTAURANTEUR

Minh Hang from Ming's Great Wall
The Joys of Owning My Own Restaurant

There are many joys to owning your own business. I myself own a Chinese restaurant called Ming's Great Wall, and I can say that I couldn't be happier. Since I own my own restaurant, I can be as creative as I want, I do not have to follow corporate designs, recipes, plating, etc., it's my choice, and the only thing I have to worry about is making my customers happy. Another positive to owning my own business is I also have a huge range of flexibility when it comes to the hours I'm open, the holidays we celebrate, where I put my restaurant, and how my operational plan is implemented. Also, being my own boss means that if I feel that I should add an item, run a promotion, change my prices, or even change the style of my restaurant, I do not have to go and ask for permission, I could do it the very next day if I wanted to. Plus, because I opened my own business, created from my own design, it's not like every chain that can be found in just about every town and city; it's unique. Being unique is one of the biggest joys I get from having my own restaurant, because I know that my ideas made it what it is today, and people like it. I know because it is unique it won't be found anywhere else because I am the one who put the time, the work, and the sweat into what it is today, and it is a symbol of how hard I worked, and everyone who comes in can see that and many appreciate it. Which leads me to another joy that comes from owning my restaurant, and that is the relationship that I can and have built with my customers. Many of them have been coming ever since I opened and have stuck with me since then, and because of that they have watched it grow and made it part of our city, and every time I hear that my restaurant is the best in town, I couldn't be happier. All of this might not sound that important from an outside view, but being able to make my own decisions, choices, rules, and getting the satisfaction from all of my customers from what I worked so hard for, brings so much joy that I know I did the right thing opening my own restaurant.

and often the property is located in an area that has difficult government regulations. For the tranquility and beauty of many of the areas in which these properties are located, owners feel it is an opportunity they cannot pass up.

Chip Conley, original owner of Joie de Vivre Hotels, notes: "We sell sleep, but we create dreams through making an emotional connection to our customers."[13] It is very difficult not to develop an emotional connection when a guest can interact with local wildlife, assist in choosing and harvesting fresh vegetables and fruit for the meals they are creating, and visit with the owners and family members during their stay.

Some independent hotels do collaborate with other independent hotels to assist with marketing and offer guest rewards systems;[14] they also can be represented in state and national government lobbying efforts.[15] In the past only brands and large associations such as the American Hotel and Lodging Association (AH&LA) employed lobbyists to help educate lawmakers on the needs and challenges of the industry. The Independent Lodging Industry Association (ILIA) founded in 2011 gives a voice to the independent hotelier. The association tracks and represents the members in state and federal issues regarding tourism, governmental regulations, and taxes to name some of the issues involved. This assists the independent hotelier in making their needs known in the world of government.

Many historic classic hotels are still independent. They have become icons in the hotel industry. One of the hotels in this classification is The Greenbrier Resort found in White Sulfur Springs, West Virginia. It is a National Historic Landmark and has been in existence since 1778.[16] It is a spectacular resort with the architecture of yesterday and the amenities of today.

Some other well-known independent properties are The Grand Hotel in Mackinac Island, Michigan, The Breakers in Palm Beach, Florida, and The Ocean Reef Club in Key Largo, Florida. These hotels have endured the test of time with graciousness and beauty.

SUMMARY

If you have the entrepreneurial spirit and drive the possibilities are endless. Independent properties thrive in many different types of locations and formats. All it takes is the passion, motivation, planning, target market, and of course financing to make it all happen. Entrepreneurs and small business people continue to provide many new jobs; this will not change. Learn all you can about the industry and see if you have the passion for working with and through your employees to create unique hospitality experiences for your guests.

RESOURCES

Internet Sites

American Hotel and Lodging Association (AH&LA): www.ahla.com/

Independent Lodging Industry Association (ILIA): www.independentlodging.org/

Kindred Resorts & Hotels: www.staykindred.com/

National Restaurant Association (NRA): www.restaurant.org

Professional Association of Innkeepers International (PAII): www.innkeeping.org/

Small Business Association (SBA): www.sba.gov

ENDNOTES

1. National Restaurant Association. (2013). *Pocket Factbook*. Retrieved from http://www.restaurant.org/Downloads/PDFs/News-Research/Factbook2013

2. Entrepreneur. (n.d.). In *Merriam-Webster Dictionary* online. Retrieved from http://www.merriam-webster.com/dictionary/entrepreneur.

3. Wagner, E. (2012). *Seven Traits of Incredibly Successful Entrepreneurs*. Forbes. Retrieved from http://www.forbes.com/sites/ericwagner/2012/06/05/7-traits-of-incredibly-successful-entrepreneurs/

4. Forbes/Opinion, (April, 2015).

5. National Restaurant Association. (2013). *Pocket Factbook*. Retrieved from http://www.restaurant.org/Downloads/PDFs/News-Research/Factbook2013

6. Kotler, P. and Armstrong, G. (2014). *Principles of Marketing*, 15th ed. Pearson Publishing.

7. NRA Factbook, 2015

8. National Restaurant Association. (2013). *Pocket Factbook*. Retrieved from http://www.restaurant.org/downloads/PDFs/News-Research/Factbook2013

9. (NRA Factbook, 2015)

10. (Intercontinental Hotel Group, March 2015)

11. Professional Association of Innkeepers International (PAII). (n.d.). *The B&B Industry*. Retrieved from http://www.innkeeping.org/?The_Industry

12. Ibid.

13. (*January, 2015 Hotel Insights, Hotel Management Best Practice Resources*).

14. Lodging Magazine. (2009). *Seven Iconic Hotels Form Kindred Resorts and Hotels*. Retrieved from http://www.lodgingmagazine.com/PastIssues/PastIssues/1459.aspx

15. Ponchione, A. (2012). *ILIA Gives Voice to Independent Hotels*. Hotel News Now.com. Retrieved from http://hotelnewsnow.com/articles.aspx/7274/

16. Greenbrier Hotel. (2013). Retrieved from http://www.greenbrier.com/

REVIEW QUESTIONS

1. Please name at least five traits of the successful entrepreneur listed in the chapter.

2. Please evaluate your own possibility of perfecting the traits listed by Eric Wagner.

3. How can independent hotels inform their potential guests about the unique aspects of their rooms and property?

4. What organization can help an independent hotel market to the public?

5. What percentage of Bed and Breakfast owners live on the premises?

6. What does the Independent Lodging Industry Association (ILIA) do for its members?

7. Please name at least one historic independent hotel.

8. What did Mr. Hang say was one of the advantages of having an independent restaurant?

© Alexander Tihonov/Shutterstock.com

CHAPTER 7

CHAIN OPERATIONS

AUTHOR

Radesh Palakurthi, PhD, MBA, The University of Memphis

LEARNING OBJECTIVES

- Learn the definition of a hospitality chain operation.
- Understand the difference between a hospitality chain and a brand.
- Know the different business models of hospitality chain operations.
- Know the advantages and disadvantages of hospitality chain operations.
- Know the big hospitality chains in the lodging and foodservice industries.

CHAPTER OUTLINE

Opening Vignette—How Hospitality Chain Operations are Created

Definition of Hospitality Chain Operations

Characteristics of Hospitality Chain Operations

Structure and Business Models of Hospitality Chain Operations

    Simple Form

    Mixed Franchise Form

    Management/Franchise Form

    Brand Management Form

Advantages of Chain Operations

Disadvantages of Chain Operations

The Big Chains in Hospitality

Summary

Brand

Brand management
  business model

Business organization

Business structure

Chain advantages

Chain disadvantages

Chain operation

Corporate hotel

Economies of scale

Franchise

Full equity business model

Hotel management company

Management/franchise
  business model

Mixed franchise
  business model

HOW HOSPITALITY CHAIN OPERATIONS ARE CREATED

© Sergey Nivens/Shutterstock.com

Joan Tortza was a bright, young, enterprising undergraduate student in Hospitality Administration at a reputable national university. Ever since Joan started the program, she had harbored a passionate desire to start her own restaurant. With her excellent culinary abilities, people skills, and superior knowledge of management techniques (gained through hard work at school and internships), she was confident that she would be successful. During her senior year, Joan put together a business plan for her proposed restaurant concept for the capstone course in strategic management. Joan's professor for the course was very impressed and offered an opportunity to present her plan to potential investors in the hospitality industry. Soon after graduating from school, Joan was making presentations to groups of investors who asked her pertinent questions about the feasibility of her business plan.

Joan was eventually able to convince one local group of investors about the soundness of her proposed restaurant concept and they agreed to convert one of their existing restaurants that was not performing up to standards into the concept proposed by Joan. After months of planning and renovation, the new restaurant opened with much fanfare. It was instantly a huge success, confirming that Joan's assessment of the need for such a restaurant concept was on the mark. In fact, the restaurant concept was so successful that the investors decided, with Joan's approval, to open a chain of additional restaurants using the same name and restaurant concept theme. Within a couple of years after graduation, Joan was overseeing four of her restaurants in the region. Needless to say, Joan was very happy with her success.

One fine day, a rich customer dining at one of her restaurants was visibly impressed with the operations and approached Joan to ask if she was interested in expanding her operations nationwide. Joan could not believe what she was hearing since the thought had crossed her mind many times before. However, she was limited by her legal contractual agreement with the original investment group and also their relatively limited resources from expanding rapidly nationwide. Additionally, the cash-flow from her four restaurants was not high enough to expand rapidly in many markets simultaneously. If she decided to use only the profits from her restaurants to expand, called organic growth, the expansion would be very slow and other people with more money to invest could beat her to the market. The customer suggested that Joan consider the franchising route instead. In such a business model, many rich individuals or investors from across the country would make the capital investment to buy the land, build the restaurant, license Joan's restaurant name and logo, and agree to operate the new restaurants according to Joan's standards. In return, Joan would receive part of the new restaurants' sales as franchise fees and royalties, even though she had not made any additional investments. She could also charge them a management fee if they decided to allow Joan's employees to operate the restaurants. While Joan was thrilled with the prospect of turning her four-restaurant concept into a national chain, she was immediately concerned with all the management issues that might crop up in the process. After all, the devil is in the details, isn't it? For example, Joan wondered if such rapid expansion would enable her to maintain the control that she now had over the quality of the restaurant products. How about the fact that she would have to deal with hundreds of investors (franchisees) from across the country, all with different personalities and financial goals? If most of the restaurants in the company were franchisee-operated, how well would she be able to manage the development and implementation of new policies and procedures for the company? Would she be able to find an adequate number of employees with the required skills to run her restaurants nationwide? What would the legal responsibilities and obligations of her company and the franchisees be in the new company? Reflecting on such critical issues, Joan sat down to do some careful planning to set the course for the future of her company.

Class Discussion Questions:

1. What are some of the benefits of growing the company organically into a chain that Joan should consider before she makes her decision?

2. What are some of the other critical issues that Joan may want to consider before she decides to pursue growth through franchising?

3. Given Joan's situation, what course of action (grow organically or grow through franchising) would you recommend she take? Discuss why you think your recommendation would be the best course of action for Joan.

The above vignette offers a scenario in developing chain operations. It describes one of the ways by which a hospitality chain operation can be created and the underpinning issues involved in growing it. The vignette also describes a chain operation without unfolding the specifics. The purpose of this chapter is to throw light on hotel and restaurant chain operations and discuss the nuances of structuring such chains.

DEFINITION OF HOSPITALITY CHAIN OPERATIONS

A **chain operation** can simply be defined as a business under one management or ownership. More specifically, chain operated hotels, restaurants, and other similar businesses are owned by the same company, and offer similar goods and services, but are found in different geographic locations. Invariably, many large hospitality companies have many chains that represent a different brand with distinct benefits and target markets. For example, The Intercontinental Hotel Group, IHG, has several chains including: InterContinental, Crowne Plaza, Hotel Indigo, Holiday Inn, Holiday Inn Express, Staybridge Suites, Candlewood Suites, EVEN™ Hotels, and HUALUXE™ Hotels and Resorts, all of which were developed to cater to a different need in the market. The chain, therefore, represents the brand and the distinct, market-segment-targeted brand is clearly displayed in all interactions with the customer. While there is no magic number in commerce that converts similar operations into a chain, generally, six similar-type operations could be considered to be a chain. The scope of a chain operation could be regional, national, or international.

A chain operation is a business under one management or ownership.

© Tupungato/Shutterstock.com

CHARACTERISTICS OF HOSPITALITY CHAIN OPERATIONS

It is prudent to understand some of the key elements related to hospitality chain operations before discussing the business models. The key elements can be described by the following variables:

Ownership. The chain could be owned by a company or an individual, a group of investors/partners, or a large parent company/corporation with a portfolio of many chains within it. A parent company may represent chains in all price segments and geographic areas or may be restricted to one or more depending on their focus and strategic intent. There are 21 hotel parent companies in the U.S. with more than 25,000 rooms. Worldwide, there are 32 other such companies. A listing of the top five parent companies and their chains is shown in Table 7.1. It should be noted that out of the top five largest hotel chains, four are based in the U.S. and one (IHG) is based in the U.K.

Table 7.1 also shows the distribution by scale category in terms of the total number of properties and the

Table 7.1	Top 5 Global Parent Companies By Chain Brands, Number of Hotel Rooms and Scale Type (As of end of 2015)						
Parent Company and Rank	**Chains**	**Scale**	**WW Props***	**% of Total Props.**	**WW Rooms***	**% of Total Rooms**
Marriott International (1)	BULGARI Hotels and Resorts	Luxury Chain	4	4.20%	207	8.37%
	Edition	Luxury Chain	5		844	
	JW Marriott	Luxury Chain	76		33,518	
	Ritz-Carlton	Luxury Chain	94		26,729	

(continued)

Parent Company and Rank	Chains	Scale	WW Props*	% of Total Props.	WW Rooms*	% of Total Rooms
Marriott International (1)	Autograph Collection	Upper Upscale Chain	93	18.86%	22,397	36.97%
	Gaylord Entertainment	Upper Upscale Chain	5		8,098	
	Marriott	Upper Upscale Chain	522		185,460	
	Marriott Executive Apartments	Upper Upscale Chain	26		3,416	
	Renaissance	Upper Upscale Chain	158		51,305	
	AC Hotels by Marriott	Upscale Chain	82	53.07%	10,359	41.51%
	Courtyard	Upscale Chain	1020		150,621	
	Residence Inn	Upscale Chain	689		84,335	
	Springhill Suites	Upscale Chain	333		39,408	
	Delta Hotels and Resorts	Upscale Chain	37		9,590	
	Protea Hotels	Upscale Chain	102		9,612	
	Moxy Hotels	Upper Midscale Chain	1	24%	162	13%
	Fairfield Inn & Suites	Upper Midscale Chain	753		69,552	
	TownePlace Suites	Upper Midscale Chain	264		26,508	
	TOTAL		**4,264**	**100.00%**	**732,121**	**100.00%**
Hilton Worldwide (2)	Curio—A Collection by Hilton	Luxury Chain	5	1.27%	3,170	3.08%
	Conrad Hotels & Resorts	Luxury Chain	24		8,091	
	Waldorf Astoria Hotels & Resorts	Luxury Chain	26		10,653	
	Embassy Suites Hotels	Upper Upscale Chain	219	18.00%	52,140	35.59%
	Hilton Hotel & Resorts	Upper Upscale Chain	560		201,047	
	DoubleTree by Hilton	Upscale Chain	410	32.07%	100,879	31.92%
	Hilton Garden Inn	Upscale Chain	618		86,095	
	Homewood Suites	Upscale Chain	360		40,128	
	Hampton Inn	Upper Midscale Chain	2,005	47.76%	198,914	28.90%
	Home2 Suites by Hilton	Upper Midscale Chain	62		6,649	
	Hilton Grand Vacation	Timeshare	44	1.02%	6,794	0.96%
	TOTAL		**4,328**	**100.12%**	**711,390**	**100.45%**
InterContinental Hotels Group (3)	InterContinental	Luxury Chain	182	3.74%	61,335	8.74%
	Kimpton Hotels & Restaurants	Upscale Chain	59	15.35%	10,672	22.04%
	HUALUXE	Upscale Chain	2		562	
	Crowne Plaza	Upscale Chain	403		112,406	
	Hotel Indigo	Upscale Chain	64		7,200	
	Staybridge Suites	Upscale Chain	219		23,866	

(continued)

Parent Company and Rank	Chains	Scale	WW Props*	% of Total Props.	WW Rooms*	% of Total Rooms
InterContinental Hotels Group (3)	Holiday Inn	Upper Midscale Chain	1,151	74.06%	209,064	64.71%
	Holiday Inn Express	Upper Midscale Chain	2,406		233,960	
	Holiday Inn Resort	Upper Midscale Chain	45		10,939	
	EVEN	Upper Midscale Chain	2		296	
	Candlewood Suites	Midscale Chain	333	6.84%	31,678	4.51%
	Holiday Inn Club Vacations	Timeshare	12	0.25%	4,256	0.61%
		TOTAL	**4,886**	**100.25%**	**701,978**	**100.61%**
Wyndham Worldwide (4)	Dolce	Upper Upscale Chain	24	4.47%	5,530	9.87%
	Wyndham Hotels & Resorts	Upper Upscale Chain	210		45,537	
	Tryp by Wyndham	Upper Midscale Chain	122		17,641	
	Baymont Inn & Suites	Midscale Chain	396	23.67%	31,480	31.01%
	Hawthorn Suites by Wyndham	Midscale Chain	101		10,053	
	Howard Johnson	Midscale Chain	403		43,803	
	Ramada	Midscale Chain	838		117,044	
	Wingate by Wyndham	Midscale Chain	148		13,450	
	Days Inn	Economy Chain	1,785	69.21%	142,613	55.66%
	Knights Inn	Economy Chain	383		23,464	
	Microtel Inn & Suites by Wyndham	Economy Chain	333		23,960	
	Super 8	Economy Chain	2,600		166,656	
	Travelodge	Economy Chain	414		30,692	
	Wyndham Vacation Ownership Resort	Timeshare	211	2.65%	24,095	3.46%
		TOTAL	**7,968**	**100.00%**	**696,018**	**100.00%**
Choice Hotels International (5)	Ascend Collection	Upscale Chain	185	3.56%	16,511	4.52%
	Cambria Suites	Upscale Chain	62		8,268	
	Clarion	Upper Midscale Chain	340	66.42%	47,100	71.92%
	Comfort Inn	Upper Midscale Chain	1,833		143,054	
	Comfort Suites	Upper Midscale Chain	673		53,281	
	Quality	Upper Midscale Chain	1,760		150,431	
	MainStay Suites	Midscale Chain	107	8.23%	6,998	7.24%
	Sleep Inn	Midscale Chain	464		32,665	
	Econo Lodge	Economy Chain	973	21.79%	58,986	16.31%
	Rodeway Inn	Economy Chain	538		30,323	
		TOTAL	**6,935**	**100.00%**	**547,617**	**100.00%**

Source: Company Annual Reports

total number of rooms. The percentage distributions give an idea about the market segments the hotel chains are targeting. It should also be noted that at the time of this writing, Marriott International acquired Starwood Hotels & Resorts Worldwide, creating a combined company that has 1.1 million rooms in more than 5,500 hotels, spanning the globe in over 100 countries. Together the company has 30 leading hotel chains representing different brands in its portfolio, easily consolidating its position as the largest hotel company in the world.

Operations. A chain hotel could be a **corporate hotel** (directly owned and/or managed by the parent company) or **franchised** (the hotel is run by a third party and the chain receives some sort of franchise fee). An independent hotel is not affiliated with any chain or parent company. Table 7.2 shows the operational characteristics of chain hotels in the world.

From the Table 7.2 it is clear that chain hotel operations are more prevalent in the U.S. compared to the rest of the world. Worldwide only about 37% of the hotels are chain-affiliated compared to about 57% in the U.S.

Other Characteristics. Hospitality chain operations are distinct in the way they are managed, represented, or marketed. A hotel within a chain could be managed by a management company. A **hotel management company** is a company with expertise in operating hotels for other hotel owners. The owners in return contractually agree to pay management fees and/or share the profits from the operations. There are 29 hotel management companies in the U.S. and 40 such companies worldwide, managing more than 7,500 rooms each. Management companies typically manage hotels across many chains, brands, and sometimes even different owners. Since a management company may be self-serving in the operation of a hotel, it becomes necessary for the hotel owner (who may have no experience in the hotel business) to have appropriate representation with an asset management company that has operational experience in hotels, including chain hotels. An additional dimension is a chain hotel's linkage with an organizational membership group or a marketing affiliation. Such linkage provides specific benefits such as marketing assistance, reservation services, and quality endorsement. Table 7.3 lists the top 10 hotel membership groups in the world.

STRUCTURE AND BUSINESS MODELS OF HOSPITALITY CHAIN OPERATIONS

While the concept of a chain operation is easy to understand, structurally, it may become more complex with increasing size. The complexity comes from the ownership and management contracts that form the basis of the relationships between the unit operators and the corporate office. Each of the business models is briefly described below.

Simple Form (Full Equity). In its simplest form, a chain can consist of a single owner/investor that has full equity stake in all the units owned by the company. In such a chain, called the simple form, or **full equity business model**, the parent company fully owns and operates all the units in its chain. All the costs and profits obtained by running the chain belong to the parent company. Usually, this type of structure is found in local or regional chain

Table 7.2	Operational Characteristics of Chain Hotels Worldwide							
Operation	**U.S. Properties**		**U.S. Rooms**		**WW Properties**		**WW Rooms**	
	No.	%	No.	%	No.	%	No.	%
Chain—Corporate	4,436	8%	883,553	18%	20,811	14%	3,605,319	25%
Chain—Franchise	25,628	49%	2,471,475	51%	35,981	23%	3,644,299	26%
Independent	22,224	43%	1,523,169	31%	96,935	63%	7,002,480	49%
TOTAL	**52,288**	**100%**	**4,878,197**	**100%**	**153,727**	**100%**	**14,252,098**	**100%**

Source: Smith Travel Research (STR), 2012 Statistics. WW=worldwide.

Table 7.3	Top WW Membership Groups	
Membership Group	**Properties**	**Rooms**
World Hotels	405	89,886
Hotelleriesuisse	1,964	88,814
Leading Hotels	421	75,855
Magnuson	1,294	71,515
Preferred Lodging	253	70,087
Historic Hotels of America	280	49,622
The Sovereign Collection	184	40,802
AHMI—RES Hotel	206	39,362
Summit	149	35,450
Hotusa	384	34,982

Source: Smith Travel Research, Inc.; Hotels' 325 Report, 2013—Hotels Magazine. WW=worldwide.

operations and they constitute a large percentage of the smaller chains in hospitality. Figure 7.1 illustrates the structure of this simple form of chain operations in hospitality.

Mixed Franchise Form. In the **mixed franchise business model**, there is a mix of ownership with some units being owned and operated by the parent company (franchisor) and the rest owned and operated by many other owners/investors (franchisees). Depending upon the size of the chain, the number of franchisees can be large, with some owning many units. It is not uncommon for some of the franchisee partnerships to own more units than the parent company. The franchisor derives their revenues through multiple revenue streams such as: franchising fees (franchise application fees and a flat fee as a percentage of gross sales), incentive fees (an additional fee based on the level of profitability of the unit operation), royalty fees (a fee for using the name, logo, and standard operating systems of the parent-company), marketing fees (an additional fee to pay for marketing the entire chain through different campaigns), and other fees (for project consulting, employee training, and inventory/supplies management). Figure 7.2 illustrates the structure of a mixed franchise form in hospitality.

Management/Franchise Form. In the management/franchise business model, the parent company (franchisor) also engages in offering professional management services for its non-company-owned

(franchised) units. The difference is that in this form, the parent company has an additional stream of revenue called "management fees," that is, fees that it charges the non-company-owned units for managing their operations. Many regional and national chain operations use this business model. The franchisees may be free to hire any other professional operations management company rather than the parent company. In such a case, the unit will be owned by an investor and managed by an outside company that will operate the business strictly by the standards established by the parent company. Figure 7.3 illustrates the management/franchise form of structure in hospitality.

Brand Management Form. When a mega-corporation owns multiple chain operations under the same parent umbrella structure, it prefers to refer to each of such chain operations as a brand to reflect the distinctive image. Such a structure is called a brand management or **mega-corporation business model** (Figure 7.4).

For example, Marriott International owns 18 hotel brands (Table 7.1), each with a distinctive market position. The Ritz-Carlton is an elegant and luxurious brand for business and leisure while the Courtyard is designed to be an upper-midscale option for travelling families and business clients. Each chain within the brand management form operates similarly to the management/franchise form in terms of the franchisor-franchisee relationships. The chain's

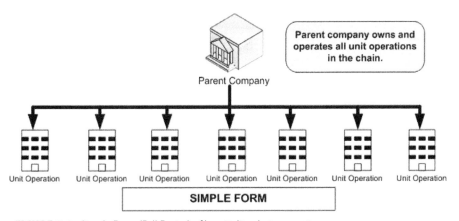

FIGURE 7.1 Simple Form (Full Equity) of hospitality chain operations

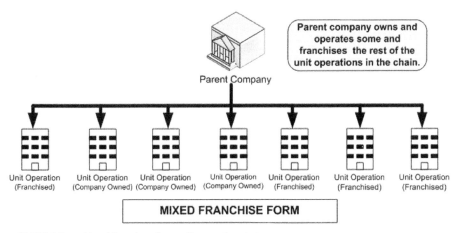

FIGURE 7.2 Mixed Franchise Form of hospitality chain operations

units may be operated by the parent company directly, sole-owners as franchisees, partnership-owners as franchisees, or a management company as a third-party operator for a franchisee. The large size of the mega-corporation may also allow it to raise funds through the financial markets and to make direct investments in real estate across the globe. The complexity is compounded when the mega-corporation enters into a joint venture or other similar partnership with a foreign entity in order to enter and expand in foreign countries.

ADVANTAGES OF CHAIN OPERATIONS

Hospitality chain operations have many advantages that can broadly be classified into the following categories:

Market Reach. How many times have we wished that one of our local favorite restaurants also traveled with us so we never have to miss the food we love? That is precisely the need that chain operations aim to fulfill by replicating a successful product in as many geographic regions as they can. In this way, chain operations have an advantage over single independent restaurants since they "reach" out to many markets with the same concept.

Economies of Scale. **Economies of scale** refers to the cost advantages that a company can derive because of its large size. Since chain operations have multiple units, all products and supplies they buy are also multiples of the requirements of a single independent unit. Therefore, a chain operation will be able to negotiate better rates for its products and supplies from vendors compared to a single owner unit. In addition, chain operations will also be able to derive cost savings through synergy (centralized marketing, human resources functions, etc.).

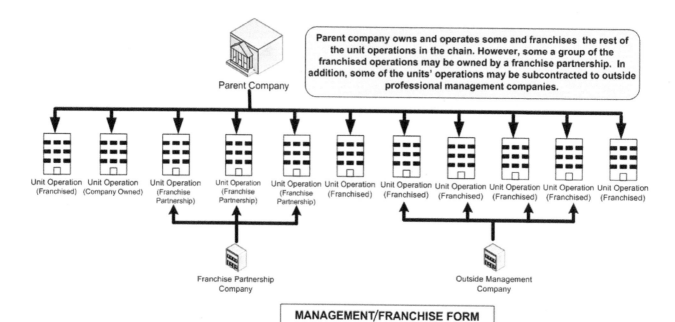

FIGURE 7.3 Management/Franchise Form of hospitality chain operations

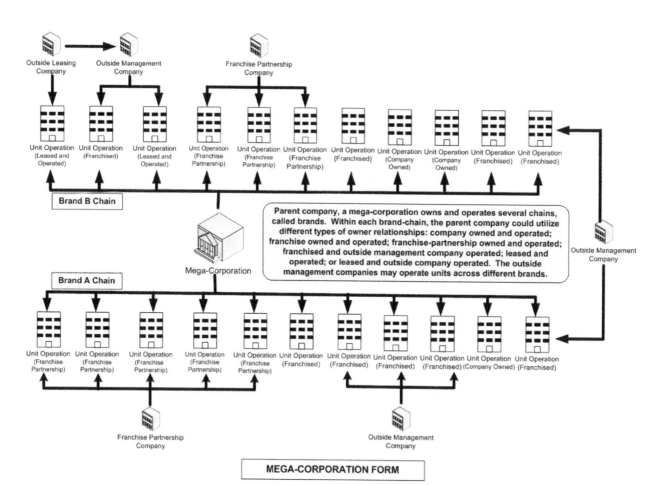

FIGURE 7.4 Mega-Corporation Form of hospitality operations

The Waldorf Astoria is one of Hilton's worldwide chains.

Streamlined Operations. Chain operations often standardize the products and services offered in order to streamline their operations. The standardization also extends to operating procedures resulting in commonly understood requirements for managing all resources (people, finances, and equipment) and performance.

Marketing Power. The marketing power of chain operations comes from increased visibility gained through greater market reach. The greater visibility allows the chain to use mass media such as TV, radio, and newspapers and to repeat successful campaigns in other regions.

Service Options. Chain operations are often able to provide additional services both to the customers and to units within the chain. Such services range from providing a reservations service, loyalty programs, and customer relations management (CRM) at the unit level to full-fledged consulting such as pre-opening services, architectural and construction plans, and employee training and certification services.

Access to Finances. The larger size of the chain operations may mean the company may have multiple options for raising money for growth. The company can borrow money from banks, savings & loans, other financial institutions (such as insurance companies and retirement savings) or even issue bonds on the stock market. All such funds raised can be used to fund operations, or make capital investments for growth.

Professional Management. Because of the enhanced legal requirements and the complexity of operations in a chain, many chain companies are realizing that it is prudent to hire professionals such as students graduating from hospitality management programs. With professionalism and specialization come a better understanding of a company's operating needs. In that regard, chain operations are becoming incubators of good management practices in hospitality.

DISADVANTAGES OF CHAIN OPERATIONS

Depending on the perspective of the owner (or the parent-company/franchisor) and the operator (or the franchises/management company), some of the advantages listed above can also be seen as drawbacks of hospitality chain operations. The disadvantages can broadly be listed under three categories as discussed below.

Operational Constraints. While the parent company may want standardized operations throughout the chain to control costs and increase efficiency, it may put a lot of restrictions on the franchisees or owners that may want to vary those operations in some small ways. For example, the ownership contracts may disallow independent marketing in the local areas by any unit operation without prior approval from the parent company. All chain operations have some form of quality-assurance program where they perform surprise inspections and repeated violation of standards may result in loss of franchising rights.

Financial Strain. Another disadvantage of belonging to a chain operation may be the strain put on the financial resources of the company. For example, if the parent company of a 300-hotel chain decides that the lighting in the guest bathrooms must be increased from 400 lumens to 500 lumens for better visibility and safety at the cost of $300 per room, each hotel will incur $75,000 in expenses and the whole chain may spend up to $22.5 million to fulfill the new needs.

Legal Forces. The complex structure of most chain operations, along with many types of owner-operator contracts and partnerships, often plagues it with legal woes. Invariably a difference of opinion or perspective on the same issues may have no other recourse than the local courthouse. For example, the enhanced lighting could be seen as a cost increment by the unit operations while the parent company sees it as enhancing safety and customer service in the long run.

THE BIG CHAINS IN HOSPITALITY

The increasing globalization of the hospitality industry is rapidly being reflected in the geographic profiles of large hospitality corporations, especially in the hotel industry. Table 7.4 lists the top ten nations in which the major hotel chains operate according to Smith Travel Research (STR Global). In many of the hotel chains, the number of hotels they operate in their home country is almost equal to or exceeds the number of hotels they operate overseas.

In addition to the countries in which the hotel companies operate, the countries in which the companies are based are also truly global in scope. Table 7.5 shows the next largest hotel companies globally (after the list shown in Table 7.1). In the list, four are American companies while five are Chinese, reflecting a growing lodging market in China.

Unlike the hotel industry, the foodservice chains are currently dominated by American quick-service restaurants. Table 7.6 lists the top twenty foodservice chains in the U.S. in 2015 according to Nation's Restaurant News' Top 100 Chains Survey. The top fourteen chains have substantial international operations with most of their growth actually coming from the overseas markets. It is interesting to note that while McDonald's Restaurants is still ranked first in terms of sales, the Subway Restaurants chain is the largest in terms of the number of units. Table 7.7 lists the fastest growing foodservice chains in 2015. Among the top fifteen largest chains, Chipotle Mexican Grill made it into the ten fastest growing chains in 2015, ranking at number two. This rapid growth also brings substantial quality control issues to light as is evidenced by the recent E. coli outbreaks in Chipotle restaurants in Washington and Oregon. Other chains such as KFC are making substantial strides and achieving rapid growth in overseas markets such as in China and India. Not unlike the hotel industry, the foodservice industry also has a penchant for franchising with some of the chains such as Subway and Dunkin' Donuts franchising almost all their restaurants.

SUMMARY

In an increasingly competitive world, chain development strategy offers an opportunity for hospitality companies to take control of costs and harness their strengths. With the short time it now takes for the diffusion of innovation and migration of ideas across the world because of rapidly evolving telecommunications and social media, the world is swiftly shrinking and creating immense business opportunities for growth globally. As people around the world share the same information and ideas, they may also develop the same preferences for hospitality products and services. In such an environment, growing through the application of chain development strategy is prudent for business. Needless to say, the concept of hospitality chain operations will only get stronger in the future.

Table 7.4 Top Ten Nations of Operation by Hotel Chains

Hilton Worldwide			Marriott International			Wyndham Worldwide		
Country	Properties	Rooms	Country	Properties	Rooms	Country	Properties	Rooms
United States	3,374	504,536	United States	3,101	500,585	United States	5,752	447,461
United Kingdom	106	22,715	China	58	22,367	China	513	64,142
Canada	86	15,419	Canada	73	14,875	Canada	494	39,564
China	33	13,751	United Kingdom	58	11,305	United Kingdom	111	9,943
Egypt	19	6,934	Spain	78	9,474	Germany	54	8,091
Germany	18	5,477	Germany	28	6,525	Spain	53	7,563
Japan	10	5,385	Mexico	22	5,410	Mexico	30	4,140
Mexico	30	5,336	India	17	4,105	Brazil	15	2,693
Turkey	21	4,838	France	18	3,858	United Arab Emirates	10	2,265
Italy	18	4,043	Russia	14	3,497	South Korea	10	2,198
InterContinental Hotels Group			**Choice Hotels International**			**Best Western Company**		
Country	Properties	Rooms	Country	Properties	Rooms	Country	Properties	Rooms
United States	3,132	372,157	France	1,382	127,630	United States	1,937	158,039
China	180	59,647	Germany	328	43,964	Germany	193	19,967
United Kingdom	294	41,262	China	114	29,987	Canada	192	17,832
Canada	164	24,037	Brazil	174	27,317	France	305	15,699
Mexico	121	19,236	United Kingdom	194	26,023	United Kingdom	281	15,673
Germany	70	14,175	Australia	175	24,271	Italy	179	13,119
Japan	30	9,274	Thailand	47	11,185	China	38	8,359
Australia	31	7,379	Indonesia	56	11,079	Sweden	84	7,125
France	51	6,327	Spain	80	9,294	Australia	163	5,844
Italy	35	5,710	Poland	48	9,124	Mexico	63	4,231
Starwood Hotels & Resorts			**ACCOR**			**Hyatt Hotels Corporation**		
Country	Properties	Rooms	Country	Properties	Rooms	Country	Properties	Rooms
United States	485	152,491	France	1,376	126,694	United States	353	92,003
China	110	39,951	Germany	327	43,892	China	19	8,465
Canada	60	17,676	China	119	30,735	India	12	3,361
India	34	8,242	Brazil	174	27,362	Japan	8	2,674
Germany	25	7,389	United Kingdom	194	26,024	Canada	5	2,344
Japan	15	6,125	Australia	177	24,854	Indonesia	5	1,980
Italy	23	5,600	Thailand	47	11,356	United Arab Emirates	5	1,807
United Arab Emirates	20	5,592	Indonesia	56	11,079	Australia	5	1,558
Thailand	20	5,572	Spain	81	9,374	Mexico	4	1,547
Mexico	25	5,142	Poland	48	9,124	South Korea	4	1,532

Source: STR Global, Inc.

Table 7.5 The Next Big Ten Global Hotel Chains

Rank	Parent Company	Headquarters	WW Rooms	WW Props.
6	AccorHotels	Paris, France	482,296	3,717
7	Plateno Hotels Group	Guangzhou, China	442,490	3,023
8	Starwood Hotels & Resorts Worldwide	Stamford, Connecticut, USA	354,225	1,222
9	Shanghai Jin Jiang International Hotal Group Co.	Shanghai, China	352,538	2,910
10	Best Western International	Phoenix, Arizona, USA	303,522	3,931
11	Home Inns & Hotel Management	Shanghai, China	296,075	2,609
12	China Lodging Group	Shanghai, China	209,955	1,995
13	Carlson Rezidor Hotel Group	Minnetonka, Minnesota, USA	172,234	1,092
14	Hyatt Hotals Corp.	Chicago, Illinois, USA	155,265	587
15	GreenTree Inns Hotel Management Group	Shanghai, China	142,038	1,580

Source: Hotels' 325 Report, 2015—Hotels Magazine. WW=worldwide.

Table 7.6 Top Twenty Foodservice Chains in the U.S.

Rank	Food Service Chain	Segment	Fiscal Year	Systemwide Sales in Billions		Sales % Change
				Latest Year	Preceding Year	
1	McDonald's	LSR/Burger	Dec. '14	$35.45	$35.86	-1.14%
2	Starbucks Coffee	Beverage-Snack	Sept. '14	$13.02	$11.86	9.74%
3	Subway	LSR/Sandwich	Dec. '14	$12.27	$12.22	0.36%
4	Burger King	LSR/Burger	Dec. '14	$8.63	$8.50	1.54%
5	Wendy's	LSR/Burger	Dec. '14	$8.57	$8.48	1.07%
6	Taco Bell	LSR/Mexican	Dzc. '14	$8.20	$7.80	5.13%
7	Dunkin' Donuts	Beverage-Snack	Dec. '14	$7.18	$6.74	6.42%
8	Chick-fil-A	Chicken	Dec. '14	$5.71	$4.99	14.48%
9	Pizza Hut	Pizza	Dec. '14	$5.50	$5.70	-3.51%
10	Applebee's Neighborhood Grill & Bar	Casual Dining	Dec. '14	$4.58	$4.52	1.34%
11	Panera Bread	Bakery-Cafe	Dec. '14	$4.26	$4.03	5.73%
12	KFC	Chicken	Dec. '14	$4.20	$4.20	0.00%
13	Domino's	Pizza	Dec. '14	$4.12	$3.77	9.17%
14	Chipotle Mexican Grill	LSR/Mexican	Dec. '14	$4.06	$3.19	27.25%
15	Sonic America's Drive-In	LSR/Burger	Aug. '14	$4.03	$3.88	3.88%
16	Olive Garden	Casual Dining	May '15	$3.76	$3.63	3.81%

(continued)

17	Chili's Grill & Bar	Casual Dining	June '15	$3.63	$3.54	2.74%
18	Little Caesars Pizza	Pizza	Dec. '14	$3.41	$3.10	9.84%
19	Buffalo Wild Wings Grill & Bar	Casual Dining	Dec. '14	$3.24	$2.78	16.31%
20	Dairy Queen	LSR/Burger	Dec. '14	$3.19	$2.96	7.84%

Source: NRN Magazine: Top 100 Chains Survey, 2015

Table 7.7 Top Ten Fastest Growing Foodservice Chains in 2015

Rank	Chain Name	2015 Profile	Rank	Chain Name	2015 Profile
1	Jersey Mike's Subs	Segment: Limited Service/Sandwich Sales growth: 29.3% Total sales: $525 million Sales rank: 81 Total units: 857 (+20.2%)	6	Yard House	Segment: Casual Dining Sales growth: 21% Total sales: $478 million Sales rank: 91 Total units: 59 (+13.5%)
2	Chipotle Mexican Grill	Segment: Mexican Sales growth: 27.3% Total sales: $4.1 billion Sales rank: 14 Total units: 1,755 (+11.6%)	7	Jimmy John's Gourmet Sandwiches	Segment: Limited Service/Sandwich Sales growth: 19.8% Total sales: $1.8 billion Sales rank: 37 Total units: 2,109 (+17%)
3	Firehouse Subs	Segment: Limited Service/Sandwich Sales growth: 24.8% Total sales: $544.4 million Sales rank: 78 Total units: 840 (+18.0%)	8	Casey's General Stores	Segment: C-Store Sales growth: 17.7% Total sales: $776.1 million Sales rank: 57 Total units: 1,880 (+4%)
4	Raising Cane's Chicken Fingers	Segment: Chicken Sales growth: 23.5% Total sales: $415 million Sales rank: 95 Total units: 208 (+17.5%)	9	Zaxby's	Segment: Chicken Sales growth: 17.2% Total sales: $1.3 billion Sales rank: 42 Total units: 658 (+11%)
5	Wingstop	Segment: Chicken Sales growth: 22.9% Total sales: $664 million Sales rank: 65 Total units: 671 (+13.9%)	10	Buffalo Wild Wings	Segment: Casual Dining Sales growth: 16.3% Total sales: $3.2 billion Sales rank: 19 Total units: 1,052 (+7.6%)

Source: NRN Magazine: Top 100 Chains Survey, 2015

RESOURCES

Hotel Chain Websites

Marriott Corporation: http://www.marriott.com

Intercontinental Group: http://www.ihg.com/hotels/us/en/

Accor: http://accor.com/gb/index.asp

Starwood Hotels & Resorts: http://www.starwoodhotels.com/

Best Western International: http://www.bestwestern.com/

Hilton Groups PLC: http://www3.hilton.com/en/index.html

Le Meridien Hotels & Resorts: http://www.lemeridien.com/

Carlson Hospitality Worldwide: http://www.carlson.com/

Golden Tulip Hospitality/THL: http://www.goldentulip.com/

Cendant Corp: http://cendant.com/

Global Hyatt Corp: http://www.hyatt.com/hyatt/index.jsp

Choice Hotels International: http://www.choicehotels.com/

Rezidor SAS Hospitality: http://www.rezidorsas.com/

Club Mediterranee: http://www.clubmed.com/cgi-bin/clubmed55/clubmed/welcome.jsp

TUI AG/TUI Hotels & Resorts: http://www.tui-group.com/en/ir/group/

Foodservice Chain Websites

McDonald's: http://www.mcdonalds.com/

Wendy's: http://www.wendys.com

Burger King: http://www.bk.com/

Subway: http://www.subway.com/subwayroot/default.aspx

Taco Bell: http://www.tacobell.com/

Pizza Hut: http://www.pizzahut.com/

KFC: http://www.kfc.com/

Starbucks: http://www.starbucks.com/

Dunkin' Donuts: https://dunkindonuts.com/

Domino's Pizza: http://www.dominos.com/Public-EN/

Arby's: http://www.arbys.com/

Sonic Drive-In: http://www.sonicdrivein.com/index.jsp

Chipotle Restaurants: http://chipotle.com/

Firehouse Subs: http://www.firehousesubs.com/

Jersey Mike's Subs: http://www.jerseymikes.com/

REVIEW QUESTIONS

1. What is the definition of a hospitality chain operation?

2. What is the difference between a hospitality chain and a hospitality brand?

3. What are the different business models used in hospitality chain operations?

4. Describe the differences between the different business models used in hospitality chain operations.

5. Describe the relationship between a franchisor and a franchisee in hospitality chain operations. When can the franchisors be more powerful than the franchisees?

6. What are the additional sources of revenue available to an owner in a Mixed Franchise Form compared to a Simple Form?

7. How would you describe a mega-corporation in hospitality? Explain how its operation is more complex than other forms of business models.

8. What are some of the advantages of hospitality chain operations?

9. What are some of the disadvantages of hospitality chain operations?

10. List the top ten hospitality chain operations in the lodging and foodservice industries.

CHAPTER *8*

FRANCHISING AND REFERRAL ORGANIZATIONS

© oneinchpunch/Shutterstock.com

AUTHOR	*Tierney Orfgen McCleary, Eastern Michigan University*
LEARNING OBJECTIVES	• Describe the role of franchising in the hospitality industry.
	• Identify the advantages and disadvantages of franchising from both the franchisor and franchisee perspectives.
	• Explain the role of referral organizations in the hospitality industry.
	• Describe the commonalities between franchising and referral organizations within the hospitality industry.
	• Identify the trends influencing franchising and referral organizations in the hospitality industry.

KEY TERMS

Franchise	Franchisor
Franchisee	Referral organization

INTRODUCTION

In previous chapters, you have learned about independent and chain operations within the hospitality industry. This chapter will explore franchising and referral organizations as other options of business operations and ownership. Both franchising and referral organizations share common functions in that these business types offer a manner of marketing and developing a product or service under an established trademark or brand name. This marketing allows for an expansion of the visibility of the business to potential customers beyond what they would have if they were competing in their market on their own.

FRANCHISING IN THE HOSPITALITY INDUSTRY

Franchising is a method of doing business. A franchise is a way existing businesses can expand the distribution of their products and/or services to customers through the creation of a business relationship with a third party, or the franchisee. A **franchise** is a contractual relationship whereby a **franchisor** allows or licenses the **franchisee** to use the franchisor's established name and/or successful business techniques in exchange for a fee. It is a proven business operation, and by replicating the success of the brand's methods, it can allow companies to expand their brand identity and market share more quickly and with less of their own capital. For the franchisee, the business model has already been demonstrated to be a success; therefore, it reduces the risk of trying to start an independent operation from scratch. Also, for the franchisee, being a part of a bigger organization with support from the franchisor can also mean a shorter path to a return on their investment, as many of the mistakes that new business owners might make are reduced by the replication of a successful model. An owner of a franchise has some advantage over an independent operator in that the franchisee does not have to "reinvent the wheel," because the franchisor provides the marketing and operational expertise to guide them toward a successful business. If problems do arise, the franchisor, as well as fellow franchisees, can offer support through their depth of knowledge and experience in the system.

In 2007, the U.S. Census Bureau estimated that over $4.2 billion dollars in sales were generated by hotel and restaurant franchises. Today, the largest franchise organization remains McDonald's. While there are many business types other than restaurants, quick-service restaurants remain one of the largest growing segments in the United States. Despite coming out of one of the toughest economic times in the United States, franchise businesses continue to grow at a slightly faster rate than other business types with regard to job creation, economic output, and contribution to the gross domestic product.[1] One reason for the continued growth is the franchise's ability to grow internationally. Many of the larger franchises have developed brand recognition to overseas markets. The top 200 franchise companies since 2000 have grown 32% domestically, while the number of their international locations have more than doubled, growing nearly 113% in number of units. The rapidly expanding economies of Asia and South America allow for growth for brands that may have reached saturation in the United States.

Franchising is a method for growing a business to sell goods or services at multiple locations under the same brand. Many hospitality businesses have used the method of franchising to widen their market share and brand recognition without having to finance or operate the business themselves. A franchisor licenses their brand name, business operations system, marketing, or their operational expertise to a third party (individual or group). This allows entrepreneurs who may even be unfamiliar or novices in the field to open and operate a successful business. This third party or **franchisee** agrees to follow the policies and procedures laid out by the franchisor in the franchise agreement. Depending on the franchise, in some cases the franchisor will provide all the necessary tools for the business, even management training. This training and offering of expertise allows for someone to become an owner and manager at a faster pace than learning the business on their own. The franchisee pays the initial fee, or franchise fee, to start up the relationship as well as continuing fees (often called royalties or maintenance fees) for the duration of the contractual relationship. These royalties are often calculated as percentages of sales and may include payment for regional and national marketing that the franchise might offer.

Table 8.1	Franchising Trends and Factoids Table
Growth franchise locations in nontraditional locations like churches, hospitals, schools, and other unexpected places. McDonald's built a location underneath the Museum of Communism in Prague and a Subway Sandwich is located inside a Toyota dealership.	
Healthier food operations are on the rise, consumers have exhibited a desire for higher quality and more sustainable procurement for products.	
There are over 1,200 franchising companies operating in the United States with more than 450,000 retail units and more than 7.8 million employees.	
Average investment in a foodservice franchise is less than $250,000.	
Average length of a contract is 10 years.	
Franchises are continuing their expansion of their market share into international markets.	

TYPES OF FRANCHISING

There are three types of franchises: product distributorships, trademark or brand, and business format. **Product or service distribution franchises** grant the right to sell their parent company's product as in car dealerships, gasoline, and insurance. **Trademark or brand licensing** allows the licensees the right to use the parent company's brand name in operating their own business. Coca Cola is a good example of trademark licensing. The product distribution or trademark franchisor provides the brand and product, but does not usually provide a business operating system.

The type of franchise that is most familiar to the hospitality industry is the business format type of franchise. **Business format franchisors** offer to their franchisees not only the right to use their product or service and brand name, they also provide the franchisor's business operations systems with initial training and ongoing support. Examples of operations that are business format franchises can range from restaurants, hotels, and convenience stores, to muffler shops, plumbing, and tax preparation services. The franchisor provides a detailed system to successfully replicate the business, including the physical structure, appearance, and facility requirements; specifics of fixtures and equipment; product and service standards; and operations manuals that outline clear policies and procedures to ensure consistency of service from one location to another. These proprietary materials provide a "business in a box," or everything that a franchisee needs to build, operate, staff, and market their new location.

These materials include business operation manuals, management guides, and promotions templates to market their franchise; and employee forms and materials to assist in recruitment, interviewing, and training, along with other human resource forms and templates. For example, Subway provides a two-week initial training program at one of their multiple training centers around the country as well as ongoing training for both owners and staff. In addition to extensive training, franchisees are required to order food from an approved food distributor to ensure that all restaurants provide consistency in quality of product and maximize savings. Brand consistency in both the quality of product and of service provided to the customer ensures the greatest business advantage for the franchisor and franchisee.

Franchise agreements can be for a single unit or for multiple units. **Single unit**, sometimes called direct unit, is a contractual agreement for the franchisee to operate one unit of the franchise by the franchisor. Most franchise agreements include an area of

Coca-Cola is a good example of trademark licensing.

exclusivity whereby the franchisee is guaranteed that the franchisor will give rights to a certain market or specified geographic area to the franchisee. In other words, franchisees are given a defined territory around their location where no other franchise location is allowed to operate; this is called a **protected market.**

Multiunit contracts allow a franchisee (individual or group of owners) to purchase additional units of the franchise. By operating multiple units of the same franchise concept, franchisees are able to grow their own business wealth with an operation with which they are familiar, which lowers the financial risk for both the franchisor and the franchisee. As the franchisee of multiunits gains more experience and expands their financial resources, they may negotiate with the franchisor for area development agreements.

Area development agreements grant the franchisees exclusive rights to a geographic area for opening new franchise locations within a certain time period.

FRANCHISOR'S ROLE

Franchisors can be large publicly traded companies like McDonald's or Wendy's or smallerprivately held companies like Biggby Coffee and are headquartered all over the world (Accor:Paris, France, or Domino's Pizza: Ann Arbor, Michigan). Franchises can be a small start-upcompany (Tony Sacco's Coal Oven Pizza: Bonita Springs, Florida) or a large consortium ofbrands (YUM! Brands, Inc.: Louisville, Kentucky). As described before, the franchisor licensesthe right to operate a business under their brand name. This brand recognition is one of thelargest advantages that the franchisor offers to potential franchisees. This brand name offerscustomers clear expectations of what to anticipate when they patronize the establishment.Franchisors also offer support to the franchisee, while they ensure control over the manner in

which the franchisee operates the franchise location to guarantee consistency of the customerexperience from location to location. Top hotel franchises don't necessarily make all the hotelsphysically the same, but rather, they aim to ensure that the guest experience is the same acrossproperties. In addition

Table 8.2
Top 10 Franchises by Number of Units

1. McDonald's
2. 7-Eleven
3. KFC
4. Subway
5. Burger King
6. Hertz
7. Ace Hardware
8. Circle K Convenience Store
9. Pizza Hut
10. Wendy's

Franchise Times *Top 200 Franchise Systems List, 2015*

to centralized reservations, franchisors must also maintain mobileapplications for smart phones that might help with marketing, reservations, and customerservice.

As described, in the business format franchise, franchisors offer more than the brand name;they provide operation methods and procedures to the franchisees in many forms, from technical and management training to operations manuals and checklists, in order to maintainconsistent levels of quality of product and service delivery. The level of detail of theseoperations procedures and training may vary from one franchising organization to another aswell as varying levels of opening and ongoing support. Franchisors are required to outline the types of support they offer and the requirements of the franchisee in the **Uniform Franchise Offering Circular (UFOC)**, so it is clear to all parties what is included and required withintheir relationship agreements.

There are several possible advantages and disadvantages to developing a franchise from an independent operation:

FRANCHISEE'S ROLE

Within the franchise business relationship, the franchisee contractually agrees to operate the franchise location under the franchisor's brand according to

ADVANTAGES OF A DEVELOPING FRANCHISE

- Allows the parent business to grow beyond the existing location with minimal financial outlay.
- Management of new locations becomes the responsibility of the franchisee,
- The structure of royalty payments, often a percentage of sales, motivates the franchisee to run their franchise profitably.

DISADVANTAGES OF DEVELOPING A FRANCHISE

- The royalty fees may be and are often less than what the franchisor could make if they operated the location on their own.
- The franchisee may not have the required management or business acumen to profitably operate the business.
- Some entrepreneurial franchisees may find the franchise business model to be constraining and limiting, as they may have varying viewpoints on how the business should be operated beyond how the franchisor proscribes in their policies and procedures.
- Must be very careful in selection of franchisees.

the approved policies and procedures and often only using approved products as outlined in the agreement. The franchisee is responsible for acquiring the capital and necessary resources for the building of the new location, the franchising fees, and operating expenses. For many franchises, the franchisee owns or leases the land and building for the new location; however, in the case of Subway sandwiches, Subway handles the leasing agreement, all their leases/locations are corporately held, and franchisees receive a sublease for their location. Though most franchisors offer support and tools for human resource functions, franchisees are ultimately responsible for activities like hiring, training, and payroll for their employees.

There are several advantages and disadvantages to operating a franchise location versus starting a business from scratch:

ADVANTAGES OF BECOMING A FRANCHISEE

- Operating a business with established name recognition gives a newcomer franchisee an edge to competing with existing independent operators in their market.
- No "reinventing the wheel," with access to proven operations and training manuals, blueprints, marketing tools, and successful store design and layout.
- Established relationship and purchasing power with existing vendors; being a part of a larger organization allows for better pricing for equipment and supplies.
- Savings of time and resources with the franchisor responsible for research and development of new products and services.
- Reduced risk in opening a new business; replication of a successful business model and procedures gives the franchisee an edge over an independent operation.
- A wealth of expertise and support available from the parent company.

DISADVANTAGES OF BECOMING A FRANCHISEE

- Franchisee has a loss of independence, as they must adhere precisely to franchisor's policies and procedures even if the franchisee disagrees with their methods.
- The reputation of the brand is influenced by other franchisees in the system.
- Income expectations must be balanced with the costs of franchising; must have profitable operations in order to pay ongoing fees.

Table 8.3   Top 10 Hotel Franchises

Rank*	Company/Brand	Franchised	Number of Rooms*
1	Wyndham Worldwide	7,585	667,000
2	Choice Hotels International, Inc.	6,300	500,000
3	IHG (Intercontinental Hotels Group PLC)	4,096	726,867
4	Hilton Worldwide	3,608	745,000
5	Marriott International, Inc.	2,882	697,000
6	Home Inns & Hotels Management	1,695	530,000
7	Green Tree Inns Hotel Management Group	1,541	123,000
8	Accor USA	1,506	465,072
9	Shanghai Jin Jiang International Hotal Group	1,503	360,000
10	Vantage Hospitality Group, Inc.	1,213	71,000

*Hotels 325, July/August 2015 www.hotelsmag.com
**Corporate websites

INDUSTRY SPOTLIGHT

Biggby Coffee, East Lansing, Michigan

In 1995, Bob Fish and Mary Roszel decided to open a coffeehouse in a building that formerly housed an Arby's in East Lansing, Michigan. They offer the traditional coffee, espresso drinks, tea and tisanes, and bottled beverages, along with assorted hot and cold food items and smoothies. They pride themselves on the quality of their coffee offerings—beans are selected from countries around the world, slow roasted, taste tested, and then distributed to stores in less than a week to ensure freshness. As they learned and mastered the operations of this coffeehouse and it gained popularity in this college town, they decided to open a second location in nearby Lansing, Michigan in 1997. With the success of the second location and growing popularity of the cafes, Fish and Roszel added Michael McFall, a former barista in the first location, to the management team, decided to develop a franchise, and founded Global Orange Development, LLC in 1998. Within four years, nine locations were opened throughout Michigan and Ohio. With rapid growth, there are currently 245 locations, and they are ranked #7 by Franchise Business Review (FBR), as one of the top food franchises to own in 2015. All of their locations are franchised.

Biggby franchisees are given a minimum of six weeks of training, both in the classroom and "on-the-job" in an existing Biggby location. Corporate provides operational assistance onsite prior to and after store opening. Franchisees and new managers are assessed and must successfully complete all training before the location can open. In the highly competitive world of Starbucks and other large coffee chains, Biggby continues to grow steadily with their ability to adapt and customize their relationships with their franchisees.[2]

REFERRAL ORGANIZATIONS

Referral organizations or associations offer similar benefits and services to business properties as franchises, though at a lower cost to both the brand and the member. Typically, a **referral organization** is a nonprofit affiliation owned by members of independently owned and operated lodging operations. Lodging properties with a referral organization share a customer reservation system (CRS), a common logo, or marketing. Being a part of the referral organization can also offer its members group-buying discounts, as well as possiblemanagement training programs for their employees. Members of the referral organization pay fees to be a part of the group, and those fees typically cover administrative expenses of the referral organization. The voting members of the referral association determine the rules, policies, and governance of the association. Further differentiating the model from a franchise, a referral organization is composed of member properties that collaborate and link themselves together for marketing purposes and often have fewer rules and regulations than being a part of a franchise. While the physical appearance of each member lodging property may be different, they will offer similar quality of products and level of service to the customer.

In combining their brand and marketing resources through a referral organization, these member properties have a wider reach in creating their brand image than they would as an independent operation. For example, Leading Hotels of the World (LHW), headquartered in New York City, is an association of 375 member hotels. These properties are all connected by a central reservation system, with 25 offices around the world providing reservations, sales, and marketing services to their member hotels. Having one central website and brand image helps these independently owned businesses compete with the bigger franchises while still maintaining their individuality. Member properties are inspected regularly to ensure that they are executing against the standards of quality and service set forth by the membership to ensure that brand image is not compromised.

The largest referral organization is Best Western International with more than 4,100 properties in 100 countries around the world. Through these referral organizations, the independent owner members band together to market their businesses under a common trademark or brand. Their combining of resources allows them to leverage their membership size in purchasing power, finding efficiencies with a combined reservation system, and sharing ideas for improving operations and service.

Referral organizations like Best Western International, Leading Hotels of the World, and Kampgrounds of America (KOA) allow members to maintain their individual property charms while ensuring that they meet the global quality standards set forth by the membership. Similar to the

The largest referral organization is Best Western International with more than 4,100 properties in 100 countries around the world.

expectations set by a franchise, referral organizations help customers generally know what to expect when they visit a property that flies the brand flag of the referral organization. A downside to a referral organization is that with the independence and relaxed policies and standards, the range of properties and rates can vary much more than those that are part of a franchise organization. This wide variance can sometimes be frustrating or confusing to customers.

SUMMARY

Franchises and referral organizations offer different methods to manage a hospitality operation. Each system, though with similar functions, operates differently to give owners of hospitality enterprises choices in how to make their business ventures more successful. Six of the top 10 franchisors are hospitality organizations; it is likely that you have patronized or even worked for a franchised operation in the hospitality industry. Franchising offers operational consistency in brand offering and service quality to both owners and customers alike. As a future hospitality professional you have a wide range of employment choices available. If owning your own business is something you are interested in, a franchise is a way to go into business for yourself without starting the operation from scratch and doing everything on your own. If adhering to the strict rules and policies laid out by a franchisor seems too limiting to your independent, entrepreneurial spirit, being a part of a referral organization might offer you the best of both worlds.

RESOURCES

Internet Sites

Hotels 325: http://bt.e-ditionsbyfry.com/article/325_HOTELS/2224891/266418/article.html

Wyndham Worldwide: http://www.wyndham-worldwide.com/category/wyndham-hotel-group

Choice Hotels: https://www.choicehotels.com/about Intercontinental

Hotels Group: http://www.ihgplc.com/index.asp?pageid=2

Hilton Worldwide: http://www.hiltonworldwide.com/about/

Marriott International, Inc.: http://www.marriott.com/about/corporate-overview.mi

Accor SA: http://www.accorhotels-group.com/en/group/accorhotels-worldwide.html

GreenTree Inns: http://www.greentreeinn.com/products.html

Vantage Hospitality:

http://www.vantagehospitality.com

Franchising Resources

www.census.gov/newsroom/releases/pdf/franchiseflyer.pdf

www.franchise.org/Franchise-News-Detail.aspx?id=59741#

http://www.franchisetimes.com/pdf/2015/2015-Top-200.pdf

http://biggbyfranchising.com

Referral Organizations

http://www.bestwestern.com/about-us/press-media/factsheet-country-detail.asp

http://www.lhw.com/corporate/fact-sheet

ENDNOTES

1. www.franchise.org/Franchise-News-Detail.aspx?id=59741#

2. http://biggbyfranchising.com

REFERENCES

Haskin, Matt. (2015). *Franchise Times Top 200*. Retrieved December 7, 2015.

Hotels. (July/August, 2015). *Hotels 325*. Retrieved November 12, 2015, pp. 23–40.

Judd, Richard J. and Justis, Robert T. (2008). *Franchising: An Entrepreneur's Guide*, 4th ed. Mason, OH: Thompson.

Seid, Michael and Thomas, Dave. (2010). *Franchising for Dummies*, 2nd ed. New Jersey: Wiley Publishing, Inc.

Sickel, Julie (2015). *2015 U.S. Hotel Chain Survey*. Businesstravelnews.com. Retrieved December 7, 2015, pp. 10–19.

Name: _____ Date: _____

1. What are the advantages to opening a franchise instead of an independent operation?

2. What are the advantages to an independent operator of joining a referral organization?

3. What are the main differences between a franchise and a referral organization?

4. Why do customers like franchised or branded hospitality businesses?

5. What are the names of some local franchise operations in the area in which you live?

6. How can someone find more information about what services a franchisor offers to its franchisees?

7. As a potential employee, what are some of the advantages and disadvantages of working for a franchise over being an independent operator?

CHAPTER *9*

© Jeerawan Soisayampoo/Shutterstock.com

CONTRACT AND ASSET MANAGEMENT

AUTHORS	*Wanda M. Costen, Northern Arizona University* *David A. Sherf, CHM Warnick*
LEARNING OBJECTIVES	• Understand the roles of owner, contractor, and asset manager. • Know the components of a management contract. • Understand the key criteria for selecting a hotel management contractor. • Understand how hotel asset managers partner with and create value for owners. • Understand asset management pricing. • Explain the roles of owner, host, client, contractor, asset manager, and self-operators. • Describe the different segments of the on-site foodservice industry. • Know the key players in the hotel management and on-site foodservice industry. • Understand the career opportunities available in contract services management.

CHAPTER OUTLINE	Introduction
	Hotel Contract Management
	    The Contract
	    Choosing a Hotel Management Company
	    Hotel Asset Management
	Contract Foodservice Management
	    The Players
	    On-Site Foodservice Management Companies

INTRODUCTION

You may not realize it, but when you stay at a hotel or motel, sometimes the company that runs or operates the hotel is not the same company that *owns* the property. Similarly, when you eat in your university's dining facilities, there is often a separate organization providing the foodservice. The organization that runs the hotel or foodservice operation is called an operator.

Over the years, real estate has been an attractive and lucrative investment. Many investment companies choose to purchase real estate, and subsequently build a lodging property on the land. These investment companies typically do not have the expertise necessary to operate a hotel or motel, and therefore hire another organization to run the property. Likewise, most businesses, universities, and hospitals do not operate their own cafeterias. They, too, hire outside organizations to run their foodservice operations. The agreement between the owners and the operators is called a contract, and thus this segment of the hospitality industry is referred to as **contract services management**.

HOTEL CONTRACT MANAGEMENT

The concept of separating the ownership and operation of a lodging property fueled much of the capital needed to fund the expansive growth of the lodging industry in the 1970s and 1980s. Investors were able to purchase land all over the country, without having to be concerned with the challenges of running a lodging property. Operators were able to grow their brands and expand into new markets, without huge capital expenditures.

Ultimately, there are three parties involved in hotel management contracts: lenders, owners, and operators. Each party has its own objectives or incentives for entering into the contract. Lenders are typically concerned with generating an adequate financial rate of return and protecting the investment. In recent years, lenders have become more involved in the negotiation of these contracts. **Owners** are primarily interested in generating cash flow, and ensuring that their capital investment grows in value. **Operators** desire an increase in both market presence and market share, maintaining control over the day-to-day management decisions, and long-term stability.[1]

There are three types of operators: brand operators, independent management companies, and self-managed. Brand operators, as the name implies, are the management arm of major hotel chains like Marriott, Starwood, Hyatt, and Hilton. In November 2015, Marriott International acquired Starwood and instantly become the world's largest hotel company with 1.1 million rooms in 5400 hotels![2] This continued trend towards acquisitions means the group of major chains is becoming smaller each year. In July 2007, Blackstone Group, a global real estate firm, purchased Hilton Hotels Corporation for $26 billion. Blackstone owns substantial interests in publicly-traded hotel companies including Hilton Hotels, Wyndham, Extended Stay America, and La Quinta. Starwood has eleven different brands today, including Sheraton, Westin, W, Four Points, and St. Regis. These brand operators have name brand recognition, a history of successful performance, and efficient operating systems.

As the largest global lodging group, Intercontinental Hotels Group (IHG) manages 772 of its 4955 hotels or about 16% of all the hotels within the IHG chain.[3] By contrast, Hyatt manages 54% of the rooms in the Hyatt chain.[4] Prior to the acquisition of Starwood, Marriott had 4,175 hotel properties, of which approximately 31% or 1,293 were managed by Marriott itself.[5] This makes it the largest chain management operator.

Independent management companies (contractors) are not affiliated with any specific brand. For example, Interstate Hotels & Resorts is the largest global hotel management company with 435 properties in eleven countries.[6] The Hotel Group manages 25 properties under brands like Double Tree, Sheraton,

Sheraton is one of the 25 properties The Hotel Group manages.

Crowne Plaza, Microtel, Best Western, Embassy Suites, and even Courtyard by Marriott.[7, 8]

Self-managed hotels are those where the hotel owner only manages the hotels s/he owns.

THE CONTRACT

The most significant change in the contract negotiating process over the past few years has been the more active involvement of lenders, and an increase in the power of the owners. Owners have developed more knowledge about hotel operations, and an increase in the number of hotel operators (i.e., competition) has shifted the bargaining power to the owners.

A management contract is a written agreement between two organizations that outlines each party's responsibilities and consequences for not fulfilling its obligations. Management contracts comprise several key provisions, which explain the contract. One key provision is **operator loan and equity contributions**. As a result of the increase in competition amongst operators, many are now choosing to make loan or equity contributions. In the past, operators were solely responsible for managing the hotel property, but today operators are willing to contribute funding, which demonstrates the operator's commitment to the success of the property.

All contracts include an initial **term** or length of the contract, and guidelines for renewing the contract. The length of the initial term for brand operators is approximately 8–10 years, with one or two 3–5-year renewals. Independent contractor (hotel management companies) initial terms are typically 1–3 years, with one or two 2-year renewals. Owners desire shorter terms, because they believe this will entice the operator to perform well in order for the contract to be renewed. Operators obviously prefer a longer contract term, because they want stability. Operators also argue that shorter-termed contracts force them to focus on short-term goals instead of a long-term strategy.[9]

Management fees, which have decreased in recent years, are paid to the operators. In general, basic management fees have been on the decline, and **incentive fees** have become more challenging for operators to achieve. These trends are a result of the increase in owner negotiating power and operator

competition. Basic management fees for brand operators of full-service hotels average 2.25% of gross revenues without an operator equity contribution, and 2.5% or more of gross revenues with an operator equity contribution. Independent management companies typically receive **base fees** of 1.5% and 2.5% of gross revenues respectively.[10]

Incentive fees are typically based upon cash flow after debt service or return on equity. Cash flow after debt service is the amount of cash that flows through the company after paying for its debts. Return on equity is the amount of profit a company makes with the money shareholders have invested. In the past, operator incentives were determined by gross operating profit, or the amount of revenue generated after the costs associated with the goods and services sold are removed. This shift indicates that owners expect operators to contribute to the bottom line profit of the venture, not just the revenue.

Another important area that must be addressed in the contract is the **brand's system reimbursable expenses**. The owner pays the brand/operator for centralized services provided by the brand through a brand license or franchise agreement. For example, brands provide comprehensive marketing and advertising programs, centralized reservations systems, frequent guest rewards programs, management information systems, purchasing services, as well as risk management and insurance. Owners pay these costs, because these systems are provided by the brand, and the property benefits from them. In addition to these costs, each franchise agreement requires an owner to pay a franchise fee for the use of the brand name. The base franchise fee for the use of the brand name ranges from 3% to 6% of room revenues, and may also include a percentage fee based on the food and beverage revenues.

Total franchise fees are a combination of all these costs, plus the brand fee. The total costs and fees range from 8% to 12% or more of room revenues. When a brand manages a property, some of these franchise costs may be reduced for hotel owners. When an independent management company manages a property, they have to pay the full brand franchise fees and costs on top of the management fees. Thus a brand-managed hotel may have the ability to charge less in total franchise and management fees than an independent management company.

As with individual employee performance, management companies must be held accountable for achieving certain outcomes. These **performance standards** are the specific criteria the operators must meet to achieve the owners' goals (e.g., a particular customer satisfaction score or a certain percentage of profit). These standards are included in the contract and are typically evaluated each year. Often the measures include year-to-year growth, based upon an initial 3–5-year gross operating profit projection. When the hotel first opens, an operator may have one or two years, or a grace period, before the performance criteria are fine-tuned. If the operator assumes control of an existing property, the operator usually has a 6-month grace period. When operators fall short of their projections due to changes in the economy or market, owners may make allowances for lower than expected performance. If the operator simply does not meet the performance criteria, they are usually required to pay the owner the difference between the approved budget and what was achieved at the hotel. Additionally, owners usually include options for terminating a contract based upon continued poor performance.

The specific conditions under which a contract may be terminated by either party is a crucial component of every contract. Once again, there is a benefit to being a brand-managed property. In general, owners cannot terminate a contract with a brand operator at any time. However, after some period of time in the contract, owners may terminate the operator, but the franchise agreement, which may be modified, usually stays in place. Owners must pay operators a termination fee, which ranges from 2–4 times the management fee for brand operators, and 0.5–2 times the management fee for independent management companies.[11]

The final component of the contract is the degree of input the owner has in decision-making related to running the hotel. Owners usually negotiate the right to have input on the annual budget and hiring the executive staff. In general, the executive staff (general manager, controller, and directors of marketing, human resources, rooms, food and beverage, housekeeping, and engineering) and hourly staff are employees of the operating company.

It is important to note that as with all contracts, each provision or component is negotiated. As mentioned earlier, today owners have gained a slight advantage in negotiating, but major brand operators are still able to influence the provisions that matter most to them.

CHOOSING A HOTEL MANAGEMENT COMPANY

Given the large number of hotel operators today, it is important for owners to develop criteria for selecting a management company. Research shows that there are several key areas that should be examined and evaluated when choosing a company to operate a hotel. First, an owner should look at the operating performance of the hotels being managed by that particular company, and obtain feedback from the owners of these hotels. Next, the owner should try to determine how accessible the operating company's senior management is. How willing is the operator's senior management to meet with the owner and work through issues, or discuss opportunities for growth? The owner should also try to get a feel for the overall integrity of the operating company. What is the operator's reputation in the industry? Does the operating company's organizational culture and values align with those of the owner's company?[12]

Brands provide tremendous expertise in lodging management. For example, Marriott International has cutting edge marketing strategies and campaigns that can drive customers to an owner's hotel. Similarly, Hilton Worldwide's General Managers have an average tenure of 15 years,[13] which means owners who partner with Hilton will have a seasoned manager leading the property. Hyatt has a corporate team of over 100 sales professionals dedicated to growing

It is important for owners to develop criteria for selecting a management company.

© Dmitry Kalinovsky/Shutterstock.com

revenue for their properties.[14] These are just some of the examples of the benefits of partnering with a brand management company.

It is important to note that hotel owners and operators must work together to create a successful hotel that delivers or exceeds the level of customer service expected by its guests. The process of negotiating a management contract is one of give and take. Each party has its own goals, but must be flexible in order to create a mutually beneficial contract.

HOTEL ASSET MANAGEMENT

Now that we've talked about management companies, it's time to discuss asset management. Modern day hotel asset management involves a hotel owner hiring someone who reports to the hotel owner, and is tasked with implementing an owner-driven strategic plan and vision. The management company and the general manager need to work together with the asset manager for the hotel to be successful. Excluding one party from the equation results in less than optimal results, and is like a boat being rowed by oarsmen rowing at different speeds. A seasoned hotel asset manager helps define the owner's short and long-term financial goals, and communicates these in an understandable and measurable way to the management company and the general manager. This process involves analyzing all areas of the hotel, and helping guide the property team to maximize and increase the value of the hotel. An asset manager may also assist the owner with different financing and sale strategies.

The Role and Scope of a Hotel Asset Manager

When a hotel is purchased, it typically already has a brand (e.g., Marriott, Hilton, Hyatt, etc.). The new owner selects a management company to operate the hotel, and the management company then selects, usually with the owner's approval, a general manager. When an asset manager is hired, two of the most important areas to evaluate are the brand the hotel should operate under, and which management company should be selected.

As mentioned earlier in this chapter, a hotel owner often does not have the business experience necessary to fully understand all the aspects of managing a hotel. Many owners do not realize that the "business of hotels" is different from the hotel business, and a quality asset manager thoroughly understands

the "business of hotels." The hotel business can be characterized as owning and operating a hotel with minimal owner engagement and involvement. The "business of hotels" is fully understanding that the hotel itself is a complex real estate investment, and to fully maximize the value of the real estate, it must have the right brand, the right management company, and the right strategy to maximize value. An asset manager orchestrates the process for all parties to understand what is necessary to maximize the hotel's value and guides them towards the timely achievement of the owner's goals. Ultimately, a hotel asset manager helps a hotel owner fully understand the investment they own and implements the owner's objectives to increase cash flow to build maximum value. The scope of an asset manager's duties includes the following areas, described in detail below.

Investment Strategy. It is critical that the asset manager understand whether the owner is investing in the hotel property for a short while, or the long-term. The asset manager also helps the owner determine whether s/he has the financial ability to endure negative changes in the economic climate. The asset manager guides the owner in calculating how much money to invest in the hotel property (e.g., to upgrade or add facilities), and the degree to which this investment might enhance the property's market position or significantly increase the property's value.

Asset managers also work with owners to determine the appropriate brand affiliation, and the costs/fees associated with branding. Sometimes the best decision for the owner may be for the hotel to be an independent. Overall, the asset manager helps the owner determine the best brand strategy for accomplishing the owner's goals and objectives.

Brand and Management Company. The next key area to explore is which brand best aligns with the market positioning of the hotel. The asset manager helps the owner understand the importance of distribution and brand loyalty. Distribution is the number of hotels, by brand, throughout the U.S. or within a particular region. This is important information for the owner to understand, because travelers who prefer a particular brand like to travel almost anywhere in the U.S., and stay at their preferred hotel brand. If a hotel brand does not have significant distribution, travelers loyal to one brand may not find that brand when seeking lodging in another city, and thus stay at a competing brand.

Distribution is a key factor in brand loyalty, and all major brands have frequent guest reward programs, where guests accrue points for staying with a specific brand. Guests are usually going to seek hotels/brands where they can quickly earn the most cumulative points, rather than earning points with several brands.

The asset manager also works with the management company to select a general manager and executive team that can best support and achieve the owner's goals and objectives. Once the management team has been selected, the asset manager works with the general manager to assess all areas of the operation, and develop a plan to address any concerns. The asset manager also works with the management company to establish a realistic marketing plan, a revenue management strategy, an annual budget, as well as formal reports. Because the asset manager has expertise in the "business of hotels," s/he also shares best practices with the management team, and works with the general manager to not only achieve (and hopefully exceed) the annual profit goals, but also to increase the hotel's cash flow. Cash flow is the amount of money available to the owner after all operating expenses (e.g., management fees, real estate taxes, insurance, interest on loans, and money set aside for replacing furniture and other building enhancements) have been deducted. The asset manager also reviews guest satisfaction and employee surveys, social media reviews, and brand inspection reports.

Since the asset manager builds relationships with both the owner and the management company, s/he often serves as a liaison between both parties, and assists with reaching consensus on difficult issues. In short, the asset manager is constantly monitoring the hotel's competitive environment, which includes economic, social, and technological changes.

Contract Administration. The asset manager reviews all of the management company's contracts, leases, and third party agreements. The asset manager also ensures strict compliance with the brand franchise agreement or management contract, in addition to reviewing the fees/costs associated with franchising or the management contract.

Capital Planning and Expenditures. Capital refers to the money the owner will invest in the hotel each year. Therefore, the asset manager helps the owner plan for these expenditures. In order for the asset

manager to assist the owner in making these decisions, s/he must understand the physical condition and limitations of the hotel, the brand standards, and the available funds the owner has to invest in the hotel. Not only does the asset manager work with the management company to develop a 5-year investment plan for the owner and general manager to review, but s/he also proposes the specific projects and associated budgets and timelines for implementation and completion. Additionally, the asset manager evaluates preventive maintenance programs needed to maintain the hotel's physical condition, as well as the occupational safety, health requirements, and compliance with the Americans with Disabilities Act.

Competitive Market Environment. As you're starting to understand, it's important for the asset manager to fully comprehend the market in which the hotel property operates. It's important that asset managers understand the key market drivers, and the degree to which these impact the property. They track the hotel's occupancy percentage, Average Daily Rate (ADR), in addition to the market mix of competitive properties. They also analyze the property's penetration rate. Finally, the asset manager prepares an annual report to the owner with the hotel's estimated value, which helps the owner determine whether to hold or sell the property.

As demonstrated above, an asset manager needs to be effective, and most importantly have the trust of both the owner and the hotel management team. An asset manager develops her/his skill set through extensive operations experience in a variety of hotels and markets, supported by a knowledge base from the asset management firm itself. Some individual asset managers have the experience and an effective network that enables them to be competent asset managers without the support of a large asset management firm.

The Relationship of the Asset Manager, the General Manager, and the Hotel Management Company. As previously discussed, it's very important that the asset manager work with both the general manager and the hotel management company to ensure the owner achieves success. Since the business at a hotel changes daily, and often hourly, decision-making requires knowledge, flexibilty, and nimbleness to respond to market conditions, while remaining on track with the annual budget. This environment dictates a strong and trusting relationship between the asset manager and the hotel general manager. Unfortunately, in years past, many asset managers were dictatorial in style, bullied the hotel team, and took credit for successes, while attributing failures to the hotel general manager. Executive teams were skeptical of, and had little respect for, an asset manager who operated under a dictatorial style. This lack of trust permeating throughout the hotel, usually results in less than optimal operating performance.

Today, the best approach to be a successful asset manager is to earn the respect of the executive team, collaboratively evaluate and embark on a business strategy, and allow the management company to take credit for the hotel's performance. An asset manager offers guidance to the hotel team to implement the strategy set by the owner, and should be able to offer expert advice gained through years of operational experience. The key to success is based on trust, which must be earned by the asset manager. If the hotel general manager or the asset manager is unwilling to share her/his thoughts, concerns, and ideas in an open manner with the other, neither will prosper. At the end of the day, final operational decisions should be made by the general manager, as s/he is responsible for managing of the hotel, and these decisions will impact her/his job and compensation. This is always a delicate area and both sides must be acutely aware of the effects of each decision.

Hotel asset management has evolved due to the increased complexity of hotel operations caused by more transparency in the sources of business, the prices consumers pay for rooms, the evergrowing multitude of revenue chanels, the competitive and market-driven need for increased customer interaction and satisfaction, employee needs, increased regulation, and more sophisticated owners. The hotel asset manager should be a trusted resource for the general manager, who responds quickly to help solve issues in a timely manner, using her/his experience, knowledge, and industry best practices.

Who Actually Runs the Hotel: The Asset Manager or the General Manager?
The asset manager has a fiduciary resposibilty to the owner to maximize the value of the hotel in accordance with the strategy set forth by the owner; however, the hotel management company and its general manager are the true operators of the hotel.

An asset manager has to let the management company and general manager do what they have been hired to do, while providing critical oversight in all areas of the operation. This is a delicate balance. While budgets, marketing and revenue plans, capital spending, and market positioning are many of the areas where the asset and general management work together, a big role of the asset manager is to question why things are being done in a particular way. For example, an asset manager would ask: Should more sales people be added? Does the ballroom need recarpeting or can it wait two more years? Should the theme of the restaurant be changed? Should the hotel begin charging for parking? Should housekeeping staff's wages be raised since there's a new hotel opening across the street that might recruit the hotel's employees? Should the hotel eliminate room service or start free airport shuttle service? What type of amenities should be given to our best customers, etc. Management's responses to these questions impact the hotel's performance, and having an asset manager to navigate the hotel through these issues is welcomed by most seasoned general managers.

A good asset manager must effectively communicate both good and bad news to the owner. There should be no surprises. How decisions are made is as important as the decisions themselves. While an owner should know the value being delivered by the asset manager, all recognition for successes should go to the property management team. Shortcomings should be reviewed, and each party should be held accountable for its part in the lack of success. Finger pointing is a quick road to a lack of trust.

Is the Brand the Right One?
The right brand for a hotel is one that delivers the right type of guests willing to pay the rates needed to support the hotel's market position and the owner's investment. Moving to a higher quality brand means being able to exit the existing contract, and finding a brand that is more attractive to consumers. Moving to a higher quality brand nearly always requires an owner to invest substantial capital (money) to upgrade many areas of the hotel, which may include adding facilities like meeting space, restaurants, and more guest rooms. An asset manager needs to quickly understand the current brand, determine if it's appropriate, and whether the contract can be terminated. If the brand is appropriate, the asset manager and general manager should meet with the corporate brand team, and gather their suggestions for improving the

The right brand for a hotel is one that delivers the right type of guests willing to pay the rates needed to support the hotel's market position, and the owner's investment.

business. If the brand is not appropriate, it may be in the best interest of the owner to shorten the term of the contract, and bring in a better brand that can more quickly attain the owner's goals and objectives.

Improved Physical Product. Most hotels will benefit from upgrading the facilities, particularly the rooms and public spaces. This entails a well thought out process that is dependent on the owner's financial ability to fund a renovation. Many factors must be reviewed to determine a renovation's short-term and long-term Return on Investment. An experienced design and construction team and brand input are critical to a successful renovation. The asset manager should take responsibilty for hiring the project team and directing, managing, and administering the renovation, in close coordination with the general manager. This allows the hotel's management team to conduct its daily business without spending the time and energy necessary to manage the renovation process.

Managing the General Manager. The asset manager is the eyes and ears of the owner, and essentially manages the general manager. This process begins with properly positioning the hotel to achieve maximum cash flow and then annually guiding the hotel to optimum results based on everchanging market and operational conditions. An asset manager helps translate the owner's vision to measurable financial goals, which becomes the annual budget. Budgets should begin with realistic revenue assumptions based upon the hotel's physical condition, the market, and the overall general economic outlook. General managers may over or under estimate the

property's competitiveness, which can result in missed budgets, or failing to achieve the hotel's true potential. Monitoring budgets and helping develop plans to keep budgets on track are an asset manager's key responsibilities.

Annual and Five-Year Capital Plan. Evaluating the annual and five year capital plan is a continuous, evolving process that serves as the basis for building hotel value. It starts with an accurate assessment of the hotel's physical condition, but also includes the hotel's ranking among its competitive set, guest feedback, preventive maintenance programs, the hotel's profitability, and the owner's ability to provide funds. The five-year capital outlook enables an owner to see how much capital may be needed and when. This plan may also help an owner determine whether to sell or keep the property.

How Asset Managers are Compensated and Typical Contract Terms

Asset managers may be hired directly by owners. If a company owns many hotels, it may have in-house asset management. An asset management firm's compensation is either a flat monthly fee or a percentage of total revenues. The negotiated fees are typically ⅓ to ¾ of a percent of the hotel's total annual revenues. There could also be an incentive fee for achieving or exceeding the annual budgeted net operating income. The fees are directly related to the amount of time an asset manager spends on hotel-related activities. The more time an asset manager is required to work on hotel matters, the greater the fee. Additionally, most asset management contracts are 1–3 years in length, and specifically identify the the asset manager's responsibilities, the required weekly or monthly financial reports they will provide, and how frequently s/he will meet with ownership.

Which Hotel Owners Utilize Asset Managers?

While nearly all hotels can benefit from an asset manager's oversight, hotels with food and beverage outlets, and revenues in excess of $5 million typically employ asset managers. All types of hotel owners employ asset managers: individual owners, municipalities with convention center hotels, public hotel companies (e.g. Marriott, Hilton, Hyatt, etc.), Real Estate Investment Trusts (REITs) (e.g., Host Hotels & Resorts, LaSalle Hotel Properties, FelCor Lodging Trust, etc.), or real estate companies that own hotels.

As previously mentioned, lodging companies like Marriott and Hilton do not own many hotels today, but they do have internal asset managers on their staff. This is also true for hotel REITs, which own many hotels and have asset managers on their staffs. Individual owners, municipalities, and real estate companies are the largest employers of third party asset managers, because they typically do not have the necessary internal expertise, and may not want to fund an asset management team. These latter three ownership categories also often own larger and more complex hotels, requiring an asset manager's expertise.

CONTRACT FOODSERVICE MANAGEMENT

The evolution of the term used to describe foodservice management contracts also explains the transition of this segment of the hospitality industry. Contract foodservice management was initially called institutional foodservice, because most contracts were with hospitals, industrial plants, and correctional facilities (prisons). The focus was on producing mass quantities of food that could be delivered quickly. Not surprisingly, quality was not a high priority. Today this segment of the foodservice industry is known as **on-site foodservice management**, or managed foodservice. The quality of food and service provided in business organizations, hospitals, schools, colleges and universities, and recreational facilities today often rivals that of top restaurants. The difference is that the foodservice is provided on-site (i.e., at the hospital, business organization, or recreational facility). Furthermore, today's providers of on-site foodservice now manage other services (e.g., copy centers, on-site childcare, company stores) as well. This segment totals approximately $230 billion of the $800 billion global foodservice industry.[15]

THE PLAYERS

In order to grasp the difference between on-site foodservice management and restaurants, one must first understand the terminology and the roles of the players. First, the *contractor* is the organization that provides the foodservice. The **host** is the organization that hires the contractor. The **client** is the person within the host organization that serves as the host

organization's representative and is responsible for monitoring the contractor's performance. In a general sense, the term client is also used to refer to the entire host organization.

Some host organizations decide to operate their own foodservice instead of hiring an outside contractor. These organizations are **self-operated**. In these situations the foodservice operation is a division of the host organization, and all of the managers and employees in the foodservice operation work for the host company. Many school districts operate their own foodservice organizations, but there is a trend toward outsourcing. It is often difficult for organizations to profitably operate two separate organizations. Until 2001, the largest and most successful self-operated on-site foodservice organization was Motorola. Its Hospitality Group generated revenues in excess of $55 million in 2001.[16] However, the pressure to reduce costs while maintaining quality and generating revenues became too challenging, and Motorola hired Compass Group North America to run its foodservice in September 2001.

ON-SITE FOODSERVICE MANAGEMENT COMPANIES

The largest on-site foodservice management company is the Compass Group. This organization is based in Britain and generated revenue in excess of $25 billion in 2015.[17] Compass operates in 50 countries with over 509,000 employees.[18] Each of its businesses operate as separate entities under the following brands: Eurest, Bon Appetit, Restaurant Associates, Medirest, Morrison, Crothall, Chartwells, Scolarest, Levy Restaurants, All Leisure, ESS, and Canteen.[19]

The next largest on-site foodservice management company is also a global company: Sodexo Group. Sodexo is based in France and generated $21.6 billion in revenue in 2015.[20] Sodexo operates in 80 countries and employs approximately 420,000 people.[21]

The third largest on-site foodservice management company is ARAMARK Corporation, which is the only major player based in the U.S. In 2015, ARAMARK generated over $14.3 billion in sales.[22] It operates in 20 countries and employs 259,000 people.[23] As the numbers indicate, these companies manage the overwhelming majority of contracts in the on-site foodservice segment of the hospitality industry.

ON-SITE FOODSERVICE SEGMENTS

The on-site foodservice industry is divided into market segments based on where the foodservice is provided. The first market segment is business and industry. Approximately 85%–90% of this segment is operated by on-site managed services organizations.[24]

In this market segment, on-site foodservice contractors operate dining facilities in corporate offices. These facilities include multiple food stations, often with different ethnic cuisines. Today the trend is toward exhibition cooking and meal replacement. Many on-site foodservice contractors prepare take-home meals for their customers. Customers can now eliminate a stop on the way home, and this increases the revenue of the operation. The focus is on providing what the customers want and exceeding their expectations, while remaining profitable. Not surprisingly, these are the same goals of a freestanding restaurant.

The education segment of the industry comprises K–12 schools, as well as colleges and universities. Approximately 60%–65% of college and university foodservice is operated by managed services companies, while only 15%–20% of K–12 foodservice is contracted out.[25]

With the reductions in federal funding, the focus in K–12 schools is on reducing costs and increasing participation. Managed services providers are also offering on-site childcare (i.e., before and after school programs). Moreover, occasionally the foodservice operator extends its services to adult daycare centers, preschools, and private schools that are nearby. Centralized production kitchens often allow the on-site foodservice contractor to serve these other organizations with little increase in costs.[26]

Foodservice operations on college and university campuses have two types of operations. One is the **board plan** and the other is termed *retail*. The board plan allows students to pre-purchase a set number of meals throughout the semester. These all-you-can-eat meals are typically offered in the campus dining halls. Retail operations resemble shopping mall food courts. Students transfer money to a debit card, which is used to purchase items in the food courts and kiosks around campus. Managed services providers use branding (which will be discussed later) to increase participation.

Heathcare is a challenge because it includes patient feeding in addition to operating on-site dining facilities.

Healthcare is probably the most challenging segment of the on-site foodservice industry, because it includes patient feeding, in addition to operating on-site dining facilities. Not only are there nutrition and dietary concerns in this segment, but patient treatment has shifted from inpatient to outpatient services, and shorter hospital stays. This shift has resulted in lower foodservice revenue projections. Managed services companies have opted to offer additional services like housekeeping and facilities maintenance to offset these reductions. This shift might also explain why only 40%–45% of this segment is managed by on-site foodservice companies.[27]

Recreation and leisure is the fastest growing segment of this industry, with 35%–40% of the business being operated by managed services companies. This segment includes ball parks, stadiums, arenas, and national and state parks. Today's sports fan can find a wide variety of menu options, ranging from clam chowder and garlic fries at AT&T Park in San Francisco to a Dodger Dog at Dodger Stadium in Los Angeles. Additionally, many of the top stadiums and arenas today have deluxe skyboxes, where gourmet meal packages are offered.[28]

Corrections or prison feeding is the final segment in this industry. Not surprisingly, only 10%–15% of this industry is managed by on-site foodservice contractors.[29] Security is only one of the challenges in this segment. Prison foodservice production facilities were not built to accommodate the recent increase in the prison population, which presents many challenges for foodservice operators. Additionally, similar to K–12 schools and hospitals, the correctional nutrition requirements pose unique challenges in designing menus. Moreover, the workers in these facilities are inmates, which can present management challenges.

BRANDING

On-site foodservice management companies have realized the importance of branding for increasing revenues. In each segment, the dining facilities include national, regional, and corporate brands. **Branding** has shifted the ambience of on-site dining from a cafeteria to a "market-style eatery."[30] National brands include fast food eateries like KFC and Pizza Hut, as well as Starbucks. Regional brands allow the management companies to bring in foods that are unique to the local area. Finally, each of the major on-site foodservice companies has developed its own in-house brands. For example, you might find a Coyote Jack's Grill next to a Burger King kiosk in a Compass account, or a Miso Noodle Bar next to a Quizno sub outlet in an ARAMARK account.

CAREER OPPORTUNITIES

Like the restaurant industry in general, there are vast career opportunities in on-site foodservice management. In operations, a recent college graduate can expect to spend 2–3 months in a comprehensive training program, followed by an assignment as an Assistant Foodservice Manager at a particular location. Within 3–5 years, an Assistant Manager can move up to a Foodservice Director position (depending on the complexity of the operation). Most foodservice operators aspire to reach a District Manager position. This position oversees on-site foodservice operations within a specific geographic region, and reports to a Regional Vice President. One of the primary benefits of a career in this segment is the hours. Typically, foodservice managers work during the hours of operation for their location. Thus, if a business and industry account operates Monday–Friday, 7:00 A.M.–6:00 P.M., the management team typically provides breakfast and lunch, and does not have to work late nights and weekends. This structure allows those with a passion for the foodservice business to also have a quality life.

SUMMARY

Contract services management allows the ownership and operation of a hospitality venue to be separated. The owner and operator enter into a binding legal contract, which outlines the nature of the relationship and each party's responsibilities. While hotel management companies are facing increasing competition, which is impacting their bargaining power, on-site foodservice organizations are gathering up more of the market. This segment of the hospitality industry offers unique, challenging, and exciting career opportunities, which provide employment options for hospitality majors. Hotel asset management is becoming an increasingly important component of lodging management. Asset managers, who are focused on maximizing a hotel's value, serve as a liaison between the owners and hotel management companies.

ENDNOTES

1. Eyster, J. (1993). The Revolution In Domestic Hotel Management Contracts. *Cornell Hotel and Restaurant Administration Quarterly*, (February), pp. 16–26.

2. Marriott International to acquire Starwood Hotels & Resorts Worldwide, creating the world's largest hotel company. (2015). Retrieved 4 January 2016 from the Marriott International website: http://news.marriott.com/2015/11/marriott-international-to-acquire-starwood-hotels-resorts-worldwide-creating-the-worlds-largest-hotel.html

3. How our business works. (2015). Retrieved 4 January 2016 from the Intercontinental Hotels Group website: http://www.ihgplc.com/index.asp?pageid=18

4. Hyatt Hotels Corporation Investor Presentation. (2015). Retrieved 4 January 2016 from the Hyatt Hotels Corporation website: http://s2.q4cdn.com/278413729/files/doc_presentations/2015/Investor-Presentation-November-2015.pdf

5. United States Securities and Exchange Commission: Marriott International, Inc. Form 10-K. (2014).

6. Global Hotel Portfolio. (2014). Retrieved 4 January 2016 from the Interstate Hotels & Resorts website: http://interstatehotels.com/portfolio/brand/ac-hotels-by-marriott/

7. Hotel Business 2015 Management Companies. (2015). Retrieved 4 January 2016 from the Hotel Business website: http://m.hotelbusiness.com/links/surveys/results/management_2015.php

8. *History*. (2007). Retrieved November 16, 2007 from The Hotel Group website: http://www.thehotelgroup.com/about_history.asp

9. Eyster, J. (1997). Hotel Management Contracts in the *U.S. Cornell Hotel and Restaurant Administration Quarterly*, (June), pp. 21–33.

10. Ibid.

11. Ibid.

12. Rainsford, P. (1994). Selecting and Monitoring Hotel-Management Companies. *Cornell Hotel and Restaurant Administration Quarterly*, (April), pp. 30–35.

13. Hilton Management Services. (2015). Retrieved 4 January 2016 from the Hilton Worldwide website: http://www.hiltonworldwide.com/development/management-services/

14. Hyatt Development Sales and Marketing. (2015). Retrieved 4 January 2016 from the Hyatt Corporation website: http://www.hyattdevelopment.com/competitive_strengths/sales_and_marketing.html

15. Reynolds, D. (2003). *On-Site Foodservice Management: A Best Practices Approach*. Hoboken, New Jersey: John Wiley & Sons, Inc.

16. Ibid.

17. Compass Group. (2015). *Full Year Results*. Retrieved January 9, 2016 from the Compass Group website: http://www.compass-group.com/documents/FY_15_Press_Release_FINAL.pdf

18. Ibid.

19. Compass Group, 2012. *Annual Report*. Retrieved May 2, 2013 from the Compass Group website: http://annualreport12.compass-group.com/our_business/focus_on_our_sectors

20. Sodexo Group. (2015). *Sodexo Fiscal 2015 Registration Document*. Retrieved January 9, 2016 from the Sodexho Group website: http://www.sodexo.com/en/Images/Sodexo-Fiscal2015-Registration-Document_v151125342-877090.pdf

21. Sodexho Group. (2013). *Sodexho in a Snapshot.* Retrieved May 2, 2013 from the Sodexho Group website: http://www.sodexo.com/en/Images/GB13ChiffresCles2012342-557885.pdf

22. ARAMARK Corporation. (2007). *2015 Results: Fourth Quarter & Full Year.* Retrieved January 9, 2016 from the ARAMARK Corporation website: http://phx.corporate-ir.net/phoenix.zhtml?c=130030&p=irol-calendar

23. Ibid., 2012.

24. Reynolds, D. (1999). Managed Services Companies: The New Scorecard for On-Site Foodservice. *Cornell Hotel and Restaurant Administration Quarterly,* (June), pp. 64–73.

25. Ibid.

26. Ibid.

27. Ibid.

28. Ibid.

29. Ibid.

30. Ibid.

REVIEW QUESTIONS 9

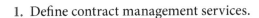

1. Define contract management services.

2. What is a hotel management contract?

3. Describe three key provisions of a hotel management contract.

4. What are some of the challenges hotel management companies face today?

5. Describe an asset manager's responsibilities.

6. Explain the relationship of the asset manager, general manager, and the hotel management company.

7. Discuss the benefits of hiring an asset manager.

8. What are the two terms used today to describe contract foodservice management?

9. Describe the market segments in the contract foodservice management industry.

10. Name the three key contract foodservice management companies.

11. What are some of the benefits of a career in contract foodservice management?

© Sorbis/Shutterstock.com

CHAPTER *10*

INTERNATIONAL COMPANIES

AUTHOR

Christina K. Dimitriou, State University of New York at Plattsburgh

LEARNING OBJECTIVES

- Discuss how hospitality chain operations and franchises differ from independent companies on an international level.
- Describe the cultural and ethical considerations when managing at an international level.
- Identify the emerging hospitality industry trends internationally.
- List the important steps in building an international career.
- Explain the value of study abroad programs and the key role that international internships play in a hospitality student's career.

CHAPTER OUTLINE

Business ethics

Franchises

Hospitality chain operations

Independent hospitality
companies

International internships

International tourism growth

Study abroad programs

AN INTERNATIONAL PERSPECTIVE TO MANAGING HOSPITALITY COMPANIES

Very large American-owned hotel companies own and/or operate properties in the U.S. and throughout the world. Large hotel companies owned by Asians, Europeans, and people of other nationalities own and/or operate properties in the U.S. and other regions of the world. It is important to understand that where these companies are in the world and how they operate does matter and can create many challenges for the people involved in running them. Cultural and ethical concerns should not be underestimated as they play a key role in international hospitality management. Therefore, hospitality students who wish to pursue an international career in the hospitality industry and who are excited about the great employment opportunities that are associated with this industry should also be aware of what is required of them in order to succeed.

MANAGEMENT/OWNERSHIP OF HOSPITALITY ORGANIZATIONS ON AN INTERNATIONAL LEVEL

In the world of international hospitality management, chain operations and franchises differ from independent hospitality companies on several levels. Apart from the clear differences related to management/ownership issues that have already been discussed in previous chapters, additional differences exist on an operational level. Hospitality chains and franchises not only consist of a significant number of properties, but they also have the same set standards, share the same operating systems and procedures, and abide by the same rules. Contrastingly, independently owned companies can consist of one or more owners who live and operate in that country and create their own rules and standards that can be very different culturally and ethically for a foreigner who must adjust to them. This is a critical piece of information that hospitality students need to know as they prepare to enter the hospitality industry. For example, if they decide to join a hospitality chain, then they will learn everything about the rules and policies that all its properties follow and be ready to work in any of them. Similarly, if they decide to switch

to another hospitality chain, the same principle will apply. However, things get more complicated when deciding to be employed by an independent hospitality company where no general rules exist and all policies are set by the general manager (GM). Another risk that hospitality students may encounter, in this case, is the possibility of having to deal with more than one supervisor who may have contradicting ideas and opinions, which can be extremely confusing. Taking the time to carefully research the details of the hospitality company they intend to work for will enable them to make the best decision for their future.

CULTURAL AND ETHICAL CONSIDERATIONS WHEN MANAGING AT AN INTERNATIONAL LEVEL

Working for a multinational hospitality organization can be very challenging not only in terms of operating in a different political, social, and economic environment, but also in terms of the cultural differences and ethical considerations that come into play. Hospitality organizations that operate around the world may have the same company standards, but the cultural norms and ethical values and beliefs within some of those countries can be significantly different. For example, in Japan, a person cannot conduct business unless he/she gives the other party a small gift. In India, hiring relatives in one's company is considered an ethical and appropriate way of conducting business. In Indonesia, bribing an official is an acceptable cost of doing business. However, all these actions are considered unethical in the U.S.

When it comes to implementing ethics abroad, there are two theories that must be considered: a) cultural relativism which dictates that no culture's ethics are better than any other's; therefore there are no international rights and wrongs, and b) ethical imperialism which directs people to do exactly as they do at home wherever they are in the world. When a hospitality manager gets a job in a country other than his/her country of origin, it is not only important to identify the cultural differences that are involved, but also to be aware of the policies and strategies that the specific hospitality company follows, especially if it is an American company operating on foreign soil. This tactic will leave no room for any potential

It is important to identify cultural differences when working in a country other than your country of origin.

misunderstandings and will clearly allow managers to present and explain to hospitality employees what is considered wrong and right in the specific working environment. In turn, this will lead to a smooth and harmonious working experience for both hospitality managers and employees, free from unexpected surprises and problems.

EMERGING HOSPITALITY INDUSTRY TRENDS INTERNATIONALLY

As the hospitality industry changes and advances, its trends that are emerging internationally include the following:

Hotel Brands with Special Focuses. A number of hotels are taking the trend of sustainability to a whole new level by introducing environmentally friendly hotel properties that are eco-conscious such as the Element by Starwood. Other hotels, such as Even Hotels by Intercontinental Hotels Group (IHG), cater to guests' needs that are health-conscious by offering healthier food choices, natural and relaxing spaces, as well as a best-in-class fitness experience through their athletic studios, in-room training zones, group classes, and sets of activities customized by highly trained staff to fit each guest's special workout needs and requirements. A number of other hotels are designed and developed with a special concentration on the lifestyle such as Home 2 by Hilton, which is an innovative all-suite extended stay hotel brand; MGallery by the French hotel chain Accor, which represents unique hotels of character for luxury stays; Venu by Jumeirah in the United Arabian Emirates, which is a contemporary lifestyle brand; etc. Other hotels focus on a youthful, more family friendly clientele and offer hotel rooms with bunk beds such as Tryp by Wyndham or Jen by Shangri-La. Certain hotels have developed a concept of tailoring their product to a specific type of traveler. For example, IHG has created the Hualuxe Hotels and Resorts, which is the first upscale hotel brand in China that targets Chinese travelers, whereas Citizen M hotels have been designed specifically to meet the needs of the Millennial traveler.

Boutiquefication of Hotels. There is a growing trend towards hotels that turn from upscale and luxurious to more sophisticated, elegant hotel properties with a style that is unique and creates its own personality. They are known as soft brands and they are becoming increasingly popular around the world. Table 10.1 below represents some characteristic examples of this emerging hotel industry trend.

Emphasis on Business Ethics. More and more hospitality companies understand the importance of conducting their business in a responsible manner after taking into consideration the negative

Table 10.1	Some Boutique Hotel Chains		
Parent	**Chain**	**Total Hotels**	**Total Rooms**
Starwood	Aloft Hotels	85	14,420
Hyatt	Andaz	12	2,437
Marriott	Autograph	61	12,383
Wyndham	Dream Hotels	5	986
Starwood	W Hotels	44	12,609
IHG	Hotel Indigo	59	6,566

Source: Hood, 2014

repercussions of ethical scandals that have plagued the hotel industry in recent years. Efforts to create ethical codes of conduct and set clear ethical standards for their management and staff has become a top priority for many hospitality organizations.

Technological Advancements. The hospitality industry is going mobile internationally. Cell phones are used by guests to make reservations, do an e-check-in, provide keyless access to their hotel rooms, and use their hotels' concierge services. Wearable technology is becoming very popular around the world and better apps are being introduced and implemented by many hotel companies across the globe. More and more hospitality companies are turning to big data analytics to drive their guest acquisition, engagement, and retention strategies. These companies and their guests are generating massive amounts of data like purchase history, profile data, browsing history, product usage patterns, and social media behavior. This valuable information is then carefully used by marketers to tailor the hospitality products and services to guests' interests and needs and make accurate forecasts and predictions for the company's future direction.

INTERNATIONAL TOURISM GROWTH

The hospitality industry is one of the fastest growing industries in the world. However, one of its major segments, the tourism industry, has experienced significant growth on an international level in recent years both in terms of volume of income and employment generated. The annual growth rate in international world tourist arrivals has been estimated to rise from 3.3% in 2000 to 4.5 by 2020. According to recent statistics, there is increased tourism development in the Asia-Pacific region, not only in terms of the infrastructure such as airports, hotels, etc., but also in terms of the new international career opportunities it generates. International travel has risen up to 5% worldwide and there has been a significant increase of up to 25% for Chinese travelers. In 2014, between the months of January and August, the number of international tourists reached 781 million, and in terms of its growth by region the percentages are as follows: Americas (+8%), Asia Pacific (+5%), Europe (+4%).

International tourism has experienced significant growth in recent years.

KEY CHARACTERISTICS THE HOSPITALITY INDUSTRY IS LOOKING FOR WHEN HIRING RECENT GRADUATES

When it comes to hiring hospitality graduates, the most important trait that hospitality companies are looking for is integrity. They want to hire people who they can trust who will perform their duties and do everything they are supposed to do even without supervision. Hospitality companies are also looking for people who are enthusiastic, confident, knowledgeable, and passionate about their job. Being sincere is another crucial qualification for which hospitality companies are on the lookout. In addition to the hospitality education that potential job candidates may have, working experience such as a job at a restaurant, a coffee shop, an internship, etc. is considered a big plus.

In customer-contact job positions such as those related to the hotel front desk, a ready smile and a kind disposition are imperative. In those positions, hospitality graduates are also expected to be able to engage in conversation with guests and show empathy.

Additionally, hospitality companies are looking for people who are characterized by the so-called "service heart." Not everybody is a customer-service person, so when they interview applicants for a job position, they expect to see clearly how these applicants could provide good quality of service upon hiring. They are also looking for team players, people who can fit well within a team and work harmoniously together to achieve the set goals and objectives. More importantly, though, hospitality companies are looking for people who care, and they prefer hospitality graduates who want a career, not just a job.

IMPORTANT STEPS IN BUILDING AN INTERNATIONAL CAREER

This section lists certain important steps that hospitality students must take, based on the author's knowledge, experience, and expertise, in order to build a successful international career in this industry. To start off, they need to be enrolled in a well-planned, well-organized hospitality management program from an accredited university to ensure that they will receive a high quality of education. An international career requires the ability to live abroad for extended periods of time and to adapt to a totally different culture. Thus, it is highly recommended they join a study abroad program and/or international internship program. To enable them to get better positions while abroad and make the most of those opportunities available to them, hospitality students need to know at least one foreign language as near to fluent as possible.

They need to familiarize themselves with the local culture, customs, and habits which will facilitate their adjustment to their new environment and surroundings and prove extremely helpful and useful for them. Additionally, during their studies, hospitality students need to attend conferences, expos, congresses, and other professional events in order to network with industry employers and professionals and keep up with the hospitality industry trends and the opportunities that this industry holds for them. Visiting establishments related to their chosen field and meeting and talking with management and staff will help them get a clearer picture of how this kind of hospitality company operates and what their representatives value most. Staying current by subscribing to hospitality industry magazines and journals will also set them apart from the competition and give them the competitive advantage of being more knowledgeable and up-to-date with current and future industry trends. Throughout this process, it is also recommended they choose a mentor who will guide, advise, and support them as they build their career. This person must be someone who knows the industry well and is an expert in the field that the hospitality student is interested in. However, the key in this case is that the selected mentor should be someone with a strong international background and contacts who will be able to share his/her valuable knowledge and experience and open the doors to the mentee for great international opportunities.

THE VALUE OF STUDY ABROAD PROGRAMS

One of the most beneficial and valuable experiences a hospitality student may acquire during their studies is participating in a study abroad program. When joining a study abroad program, students have the ability to see the world and be with students from various ethnic and cultural backgrounds who speak different languages, have different beliefs, but share the same dream of building a successful career in the hospitality industry. They have the opportunity to smoothly adjust to a different setting and lifestyle away from home. Through this cultural exchange and engagement in a multicultural community, students absorb an experience that is critical in their success as future leaders within the global village. Furthermore, the benefits of working together and communicating with people from different origins are immense. This gives hospitality students the opportunity to connect with others and make lifelong friendships that are not only precious on a personal level, but can also serve as useful networking tools on a professional level in the long run. Hospitality students can use a study abroad program as an opportunity to grow, learn, and enhance their personal development which will allow them to explore the excitement of living in a foreign country and give

Study abroad programs are extremely beneficial to hospitality students.

them the confidence they need to travel and pursue other career opportunities in the future.

Study abroad programs expose hospitality students to different styles of education that can be very different in the host country compared to the student's country of origin. Therefore, it is extremely important to choose carefully the right school that will best meet the hospitality student's needs. Upon completion of the study abroad program, hospitality students return home with a new perspective on culture, language and communication skills, and a high level of education that is very appealing to industry employers and opens doors to great international career opportunities. Recent statistics show that 97% of study abroad students found employment within 12 months of graduation, when only 49% of college graduates found employment in the same period. Study abroad students earn 25% higher starting salaries than those college graduates who do not study abroad. Additionally, 84% of study abroad alumni felt their studies abroad helped them build valuable skills for the job market, 80% of study abroad students reported that study abroad allowed them to better adapt to diverse work environments, and 59% of employers said that study abroad would be valuable in an individual's career later on with their organization.

THE KEY ROLE OF INTERNATIONAL INTERNSHIPS

One of the best strategies to acquire hands-on experience in the job hospitality students want and set the foundation for their successful international career is having an international internship opportunity. Many hospitality companies that operate internationally, such as Marriott, Hyatt, and Starwood, offer and support internship programs that are designed to train and prepare students and young industry professionals for management careers in the hospitality industry. Students are guided and monitored by experts throughout their internships. Sometimes they are asked to fill out detailed reports related to their internship experience and the nature of the management style of the establishment where they completed their training. Other times they are assessed by employers on their performance, behavior, and professional attitude.

Similar to the study abroad programs, internships expose students to global experiences that are hugely beneficial for them in terms of both personal and professional career growth including: language, culture, international friendships, and international work experience. Students have the ability to put into practice what they learned in theory, develop a high level of professionalism and a deep understanding of their chosen field, and grasp how hospitality companies not only perform their daily operations, but also how they create their long-term strategic direction and expansion. For example, the Hyatt Hotels and Resorts internship program was created to generate student interest in hotel management and give students the opportunity to experience the culture of a hospitality leader.

A major advantage that derives from pursuing an international internship is that students get to familiarize themselves with the organizational culture, policies, and rules of one of the branches or brands of the hospitality company they selected and decide if that hospitality company matches their own personal values and is the right career fit for them. In fact, on numerous occasions hospitality companies made an official offer to interns to stay with the company and work as actual hospitality employees upon completion of their internship program.

SUMMARY

Hospitality students who want to pursue an international career should choose to do their international internship in a hotel chain. Prior to the start of their employment in the hospitality company of the foreign country of their choice, hospitality students need to be aware of how their future employer addresses ethical and cultural considerations at the locality. It is also important for hospitality students to stay current with the international industry trends in order to remain competitive and marketable. The key is to start their path to an international career early and make sure to take the steps needed to keep developing on a personal and professional level. As they plan their future, hospitality students must bear in mind that study abroad programs and international internships are valuable to them as they broaden their minds and set the foundation for great international opportunities.

RESOURCES

Internet Sites

Study abroad statistics: https://studyabroad.ucmerced.edu/study-abroad-statistics

Career benefits of studying abroad: http://www.iesabroad.org/study-abroad/why/career-benefits

Intern abroad: http://www.goabroad.com/intern-abroad

Even hotels: http://www.ihg.com/evenhotels/hotels/us/en/reservation

Element hotels: http://www.starwoodhotels.com/element/experience/index.html

Venu by Jumeirah: http://www.jumeirah.com/en/jumeirah-group/press-centre/press-releases/press-releases-for-2014/jumeirah-launches-new-contemporary-lifestyle-brand-venu/

Trip by Wyndham: https://www.tryphotels.com/en/about-tryp-by-wyndham/

MGallery by Accor: http://www.mgallery.com/gb/home/index.shtml

Shangri-La Hotels and Resorts: http://www.shangri-la.com/corporate/about-us/our-brands/hotel-jen/

REFERENCES

Datameer, K. H. (2014). Tapping big data analytics to acquire, engage and retain customers. *Information Week: Bank Systems & Technology*. Retrieved from http://www.banktech.com/data-and-analytics/tapping-big-data-analytics-to-acquire-engage-and-retain-customers/a/d-id/1296950?

Dimitriou, C. K. (2013, October). *Factors influencing the ethical behavior of hotel employees*. Paper presented at the 31st EuroCHRIE Conference, Freiburg, Germany.

Donaldson, T. (1996). Values in tension: Ethics away from home. *Harvard Business Review, 74*(5), 48–62.

Goldner, C. R., & Ritchie, J. R. B. (2012). *Tourism: Principles, practices, philosophies* (12th ed.). Hoboken, NJ: John Wiley & Sons Inc.

Greenberg, J., & Baron, R. A. (2008). *Behavior in organizations* (9th ed.). Upper Saddle River, NJ: Pearson-Prentice Hall.

Hayes, D. K., & Ninemeier, J. D. (2006). *Foundations of lodging management*. Upper Saddle River, NJ: Pearson-Prentice Hall.

Hood, S. (2014). *Future trends in hospitality & tourism*. Keynote speech conducted at the 32nd EuroCHRIE Conference 2014, Dubai, United Arab Emirates.

Kastarlak, B. I. & Barber, B. (2012). *Fundamentals of Planning & developing tourism*. Upper Saddle River, NJ: Pearson-Prentice Hall.

Panel discussion (2015, October 16). *Hiring recent graduates*. Panel discussion conducted at the 34th International Society of Travel & Tourism Educators (ISTTE) Conference 2015, Charlotte, NC.

University of California, Merced. (2015). *Study abroad statistics*. Retrieved from https://studyabroad.ucmerced.edu/study-abroad-statistics

Walsh, K., Sturman, M. C., & Carroll, B. (2011). *Preparing for a successful career in the hospitality industry*. In the Scholarly Commons, Cornell University, School of Hotel Administration. Retrieved from http://scholarship.sha.cornell.edu/articles/241

Name: _____ Date: _____

1. What is the important difference between hospitality chains and franchises and independent hospitality companies on an operational level?

2. What are the two theories that must be considered when implementing ethics abroad?

3. Describe the emerging hospitality industry trends internationally.

4. What do recent statistics show regarding international tourism growth?

5. Name at least three key characteristics that the hospitality industry is looking for when hiring recent graduates.

6. List the important steps in building an international career in the hospitality industry.

7. Explain the value of study abroad programs.

8. Describe the key role that international internships play in helping hospitality students build an international career in this industry.

© ariadna de raadt/Shutterstock.com

PART 3

HOSPITALITY OPERATIONS

© g215/Shutterstock.com

CHAPTER *11*

LEADERSHIP AND ETHICS

AUTHORS	*Dr. Richard J. Mills Jr., Robert Morris University* *Dr. Denis P. Rudd, Robert Morris University*
LEARNING OBJECTIVES	• Identify the importance of operations management. • Define the role of the manager in the hospitality industry. • Understand the differences between managing change and exploring change. • Outline the four elements that create a sense of integrity. • Identify the levels of morality. • Define leadership. • Discuss why leadership qualities are important to hospitality operations.

CHAPTER OUTLINE	Hospitality and Tourism Management Perspectives
	    What Is Hospitality Operations Management?
	    The Hospitality Manager's Role
	    Managing Change
	    Integrity and a Sense of Ethics: Four Key Elements for Success
	    Levels of Morality
	Leadership, Ethics, and Hospitality Operations
	    Leadership Defined
	    Explore Change
	    Leadership Qualities and Hospitality Operations
	    Why People Follow the Leader

CHAPTER OUTLINE
(Continued)

Future Concerns for Hospitality and Tourism Management
  Enthusiasm for the Industry
  Developing Your Own Style of Leadership
Summary

KEY TERMS

Empowering   Management
Ethics   Moral development theory
Leadership   Vision

HOSPITALITY AND TOURISM MANAGEMENT PERSPECTIVES

WHAT IS HOSPITALITY OPERATIONS MANAGEMENT?

Students considering a career in hospitality and tourism management must first identify the meaning of management, and second, identify the meaning of operations. It is equally important for them to understand the work of operations managers and supervisors. The word management has two meanings. First, management is used as a collective noun to identify those in charge of directing business affairs. Management is a group of persons or individuals who receive their authority and responsibility from ownership or a directive from organizations to oversee the entire operation. Managers use this authority, along with the resources that are supplied from the business, to produce a product or service that creates an operation. Second, management becomes a service. From the sale of products and services, the operation itself becomes an additional product that engages management compensations, employee wages, and dividends paid to owners. Therefore, operations management becomes an act, the job that management does.

One distinguishes management and operations into categories of managing itself, consulting, or just doing routine operative tasks. Therefore, as a student, the first task at hand is to define what management *does*, and second, how these managerial tasks are learned, applied, and implemented. This defines the different operations that encompass the hospitality and tourism industry today. To be successful in the hospitality and tourism industry, it is imperative that students have a basic understanding of what management actually *performs* and why particular managerial styles, leadership skills, and personal qualities enhance the direction and overall outcome of any operation.

THE HOSPITALITY MANAGER'S ROLE

There have been many definitions applied to the term management, but the one that seems to get directly to the point is: **Management** *is the process of getting tasks accomplished through people.* A manager is a person who is responsible for the work of others,

Management identifies those in charge of directing business affairs and produces a product or service that creates an operation.

© Saklakova/Shutterstock.com

deciding the tasks people should perform, and ultimately how they can accomplish these goals. It is strongly suggested that managers accomplish their goals by acquiring skills and knowledge and passing these qualities on to employees.

Identifying *who management* is may be easier than defining *what management does*. The products of management are not easily recognizable. The products are not readily visible, such as a hamburger or an ironed tablecloth, but management is responsible for both. The average employee may not see what management *does*, but management does produce. The production success of management is evident in a successful business, and often, in the failure of another, even though both have equal resources. It is well recognized that the value of a business is based on its management talent as well as its physical assets.

Supervision, in a service business, is more complex than that in a factory, and for this reason, hospitality supervisors face a unique challenge. Manufactured products and labor drive the hospitality manager. Often, the workers are fatigued and dull working under different conditions. Service employees work under different conditions. The "product" of their work is a satisfied guest. In turn, the guests force employees to react to them. The work situation changes from guest to guest and changes with each individual guest. This keeps the supervisor under pressure because of unpredictable reactions.

MANAGING CHANGE

Management is a very modern institution, and ultimately, it must view the problems of work in an expanding and increasingly wealthy society. This new way of viewing problems has become one of the strongest forces in the last 100 years of the development of civilization. Because of rapid development in this period, our view of management problems has changed dramatically. Management continues to change or adapt itself to the dynamic society in which it operates, and those who aspire to a career in management must be prepared to adjust to these changes.

Management styles change with the fluctuations in society. There is a different set of rules for managing today's workers. Today's managers do not have the same set of rules that were evident in Colonial America or the sweatshops in the Industrial Revolution. These rules would be intolerable for today's managers housed in computer-age, air-conditioned, sanitary workplaces.

INTEGRITY AND A SENSE OF ETHICS: FOUR KEY ELEMENTS FOR SUCCESS

Organizational communication is not unlike any other entity in its ethical responsibilities. There are four key components for ethical balance and success for an organization. The first is the story: the organization is ultimately recognized for its message or story. The story is the *meta narrative* or big story of the organization and encompasses all of the qualities needed for success. Messaging must be consistent in order for the company to create an identity or brand. In contrast to the meta narrative is the emergence of a petite narrative or a series of little stories that do not tell the whole story of the organization and often complicate the meta narrative.

The second is *inclusion vs. exclusion*: inclusion is essential for an organization to proceed in an ethical manner. Inclusion is ultimately achieved by including participants in a conversation or exchange of ideas. The leader must recognize the best ideas to maintain an ethical balance. Exclusion is often the downfall of ethical communication as subjects become disenfranchised and discouraged; **empowering** others is powerful communication as the organization shares in the successes and, also, the failures.

The third ethical consideration is *private vs. public*. There are two voices with ethical connotation; one is the private voice and the second is the public voice. The ethical image of an organization is demonstrated through the public image and, also, the public voice.

The under story or back story of an organization should be kept private. When private emerges over public, chaos can ensue as the overall image and story of the organization is clouded with "noise" rather than message.

The fourth phase of ethical practice is *civility vs. cynicism*. Once again we are faced with an ethical dilemma if the message of the organization is laced with cynicism rather than civility. The big story is affected, but, in addition, the story within a story, the structure within the organization, is damaged. It is very important for a leader to promote a climate of civility within the organization and, also, to the public. The ethical balance for an organization can be achieved through these four practices.

LEVELS OF MORALITY

A person's level of morality is imperative and determines whether the leader is respected. Social psychologist Lawrence Kohlberg explains that each person makes ethical decisions according to three levels of **moral development**. Level I *Preconventional Morality*: the individual is aware of cultural prescriptions of right and wrong behavior. Response is based on two concerns: will I be harmed (punishment): Will I be helped (pleasure)? Level II *Conventional Morality*: Morality is characterized by group conformity and allegiance to authority. The individual acts in order to meet the expectations of others and to please those in charge. Level III *Postconventional Morality* is the most advanced level of moral development. The individual is concerned with right and wrong conduct over and above self-interest, apart from the views of others and without regard to authority figures. Ethical judgments are based on self-defined moral principles.

An organizational manager must have a set of principles or **ethics** to enhance interaction with others. Ethics should govern the general behavior of managers and guide them in making business decisions. The quality of one's integrity manifests itself in many ways, but the honesty and sincerity of an effective organizational manager must be unquestionable. This quality applies to *true leaders* and must not be compromised. Operational managers are responsible for the ethical treatment of five different groups of people: customers, employees, suppliers, owners, and the community at large. Basically, ethical behavior means fair and consistent treatment towards members of each of these groups. A personal code of ethics is imperative for a qualified organizational manager to ensure truth, a lack of bias, consistency, and respect when interacting with others.

LEADERSHIP, ETHICS, AND HOSPITALITY OPERATIONS

LEADERSHIP DEFINED

Leadership has historically been defined as the relationship among the leader, follower, and environment. It is suggested that the voice of the stakeholder should be included in management decisions and overall future of the hospitality industry. Understanding the environment is essential to good management practices. Successful management can be enhanced by incorporating a leadership vision of the future and translating this **vision** into the organization.

In many instances, leadership is associated with power. It is essential that a leader not exert his/her power over others but create a relationship with others. Power can be evaluated in a context of human motives and physical constraints. If we come to realize that power is persuasive, we can hope to understand the true nature of leadership. All leaders are actual or potential power holders, but in contrast, not all power holders are leaders. What is crucial is the purpose of the power holder and the purpose of the leadership. In management, the goal is twofold: the leader must exert an ideology that is for the common good of the company, and thus, create an environment in which the followers engage in common goals. A true leader has the skills to utilize his/her power and motivate others to achieve success for the establishment/company. Several traits are important for a leader to possess: 1) a leader acts by example and demonstrates to others a willingness to contribute to the project; 2) a leader listens to others and entertains an exchange of ideas for the common good; and 3) a leader uses persuasion and power as positive tools for the advancement of the project.

In the environment of organizational leadership, the leader must hold all of the above skills. Leading by example is often the key to success, as others see the leader in a role similar to their own and a willingness to "roll up their sleeves" for the good of the organization. A good leader listens to ideas from others and

A good leader listens to ideas from others and encourages inclusion versus exclusion for the success of the organization.

encourages inclusion versus exclusion for the success of the organization. The final point and likely the most important is that the leader should use their power within the role of leader in a positive way to assure a positive result.

In conclusion, a leader must show strength, compassion, and have excellent communication skills. The skills manifested by leadership should lean to altruism rather than advancement of self. These traits and skills have not changed over the years but are more evident today as industry requires leadership to show success and results. The consequences of poor leadership are often recognized in the "bottom line" or end result. It is in the best interest of the leader to show ethical and inclusive practices for him/herself and, ultimately, for the good of the company or organization. Strong leadership is not necessarily powerful leadership but demonstrative leadership with the ultimate goal being success.

EXPLORE CHANGE

It is essential that the leader understand the emerging changes happening within the industry. In order to accomplish this, the changes must be identified through a system of intelligence gathering, trend analysis, predictions, and conversations with others. This requires excellent communication skills and information-gathering techniques. This may be done through *analyzing and synthesizing* pertinent information. A leader with good communication skills can and should direct others to gather information and give feedback to management. This is an essential model for predicting what changes will ensue because of a changing environment.

LEADERSHIP QUALITIES AND HOSPITALITY OPERATIONS

An organizational manager must instill ideals and influence others for the purpose of channeling their activities toward assisting the hotel or restaurant's goals. Leadership can be viewed as having two separate components or elements: success and effectiveness. A successful leader demonstrates a quality that followers want to emulate; an effective leader instills a desire to follow in the right direction. As mentioned previously, leadership may be defined in several ways, and often, these qualities consist of the leader, the group, and the situation. Leadership is a *personal* and a *human* experience, as animals and computers cannot lead. Leadership is both an *art* and a *science* and is subjective in nature. There are fundamentals of leadership that can be learned and are based on research and observation. Leadership is *active*, as leaders must do something; leadership is one element of a three-part dynamic; the leader, the group, and the situation are always in *interaction* and tension with one another.

WHY PEOPLE FOLLOW THE LEADER

People enter an organization and perform their work for various reasons. They follow the leader of the organization for the purpose of being financially and socially successful. The most basic reason that people work is to provide themselves and their dependents with food, shelter, and clothing. This is often identified as a *selfish* reason for working. In contrast, there is a more positive motive for *following the leader*. This is most evident when people seek work for societal goals. Making enough money to achieve both needs and wants supports the aspirations of the worker. Personal satisfaction is therefore necessary for individuals to pursue work. Through hard work and diligence, one is rewarded with independence, encouragement, praise, and recognition.

Followers must freely accept the efforts of the leader for leadership to occur. Followers must voluntarily align their will with that of the leader. A leader must manifest good qualities, without threats of discipline or punishment, for followers to function within their own free will. It is only when followers make a true choice to follow the leader that true leadership occurs.

A manager must first be enthusiastic and second, confident.

© Kzenon/Shutterstock.com

FUTURE CONCERNS FOR HOSPITALITY AND TOURISM MANAGEMENT

ENTHUSIASM FOR THE INDUSTRY

An enthusiasm for the industry is often identified as having the business "in their blood." For the purpose of developing a desire to work in this industry, it may be necessary to have a passion for the business. Leaders are the best "cheerleaders" for their organization and their people. They display enthusiasm or passion and instill it in others. They possess poise, stability, clear vision, and articulate speech. Their enthusiasm is often described as *infectious* and motivates workers who are in their presence.

Successful managers are confident that their abilities are up to the task of their actions and are able to gain the trust and support of workers. A manager must first be enthusiastic, with a passion for the position, and second the manager should be confident. It is obvious when these qualities are displayed; self-confidence helps the manager adjust to the ever-changing direction of the industry.

DEVELOPING YOUR OWN STYLE OF LEADERSHIP

We are impressed and often amazed with the ability of certain managers and their leadership style. All are unique, and top managers are uncommonly different; they are extraordinary people who can adjust from one role to another without losing momentum or hesitation in thought or action. The roles of managers may also reflect the styles of the managers. A leader possesses standards and values within the organizational culture. The manager is responsible for what happens in the organization in such areas as personnel choices, marketing, financial, and public affairs decisions. The manager is the chief tactician, strategist, spokesperson, negotiator, observer, and the one who ultimately represents the organization beyond whom decisions do not pass without a final determination.

SUMMARY

There is an interrelated set of functions carried out by managers at all levels of the organization, and also with the organization's workers. Leadership is relatively new and has emerged as a field of study only in the last 100 years. As a separate practice, leadership grew up to meet the changing needs of society and eventually affect several areas including the hospitality industry.

Future events will transform the nature and structure of the hospitality industry, but one fact remains even in an environment of constant and rapid change: both leadership and ethics will continue to be in high demand. The future is in the hands of the future leaders within the industry, through a collective experience and wisdom. Leaders must find solutions to meet the needs of an ever-changing society and industry. The future leaders will plan and implement strategies to deal with them successfully and introduce the new, while holding on to the best of the old.

Leadership is both an old and new profession with a body of knowledge gained through practical application of leadership principles. Excellent leadership means better individual communications and operational leadership, and therefore, a better and more efficient industry. The destiny of the industry is in the hands of competent, passionate leaders with exemplary leadership skills and professionalism. Hospitality leaders must keep pace with the dynamics of the society.

REFERENCES

Brymer, Robert A. *Hospitality & Tourism.* 11th Edition. Dubuque, Iowa: Kendall/Hunt Publishing, 1977.

Fisher, William P. & Muller, Christopher C. *Four-Dimensional Leadership.* Upper Saddle River, New Jersey: Pearson Prentice Hall, 2005.

Nykiel, Ronald A. *Hospitality Management Strategies.* Upper Saddle River, New Jersey: Pearson Prentice Hall, 2005.

Powers, Thomas F. Ph.D. *Introduction to Management in the Hospitality Industry.* Second edition. NewYork/Chichester/Brisbane/Toronto/Singapore: John Wiley & Sons, 1979.

Powers, Tom and Barrows, Clayton W. *Management in the Hospitality Industry.* Eighth Edition. Hoboken, New Jersey: John Wiley & Sons, 2006.

Vallen, Jerome J., Ph.D., Cha & Abbey, James R. Ph.D., Cha. *The Art and Science of Hospitality Management.* East Lansing Michigan: The Educational Institute of the American Hotel & Motel Association, 1987.

REVIEW QUESTIONS

1. How has management changed historically?

2. What five groups should managers be concerned with when ethics is applied?

3. List some basic reasons why people follow. And what role does leadership play?

4. From the authors' perspective, why is enthusiasm for the industry important?

5. What is meant by developing your own leadership style?

6. How do the authors define ethics and integrity?

7. What are Kohlberg's three levels of moral behavior development?

8. What are some future concerns for operations managers?

9. What five key ingredients are needed for leaders to implement a strong and welcoming vision?

© Yuri Yavnik/Shutterstock.com

CHAPTER *12*

MARKETING

AUTHOR

Randall S. Upchurch, PhD, Florida Gulf Coast University

LEARNING OBJECTIVES

- Understand the role of marketing and its meaning to hospitality organizations.
- Explain the key elements of marketing mix.
- Understand the importance of co-aligning marketing efforts with consumer needs, wants, and expectations.
- Comprehend the concept of addressing customer attitudes, interests, and opinions.

CHAPTER OUTLINE

Introduction to Hospitality Marketing

Marketing Mix Elements: Elements of Success

    Product Orientation

    Price Orientation

    Place Orientation

    Promotion Orientation

Consumer Analytics: Emergence of a New Field of Integrated

  Hospitality Data Mining

    Big Data Analytics

Social Media: A Promotional Gateway

Summary

KEY TERMS

Attitudes, interests, and opinions

Customer loyalty

Marketing mix

Price orientation

Product orientation

Promotion orientation

Public relations

Sales promotion

INTRODUCTION TO HOSPITALITY MARKETING

In today's economic climate there is no doubt the hospitality industry continues to be a major contributor to local, regional, national, and international economies. To highlight this statement, the World Travel & Tourism Council estimated the 2015 employment of the combined travel and tourism industries, of which hospitality is a subset, was approximately 14 billion employees. Moreover the economic impact of those respective industries was estimated to be 1.5 billion dollars in terms of gross domestic product (GDP) for the United States of America. The art of achieving such commanding accomplishments is directly related to a very intricate deployment of governmental economic development policies, corporate strategies, and the implementation of business level strategies that are specifically aimed at attracting the right customer for a company's product and service offerings. The latter point is, of course, pertinent to operating a successful hospitality business.[1]

What does this "state of the industry information" mean for the hospitality manger? At a very fundamental level, the unit manager (i.e., hotel manager, restaurant manager, marketing manager, etc.) must remain highly focused on creating value for their consumers in ways that create sustained satisfaction, foster loyalty, and prompt this target market to share their entire experience with friends, peers, business acquaintances, and family...again, again, and again! In short, there is an art to creating "wow" service. Once accomplished, the customer sees their needs as being met, and in turn they return to spend more and they share more, and, as a result, company profits continue to escalate, thereby contributing more to the hospitality operator's "bottom line."

This preface indicates that marketing is, and always has been, a critical business development tool for hospitality businesses. It is a highly recognized fact that the competition is intense for leisure, transient, business, and association and other pertinent consumer dollars for all segments of the travel and tourism industries...of which segments include lodging providers, foodservice operators, convention centers, entertainment facilities, sport complexes, and many other hospitality service providers. This competition, at times, is incredibly intense and spans from local and national to international arenas; thus stressing the importance of deploying marketing tools which reach out to the right target market, at the right time and the right price, and, once deployed, leads to a consumer experience that exceeds their expectations. The purpose of operating a hospitality business therefore is twofold: first, to create and operate a business that appeals to an intended target market; and second, is profitable for that business operator.

To clarify the role and importance of marketing to a hospitality operator you will be exposed to: a) the concept of marketing, b) the marketing mix toolkit, c) the concept of consumer "big data" analytics, and d) emerging social media tools.

THE MARKETING MIX: ELEMENTS OF SUCCESS

The historical approach to marketing delineates the marketing mix to be composed of product, price, place, and promotion. These traditional "P's of marketing" remain a critical part of the hospitality business operator's toolkit for achieving market success. The challenge, however, for the hospitality industry, and for many service industries, is that these four elements require an interplay between the service provider and consumer. This service-based interaction requires an interactive analysis of the intangible components that result from a single or multiple service transactions. It is indeed this service interplay that is unique to the hospitality industry.

To paraphrase the American Marketing Association, **marketing** is the actions...and processes designed to create, communicate, deliver, and exchange "offerings" that have value for customers, clients, partners, and society at large.[2] For the hospitality marketing manager this means there must be a) constant attention devoted to ensuring that all business strategies are deployed, b) they are administered on time, c) those programs are monitored for attainment of objectives, and, d) of course, the projected level of profits is attained as well. The fundamental question of concern is twofold: first, who is our intended target audience; and second, how can we best satisfy their needs, wants, and expectations?

The marketing mix toolkit available to non-hospitality businesses can, and should be, leveraged by hospitality operators. However, given the exchange-based and dynamic nature of changing consumer needs, along with the intense competitive environment, the tools utilized by hospitality businesses have extended past the traditionally known *4 P's* of marketing (product, price, place and promotion). The **marketing mix** for hospitality business operators is composed of product, pricing, promotion, place, people, and for the purpose of this chapter what is known as passage of those business strategies onward to the intended customer, planning relative to business strategy deployment, and perpetual analysis of emerging consumer trends. In spite of the personal passion and financial investment put into a business concept, the overriding message is that without satisfied customers a hospitality operation will certainly close its doors due to cash flow issues… this stresses the importance of the marketing manager's role in enticing individuals to seek out their products.

PRODUCT ORIENTATION

The roots of the traditional product-oriented approach to moving a product to the market stems back to the Industrial Era, the 18th to 19th centuries, when mechanized production lines replaced a largely agrarian economy with massive factories aimed at mass production of textile, iron, and steel products. This shift to mass-market production therefore represented a shift away from personalized craftsmanship for the masses. As such, mass-market production and distribution of products was aimed exclusively for general public consumption as opposed to a tailored and personalized approach, which was reserved for the upper classes. What this indicates is that, over time since the Industrial Era, the cachet associated with tailored, personalized products combined with the entrance of many different manufacturers created increasing consumer demand for personalized products and paved the way for differentiated products.

On that note, it should also be understood that this trend toward consumer demand for differentiated products and services is not new to the hospitality industry. For instance, the lodging industry also grew during this same era in terms of geographical locations, types of lodging accommodations, and

lodging companies dominating the market ranging from recognized brands such as Holiday Inn, Statler, Marriott, and Hilton. The evolution of the lodging industry is therefore an excellent example of refinements in travel products as reflective of changing consumer travel needs. For example, the roadside motel of the 1950's and 1960's, although still in existence at that time, was not the only lodging product line available. Over time the depth of lodging product offerings expanded to downtown areas via luxury high-rise hotels, airport properties, ski resorts, casinos, convention hotels, conference centers, extended stay units, bed and breakfast properties, luxury hotels, all-suite properties, condominiums, timeshare properties…just to name a few.[3] Again, this differentiated approach to lodging accommodation lines is directly proportional to the available supply of other lodging properties in the immediate geographical area as associated with increasing consumer demand for those products.

PRICE ORIENTATION

Pricing is decidedly different than the other marketing mix components in that price generates *income* while the other elements are considered *cost* generators. What this means from a financial planning perspective is that pricing has to be set at a sufficient level to cover all production, advertising and promotion, and distribution costs associated with product offerings…while yielding an acceptable amount of profit for the company. Therefore the art of monitoring supply and demand characteristics and perceived consumer value for products/services within the context of actual value for the products/services is a dynamic and ongoing process for a hospitality company and therefore the marketing manager.

The biggest challenge is in setting the *selling price* at a level that has perceived value, leads to sufficient company revenues, is based on thorough consumer and competitor research, and is co-aligned with the company's strategic goals, both short term and long term. Clearly this is a delicate process that requires a keen eye toward competitive analysis and consumer attitude, interests, and opinions. Imagine the consumer outcry that could result from starting with a pricing strategy which is below an estimated consumer-pricing threshold…and then later a decision is made to raise the price to a higher level. The resultant backlash could be devastating in terms of consumer retention and it would have significant negative impacts on company profits. So, without proper communication to the consumer concerning pricing fluctuations, the consumer can become perplexed, if not irritated, and as a result switch to a rival product. The latter result would lower profits for the hospitality company and certainly damage the customer's perception of the hospitality company as being a fair and equitable operator...which raises the issue of the long-term impact associated with negative word-of-mouth consumer campaigns, and especially so in the present age of social media. The reach of such social media websites is very extensive, which stresses the strategic importance of aligning all marketing mix elements. Why? So that a consistent and deliberate message may be achieved. Examples of pricing strategies are numerous ranging from a low cost leader such as Motel Six where the product offerings are very standardized, the amenity offerings are economical, and the facility layout is very standardized from property to property. Conversely, high-end luxury lodging providers, such as Mandarin Oriental, Four Seasons, and J.W. Marriott, offer a collection of luxury resorts inclusive of holistic spas, authentic Asian-style services, meeting spaces, and award winning restaurants, thus being highly differentiated in their product and service offerings.

PROMOTION ORIENTATION

The promotional mix serves to inform, persuade, or remind the consumer of available locations, products, and services that are available for their recreation, leisure, business, and other related travel. The promotional tools available to the hospitality operator include advertising, direct marketing, personal selling, public relations, and sales promotions.

Advertising

Advertising is defined as a paid form of non-personal communication and promotion of an idea, product, or services by an identified entity. In perspective of the other marketing mix elements, advertising stands out as being the most "visible" within mainstream media such as television. A driving reason for such visibility is the mature nature of the hotel, restaurant, and travel industries, which makes the quest for market share to be a primary directive for all hospitality businesses. For example, those inclined to take cruise line vacations will likely find

Burger King uses advertisements to inform, raise awareness, persuade customers to purchase, and increase profits.

television advertisements on major network affiliates from Carnival Cruise Lines, Royal Caribbean Cruise Lines, and Norwegian Cruise Lines. Another example taken from the restaurant industry would be quick-service advertisements from McDonald's, Burger King, Wendy's, Subway, and Chipotle... all with the intent to inform, raise awareness, persuade consumers to purchase, and increase profits. The desired result is an increase in market share by distributing advertisements through network media to audiences that fit consumer profiles set by these respective companies.

The reader should be aware that there are differences in leveraging national advertising as just described in that corporations typically have the financial ability to invest in this type of advertising while local operators, franchisees, or independent operators must focus instead on more regionalized advertising efforts. Furthermore, in the 21st century the use of network-televised media continues to be scrutinized by hospitality companies from a return-on-investment perspective due to generational preferences for Internet services relative to their educational, recreational, and leisure needs. In essence, the trend in the hospitality industry is to steer from 30-second network commercials to Internet based, target audience focused, cost-effective, and personalized media, which is then distributed to a wide variety of mobile devices or Internet services. According to researchers, this trend to leveraging promotional campaigns via the Internet and mobile devices is being driven by generational preferences whereby those within younger generations prefer to search for their information either on the Internet or mobile devices.

Direct Marketing

Direct marketing campaigns are designed to inform and persuade existing and potential customers to purchase or to cultivate a relationship with the hospitality company. The channels for direct marketing efforts are expansive in scope and range from mailed leaflets or flyers, e-blasts, telephone campaigns, and information booths (manned or non-manned kiosks), to the Internet. The key with direct marketing campaigns is that they are aimed at specific consumer demographic or **psychographic** (values, interests, and opinions) characteristics, thus making such campaigns very effective and efficient in terms of analyzing consumption patterns and trends. For example, a hospitality operator could test market a loyalty program by requesting the recipient to visit a specific webpage; thus enabling the hospitality operator to determine level of interest in the promotional program. For this example, the intent of the message is to inform the customer of the program's features and then persuade them to enroll in the program components.

Personal Selling

At the foundation of the hospitality industry is the art of selling. **Personal selling** consists of a transaction between at least two individuals whereby one of those individuals, known as the sales representative, by means of a structured transactional process, attempts to incite the other person, known as the prospect, to participate in a product or service, and then to build a lasting relationship by means of converting the prospect into a loyal customer.

The steps of the selling process vary depending on the sales consultant model followed. However, the basic steps of the personal selling process are a) greeting, b) credibility, c) prospecting, d) presentation, e) overcoming objections, f) trial close/close, and g) follow-up. The key is that this interaction is highly personalized and involves strong listening, empathy skills, a high degree of professionalism, product knowledge, and emotional intelligence.

GREETING

This is the initial phase of the interaction, which requires the sales representative to "break the ice" with the prospect. It is, however, a common practice for the sales representative to have already reviewed

The greeting phase requires the sales representative to 'break the ice' with the prospect.

© Syda Productions/Shutterstock.com

personal or company information beforehand so that a baseline understanding is known about the possible needs of the individual or business.

CREDIBILITY

It is within this stage that the sales representative brings to the foreground the company's reputation, company history, corporate social responsibility, industry ratings such as Michelin ratings and TripAdvisor (for hotels), Travelpost, Zagat rating, and Yelp (for restaurants). Another practice is for the sales representative to discuss their credentials, degrees, or awards in an effort to establish personal credibility during this step of the selling process with the prospect.

PROSPECTING

This stage can be in the form of "cold calling" or "warm calling" with the former meaning that the sales representative has little if any previous information to review prior to their first interaction with the prospect. This mere fact commonly means that cold calling takes much more time and effort to yield established sales targets. Warm calling, on the other hand, is based on a pre-established relationship with a company or association, which offers the sales representative a preview of the needs and wants of the individual or company being pursued. A critical step during this stage for the hotel or restaurant sales representative is the determination of the individual's or company's estimated room night generated, foodservice, meeting rooms needed per year, location needs, financial ability of the person or company, and an estimate of future needs.

PRESENTATION

For the purpose of this chapter the premise is that the sales representative has already approached the individual or company in advance and therefore a foundation has been established in terms of the prospect's needs. The next logical step then is to invite the individual to the property for a review of the products and services (e.g., for a hotel that would be meeting rooms, guest rooms, business center, recreational facilities, meeting rooms, exhibition halls, and introduction to appropriate executive personnel). However, the advancement of digital technologies has enhanced the demonstration phase of this process by allowing hospitality companies to stream "virtual tours" of their properties on the Internet thus allowing the prospect to seek out preliminary information prior to their on-site visit. The key is that deployment of "virtual tours" and "informational tours" or on-site demonstrations remain exclusively focused on the prospect's needs.

OVERCOMING OBJECTIONS

There is a common saying in the sales world that "salesmanship begins when the sales agent hears the word *No* from the prospect." Perhaps this is the phase that is the most exciting and challenging for the sales representative because it is at this point that the sales representative converts the prospect into a customer either on that very day or a later day. The pivotal point is to determine the reason for the prospect's objection, which can range from rational (e.g., cost-benefit) to emotional in nature. Regardless of the reason it is not productive for the sales agent to become defensive; instead he or she should remain focused on finding what it would take to overcome the objection by packaging the offer in a way that is legitimate, obtainable, profitable, and acceptable to both parties.

CLOSING

During this phase of the sales process the sales agent reviews the main points of interest, revisits any objections, and then asks for the sale. Depending on the hospitality product being sold, the sales agent may be the one issuing the contract and therefore reviews all the legal terms and conditions stated within that contract. However, it is not unusual for the contracting process to be handled by either a senior sales manager or contracting officer as means of additional verification of the prospect's sustained desire to enter into an agreement with the hospitality company. For instance, in the timeshare industry it is at this phase that a contract verification officer handles the review and signing of contractual elements. This contract in turn is then filed with the appropriate state government entity for deed or leasehold processing relative to real estate and consumer protection legislation.

FOLLOW-UP

For all hospitality operations, this step is mandatory and must be perpetual in nature. Up to this point, the marketing process has been a personalized process…and this personal selling phase is no exception. The sales representative should maintain personal contact with the customer to ensure that what was promised was delivered, and that future needs are met. In short, this unknown individual has become part of the hospitality family and the act of exceeding their expectations is a task of utmost importance. In essence, the selling process is the beginning of a long-standing relationship…a relationship of reciprocal loyalty among the sales representative, the hospitality business, and the guest.

Public Relations

Public relations is the process of establishing a climate of goodwill with the general public, customers, community leaders, and other stakeholders of the company. For example, a restaurant could promote a holiday package to induce sales, a hotel could offer weekend getaway packages during the off-season, or a theme park could offer residents a promotional Internet rate for annual members as a gesture of goodwill. In such cases the reach of paid advertising is highly targeted, traceable, and is leveraged to inform the public of existing and new services, persuade them to participate, or remind them of the hospitality business presence. For the latter, television advertisements placed by McDonald's are aimed at reminding the public of their presence in the community versus intentionally focusing on persuading a purchase. Such would definitely be the case when McDonald's nationally broadcasts their involvement and support of the Ronald McDonald House, a charitable organization that creates, finds, and supports programs that improve the health and wellbeing of children.[4]

Non-paid advertising is more challenging in that the hospitality operator often does not have direct control over the content nor the timing of the advertisement's release. For example, a restaurant operator could volunteer time to a local charity, such as United Way, Give Kids the World, or the Harry Chapin Food Bank, which in turn could be picked up by a local radio, television station, or either's associated webposting. This gesture of goodwill offered by that restaurant's employees would be viewed by hundreds of thousands of individuals thus reminding them of the civic consciousness of that operator.

Sales Promotion

A sales promotion is the deployment of a limited time incentive for the purpose of stimulating consumer purchase of a product or service. The array of promotional techniques includes coupons, trade show exhibits, product demonstrations, samples, loyalty rewards, and contests. Relative to promotional coupons, a startup company named Groupon offers Internet-based coupon services that can be refined to the local market you are interested in… all of which can be searched and retrieved from your personal mobile device. According to Groupon they offer a service that "provides a great way for customers to shop local in an expansive online marketplace." Another example of leveraging the Internet took only one quick Google search using the keywords… McDonald's contest. What popped up was a "join our email list" for news on events, including contests/sweepstakes, and promotional offerings. Continuing onward, and relative to a loyalty program, a quick Internet search for Honors members yielded a limited time offering for Hilton Honors Members to get double points or miles from January to April.[5]

In terms of trade show exhibits, there are numerous examples ranging from state fairs to industry specific shows such as the American Hotel & Lodging Association, the National Restaurant Association, and more specialized "regional" shows such as the one held by Cheney Brothers for the purpose of demonstrating the newest and best food, beverage, and equipment ideas.[6]

CONSUMER ANALYTICS: EMERGENCE OF A NEW FIELD OF INTEGRATED HOSPITALITY DATA MINING

As noted earlier in this chapter, there is no doubt that emerging technologies have increased the amount of information available to consumers. This ability to search and retrieve information and make purchase decisions based on the availability of this information continues to have a significant impact on the hospitality industry. Imagine how powerful it would be for a hospitality company to extract consumer spending patterns *along with* their lifestyle, values, and opinions of *existing* and *future* products and services. Is this "looking glass" concept that far off for the hospitality industry? From an operator's perspective, it is pretty easy to visualize the refinement of services, project feasibility enhancements, geographical markets pursued, and refinement of marketing mix activities associated with generational differences, attitudes, interest, and opinions that would ensue.

BIG DATA ANALYTICS

A term that is frequently tossed around the hospitality, travel, and tourism industries is that of big data analytics. What is big data analytics, or predictive analytics? Why is it so important to the hospitality, travel, and tourism industries?

Big data analytics is a strategic business tool that leverages the analysis of large data sets containing a variety of data from often separate sources. The concept behind the analysis of "big data" resides with uncovering underlying patterns, projected consumption patterns, market trends, and other business information that is aimed at market penetration, market share gains, and design of products and services to meet future consumer needs.

At a strategic planning level the appeal in analyzing "big data" is quite promising for the hospitality operator in terms of deciphering massive amounts of data for two specific purposes. First, is to devise products and services aimed to improve already existing *high caliber* services. Second, to personalize marketing campaigns using targeted social media channels, thus inciting consumers to partake in the newly devised or future products and services at a price that achieves the company's pricing strategy and then exceeds consumer expectations.[7]

An example of applying the results gleaned from "big data" crunching at the property level might allow a hotel concierge to recommend local site tours, museum tours, or Broadway plays to their guests as based on their booking history, travel history, and entertainment profile. Another example of particular interest to the lodging industry concerns the practice of yield management. The yield manager could elevate sales forecasts to the next level by reflecting upon the local weather, world travel advisements, and area events, thus enabling the yield manager to set room rates and to push out personalized promotional messages to social media sites of interest to those consumers. Another more realistic example would be for the yield manager to set room pricing by extracting information from sources such as Yelp, TripAdvisor, Expedia, Facebook, Instagram, or Orbitz in tandem with their company's customer profile database. Therefore, from a management perspective, the act of combining information from varying data sources enables the hospitality manager to gain a deeper understanding of their customer's likes and dislikes specific to travel, food and beverage, room accommodations, experiences, spa, meeting, and entertainment preferences. The challenge is that the sharing of this data requires collaboration between the hospitality corporation/company and the Internet companies which house this customer information, which naturally resides within cookies, computer history files (logs), and third party companies which house this consumer information.[8]

Furthermore, at the property level, a hotel, restaurant, casino, or entertainment complex could provide their staff with real-time consumer information concerning guest room preferences, booking histories,

amenity offerings, nutritional preferences, or beverage preferences. Although this requires a deeper analysis of guest information from separate databases, the act of placing predictive analytics in the hands of frontline employees will definitely improve customer satisfaction. There is no doubt that the future of the hospitality industry resides in the ability to coalesce this data in a manner that enhances the consumer's experience.

SOCIAL MEDIA: A PROMOTIONAL GATEWAY

The old adage that word-of-mouth marketing is a powerful tool if properly harnessed has been a truism for quite some time. In the present day, the strength of word-of-mouth communication becomes drastically amplified by the act of promoting services through social media tools. Why? Because with a simple key stroke, or perhaps a *tweet*, an individual can communicate with thousands of others who in return share that same message with countless others, which in turn renders the business operator helpless when it comes to controlling the frequency and occurrence of the message. Or does it? It is quite possible that the hospitality business can leverage their social media channels in a way that enhances property-to-consumer interactions, business-to-business interactions, and consumer-to-consumer dialogue. If this is the case, which is a notion supported by researchers, then it is in the hospitality operator's best interest to become versed in blogs, social networking sites such as *Meetup.com* and *Facebook.com*, video sharing services, photo sharing services, podcasting, *YouTube, Twitter, Flickr,* and

The hospitality industry can use social media channels for its benefit.

Table 12.1 Social Media Resources

Social Networking	Consumer Evaluations	Multimedia Sharing
Facebook	Gayout	Flickr
Faceparty	OpenTable	Pinterest
Google+	Oyster	YouTube
Linkedin	Raveable	
Meetup	Travelpost	
MySpace	TripAdvisor	
Twitter	Yelp	
	Zagat	
	Zomato	

other third party sites that rate and pertain to their business products and services. Further evidence of the importance of leveraging social media sites as a customer relations tool is the fact that researchers are finding that consumers no longer rely on traditional channels of advertising when making travel decisions...thus elevating the importance of monitoring, communicating, and analyzing social media outlets concerning the deployment of products and services for now and long into the future.[9]

As a business planning tool, the tracking and analysis of social media content is extremely important to the hospitality operator due to promotional effects associated with the information, both positive and negative, shared via those media outlets. However, those websites do not encompass all possible Internet space. It is important for the hospitality business to effectively monitor, rebut, manage, and compete with social media for consumers' attention. The key point is that effective management of social media is indeed a marketing activity that must be part of the business operator's daily process, which in turn will allow the marketing manager to tap into the social information space by understanding what drives a consumer to use, and to continue to use, their products and services. Table 12.1 is a listing of some of the more common social media sites of specific relevance to hospitality operators.

SUMMARY

The hospitality business manager has an overarching goal to produce a maximum level of revenue by filling the hotel, filling all restaurant tables throughout daily operation, airline seats, theme park handling capacity, etc., by attracting a mixture of customers as differentiated by price points, needs, and interests. Marketing plays a critical part in achieving that goal.

Hospitality marketing is a robust and rewarding career path to pursue. The fact is that many line level positions (front desk, waiter/waitress, banquet server) engage in the personal selling and marketing of items to guests. This face-to-face exposure prepares them for future careers in marketing at the property level, multiunit level, district level, or national level. To be adequately prepared, these line level personnel must be eager and willing to learn and management must train them in the competencies that will take them to that next level within their career.

As noted within this chapter, marketing professionals must be competent in consumer analytics (attitudes, interests, and opinions) market research (supply and demand patterns), consumer segmentation, targeting of consumers, and positioning of products and services to meet the aforementioned competencies.

ENDNOTES

1. World Travel & Tourism Council (2015). Travel & Tourism Economic Impact 2015. United State of America.

2. https://www.ama.org/AboutAMA/Pages/Definition-of-Marketing.aspx

3. Walker, John (2013). Introduction to Hospitality. 6th edition, Pearson Publishing.

4. http://www.rmhc.org/

5. http://hhonors3.hilton.com/en/index.html

6. http://www.cheneybrothers.com/food-show.php

7. SAS White Paper (2012). Big Data Meets Big Data Analytics. SAS Institute Inc.

8. Xiang, Zheng and Gretzel, Ulrike (2010). Role of Social Media in Online Travel Information Search, *Tourism Management*, 31, 179–188.

9. Leung, Daniel, Law, Rob, van Hoof, Hubert, Buhalis, Dimitrios (2013). Social Media in Tourism and Hospitality: A Literature Review, Journal of Travel & Tourism Marketing, 30. DOI: 10.1080/10548408.2013.750919.

REVIEW QUESTIONS 12

1. What are the P's of marketing? Why are they important to the hospitality marketing manager?

2. What subcomponents comprise a company's promotion strategy? Refer to specific examples as to how these subcomponents are leveraged by the hospitality business manager.

3. Why is it important to determine the attitudes, interests, and opinions of the consumer? How do these relate to the design of a marketing plan? Explain.

4. Describe what is meant by big data and predictive analytics. What role do they play in the deployment of business strategies?

5. Briefly explain how social media has impacted the hospitality industry.

CHAPTER *13*

MANAGING REVENUE AND EXPENSES

© dmitry_islentev/Shutterstock.com

AUTHOR

Lisa Y. Thomas, PhD, DePaul University

LEARNING OBJECTIVES

- Know how to reduce costs for hospitality organizations.
- Explain how to improve revenue for multiple segments of the hospitality industry.
- Be able to calculate and use ratios that are commonly utilized in the hospitality industry.
- Enact strategies to maximize sales through the different distribution channels available.

CHAPTER OUTLINE

Overview of Hospitality Revenue and Cost Control

Hotel Industry

    Hotel Supply

    Hotel Demand: Occupancy

    Hotel Average Daily Rate (ADR)

    Revenue Per Available Room (RevPAR)

    Hotel Revenue Management Pricing

    Hotel Channel Distribution

Restaurant Revenue Management

    Capacity Management

    Time Management

    Menu Management

    Price Management

KEY TERMS

Average daily rate (ADR)

Brand.com

Capacity management

Channel distribution

Complimentary (comp)

Cost control

CRS/voice

Cruise cabin pricing

Food cost per customer

Food cost per meal

Food cost per menu item

Global distribution system (GDS)

Key performance index (KPI)

Menu item contribution margin

Occupancy ratio

Onboard revenue management

Online travel agent (OTA)

Port of call revenue management formula

Property direct

Ratios

Revenue management

Revenue per available room (RevPAR)

Revenue per available seat hour (RevPASH)

OVERVIEW OF HOSPITALITY REVENUE AND COST CONTROL

While the hospitality industry is in the people pleasing business, it is also in the moneymaking business. Revenue management and cost control are important to all types of hospitality businesses, whether it is managing hotel beds, menu items, or hospitality employees. When these revenues and costs are efficiently controlled, then a hospitality company can maximize its profits. Better financial results lead to increased wages, company growth, and better careers.

Revenue and cost management have evolved into an important position within hospitality organizations. **Cost controls** include policies for purchasing, receiving, storage, preparation, sales, payment, efficient systems, and supervision. Hospitality managers can't see everything so they use ratios to identify areas where they should focus their attention. Managers review each day's ratios and compare them against previous months' or past years' results. Managers can then take action to improve areas that are not reaching their potential.

Besides controlling costs, ratios can also identify revenue-increasing opportunities. Ratios are often the best opportunity for improving profits in the revenue generating areas of the hospitality businesses. **Revenue management** is the art and science of predicting customer demand and then setting prices to match consumer demand. It is an approach for persuading consumers to purchase products during decreased-use time periods in order to increase their desire for the hospitality products and services along with boosting the average dollar amount spent. Revenue management practices help managers identify industry trends and determine the right price for hospitality services with the goal of maximizing profits. Effective revenue management is also critical for accurate forecasting, which requires skilled staff and sophisticated technology to analyze past data to accurately predict future consumer behavior.

Let's take a more in-depth look at some of the cost and revenue control approaches of different segments of the hospitality industry.

HOTEL INDUSTRY

HOTEL SUPPLY

The U.S. lodging industry consists of almost 55,000 hotel properties, for a total of 5 million hotel rooms. This is tremendous growth from 1990 when the U.S. hotel room supply was 3.3 million. The next top hotel markets are China with 9,000+ hotel properties and 1.7 million hotel rooms, and Germany with over 9,500 hotel properties and 580,00 hotel rooms. Which U.S. cities have the most hotel rooms? Las Vegas, NV has over 168,000 hotel rooms, followed by Orlando, FL with 121,000 hotel rooms. New York City has 113,000 rooms, with Chicago (110,000 rooms) and the metropolitan Washington DC area (107,000 hotel rooms) not far behind.

This type of hotel data is tracked by Smith Travel Research (STR), the leading authority on hotel trends. They gather and analyze global lodging industry supply and demand data. This data is used to calculate key performance index (KPI) measures of occupancy percentage rates, average daily rates (ADR), and revenue per available room (RevPAR).

HOTEL DEMAND: OCCUPANCY

The U.S. hotel occupancy rates peaked at approximately 65% in 1995 and remained stable until the early 2000s recession, which saw occupancy rates dip to 58%. Occupancy returned to the mid 60% range until the severe economic downturn in the late 2000s, which drove occupancy rates to historic lows of 54% in 2010. Occupancy rates have steadily grown

Occupancy ratios show how efficiently hotel rooms are sold each day.

to just over 65% due to the strong demand for hotels by corporate, vacation, and group travelers.

Occupancy ratios give managers a measure of how efficient they are at selling the hotel rooms they had available on a given day. This ratio looks at rooms sold as a proportion of rooms available.

$$\text{Rooms Occupancy \%} = \frac{\text{Rooms Sold}}{\text{Rooms Available}}$$

HOTEL AVERAGE DAILY RATE (ADR)

Average daily rate (ADR) is a measure of the average rate that guests paid for rooms sold during a specific time period. It is calculated by dividing the room revenue by the demand (rooms sold). ADR is expressed as a dollar amount.

$$\text{ADR} = \frac{\text{Room Revenue}}{\text{Rooms Sold}}$$

REVENUE PER AVAILABLE ROOM (REVPAR)

Revenue per available room is the most widely used hotel performance ratio. It is a measure of a hotel property's revenue in terms of each hotel room that is available for sale. Its reported dollar amount and movement over time can assess the health of individual hotels and the lodging industry overall. It differs from ADR because RevPAR is affected by the amount of unoccupied rooms, while ADR only shows the average rate of rooms actually sold.

RevPAR is calculated by dividing the room revenue by the total number of rooms available, known as the hotel's supply. RevPAR is expressed as a dollar amount.

$$\text{RevPAR} = \frac{\text{Room Revenue}}{\text{Room Supply}}$$

HOTEL REVENUE MANAGEMENT PRICING

Hotel revenue management uses past consumer purchase data to forecast future hotel night bookings. It also helps determine future hotel prices. Knowledge of the financial contribution from each type of hotel booking helps optimize revenues.

Revenue management is selling the right hotel room, to the right customer, at the right time, for the right price. To do this profitably, a revenue manager must control three strategic levers to manage room demand. The first lever, price, refers to the revenue manager's ability to set and control prices. The second lever is duration, a reference to managing hotel guests' length of stay at the property. The final lever is reach, which means finding the best avenues to market and eventually sell hotel rooms to prospective guests. By controlling each of these three levers, this type of strategic revenue management has helped the hotel industry increase revenues.

Revenue managers use several marketing methods to reach and attract customers to their hotel. One method is to use the data from the hotel loyalty program, which is composed of a database of past customers and their purchase and travel patterns. This data is used to create enticing email offers. These special offers often include bundling, which is a discounted price of a hotel room combined other hotel services, like free breakfast, Wi-Fi, or spa services.

Many consumers use search engines to research potential destinations and the hotels located there as their first step. Hotels like to ensure that they have prime placement on the search engine results. Hotel revenue managers determine the hotel room pricing used for marketing campaigns via online search engines, such as Google or Yahoo, for advertising links to reduced hotel room prices or special bundled hotel packages. Revenue managers also work with the hotel's sales teams to offer attractive group hotel room rates for sports events or weddings.

HOTEL CHANNEL DISTRIBUTION

It is rare for a hotel to sell all of its rooms through its own website, call center, and sales staff. Hotels need to distribute their hotel rooms by using **distribution channels** (see Table 13.1) in order for hotel rates to be available to consumers when they are shopping for travel.

Each of these distribution channels has different costs, whether it is commissions associated with the hotel booking (OTAs and GDS) or labor and technology costs (CRS, brand.com, property direct). Therefore, hospitality companies need to periodically review where and how their hotel rooms are sold to ensure that they are effectively marketing

Table 13.1	Hotel Distribution Channels
Distribution Type	**Distribution Definition and Example**
Brand.com	Hotel's own website, such as Hilton, Marriott, or Wyndham Worldwide, or Intercontinental Hotels Group.
CRS/Voice	Central reservation system handled by a call center with a toll-free number.
GDS	**Global distribution system** for their hotel rooms to be available to sell to the estimated 165,000 travel agents using them. The four main GDS systems are Amadeus, Galileo, Sabre, and Worldspan. The first electronic channels for hotel and airline reservations are now used primarily by managed corporate accounts through travel agencies such as American Express Travel and AAA Travel.
OTA	**Online travel agency**, such as Expedia, Travelocity, Booking.com, and Priceline.
Property Direct	Sales activity by the front desk (walk-ins) and hotel sales managers (groups, meetings, and contract sales).

their product in a profitable manner. Many hotels' revenue managers advertise their hotel's rates with online travel agents (OTAs) to reach consumers who are attracted by low prices. These price-sensitive customers are motivated to book a hotel room when they feel they are saving money.

RESTAURANT REVENUE MANAGEMENT

Restaurants can improve their revenue by increasing the number of customers they serve and/or the amount of money that each customer spends. Revenue management for the restaurant segment of the hospitality industry means selling the right seat, to the right customer, at the right price, and for the right duration. Determining what is *right* means attaining the largest contribution possible for the restaurant while delivering the greatest value to the customer.

CAPACITY MANAGEMENT

The ability to change four-person tables to two-person tables to accommodate more customers quickly is important, especially during peak periods. Based on past consumer data, restaurants may determine the common sizes of customer groups during certain times of the day and set up their tables accordingly. Examples of restaurant efforts to increase their capacity to serve more customers include extending operating hours, increased seating capacity (such as outdoor seating), drive-thru windows, and/or delivery.

TIME MANAGEMENT

The time customers spend in the restaurant is important, along with how quickly a table is ready for the next customer. This is tracked through the **ratio revenue per available seat hour (RevPASH).**

$$RevPASH = \frac{Total\ Outlet\ Revenue}{Available\ Seats \times Opening\ Hours}$$

MENU MANAGEMENT

The production cost of each menu item is different because of the varied ingredients and employee preparation time. The most commonly used ratio for assessing effective cost control in restaurants is the **food cost percentage**. This helps determine which menu items are regarded as more profitable than other items.

The time customers spend in a restaurant is important, as well as how quickly the table is ready again.

$$\text{Food Cost per Menu Item} = \frac{\text{Total Cost of Menu Item}}{\text{Menu Price}}$$

Other important ratios are the cost of food and/or beverage per customer and the cost per meal.

$$\text{Food Cost per Customer} = \frac{\text{Total Food Cost}}{\text{Number of Customers}}$$

$$\text{Cost per Meal} = \frac{\text{Total Cost for Meal}}{\text{Number of Meals Sold}}$$

$$\text{Menu Item Contribution Margin} = \text{Menu Item's Price} - \text{Menu Item's Food Cost}$$

While these ratios are useful tools, they do not take into account the restaurant's service capacity and the time issues. To maximize a restaurant's profitability, menu engineering should be applied to the restaurant's revenue management strategy. During peak hours when restaurants have more customers than service capacity, restaurants may want to heavily promote their superstar menu items. A superstar refers to popular menu items that have a high contribution margin and take less time to prepare and be consumed by customers.

PRICE MANAGEMENT

Restaurants should not offer discounts during peak hours. Instead, discounts are offered during off-peak hours to increase demand. Menu items can also differ in terms of the serving size or the accompanying side dish. Differentiating the menu for lunch and dinner is often perceived as fair pricing. Offering discounted food items on low demand days, such as Monday $1 burger nights, are ways to shift demand to off-peak days by attracting customers looking for value. Framing demand-based pricing as discounts instead of surcharges helps consumers perceive revenue management practices to be fairer.

CRUISE INDUSTRY

The major difference between a hotel and a cruise ship vacation is that a cruise ship travels to multiple destinations and typically includes all of the dining while onboard the ship. Like the hotel industry, cruise lines price their itineraries, cabins, and onboard services based on supply and demand. Cruise lines promote and sell their product through multiple distribution channels.

CRUISE ITINERARY PRICING

A cruise itinerary is a mix of key destinations that entice customers to purchase a cruise vacation. The first consideration when creating a cruise itinerary is the itinerary's homeport, such as Miami, FL. A desirable homeport is one that can facilitate the movement of thousands of guests on and off the ship in a short time period, along with reasonable port charges. Another important feature of an itinerary is appealing shore excursions with sufficient daylight time to maximize shore excursion revenue. A final consideration is that there must be enough time at sea for the cruise line to maximize the onboard revenues from the ship's facilities, with the entire trip having a moderate fuel cost. Therefore, an ideal port of call from a revenue management point of view is when the shore excursions less the port charges are greater than the onboard revenues minus the fuel costs.

IDEAL PORT OF CALL FORMULA

The **port of call revenue management formula** is: shore excursions – port charges > onboard revenues – fuel costs

There are multiple itinerary choices. Popular cruise itineraries include the Caribbean, Alaska, Europe, or Asia. Luxury cruise lines offer around-the-world cruise itineraries that give guests the opportunity to sail to worldwide destinations, with the cruise often taking 100 days to complete exotic world cruise ports of call.

CRUISE CABIN PRICING

There are multiple cruise cabin types, each with different prices to help increase the ship company's revenue. Inside cabins do not have a window and outside cabins have a window. There are larger cabins, such as suites, which often include a balcony. Each cabin type has a unique price to attract different segments of travelers. As the demand for a certain cabin increases, so does the price. If a specific cabin type is

There are multiple cruise cabin types, each with different prices to help increase their revenue.

decreasing when comparing the demand to previous sales levels, the price is often decreased to stimulate demand and fill the ship.

ONBOARD REVENUE MANAGEMENT

Besides cabin pricing, onboard revenues are particularly important for maximizing revenues in this segment of the hospitality industry. Key onboard revenue drivers are duty-free shopping, casino gambling, spa treatments, bars, and shore excursions. What is the top onboard revenue maker? The photo department, which displays guests' photos taken by the ship's photographers.

CASINO INDUSTRY

REVENUE MANAGEMENT

It is critical for casino managers to practice basic revenue management principles to market to the right customers and price their product to ensure a consistent stream of revenues. Each department in a casino resort has unique profit margins. Here's an example of pricing casino hotel rooms. If it costs $40 to maintain a hotel room and you can get $45 per night for the hotel stay, you are making a $5 profit. Multiply the $5 by 200 rooms and you can increase your room department profit by $1000. If you charge $50, you are doubling your profits to $2,000. Multiply that $10 per room (for 200 rooms sold) by 365 nights a year and that $730,000 from the rooms department could boost your casino resort's bottom line. If you are managing a large 1,000 or more hotel room casino

resort, such as those in Las Vegas or Macau, the $10 profit per room could mean an additional $3.65 million each year.

While one casino resort guest may spend $500 gambling, another guest spends $500 on spa treatments, while a third may spend $500 going to an elegant dinner and a show. At the same time, there are many casino guests who spend $1,500 while doing all three activities. This means each casino resort guest has a different value. Because casino resorts have different profit margins for each department where the guest spends money, revenue managers use technology to understand each guest's value. This daily value is used to determine how much should be spent to entice guests to return to the casino, known as **customer retention.**

CUSTOMER RETENTION COSTS

The types of casino customer retention strategies can include discounted or free drinks, dinners, shows, spa treatments, or hotel room nights, with each having a unique cost to the casino resort. These costs may also be different based on the day-of-the-week demand. For example Wednesday nights have a lower demand rate than Friday nights. Consequently, it costs the casino resort less to offer **complimentary items**, known as **"comps"** on Wednesdays. But some customers may want to come to the casino on a Friday night, so offers vary by guest.

Because of the multiple options and costs involved with each casino guest, casino managers use a sophisticated computer system to analyze their customers' spending behaviors. This computer database system determines each guest's value to the casino and how to motivate the guest to return to the casino in the future. Besides "comps," other strategies to encourage casino patrons to return and gamble in the casino include invitations to slot tournaments and special events, such as a Super Bowl party. These events are unique experiences for invited guests, as they feel valued by the casino.

The casino's computer database is also important for creating a revenue management model that is used for creating a demand forecast. Using past consumer gaming and spending behavior to forecast future consumer demand helps casino managers determine what the hours of operation should be for restaurants

Casino managers use a sophisticated computer system to analyze their customers' spending behaviors.

and spas, when to invite guests to the casino's special events, and how many employees to staff in each department daily.

SUMMARY

Revenue and cost control is important to all types of hospitality businesses. When these revenues and costs are efficiently controlled, then the hospitality company can maximize its profits. Ratios are used to identify problems when strategies are not reaching their goals. When efficient control mechanisms are in place, the way to further improve profits is to maximize revenue opportunities by finding ways to encourage guests to spend more money through revenue management.

Revenue management is selling the right hospitality product to the right customer, at the right time, for the right price. The cost and revenue control approaches of different segments of the hospitality industry are reviewed including the key ratios and opportunities for maximizing revenues. Revenue management has evolved into an important position within a hospitality company for determining multiple strategies for generating demand and ensuring profitability. In fact, many revenue managers are now responsible for multiple aspects of business strategy

development, e-commerce, and applying knowledge to social media and mobile pricing. Understanding these analytical functions makes for exciting hospitality career opportunities.

RESOURCES

Hospitality Associations

American Hotel & Lodging Association: www.smartbrief.com/ahla/index.jsp

Hospitality Financial and Technical Professionals (HFTP): www.hftp.org

Hospitality Sales and Marketing Association International: www.hsmai.org

AH & LA and Smith Travel Research Certified Hospitality Industry Metrics and Analytics certification:

www.ahlei.org/chia/

www.ahlei.org/Newsletters/Articles/STR-and-EI-Offer-Training-for-New-Certification-in-Hotel-Industry-Analytics/

www.str.com/products/CHIA

National Restaurant Association: www.restaurant.org

Hospitality Research and Consulting Firms

Smith Travel Research: www.strglobal.com

Hospitality Financial & Technology Professionals: www.hftp.org

Hospitality Valuation Services: www.hvs.com

PKF Consulting: www.pkfc.com

Hotel Industry

Hotel News Now: www.hotelnewsnow.com

Skift: Global Travel Industry Intelligence: skift.com

Hotel Business: www.hotelbusiness.com

Hotels Magazine: www.hotelsmag.com

Hotel Online: www.hotel-online.com/News/Subs/mailme.html

Hotel Management: www.hotelworldnetwork.com

Global Travel News: www.traveldaily.co.uk

Hospitality Net News: www.hospitalitynet.org

Hotel Resource: www.hotelresource.com

Hotel Real Estate: www.lodgingeconometrics.com

STR Hotel Stock Index: www.hotelstockindex.com

Restaurant Industry

Restaurant Hospitality: www.restaurant-hospitality.com

Restaurants and Institutions: www.rimag.com

Nation's Restaurant News: www.nrn.com

Restaurant Report: www.restaurantreport.com

NRA Performance Index: http://www.restaurant.org/News-Research/Research/RPI

ONLINE EXERCISES

1. Visit website for either Carnival Cruise Line or Royal Caribbean International. Choose a cruise sailing itinerary that is over your birthday. What is the per person price for an oceanview cabin? What are the ports of call on the itinerary? What makes this sailing appealing to you?

2. Go online and enter your dream vacation destination in the search field to see what hotels are on the first page of results. Which of these hotels is appealing to you? Click on that hotel weblink. Is the hotel being promoted by the hotel brand or an OTA? Try to book the hotel for a week stay over spring break. What are the prices? Try another search for prices for that hotel on a different OTA or on the hotel brand's website. What are the hotel rates? Are there price differences between the two websites?

REFERENCES

Burgess, C. (2014). *Essential financial techniques for hospitality managers: A practical approach, 2nd ed.* Oxford: Goodfellow Publishers Ltd.

Green, C.E., & Lomanno, M.V. (2012). *Distribution channel analysis: A guide for hotels.* Los Angeles: Hospitality Sales & Marketing Association International (HSMAI) Foundation.

McGuire, K.A. (2016). *Hotel pricing in a social world: Driving value in the digital economy.* Hoboken, NJ: Wiley.

Raleigh, L.E., & Roginsky, R.J. (2012). *Hotel investments: Issues & perspectives, 5th ed.* Lansing, MI: American Hotel & Lodging Educational Institute.

Thomas, L.Y., Thomas, N.J. & Ollstein, B.W. (2015). Exploring casino special events: An empirical analysis for determining which themed celebrations and tournaments have an indirect effect on increasing slot volumes. *Journal of Convention & Event Tourism, 16*(4), 310–337.

REVIEW QUESTIONS

1. List three cost control ratios that help hospitality companies.

2. What is revenue management?

3. How does revenue management differ between hotels and restaurants?

4. What are the five revenue and cost considerations that must be reviewed when creating a cruise itinerary?

5. How does revenue management differ between cruise lines and casinos?

6. Why is it critical for casino managers to practice basic revenue management principles?

CHAPTER *14*

HUMAN RESOURCE MANAGEMENT

© T photography/Shutterstock.com

AUTHORS	*Nicholas J. Thomas, DePaul University* *Eric A. Brown, Iowa State University*
LEARNING OBJECTIVES	• Describe how regulations influence human resource management. • Recognize the importance of workforce planning, staffing, and training and development. • Identify methods of managing employee performance and dealing with poor performers. • Identify common types of compensation and benefits. • Recognize the role everyone plays in the health and safety of employees.
CHAPTER OUTLINE	Human Resources: An Introduction Regulatory Issues Workforce Planning Staffing Training and Development Managing Employee Performance Turnover Compensation and Benefits Health and Safety Summary

KEY TERMS

- Development
- Direct compensation
- Employer of choice
- Equal Employment Opportunity
- HR department
- Human resource management
- Indirect compensation
- Job analysis
- Job description
- Job design
- Job specifications
- New hire orientation
- Progressive discipline policy
- Recruiting
- Selection
- Training
- Training cycle
- Turnover
- Workforce planning

HUMAN RESOURCES: AN INTRODUCTION

From Beijing to Boston, to be successful in today's global hospitality industry, owners and operators of hospitality organizations must realize that their employees are a major key to success. The various functions related to the management of these employees is referred to as **human resource management.**[1] Human resource management refers to the practices undertaken in the management of employees in order to meet the strategic goals and objectives of an organization. Because all the employees in a hospitality business are an integral part of the service offered to guests, every employee in the organization, particularly those in supervisory/management positions, influences human resources (HR).

While not all hospitality organizations have an HR department, for purposes of this chapter, the **HR department** will refer to those responsible for the HR management within their organization. Today, HR has evolved into a department, or group of people, that create, implement, and manage policy related to functions such as recruiting, selection, training and development, regulatory compliance, and compensation. HR now has a seat at the table in decision-making in the short-term, as well as the strategic plans for the long-term.

Good human resource management practices have a positive impact on employees and lead to increased levels of job satisfaction and loyalty of a workforce. As these two metrics increase, employees tend to

© Konstantin Chagin/Shutterstock.com

Human resource management refers to employee management in an effort to meet the strategic goals of an organization.

consistently provide better service to their customers. This cycle of happy employees leading to happy guests allows hospitality organizations to be more successful. Through their experience, Williamson and Tharrett determined that in order to run the best performing organization, in their case a private club, "you have to begin by creating a workplace environment that engages its employees and engenders employee happiness.[2]"

REGULATORY ISSUES

When President Lyndon Johnson signed the Civil Rights Act of 1964, he created a new standard in managing employees that was needed to combat a long history of workplace discrimination. Title VII of this law prohibits workplace discrimination on the basis of race, color, religion, sex, or national origin and launched the **Equal Employment Opportunity** regulatory landscape that exists in today's hospitality industry workplace within the United States. Equal Employment Opportunity is a framework of laws and practices that aim to mitigate discrimination in the work place. Table 14.1 includes a summary of some of the major legislation that is currently enforced at the federal level. Some laws only apply when an organization has a minimum number of employees, such as Title VII of the Civil Rights Act, which only applies when an organization has 15 or more employees.

Human resource departments, and those responsible for managing employees, should be aware of various federal, state, and local laws, regulations, court decisions, and mandates regarding the management of employees. Being unaware of a law is not a defense against a lawsuit or fine. In addition to understanding each law, those responsible for managing employees should be familiar with various

"How we treat [employees] influences how they feel when they're here. If they feel good, it creates motivation and passion, and the guests are the [beneficiaries]. Fundamentally, and truly, everything we do is based on that truth."[3]

—Erin Haid, Associate Director of Talent Development at Starwood Hotels & Resorts Worldwide, Inc.

Table 14.1

Legislation	Summary
Equal Pay Act (EPA) of 1963	This act requires equal pay for equal work regardless of the sex of an employee.
Title VII of the Civil Rights Act of 1964	This makes it illegal for employers to discriminate in employment based on race, color, religion, sex, or national origin.
Age Discrimination in Employment Act (ADEA) of 1967	This act prohibits discrimination based on age of anyone 40 years of age or older.
Pregnancy Discrimination Act (PDA) of 1978	An amendment to Title VII of the Civil Rights Act, this prohibits sex discrimination based on pregnancy.
Immigration Reform and Control Act (IRCA) of 1968	This act made it illegal for employers to knowingly employ illegal immigrants and requires employers to confirm employment eligibility of employees using the I-9 form (employment eligibility verification).
Americans with Disabilities Act (ADA) of 1990	This act made it illegal to discriminate based on an employee or applicant's disability. Employers are required to make reasonable accommodations for those with disabilities as long as it will not cause an undue hardship to the organization.
Family Medical Leave Act (FMLA) of 1993	This act requires employers to provide employees with unpaid leave for specified family or medical reasons without fear of losing their job.
Affordable Care Act (ACA) of 2010	This act outlines the responsibilities and benefits for employers to offer health insurance to their employees.

federal agencies that have been established to enforce and track compliance of these laws. These include the Equal Employment Opportunity Commission (EEOC), Occupational Safety and Health Administration (OSHA), Department of Labor (DoL), and the Immigration and Naturalization Service (INS). Additionally, state and local governments have agencies that enforce employment law and are available for HR professionals as a resource for more information, suggestions for compliance, and other operational needs.

WORKFORCE PLANNING

Human resource departments are a great resource for a variety of stakeholders, such as department heads and top management, as they conduct **workforce planning**. This often overlooked, yet critical HR function refers to actions undertaken to determine and respond to current and future workforce trends. Simply put, workforce planning means having the right number of people, in the right job, at the right time. HR departments can also help assess if an organization is an employer of choice. An **employer of choice** is a business that has practices, policies, and benefits that ensure employees would rather work for them as opposed to a similar organization. Before organizations can ensure they have adequate staff, they must first ensure they know what tasks must be done, how those tasks should be accomplished, and what skills are needed to complete the task.

Prior to determining how many employees will be needed to meet their needs, organizations will conduct a **job analysis**. A job analysis is a process that focuses on a particular job in identifying what tasks need to be accomplished. The end results of a successful job analysis are two fold, the **job description** and the **job specifications**. A job description is a written summary of the tasks, duties, and responsibilities of a specific job. This can be useful in getting a sense of what someone would do in a typical day on the job. Job specifications are the knowledge, skills, and abilities (KSAs) needed to successfully complete the tasks of a job. Both the job description and the job specification are used extensively in both the human resource management functions of recruitment and selection.

In addition to the above-mentioned aspects of workforce planning, there is still a need to determine how a job should be completed in an ideal scenario. This is referred to as a **job design**. A job design is useful in meeting organizational goals related to performance and also allows the employee to increase their motivation and morale. There are five common strategies in job design: a) job simplification; b) job enlargement; c) job enrichment; d) job rotation; and e) team building.

Job Simplification	Reducing the number of tasks or responsibilities of a specific job with the intent of making the job simpler.
Job Enlargement	Increasing the number of tasks or responsibilities of a specific job with the intent of making the job more challenging.
Job Enrichment	Designing a job so it is more challenging and less repetitive.
Job Rotation	Having employees cycle through different tasks or responsibilities with the intent of reducing boredom.
Team Building	Treating employees as part of a group with the intent of increasing cohesiveness among employees.

STAFFING

Both recruiting and selection are important aspects of human resource management that aim to make sure open positions are filled with qualified employees. **Recruiting** is a process by which an organization attempts to attract individuals from within or outside the organization to apply for an open job position. Recruitment can be internal (within the organization) or external (outside of the organization) in nature. If recruiting efforts are successful and the organization has a pool of applications, they can begin the process of **selection**. In selection, the organization chooses the applicant they believe will be the most successful in the open position.

TRAINING AND DEVELOPMENT

Once an employee starts working for an organization they should start to receive **training**. Training refers to the process of giving employees the knowledge, skills, and abilities to complete their current job. One of the first trainings that an employee goes through is the **new hire orientation**. This training, which is commonly facilitated by the HR department, gives the employee an overview of the company, and allows the new hire the chance to learn how they fit into the organization. Additionally, this training allows new employees to form bonds with one another, a critical aspect for a hospitality organization if they want to be successful in delivering great service to their guests. Once new hire orientation is completed, the new employee goes to their respective department for more job-specific training. The length of training varies depending on the position.

HR departments also lead and assist other hospitality departments in the training and development of existing employees, not just those who are new. Ongoing training is important to ensure that employees are consistently completing the essential functions of their jobs to meet the goals of the

organization. In some cases, assistance is needed to help develop employees for tasks, duties, and responsibilities they may need later. This preparation of employees for jobs they may have in the future, for example, a promotion to a supervisor or manager position or even a position outside the organization, is referred to as **development**. Aspects of development that improve an employee's ability to take on a supervisory or managerial position may be conflict resolution, effective communication strategies, and strategies for managing employee performance.

To assess needs for training in an organization, HR departments may use the **training cycle**, outlined below.[4]

1. Develop and conduct a needs assessment to determine where training is needed.
2. Identify training objectives that are clear and measurable.
3. Establish training criteria that will be a benchmark for measuring what will be learned or gained.
4. Select trainees who will participate in the training.
5. Pretest trainees to identify current knowledge related to the training topic.
6. Choose the training method that is most appropriate based on the trainees.
7. Implement the training program and deliver it to the trainees.
8. Evaluate the training program based on the training objectives to ensure that learning has occurred and there is a positive change in behavior within the work environment.

MANAGING EMPLOYEE PERFORMANCE

Once initial employee training is completed, organizations must continue to manage the performance of these employees. When employees are doing well in completing their assigned tasks, this performance should be acknowledged. When employees are not meeting the established performance criteria, they should receive prompt and constructive feedback in order to improve. In the event that it is needed, some employees may receive re-training.

Feedback on what an employee is doing well and/or what they need to improve can be done informally through real-time verbal interactions between an employee's supervisor and the employee. Additionally, more formal feedback can be done at regularly scheduled (90-day, 6-month, annual) feedback sessions between the employee and their supervisor. In these sessions, the supervisor often uses a standard evaluation form created by, or with the assistance of, the HR department. These sessions should be used not only to discuss the employee's performance, but also to set future goals for the employee. Employees who feel confident about their ability to grow within an organization are more motivated and have higher levels of job satisfaction. Future goal attainment by an employee should be realistic and measurable.

When an employee does not meet the performance standards of their supervisor or the organization, it may be necessary to utilize a **progressive discipline policy**. Progressive discipline is a method of discipline where an employee receives incrementally more rigorous discipline for repeated infractions of organizational policy and procedures. Progressive discipline may start with a verbal warning, and then be followed by a written warning, suspension, and eventually termination. Every organization has a different standard when it comes to discipline, and the HR department is a great resource to assist supervisors and managers.

INDUSTY INSIGHT

The restaurant and accommodation sector has almost a 50% higher annual turnover rate than the total private sector.

—According to the Department of Labor as reported by the National Restaurant Association[5]

Employees who get feedback on their performance tend to have higher levels of job satisfaction.

TURNOVER

Research has shown that employees have higher levels of job satisfaction when their managers provide them with feedback on their work performance. Job satisfaction is very important because when employees are less satisfied and their job satisfaction decreases, employers tend to see higher turnover amongst their employees. Turnover is the name given to the occurrence when an employee leaves an organization by choice (voluntary) or by decision of their employer (involuntary).

COMPENSATION AND BENEFITS

The compensation and benefits strategy of a hospitality organization is traditionally overseen by the HR department and is a key variable in determining employee motivation, morale, and job satisfaction. There are a variety of things that influence compensation and benefits strategies. They include, but are not limited to, cost of living, labor market trends, collective bargaining agreements between an organization and a labor union, and regulatory issues. All supervisors and managers should be aware of their hospitality organization's compensation and benefits program.

Direct compensation is often used to describe the payment an employee receives for work they complete. This includes base pay, merit pay, incentive pay, and bonuses. Hospitality employees often receive **indirect compensation**, which is the term used to describe compensation that is given as a condition of employment as opposed to compensation for work completed. This includes payment for time not worked, which can come in the form of vacation, holidays, sick leave, jury duty, and other similar scenarios.

There are both mandatory and voluntary benefits. Mandatory benefits are enforced by federal, state, and local governments. Mandatory benefits include Social Security, workers' compensation, and unemployment compensation insurance. There are myriad voluntary benefits that a hospitality organization could choose to offer in their efforts to become an employer of choice. Examples of voluntary benefits include life insurance, health insurance, retirement plans, employee assistance programs, and payment for time not worked.

HEALTH AND SAFETY

Another important aspect of the HR department is the processes designed to make sure employees are healthy and safe in their working environment. Much of this focus on health and safety is interwoven into training, development, and day-to-day practices in an organization. While HR is often the department that oversees this, each employee is responsible for their own health and safety, as well as that of their colleagues and customers. This means all employees and managers within an organization have the responsibility to report unsafe or hazardous working conditions.

SUMMARY

Those responsible for managing human resources in hospitality organizations have a lot of influence and power within the organization. In order to avoid lawsuits, they need to understand the regulatory issues. However, one of the most important responsibilities of a human resource manager is to ensure they recruit, select, train, and develop people who will help achieve the goals of the organization. In an industry where turnover is high, managers may fall into the mindset that employees will not be around long, so they hire whoever they can and spend as little money as possible on training. Managers should be cautious of putting unqualified or improperly trained employees in a position to interact with customers and ultimately be responsible for delivering hospitable service.

The assistance managers have can range from doing all human resource activities alone to having a fully staffed human resource department or division. Regardless of how much assistance is provided, managing human resources is ultimately the responsibility of anyone who manages or supervises employees. In an industry where customers are paying for service, an organization with well-managed human resources can have a significant competitive advantage.

RESOURCES

Internet Sites

Society for Human Resource Management (SHRM): www.shrm.org

U.S. Department of Labor (DOL): www.dol.gov

Equal Employment Opportunity Commission (EEOC): www.eeoc.gov

O*NET OnLine: www.onetonline.org

ENDNOTES

1. http://www.shrm.org/templatestools/glossaries/hrterms/pages/h.aspx

2. Williamson, M., & Tharrett, S. (2013, May). Create a climate that encourages employee engagement, happiness. *Club Industry*, pp. 36.

3. Keep your hotel employees happy and engaged. (2014, December 8). Retrieved from http://www.hoteliermagazine.com/keep-your-hotel-employees-happy-and-engaged/

4. Woods, R.H., Johanson, M.M., and Sciarini, M.S. (2006). *Managing Hospitality Human Resources*, 5th ed Lansing, MI: American Hotel and Lodging Association.

5. Hospitality employee turnover rose in 2014. (2014, March 11). Retrieved from http://www.restaurant.org/News-Research/News/Hospitality-employee-turnover-rose-in-2014

Name: _____ Date: _____

1. What is human resource management and who is responsible for the management of human resources within an organization?

2. How did the Title VII of the Civil Rights Act of 1964 change how employees are treated?

3. Why is it important for anyone who manages employees to understand the employment laws in their area?

4. What is the difference between job analysis and job design?

5. What is the difference between job enlargement and job enrichment?

6. What is the goal of recruitment and selection?

7. What is progressive discipline?

8. Identify turnover and discuss the difference between voluntary and involuntary turnover.

9. What is considered direct compensation? Indirect compensation?

10. Why is it important that all employees and managers be aware of health and safety issues? What is progressive discipline?

© Anna Azimi/Shutterstock.com

CHAPTER *15*

FACILITIES, SAFETY, AND SECURITY

AUTHOR

Robert A. McMullin, East Stroudsburg University

LEARNING OBJECTIVES

- Introduce the importance of the physical plant of a hospitality property.
- Understand the value of curb appeal.
- Develop an understanding of the importance of communication between hospitality managers, independent contractors, and corporate property facility personnel with regard to property renovations, maintenance, and repairs.
- Introduce the need to apply human resources with regards to managing the facilities department.
- Identify the financial relationship between repairs and cost.
- Introduce the major engineering systems, types of maintenance repairs, safety, security and the Americans with Disabilities Act.
- Connect the need and importance of physical plant management with the relationship to guest satisfaction.

CHAPTER OUTLINE

Manager Roles and Responsibilities

Engineering Systems

    Water and Wastewater Systems

    Refrigeration Systems

    Heating, Ventilation, and Air Conditioning Systems

    Electrical Systems

    Emergency Maintenance

CHAPTER OUTLINE
(Continued)

Maintenance
    Regular Maintenance
    Preventative Maintenance
Safety
Security
Americans with Disabilities Act
Summary

KEY TERMS

Alternating current (AC)

Americans with Disabilities Act (ADA)

Ampheres

Capital expenditures (CAPEX)

Contract maintenance

Curb appeal

Engineering systems

Furnishing, fixtures, and equipment (FF&E)

Guest room maintenance

Heating, ventilation, and air conditioning (HVAC)

Lifecycle costing

Preventative maintenance (PM)

Property operation and maintenance (POM)

Refrigerant

Routine maintenance

Soft target

The hospitality industry places great emphasis on service, marketing, human resources, and profitability for competitiveness. However, one salient facet of the industry, which is often overlooked, is "**curb appeal**," or attractiveness of the physical operations. Many potential guests see the attractiveness of hospitality properties from Internet websites, virtual tours, and social and/or broadcast media. Other potential guests perceive a mental picture of the facility before making a reservation or purchasing decision. Consequently, the traveling public can be fickle in choosing to patronize a hospitality entity. Quite often, they judge the quality of the potential experience based on what they think of the physical or visual appeal. Along with the physical attractiveness of the facilities, the physical operations enhance guest satisfaction. How clean and attractive the property is also impacts the perception of the guest. Therefore, learning and understanding the physical plant or facilities operations are imperative for hospitality management. The maintenance and design of a good, well working property can affect the service you deliver, or how your facility is marketed, ultimately having a great impact on profitability.

Primarily, the physical plant is composed of landscaping, grounds, exterior and interior building structure, building systems, and **furnishings, fixtures, and equipment (FF&E)**. Landscaping and exterior appeal (curb appeal) sets the tone of attractiveness of a hospitality facility. Many hospitality organizations spend large sums of cash resources in marketing to or luring guests, but one of the most important aspects of the business is visual appearance. Hospitality properties should have clean, bright, and well-lit signage to allure travelers in conjunction with attractive landscaping.

Other elements of the physical plant that guests experience include plumbing, electricity, and heating, ventilation, and air conditioning (HVAC). Managers of hospitality properties need knowledge and experience in understanding the effects of the physical plant and the actual (financial) outcomes to guests if equipment fails. In addition, management needs to be able to communicate with contractors, maintenance, and/or engineering staff to effect proper repairs without jeopardizing the guest's stay.

MANAGER ROLES AND RESPONSIBILITIES

The scope and depth of the knowledge a facility manager must have depends on the type and size of the property. Budget and economy lodging operations have relatively small and simple physical plants, whereas convention, resort, and luxury properties may have complex engineering systems that may resemble small cities. Other hospitality enterprises like restaurants and country clubs may rely on the property's general manager's communications with independent contractors or corporate personnel to repair their facility. Therefore, depending on the facility, there are many different backgrounds a physical plant manager must possess.

The role and responsibilities of the hospitality facility manager or maintenance engineer typically include detailed knowledge about the following areas:

1. Systems and Building Design
2. Building and System Operations
3. Guest Room Furnishing and Fixtures Maintenance
4. Equipment Maintenance and Repair
5. Equipment Selection and Installation
6. Contract Management
7. Utilities Management
8. Waste Management
9. Budget and Cost Control
10. Safety
11. Security
12. Contractual and Regulatory Compliance
13. Parts Inventory and Control
14. Renovations, Additions, and Restorations
15. Staff Training
16. Emergency Planning and Response

The aforementioned responsibilities present challenges for many hospitality facilities managers or maintenance engineers. Each skill level varies depending on work experience and educational background. For example, the facilities manager may have to work with various contractors when the decision is made to renovate or restore his or her facility.

In many hospitality maintenance and engineering situations, the facilities manager will have some detailed technical background from contracting firms, trade or technical schools, or other related employment. Although a technical background in plumbing, electrical, or HVAC equipment is good, a facilities manager new to the hospitality industry may have little conceptual knowledge of the relationship of repair versus guest service. This can create problems with communication, as various hospitality departments attempt to communicate guest service repair problems, and facilities managers fix equipment so the guest's experience is not jeopardized. If a guest reports a plumbing issue like a leaky faucet, running toilet, or low water pressure in the shower, facilities managers need to be responsive and efficient with repairs, or the lodging property may have to provide a refund. Housekeeping attendants or front office employees may have difficulty communicating guest room problems to facilities managers or maintenance employees who are responsible for fixing the problems. In some cases, it may feel like each department is speaking a different language, and in some ways they are. This can place an additional burden on the management staff, because the facility manager needs to work closely with the executive housekeeper, front office manager, and food and beverage manager. Bridging the communication gap is an important task for the general manager of a property, because the property can lose revenue, attractiveness, and desirability from the guest.

In addition to working closely with other departments, the facilities manager must understand the financial relationship between maintenance repair and cost. For example, the facility manager needs to track energy costs while trying to find ways to decrease this expenditure. This position requires the need to analyze energy bills like gas and electric, track the nature and frequency of work orders, review the equipment data cards, record equipment repair history, examine architectural plans, and conduct warranty analysis. The facility manager needs to evaluate the cost of a repair while remaining committed to bringing cost within or below budget. In accounting terms, the action of the facility manager is reported on the line item of the income statement called **property operations and maintenance (POM)**. The challenge for the facility manager is to improve the quality of the physical plant while using minimal financial resources. Meanwhile, the facility manager has to study the relationship of how equipment is used, and the consumption of energy usage from utility bills like electric, gas, and water. Therefore, the facility manager must work closely with the property controller too. If the facility manager can maintain the same level of property energy efficiency, or even enhance efficiency levels, while finding ways to reduce costs, this would have a positive effect on the hospitality property's financial statements. When fewer maintenance problems are coupled with a well kept, landscaped property, the result is often improved guest satisfaction, repeat patronage, and an increase in profits.

Another significant financial responsibility of the facility manager is the evaluation of capital projects. These projects require a major cash outlay when either replacing or acquiring new equipment. The facilities manager, along with other key hospitality management, must judge the initial cost, durability, safety, and energy consumption of capital equipment purchases. There are other accounting concerns like depreciation and tax implications. The process of judging, selecting, and analyzing capital projects is called **lifecycle costing**, which considers the following:

- **Initial Costs:** The cost of the item itself, including costs of installments, interconnection, and modification of supporting systems or equipment.
- **Operating Costs:** The costs of energy or water to operate the equipment and supporting systems, or those systems affected by the equipment, maintenance, labor, and supplies, or contract maintenance services.
- **Fixed Costs:** Insurance, depreciating and/ or property tax changes resulting from the equipment or system.
- **Tax Implication:** Income taxes and tax credits such as investment, tax credits, and depreciation deductions.[1]

Technology is now available to assist the facility manager in organizing and operating vital management services. Mintek Mobile Data Solutions, www.mintek.com, enables hotel owners and operators to manage five important processes: preventative maintenance (PM), asset management, capital expenditure (CAPEX) planning, work orders, and document and contract management. This technology features opportunities to control a property's assets with a detailed database for monitoring, scheduling, warranties, architectural design, and maintenance contracts.[2]

ENGINEERING SYSTEMS

Management in the hospitality industry needs to understand the basic design and operations of the various **engineering systems**. This improves the communication between the facility manager and the rest of management. Having direct daily communication is imperative to relay any information on malfunctioning equipment so it can be repaired, while not disturbing the patrons or interrupting other management in completing their own tasks. The facility manager must take a proactive stance to manage communications with maintenance, housekeeping, front office, foodservice, and marketing and sales departments. For example, a planned electrical outage to repair a major piece of equipment, such as an elevator, can effect the immediate daily activities of housekeeping staff, bell staff, and room service.[3] The basic elements of the engineering systems include several areas.

Management should know the basic operations of water and wastewater systems, refrigeration systems, heating, ventilation, air conditioning systems, on-site power production, and safety and security systems, so they can intelligently explain what needs to be accomplished by the facilities management team.

WATER AND WASTEWATER SYSTEMS

A water supply is necessary for food and beverage and lodging establishments. Management should be familiar with where the water cut-off valve is located in case of an emergency. Additional knowledge of the operations of backflow devices to prevent unwanted water from re-entering a building is similarly helpful. Other relevant systems to understand include a storm sewer system for the disposal of rainwater, and a sanitary sewer system for the removal of waste

© wavebreakmedia/Shutterstock.com

Water supply is essential for food and beverage and lodging establishments.

products. A key system for restaurants is a grease separator or grease trap. Grease needs to be separated from wastewater to prevent water backup.

REFRIGERATION SYSTEMS

Hospitality managers should be knowledgeable about refrigeration systems. In the compressive refrigeration systems, undesired heat is picked up in one place and carried to another place, where it is dumped or deposited. In many lodging establishments individual heating and air conditioning units are in each room. These are self-contained units that need to be maintained on a regular basis for guest comfort. Heat pumps present in residential properties work in a similar process, except the unit is outside the room. The major components of the refrigeration cycle are:

1. **Refrigerant**, which is a fluid with a low boiling point that starts as liquid, absorbs heat, and becomes a gas, and then is placed under pressure to become a liquid again.

2. The evaporation is the section of the circuit in which the refrigerant evaporates or boils to soak up heat.

3. An expansion valve allows the refrigerant to soak up heat, allowing pressure to be lowered, aiding the refrigeration cycle.

4. A compressor is a pump supplying the power to move the refrigerant through the system.[4]

HEATING, VENTILATION, AND AIR CONDITIONING SYSTEMS

Heating, ventilation, and air conditioning (HVAC) systems provide levels of temperature comfort based on heating, cooling, and humidity for guests, staff, and management. The key components of an HVAC system are pipes (hollow cylinders or tubular passes through which a substance, especially a fluid, is conveyed), pumps (machines or devices for transferring a liquid or gas from a source or container through tubes or pipes to another container or receiver), thermostats (instruments that convert the temperature into a signal that is sent to the HVAC unit conditioning the space), and valves (devices that regulate the flow of gases, liquids, or loose materials through structures, such as piping or through apertures by opening, closing, or obstructing parts of passageways). Systems can be decentralized and operate as individual units, or they can be centralized as one system working collectively.

ELECTRICAL SYSTEMS

Some hospitality properties operate an on-site power production, but most operations have electricity delivered by local utilities. In either case, hospitality managers should have a familiarity with electrical systems, because they may experience brownouts (partial loss of electricity) or blackouts (total loss of electricity) that could disrupt the electrical service. Furthermore, management needs to understand electrical utility rates for cost control. The utility is responsible for providing power at a correct voltage and frequency. The utility provides power tracked through an electric meter that measures the rate and amount of power consumed, which generates the electric bill. The measure of the use of electrical energy is a watt. An **amphere** measures the rate of electrical flow through a device or appliance. The volt is the unit of electrical potential. Hospitality properties are supplied with **alternating current (AC)** from the local utility company. If you do not have sufficient current, your property may experience lights flickering or reduced illumination. Why do you need to know this? The goal of the facility manager is to provide a suitable level of guest comfort while reducing electrical use and costs.

EMERGENCY MAINTENANCE

Emergency and breakdown maintenance occur when equipment fails based on unforeseen occurrences like severe weather. Hospitality properties cannot prevent equipment breakdown, but they can use preventative maintenance procedures to help limit the occurrence of breakdowns. However, having contingency plans can aid when a breakdown or power outage occurs. For example, when there is a power failure, tested backup electrical and/or battery generators can keep guests calm so that they can get to safety. Especially on the day of a big banquet, the kitchen staff does not want to find out the refrigeration unit died, and the food product is slowly defrosting without a backup refrigeration unit available. Or, during a heat wave, guests and staff will not appreciate the higher, uncomfortable temperatures without a tested emergency air conditioning backup unit. Therefore, planning for all emergencies is imperative.

Many hospitality establishments have been rethinking their disaster plans because of major weather events like Hurricane Katrina (2005) and Hurricane/Super Storm Sandy (2012). Emergency maintenance has become a major part of planning and preparation for all hospitality operations.

Contract maintenance is necessary for certain equipment needs when repairs are beyond the skill level of your facility staff. Some contractors can be on retainer where they promise to handle emergencies as they happen, for an annual fee. Cases for this type of contract might be refrigerators and freezers for the kitchen, and washers and dryers for housekeeping. Another contracted group is for the computers, property management system, and point of sale systems. There are other contracts for specific visits on a routine basis such as pest control. Some contracted arrangements can be available to assist in emergency or breakdown situations.

MAINTENANCE

REGULAR MAINTENANCE

Hospitality buildings and interiors are heavily used 24 hours of every day, 7 days a week by guests, staff, and management. Each facility should have budgeted funds, such as a **capital expenditure** fund (CAPEX)

© photomatz/Shutterstock.com

Regular maintenance could include cleaning pools, emptying trash, or shoveling snow.

to reinvest in their property. Equipment will wear down, break down, and become obsolete. Facilities management should have a tier plan to keep the property running efficiently.

- **Routine maintenance** is the general everyday duty of facility staff, which requires relatively minimal skills or training. Examples of these duties include picking up litter, emptying trashcans, raking leaves, and shoveling snow.

PREVENTATIVE MAINTENANCE

- **Preventative maintenance**, sometimes referred to as **PM**, requires more training and advanced skills of facility personnel. Examples of PM include inspections, lubrication, minor repairs or equipment adjustments, and work order investigation.
- **Guest room maintenance** is an activity applied to guest rooms of a lodging establishment. This is a form of prevention in ensuring guest comfort. Usually, trained facilities personnel will remove several rooms a day from the room inventory to inspect them for the following:
  1. Change of filters in HVAC systems.
  2. Test operation of TVs, electronic equipment, plumbing, and electrical equipment.
  3. Ensure the guest room is free of any maintenance issues.[5]

When a facilities manager makes plans, he or she must take into consideration scheduling regular maintenance, which requires advance planning,

a significant amount of time to perform, specialized tools and equipment, and coordination of the departments affected. Each task should be assigned as part of each employee's schedule every day so that it does not get lost or forgotten when problems occur.

SAFETY

Employee, guest, and management safety programs are another key responsibility of hospitality management, which is usually implemented and maintained by the Facilities Department or Human Resources. The entire hospitality staff should be committed to a safe and secure environment to protect guests, staff, and management. This can be accomplished by communicating safety and security needs at management staff meetings, and developing safety committees composed of various employees of each department of the hotel and/or restaurant. One of the major concerns in this area is protecting people and hospitality assets. Upon check-in, guests should be made aware of their physical surroundings and encouraged to use all protective devices a room has installed. Most hospitality lodging establishments have two to three locks to each guest room door, which include a lock on the door latch, a deadbolt, and a chain/throw-bar. Guests should be informed that all locks should be used, along with a door port viewer to prevent room invasions by potential criminals. Guests should be informed to never open doors to strangers, and always contact the front office with any concerns. Once again, it is facilities management responsibility that all locking devices are working properly as part of an effective preventative maintenance program. These check-in and rooming procedures should always be reviewed and enhanced as technology and human intervention improves.

The guestroom design provides safety concerns such as the guest bathroom. These safety concerns include hot water temperatures, slip resistant bathroom features, and electric shock. Water temperature should not exceed 120 degrees Fahrenheit or 49 degrees Celsius to prevent scalding of guests. Slip resistance features include, but are not limited to, using the correct detergents to prevent falling. Also grab bars should be located generously around the bathtub and shower to aid the guest. With bathroom amenities like electric hair dryers, curling irons, and coffee makers, the cords should be short to prevent a guest from dropping the appliance into a water-filled sink or bathtub. Careful planning of guestroom amenities should aid in the prevention of accidents in the guestroom.

In restaurant operations, slips and falls are a major concern for everyone. When water is spilled it should be cleaned up immediately with proper signage. If a guest falls, there needs to be complete and thorough documentation that demonstrates concern for the guest while protecting the hospitality operation from legal issues. Meanwhile, an employee may be injured, miss work, and possibly collect workers compensation. Another employee will need to fill in for the missed duties of the injured employee and may incur overtime as an additional cost to the employer. These concerns require proactive responsibility of all employees in the hospitality industry.

Hospitality managers, along with facilities managers, should know the operations of fire equipment, including detection, notification, suppression, and smoke control systems. By knowing these procedures, hospitality employees can aid in the deterrence of fire emergencies. Just as important is to have a fire safety plan in place for the trained employees to execute and communicate to guests. At a minimum, each room should be equipped with smoke detectors that are hard wired to a central communication system. These smoke detectors should be tested regularly and up to date records of all tests should be documented. Floor plans should be prepared for evacuation with a minimum of two escape routes. All employees should be tested in the use of fire extinguishers and on fire alarm locations. A fire communication plan should be developed with a designated area for all guests and employees to evacuate to when an emergency occurs. In-room guest lists should be printed to make sure all guests are being evacuated. Employees should be dispatched to rooms where guests need assistance. Finally, all these procedures should be reviewed to insure they are in keeping with the local fire code regulations, and fire drills should be scheduled regularly in coordination with the local fire/emergency service.

Another key is knowing how to use security systems, such as electronic lock systems, closed-circuit televisions, elevator controls, and exit alarms. These procedures aid in protecting the guests from unwanted intruders, and in safely evacuating guests if an emergency arises. All departments in a lodging facility should develop, practice, and review procedures in case evacuation is necessary. Facilities and security staff need to develop and practice plans in case of terrorist acts, bomb scares, robberies, and extreme weather situations such as blizzards, earthquakes, hurricanes, and tornadoes.

SECURITY

Generally, in the lodging industry, we welcome guests to our properties, have them lower their guard, and have them relax and feel at home. However, it is not always possible to know when a person is a welcomed guest or a stranger who is pretending to be a guest. Without security measures, strangers could enter a property unchallenged by staff and attempt to enter or break into guest rooms. Yet, lodging facilities are public buildings, and so, guests need to be aware of safety measures as well. Many establishments provide "Traveler Safety Tips" upon check-in or in the room. Again, the lodging employees, especially housekeeping and maintenance staff, during their routine activities should monitor any suspicious activities, and request to see guest room keys and let guests know this is for their own protection. Any guest who refuses should be asked to leave, while informing security.

However, in addition to guests' awareness, equipment can be in place to increase security. These security enhancements should be installed and maintained by the facilities department. Guest rooms should be equipped with phones to enable guests to place emergency phone calls in case of a cell phone malfunction like a low battery or signal. Many hotels place phones by elevators or in hallways to ensure guests have access to hotel personnel. The facilities staff should install guest room doors that self-close and lock automatically. Doors should be equipped with deadbolts, view ports, security door chains, or throw-bars. Windows and sliding glass doors should be able to open, but not wide enough for an intruder to enter. In many cases, facilities can place a bar that fits into the floor track of a sliding glass door to ensure guest safety.

Guests should be encouraged to use in-room safes or safety deposit boxes available at the front desk. This provides an extra level of security for guest valuables.

All lodging facilities should have a strong key control system for both manual and electronic locks. When keys are lost, stolen, misplaced, or not returned, the lock system should be evaluated. One approach is referred to as the "Five R's of Key Control":[6]

- **Rationale:** Criteria used to develop the key scheduling and to identify who will have various levels of access.
- **Records:** Involve guest information with regard to occupancy, status, and access.
- **Retrieval:** Actions by staff to recover keys from employees and guests.
- **Rotation:** Involves moving locks from room to room as a preventative security plan.
- **Replacement:** As keys are lost or locks compromised, replacement is necessary.

Historically, older lodging properties with manual locks need to follow the aforementioned procedure. Even electronic locks have been compromised, which means lock systems should be evaluated from time to time by facilities, security, and room division management.

As technology improves, hybrid keys have become the norm. These include smart cards, contactless locks with microchip key access, cell phone access, and other devices using radio frequency identification (RFID). RFID provides an electronic audit trail of who has gained access, with dates and times. Upon checkout, the new check-in will have a completely different access code with an electronic signature assigned. In some cases, the guest will have the access to the guestroom streamed to their electronic media for guestroom access so they may bypass the check-in process. The new electronic features have improved guest services by enabling mobile guestroom access and billing and enhancing security.

Unfortunately, the travel and tourism industry, including lodging properties and restaurants, has become a "**soft target**" for terrorism. Mass casualty attacks using but not limited to automatic weapons, vehicle bombs, suicide vest bombs, and explosive luggage have occurred. Two recent examples include the JW Marriott and Ritz Carlton bombing on July 17, 2009 in Jakarta, Indonesia, and the gunmen who stormed the Radisson in Mali, West Africa on November 20, 2015. Guests, employees, and management need to be aware of any questionable activity on the lodging premises. Some of the protective measures include: encouraging personnel to be alert to suspicious behavior, using vehicle barriers, controlling or restricting access to buildings, having some security cameras visible (other cameras hidden), paying attention to the clothing being worn by guests (loose fitting or wrong clothing for the weather may be concerning), and regularly training personnel on terrorism prevention.[7] When emergencies occur, the hospitality property needs to be proactive in coordinating their response (phone numbers with emergency contacts) with the police department, fire department, bomb squad, electric company, gas company, rescue squad, Red Cross, and owner and general manager of the property.

Hospitality management and facilities staff should work together to provide the highest means of safety and security to the guests and their own staff. This provides a safe work environment for employees and allows the guests to enjoy their visit in a secure setting.

AMERICANS WITH DISABILITIES ACT

An important consideration in the hospitality industry is the **Americans with Disabilities Act (ADA)**. Since July 26, 1990, the law has required commercial and government buildings to ensure that their physical surroundings allow disabled people to enter and use the facilities. It also called for a change in behavior. Policies and procedures that effectively denied access to the disabled were no longer legal.[8]

This Act spells out reasonable accommodations for individuals with disabilities. Most people believe that the ADA is only for those with physical handicaps or sensory impairments. However, think about other people who could use some help. Wouldn't it be easier for your grandmother who is healthy to use a ramp instead of steps to gain entry into a building? Wouldn't a railing by the bathtub make it easier to get in and out if you broke your leg and had a cast? And wouldn't it be easier for you to use a wheelchair for improved mobility throughout the hospitality property rather than using crutches? The Act requires a percentage of guest rooms to have special accommodations and equipment for guests who have special circumstances that make an ADA room appropriate.

To accommodate transportation needs, vans are equipped to allow wheelchair entry, and wider parking spaces are needed to accommodate someone exiting from the side of the van. For people with hearing and visual impairment, the ADA covers emergency situations like visual and audible alarms including strobe lights. Many individuals believe that complying with ADA standards is expensive. However, many accommodations have inexpensive alternatives. If a hospitality establishment has a few steps that lead to the entry of the building, the use of a temporary metal ramp that can be folded to store nearby may be an inexpensive alternative. Some hospitality facilities will have consultants to evaluate their facility to ensure their compliance with ADA laws.

SUMMARY

The facilities management and its staff are critical components of a hospitality enterprise. The way the property looks, how it works, its safety, and the comfort of the guest are critical. Preventative maintenance and repairs will help ensure repeat business and guest satisfaction. If facilities issues are not remedied to ensure guest comfort, safety, and security, you may find yourself in financial and legal problems.

MORE RESOURCES HERE

American Hotel & Lodging Association (producer). *Curb Appeal: Creating Great First Impressions* (Videotape). Available from the American Hotel & Lodging Association, P.O. Box 1240, 1407 S. Harrison Road, East Lansing, MI 48826-1240.

Bardi, J. A. (2011). *Hotel Front Office Management*, 5th ed. New Jersey: John Wiley & Sons.

Borsenik, F. D. and Stutts, A. D. (1991). *The Management of Maintenance and Engineering Systems In the Hospitality Industry*, 3rd ed. New York: Wiley.

Jones, T. and Zemke, D. (2010). *Managing the Built Environment in Hospitality Facilities.* Upper Saddle River, NJ: Prentice Hall.

Palmer, J. D. (1990). *Principles of Hospitality Engineering.* New York: Van Nostrand Reinhold.

Stipanuk, D. M. (2006). *Hospitality Facilities Management and Design*, 3rd ed. East Lansing, MI: Educational Institute of the American Hotel and Lodging Association.

Stipanuk, D. M. (2015). *Principles of Hospitality Management and Design*, 4th ed. East Lansing, MI: Educational Institute of the American Hotel and Lodging Association.

Usiewicz, R. A. (2004). Physical Plant Management and Security. In R. A. Brymer (ed.), *Hospitality & Tourism, An Introduction to the Industry*, 11th ed., pp. 147–156. Dubuque, IA: Kendall Hunt Publishing Company.

RESOURCES

Internet Sites

American Hotel & Lodging Association: www.AHLA.com

PM Engineer: www.pmengineer.com

International Facilities Management Association: www.Ifma.com

Tradeline: www.tradelineinc.com

Buildings Magazine: www.buildings.com

Burnham Commercial Boilers: www.burnhamcommercial.com

American Solar Energy Society: www.ases.org

Green Globe 21: www.greenglobe21.com

National Fire Protection Association: www.nfpa.org

Water Web: www.waterweb.org

Water Online: www.wateronline.com

Electric Power Research Institute: www.epri.com

Laundry Today: www.laundrytoday.com

National Gardening Association: www.garden.org

American Institute of Architects: www.aia.org

Mintek Mobile Date Solutions: www.mintek.com

Building Owners and Managers Association: www.boma.org

Energy User News: www.energyusernews.com

Facilities Net: www.facilitiesnet.com

FM Link: www.fmlink.com

International Society of Hospitality Consultants: www.ishc.com

Association of Energy Engineers: www.aeecenter.org

Energy Star: www.energystar.gov

U.S. Green Building Council: www.usgbc.org

Project Planet: www.projectplanetcorp.com

National Renewable Energy Laboratory: www.nrel.gov

U.S. Department of Labor—Occupational Safety & Health Administration: www.osha.gov

American Water Works Association: www.awwa.org

Association of Pool & Spa Professionals: www.theapsp.org

American Society of Heating, Refrigerating and Air-Conditioning Engineers: www.ashrae.org

Gas Technology Institute: www.gastechnology.org

HVAC Toolbox: www.hvac-toolbox.com

American Gas Association: www.aga.org

Commercial Food Equipment Service Association: www.cfesa.com

Foodservice Consultants Society International: www.fcsi.org

Underwriters Laboratories Inc.: www.ul.com

North American Association of Food Equipment Manufacturers: www.nafem.org

National Association of Elevator Contractors: www.naec.org

National Roofing Contractors Association: www.nrca.net

ENDNOTES

1. Usiewicz, R. A. (2004). Physical Plant Management and Security. In R. A. Brymer (ed.), *Hospitality Tourism*, pp. 148–140. Dubuque, IA: Kendall Hunt Publishing Company.

2. Bardi, J. A. (2011). *Hotel Front Office Management*, 5th ed. New Jersey: John Wiley & Sons, p. 449.

3. Ibid.

4. Stipanuk, D. M. (2006). *Hospitality Facilities Management and Design*, 3rd ed. East Lansing, MI: Educational Institute of the American Hotel, Lodging Association, p. 247.

5. Ibid., pp. 38–39.

6. Ibid., p. 153.

7. Stipanuk, D. M. (2015). *Hospitality Facilities Management and Design*, 4th ed. East Lansing, MI: Educational Institute of the American Hotel, Lodging Association, p. 164.

8. Jones, T. and Zemke, D. (2010). *Managing the Built Environment in Hospitality Facilities*, Upper Saddle River, NJ: Prentice Hall, p. 66.

Name: _____ Date: _____

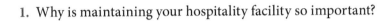
1. Why is maintaining your hospitality facility so important?

2. What comprises the physical plant?

3. What is curb appeal? Discuss why it affects your property's image.

4. What are the responsibilities of the physical plan manager or maintenance engineer?

5. What is the relationship between the general manager and maintenance engineer with regard to the physical property?

6. What is the financial relationship between repair, guest satisfaction, and cost?

7. Name and discuss the engineering systems.

8. Name and define three types of maintenance.

9. What is life cycle costing? Why is it important?

10. Why is safety so important to the guests? Employees?

11. Why is security so important to a hospitality facility?

12. What is the importance of the Americans with Disabilities Act?

CHAPTER *16*

© Bucchi Francesco/Shutterstock.com

TECHNOLOGY

AUTHOR

Kathleen E. King, Northern Arizona University School of Hotel and Restaurant Management

LEARNING OBJECTIVES

- Identify the components of hospitality technology.
- Define the terms property management system and point-of-sale system.
- Describe trends in hospitality technology.
- List the challenges technology holds for the hospitality industry.

CHAPTER OUTLINE

The Property Management System
The Point-of-Sale System
Technological Expectations of Hospitality Guests
Challenges of Technology in the Hospitality Industry
Trends in Hospitality Technology
Summary

KEY TERMS

Guest room technologies
Keyless lodging entry
Meal pacing system
Point-of-sale system

Property management system
Self check-in kiosk
Tableside restaurant technology

THE PROPERTY MANAGEMENT SYSTEM

Whether a lodging property is a small operation like a bed and breakfast or a mega casino in Las Vegas, they all require a system to keep track of reservations, rates and availability, and many other operating functions of the property. A **property management system** (PMS) is a central computer system that allows this to happen. It is defined by a company called All Property Management as "an online program or software designed for residential or commercial property management. However, more often it refers to software used in the hospitality industry to manage the day to day requirements of running a hotel or resort."[1] The PMS is used by a wide variety of departments at the hotel. The front desk will use it to answer a customer's questions about what rooms are available on a specific date and what rate is available. The housekeeping department will be able to access what rooms have customers checking out versus staying an additional night so that they can clean them accordingly. Accounting departments use the PMS to bill customers with accounts, and human resources keeps track of employee information. The PMS is the heart of the hotel's technology.

A PMS can be one that has all the data stored on site and is backed up frequently by an information technology manager, or it can be a cloud-based system that has the memory housed off-site by a third party. In either case, easy access to information is necessary for the smooth running of the operation. Cost varies on whether you have all the hardware and software on site or have the software hosted in a cloud system. Managers and technology professionals have many vendors to choose from and must match the product to the needs of their lodging property. A company called Capterra helps the property match their needs with the property management systems available. This information can be invaluable when dealing with new technologies and budgetary restraints. As you can see, property management systems are the heart of the lodging property and need to meet the needs of many departments. When built and maintained correctly, they allow the hotel to run smoothly and therefore guests to get the prompt customer service they desire.

THE POINT-OF-SALE SYSTEM

As lodging establishments need a PMS to help successfully run their operations, food and beverage establishments also need a centralized, useful system. The system used is called the **point-of-sale system** or POS. "A POS system is a network of cashier and server terminals that typically handles food and beverage orders, transmission of orders to the kitchen and bar, guest-check settlement, timekeeping, and interactive charge posting to guest folios."[2]

Both the front-of-the-house and back-of-the-house portions of foodservice operations utilize this system. Servers will input orders that the POS system sends to the kitchen where staff will prepare the food and then notify the servers when the orders are ready. Some POS systems have software called the **meal pacing system**. Darden Restaurants uses this system, which sends the pieces of a guest's order to the kitchen based on cook times, to increase customer satisfaction and increase the number of table turns (number of times the table is used by different guests during a specific time frame). According to an article in *Chain Store Guide*, this system worked so well with Olive Garden and Red Lobster that it was rolled out to other brands within the Darden Chain.[3] Recipes can be stored in the POS system so that new employees always have the ability to properly make a dish. This also allows servers to answer questions from their guests in detail regarding what goes into a particular meal. Customers with food allergies or sensitivities can feel secure that a particular foodservice establishment is a good one for them to choose when this option is available.

The POS hosts all the human resources information for an establishment as well. Payroll, reviews, scheduling, and timekeeping are also handled through the POS system. Applications can be connected to the POS system to help with scheduling and modifying existing schedules as the business needs dictate. All these components combined assist a foodservice business in running a profitable, customer-oriented business.

TECHNOLOGICAL EXPECTATIONS OF HOSPITALITY GUESTS

Hospitality guests have expectations today that each operation must attempt to uncover and then meet to the best of their ability. As such, each owner or general manager must be familiar with the technology that is available and required for their respective businesses in addition to finding those cutting-edge products and applications that will give them a competitive edge within their segment of the hospitality industry.

As our customer base becomes more and more tech "savvy" so should our hotels, restaurants, cruise ships, airlines, etc. Wi-Fi is expected to be available with a preference for being free to guests. Hotel guests desire a fast check in and the ability to easily use the technology that is available in the guest room. Restaurants are using **tableside restaurant technology** for ordering and check payments to assist in smooth delivery for customers. Servers have access to complete ingredient lists for those who request the information for dietary or allergy needs. Regardless of the location, hospitality guests want the same ease of access to information that they have at home. This expectation means that all professionals in the industry must not only be excellent at reading customers and providing the service they desire but also at learning the technology that is a part of their location.

Today, hotel guests expect Wi-Fi, preferably for free.

CHALLENGES OF TECHNOLOGY IN THE HOSPITALITY INDUSTRY

Every hospitality establishment wants to have the best and most advanced technology that suits their guests. Obviously, the type of hotel or restaurant determines what technology is appropriate. Meeting our customers' needs is a very challenging part of the industry. It can be costly, difficult to anticipate trends, hard to determine what your customers truly want, and a challenge to place in existing buildings.

Technology is costly. A new, state of the art PMS could cost a hotel tens of thousands of dollars just for the software. And if a cloud-based system is what you choose, there are monthly fees to be paid as well. A company call INNROAD has systems where guests can have an iPad in their room that allows access to the front desk, valets, and room service, and can even control the lighting, temperature, and entertainment. It would cost a hotel $1600 per iPad to have it ready to go. For a 200-room hotel, that is approximately $320,000.[4] POSs offer the same choices (software and cloud-based systems, hardware and locally stored information) all at a substantial cost. If you want your servers to have tableside tablets or iPads, those must be purchased.

Trying to anticipate trends in hospitality technology is a very challenging task. Just like when you are buying a new car, a manager will need to look at the cost, what the establishment truly needs, and what the customers may want. Another issue to take into account is that fact that, as soon as you install the technology in your property, there will be something on the market that is newer and "better." Having qualified people on staff who are very information technology literate or having an information technology manager as an employee can reduce the risk of making poor purchasing decisions.

Knowing your customer base will be the biggest asset to choosing technology for your hospitality business. For example, property management systems are available with **self check-in kiosks**. Similar to a self check-in at the airport, a guest can go to a kiosk and, choosing the correct menu options, check themselves in, get a key and room assignment, and begin their stay at your hotel. This technology helps with speed of check-in and labor costs (not as many front desk agents needed on any one shift). However, let's look at this from a luxury resort hotel perspective. These customers have service expectations based on the price they pay for their room. Do they want to have to check themselves in? Or do they prefer to have a front desk agent greet them and take them through the process? Before management spends money on any new technology, they really need to see just what their customers expect from a stay at their hotel or a meal at their restaurant. Putting the newest and most exciting cutting edge technology into the establishment won't always make the customers happy and want to return. The Hyatt Andaz brand has actually done away with the front desk at some of their properties. Instead agents greet the customers at the door with an iPad and check them in while seated in a comfortable lobby. This is an example of new technology working with the customers' expectations. Lastly, the building itself needs to be taken into account when determining what technology will be placed in a hospitality establishment. Wi-Fi is a wonderful thing to offer customers but some buildings have thick walls and dead spots that won't allow a signal to completely pass through. If customers have expectations that aren't met, you have potential issues. If there isn't space to run cabling or place wireless access points (WAPs) then signal strength or the ability to have terminals where they are needed becomes a concern.

TRENDS IN HOSPITALITY TECHNOLOGY

Looking at the current and future potential for technology in hotels, restaurants, cruise ships, airlines, and other hospitality businesses is exciting. Deciding what to choose and where to spend money can be a daunting task, but if done thoughtfully and purposefully it can really take the business to a new level. Here are some of the **guest room technology** trends that are emerging.

Disney Cruise Lines Imagineering Department wanted to enhance the guest experience. One place they thought would be great to improve were their

Disney Cruise Lines constantly updates technology to enhance guest experiences.

ships' interior staterooms. They designed magical portholes for their guests. Cameras located on the port, starboard, aft, and front of the ships project actual images to the rooms of the sea and skyline. But, they didn't stop there. Also projected are images of Disney characters such as Ariel and Princess Jasmine floating by the portholes, stopping and waving hello. Each room has a different sequence of characters and the images can be turned off if the guest wishes to do so. Vingcard Hotel Locks are a state of the art RFID system that allows hotel guests to enter their room without using a hotel key. This **keyless lodging entry** allows the customer to use their smartphone (either android or iOS) through Bluetooth technology to open their hotel room door. There is an anti-cloning solution for added guest security.[5]

Tech trends for restaurants are also a booming business. According to the National Restaurant Association's News and Research division, there were five big trends seen at the NRA Show in Chicago in May of 2015.[6] Digital menus place all the information in the customer's hands. Changes can be made quickly and over time cost is reduced because reprinting is not necessary. Guests still get the personal experience expected from a restaurant and have easily accessible, visual menu information. Personalized marketing is also a way restaurants can provide a better experience to their customer. Past history can lead to specific ads for a guest that can show up via text, email, or through social media. Media integration will allow restaurateurs to handle multiple systems, such as menus, social media, automated order taking, and signage all through one system. This can even be done without the use of a PC. Simplifying things allows for the operators to spend time on other things, like their guest experience. Electronic scheduling allows the restaurant to make changes as needed via applications on smartphones. Shifts can be swapped, people can call in sick, shifts can be added, and schedules can be released easily to the employees. No need for Excel or paper schedules.

Data security is another huge issue for retailers and hospitality professionals. A California based company called MegTek has a system that can tell if a card is or might be fraudulent. When a server swipes the card the system will send a message to "examine this card carefully. It might be a counterfeit." This added measure takes some pressure off the servers and can make guests feel more secure about using their card at this particular location.

Trends in the hospitality industry are as fast paced and ever changing as the rest of the world. However, since our job is to meet and sometimes anticipate the needs of our guests, managers need to be up to date on what is available or soon will be available. Whether it is a hotel room locking system, upgrades to cruise ship staterooms, or security at a restaurant, good hospitality professionals will know what they need and work toward getting it so their guests have the best experience possible.

SUMMARY

Technology in this industry is like that of any other, it's fast paced and necessary. We as professionals need to know the basics that are required. A property management system for a lodging establishment and point-of-sale system for a foodservice location are the basic building blocks of running the business. They keep track of much of what the hotel or restaurant does and forecast what is to come. In-room guest technologies and tableside technologies allow establishments to embrace and meet or exceed customers' expectations. Having valued employees who are able to look at the challenges, meet them, and then surpass the expectations of their guests helps a business truly make its mark in the industry. And looking to the future, budgeting for and purchasing the "next best thing" will keep each business in the mix with the best that is out there. Technology is a part of every industry and we must understand and embrace it.

RESOURCES

Internet Sites

Andaz Hotels by Hyatt: http://www.andaz.hyatt.com/en/andaz.html

Disney Magical Porthole: https://www.youtube.com/watch?v=YqQ8W2igX9w

https://www.innroad.com/

National Restaurant Association (NRA): www.restaurant.org

ENDNOTES

1. All Property Management 2016
2. Collins et al., 2013
3. Chain Store Guide, 2011
4. Innroad, 2016
5. Assa Abloy Hospitality, 2016
6. NRA, 2015

REFERENCES

All Property Management, *What is a property management system?* 2016. Retrieved from: http://www.allpropertymanagement.com/faq/property-management-system_p69.html\

Assa Abloy Hospitality (2016) *Ving Card Classic RFID Locks* Retrieved from: http://www.assaabloyhospitality.com/en/aah/com/products/hotel/locks/classic-rfid/

Capterra (2016) Retrieved from: http://www.capterra.com/hospitality-property-management-software/

Chain Store Guide (2011) *Darden Does It Right* Retrieved from: http://newsroom.chainstoreguide.com/2011/10/darden-does-it-right/

Collins, G., Cobanoglu, C. and Bilgihan, A. (2013) *Hospitality Information Technology*, 7th Ed. Kendall Hunt Publishing

Disney Magical Portholes (2014) Retrieved from: https://www.youtube.com/watch?v=YqQ8W2igX9w

Hyatt Andaz (2016) Retrieved from: http://www.andaz.hyatt.com/en/andaz.html

InnRoad (2016) *In Room Technologies* Retrieved from: https://www.innroad.com/

National Restaurant Association (2015) News and Research, *5 Tech Trends from the NRA Show* Retrieved from: http://www.restaurant.org/News-Research/News/5-tech-trends-from-the-NRA-Show

Property Management System https://en.wikipedia.org/wiki/Property_management_system

Name: _____ Date: _____

1. List three components of a property management system.

2. What are three technology trends in the hospitality industry?

3. Disney's Imagineering Department created what special feature for their interior staterooms? What does this provide to the guests?

4. List and describe two challenges of having technology in a hospitality business.

5. What does POS stand for? Name three components of a POS system.

6. Identify and define three technology trends in the foodservice industry.

CHAPTER *17*

LAW

© Maridav/Shutterstock.com

AUTHOR	*Diana S. Barber, J.D., CHE, CWP, Georgia State University*
LEARNING OBJECTIVES	• Explain basic principles of law and differentiate their applicability in a hospitality context.
	• Analyze basic prevention techniques to reduce liability in a hospitality business.
	• Summarize basic responsibilities of a manager/owner with regard to employment matters.
	• Explore industry periodicals as management resources for supporting the practical impact of current events on hospitality businesses.
CHAPTER OUTLINE	Hospitality Law
	Preventative Approach
	Legal Procedures
	Alternative Dispute Resolution
	Governmental Compliance
	Local
	State
	Federal
	Hospitality Agreements
	Theories of Liability
	Torts
	Employment
	Contractual

CHAPTER OUTLINE (Continued)

Food and Beverage Laws
   Truth in Menu
   Alcohol Liability
Safety and Security
   Crisis Training
   Media

KEY TERMS

Answer	Litigation
Arbitration	Mediation
Complaint	Negligence
Damages	Plaintiff
Defendant	Torts
Dram Shop Act	

HOSPITALITY LAW

Every hospitality leader, executive, manager, supervisor, and line employee will make day-to-day decisions about the hospitality business that have legal implications. Some of these decisions will have minimal risk. Other decisions could have devastating consequences and hospitality personnel need to know just how these decisions will impact the business. Hospitality law covers a wide range of topics. A full course on the subject is available in collegiate hospitality programs to assist students with the knowledge they need in order to be successful and, more importantly, to recognize when it is time to reach out to a specialist for more information and assistance. This chapter will address some of the more common legal issues in the hospitality industry; however, this chapter is not intended to replace a full course on the study of hospitality law nor the expertise of a well-trained lawyer.

PREVENTATIVE APPROACH

The number one goal of the preventative approach is to reduce injuries, **damages**, and risk to all those who touch the hospitality business such as owners, guests, patrons, managers, employees, suppliers, and vendors. The philosophy that many lawyers and business professionals take is that proper and continuous training is one key that will help prevent lawsuits. Some maintain that selecting the right employees for the right job, rather than just hiring anyone, is the key to limiting liability. Both approaches are helpful; however, no matter how much one does to prevent liability it is impossible to eliminate all lawsuits. Our society is litigious and one must not only be aware of this phenomenon, but also anticipate ways to lessen the potential liability of the business. Every manager will be faced with some aspect of **litigation** in his/her career at some point; either by instituting a lawsuit, by being a witness in a case, or by defending a claim brought by a customer, a supplier, a vendor, or an employee. Continuous employee training and corresponding follow up assessment on the training, coupled with good, sound employee selection tools are important keys to reducing claims against a hospitality business. All claims against the business require a certain amount of time by the hospitality staff to prepare defenses to the claims. Furthermore, it can be very expensive to hire lawyers to defend a business on legal issues that could truly have been avoided through proper training with keen management oversight. A hotel or restaurant operator will also have the added value of avoiding undue litigation, out of court settlements, bad publicity, and increased insurance premiums.

LEGAL PROCEDURES

There are numerous procedures that must be followed in the legal arena. Many procedures are so complicated that they are best left to the professional, well-trained lawyers. The main issue that hospitality managers need to know is that the action and/or omission that one takes as a manager in real time can set the tone for potential litigation in the near future, even with the best legal team. Many claims are lodged as a result of managers not being consistent with their handling of matters such as playing favorites with certain employees over other employees. Supervisors and managers must be held accountable to perform in a consistently fair and dignified manner with each and every employee. Another area that needs focus is documentation. Many managers have a mantra that if something isn't documented, then it didn't happen. Not being able to prove a conversation took place or the statements of witnesses to an incident will be difficult to recreate once memories fade and knowledgeable employees move on to other positions. Lack of documentation can be costly because advocates and lawyers need to have the proof (i.e., testimony or documents) to convince a judge or jury of the facts supporting the hospitality business's positions on the issues. Smart managers need to know the basics of legal procedures and to understand that the legal system and procedures must be followed. For example, ignoring a claim or a situation with a disgruntled employee will not make the issue go away. Being able to anticipate when a situation needs to be handled carefully and fully documenting the incident is a learned behavior that comes with time and experience. Learning how to avoid legal matters can certainly help to reduce the liability of the business and should be a constant thought when making decisions. A manager should educate him or herself as to the basics of legal procedure and its importance with a view towards handling litigation in the future. For instance, if a process server (one who is serving legal papers to someone or a company) delivers a **complaint** (formal legal document that initiates a lawsuit) to the business, the time for responding to the complaint begins immediately upon acceptance of the complaint. In most jurisdictions, a **defendant** (the one being sued) has 30 days to respond to a complaint with a formal legal document known as an **answer** once it is served upon the defendant. If no response is made, a default judgment may be entered on behalf of the **plaintiff** (the one doing the suing). The defendant would lose before even having the time to defend its case in court. To move the lawsuit paperwork to another in-box full of papers with the good intention to address and deal with it later can have substantial damaging legal results.

ALTERNATIVE DISPUTE RESOLUTION

In addition to costly litigation, the parties to a lawsuit may use alternative formats to resolve differences. Many times parties will use **arbitration** or **mediation** to help with disputes. Arbitration is used in many circumstances as a way to resolve disputes quickly and more cost effectively. Arbitration occurs when a panel of independently appointed individuals hears both sides of a dispute and then makes a decision as to who prevails. In some cases, the decision is binding; but it can be non-binding if the parties agree in advance of a decision. Anyone who has a credit card, cell phone contract, or iTunes account has already agreed to resolve disputes with the provider by arbitration. This language is in the fine print of your agreement with the provider and you may not even be aware that you agreed to this type of dispute resolution. Mediation is a mechanism whereby the parties tell their respective positions to an independent mediator who assists the parties in coming to a mutual agreement. If the mediation is successful and the parties agree, then the decision is binding on both parties. If the parties cannot agree, then litigation would be the next step toward a resolution.

GOVERNMENTAL COMPLIANCE

Hospitality businesses are forever being regulated and subject to oversight by governmental agencies to make sure working conditions are safe, employees are treated with respect and dignity, food handling procedures are being followed, and ensure compliance in many other areas of the hospitality business which all have legal consequences. It is essential for a hospitality manager to be familiar with these agencies, as well as the laws, codes, and ordinances on a local, state, and federal level, to make sure they stay on top of regulations and any alleged violations.

LOCAL

Local governmental agencies may include the public health and sanitation department, tax assessor's office, and other municipal, city, or county agencies. Requirements for permits and those necessary to operate a business in compliance with local codes, whether for the sale and service of alcoholic beverages, transportation of guests, cigarette sales, or even soft serve ice cream will differ as to the various areas where the business is located. Ignorance of the law is not a defense, nor a good excuse. Following whatever another hotel or restaurant has done in the past, even within the same area or under the same parent company, without obtaining the required permits for that particular business is not a sound legal defense. A business operator must research and obtain the required permits to avoid hefty fines or loss of an important service to guests.

STATE

There are many state agencies that regulate hospitality businesses as well. The Alcohol Beverage Commission is one that will be essential if your business is selling and serving alcoholic beverages. In addition, the Department of Transportation, the Treasury Department, building and zoning agencies, as well as state regulated employment agencies will all affect the hospitality business's day-to-day operation. Compliance with such regulations is required and essential for a successful business. Managers need to be aware of all state rules as they pertain to the business.

FEDERAL

Many federal agencies will also be seeking your compliance with the appropriate federal rules and regulations. Some of the most common ones that regulate the hospitality industry include the Occupational

Safety and Health Administration (OSHA), Equal Employment Opportunity Commission (EEOC), Environmental Protection Agency (EPA), and the Department of Labor (DOL). It is not a requirement that all hospitality managers know each and every thing about these federal agencies, but it is in your best interest to have someone on the team, such as a human resource manager for EEOC, OSHA, and DOL issues, who is very familiar with the existing laws and keeps current with any changes. The engineer of a hotel should be up to speed with all EPA regulations. The Civil Rights Act of 1964, as amended, is a law with which all hospitality managers should be familiar even if one is not part of the human resource department.

HOSPITALITY AGREEMENTS

The backbone of any hospitality business is composed of the myriad agreements entered into on a daily basis—some in writing and some verbal. These agreements provide the essential services to all guests. There are circumstances when a valid agreement may be unenforceable; such as one signed under duress, a party to a contract who is a minor, mental incapacity, an illegal subject matter of the agreement, or the agreement must be in writing as a matter of law, to name a few. All hospitality agreements should be documented because, if there are legal disputes, documentation will enable your legal team to adequately represent the business's best interest. Only those in the business who have the authority should execute agreements and copies should be kept on file at all times. Hotel and restaurants will engage in many contracts, including these types of agreements: employment, vendor, service, consulting, construction, and the like. Some of the major hospitality agreements include franchise, operating or management, and group sales for booking functions.

THEORIES OF LIABILITY

One area of law that has developed over time has created certain legal obligations for businesses requiring them to use reasonable care in operating the business. The term reasonable care, an obligation or duty of the business, is defined as the standard used in determining legal liability of what the reasonable person would do in any given situation. Case law, statutes, and industry standards help develop what is deemed reasonable, usually resulting from jury decisions and/or case settlements. Many customers will believe that all injury or damage whatsoever that occurs within a hospitality business is the full responsibility of the business. From a customer's viewpoint, it may make sense. We are taught that the guest is always right. As business professionals, we want the guest to be happy and, of course, become a loyal customer. The liability, however, may not rest with the business if the injury or damage is caused by other factors or events not within the duty of care of the business. Below are some of the more common liability situations in hospitality.

TORTS

Torts are civil claims for injury and/or damage to someone or their property that may be the responsibility of the business, which results in liability to the business. Torts are civil wrongs and are different than criminal offenses. Some common torts that may occur in a hospitality setting include **negligence**, defamation, and intentional infliction of emotional distress. In a negligence case, all four of these elements must be proven for the plaintiff to prevail: 1) a duty of care owed to a guest, employee, or someone invited onto the hospitality property such as a vendor; 2) a breach of that duty of care by the business; 3) the action or omission was foreseeable to create harm, also described as the proximate cause of the harm; and 4) injury or damage has occurred as a result of the foregoing.

EMPLOYMENT

Employment claims seem to take center stage when it comes to the number of claims and active litigation in the hospitality industry. This is true because we are in a people industry and it takes people to provide great service to our wonderful guests. Because we work hard and long hours, relationships can become strained and misunderstandings may occur. It is very important for all managers to receive the necessary training to understand human behavior and to know how to deal with employees effectively. Training is critical for not only the manager and supervisor, but also for all the line employees so they know how to treat each other with respect and dignity.

Hostile work environments, workplace discrimination, and harassment can certainly be avoided, but often happen due to lack of training. The workplace is not the location to test out new jokes, which may be offensive to an employee who overhears the joke not intended for that person to hear, to touch co-workers whom you don't know well, or to make others feel uncomfortable. It is important to be professional at the workplace at all times. It is everyone's job to treat people fairly and with respect and dignity.

CONTRACTUAL

In business, disputes are going to happen. Contracts can be created and signed where both parties have different understandings of the expectations and desired outcomes. It is imperative that the parties anticipate the behavior of others and write down their expectations. Copies of all written contracts should be kept in a safe place and referenced from time to time. The most important aspect of dealing with vendors and service providers, however, is the relationship. Nurturing a business relationship can take time, but will be very beneficial in the event of conflict. Absent a smooth relationship and during the times of disagreement, the contract should provide protection in the form of an indemnification and insurance in order to shift the burden of business risks.

FOOD AND BEVERAGE LAWS

There are numerous duties of care of which one must be aware when operating a restaurant as it pertains to liability. Preparing and serving food safely is number one. From a preventative approach, a business operator must train the staff to understand the issues surrounding food-borne illness and cross-contamination, as well as how to avoid them. Having a diner who becomes ill due to food served in your restaurant can have devastating consequences and can even ultimately shut down the business. Many of you may not recall the popular Mexican restaurant known as Chi-Chi's Mexican Restaurant. The business had financial troubles and eventually went bankrupt. Just after filing bankruptcy, the business was sold in November 2003 following an outbreak of hepatitis A, one of the worst outbreaks in

Preparing and serving food is a huge liability if not done safely.

© purplequeue/Shutterstock.com

American restaurant history. During the outbreak, four people died and 660 others contracted hepatitis A. The outbreak was eventually linked to contaminated green onions.[1] The restaurant name still operates overseas, and in the U.S. some grocery stores carry products using the CHI-CHI's brand name for tortillas, sauces, and salsa.[2] When a patron finds a foreign substance in their food or anything that is not reasonably expected to be in the food product, and as a result the customer is subsequently harmed, a restaurant operator will need to anticipate that a claim may likely arise. Contacting the insurance company to put them on notice of a potential claim is a wise idea. Likewise, a call to the local health department may be in order depending on the number of calls a restaurant has concerning ill patrons near and around the same time period. It is essential to a restaurant business to keep patrons safe from food-borne illnesses. Allergens are another hot topic that restaurant operators need to be familiar with to avoid ill patrons.

TRUTH IN MENU

The Nutritional Labeling and Education Act of 1994, as amended,[3] defines many terms used in menus so it is imperative that one knows and understands the verbiage and wordsmithing on menus necessary to be in compliance with federal law. The main issue is to remember that if you say it on a menu, you must serve it. If the menu calls for grilled chicken, purchasing the frozen chicken breasts with the grill marks on it will not be in compliance. If you say grilled chicken, then it must be chicken that has been grilled.

ALCOHOL LIABILITY

Most states have adopted a form of law that is widely known as the **Dram Shop Act**. This law places the responsibility on the seller and server of alcohol in the event 1) service is made to an underage patron or 2) service is made to someone who is noticeably intoxicated and injures a third party (someone who is not the drinking patron or the bar serving the alcohol). Devastating and lasting damage could and does occur when alcohol is combined with driving, as do large settlements and high jury verdicts. There are many training resources that should be used to educate employees in order to reduce the legal liability associated with alcohol service. Best practices suggest that all employees undergo training, even those not serving the alcohol to patrons, in order to assist the business with legal compliance.

SAFETY AND SECURITY

Premises liability is a big part of operating a hospitality business. Even if a business has a loss prevention department, safety and security is the responsibility of all employees. Each employee should be trained to be observant and reach out to management for help if anything is the least bit suspicious. There will be guests who slip and fall and are otherwise injured on the premises. Care must be taken to assist with first aid and to contact medical and law enforcement authorities, as necessary. Employees should always follow company policies and protocol for handing medical issues or rendering first aid. Negligence cases can occur if the hospitality company has not delivered on its duty of care by providing a safe environment, training all employees, serving food and beverages safely, and terminating employees who pose a threat to others.

CRISIS TRAINING

Life safety of guests, employees, and all others on the property is paramount in any business setting. All employees should undergo continuous crisis training and be alerted to the steps necessary to take in the event of an Act of God (hurricane, tornado, earthquake, and the like), bomb threats, terrorist attacks, and other events causing or potentially causing harm to people and property. Training on active shooters in the workplace should also be addressed; there are several good online films that can assist with this necessary training.[4] Crisis manuals need to be created, disseminated to all employees, practiced regularly, and revised accordingly to stay current and up to date on the latest threats to the business.

MEDIA

It is important to be prepared for statements provided to the media if a crisis occurs in your hospitality business. Pre-prepared information pages for the company's website need to be ready to upload at a moment's notice since that is where the media will go first for information. The role of spokesperson for the business should be delegated to only one person in order to maintain control and consistency over the message disseminated. Businesses should refrain from using the hollow phrase "no comment" approach to media inquiries, as the implications will not be well received by the public who may interpret such a response as hiding information or mere carelessness on the part of the business. Best practices suggest initially addressing media inquiries with a statement that reiterates the company's philosophy that the concern and safety of all employees and guests must take precedent. In addition, preservation of the asset (the physical building) also needs attention to provide employees with a safe workplace to return to after the crisis.

SUMMARY

Hospitality law is a unique aspect or niche area of the hospitality industry. Some may think dealing with lawyers and courts is a complex arena to be avoided at all costs. Litigation and dispute resolution is only one aspect of hospitality law. Most of the time, litigation and courts are not involved. As you've learned, a successful hospitality business is built on good, solid professional relationships and trust. The fact is that almost every decision a hospitality manager makes could turn into a legal claim if it is not executed with a very thoughtful decision making approach coupled with the proper respect and dignity for all involved. What a hospitality manager needs to know about legal issues is that continuous education on legal issues is a prerequisite for reducing liability and growing a thriving business. Taking a preventative approach to management will limit the time needed to prepare and defend claims, and allow your employees and management staff to focus on the real purpose of providing hospitality: to create a memorable experience for all guests and achieve loyalty on their behalf. Resolution of legal issues can be challenging but very rewarding and provide a tremendous asset to a hospitality business.

RESOURCES

Internet Sites

http://www.hospitalitylawyer.com

https://www.smartbrief/nra.com

https://www.smartbrief/ahla.com

http://ahla.com

http://www.restaurant.org

https://www.servsafe.com

https://www.ahlei.org/Alcohol-Awareness

http://www.fda.gov/Food/GuidanceRegulation/ GuidanceDocumentsRegulatoryInformation/ LabelingNutrition/ucm2006828.htm

ENDNOTES

1. Journal Times Staff Writer (2008). Glad You Asked: What happened to Chi-Chi's? Why did they close? *The Journal Times.com*. Retrieved from http://journaltimes.com/news/local/glad-you-asked-what-happened-to-chi-chi-s-why/article_fea637c0-075e-5912-b5bb-34ccead84f1a.html

2. Hormel Foods, LLC (2015). *FAQ 1. General Questions. Are CHI-CHI's ® products affiliated with the Chi-Chi's Restaurants?* Retrieved from http://www.chichis.com/content/faq.

3. U.S. Food and Drug Administration Protecting and Promoting Your Health (2015). *Nutritional Labeling and Education Act (NLEA) Requirements (8/94–2/95)*. Retrieved from http://www.fda.gov/iceci/inspections/inspectionguides/ucm074948.htm

4. City of Houston Mayor's Office of Public Safety and Homeland Security (July 23, 2012). *Run>Hide>Fight>> Surviving an Active Shooter Event*. Retrieved from https://www.youtube.com/watch?v=5VcSwejU2D0

Name: _____ Date: _____

1. Name the two basic keys to the preventative approach to managing legal claims.

2. Describe the differences between litigation, arbitration, and mediation.

3. Name several federal governmental agencies that oversee the hospitality industry.

4. Name the three major agreements used in the hospitality industry.

5. List the four elements of a negligence claim.

6. What are the elements of the Dram Shop Act?

7. Why is it important to preserve the physical asset of the hospitality business after a crisis?

© pkproject/Shutterstock.com

PART 4

HOSPITALITY COMPANIES

CHAPTER *18*

CAREER EXPECTATIONS AND REALITIES

© Artur Ish/Shutterstock.com

AUTHORS

Melvin Weber, East Carolina University
Seung Hyun (Jenna) Lee, East Carolina University

LEARNING OBJECTIVES

- Explore the positive and negative aspects of a hospitality career.
- Understand the skills and traits needed to become successful in the hospitality industry.
- Develop an understanding of the size and scope of hospitality careers.
- Understand the advantages and disadvantages of internships.
- Develop résumé building skills and interview strategies.

CHAPTER OUTLINE

The Myths and the Realities
The Career: The Advantages and the Disadvantages
    The Advantages
    The Disadvantages
The Skills and Qualities Needed for Success
Salaries and Wages
The Career Pursuit
    The Internship
Career Portfolio
    The Résumé
    The Cover Letter
    The Interview
    The Thank You Letter
Summary

KEY TERMS

Career fair	Interviewer
Emotional labor-intensive business	Myth
	Organization's culture
Internship	Relocation
Interview	Résumé
Interviewee	Social networking

Are you interested in getting paid to help people have fun? Do warm sunny beaches, majestic mountain views, or far away places spark your interest? How about being around delicious food in exotic restaurant locations, working on a cruise ship, coordinating events for country clubs, or owning your own foodservice or lodging establishment?

The hospitality industry is based on two major components: the complexity of the product, and the amount of service that is required. This is referred to as the product continuum (from products prepared with minimum effort, to those that require extensive preparation), and the service continuum (extending from vending machines to luxury resorts with outstanding service).[1] Whether it is a weekend getaway, a month long backpacking trip, or simply going out to dinner at a local restaurant, workers in the hospitality industry become a part of these memorable experiences. In a fast paced environment, hospitality workers must act as experts in ensuring guest satisfaction, solving problems, and communicating effectively with guests, clients, and other departments.

Choosing a career that fits your personal characteristics and goals can be challenging. To find this out, one must explore different options in the industry. The hospitality industry offers its employees the opportunity to work in an environment that is best suited to their talents.

THE MYTHS AND THE REALITIES

Like other service sectors, hospitality careers are often stereotyped as low-wage and entry-level with little opportunity for advancement. Consequently, would-be workers, especially youth, are unaware of the range of hospitality careers available. Do you have a realistic view of the hospitality industry? Where do you see yourself in the future? Will you find your career enjoyable and fulfilling, and will you look forward to going to work each day? Will you like the people who work with you? You may have preconceived notions about a career in the hospitality industry. Do you know the difference between the myth and the reality?

Myth: There is a shortage of hospitality job opportunities.

Reality: There is a shortage of qualified hospitality employees because it is one of the fastest growing industries. Across the world, the travel and tourism industry encompasses 277 million jobs, and contributes 9.8% of gross domestic product (GDP) globally. With travel and tourism sector growth forecast to expand by 3.6% during 2016, the sector will be increasingly recognized as a key driver of economic growth at the local, regional, and global level.[2]

Myth: Anyone can become a successful hospitality manager.

Reality: A career in hospitality management is not suitable for every individual. The industry is people- and service-oriented. A career in this field is rewarding for those seeking responsibility, opportunity for advancement, salary growth, and personal satisfaction. As a hospitality manager, one must always try to meet and even exceed your potential, treat others as you would want to be treated, work hard, learn from your mistakes, listen to your employees, and be excited about your job. A college education and industry experience are needed for a successful hospitality career.

Myth: I will spend most of my time sitting at my desk.

Reality: The hospitality industry is too fast paced to sit at a desk. Every day brings a new set of guests and with them a new set of challenges.

Myth: There is limited career advancement.

Reality: The potential for advancement is excellent for the capable individual who is willing to work hard. In the hospitality industry, there is a critical need for people with general management skills to manage all aspects of a complex industry. The growth of the field has translated into exceptional opportunities for graduates. The hospitality field employment outlook is excellent for people from every race and ethnic background.

Myth: Starting salaries are low.

Reality: Starting salaries are competitive, and after a few promotions, the compensation package is tremendous.

Hospitality employees enjoy the novelty of every day.

Myth: Graduating with a degree in hospitality is all I need to be successful.

Reality: Hospitality management degrees are a valuable credential in a fast-paced industry and provide you with a platform for entry. However, a degree by itself is not enough. A college education combined with relevant work experience is essential for success. Professionals who have education and experience are best positioned for faster promotions.

Myth: A job in the hospitality industry is boring.

Reality: Hospitality employees have fun! Every day is different as workers try to meet the expectations of people from different backgrounds.

THE CAREER: ADVANTAGES AND DISADVANTAGES

The hospitality industry has a long history of providing meaningful employment in a variety of career fields. According to the Council of Hotel, Restaurant, and Institutional Educators (CHRIE), the hospitality industry is composed of five major career fields: food, lodging, event, tourism, and recreation management. These areas include many diverse and exciting career opportunities. Examples of career opportunities include but are not limited to club management, foodservice, parks, lodging, resorts, casinos, catering companies, conference centers, wedding planning, attractions management, marinas, and college/university and school foodservice. The hospitality industry offers many advantages to employees, but just like any other industry, challenges exist. Analyzing the categories offered allows you to increase your knowledge of the industry's good and bad points, thus reducing mistakes that could cost you resources, whether in money, time, or effort.

ADVANTAGES

Some of the advantages of a career in the field are:

1. Extensive list of career options
2. Creative opportunities
3. Varied work environment
4. Career growth
5. Social networking

Extensive List of Career Options. The hospitality industry offers an abundance of management opportunities. You may choose a 500-room property or a 10-room bed and breakfast, an international franchise company or a local eatery, a final destination theme park or a city amusement park, a metropolitan convention center or a privately owned catering company, a night club, or an assisted living facility. Hospitality career possibilities are endless. So, there are choices.

Creative Opportunities. Hospitality managers may design new products or remodel foodservice and lodging facilities. Managers may be asked to develop training programs or implement new marketing strategies. Especially if you work at a smaller firm or own your firm, you can be creative and flexible in developing your own themes, menu items, and strategies.

Varied Work Environment. Hospitality careers are fast-paced, and each day begins a new work environment. Power outages, severe weather, equipment failures, a busload of guests, and staff shortages are some of the challenges that provide variety and excitement. Quality customer service and meeting and exceeding guest satisfaction cannot be obtained from merely hiding in your office. Hospitality employees should consider the entire facility as their "office" and seek the opportunity to interact with guests on a daily basis. Although most hospitality positions are not desk jobs, there are sufficient opportunities where you can still pursue your career in the hospitality field. If you desire a 9-to-5, five day a week career, you may find a position working in the department of finance, accounting, marketing, human resources, or engineering.

Career Growth. The hospitality industry is widely based. You can work almost anywhere in any setting, from a small country town to a metropolitan city, from a warm sunny beach to a deep powder ski resort, from a small bed and breakfast to a casino resort, from a small town in Kansas to a foreign country. Across the nation and around the world career opportunities abound for people of all ages, education levels, and backgrounds. No other industry offers the chance of working almost anywhere you choose, with interesting work, a chance for advancement, people contact, and stability of employment.

Social Networking. Meeting people is a major component of your career. You build your social networking in the field by meeting, getting to know, and spending time with people who work in the industry. You will have the opportunity to meet people from all over the world and from all walks of life, including celebrities, political figures, wealthy clientele, top executives, professional athletes, and local community members. How do you start networking? You expand your base of contacts by attending **career fairs**, and by joining alumni associations, student organizations, and professional organizations.

DISADVANTAGES

Like all work environments, there is a downside, which must be put into perspective. The challenges of a career in hospitality include:

1. Emotional labor-intensive business
2. Hours of work
3. Relocation

Emotional Labor-Intensive Business. Within the hospitality industry, employees constantly interact with guests and must exude positive emotions such as friendliness, compassion, or warmth, even in emotionally negative situations.[3] While hospitality firms focus on delivering customer service, employees are often called on to suppress displaying any form of negative emotion during customer interactions. This may result in a stressful work environment.

Hours of Work. The hospitality industry is open 365 days a year, 7 days a week, 24 hours a day. Most managers work 10–12 hour days and 60+ hours a week, weekends, and holidays. This is an industry where most people spend long hours on their feet and spend

each day making complete strangers feel welcome and happy. These long hours can limit the time you have available for family, friends, and your social life. A common cliché is "employees in the hospitality industry work while others play."

Relocation. Relocation can be defined as the act of moving from one place to another for employment advancement. You may have to consider relocating several times, since hospitality organizations have facilities in a variety of geographic locations. Larger chains may offer better opportunities than small, but relocation every several years is often necessary. A willingness to relocate often is essential for advancement. The decision is difficult: 1) remain in your current area, 2) return home, or 3) relocate? However, many people find relocation exciting and a benefit of a hospitality career.

THE SKILLS AND QUALITIES NEEDED FOR SUCCESS

A desire to serve others is characteristic of successful people in this industry. Wanting to give guests a quality experience is an important trait. It comes down to something as simple as wanting to help, whether it is giving them directions to an area attraction or clearing and cleaning a table so they can be seated in a restaurant. Liking people and a desire to interact with them is something intrinsic to most positions in this business. Being friendly, sincere, patient, and a good listener are critical skills for anyone contemplating success in this field. Now, these skills take time and practice to develop and there will be days when they will be tested to the limit. However, there are essential skills and qualities you will need in order to perform to the best of your ability. Some of these are:

1. Conceptual skills (planning, problem solving, and decision making)
2. Communication skills (verbal and nonverbal)
3. Flexibility
4. Leadership skills and qualities (supervising, team building, organization)
5. Personality skills (outgoing, ethical, sense of humor, energetic, like to work with people, don't like to sit behind a desk, creative, problem solver, service oriented, ambitious)

SALARIES AND WAGES

If you possess these skills and qualities, your earning potential can be enhanced. *Don't price yourself too high or too low; strive for the correct price based on your value.* Salaries vary depending on the size of the hospitality firm you work for and the area or region in which it is located. A general manager of a five-star hotel in New York City will earn a higher salary than the general manager of a local boutique hotel in a small town. In addition to base salary, many jobs have a commission, shared gratuity, or bonus plan that pays up to 40% of salary as incentive compensation. Hospitality is an industry where pay for performance and career opportunities are especially strong. *Should you accept a position with a lower salary than you expected? The decision is up to you.*

The American Hotel & Lodging Educational Institute (AH&LA) publishes compensation and benefits information for the hospitality industry every year.

The median salary compensation for management positions in the industry includes:

- Sales and Marketing Director: $80,400
- Controller: $73,800
- Senior Sales Manager: $56,000
- Personnel/HR Director: $61,600
- Sales Manager: $38,500

In addition, according to the National Restaurant Association (NRA), the following table details potential earnings based on job positions within the hospitality industry (Table 18.1).

THE CAREER PURSUIT

There are several key questions that you will need to address for yourself. First, what segment of the industry is right for you, and secondly, who are the better employers in each sector? You may not be able

Table 18.1 Earning Potential in the Hospitality Industry		
Career	**Average**	**Required Education**
President/Chief Executive Officer	$50,000–$350,000+	Bachelor's/Master's degree
Owner	$35,000–$200,000+	Bachelor's/Master's degree
Chief Financial Officer	$45,000–$200,000+	Bachelor's/Master's degree
General Manager/Chief Operating Officer	$42,000–$200,000+	Bachelor's/Master's degree
Director of Operations	$40,000–$150,000+	Bachelor's/Master's degree
Regional Manager	$40,000–$100,000+	Bachelor's/Associate's degree, or on the job training
Food and Beverage Director	$35,000–$85,000+	Bachelor's/Associate's degree, or on the job training
Director of Purchasing	$35,000–$100,000+	Bachelor's/Associate's degree, or on the job training
Director of Training	$35,000–$100,000+	Bachelor's/Associate's degree, or on the job training
Unit Manager	$30,000–$70,000+	Bachelor's/Associate's degree, or on the job training
Chef	$40,000–$65,000+	Associate's degree or on the job training
Catering Manager	$39,000–$57,000+	Associate's degree or on the job training
Kitchen Manager	$39,000–$57,000+	Associate's degree or on the job training
Server	$12–$21 per hour including tips	On the job training
Cook	$10–$14 per hour	On the job training
Bartender	$15–$25 per hour including tips	On the job training
Host	$8–$9.50 per hour	On the job training
Housekeeper	$9 per hour	On the job training

Data from the National Restaurant Association. www.nraef.org/hba/hba_career_ladder.asp
Data from the National Restaurant Association, http://www.nraef.org/Public/NRAEF_RestaurantWorkforce
Data from the American Hotel and Lodging Association, http://www.ahla.com/uploadedFiles/AHLA%20Survey9.4_730pm.pdf

to find answers to these questions until you have experienced a variety of employment settings. Start becoming a student of the industry now. Read various trade publications. Track different company performances and histories during your time in school. Attend open houses and talks given by hospitality employers. Attend annual career conferences. Be sure to talk to employer representatives even if you are not looking for work at that time. Networking is a good skill to practice so you are comfortable with that format when it really counts. Definitely take advantage of the resources your school offers, whether they are your advisor or the career services office. A career in hospitality may take you on an adventure around the world, leading you on a successful journey of personal and professional satisfaction.

THE INTERNSHIP

To gain experience, most colleges/universities encourage or require **internships** as part of a hospitality student's major program of study. Internships help students gain a better knowledge of the tasks and practices performed by industry professionals and also develop job skills, problem-solving skills, and decision-making skills in the actual business setting. Internships provide not only enhanced employment and professional growth opportunities, but also the ability to network within the industry by creating personal contacts. Having internship experiences on résumés makes for more marketable post-graduation employment. It can be a base upon which you can develop future job opportunities. You will observe various management styles in action;

Internship opportunities help students learn tasks and practices from industry professionals.

some that you will want to adopt and many you will want to avoid. It may even bring a job offer for after school. This way you and the employer will be in a better position to make an informed decision regarding your suitability for the job and your fit within their **organization's culture.**

Internship programs for hospitality management students have been recommended by a variety of authors. Saunders (2004) reported that leadership skills in hospitality are developed by practice in day-to-day operations. Immersion in the day-to-day operation of a hospitality company is a major expectation of hospitality internships. An additional method used to help develop leadership skills according to Saunders (2004) is mentoring.[4] Zopiatis and Constani (2012) include a recommendation that a mentor to be assigned to students during the internship program. These authors highlighted that the mentor has the potential to influence the student's management and leadership styles. Most hospitality management internship programs are designed to require mentoring for students while completing the experience. These two components of hospitality internship programs are critical for successfully developing leadership skills in students.[5]

Some significant challenges face hospitality internships. Kay and DeVeau (2003) state that internships are designed for academic purposes and are carried out in non-academic environments. Host organizations are usually in the service industry, and many times interns fall through the cracks if the work experience is not well-tested within an industry-agreed-upon internship program.[6] Students have also commented that they face problems in relating and applying theory to realistic situations.[7] Zopiatis (2007) stated that poor internship experiences can alienate students from a career in hospitality when expectations do not meet reality.[8]

CAREER PORTFOLIO

A career portfolio sets you up to become a professional in the workplace. It contains evidence of who you are and what you hope to become. It presents you in a positive light. It includes interview strategies, a résumé, and a thank you letter.

THE RÉSUMÉ

A **résumé** is a written document that lists an individual's personal and professional qualifications; it is submitted when someone is applying for a position. The purpose of a résumé is to provide information to people about who you are and what skills you have. Because every individual is unique, there is room for individuality and creativity when writing a résumé. In reality, it is your "personal advertisement."

Writing a résumé during your first year of college helps you to answer questions about yourself. By documenting your career objective, your past and present education, and past and present work experiences, it enables you to see what you have

---

NAME

| 299 CHERYL CIRCLE | Phone # | 199 PAR DRIVE |
| GREENVILLE, NC 27858 | E-MAIL: email address | HENDERSON, NC 27536 |

OBJECTIVE

To obtain an internship, which will allow me to utilize my professional and educational experience, fulfilling my ultimate goal of employment within the lodging industry

EDUCATION

East Carolina University - *Greenville, North Carolina*   GPA: 3.23
Major- Hospitality Management   Minor - Business Administration
Concentrations – Lodging Management/Special Event & Convention Management
Graduation in December 2012

WORK EXPERIENCE

PARKER'S PEACE PARK - *EVENTS COORDINATOR*   9/10 – PRESENT

- Coordinate all special events for the park
- Collect pre-event information to ensure adequate space, personnel, and equipment is available
- Oversee and monitor operations during events
- Track and process event expenditures while, adhering to the budget set forth by the board of directors
- Utilize social media such as Facebook and Twitter to promote and coordinate special events

PARKER'S PEACE POOL - *ASSISTANT MANAGER*   9/09 – 8/10

- Supervised pool staff and pool operations
- Imposed rules and regulations for staff and patrons as set forth by the board of directors
- Maintained pool chemical records, testing, and made adjustments as needed
- Assisted in preparing schedule for guards
- Managed a staff of 13 employees

PARKER'S PEACE POOL - *LIFEGUARD/LEAD LIFEGUARD*   5/03 – 5/09

- Maintained constant surveillance of patrons in the pool
- Enforced rules and regulations for patrons as set by pool board
- Completed various maintenance duties as directed to maintain a clean, safe facility
- Handled cash transactions from customers

SKILLS

- Computer-literate with extensive software proficiency covering wide variety of applications
- Innovative problem-solver who can generate workable solutions and resolve complaints
- Highly motivated self-starter who takes initiative with minimal supervision
- Resourceful team player who excels at building trusting relationships with customers and colleagues

HONORS AND ACTIVITIES

- Member of the Phi Eta Sigma Honor Fraternity
- CVent Certified, ServSafe Certified
- Dean's List
- Active member of National Society for Minorities in Hospitality Service Committee

References: Available upon request

FIGURE 18.1 An example of a résumé

accomplished and where you are going. It should be well organized, concise, and written in a focused manner. A well-written résumé also aids you in obtaining scholarships, internships, and professional job positions. *Your résumé may be 1 out of 100 résumés received for a single open position. Make sure all the information on your résumé is accurate, as one mistake may cause you to lose your dream.* There are certain headings and information that should be included in your résumé:

1. Current contact information
2. Career objective
3. Education
4. Internship(s)
5. Work experience(s)
6. Special skills and abilities
7. Awards and recognitions
8. References (people who are willing to speak with a potential employer about your personal and professional experiences; usually listed on a different document)

THE COVER LETTER

Included with your résumé should be a cover letter. This letter should be written to introduce yourself to your potential employer. The content should include highlights of your personal and professional experiences (talents) and a request for an interview. Many potential employers will only review your résumé if your cover letter sparks their interest. *You do not want to get a big red "X" and be eliminated from the search.*

THE INTERVIEW

The goal of your résumé and cover letter is to get you an interview with an employer of your choosing. An interview can be defined as a formal meeting between two or more individuals. Interview etiquette includes dressing in a professional manner, introducing yourself, offering a firm handshake, maintaining eye contact, responding to questions, never saying anything negative, asking questions, smiling, and being enthusiastic. Enthusiasm is the single most important quality. Remember the saying "you only get one chance to make a first impression."

Remember that you only get one chance to make a first impression.

During an interview, the **interviewer**(s) asks the **interviewee** questions in order to determine their ability to meet the expectations of a position. The Council of Hotel Restaurant Institutional Educators (CHRIE) offers the 10 most common interview questions and offers suggestions on how to answer the questions on their website. Questions include: What are your weaknesses? Why should we hire you? Why do you want to work here? What are your goals? Why did you leave (are you leaving) your job? When were you most satisfied in your job? What can you do for us that other candidates can't? What are three positive things your last boss would say about you? What salary are you seeking? If you were an animal, which one would you be, and why?

Today in many interviews the employer wants to understand how you will perform on the job under certain circumstances. To get at this they will present you with a series of lifelike events that happen daily on the job and ask how you would respond to them. In some cases you may have had actual experience in dealing with similar situations earlier in your work life and will feel comfortable answering such inquires. Other questions may represent your first exposure to a certain situation. The key is to remain calm and think through how you would answer the question.

Remember, an interview is a two way street. The goal of both interviewer(s) and interviewee is to get enough information about each other to make an informed decision. Making a quality decision about whether to work (or not) for a particular employer is just as important for you as it is for the employer. You should develop a list of questions that you want

999 First Street

sam.embree@gmail.com

Greenville, NC 27834

(111)-222-3333

Ms. Jane Doe,

Owner

A Touch of Gold Events

99 Eastern Street

Greenville, NC 27858

Dear Ms. Doe:

"Something old…" is all most women need in order to finish this historical wedding superstition. These four seemingly unrelated items have been incorporated into weddings since the late 1800s and continue to be an integral part in modern ceremonies. As your new event coordinator, I have attributes that relate to this traditional rhyme, and can use them in order to create a special day for each and every couple.

Something Old: I keep the integrity of wedding traditions that are important to the couple.

Something New: I am able to be innovative and creative with design and execution.

Something Borrowed: The information I have learned in my previous work experience has provided me with invaluable insight and ability.

Something Blue: My capability to stay calm in high-pressure situations makes me a valuable asset.

I am excited about this opportunity in your company and would be very appreciative of the chance to show you how many more skills and talents I possess. My résumé is enclosed with this letter and I thank you for taking the time to consider my application. I look forward to meeting you in person to discuss how I would be an outstanding addition to your company.

Sincerely,

Samantha Embree

Samantha Embree

FIGURE 18.2 An example of a cover letter

answered prior to the interview. At some point toward the end of the interview, you may be asked if you have any questions for the employer. There is nothing wrong with pulling your list out at this point and reviewing it to see if there are any unanswered questions. This shows the employer you are prepared and an active participant. Ideally you should have some idea of the salary range for the position after the first interview. There are different schools of thought about asking about salary in the initial interview.

Joe S. Student
17 Apple Court
Pittsburgh, PA 15102
412-555-1212

Ms. Lee Thomas
Hilton Hotel Corporation
Runway Road
Pittsburgh, PA 15120

Dear Ms. Thomas:

Thank you for taking the time to discuss the internship opportunities at Hilton Hotel Corporation with me. I really appreciate that you took so much time to acquaint me with the company. It is no wonder that Hilton Hotel Corporation retains its employees for so long. I feel I could learn a great deal from you and would certainly enjoy working with you.

After meeting with you and observing the company's operations, I am further convinced that my background and skills coincide well with your needs. In addition to my qualifications and experience, I promise to bring excellent work habits and judgment to this position. With the countless demands on your time, I am sure that you demand trust in the people you delage to carry out their responsibilities with minimal supervision.

I look forward to hearing from you concerning your hiring decision. Again, thank you for your time and consideration.

Sincerely,

Joe S. Student

FIGURE 18.3 An example of a thank you letter

During an interview you will be challenged mentally and sometimes even physically. You must overcome your fears and not be afraid to answer questions and prove yourself to be better and stronger than everyone else. Send a thank you note to the interviewer. This is not often done and can leave a lasting impression.

THE THANK YOU LETTER

After completing an interview, it is important for you to write a thank you letter to the interviewer(s). This personalized handwritten letter should be written and mailed the same day as your interview. *A well written thank you letter can make you stand out from the other contestants, thus revealing your true voice.*

SUMMARY

You are about to embark on a journey that can lead to a long-term successful career in a dynamic and thriving industry. The hospitality industry is a very unique industry, and it demands certain skills and qualities, such as strong interpersonal skills, attention to detail, and the desire to be a problem solver. While the industry has different hours than most, it has many rewards to offer someone who is willing to work hard and "earn their stripes."

Your number one priority over the coming years is to be a student; a good student. This is both from an academic skills standpoint and from the standpoint of understanding this industry. Build your resume now while you are in school. Develop a variety of experiences that will help you land a great starting position when you finish your schooling. Definitely pursue one or two internship experiences to add to your portfolio. Utilize all the services of your school's career office and your department to assist you in the interviewing and the job acceptance process as you finish your studies. Be prepared to take the good work and study habits you developed during school with you into the hospitality industry so that you are ready to advance your career. *Aim high, pay attention to detail, perform the steps correctly, don't miss a beat, and you too can be dancing with the stars.*

RESOURCES

Internet Sites

Council of Hotel, Restaurant, and Institutional Educators: www.chrie.org

American Hotel & Lodging Association: www.ahla.com

Hospitality Career Net: www.hospitalitycareernet.com

Hospitality Jobs Online: www.hospitalityonline.com

Hospitality Net: www.hospitalitynet.org

Hospitality Careers: www.hcareers.om

National Restaurant Association: www.restaurant.org

National Restaurant Association Education Foundation: www.nraef.org

ENDNOTES

1. Dennison, D. & Weber, M. (2015). Strategic hospitality human resource management. Upper Saddle River, NJ: Pearson.

2. World Travel & Tourism Council. Retrieved from: http://www.wttc.org/-/media/files/reports/economic%20impact%20research/economic%20impact_midyear%20update_161115%20%282%29.pdf

3. Diefendorff, J. M., & Richard, E. M. (2003). Antecedents and consequences of emotional display rule perceptions. *Journal of Applied Psychology, 88*(2), 284.

4. Saunders, R. E. (2004). Leadership training in hospitality. FIU Hospitality Review, 22(1), 30–40.

5. Zopiatis, A., & Constanti, P. (2012). Managing hospitality internship practices: A conceptual framework. Journal of Hospitality & Tourism Education, 24(1), 44–51.

6. Kay, C., & DeVeau, L. T. (2003). A survey of lodging executives' views on internship programs and cooperatives. Journal of Hospitality & Tourism Education, 15(2), 24–29.

7. Lam, T., & Ching, L. (2007). An exploratory study of an internship program: The case of Hong Kong students. International Journal of Hospitality Management, 26(2), 336–351.

8. Zopiatis, A. (2007). Hospitality internships in Cyprus: A genuine academic experience or a continuing frustration? International Journal of Contemporary Hospitality Management, 19(1), 65–77.

Name: _____ Date: _____

1. Discuss several advantages and disadvantages of working in the hospitality industry.

2. List skills and qualities necessary to become a successful manager.

3. What are the advantages and disadvantages to internships?

4. What are some common interview questions, and how would you answer them?

5. What are three questions you could ask a potential employer while being interviewed?

6. Develop a resume, cover letter, and thank you letter for a position offered in your local newspaper.

CHAPTER *19*

LODGING INDUSTRY

© Yulia Grigoryeva/Shutterstock.com

AUTHORS

Sherie Brezina, Florida Gulf Coast University
Marcia Taylor, Florida Gulf Coast University

LEARNING OBJECTIVES

- Describe the different types of lodging available.
- Explain how lodging segments are classified.
- Outline the common and unique characteristics of each lodging segment.
- Identify the target guest market for each lodging segment.
- Explain the services and amenities typically provided in each lodging segment.

CHAPTER OUTLINE

Lodging Segments
    Classic Full-Service Hotels
    Limited-Service
    Select-Service Hotels
    Long-Term/Extended Stay Hotels
    Bed and Breakfast Hotels
    Resorts
Other Lodging Segments
    Vacation Ownership and Rentals
    Casino Hotels
    Convention and Conference Hotels
    Boutique/Lifestyle Hotels
    Senior Service and Residential Hotels

KEY TERMS

Bed and breakfast

Boutique hotel

Classic full-service hotels

Lifestyle hotel

Limited-service

Long-term stay

Luxury hotel

Peer-to-peer sharing economy websites

Recreational amenities

Resort hotel

Spa resort

Vacation ownership/timeshare

LODGING SEGMENTS

The lodging industry is characterized by an array of lodging alternatives to meet the demands of people traveling for business or leisure. At the core, lodging provides a place for one to sleep. Beyond the basic product, typically a room with a bed, the mix of all other products provided to satisfy guests—food and beverage, room, quality, standards, service, amenities, and parking—are often variable and determine the lodging category. Lodging properties are classified in numerous ways. The most common classifications are by price or rate (budget, midscale, luxury, boutique), location (urban, suburban, airport, destination), room type (standard rooms, suites, vacation condo units), market (business or leisure), size (small, medium, large, megaresort), and key attraction or amenity (spa, golf, convention, casino).[1]

Regardless of classification, all lodging segments share these common characteristics:

- The tangible product is rooms with beds for the traveling public to sleep.
- The product is perishable, consumed on site; meaning if it is not consumed or sold for the day, the revenue is lost, and cannot be recovered.
- Lodging is labor-intensive, with the traveling public willing to pay for services provided by people to meet their needs.
- The level and quality of hospitality courtesy and services distinguishes the lodging property.
- Buildings and grounds must have continuous maintenance and upkeep.
- Common laws of inn keeping apply, emphasizing safety, security, and cleanliness.[2]

This chapter describes the key lodging segments, and the unique characteristics, services, and target guest market of each segment.

CLASSIC FULL-SERVICE HOTELS

The **classic full-service hotel** is best defined in the context of historical standards of accommodation and service tradition developed through experiences and refinement up to present times.[3] The full-service hotel market may be classified as midscale, upscale, or luxury according to the services and amenities offered, the pricing structure, and the location. Classic full-service hotels in urban areas of commerce cater to transient business travelers' needs of time and efficiency.

The amenities and location of full-service hotels also make them appealing to vacation and leisure travelers. Baby Boomers continue to make up the largest spending segment of travelers and are loyal to brands with reliable and comfortable services. Millennial and Generation Y, 20- to 30-year-olds, make up the fastest growing hotel customer segment and represent the future consumer. This generation spends less time in their hotel rooms than previous generations and seeks out innovation and social space to engage with technology in their lodging preferences. In recent years, the hotel industry has begun to court the younger generation by remodeling existing hotels or creating new ones that offer free hotel-wide Wi-Fi connections, social space lobbies with plush furniture, stylish bars, fitness areas, and power consoles in rooms. Classic full-service chain hotels represented in this segment can include Hilton, Hyatt, Marriott, Sheraton, Intercontinental, Le Meridian, Ritz Carlton, Loews, Radisson, and Four Seasons.

Midscale. Also referred to as midpriced hotels, they are attractive to guests because of the rates, which are slightly higher than limited-service hotels and below luxury hotels. They offer the basics in full service such as food and beverage outlets, including room service and uniformed guest service. They appeal to the largest segment of travelers, but cater mostly to business and individual travelers and families. Because they offer fewer services, they appeal to guests desiring some hotel services, but not the full range of luxury services offered by an upscale hotel. They are located in cities and suburban areas. Hotels in midscale classification can include Holiday Inn, Radisson Hotels, Courtyard by Marriott, and Hampton Inn.

Luxury/Upscale Hotels **Luxury hotels** are the ultimate lodging experience. The meaning of luxury or upscale is subjective, and in the hotel industry, constantly evolving. Common to understanding the product is providing extraordinary experiences

Luxury hotel rates are high, which is justified by the level of personalized service offered.

that exceed customer expectations, and in many instances the term ultimate luxury conveys the idea of creating lifelong memories.[4] Although they are a small hotel segment in terms of number of properties, these hotels enjoy high profile status within brands and with customers. They are luxurious properties with an emphasis on service. Services and amenities offered include larger rooms, plush bath towels, upgraded amenities, and multiple food and beverage facilities, including fine dining or signature restaurants. As with the food world, creating high impact experiences by showcasing hyper local trends is gaining popularity in the luxury hotel market. Standard to luxury hotels are turndown service, valet service, 24-hour room service, concierge service, a swimming pool, and a spa. Luxury hotel rates are high, which is justified by the level of personalized service offered and the ratio of employees to guest, which usually averages at least two employees per guest. This high ratio enables the hotel to offer an extensive variety of amenities and unique services.[5] Examples of brand hotels in the upscale category can include J.W. Marriott, Hyatt Regency, Westin, St. Regis, and Omni. Brand hotels in the luxury category can include Marriott Marquis, Jumeirah, Ritz-Carlton, Four Seasons, Hilton Towers, and Forte Hotels.

LIMITED-SERVICE HOTELS

The first limited-service hotels–Motel 6, Days Inn, and La Quinta—were built in the 1960s as an alternative to full-size hotels. They were able to offer low prices by not having the amenities of the full-size hotels, such as restaurants, lobby, and meeting space. Today, **limited-service** hotels, as the name implies,

provide a limited number of services to the guests—a clean room, at a low price, in a secure environment. Usually, limited-service hotels have the lowest operating cost because of the lack of extras. The original idea was to meet only the basic needs of guests; however, in recent years additional amenities such as business centers, small gyms, and swimming pools have been added to create a more upscale ambience and appeal to a broader budget conscious market. Limited-service hotel sizes vary between 50 and 150 rooms, although some of the newer properties are larger, with 200 or more rooms. The size of the rooms are usually smaller than full-service hotels, but some limited-service hotels are suite hotels, and therefore offer more space than a traditional hotel.

In addition, they use modular and prefabricated construction materials, which keep the building costs low. This makes it more profitable at lower occupancy levels. Not only does this allow guests a less expensive alternative but it also creates a segment that is more affordable to purchase, and hence attractive to first-time hotel buyers. The entry barriers to the economy segment are relatively low; less than $2 million, with minimal equity requirements, for a 40- to 50-room economy property. As a result, this segment experienced tremendous growth historically, and is now the segment of the lodging industry with the largest number of rooms.

The limited-service hotel category is divided into three different segments and offers three different levels of limited service:

- Budget/economy hotels offer low-priced, clean, and safe rooms in convenient locations.

Limited service hotels provide a clean room at a low price in a secure environment.

- Midscale limited-service is priced higher than the economy level and offers amenities just below full-service hotels.
- Upscale limited-service without food and beverage, the highest priced segment in the category, offers a higher level of comfort, such as upgraded décor and furnishing and hot breakfast.

Staffing is dependent on the number of rooms and the additional amenities. The role of the general manager is usually dependent on the size of the property and the level of service.

SELECT-SERVICE HOTELS

Select-service hotels, a segment developed over the past two decades, are described as a hybrid between full-service and limited service hotels. It is the fastest growing segment in the hotel industry due to the need for affordable accommodations, with the amenities of a full-service hotel. Select-service hotels are similar to limited-services, except in the additional services and amenities offered. They combine the fundamental services offered by limited-service hotels, with a selection of the services and amenities offered by full service-hotels.

The additional services and amenities offered by select-service hotels differ from property to property and at a smaller scale than full-service hotels. The amenities and services may include a restaurant, small meeting/banquet space, fitness room, business center, and indoor and/or outdoor pool. The in-room amenities usually equal that of a full-service hotel. The restaurant offers a limited menu and usually opens only for breakfast and dinner.

Examples of select-service hotels: Courtyard by Marriott, Holiday Inn Select, Hilton Garden Inn, Four Points by Sheraton, Hyatt Place, DoubleTree Club, Wyndham Garden Inn, Hotel Indigo, and Ramada. The select-service segment is highly driven by competition, mostly because of the increase in the numbers as chains continue to release more prototypes. With major chains introducing prototypes, identifying select-service-hotels sometimes becomes difficult because of the increase in amenities, competition, and the number of brands.

LONG-TERM/EXTENDED STAY HOTELS

Long-term stay hotels, also called extended stay, are defined as a lodging facility where all guest rooms include a kitchenette and provide clean, comfortable, inexpensive rooms that meet the basic needs of the guests staying for business, leisure, or personal necessity. They are designed to offer a home-away-from-home atmosphere. The guests' rooms are apartment style, with a living and dining area and a separate bedroom. The bedrooms, living, and dining areas are spacious, and the kitchen is fully equipped with dishes and kitchenware. In addition, limited housekeeping services, grocery shopping services, business services, self-service laundry and valet, continental breakfast, manager's reception, and limited exercise and recreational facilities may be provided. Rooms are rented by the day, week, or month. The more nights a guest stays at the hotel, the lower the rate typically. The typical long-term stay guests are business travelers on extended assignments, individuals relocating between jobs, corporate trainees, consultants, construction crews, occasional leisure travelers who are visiting relatives/friends, and families needing temporary housing.

The concept emerged as an alternative to the more traditional lodging for business and leisure travelers who needed a place to stay for seven or more days. The popularity and growth of this segment has continued, due in part to a significantly higher occupancy average within other segments. The number of rooms represents approximately 5% of total hotel rooms in the United States. Further, marketing properties within this segment is unique. Direct mail and advertising on Internet sites, such as rent.com and homebuyers.com, are common. Marketing the property is more akin to leasing apartments than selling hotel rooms.

BED AND BREAKFAST HOTELS

Bed and breakfast hotels, or B&Bs, offer an alternative lodging experience to the traditional hotel and limited-service hotels. They were first introduced in Europe and experienced explosive growth in the United States in the 1970s. Today, it has been estimated that the industry has grown to over 20,000 bed and breakfast hotels in the United States, catering to more than 40 million guests. The average B&B has nine guest rooms, but two-thirds have fewer than eight guest rooms, and one-third have fewer than four guest rooms. B&Bs are usually independently owned and operated, with the owner and his/her family living on the premises. However, some websites refer to three different categories of B&B facilities:

1. **Bed and Breakfast**—a small lodging establishment in a private residence, with one to seven guest rooms.

2. **Bed and Breakfast Inn**—larger and more commercialized facilities with 8 to 15 rooms.

3. **Bed and Breakfast Hotel**—16 to 30 rooms, and operates more like a hotel, but only serves breakfast.

B&B guest rooms offer variation in size, attractive appointments, and intimacy in a relaxing home-away-from-home atmosphere. No two B&Bs are the same. Each room is decorated to match the architecture and era of the building or to match a particular theme. They are smaller than regular hotels, are personal in nature, have a quiet private atmosphere, and typically provide extraordinary personalized service—catering to needs of the individual guests.

Although breakfast is traditionally the only meal provided, at some B&Bs afternoon tea is served, and dinner is optional—served at the discretion of the owners. The addition of full-scale, gourmet, or specialty restaurants and cooking classes for their guests has become the main attraction of some B&Bs.

With the increase in the number of B&Bs came an increase in competition. Traditionally, B&Bs cater to the leisure market, so occupancy is highest on the

weekends and holidays. The typical B&B guests are the older, affluent, well-educated travelers, who seek shorter vacations relatively close to home. They are looking for variety in accommodation—not the location—and stay an average of 2 to 4 nights. There is a move toward catering to the business market for meetings and the occasional business traveler, which helps the midweek occupancy. Wedding groups are also a major market, because of the quaintness of some facilities and attractive locations.

RESORTS

Resorts are the fusing of traditional food, beverage, and lodging hospitality facilities with recreational amenities that offer activities to guests. The variety and complex nature of the food, beverage, lodging, and recreational amenities found at resorts demand sophisticated management practices to be successful.

Resorts can be characterized in terms of the:

- Location relative to the primary market—how far guests travel and by what means (i.e., car, airplane, or train).
- Primary amenities, setting, and climate.
- Mix of residential, lodging, and community properties.[6]

Location is critical to both destination and non-destination types of resorts. The surrounding scenery, environment, or close proximity to the region's natural or man-made attractions that provide recreation offerings are the experiences that motivate people to travel and stay at resorts. Resorts, particularly those referred to as megaresorts, are associated with specific types of **recreational amenities** and are identified by activities such as golf, tennis, skiing, mountain climbing, fishing, health, and wellness. Premium facilities for sports, exercise, gaming, equestrian, and entertainment activities create unique reputations and images for resort destinations. In many instances, the resort is the destination because of the recreation amenities it offers.

At most resorts across the United States, high season is usually a 90- to 120-day period. Weather and climate dictate what is considered "high season," depending on the nature of the recreational activity that drives guest demand. Much marketing effort

© Robynrg/Shutterstock.com

B&Bs offer an alternative lodging experience to the traditional hotel.

Resorts are associated with specific types of recreational amenities such as skiing.

is given to boost occupancy levels during "shoulder season," those months that book-end high season, but do not have as high of occupancy levels as peak season. Full capacity is the norm during high season. It is in the off-season that a good marketing strategy can bring needed guests to the resort, extending the year and the profitability of the resort. Resort hotels often extend their season and fill the property in the months on either side of high season with group business.

Resort guests have always been and continue to be consumers that are more sophisticated and have higher expectations of service and quality standards. Resorts cater to repeat guests, annually or several times a year. Often the yearly traditions and festivals attract and keep guests returning time after time to the resort. This must be incorporated with new offerings that keep the experience fresh for the guest.

The time and money that guests spend at a resort is discretionary, meaning freely chosen. Because of this, resorts are affected by demand elasticity to a much greater extent than traditional commercial hotel properties. This means management strategies must be always knowledgeable of economic, political, or social changes that may affect the resort's projected revenues and expenses in the short and long term.

Resort hotels attract guests that are seeking relaxation and an array of recreational and leisure activities. These properties are also popular choices to host business meetings because the property and location have marketing cachet, and the self-contained environment provides everything needed for a successful meeting, including recreational activities with few outside distractions to pull the attendees away from the business meeting. Resorts offer dedicated function space for meetings and events.

Resorts are found in all size categories, from a few rooms or bungalows up to hundreds of rooms, suites, or housing units.

- Small resorts with 25 to 125 lodging units are often specialty "boutique" resorts, catering to a small upscale market niche.
- Midsize properties of 125 to 400 rooms are typically chains and located in megaresort areas, offering more space and amenities than the traditional commercial brand hotel.
- Large resorts have more than 400 rooms and are often located in primary resort locations, offering ski facilities, beach frontage, theme parks, gaming, spa, golf, or a combination of these amenities.[7]

Further, resorts often offer a combination of facilities, including spa and wellness centers, and residential single or multifamily homes known as multiuse resorts. The recreational amenities are available to all owners and visitors to the resort.

Residential Resort Lifestyle Communities— Second-Home Developments

Fee simple, individually or family owned attached, detached, or multifamily homes are often found in resort second-home development communities. These are best combined with primary and retiree residences to provide a mix of full- and part-time residents. These resort communities may be characterized by high-rise condominiums on beachfront locations, midrise low-density residential communities near lakes or ski areas, single-family developments with golf courses and a clubhouse, or large planned communities with a variety of housing types and recreation activities. For property owners, resort living becomes a lifestyle.

The **spa resort** is distinct from the spa found at a resort that is part of many amenity offerings available to guests. Sometimes referred to as a destination spa, the spa resort accommodations and amenities are designed to target the spa guest, providing treatments and health and wellness programming. The spa resort markets to a distinct and affluent niche, providing luxury, pampering, and programming to guests. The spa resort may not be open to outside guests. Memberships are sometimes sold to use spa facilities.

OTHER LODGING SEGMENTS

VACATION OWNERSHIP AND RENTALS

Shared ownership or timesharing was introduced to the United States in the 1970s. The term **timeshare** is defined as "the right to accommodations at a vacation development for a specified period each year for a specified number of years or for perpetuity."[8] Owners of timeshares purchase a time period, or fraction of a unit in the resort development, either by a lump sum payment or financed over a number of years. Timeshare owners pay a yearly maintenance, management, and operation fee. Many timeshares allow the purchaser to exchange or trade the timeshare through exchange companies. Over time, the timeshare option has evolved from a set week that was purchased, to the addition of floating week options, and most recently, the more flexible option of vacation club points, which are purchased and can be redeemed at resorts within the brand or a vacation time period.[9]

The development of the timeshare concept grew out of the desire to finance property development of hotels and resorts. Timeshare units that can be sold prior to development have a much quicker return on investment (ROI) for the project's investors than traditional long-term finance options.

In recent years, most major hotel companies have developed timeshares. Marriott, Hyatt, Hilton, Wyndham, and Disney are examples of hotel companies that entered the timeshare market. Having well-known brands involved has helped to bolster consumer confidence in the timeshare product.

Although some brands have recently backed away from further expansion of vacation ownership developments or sold their interests, the timeshare concept continues to evolve, offering a wider range of products and choices for consumers.

Condominium hotels have become very popular with major hotel brands over the past few years. The condominium hotel has marketing appeal to the buyer as an investment and upscale vacation option, to the developer in securing investment funding upfront, and to lenders for minimizing investment risk. Condominium hotels combine hotel style amenities such as public spaces, housekeeping, spa privileges, beach, golf, tennis, and skiing access with the lodging appeal of a condominium unit. The condominium hotel touts all the comforts of home, in a hotel resort atmosphere with none of the upkeep associated with owning a second home property. Structure and time options vary; however, each unit is individually owned, and the owner has a specified right to occupy the unit. When not in use by the owner, the unit is part of the hotel's rental program and is booked and rented to guests who want to stay at the property.[10]

At many resorts and lodging properties, the distinction between hotel rooms, timeshare units, and condominium hotels is becoming blurred. The consumers' expectation is that resort lodging includes the availability of units with full kitchens, separate bedrooms, bathrooms, living rooms, and patios. Management of resort timeshare units or condo hotels is particularly complex. The manager is often responsible for three or four stakeholders, the developer selling the units, the owner of the units, the owner of the hotel or shareholders, the timeshare association board, which governs the timeshare community, and the guest who is renting the unit.

Current demographic and vacation trends suggest that the timeshare and condo hotel concept is filling a market need for people desiring a resort or second home experience. This consumer does not want the financial or maintenance responsibilities of year round ownership, because they only plan to spend a few weeks or long weekends on vacation. With the flex point system, vacations are not restricted to one location, and the desire to experience new places is appealing to many people. The United States dominates the timeshare market worldwide. Despite economic highs and lows, the long-term outlook for the vacation ownership segment is positive.

© Leonard Zhukovsky/Shutterstock.com

Casinos have developed opulent mega hotel resorts.

CASINO/GAMING HOTELS

As the gaming industry continues to grow around the world, casino hotels have proliferated to accommodate the gaming public. Most casino hotels offer full-service accommodations, several food and beverage offerings, entertainment, and shopping opportunities.

In recent years, casinos have developed opulent mega hotel resorts with thousands of rooms. In addition to a large casino gambling space for the gaming consumer, large casino hotels usually have dedicated meeting facilities to market the hotel to conventions and large groups, meetings, and associations. For additional information on the unique characteristics of the casino hotel industry and entertainment, refer to the chapter on casinos.

CONVENTION AND CONFERENCE HOTELS

The large and small group meeting and convention market is a significant economic contributor of revenue to host destinations and meeting venues. Hotels designed to attract and serve this market are in all major cities. Convention hotels range from 300 to 3,500 or more rooms. Conference hotels target smaller groups and usually have 300 rooms or less.

These hotels either have their own exhibition ballroom space or are located in close proximity to a large meeting exhibition (trade show) center, typically found in urban centers. The facilities offer ample function and entertainment event space, breakout rooms of varying sizes, up-to-date technology, audiovisual equipment to support many simultaneous meetings, and large capacity dining facilities. Reliable transportation to and from the nearby airport and area attractions, as well as on-site parking and concierge services, are found at convention and conference hotels. The marketing and services of these hotels is oriented to group business. The acronym for the targeted guest group business activity is MEEC (meetings, expositions, events, and conventions) or MICE (meetings, incentives, conventions, and exhibitions).

BOUTIQUE/LIFESTYLE HOTELS

The first boutique hotel, the Bedford Hotel in San Francisco, opened in 1981. Today, boutique hotels can be found in most major cities in places such as Europe, Asia, and South America. The growth of this segment is associated with travelers' search for a more unique or special hotel. **Boutique hotels** can be independently owned and operated, or they may belong to a group or collection of properties. They are located in major cities, usually in upscale/elite neighborhoods, and are traditionally housed in older, renovated buildings. Today, there are over 25,000 boutique hotels worldwide. The popularity has sparked the interest of major chains that are entering the boutique hotel market, building prototypes. The concept behind boutique hotels, and also associated with the popularity of the segment, is the growth in travelers' interest in history, art, culture, and design.

Boutique hotels are small, uniquely designed hotels with 100 rooms or less, and are described as contemporary, designed-led hotels, which offer unique levels of personalized service and high-tech facilities. Other descriptions of a boutique hotel are avant-garde, intimate, charming, distinctive, cutting edge, trendy, and classic, and with incredible attention to detail and a high level of personal service. The majority of boutique hotels are described as small luxury hotels offering fewer amenities than luxury hotels. This distinguishes them from other hotels, because each hotel has a unique design, with a specific focus on style. The rooms are usually furnished in a theme, and are stylish and/or inspirational. Some boutique hotels do have a dining room, and the majority have bars and lounges. Those without food and beverage services are in areas with a wide variety of restaurants in close proximity.

In recent years, the boutique hotel concept has morphed into **lifestyle hotels**. These hotels are the hotel chains' answer to using the best of the boutique concept to create "branded boutiques." The major hotel groups all are expanding into the lifestyle market segment. Examples of lifestyle hotels are: Andaz (Hyatt), Aloft, and Edition Hotels (Marriott). Similar to boutique hotels, the emphasis is on contemporary styling and style, and expands this to the latest technology amenities and service focused on wellness and life enrichment.

Boutique and lifestyle hotels target customers from the early 20s to the 50s, with mid-to-upper-income averages, who are creative, fashionable, and hip, and those who are looking for something different. Most guests will stay in a boutique hotel because of the uniqueness of the hotel more than the services offered. The majority of boutique/lifestyle hotels' services are at the four-star level, and distinguish themselves by providing personalized accommodation and services. They are known for offering a more unique guest experience than the typical large, corporate, and chain hotels.

SENIOR SERVICE AND RESIDENTIAL HOTELS

Senior service or senior living hotels, sometimes referred to as life care facilities, are designed for the affluent seniors and targeted to the specific residential and lifestyle needs of the 50+ age group. They are marketed to active seniors, and provide varied daily leisure programming activities, health, and medical facility access. Residents can buy or rent small studios, one- or two-bedroom apartments with kitchens, and have the daily convenience of hotel services. Meals may be provided as well as concierge services. Though a small part of lodging, this segment has gained renewed interest in the past few years, as affluent retirees prefer hotel living convenience to home ownership responsibility. Major hotel chains have entered this growing market segment, operating and managing senior housing facilities.[11]

AIRPORT HOTELS

Airport hotels provide guest rooms and meeting and hotel service facilities near airports. Airport hotels target the traveling public and are in high demand during the workweek, when airport traffic volume is highest. Airport hotels have added meeting rooms and conference facilities over the past few years to accommodate the needs of industrial park businesses that have developed around the airport. The convenience and cost efficiency of holding a meeting or staying overnight at the airport hotel is appealing to the busy business executive or salesperson. These hotels provide a crucial service to the traveling public in times of foul weather, overbooked or delayed flights, and air travel shutdowns.[12]

MOTELS

Motels are basic room accommodations, built along highway corridors to provide overnight rest stops for the traveling public. In recent years, the motels that have been added to the market are managed by reputable lodging franchise chains, and have customized the design and amenities of the motel to have consistent quality standards. The guest target market has expanded from the roadside leisure traveler to the traveling businessperson and local meetings market. The provision of a clean comfortable room, parking, limited exercise facilities, a pool, and often a limited-service restaurant at reasonable rates, make the motel segment popular.

PEER-TO-PEER SHARING ECONOMY LODGING ACCOMMODATIONS

Over the past decade the emergence of the Internet-based economic system where consumers share resources, typically with people they don't know, and often in exchange for money, has led to widespread market disruption. In the hotel industry this is evidenced in the rise of **popular peer-to-peer sharing economy websites** such as Airbnb, Homeaway, VRBO, Flipkey, and others that allow residents of homes, apartments, and condos (called hosts) to rent out accommodations on a short term basis to visitors, directly through the website.[13] On a global scale, hundreds of thousands of rental room products have become available to travelers, outside of the traditional hotel/lodging marketplace. There are now more rooms available for rent worldwide through the shared economy, than all the hotel brand chain room stock combined.

The most widely recognized company in this accommodations' segment is Airbnb, which started in 2008, during the recession, and was designed to give ordinary people the opportunity to earn extra income by renting space in their homes to travelers seeking affordable accommodations. Airbnb reports that they have over two million listings worldwide in over 190 countries and 34,000 cities. Airbnb is a regulation-free segment of the lodging industry, referred to as "a trusted community market place" where individuals can list, discover, and book unique accommodations around the world. It is described as "a people-to-people platform—of the people and for the people...." It is also viewed as a lodging segment that includes a wide variety of accommodations, from apartments to castles, and as an alternative-lodging segment.

The Airbnb community consists of individual property owners or hosts, who rent space within their homes, or in some cases individuals renting extra space, to travelers looking for affordable short-term accommodations. The space can be rented with or without the owners being present. The hosts who supply the accommodation see themselves as participating in a market, not a community.

Airbnb's impact on the hotel market is evident in the reaction of chain-scale brand hotels and, its greatest competitors, boutique hotels. Airbnb accounts for 1 to 2% of hotel demand in the U.S., while Airbnb listings make up 2 to 4% of hotel room supply, and 8 to 15% of the supply in large markets. The growth of Airbnb is evident in major cities where it is estimated to account for approximately 13% of bookings in the top ten markets (STR). Airbnb is also recognized as a distribution channel, where travellers can go to book reservations, and where they are taught how to shop for lodging. One of the key challenges confronting Airbnb and other accommodation sites is how to assure that hosts as well as travellers using the site are educated with regard to typical hospitality accommodation standards, protocol, and sanitation. With this rapid development, hotel companies are seeking avenues to partner with the websites to share in the segment growth and develop hospitality management and standards for this new lodging segment.

SUMMARY

The lodging industry is experiencing a dynamic and changing landscape. It continues to experience the expansion of distinct segment differentiation and characteristics to meet ever-changing consumer market demand. Select service hotels, senior service hotels, and peer-to-peer accommodations are just some of the latest additions as the industry continues to expand. The industry is currently characterized by large hotel brand mergers, acquisitions, and partnership initiatives, which are adding to the expansion and addition of brands and offer distinct lodging segmentation.

RESOURCES

Internet Sites

Airbnb.com

American Hotel & Lodging Association: www.ahla.com

American Resort Development Association: www.arda.org

B & B Industry Reports Healthy Figures, August 2009: www.innkeeping.org/news/28875/BB-Industry-Reports-Healthy-Figures.htm

Boutique and Lifestyle Association: www.blla.org

Hotel Magazine: www.hotel.org

Hotel News Now Research, 2016: www.hotel-newsnow.com

International Resort Managers Association: www.resortmanagers.org/resort_links.htm

Luxury Travel Magazine—The A list, 2016: www.luxurytravelmagazine.com

STR Global, 2013: www.strglobal.com/

U.S. Hotel Appraisals: www.ushotelappraisals.com/services/select:servoce-hotels/

ENDNOTES

1. Gee, C. Y. (2010). *World of Resorts, from Development to Management*, 3rd ed. Orlando, FL: Educational Institute of American Hotel & Lodging Association, p. 23.

2. Ibid., p. 24.

3. Ibid., p. 5.

4. Greenwood, G. (June, 2007). *How Do You Define Luxury*. Arabian Business.com.

5. Kasavana, M., et al. (2008). *Managing Front Office Operations*, 6th ed. Lansing, MI: Educational Institute.

6. Ibid.

7. Ibid., pp. 10–11.

8. American Resort Development Association. (1997). *The United States Timeshare Industry: Overview and Economic Impact Analysis*. Washington, DC: American Resort Development Association, p. 5.

9. Ninemeier, J. D., et al. (2008). *Discovering Hospitality and Tourism: The World's Greatest Industry*, 2nd ed. Upper Saddle River, NJ: Pearson Education, Inc., p. 170.

10. Baughman, M. A. (May, 1999). New Points System Points Industry In Right Direction. *Hotel and Motel Management*, 22.

11. Gee, C. Y. (2010). *World of Resorts, from Development to Management*, 3rd ed. Orlando, FL: Educational Institute of American Hotel & Lodging Association, p. 19.

12. Walker, J. R. (2006). *Introduction to Hospitality*, 4th ed. Upper Saddle River, NJ: Pearson, Prentice Hall, pp. 149–150.

13. http://wwwhotlenewsnow.com Source: (2016) Hotel Now Research

REFERENCES

Small But Exclusive Property That Caters to the Affluent Clientele with an Exceptional Level of Service At Premium Prices. Retrieved July 19, 2010 from http://www.businessdictionary.com/definition/boutique-hotel.html and http://www.hotelmotel.com/hotelmotel/ArticleStandard

Top 10 Trends from Boutique Hotel Experts, Luxury Travel Magazine, Luxury Travel Media 2016. Retrieved January 8th, 2016 from http//wwwluxurytravelmagazine.com

Anhar, L. *The Definition of Boutique Hotels—HVS International*. Hotel, Sales and Marketing Association International: www.HSMAI.org. Retrieved July 15, 2010 from http://www.hospitalitynet.org/news/4010409.search?query=lucienne+anhar+boutique+hotel

Barsook, D. (2010). With the term boutique thrown around, we ask what is a true Boutique hotel?: Interview with Frances Kiradjian for the *Hotel Yearbook 2010*. Retrieved July 15, 2010 from http://dbarsook@boutiquelodging association.org

Elder, C. *An Overview of Hotel Asset Classes: part 2 of 3: Select-Service Hotels. U.S. Hotels Appraisals*: Retrieved January 8th, 2016 from http//www.ushotelappraisals.com/services/select-service-hotels/

Higley, Jeff. *W at 15*. April 29, 2013, Hotel News Now. Retrieved July 19, 2010 from http://www.hotelnewsnow.com/Articles.aspx/10376/W-put-lifestyle-on-map-15-years-ago

Morrissey, Janet. (March 12, 2012). *The Millennials Check In*. New York Times, Business Daily.

Stellin, Susan. *Hotel as Lifestyle, 2007.* Retrieved from http://www.nytimes.com/2007/05/15/business/15brands.html?_r=0&pagewanted=print

Weiner, Escalera, K. *Top Ten Luxury Travel and Lifestyle Trends 2008.* Retrieved from http://www.hotelmarketing.com/index.php/content/article/071204_top_ten_luxury_travel

REVIEW QUESTIONS

1. How are lodging segments classified?

2. Explain the difference between bed and breakfast, limited-service, and long-term stay facilities.

3. Describe the different target markets for bed and breakfast, limited-service, and long-term stay facilities.

4. Explain the difference between midscale, upscale, and luxury lodging.

5. What are the advantages of being a four-season resort?

6. Explain the appeal of the timeshare or vacation ownership/club to the purchaser.

7. How is the hotel industry changing to appeal to the younger travel market?

8. What fundamental needs are resort guests seeking?

9. How do resorts differ from traditional hotels?

10. How are current trends impacting the lodging industry?

CHAPTER *20*

© IM_photo/Shutterstock.com

HOTEL OPERATIONS

AUTHOR

Michael D. Collins, University of San Francisco

LEARNING OBJECTIVES

- Identify the three (3) distinct business foci within the hotel industry.
- Outline the priorities and focus of a successful hotel management team.
- Identify the various divisions and operating departments within a full-service hotel.
- Draw an organization chart that illustrates the structure of a hotel's management team.
- Explain how each department contributes to a property's ability to meet or exceed the expectations of the hotel's guests as well as the hotel's profitability.

CHAPTER OUTLINE

Three (3) Business Foci Associated with the Hotel Industry

Management Priorities and Focus

Services Provided by a Full-Service Hotel

Organizational Structure

Rooms Division

    Guest Services Operations (Front Office)

    Revenue Management (Reservations)

    Housekeeping and Laundry Operations

Food and Beverage (F&B) Division

    Food and Beverage Outlet Operations

    Catering Sales

    Banquet Operations

CHAPTER OUTLINE (Continued)

- Beverage Operations
- Culinary Operations
- Sales and Marketing
  - Group Sales
  - Individual Traveler Relationships
  - Advertising
  - Public Relations
- Administrative and General
- Engineering, Property Operations, and Maintenance (POM)
- Management Structure
- Summary

KEY TERMS

- Administrative & General (A&G) department
- Banquet department
- Beverage department
- Catering sales department
- Contribution margin
- Culinary (food production) department
- Engineering, property operations, & maintenance (POM)
- Executive Operating Committee (EOC)
- Food & Beverage (F&B) division
- Guests
- F&B outlet
- Guest services department (front office)
- Hotel management triangle
- Housekeeping department
- Linen par
- Moments-of-truth
- Operating costs
- Operating divisions
- Profitability
- Revenue
- Revenue management (reservations) department
- Sales and marketing department

THREE (3) BUSINESS FOCI ASSOCIATED WITH THE HOTEL INDUSTRY

There are three (3) separate and distinct business functions associated with the hotel industry. They are branding, hotel ownership, and hotel management, as illustrated in Figure 20.1.

When thinking about companies that operate businesses within the context of the hotel industry, the major hotel chains are the first organizations that typically come to mind—companies including Hilton, Hyatt, Marriott and Holiday Inn, just to name a few. While these companies are involved in all aspects of the hotel industry, including the development and construction of hotels, hotel financing and ownership, as well as day-to-day operations, their focus is largely on branding. The goal of a hotel chain is to establish and maintain a family of brands that is attractive to a variety of customer segments and then to ensure that each brand is represented in key markets. The major hotel chains work in partnership with well-capitalized commercial real estate investors, such as FelCor Lodging Trust and Hospitality Properties Trust, in an effort to grow their family of brands. At the same time, the hotel chains work to maintain the quality and reputation of their brands through an in-house management services division and/or franchise agreements with hotel management firms. More details on these strategies may be found in Chapter 7, Chain Operations, and Chapter 8, Franchising and Referral Organizations.

Whether a hotel is an independent, non-branded operation, or operated under a franchise agreement as part of a hotel chain, a well-managed hotel operation is critical to the success of an individual hotel property. Consequently, the day-to-day operations of hotels are typically managed by professional hotel management firms, such as Interstate Hotels & Resorts (www.interstatehotels.com) and Winegardner and Hammonds (www.whihotels.com). Hotel management firms gain control of hotel assets by virtue of management contracts or agreements with hotel owners, as discussed in Chapter 9, Contract and Asset Management. The focus of this chapter is on hotel operations, which includes a discussion of the activities critical to the success and profitability of a hotel, as well as its organizational structure.

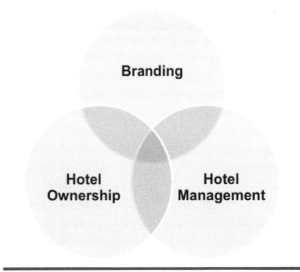

FIGURE 20.1 Three (3) distinct hotel business functions associated with the hotel industry.

MANAGEMENT PRIORITIES AND FOCUS

Hotels employ a diverse team of hospitality professionals to ensure that the guests' needs are fulfilled and that the business is successfully operated. Hotel managers must focus on the following three (3) key constituencies in order to achieve the hotel's business objectives: hotel guests, employees, and investors. Hotel guests must be a primary focus of hotel managers and associates. Without satisfied guests, the source of a hotel's revenue, a hotel cannot possibly operate profitably; however, without investors a hotel would not exist. Ultimately, a hotel is a real estate investment. Consequently, a hotel's success, from a business perspective, is dependent upon its ability to generate a significant return for the hotel's owners. In order to operate profitably and meet the objectives of the hotel's owners, a hotel requires a dedicated team of productive, customer-focused employees that consistently meet or exceed guest expectations. As a result, the role of hotel management is to ensure that the needs of these three (3) key constituencies, as illustrated in Figure 20.2, are met.

The hotel industry is a very labor-intensive industry and customer experiences are determined, in large part, by the **moments-of-truth**, or interactions, that occur between hotel employees and guests. Consequently, hotel managers that focus on fulfilling the needs of their associates and driving employee satisfaction levels will enjoy higher levels of employee

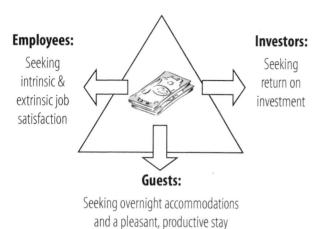

Employees: Seeking intrinsic & extrinsic job satisfaction

Investors: Seeking return on investment

Guests: Seeking overnight accommodations and a pleasant, productive stay

FIGURE 20.2 Hotel Management Triangle
A successful hotel management team fulfills the needs of three (3) key constituencies—hotel guests, employees, and investors.

Guest room bathrooms are typically equipped with a full range of personal care items.

productivity, which lowers **operating costs**, and a higher level of guest satisfaction, which drives **revenues**, resulting in higher **profitability**—the dollar amount by which revenue exceeds expenses or operating costs. As J.W. "Bill" Marriott, Jr., Executive Chairman of Marriott International, Inc., states, "Take care of your employees and they will take care of your customers"[1]; this is essential to achieving profitability.

SERVICES PROVIDED BY A FULL-SERVICE HOTEL

Hotels are, primarily, in the business of providing overnight accommodations for travelers, with full-service hotels providing a wide range of additional supplementary services including prepared food and beverages and meeting facilities. Within a hotel's guestrooms, which typically range in size from 250 square feet for a traditional hotel room to as large as 600 square feet per unit in an all-suite facility, hotel guests are provided with one or two comfortable, oversized beds with ample pillows and fresh, clean linens; a functional work/dining area with Internet access; telephone access; an alarm clock/radio; as well as an oversized television with a free-to-guest selection of network and premium cable television programming coupled with pay-per-view viewing options. Bathrooms, within the guestrooms, are typically equipped with a full range of personal care items, including a selection of soaps, shampoo, conditioner, and hand lotion, a hair dyer, and appropriate bathroom linens. A coffee maker, with appropriate supplies, iron and ironing board, and wooden suit and skirt hangers, are also typically provided within the guestrooms. Housekeeping services are provided on a daily basis within the context of a full-service property.

Full-service hotels also provide food and beverage services, meeting facilities, and a variety of support services necessary to fulfill the anticipated needs of the hotels' guests. Full-service hotels include, at a minimum, a three-meal restaurant coupled with in-room dining (room service) for the convenience of their guests; many full-service hotels may also feature a specialty or fine-dining restaurant. A lobby bar, sports bar, or entertainment lounge that provides a full complement of wine, beer, and alcoholic beverages is also available to guests. In addition, full-service hotels provide meeting space, a complete range of meeting support services, and the availability of catered meals within the property's meeting facilities. Exercise facilities, a swimming pool, a well-equipped business center, and a gift and sundry retail store typically round out the offerings found within full-service hotels. In airport locations, as well as many suburban locations, hotels often provide airport transportation or transportation services to key demand generators within close proximity to the hotel, including office buildings/parks, shopping malls, cultural facilities, and/or recreation areas.

Operating Divisions		**Support Departments**

Rooms Division	**Food & Beverage Division**
Guest services department	F&B outlets
Bell services	Three-meal restaurant
Guest transportation	In-room dining
Front desk	Specialty restaurant
Night audit	Bar or lounge
Concierge	Catering department*
Communications	Meeting/convention services
Revenue management*	Catering sales managers
Housekeeping department	Banquet department
Guestroom services	Banquet services
Public area cleaning	Meeting/convention set-up
Turndown services	Beverage department
Laundry operations	Culinary department
	Garde-manger
	Outlet food preparation
	Banquet food preparation
	Pastry
	Stewarding

Sales & Marketing

Individual business travel
Group sales
Advertising
Public relations

Administrative & General

General Management

Accounting
  Income audit
  Accounts receivable
  Accounts payable
Human Resources
  Employment
  Training & development
  Benefits & compensation
Security & loss prevention

Engineering & Maintenance

Guestroom & building maintenance
Major equipment maintenance
Energy & utility management
Sustainability

*may be part of the Sales & Marketing team in some hotel organizations.

FIGURE 20.3 Operational structure of a full-service hotel

ORGANIZATIONAL STRUCTURE

Full-service hotel operations are organized into two primary **operating divisions**: the rooms division and the food and beverage division. These two operating divisions are supported by an administrative team, sales and marketing professionals, and an engineering department. The organizational structure of a typical full-service hotel is illustrated in Figure 20.3.

ROOMS DIVISION

The rooms division includes all areas of the hotel operation related to providing overnight accommodations to guests. This includes the guest services department, **revenue management** or reservations department, housekeeping, and laundry operations. It should be noted that the rooms division is the most profitable area of a hotel operation. The rooms division is typically managed by a rooms division manager, assistant general manager, or director of operations. The rooms division includes the following operating departments:

GUEST SERVICES OPERATIONS (FRONT OFFICE)

The primary responsibility of the guest services department is to build positive, mutually rewarding relationships with the hotel's guests by engaging in friendly, efficient, and productive interactions with the hotel's clients. Doormen and bellmen are typically the first to greet all guests arriving at a hotel and the last to wish the guest a fond farewell as they depart the property. Guest service agents provide registration services at the hotel's front desk and assist in maintaining guest accounts. Guest service agents are a central information source for hotel guests and must be aware of all events taking place within the hotel as well as the local area. Finally, guest service agents check guests out as they settle their accounts upon departure. In large hotels (over 400 rooms), the guest service agents may be supported by PBX (Public Broadcast eXchange) operators that answer all incoming telephone calls, log all guest requests, follow up with the appropriate departments as well as the guests in an effort to ensure the timely fulfillment of these requests, and coordinate the delivery of mail and packages that are received for guests. High-end and luxury hotels may also employ a concierge staff, which provides a wide variety of assistance, advice, and support to hotel guests regarding area activities, local attractions, cultural sites, and

The bell services team make a significant impact on the guest's perceptions of the hotel service level.

area restaurants; an effective, well-connected concierge has close relationships with popular restaurants and attractions, often obtaining access to these facilities on short notice to the hotel's guests. Night auditors work the overnight shift and perform all of the duties of a guest service agent while also completing a number of essential accounting tasks. Each night, the night auditors update all guest accounts by charging guests the appropriate room rental and tax charges for their accommodations; they also post banquet charges to group accounts, reconcile credit card receipts, run a trial balance, and roll the data in the information technology systems during the early morning hours while guest traffic is minimal.

REVENUE MANAGEMENT (RESERVATIONS)

A guest's interaction with the hotel often begins with a call to a hotel's reservation sales agents, unless the reservation is booked online or through a travel agent or other intermediary. Reservation sales agents are responsible for assessing guests' needs and selling accommodations that fulfill these needs at the appropriate price. Hotels offer rack rates, available to the general public, as well as a variety of discounted rates for which a guest must qualify. The revenue manager is responsible for overseeing the activities of the reservation sales agents as well as the availability of the various guestroom rates and the sale of guestrooms through the various electronic distribution channels. The revenue manager also provides updated hotel occupancy forecasts each week that are critical for the proper scheduling of hotel personnel. Consequently, the revenue manager has a significant impact on a hotel's profitability since he/she is responsible for optimizing revenue as well as forecasting, which impacts labor or payroll costs—typically a hotel operation's largest variable expense.

HOUSEKEEPING AND LAUNDRY OPERATIONS

The housekeeping department is responsible for maintaining the cleanliness of the hotel's public areas and the daily servicing of the guestrooms. The housekeeping operation is managed by the director of housekeeping or executive housekeeper. Obviously, maintaining a clean facility is critical to ensuring guest satisfaction. Each day, guestroom attendants clean and re-stock guest supplies and linens in each

The housekeeping department is responsible for maintaining the cleanliness of the hotel.

occupied guest room with support from the housemen. Public area attendants maintain the cleanliness of the public areas of the hotel including the lobby, meeting room pre-function areas, exercise facilities, swimming pool deck, and public restrooms. Many upscale and luxury hotels may also offer evening turndown service, in which the bed linens are turned down, the curtains are drawn, used bathroom linens are refreshed, soft music is turned on, and the guestroom lights are dimmed; a card from the hotel staff and specialty chocolates may also be placed on the guests' pillows to wish them a pleasant night's rest. Housekeeping management also oversees the laundry operation, which may process thousands of pounds of laundry on a daily basis. Because the laundry operation also services all food and beverage linen, an appropriate portion of the department's costs is allocated to the food and beverage division with the bulk of the expense absorbed by the rooms division. If an adequate guestroom **linen par** is not maintained, typically a triple (3) par (sufficient linen, including bed sheets and terrycloth items, to service all guestrooms in the hotel three (3) times), the productivity of housekeeping and laundry associates will decrease, which will negatively impact profitability since housekeeping labor is the rooms division's largest variable cost.

FOOD AND BEVERAGE (F&B) DIVISION

The **food and beverage** division provides meals and beverage service to guests as well as meetings and convention support services to in-house groups.

Because **contribution margins** (the dollar amount by which revenue received for a product or service exceeds the direct costs associated with providing the product or service) on food and beverage services are much lower than in the rooms division, it is often the most challenging division to operate profitably. The food and beverage division is typically managed by a director of food and beverage, assistant general manager, or director of operations. Outlined below is a description of the role that each department within the food and beverage division fulfills:

FOOD AND BEVERAGE OUTLET OPERATIONS

Food and beverage outlets refer to any retail outlet within the hotel that provides prepared food and beverage services to guests upon request; this includes the three-meal restaurant, specialty restaurant(s), bar(s) or lounge(s), coffee kiosk(s), and the in-room dining (room service) operation. The various outlets employ restaurant greeters, food servers, bussers, cashiers, expediters, bartenders, and cocktail servers, as appropriate, in order to efficiently provide quality food and beverage services to hotel guests and other outlet patrons. Menus are designed to provide both comfort foods that allow guests to feel at home, as well as specialty items that are traditionally found in the property's specific destination or that support a specialty restaurant's theme. Breakfast is typically the highest volume meal within the context of a full-service hotel. In-room dining (room service), if provided, offers a unique set of challenges that must be overcome including the challenge of delivering freshly prepared food, at the correct serving temperature, to guestrooms that are often located a considerable distance from the food preparation area.

CATERING SALES

The **catering sales department** is staffed by meeting or convention services managers and catering sales or special event managers. Meeting or convention services managers manage all of the operational details and sell food and beverage services to groups that have contracted through the sales department to hold their meeting or convention at the hotel. Catering sales managers work with clients that are interested in planning meals and events in a hotel's meeting space that do not include a significant block of overnight guestrooms—typically, social and local

Special events managers work with clients interested in planning events such as wedding receptions in a hotel's meeting space.

corporate events. Because guestroom revenue has a much larger contribution margin than catering revenues, hotel management is very selective regarding the catering only business that it will accept.

BANQUET OPERATIONS

The **banquet department** ensures that meeting rooms are properly set to the clients' specifications and that scheduled breaks, planned meals, and events are properly served and executed. Convention housemen are responsible for setting up all meeting rooms as well as breaking down and cleaning the meeting rooms following an event; much of this activity takes place overnight while the meeting rooms are not in use. Banquet servers are responsible for all aspects of the meal service within a hotel's meeting space. Many convention and meeting guests will require audiovisual services including projectors, video monitors, microphones, and amplifiers; most hotel operators contract this service out to a subcontractor that pays the hotel a substantial commission.

BEVERAGE OPERATIONS

The control and distribution of alcoholic beverages within a hotel operation presents customer service, cost, and liability concerns. Consequently, this responsibility is typically assigned to one specific manager—either a dedicated beverage manager, in a large property, or one of the outlet managers. The beverage manager receives all beverage deliveries and stores all alcoholic beverages in storage space that has tightly controlled access. Banquet bars are issued stock based upon anticipated consumption just prior to a scheduled event, as outlined in the banquet event orders, and then inventoried upon return to the liquor storeroom so that actual consumption can be determined and the group charged appropriately. The beverage manager is responsible for staff training relative to the safe serving of alcohol, which represents a significant potential liability for the hotel operator.

CULINARY OPERATIONS

The executive chef is responsible for food production within the hotel. Typically, the executive chef is assisted by two (2) or more sous chefs, which oversee cold food preparation, outlet food preparation, banquet food, and bakery and pastry items, as well as an executive steward. The *garde-manger* oversees preparation of all cold food items including salads, dressings, vegetable crudités, deli trays, etc. in addition to preparing *mis-en-place* items for use in hot food preparation. The outlet sous chef oversees the food production cooking line that produces food for the restaurant(s), in-room dining, and lounge while the banquet sous chef is responsible for banquet food preparation. A pastry chef may also be employed to provide all baked, pastry, and dessert items. The executive steward and stewards wash all dishes, glassware, serviceware, and pots and sauté pans; maintain all inventories of these items; ensure the cleanliness of the kitchen and food production areas; and deliver banquet food to the meeting service areas for the banquet servers to serve.

In developing menus, the executive chef works closely with the director of food and beverage, the outlet

The executive chef is responsible for food production within the hotel.

manager, and the director of catering, as appropriate, to ensure that guests are provided with a variety of attractive, nutritious menu options while at the same time making certain that a manageable number of ingredients is maintained in the food inventory in order to produce the various menu items. Food preparation is very labor intensive. Although today's chef must have strong culinary skills, a chef must also be an effective manager. Managing food and labor costs, and a wide variety of employee issues including employee training and development, are critical to a chef's ultimate success.

SALES AND MARKETING

The **sales and marketing department** is responsible for driving revenue by attracting meetings, conventions, and individual guests to the hotel. The director of sales and marketing oversees a team of account executives and sales managers that are each responsible for contracting business in a specific market segment. Sales managers obtain business leads from a variety of sources, including the local chamber of commerce and convention and visitors bureau as well as the chain's national sales offices, and then follow up on these leads by assessing the clients' needs and preparing proposals to provide prospective clients with an appropriate array of hotel services that meet the specific needs of each client. All potential business is reviewed to ensure that it meets the targeted revenue goals of the hotel for the required dates prior to a proposal being sent to the client. It should be noted that the revenue management (reservations) and catering sales departments are supervised by the director of sales and marketing in many hotel organizations. The director of sales and marketing also oversees the advertising and public relations activities of the hotel, although the bulk of hotel advertising, particularly for brand-affiliated hotels, is controlled at the corporate level. Many hotels engage in a number of public relations activities, such as hosting charitable events, in an effort to cultivate a reputation of being a good corporate citizen, and the hub of local business and social activity.

ADMINISTRATIVE AND GENERAL (A&G)

The general manager of the hotel is responsible for the overall success of the property. He/she is ultimately responsible for all areas of the hotel's operation and serves as the interface between the hotel and the corporate office, the franchise organization (if applicable), and the hotel's investors. The general manager's administrative assistant often serves as the clearinghouse for all customer feedback including guest surveys and guest correspondence. Following up on guest feedback internally with the appropriate hotel personnel, as well as directly with the guest, is critical to maintaining a strong guest focus among the hotel's staff and a positive reputation with the hotel's clientele.

The A&G department also includes any accounting, human resource, and loss prevention personnel employed by the hotel. The accounting office, supervised by the controller, is responsible for accounts payable, accounts receivable, financial reporting, and assists with cost control procedures. Accounting functions are becoming increasingly centralized (performed in corporate or regional offices) by hotels through the use of information technology. While the hotel's operating managers are ultimately responsible for hiring, coaching, scheduling, training, and evaluating employees, a large hotel often employs a team of human resource specialists, supervised by a director of human resources, which assists hotel managers and ensures compliance with labor laws and regulations. The human resource department also spearheads employee relations efforts, administers employee benefits programs, and manages unemployment and workers' compensation claims. Loss prevention is charged with maintaining the safety and security of hotel guests and employees while protecting the property's assets. Since a hotel has a variety of egresses, often experiencing a steady flow of guests, meeting attendees, and employees through the facility, it is important that a hotel has a comprehensive loss prevention plan.

ENGINEERING, PROPERTY OPERATIONS, AND MAINTENANCE (POM)

The director of engineering or chief engineer oversees the maintenance of the hotel. Hotels typically employ a range of specialized technicians within the engineering department including carpenters, electricians, HVAC (heating, ventilation, and air conditioning) technicians licensed to work with refrigerants, a kitchen equipment mechanic, painters, and plumbers in addition to shift engineers that respond to any guest concerns or immediate needs. A strong preventative maintenance program, to maintain all operating equipment, guestrooms, and public areas, helps ensure positive guest experiences. The director of engineering also chairs the energy management and sustainability committee; this committee is charged with the responsibility of determining strategies that may be employed to reduce utility expenses or improve the sustainability of the hotel's operation.

MANAGEMENT STRUCTURE

The senior management team at a full-service hotel property is often referred to as the **Executive Operating Committee (EOC)**; this committee is composed of the rooms division manager, director of food and beverage, director of sales and marketing, controller, as well as the director of human resources and is overseen by the general manager. In some organizations, the executive chef also serves on the EOC. The next level of management is composed of the department heads; this includes the director of guest services, executive housekeeper, revenue manager, director of catering, food and beverage outlets manager, and executive chef (if not serving on the executive operating committee). A typical full-service management structure is illustrated in Figure 20.4.

SUMMARY

There are three (3) business functions associated with the hotel industry—branding, hotel ownership, and hotel management. The day-to-day operation of a hotel is typically managed by a professional hotel management firm under contract with the hotel owner. A full-service hotel provides a wide range of services to its customers including overnight accommodations, prepared meals and beverages, as well as facilities and services for conventions, meetings, and social events. Consequently, a full-service hotel employs a wide range of hospitality industry professionals to support its operations. A successful hotel management team must ensure that employees have the training, tools, and support necessary to meet and exceed guests' expectations so that the financial goals of the hotel investors may be achieved and, if applicable, the brand standards maintained.

RESOURCES

Internet Sites

www.hilton.com

www.hyatt.com

www.marriott.com

www.felcor.com

www.hptreit.com

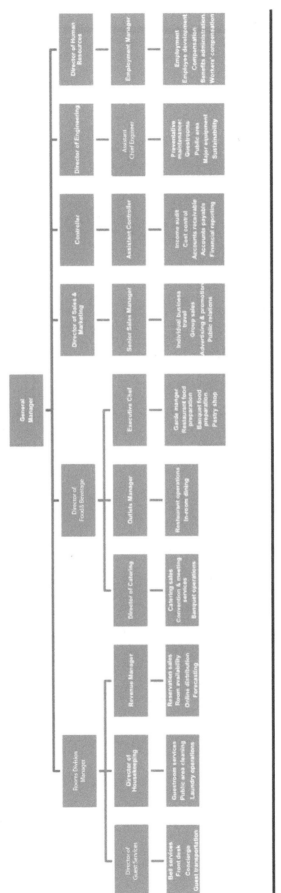

FIGURE 20.4 A typical full-service hotel management structure

ENDNOTES

1. Marriott, Jr., J.W.; Brown, K.A. (1997). *The Spirit to Serve: Marriott's Way*; HarperCollins Publishers, New York, NY, p. 34

REVIEW QUESTIONS

1. What are the three (3) distinct business functions, often performed by separate hotel firms, associated with the hotel industry?

2. What is the primary product or service provided by a full-service hotel?

3. What additional supplementary products or services are typically provided by a full-service hotel?

4. What are the priorities of a successful hotel management team?

5. Why must a successful hotel manager focus on the needs of hotel employees?

6. What are the two primary operating divisions of a full-service hotel and what departments are found in each of these two divisions?

7. What is the role or function of each of the following departments:

   a. Guest services (front office)

   b. Revenue management (reservations)

   c. Housekeeping

   d. F&B outlets

   e. Catering sales

   f. Beverage department

   g. Culinary department

8. What are the various departments that support the operating divisions and what are their roles?

9. Draw an organizational chart for the management team of a typical full-service hotel.

CHAPTER *21*

© POM POM/Shutterstock.com

FOODSERVICE INDUSTRY

AUTHORS	*George B. Ruth, The Pennsylvania State University* *Michael J. Tews, The Pennsylvania State University*
LEARNING OBJECTIVES	• Understand the importance of food service within the hospitality industry. • Differentiate between commercial and non-commercial foodservice establishments. • Identify segments within commercial food service and the factors used to differentiate segments. • Identify segments within non-commercial food service and the unique features of each segment. • Describe key trends impacting foodservice establishments. • Articulate professional career options within food service.
CHAPTER OUTLINE	Food Service in the Hospitality Industry Commercial Food Service Non-Commercial Food Service Trends and Emerging Issues in Food Service Professional Careers in Food Service Summary
KEY TERMS	Casual restaurants Non-commercial food service Casual upscale restaurants Quick casual restaurants Commercial food service Quick service restaurants Family restaurants Theme restaurants Food trucks/street food Upscale/fine dining restaurants Hyper-local sourcing

© Kendall Hunt Publishing Co.

FOOD SERVICE IN THE HOSPITALITY INDUSTRY

Food service is a dominant segment of the hospitality industry that represents a significant proportion of the economy. The National Restaurant Association estimated that 2015 restaurant industry sales were in excess of seven billion dollars and that the average U.S. household spent 47% of its food dollar in restaurants.[1] Food service is also significant employer. Over fourteen million individuals are employed in foodservice establishments, and 10% of the U.S. workforce is employed in restaurants. In 2014, there was 3.1% job growth in food service, compared to 1.9% growth in total U.S. employment. It is estimated that over one million foodservice establishments exist in the U.S. This statistic is noteworthy in and of itself, but also in comparison to the 53,000 U.S. lodging establishments.[2]

Given its dominance and importance, students of hospitality management should possess a working understanding of the foodservice segment of the hospitality industry. As such, the purpose of this chapter is to educate the reader on different segments in food service. Most of this chapter is devoted to discussing *commercial* foodservice establishments. A **commercial foodservice** establishment's main purpose is creating and selling food and beverage. *Non-commercial* foodservice establishments are discussed later in the chapter. A **non-commercial foodservice establishment** is embedded in an organization where food and beverage is not the primary business focus, such as in healthcare, the military, and transportation. Food service is continually evolving, and this

Food service is a dominant segment of the hospitality industry that represents a significant proportion of the economy.

chapter will highlight some of the notable trends and emerging issues. Finally, this chapter will discuss a variety of career options that might be of interest for those seeking to pursue a professional career in food service.

COMMERCIAL FOOD SERVICE

The majority of foodservice establishments are in the commercial sector. These establishments vary in numerous respects, and it is not an easy task to categorize the vast array of establishments into neatly defined segments. There were once clearly defined segments, but today the lines between segments are blurred in many respects. These limitations notwithstanding, we will discuss eight primary segments: 1) quick service, 2) food trucks/street food, 3) quick casual, 4) family, 5) casual, 6) themed, 7) casual upscale, and 8) upscale/fine dining. Each segment will be differentiated by service level, quality of menu offerings, and price point. These attributes will be discussed within each segment along with other unique characteristics.

With McDonald's alone spending nearly one billion dollars on advertising each year, readers are certainly familiar with the quick service segment. **Quick service restaurants (QSRs)**, commonly known as fast food by the general public, are those where the customer orders at a counter, pays prior to receiving the product, and picks food up at the counter. Drive-thru service is also commonplace in the QSR segment. Service level is minimal, fast, and efficient. The food quality is low cost value with average checks under $8.00. QSR establishments may be open for all three meal periods (breakfast, lunch, and dinner) with some operations providing 24-hour service. In 2015, McDonald's began offering breakfast all day, although the verdict on the success of this rollout is still out. QSR establishments are unquestionably chain dominated, and they are child friendly with specific children's menus. Most "pizza shops" fall into the QSR segment as well. Some establishments may be coined *QSR-Plus*, such as Chick-fil-A, Five Guys Burgers and Fries, and Shake Shack, which provide higher quality offerings and realize higher check averages. Traditionally, McDonald's, Burger King, and Wendy's dominated the QSR segment, but dominance has begun to shift. In 2015, *Nation's*

Food trucks are similar to QSR establishments, but typically have a limited, specialized menu.

Restaurant News identified McDonald's as still occupying the number one position with $35.4 billion in sales, but the number two and three spots went to Starbucks and Subway, respectively, with $13 billion and $12.3 billion in sales.[3] Subway topped the list with the highest number of units/restaurants. Today there is more competition among key players within QSR, and QSR establishments are competing with the quick casual segment as well.

A mere ten years ago, food trucks and street food vendors would not have been included in a textbook chapter, but today they are a popular and steadily growing segment. The famous Halal Guys food cart on 53rd Street and 6th Avenue in New York City is rumored to generate over one million dollars in annual sales. Similar to QSR establishments, **food truck/street service** is counter-based and limited, due to their small street-side presence. Patrons order and pay at the counter, take their food away, eat right on the sidewalk, or may sit at a few tables nearby. These operations typically have a limited menu; they find a few things to do very well (e.g., falafel, grilled cheese, or crêpes). These establishments are not necessarily the hot dog and pretzel stands they once were with a reputation of serving poor quality food ("roach coaches"). Some may still provide lower quality food, but others provide a higher-end menu, sometimes with gourmet offerings. In fact, the trend in food trucks/street food is toward the higher end. Check averages reach over $20. Pepe, a Washington DC based food truck inspired by José Andrés, a Spanish trained chef who worked at elBulli, the number one ranked restaurant in the world for several years, offers a sandwich priced at $20. Unlike QSRs, food trucks/street food vendors are typically independents, but chains are beginning to emerge, such as The Taco Truck in New York, Massachusetts, and New Jersey. Food trucks and street vendors have been innovative in using social media as a marketing strategy. Kogi is a famous taco truck in Los Angeles that has utilized social media to amass a cult-like following by tweeting their various locations numerous times throughout a day.

The **quick casual restaurant** (also known as fast casual) segment is fast growing, exciting, and is taking market share from QSR. Much of the growth in this segment can be attributed to dominant players such as Chipotle and Panera. Other key players in this segment include Noodles and Company, Pei Wei Asian Market, and Shop House Asian Kitchen. Service is limited, similar to QSR. One of the major points of distinction of quick casual vis-à-vis QSR is the quality of their menu. Chipotle uses fresh and raw ingredients and prepares items like guacamole from scratch. Panera offers high quality sandwiches, soups, and salads and fresh baked goods daily. An emphasis is placed on freshness, and many items are prepared in front of the customer. These establishments often have metallic versus plastic cutlery, ceramic plates and bowls, and more upscale and trendier décor to further differentiate themselves from QSR. Millennials and other customers are demanding higher quality food, and they are willing to pay a little more for it, choosing quick casual over fast food. Average guest checks for quick casual

Panera is one of the dominant players in the quick casual segment.

typically span $8.00 to $12.00. The quick casual segment is largely dominated by chains.

The five segments to be discussed next are full-service establishments. Customers no longer order at a counter and take their own food to a table. Rather, they are seated, typically receive menus, and are waited on by servers, who are central in orchestrating the dining experience. Food may now be delivered in courses (appetizer, main course, and dessert). Payment occurs at the end of the meal, and gratuities (tips) are now expected. We see alcohol served in many full-service establishments, although in some states alcohol is served at Chipotle.

Family restaurants include a mix of chain and independents. Notable examples of family restaurant chains include Bob Evans, Cracker Barrel, Denny's, Friendly's, IHOP, and Perkins. You will also find many independent restaurants, local diners, and "mom and pops" in this segment. Home style cooking dominates this segment, and family style restaurants are typically open for breakfast, lunch, and dinner. With respect to family restaurant chains, there is limited or no alcohol service, most offer breakfast all day, and many are open 24 hours. These establishments focus on value, and average checks range from $6.00 to $12.00. Buffet restaurants can also fall into this category. With the increasing popularity of quick casual restaurants and greater health consciousness among many Americans, buffet restaurants have been declining in certain regions of the U.S. While Americans once valued the all-you-can-eat for a fixed price concept, they are now more health conscious than ever before.

In turn, **casual restaurant** establishments position themselves with a relaxed atmosphere (relative to upscale establishments), moderately priced food, and higher quality than QSR. Typically, lunch and dinner are served in casual restaurants, but not breakfast as with family-style establishments. Alcoholic beverages are now introduced broadly in this segment. Popular casual chain restaurants include Applebee's, Chili's, Olive Garden, Outback Steakhouse, Red Lobster, Red Robin, and TGIF. On the independent side, many ethnic restaurants, such as Chinese and Mexican, and sports bars fall within the casual restaurant segment. Casual restaurants focus heavily on tabletop marketing pieces to entice

patrons to order appetizers and specialty alcoholic beverages. In a similar vein, servers are trained and encourage to "up-sell" appetizers, desserts, and alcoholic beverages. Average guest checks are generally in the range of $8.00 for lunch and $15.00 for dinner. While popular, casual restaurants are losing market share to quick casual establishments. Moreover, casual restaurants are expected to realize only modest sales gains of 0.6% in 2015.[4]

Theme restaurants are an extension of casual restaurants with the major distinction being that theme restaurants focus on a specific theme. For example, Hard Rock Café focuses on rock-and-roll memorabilia, Rainforest Café centers on a jungle theme, and T-Rex is a prehistoric themed restaurant. These restaurants are chain dominated, but there are a few independents, such as the Jekyll & Hyde Club in New York City. These establishments do serve alcohol, but many are child-focused given their themes. A major focus is on décor and architecture over food and beverage. In fact, some of these establishments cost as much as $15 million to build. These restaurants are often found in major shopping malls and major tourist areas so they can draw on high volume. Given the high costs to building these restaurants and the high cost of real estate, theme restaurant check averages are notably higher than casual establishments (in the range of $13.00 for lunch and $23.00 for dinner).

The casual upscale (also known as polished casual) segment is a minor step below upscale restaurants. This segment is arguably one of the most difficult segments for individuals to grasp conceptually. Restaurants in this segment are similar to upscale

Hard Rock Café is a theme restaurant that focuses on rock-and-roll memorabilia.

restaurants in service and food quality with average checks in the range of $16.00 for lunch and $50.00 for dinner. A major distinction is that they turn tables quickly in comparison to upscale restaurants where the dining pace is more leisurely. **Casual upscale restaurants** generally serve lunch and dinner; whereas upscale fine dining restaurants typically only serve dinner. Casual upscale establishments have expensive decor, some may use linen, they have a full bar and a high quality wine list, and most items are prepared from scratch with highest quality ingredients. There are numerous independently owned and operated casual upscale restaurants. However, the major players in this segment are chains, including Great American Restaurants, Hillstone Restaurant Group, and J. Alexander's. For the most part, chain restaurants in this segment do not want to be recognized as part of a chain, but would prefer to be perceived as unique, independent restaurants. Hillstone Restaurant Group, for example, varies the names of its restaurants (e.g., Houston's, Bandera, and R+D Kitchen), menu, and décor based on location to help achieve a unique, independent feel.

Upscale fine dining establishments are at the top of the restaurant food chain. Upscale fine dining restaurants have a strong focus on providing the highest level of product and service, and their décor has an expensive look and feel. Upscale restaurants will often have a wine cellar to meet guests' expectations. (Some wine cellars are rumored to have more than $7 million worth of inventory.) Upscale establishments employ highly trained professional servers who are typically only responsible for one or two tables at a time. Average checks can easily exceed $500.00. Unlike casual upscale, independents dominate the upscale fine dining segment. High end steakhouses, such as Pappas Bros. Steakhouse and Peter Luger fall into this segment. Many restaurants in this segment have an à la carte or a fixed price (prix fixe) menu. An à la carte menu prices each item separately; whereas everything is included for one price with a fixed price menu. Tomas Keller's The French Laundry fixed price menu is $295 per person at the time of writing this chapter. The French Laundry menu also has several "add-ons" that could easily extend the average check to over $500, excluding alcohol. Many upscale dining establishments and their chefs strive to earn a coveted Michelin Star, a top spot in one of the several international rating lists, or a positive review online.

Such accolades help these establishments maintain their exclusive status in a highly competitive business environment.

NON-COMMERCIAL FOOD SERVICE

Non-commercial food service can be defined as foodservice operations where food and beverage are not the primary focus of a business, but where food and beverage is present to support or supplement a "host." A variety of labels have been used for this segment over the years, including *institutional, non-commercial, contract feeding, on-site food service,* and most recently *managed services.* Organizations can choose to manage food service themselves, which is referred to as self-operated (self-op), or they can contract food service out to a company that specializes in feeding and related services. Three of the dominant players today in non-commercial food service are Aramark, Compass, and Sodexo. While the success of a commercial restaurant is often determined by its sales volume in dollars, non-commercial success is often rated by participation (volume of people). This is especially true in cases where food is free or partially subsidized by the host company for its employees.

The segment is somewhat misunderstood and sometimes has a connotation of only serving school lunches, hospital food, and meals in a nursing home. This segment does serve these operations, but is more diverse and spans everything from elementary school lunches to fine dining. This segment also sometimes has had a reputation of only serving uninspired food. However, companies like Google have highly

Non-commercial food service companies such as Sodexo determine success by rating participation.

trained chefs that prepare and serve very high quality food. They focus on local, organic, and sustainable offerings. Apple Inc. recently announced that its new multi-billion dollar headquarters will feature a garden where chefs will be able to select fruit, vegetables, and herbs from the property. This emerging trend has been coined **hyper-local sourcing.**

A wide variety of business and other organizations house non-commercial foodservice operations. Below we briefly discuss these segments.

- *Business and industry (B & I).* When we think B & I, employee cafeterias may come to mind. Clients range from manufacturing plants, remote site feeding (e.g., oil fields on the North Slope in Alaska), to Goldman Sachs in New York City. Services may include vending, self-service convenience stores, feeding hourly employees, feeding managerial and other white-collar employees, and upscale catered events.

- *Healthcare.* Healthcare feeding in a traditional hospital setting includes patient feeding, employee feeding, and guest feeding. Hospitals may also have catering that can range from casual to large upscale fundraising events. The size and scope of offerings largely depends on the size and location of the hospital. Rehabilitation clinics and traditional nursing homes also provide patient feeding.

- *Corrections.* Correctional facilities must feed inmates and employees, and they typically forbid individuals from bringing food into a facility from the outside. Accordingly, non-commercial food service is an important component of a jail or prison system. Furthermore, food plays an important role in maintaining inmate morale in this environment.

- *Continuing care retirement communities (CCRCs).* CCRCs are a relative newcomer and are becoming more important with the Baby Boomers at or nearing retirement age. Nursing homes may come to mind when you think of CCRCs, but a CCRC is closer to a resort. Many guests are still very active, and CCRCs fulfill individuals' needs for activities, accommodations, and fine food. There is a growing need for talent management in CCRCs, and many hospitality programs are adding courses in this area in their curricula.

- *Military.* This segment involves feeding military troops and affiliated support organizations. While much of the feeding is in "mess halls," there are more upscale dining options offered in officer's clubs. There are also balls and galas that can be upscale in nature as well. Higher ranking officers such as generals are often assigned their own culinary team to prepare daily meals and cater special events.

- *Airline.* The airline industry has food service in the airports, ranging from fast food to casual sit-down restaurants. The Burger King or Subway in the airport is most likely managed by a contracted foodservice company. In-flight food service is of course another area that falls in this category. Two of the major in-flight foodservice providers are Gate Gourmet and Sky Chefs.

- *Trains.* Onboard dining options can range from snacks to full-service meals in the dining car, often requiring reservations. On many long distance trains there may be an attendant with a snack cart who travels from car to car.

In-flight food service is a non-commercial food service.

Bar-buffet cars are a unique part of the train experience, where the quality of the food and wine can rival that of a gourmet restaurant.

- *Cruises.* One of the first questions asked of someone returning from a cruise is, "How was the food?" Dining on cruise ships has evolved over the years to allow for more options and flexibility with some outlets open 24 hours. Royal Caribbean's *The Allure of the Seas* is currently the world's largest cruise ship with more than 20 dining options, ranging from casual snacks to fine dining (and everything in between). We are now also seeing branding on cruise ships with concepts like Starbucks.

- *K-12 education.* Kindergarten through twelfth grade food service primarily involves providing lunches in both public and private schools. These programs are subsidized to various degrees by the U.S. federal government, and nutritional values must meet federal guidelines to receive federal dollars. Many schools also offer breakfast and snacks (for students who qualify) to take home to ensure nourishment throughout the day. School food service may either be self-operated or contracted out.

- *College and university.* The amount and types of foodservice operations in higher education depend on the size and type of school. Traditionally universities had dining halls where students would move along cafeteria style filling up their trays as they went through the line. Now there are more options, more stations, and more made-to-order food. We

Kindergarten thorough twelfth grade food service primarily involves providing lunches in both public and private schools.

also see smaller tables to mimic eating in a restaurant. Many universities use foodservice operations as a recruiting tool to lure prospective students, and it is not uncommon for students and parents to tour state-of-the-art foodservice facilities during campus tours. In the past, different dining halls on the same campus were basically the same. Today, dining halls try to differentiate themselves and compete for student patronage. Universities can be self-operated, or they may contract out their foodservice operations. Many universities also have food courts similar to a mall where students can find many familiar QSR brands.

- *Sports and entertainment arenas.* Sports and entertainment arenas typically contract out their foodservice operations. Offerings range from popcorn and peanuts to fine dining full-service restaurants. There may also be catering in the box suites. Often the food at an arena mimics an area's most popular and unique items. In Pittsburgh's Heinz Field for example, you can find the famous Primanti Bros. sandwich which is stuffed with coleslaw and fries. AT&T Park's $8 Gilroy garlic fries in San Francisco have become famous in their own right. For the Olympics, Aramark is the foodservice provider, feeding athletes, coaches, staff, officials, and the press. This is food service on a grand scale serving over 3.5 million meals and 10,000 people per hour with diverse dietetic and cultural needs.[5]

- *Parks and recreation.* U.S. national parks such as Yellowstone and Yosemite contract their food service out to companies like Aramark, Sodexo, or Xanterra, which is the largest operator of park-based hotels, restaurants, and stores. Concessions, upscale dining, and catering are commonly found at most parks. There is an emphasis on sustainability and fitting in with the overall look and feel of a park. Food service at theme and amusement parks may be self-operated or contracted out. Their offerings are as varied as the parks themselves, but typically include snack food or "park fare," casual sit down dining, and upscale formal restaurants.

TRENDS AND EMERGING ISSUES IN FOOD SERVICE

Menus and food preferences are always evolving. Today guests are more knowledgeable about food and more adventurous than ever before. This trend is due in part to the proliferation of television programming specifically tailored to food and celebrity chefs (e.g., the *Food Network*). In line with this trend, we now see more adventurous items on today's menus, such as bone marrow gratin and pig's blood pappardelle, just to name a few. The National Restaurant Association highlights that we now see a focus on the sustainability, quality, wholesomeness, and calorie content of menu offerings.[6] As an example, Sweetgreen is a concept built around serving high quality organic and sustainable products. Sweetgreen promotes its brand by asserting, "we source local and organic ingredients from farmers we know and partners we trust, supporting our communities and creating meaningful relationships with those around us."

While the human element is still very important in service delivery, technology is continually reshaping the experience. For example, many restaurants already offer services such as mobile payments. Mobile payments enable customers to use their smart phones to pay their bills. Currently, 35% of QSRs offer mobile payment options, while 11% of upscale restaurants offer this service.[8] Radio frequency identification (RFID) is another type of technology being used at various resorts. Disney uses RFIDs in the form of *MagicBands*, which allow guests to leave their wallets elsewhere because everything from bill paying (charging) capabilities to food preferences will be orchestrated through the RFID chip embedded into a wrist band.[9] In addition, many restaurants are using electronic tablets for payment and ordering tableside. The ability to pay the bill at the table speeds up the service cycle and helps to ensure privacy of credit card data.

A hot topic in restaurants is no tipping for front-of-house employees. Danny Meyer, CEO of Union Square Hospitality Group (which includes Union Square Cafe, Gramercy Tavern, Blue Smoke, Jazz Standard, and The Modern) recently introduced a "hospitality included" policy in select restaurants. Danny Meyer sought a way to achieve greater pay equity between front-of-house and back-of-house employees. At Meyer's restaurants, the tip is now built into the price of each and every menu item. Criticism notwithstanding, other restaurants have begun to follow suit. For example, Joe's Crab Shack has recently announced that it will pilot a no-tipping concept in 18 of its restaurants.

Another hot topic is having restaurant patrons purchase tickets for their dining experience. For the most part, restaurant pricing is the same on a Monday as it is on Saturday regardless of demand. Hotels, airlines, and plays all charge different amounts based on supply and demand. Nick Kokonas, cofounder of Alinea and Next, developed Tock Tickets, a company that handles the ticketing process for restaurants.[10] With Tock Tickets, patrons pay in advance for their reservation much like they would for a concert or Broadway show. The ticket prices vary depending on the time of day, or day of the week. This concept enables restaurants with a high demand to maximize their revenues and minimize "no-shows."

PROFESSIONAL CAREERS IN FOOD SERVICE

Given the diversity of segments within commercial and non-commercial food service, there are a variety of career options available to students. The most common upon graduation are restaurant manager or assistant manager in a standalone restaurant. Usually entry-level management positions are divided into front- or back-of-the house. One can also pursue entry-level management positions in a hotel or resort

The most common food service jobs upon graduating are restaurant manager or assistant manager.

© barang/Shutterstock.com

as a restaurant, bar, food and beverage, or banquets manager. Individuals then progress toward becoming a general manager in a restaurant or a director of food and beverage in a hotel or resort setting. The next step would be an area or regional manager, followed by an executive position in a corporate office. Many also choose to become restaurant entrepreneurs where they can create and implement their own ideas and philosophies.

There are also various options for students who choose not to work in restaurant or foodservice operations. Micros, which is now owned by Oracle, provides many of the point-of-sales terminals throughout the U.S. and worldwide. Micros often hires recent graduates to work in a sales/support role. Ecolab is another company that is often behind the scenes in many restaurants by supplying cleaning and sanitizing equipment and chemicals. Ecolab also typically hires recent graduates to work in a sales/support role. Sysco is the largest foodservice food supplier in the U.S. with over 425,000 customers.[11] Recent graduates may begin a career with Sysco in either a sales or sales trainee role to promote Sysco's various products and services.

SUMMARY

Food and beverage without question is a key component of the hospitality experience. Moreover, food-service establishments are dominant players in the U.S. economy. As this chapter highlights, there is great variety in establishments and segments within commercial and non-commercial food service. These different segments provide unique experiences for customers and guests, and they offer a wealth of career options for those seeking a career in food and beverage. Food service is a challenging and exciting business, and we hope this chapter has provided a useful overview of the breadth of the diversity in foodservice establishments.

REFERENCES

1. http://www.restaurant.org/News-Research/Research/Facts-at-a-Glance

2. https://www.ahla.com/content.aspx?id=36332

3. *Nation's Restaurant News*, June 15, 2015

4. *2015 Restaurant Industry Forecast*, 2015, National Restaurant Association

5. http://www.news.cornell.edu/stories/2008/08/alum-has-herculean-task-feeding-olympic-athletes

6. *2015 Restaurant Industry Forecast*, 2015, National Restaurant Association

7. http://sweetgreen.com/our-story/

8. *2015 Restaurant Industry Forecast*, 2015, National Restaurant Association

9. http://www.wired.com/2015/03/disney-magicband/

10. http://www.fastcompany.com/1686639/how-nick-kokonas-shaking-fine-dining

11. http://www.sysco.com/about-sysco.html

Name: _____ Date: _____

REVIEW QUESTIONS

1. What is the difference between commercial and non-commercial food service?

2. What are key segments within commercial food service? What are examples of restaurants within each segment? What factors can be used to differentiate each segment?

3. What are examples of establishments within non-commercial food service?

4. What are key trends impacting foodservice establishments today?

5. What are examples of professional careers within food service?

CHAPTER *22*

RESTAURANT OPERATIONS

AUTHORS

LEARNING OBJECTIVES

Thorir Erlingsson, Kennesaw State University

- Identify different restaurant operations.
- Describe the various departments and positions within a restaurant.
- Identify functions and responsibilities associated with management positions.

CHAPTER OUTLINE

Introduction

Management

Restaurant Structure

    Back of the House

    Front of the House

Summary

KEY TERMS

Back of the house (BOH

Bartender

Busser

Cost control

Executive chef

Food cost

Front of the house (FOH)

General manager

Host

Line cook

Point-of-sale system

Restaurant types

Server

Sous chef

INTRODUCTION

Most college students today have been dining out since they were young kids. Their favorite restaurant in early childhood was likely a fast-food restaurant with an area in which to play. As you grow, you learn to enjoy different restaurant types without always understanding the different structure that exists across restaurant operations. In this chapter you will learn about different levels of restaurants. The levels of restaurants are most commonly broken down into fast food, fast casual, casual dining, and fine dining.

Fast-food restaurants emphasize speed. Usually you order from a counter, and the food is delivered to you across the same counter. Most fast-food restaurants also offer drive-thru service. Operations vary from an individual food truck to multi-million-dollar operations like MacDonald's, Burger King, and Subway.

Fast casual is the fastest-growing sector in the restaurant industry today. Fast casual promises a higher quality of food than fast-food restaurants. More of the food is made from scratch at the location than in fast-food restaurants. Some examples of fast casual companies are Moe's, Chipotle Mexican Grill, and Panera Bread.

Casual dining restaurants include TGI Friday's and Chili's. Most casual dining restaurants are chain restaurants operating in many states and even worldwide. A lot of family-style restaurants also fall into this category. In casual dining you are served at the table by a server who seeks to provide you with a great experience.

The goal of most restaurants across the categories is to deliver great service, great food, and a wonderful experience, but in fine dining this promise takes on a new meaning. Some of the best chefs in the world work in fine dining establishments where they focus on creating a new experience for the guest, with outstanding food and flawless service. Around the world, fine dining restaurants are usually single units operated by a team of highly trained chefs and servers. Most restaurants today use some versions of the brigade system created by Escoffier. Under this system every position has a station with defined responsibilities. Fine dining operations mostly use

Most casual dining restaurants are chains operating in many states, such as TGI Friday's.

the French names established by Escoffier with the brigade system, while casual dining restaurants tend to use the English terms.

MANAGEMENT

Being a general manager for a restaurant is not for everyone. To run a restaurant you have to be ready to come to work every day without knowing how your day is going to be. To manage a restaurant you have to be organized but flexible, and ready to deal with new issues on a daily basis. The industry is fast paced, and a restaurant that is popular today can be closed next week.

The **general manager (GM)** runs the day-to-day operation and needs to understand every aspect of the restaurant. Some of the responsibilities for the GM are budgeting, marketing, hiring and firing employees, and being the contact person for the restaurant. One of the main responsibilities is **cost control**, which includes keeping control of food and labor costs. The GM works closely with the executive chef to keep food cost within the budget. There are many ways to keep **food cost** in control. Some things you can do include negotiating with different vendors to get the right price and changing your menu to get the food cost where it should be. It is also important to serve the correct sizes of each menu item as the cost of each course is calculated from the standard recipe—by increasing the amount of food for each course.

Controlling labor costs can be challenging as well. You need to have the right number of staff members working for each time of the day, every day of the week. One easy way to control labor cost is by cross training your staff. The more staff members that are trained for different jobs in the restaurant, the more flexibility the GM has in scheduling shifts. Some ideas for cross training include training your prep cook to handle the grill, training your hostesses to work as back-up servers, and training your bussers to help run food to customers. One of the challenges managers face is having too few employees working at one time. It generally results in bad service. However, having too many employees can also result in bad service.

The GM works with the owners, staff, and customers to create good experiences and a profitable restaurant. **The point-of-sale system (POS)** is used to acquire and store the restaurant's important information, including sales, hours worked per employee, and number of guests. Some of the details the GM can "pull" from the system are sales and labor cost per hour of the operation. The POS system, when used correctly, gives the GM the information he or she needs for future planning.

Some of the future challenges for restaurant operations and their management teams are to become more sustainable. The challenge for management will be in updating the restaurant and training the employees in sustainable behavior (like sorting trash and using water and electricity responsibly).

RESTAURANT STRUCTURE

BACK OF THE HOUSE

The **back of the house**'s responsibility is to deliver everything on the menu to the front of the house so they may serve the customer. In fine dining operations, the **executive chef** is in charge of all kitchen operations. He or she designs the menu, sets the standards for the kitchen (including safety and sanitation), and hires and trains the kitchen employees. He or she is also responsible for portion control and purchasing everything for the kitchen. The executive chef's reputation is also often an attraction or marketing tool for the restaurant.

The executive chef is in charge of all kitchen operations.

© wavebreakmedia/Shutterstock.com

The **sous chef** is second in command; she or he fills in for the chef, sometimes takes care of scheduling, and works with the station chefs as necessary. Station chefs have responsibility for their station, which can vary between operations. In larger operations most of these stations will appear: saucier (sauce station chef), poissonnier (fish station), grillardin (grill station), friturier (fry station), rôtisseur (roast station), potager (soup station), légumier (vegetable station), entremetier (hot appetizers), garde manger (pantry station, cold food), boucher (butcher station), tournant (swing cook), pâtissier (pastry chef), glacier (cold desserts), boulanger (bread baker), confiseur (candy and confections chef), and aboyeur (expediter and announcer).

In smaller operations, some of these stations are combined as needed, based on the size of the operation, skillset of the chefs, and equipment in the kitchen. In most casual dining operations, you will find a grill station, fry station, sauce station, cold food station, prep station, and expediter.

In casual dining, fast casual, and fast-food operations, the menus are usually provided by the corporate office and are created by the corporate chef. Chain restaurants usually have the same menu in every location, but there might be some differences between states or countries. Chain operations usually have kitchen managers who have the responsibility to follow the corporate executive chef guidelines. Chain restaurants also have **line cooks** that have responsibilities for their station.

The dishwasher is a crucial job in any restaurant.

One similarity between chain and fine dining is that the executive chef/kitchen manager takes care of ordering for the kitchen. In larger establishments, you might have a purchasing manager instead, who works with the chef to get orders in on time.

In every restaurant, the dishwasher is arguably the most important person in the operation. He or she cleans everything for the kitchen throughout the service, as well as ensuring cleanliness and sanitation of china, silver, and glassware to serve food and drinks to the guest. Without the dishwasher, there is nothing on which or with which to eat.

Cleanliness is very important for every restaurant operation and most chefs take pride in a clean kitchen.

FRONT OF THE HOUSE

Just as in the BOH, the **front of the house (FOH)** uses the brigade system, or its own version of it. In the original dining room the brigade system had a

maître d'hôtel (dining room manager), chef de vin (wine steward or sommelier), chef de salle (head waiter), chef d'étage (captain), chef de rang (front waiter), and demi-chef de rang (busser). The French names are not used as frequently in the front of the house as they are in the back of the house. In most fine dining establishments, the maître d'hôtel holds the most responsibility. He trains all service personnel, schedules FOH staff, works closely with the executive chef on menus, and orginaizes seating throughout service.

The sommelier is responsible for all aspects of the operation of the wine service, including creating a wine menu, purchasing the wines, and assisting guests with their wine selection. If the restaurant does not have a sommelier, his or her responsibilities usually transfer to the dining room manager.

The waiter (captain/chef de rang) or **server** deals directly with the customer, explains the menu, answers all questions, and takes the order. The **busser** clears the plates, fills the water glasses, and cleans the tables to prepare them for the next guest. Some of the other positions are often combined into a single position or are not used in modern restaurants.

Bartenders are an important part of the FOH. The **bartender** prepares all the drinks, both for the bar area and the dining room. Bartenders have to be knowledgeable about drinks because guests frequently ask for drinks that may not be on the menu. Sales of alcoholic drinks in restaurants have decreased in the last few years due to a new and different clientele.

The sommelier handles all wine for the restaurant.

The **host** is the person who welcomes you when you walk into a restaurant and guides you to your table when it is ready. The host is ordinarily the first person you see upon arriving at a restaurant and is commonly the last person you see before you leave. Therefore, having a well-trained host is critical for every restaurant. The host's greetings can shape your experience at the restaurant and at the same time make your visit more or less enjoyable.

One of the main differences in service between fine dining and casual dining is the speed of the service. In fine dining operations, guests generally make reservations; whereas in casual dining, guests are customarily served on a first-come, first-served basis. Generally this means that fine dining restaurants have no more than two seatings per night and the guests have time to enjoy and relax. In casual dining operations, on the other hand, the goal is to seat every table as many times as possible every night. This is known as turning a table.

SUMMARY

Today we have many different levels of restaurants, all of which have one goal: serving good food and creating a great experience for their guests. One of the tools all restaurants use to ensure success is the brigade system. The brigade system was created by French chef Georges Auguste Escoffier in the late 19th century. The fast-paced restaurant industry brings management and staff new challenges to deal with daily and the brigade system helps them to tackle these challenges with speed, confidence, and efficiency. All the different levels of restaurant use some version of the brigade system in their operations to create a structured workflow and enjoyable time for their guests.

WEBSITES

http://www.restaurant.org/Home

http://www.acfchefs.org/

Culinary Institute of America. (2011). *The professional chef: 9th Edition*. John Wiley & sons.

REVIEW QUESTIONS

1. What is one of the main differences between fine dining and casual dining?

2. Describe the general manager's responsibilities.

3. Explain how the executive chef works with the general manager.

4. What position in the restaurant works most directly with the customer? Please explain.

5. Calculating food and labor cost is important. Explain why.

CHAPTER *23*

© Taras Vyshnya/Shutterstock.com

CULINARY ARTS

AUTHORS

James E. Griffin Ed.D., CEC, CCE, Johnson & Wales University

LEARNING OBJECTIVES

- Define the six types of chefs in a typical kitchen.
- Describe three duties a typical chef performs.
- Identify at least three factors that help make a chef successful.
- Describe the three pathways to becoming a chef.

CHAPTER OUTLINE

CHAPTER OUTLINE (Continued)

- Chef Michael Voltaggio
- Chef Barbara Lynch: An Inspired Chef and Restaurateur
- Summary

KEY TERMS

- Brigade de cuisine
- Chef de cuisine (head chef)
- Chef de partie (station chef)
- Commis (line cook, apprentice)
- Culinary apprenticeship and coordinated on-the-job training
- Culinary arts
- Executive chef (highest ranking chef)
- Formal culinary education
- Independent on-the-job training
- Mise en place
- Pastry chef (leader of baking and pastry)
- Sous chef (under-chef, second in charge)

The culinary profession is a rapidly growing part of the hospitality industry.

INTRODUCTION TO THE CULINARY PROFESSION

The culinary profession is a rapidly growing and attractive part of the hospitality industry. A vast majority of hospitality operations include some sort of food service as part of their overall operation, whether it is via a formal full service restaurant or something as simple as onsite vending. Food is a core feature of the hospitality experience we all seek to provide.

The **culinary arts** industry also represents a career option for millions of workers in the United States. This increased interest and employment is driven in part by the public's growing interest in eating away from home paired with a continually expanding promotion of the food service industry in feature films, on television shows, and online as a form of entertainment. According to the U.S. Department of Labor, there are more than 127,000[1] chefs and head cooks in the United States and more than 2,290,000 line cooks currently employed. Employment of chefs and head cooks is expected to grow 9 percent from 2014–2024 and this growth is faster than average compared to all other professions.[2] Thus, based on Department of Labor projections, it is a good time to pursue a career path as a chef or head cook.

The National Restaurant Association reports that restaurant industry employment in the U.S. topped 14,000,000 in 2015. By 2025 total employment is projected to grow to 15,700,000 jobs.[3] This projected job growth is due in part to expanding restaurant sales nationally. From 2010 to 2015 restaurant industry sales grew from $586.7 billion to $709.2 billion[4] across all industry sectors. That's more than $120 billion in sales growth over that five-year span of time. Growth is projected to continue through 2025 and job growth is expected to follow this expansion in sales. As the foodservice industry grows it is expected to attract more and more talented employees to the industry.

THE ROLE OF A CHEF

Chefs manage the production of food on a daily basis at restaurants and foodservice outlets across all sectors of the foodservice industry.[5] Chefs develop recipes; create menus; purchase and receive food product; engage in food production and service; assure food safety and nutrition; manage food costs and inventory; manage labor costs; assure proper pricing and profit; hire, train, and supervise staff; employ technology to manage operations; and promote the business. The culinary profession is dynamic and constantly changing as customer preferences shift. The most successful chefs have a deep passion for the industry and love what they do. It takes years to develop the competencies required to be a professional chef—but with experience and dedication the profession offers excellent career opportunities.

Chefs are in charge of a number of tasks including the development of recipes and menus, and managing costs.

SIX THINGS GREAT CHEFS DO

Though the path to becoming a professional chef has changed since the time of Escoffier, a handful of fundamental considerations has remained constant. A professional chef must have the skills, knowledge, and attitude to perform at a high level in a physically demanding work environment. There are six things great chefs do: 1) Work hard: the culinary profession is extremely physical and requires long hours and hard work often while moving and standing. 2) Master culinary methods and techniques: the best chefs take time to master culinary methods and techniques before taking on supervisory responsibilities. This often includes earning a formal culinary degree or credential and subsequent employment under a qualified chef de cuisine. 3) Maintain professionalism: the most successful chefs continue to develop and strengthen their professionalism throughout their career. Professionalism includes leading and managing ethically and with integrity. 4) Master food safety: today, more than ever, chefs must master food safety and safe food handling procedures. 5) Lead and manage people: no chef can achieve excellence alone. The best master the process of leading and managing people. 6) Effectively manage costs and finance: the very best chefs know how to manage costs and assure operations are profitable. Achieving financial success is as important as producing excellent food—the two go hand in hand.

KITCHEN ROLES AND POSITIONS

For those considering a career path in culinary arts, it helps to have a basic understanding of the structure of a commercial kitchen. Workers in the culinary profession are usually placed within a hierarchy based on the **brigade de cuisine** (also known as the kitchen brigade) established by 19th century chef Auguste Escoffier. Georges Auguste Escoffier[6] (1846–1935) was a French chef famous for serving as executive chef of the Savoy Hotel in London, Ritz Hotel in Paris, and Carlton Hotel in London during the late 19th and early 20th century and for writing multiple books including *Le Guide Culinaire* (1903). In the late 1800's, Escoffier created a brigade de cuisine (kitchen brigade) in an effort to organize the roles and flow of work in large commercial kitchens. His kitchen brigade is one of the first culinary organizational charts to be widely adopted. Kitchens around the world continue to use a modified version of Escoffier's kitchen brigade.

There are six types of chefs in a typical kitchen:

1. **Commis** (line cook, apprentice): an entry-level cook responsible for basic food preparation and production.
2. **Chef de partie** (station chef): a line cook one level above a commis responsible for a station or specific area of responsibility as assigned by a supervisor.
3. **Sous chef** (under-chef, second in charge): a supervisor just below the chef de cuisine in charge of an assigned area of kitchen operations. Organizations may have one or more sous chefs.
4. **Pastry chef** (leader of baking and pastry): a supervisor just below the chef de cuisine in charge of baking and pastry.

Pastry chefs are in charge of baking.

© erwinova/Shutterstock.com

5. **Chef de cuisine** (head chef): a senior supervisor in charge of all kitchen operations. If no executive chef is part of the organization, the chef de cuisine is the senior-most culinary professional on staff.

6. **Executive chef** (highest ranking chef): The senior-most culinary position in the organization.

LINE COOK SKILLS, KNOWLEDGE, AND ATTITUDES

Most workers new to the culinary profession begin their career as a line cook (commis). Line cooks are responsible for daily food preparation (prep) and menu production. Success is dependent on an individual's skills, knowledge, and attitude. Line cooks must have basic culinary skills, including the ability to perform fundamental cooking methods like roasting, baking, sautéing, broiling, grilling, poaching, simmering, boiling, and frying. A line cook must also be adept with a knife and efficient in producing mise en place.

Required knowledge includes ingredient identification and handling, food safety and hygiene, efficiency, and organization. The ability to recognize and properly handle various types of fresh, frozen, packaged, canned, and dry ingredients including vegetables, fruits, poultry, beef, veal, seafood, and dairy products is essential. Every line cook must have a superior knowledge of food safety practices and demonstrate impeccable personal hygiene while engaged in food production. The best line cooks are efficient, organized, and coordinate production by using prep-lists and knowing cook times.

Attitude is one of the most important line cook attributes. A majority of executive chefs consider a positive and professional attitude the number one trait sought in entry-level line cooks. This is not an understatement. A positive and professional attitude includes arriving to work on time and in a clean uniform. It also includes a personal commitment to work hard, being team-oriented, and a willingness to perform all duties as assigned. Finally, the best line cooks have customer service at heart and work hard to satisfy guests. If a positive attitude is present,

many chefs believe additional skills and knowledge can be taught on the job.

THE FIVE CORE LINE COOK DUTIES

Most line cooks are required to engage in five core duties on a weekly basis. They are: 1) Prepare daily **mise en place**: create daily prep-lists, gather ingredients, produce mise en place. 2) Organize work station for service: assure all mise en place for the station is in place and at the proper quantities for service. Gather and secure small wares, utensils, pots, and pans. 3) Perform production: Produce menu items during service hours, respond to guest requests, and coordinate station output with the team. 4) Maintain food safety: assure all phases of production are compliant with food safety standards. Maintain impeccable personal hygiene. 5) Continue professional development: pursue development on a weekly basis.

THE CULINARY WORK ENVIRONMENT

Chefs and cooks work in food production facilities across all segments of the food service industry. These range from large commercial kitchens in hotels, conference centers, cruise ships, and restaurants to small kitchen facilities on yachts or in private homes. Most professional food production facilities are designed to match expected volume and food production output required to serve customers based on operating hours. Aside from the budget available for construction, the two most important factors that

© Sergey Mironov/Shutterstock.com

Line cooks are required to produce menu items during service hours.

This hotel kitchen has been designed to match to expected volume and food production output required to serve customers.

go into planning a commercial kitchen are the type of menu items offered and the number of customers to be served. Professional kitchens employ large and often expensive pieces of commercial food production and refrigeration equipment. Kitchens can be loud and active work environments with multiple cooks performing duties and tasks concurrently in an effort to serve customers while being productive, sanitary, and efficient.

WORK HOURS

The work hours required of chefs and cooks varies depending on the type of establishment and foodservice segment being served. Work hours vary depending on the type of foodservice facility and include evening shifts, day shifts, overnight shifts, and monthly contracts that require work 6 or 7 days per week. A high percentage of chefs and cooks work an evening shift, particularly at full-service restaurants, since that is when demand is highest. However, many non-commercial foodservice operations offer employees a day shift since peak demand occurs during normal business hours (8:30 am–4:30 pm, M–F). The range of work hours is truly dependent on the type of establishment.

THREE PATHWAYS TO BECOMING A CHEF

There are three typical pathways to career success in the culinary profession. The first is through completion of a formal degree in culinary arts at one of the many accredited culinary institutions in the U.S. The

second is through completion of a formal **culinary apprenticeship program and coordinated on-the-job training**. The third and final typical pathway is through **independent on-the-job training**.

FORMAL CULINARY EDUCATION

According to the National Center for Education Statistics (NCES), there are more than 300 institutions granting associate degrees in culinary arts and culinary related services in the United States today[7]. These institutions combined produce over 19,000 graduates in a year. The number of graduates produced each year has never been higher and enrollment in formal culinary programs remains extremely popular. Most culinary programs offer students both technical training and academic courses that provide the skills, knowledge, and attitudes required for entry-level (line cook) positions in the foodservice industry. Culinary programs are offered by many types of institutions including those that are private and not-for-profit, those that are public (state run), and those that are for-profit.

Programs at Johnson & Wales University and the Culinary Institute of America remain recognized as the best in class in the private, not-for-profit category. There are many public institutions that offer outstanding quality including programs at community and state colleges throughout the country including Schoolcraft College in Michigan, Hocking College in Ohio, and the John Folse Culinary Institute at Nichols College in Louisiana. Kendall College in Chicago is recognized as one of the best for-profit institutions offering culinary programs. Each institution has its own academic focus or approach to culinary education. When exploring culinary schools it's best to visit the institution to ensure that the programming and academic culture are a good fit for you and that you fully understand the costs associated with enrollment.

CULINARY APPRENTICESHIP AND COORDINATED ON-THE-JOB TRAINING

Apprenticeship in culinary arts has been around for hundreds of years. It is one of the oldest forms of formal on-the-job training offered. The apprenticeship approach requires cooks to work under a qualified supervising chef while completing a formal series of competencies through the duration of the program (usually two or three years). Today most apprenticeship programs also require formal academic courses be completed concurrently with on-the-job training. The American Culinary Federation is recognized for its oversight of apprenticeships in the culinary arts in the United States through the American Culinary Federation Educational Foundation (ACFEF). Apprenticeship is a combination of on-the-job training and related classroom instruction. ACFEF created a set of national guidelines for apprenticeship standards that were originally registered with the U.S. Department of Labor in 1979 and are continually updated to remain pertinent. At present, the ACFEF lists culinary apprenticeship programs in 25 states. When seeking an apprenticeship program, be sure the program is affiliated with an outstanding culinary operation (hotel, resort, etc.), academic institution (usually a community college), has been in existence for five or more years, and has produced successful alumni.

INDUSTRY EXPERIENCE: INDEPENDENT ON-THE-JOB TRAINING

Of the three recognized pathways to career success, on-the-job training is the most common and the least expensive. More people learn to be professional chefs through on-the-job training than through culinary schools and apprenticeships combined. This pathway involves gaining entry-level employment in the culinary industry and learning the craft over the years through direct work experience. When choosing this path, it is critically important to select an excellent employer with a culture of training and development.

CULINARY CERTIFICATION

The American Culinary Federation administers the most recognized chef's certification program in the country. The organization offers 14 different certification levels and types starting with an entry-level Certified Cook (CC) designation all the way to the highest level certification: Certified Master Chef (CMC). The Certified Cook designation requires two years of experience as an entry-level culinarian. Candidates with a one-year culinary arts program certificate from an accredited institution are required to complete one year of entry-level work experience prior to applying. Candidates with an associate's degree in culinary arts from an accredited institution

are not required to have additional work experience and may apply for certification upon completion of their degree program. Certification through the American Culinary Federation demonstrates skill, knowledge, and professionalism to the foodservice industry and is an excellent way to validate culinary and career competency.

EXAMPLES FROM THE PROFESSION

CHEF MARK LADNER: A ROLE MODEL PROFESSIONAL CHEF

Chef Mark Ladner's career includes completion of a formal culinary degree early in his development. He is a role model for how to leverage a formal culinary education. His dedication to hard work and to gaining the skills, knowledge, and attitude to succeed in culinary arts is inspiring. He is known to be one of the nicest people in the profession. Ladner opened Del Posto with Mario Batali and Joe and Lidia Bastianich in the fall of 2005. The restaurant received a four-star *New York Times* review in 2010 and was recently honored with a Michelin star, the Relais & Chateaux Grand Chef distinction, The Grand Award from The Wine Spectator, and the Five Diamond from AAA.

Chef Ladner's education began in Cambridge, MA at independently owned and operated pizza counters, followed by formal culinary training at Johnson & Wales University in Providence, Rhode Island. Ladner has since opened Lupa Osteria Romana (1999), Otto Enoteca Pizzeria (2002), and Del Posto (2005) as chef/partner at each restaurant. Mark co-authored *Molto Gusto* (Ecco, 2010) with Mario Batali. In 2015 Ladner experienced a career highlight by being awarded "best chef New York City" by the James Beard Foundation—known as the Oscars of the food profession. Mark Ladner is an inspiration for all culinary professionals and a role model for how to properly and professionally leverage a culinary education.

CHEF CHARLES CARROLL: A GLOBAL CULINARY LEADER AND AUTHOR

Chef Charles Carroll, CEC, CCE, AAC started his career in foodservice at an early age, enrolled in the Culinary Institute of America and graduated in 1985. He is the award-winning author of *Leadership Lessons From A Chef: Finding Time To Be Great* and *Tasting Success: Your Guide to Becoming a Professional Chef.* Chef Carroll is currently the executive chef of River Oaks Country Club in Houston Texas. River Oaks Country Club enjoys the reputation of being rated the number four country club in the United States. The Club has 1500 members and 61 culinary team members.[8] He also serves as global president of the World Association of Chefs Societies (WACS) World Association of Chef's Societiesan organization founded by Chef Auguste Escoffier in the early 20th century (Escoffier was its first president). WACS membership includes over 100 countries and more than 10,000,000 chefs. Few chefs have achieved the success that Chef Charles Carroll has. From humble beginnings he has developed into one of the most influential culinary professionals in the world.

CHEF MICHAEL VOLTAGGIO

Chef Michael Voltaggio is the owner and chef at Ink Restaurant in West Hollywood, CA. He began working in the kitchen at 15 years of age. Unlike many chefs, Voltaggio chose to pursue development of his culinary skills and knowledge by enrolling in a formal culinary apprenticeship program. He completed his formal culinary apprenticeship at the ACFEF-approved Greenbrier Hotel in West Virginia. Upon completion of the program, he was immediately hired to work at the Ritz Carlton in Naples, Florida where he first immersed himself, under the tutelage of Chef Arnaud Berthelier, in what were then considered unconventional techniques. After the Ritz, Voltaggio would go on to successfully helm the kitchens for a number of esteemed chefs and restaurants, including Charlie Palmer's Dry Creek Kitchen in Healdsburg, CA where he earned a Michelin star and The Bazaar by José Andrés in Beverly Hills where he was rewarded with a 4-star review.[9] Chef Voltaggio is also known for his appearances on *Top Chef* in the U.S. and in Canada—having won in the sixth season. In 2011, Chef Voltaggio opened Ink, his own restaurant

in West Hollywood, CA. He is a role model for where a formal culinary apprenticeship can take a graduate professionally.

CHEF BARBARA LYNCH: AN INSPIRED CHEF AND RESTAURATEUR

Chef Barbara Lynch's personal story is one of the most inspirational of any chef today. She is regarded as one of Boston's—and the country's—leading chefs and restaurateurs. Chef Lynch did not attend culinary school or complete a formal apprenticeship; her career path began with independent on-the-job training (what she jokingly calls the "school of hard knocks"). While growing up in South Boston, Barbara, at the age of 13, got her first kitchen job cooking at a local rectory. It was in high school, however, that an influential home economics teacher and a job working with Chef Mario Bonello at Boston's esteemed St. Botolph Club piqued her interest in one day becoming a professional chef. During her early twenties, Barbara worked under some of Boston's greatest culinary talents. After working with Todd English for several years at Michaela's and Olives, Barbara traveled to Italy where she learned about the country's cuisine firsthand from local women. Though Chef Lynch did not attend culinary school she did focus her efforts on developing the skills, knowledge, and attitude to be successful in her chosen profession. She also was strategic in selecting the people she worked with early in her career and exhibited the strength and fortitude to endure the long hours and harsh environment of the culinary profession while her career was advancing. Today she is an inspiration for thousands of cooks and chefs around the world. Her Boston based restaurants—which include No. 9 Park, B&G Oysters, The Butcher Shop, Stir, Drink, Sportello, 9 at Home, and Menton—cover the full range of restaurant types from casual to fine dining. Menton, her flagship fine dining restaurant, is regarded as one of the top restaurants in the Northeast. The foodservice industry provides opportunity to all who commit to developing the skills, knowledge, and attitude required to be successful.

SUMMARY

The culinary profession is a wonderful and rapidly growing part of the hospitality industry. In the coming years thousands of new culinary-based supervisory positions will be created and demand for culinary managers will continue to grow. Individuals seeking to enter the profession have multiple career opportunities across the culinary brigade including positions that start at entry level and progress to highly advanced. The pathway to a culinary career can be formal such as at a culinary school, a hybrid though an apprenticeship program, or less formal through independent on-the-job training. There's a position and approach to professional development to meet any career path or preference. Multiple examples of chefs who have succeeded via each of these three pathways can be found in industry. This is one of the best times ever to join the culinary profession.

ENDNOTES

1. http://www.bls.gov/ooh/food-preparation-and-serving/chefs-and-head-cooks.htm#tab-6

2. http://www.bls.gov/ooh/food-preparation-and-serving/chefs-and-head-cooks.htm#tab-6

3. https://www.restaurant.org/Downloads/PDFs/News-Research/research/Factbook2015_LetterSize-FINAL.pdf

4. https://www.restaurant.org/Downloads/PDFs/News-Research/research/Factbook2015_LetterSize-FINAL.pdf

5. http://www.bls.gov/ooh/food-preparation-and-serving/chefs-and-head-cooks.htm#tab-2

6. https://en.wikipedia.org/wiki/Auguste_Escoffier

7. https://nces.ed.gov/ipeds/cipcode/cipdetail.aspx?y=55&cip=12.05

8. http://chefcharlescarroll.com/chefs-bio/

9. https://en.wikipedia.org/wiki/Michael_Voltaggio

REFERENCES

Bureau of Labor Statistics, U.S. Department of Labor, *Occupational Outlook Handbook, 2016–17 Edition*, Cooks, on the Internet at http://www.bls.gov/ooh/food-preparation-and-serving/cooks.htm (visited *December 30, 2015*).

Carroll, C.M. (2011). *Tasting Success: Your Guide to Becoming a Professional Chef*. Hoboken, NJ: John Wiley & Sons.

Cullen, N. (2000). *The World of Culinary Supervision, Training & Management*. Upper Saddle River, NJ: Prentice Hall

MacLauchlan, A. (1999). *The Making of a Pastry Chef*. New York: John Wiley & Sons.

McVetty, P. (Ed.). (2015). *Culinary Fundamentals*. Providence, RI: Johnson & Wales University

Dornenburg, A., Page, K. (2002). *Becoming a Chef*. Hoboken, NJ: John Wiley & Sons.

Draz, J., Koetke, C. (2010). *The Culinary Professional*. Tinley Park: IL: Goodheart-Willcox

National Restaurant Association. (2015). 2015 Restaurant Industry Fact Book. Retrieved December 1, 2015 from https://www.restaurant.org/Downloads/PDFs/News-Research/research/Factbook2015_LetterSize-FINAL.pdf

Summary Report for Head Chef's and Cooks (n.d.). In O*Net OnLine. Retrieved December 30, 2015, from http://www.onetonline.org/link/summary/35-1011.00

Name: _____ Date: _____

1. At what percent will Chef and Head Cook positions grow in the U.S. through 2025?

2. What is the title assigned to the position just below Executive Chef in a typical working kitchen? What role does this position perform?

3. What is the difference between a Chef de Partie and a Sous Chef? Which of the two ranks higher in a kitchen?

4. List and describe three of the six things great chefs do.

5. What does the term mise en place mean? Why is it so important to food production?

6. List and describe three of the five duties of a typical line cook.

7. Who was Auguste Escoffier? Why was he important?

8. What national organization is responsible for administering culinary apprenticeships in the United States?

9. List and describe the three potential pathways to career success in the culinary arts.

10. List the names of each of the three 30-hour courses required by the American Culinary Federation. Why do you think these three courses are important to certification?

11. List and describe the three types of culinary schools.

12. When do cooks typically work?

© JeniFoto/Shutterstock.com

CHAPTER *24*

BEVERAGE INDUSTRY

AUTHOR

LEARNING OBJECTIVES

Christian E. Hardigree, J.D. Kennesaw State University

- Become familiar with the overall beverage industry and the economic impact of the industry.
- Describe the different segments within the beverage industry.
- Discuss the different products available under the two main segment classifications.
- Explain the two-tier and three-tier systems used in alcohol distribution.
- Define and give examples of beverage tourism.
- Identify and evaluate upcoming trends in the beverage industry.
- Identify career pathways in the beverage industry.

CHAPTER OUTLINE

Introduction: What is the Beverage Industry?

What are the Segments and Subsectors of the Beverage Industry?

    The Nonalcoholic Segment

    The Alcoholic Segment

What are the Important Trends in the Beverage Industry?

    Sustainability

Career Opportunities for the Future in the Beverage Industry

Summary

KEY TERMS

Alcoholic beverage	Malt beverage
Beer	Nonalcoholic beverage
Beverage industry	Sparkling water
Carbonated beverages	Still water
Craft brewer	Wine
Distilled spirits	

Americans drink an average of 3 cups of coffee each day.

INTRODUCTION: WHAT IS THE BEVERAGE INDUSTRY?

The **beverage industry** is a global industry made up of companies that manufacture, sell, and/or distribute a variety of beverages—alcoholic and nonalcoholic. It is often difficult for students to appreciate the vastness of this industry because the main segments (nonalcoholic and alcoholic) seem so easy to remember. A few facts can illustrate how complex the industry can be, as well as how innovative and ever-evolving:

- One of the largest companies in the nonalcoholic segment, Coca-Cola®, offers over 3,600 beverages around the world. In 2014, Coca-Cola® introduced over 400 new beverage options, over 100 of which were reduced-, low-, or no-calorie options.

- Americans consume 3.6 billion gallons of tea annually, and supermarket sales of tea top $2 billion according to the Tea Association of the USA. Ready-to-drink tea sales are estimated to exceed $5.2 billion annually.

- The U.S. spends $40 billion annually on coffee, with Americans drinking an average of 3.1 cups per day with a cup size of 9 ounces. In 2013, Americans paid an average of $2.98 per coffee drink, in 2015 that increased to $3.28.

- The U.S. alcohol beverage industry generates over $400 billion in U.S. economic activity, approximately a third of which is from distilled spirits.

As these facts illustrate, the beverage industry is dynamic and evolving, and a critical element to the hospitality sector. Some of the greatest margins (profits) for a restaurant or hotel come from the beverage sales, either accompanying a meal or sold in the bar. Markup on bottles of wine may be 300–400% over what they would sell for at retail. The sale or service of beverages is not limited to restaurants or hotels; in fact, we serve and/or sell beverages in all other industry sectors—hospitals, cruise ships, golf courses, amusement parks, assisted care facilities, airlines, and virtually every workplace. We also purchase beverages for service at home. As such, the beverage industry's reach is beyond merely the industry, continuing into an individual's personal life, making the beverage industry one with significant impact.

WHAT ARE THE SEGMENTS AND SUBSECTORS OF THE BEVERAGE INDUSTRY?

There are two main segments to the beverage industry—nonalcoholic and alcoholic. While that sounds simple, each segment has a variety of subsectors that are complex and diverse. For example, the nonalcoholic segment includes sparkling (**carbonated**), fruit juices, energy drinks, coffees, teas, milk and milk products, and waters. The alcoholic segment includes spirits, beers, and wines.

THE NONALCOHOLIC SEGMENT

The **nonalcoholic beverage** segment—sometimes referred to as liquid refreshment beverages—accounted for approximately $1.07 trillion U.S. dollars in worldwide sales in 2014. This illustrates an increase of almost $80 billion US dollars since 2012 (See Figure 24.1).

Coca-Cola and Pepsi have long been two giants in the nonalcoholic beverage industry, with Coca-Cola commanding approximately 42.3% of the market, and Pepsi with 27.5%. However, both companies have struggled with an evolving consumer—one who is increasingly concerned about the health benefits of their beverages, and whose taste is evolving to prefer different flavor profiles. Sales of carbonated soft drinks have dropped consistently for the past 10

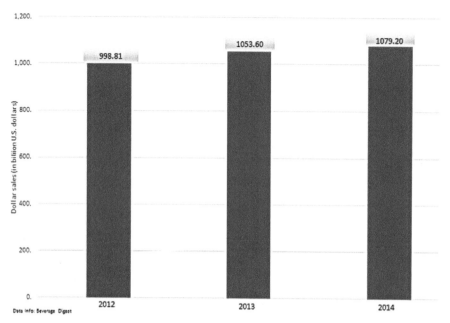

FIGURE 24.1 Dollar sales of nonalcoholic beverages worldwide from 2012-2014 (in billion U.S. $)

years, losing approximately 1.4 billion cases in volume since 2004. As global companies struggle with the brands that were more popular many years ago, they also have to expand their portfolios to offer new products to match consumer needs. Much of the expansion has been in the other subsectors of the nonalcoholic segment—particularly juices, energy drinks, coffee, tea, and **water (sparkling and still)**.

Coca-Cola and Pepsi have long been two giants in the nonalcoholic beverage industry, with Coca-Cola commanding approximately 42.3% of the market, and Pepsi with 27.5%. However, both companies have struggled with an evolving consumer—one

Coca-Cola and Pepsi have been two giants in the nonalcoholic beverage industry for years.

who is increasingly concerned about the health benefits of their beverages, and whose taste is evolving to prefer different flavor profiles. Sales of carbonated soft drinks have dropped consistently for the past 10 years, losing approximately 1.4 billion cases in volume since 2004. As global companies struggle with the brands that were more popular many years ago, they also have to expand their portfolios to offer new products to match consumer needs. Much of the expansion has been in the other subsectors of the nonalcoholic segment—particularly juices, energy drinks, coffee, tea, and **water (sparkling and still)**.

To illustrate the complexity of each subsector, we can look at one example: water. The water subsector may sound simple enough—after all, it's just water, right? In 2014, approximately 10.9 billion gallons of water were packaged/sold as bottled water, totaling over $13 billion, with sales expected to make it the number one packaged drink by 2016. In 2014, Coca-Cola® alone had over 30 *different* water brands in its portfolio. Despite a robust number of options, Coca-Cola® does not have a stronghold in this subsector of the market—they are not one of the "giants" of water, despite having over 40% of the entire nonalcoholic beverage market. The U.S. sparkling water segment posted a 26% increase in 2015, with sales of just over $682 million. LaCroix, Perrier, and San Pellegrino (the latter two owned by Nestle) compose 57% of the market in sparkling sales, with Coca-Cola's Dasani sparkling only holding 6% of the market share. As consumer tastes and expectations change, so will the leaders in the subsectors of the nonalcoholic market.

As these facts demonstrate, the nonalcoholic segment is robust and complex, and comprises a significant portion of the beverage industry. Entire units of corporations, comprising hundreds of individuals, are dedicated to the different subsectors within this market, which means there are a variety of career opportunities for the future.

THE ALCOHOLIC SEGMENT

The total **alcoholic beverage** sales in the U.S. in 2014 exceeded $211 billion, with worldwide sales exceeding $1 trillion. The alcohol segment is composed of three subsectors: beer (malts), wine, and spirits. In the U.S., alcohol is closely regulated for taxation and distribution purposes at a variety of government levels. Largely, alcohol distribution and sales are determined at the state level, where the federal government oversees many of the definitional decisions of which classifications different beverages fall under based upon their qualities (ingredients, alcohol content, etc.), which also impacts labeling requirements. The rules and regulations of alcoholic beverages can become quite complex, and for the purposes of this chapter, have been discussed in only a general sense.

DISTILLED SPIRITS

Basically, **distilled spirits** are alcohol products that are first fermented, then distilled. The distillation process increases the concentration of ethyl alcohol above the original fermentation mixture. The product may subsequently be bottled, or blended and then bottled, to create a finished product. The details of the final product—the percent of alcohol by volume, the ingredients, and/or the flavor profile, are matched to classifications identified by the government for the purposes of taxation.

Market share growth in the spirits subsector has grown from 29% in 2000 to over 35% in 2014, and is predicted to continue to grow over the next 10 years. In 2014, retail sales of distilled spirits in the U.S. market was almost $70 billion, generating over $20 billion in tax revenue for all levels of government. The popularity of U.S. spirits has also impacted the export industry, with other countries seeking to purchase U.S.-produced distilled spirits. Since 2000, export of distilled spirits has increased from approximately $500 million to over $1.56 billion in 2014, with bourbon and Tennessee whiskey comprising over 65% of the total distilled spirit exports.

BEER (MALTS)

Basically, **beer** is an alcoholic beverage made from brewing and fermenting cereal grain, usually malted barley, and flavoring with hops, and sometimes other ingredients. Some brewers will substitute malted barley for rice or corn, which impacts the legal definition of the final product being a "beer" versus a **"malted beverage."** The recipe used for brewing the beverage can impact the classification provided to it by the government.

In 2014, the overall beer market accounted for approximately $101.5 billion in sales, with the craft beer subsector responsible for $19.6 billion, representing a 22% dollar sales growth from the previous year.

A **craft brewer** is defined as someone whose annual production is 6 million barrels or less. Craft brewers account for about 3% of U.S. annual sales, providing more than 424,000 jobs. Craft brewers are responsible for the most innovation in the beer industry, with new recipes and flavors, small batch brewing, and more regional influence. As a result, new segments of industry have appeared in the past few years,

Beer is made from brewing and fermenting cereal grain, malted barley, and flavoring with hops.

Different types of grapes are pressed and fermented to make different types of wine.

including microbreweries, brewpubs, and contract brewing companies.

WINE

Wine is an alcoholic beverage made from fermented juice from various fresh grapes, usually containing 10%–15% alcohol by volume. Different types (varietals) of grapes are pressed and fermented in order to make different types of wine (like Chardonnay or Cabernet Sauvignon), and can be blended to create other wine profiles. The United States is responsible for approximately 13% of the world consumption of wine, with France (11%), Italy (8%), and Germany (8%) the next highest consumers. It should

be noted that those three countries are significantly smaller than the U.S., and thus their consumption per capita (per person) is higher. In recent years, China has become a major consumer of wines at 6%. In the U.S., an estimated $37.6 billion in retail sales occurred in 2014, representing 22 consecutive years of volume growth. California produces 90% of all U.S. wine, with states like Washington, New York, Oregon, Texas, and Georgia making great strides in their productions.

WHAT ARE THE IMPORTANT TRENDS IN THE BEVERAGE INDUSTRY?

SUSTAINABILITY

Sustainability is no longer a buzz phrase or an add-on. Instead, it represents beverage manufacturers' and suppliers' need to find a responsible approach for sourcing materials in light of climate change and shrinking resources. As more consumers are concerned about the origins of their foods and beverages, as well as the environmental soundness of the production process, more producers seek to insure the credibility of their raw materials in the supply stream. For the beverage industry, this means sustainable sourcing of sugars (sugar beets, sugarcane),

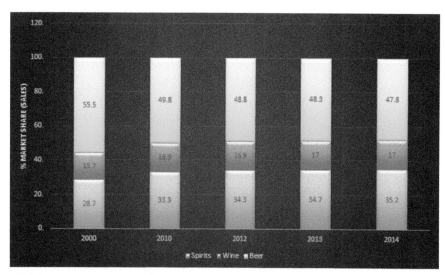

FIGURE 24.2 U.S. alcohol industry by beverage 2000–2014 (market share).

fruits, dairy, coffee beans, and more, as well as sustainable sourcing of the packaging materials.

To demonstrate concerns of sustainable sourcing, consider tea. Consumption of tea, particularly in the U.S., has increased significantly over the past 20 years, with over 80 billion servings (3.6 billion gallons) being served in 2014, to the tune of $10.8 billion dollars in estimated sales. According to the Tea Association of the USA, approximately 87% of Millennials drink tea. With climate change impacting rainfall and temperature, the cultivation of tea in China has been impacted as those factors alter the aroma and taste of the tea, as well as the potential health benefits. For the tea market to continue to grow, growers must ensure the sustainability of the growing regions.

Other sustainability concerns that will impact the industry in the upcoming 10 years include:

- Sustainable packaging, particularly recycled plastics and plant based fibers;
- Water stewardship and watershed management;
- Energy efficiency, particularly in supply chain, manufacturing, and distribution;
- Low emission trucks for distribution of beverages; and
- Concentrated beverages where the water is added at the sales point, not in the distribution cycle.

CAREER OPPORTUNITIES FOR THE FUTURE IN THE BEVERAGE INDUSTRY

The beverage industry has career opportunities in a variety of different segments, and a multitude of subsectors. Career opportunities range from working in manufacturing to designing recipes, blending wine, and marketing and sales, and from importing/exporting to recruiting and human resources. Taken as a whole, the integrated industry has opportunities for students with a variety of interests.

SUMMARY

This chapter is merely a glimpse into the dynamic and exciting beverage industry. For a student in the hospitality, foodservice, restaurant, or other related field, there are exciting opportunities for internships and work experience in the beverage industry, as well as a cadre of permanent career pathways within the different segments. Because beverages play such an important role in the profitability of a restaurant, hotel, or other facility, it is essential that a foodservice or hospitality professional understand the basics of the industry—from production to distribution to sales. As the industry moves forward, finding new beverages and new flavor profiles will continue to be a focus of the nonalcoholic beverage industry. Sustainability will also continue to be a central focus, particularly as it relates to the economic advantage that saving water and energy provides to a business.

REFERENCES

Alcohol and Tobacco Tax and Trade Bureau at http://ttb.gov/ and Classifications of Distilled Spirits at http://www.ttb.gov/spirits/bam/chapter4.pdf

Brewers Association at https://www.brewersassociation.org/statistics/economic-impact-data/

Coca Cola 2014-15 Sustainability Report at http://www.coca-colacompany.com/content/dam/journey/us/en/private/fileassets/pdf/2015/09/2014-2015-sustainability-report.pdf

International Bottled Water Association http://www.bottledwater.org/economics/bottled-water-market

Tea Association of the USA http://www.teausa.com/14655/tea-fact-sheet

Wine Institute at http://www.wineinstitute.org/resources/statistics

REVIEW QUESTIONS

1. What are the two main segments in the beverage industry?

2. Give an example of beverage subsectors under each of the two main segments.

3. Explain some of the reasons that companies are changing their beverage portfolios, and why new beverages are being introduced into the market.

4. Why are companies seeking to ensure sustainability for their ingredients and packaging?

5. One of the growing trends in the beverage industry relates to transportation costs—moving the beverages from the point of manufacturing to the point of sale. Explain some ways a company could save money in their transportation costs.

6. Compare wine, beer (malts), and spirits in terms of market share. Predict what you might see in this area in the next 10 years, and explain what your prediction is based upon.

© f11photo/Shutterstock.com

CHAPTER *25*

BAR AND BEVERAGE OPERATIONS

AUTHORS

Kirsten Tripodi, Fairleigh Dickenson University

LEARNING OBJECTIVES

- Define terms used in bar and beverage operations.
- Demonstrate familiarity with career opportunities in bar and beverage operations management.
- Understand and be able to articulate the importance of responsibility regarding the sale of alcoholic beverages.
- Appreciate the profitability and cost factors involved in beverage sales.
- Understand trends in beverage management.

CHAPTER OUTLINE

Introduction
Trends
    Quality Ingredients
    Marketing and Location Selection
Products
Glamour
Harsh Realities
    Alcohol is a Drug
    Legal Responsibilities
    Managing a Cash Business
    Theft
    Licensing

CHAPTER OUTLINE
(Continued)

Career Opportunities
    During School
    After Graduation
Profitability
    Cost Control
    Pricing Trends
Summary

KEY TERMS

BYO	Liability insurance
Core competencies	Mini bar
Corkage	"On the floor"
Cost control	POS terminal
Common law	Profitability
Dram shop legislation	Shot
Draught beer	Social responsibility
Duty of care	Sommelier
In-house training	Spirits
Inventory reconciliation	

INTRODUCTION

Political bars? Believe it or not, most political movements were born in bars. Taverns and pubs in Europe were gathering and meeting places from the times of the Middle Ages. This activity was not lost on the long trip to the New World. The first inns in Europe were gathering places for the locals and sometimes for a traveler or two; these taverns were arguably the first hospitality establishments. Today's bar and beverage operations are still places where people meet, but like other hospitality operations this part of the industry has developed many niches offering distinct entertainment and consumption opportunities for the general public.

Bar and beverage management is considered by many to be the most interesting, challenging, and profitable area of hospitality management. Many types of hospitality operations have a bar or beverage operation as part of their service offerings to their guests or members. For the hospitality student, exciting opportunities are available in the form of internships, work experiences during school, and permanent management positions upon graduation. Due to the substantial profit margin for the sale of alcoholic beverages, beverage operations are often very lucrative. Many food and beverage operations rely on beverage to increase profits and attract guests. Beverage knowledge is an essential tool for many careers in hospitality, such as banquet manager, restaurant manager, and room service manager, and in as diverse operations as private clubs, corporate food service, airlines, stadium food service, hotels, casinos, and cruise lines.

TRENDS

Today there are all kinds of beverage operations where guests and members can enjoy themselves. Trends in these operations in many ways mirror the trends in the hospitality industry overall. Healthy and more sustainable options are increasingly demanded by the public. In general, the trends we see in food and culinary operations are similar to those in bar and beverage operations. Fine ingredients, interesting combinations of flavors and textures, farm to table (farm to glass), and even molecular gastronomy are on the menu for the bar business. Interesting locations, especially the unexpected, have become all the rage in major cities (think rooftops and secret locations).

QUALITY INGREDIENTS

The craft cocktail movement is the beverage reaction to the culinary trends of molecular gastronomy. Craft bartenders use interesting ingredients in ways similar to the culinary gastronomists—smoke, foams and unique combinations of textures, temperatures, and flavors (Harrison, 2015). Talented and creative professionals have become cult figures and these talents are recognized by their peers at events and competitions ("Tales of the Cocktail's 2015 spirited awards winners," n.d.). More importantly, these talented professionals draw a lot of patrons into their establishments, which makes their operations very successful. These operations are successful in major markets (Simonson, 2015; Harrison, 2015), and are also gaining momentum in less expected places (Dowling, 2014).

One important trend in hospitality is increased choices. Spirits, wine, and even beer producers are creating and selling products for every taste (Allan, 2015); it seems impossible to keep up with all of the options. The beer business offers similar choices based on quality ingredients and boutique breweries, often with on-premise operations (Dunn & Wickham, 2015).

Keeping up with all of these innovations can be daunting. A savvy bar and beverage manager will keep up by attending events and trade shows. One of the most interesting new trends at these events is the focus on ice (all shapes for distinct purposes).

MARKETING AND LOCATION SELECTION

Location, location, location!! One of the first things a new hospitality student learns about is the genius of E.M. Statler and his mantra for site selection. For decades this has proven to be the most important consideration when deciding where to build and open a hospitality business. Interestingly, of late the bar and beverage business has opened establishments in new and even counterintuitive locations.

Rooftop bars have become very popular in beautiful cities where the view of the city is part of the

Rooftop bars have become very popular in beautiful cities.

Due to the substantial profit margin for the sale of alcoholic beverages, beverage operations are often very lucrative.

entertainment (Terrero, 2013). In general, locations are selected so that the public can easily locate and access them. We want to make it very simple for people to spend their money in our establishment. Clear signage and easy access are indicators of a great location. A counterintuitive location strategy is the secret bar—no signage, you have to know someone to get in—surprisingly, these bars are gaining in popularity (Harrison, 2015; Tirola, 2013).

PRODUCTS

Many different products are sold in beverage operations. As with sales positions in any other industry, the most knowledgeable sales persons can offer the best information and service to their guests (Grossman & Lembeck, 1983; Dias-Blue, 2004). Product knowledge separates great operations and salespeople from all others and, again, the bar and beverage business is no exception to this rule. In addition to alcoholic beverage bars, juice bars (raw foods), and coffee and tea bars are increasing in popularity.

GLAMOUR

Bar and beverage operations are connected to entertainment in many ways. Indeed, the act of going to a bar is a form of social entertainment. Many bars offer entertainment that may be as simple as darts, or as complicated as full-blown live entertainment productions of world famous artists. The bar business has a glamorous side that can be enticing. Working at night in a fast-paced part of the industry that caters to (and often hires) beautiful people who have

disposable income can be very exciting. Often, a lot of cash is changing hands and, for tipped employees, there is certainly a great deal of money to be made. Contact with entertainers and interesting promotional possibilities are perks. Due to the unique nature of alcoholic beverages, the legal implications and the control issues involved in their sale make this area of hospitality particularly challenging. Success, given these challenges, is a sign to future employers that you have exhibited all of the skills of a great hospitality manager in a fast-paced and competitive environment; that is to say, it is a great proving ground.

Like other segments of the hospitality industry, many students and the public are familiar with bar and beverage operations as guests. We see the entertainment and fun to which guests are exposed. Bar and beverage managers, like most other hospitality managers, are often too busy to enjoy the environment at work that they might otherwise enjoy as a guest.

HARSH REALITIES

ALCOHOL IS A DRUG

Many bar and beverage operations depend on the sale of alcoholic beverages. Alcohol is a legalized drug which can very much alter a person's perception of reality. Alcohol can be addictive and certain ingredients in some alcoholic beverages have hallucinogenic properties (absinthe, gin, and tequila). As a host in your home, you would never put a guest into a situation in which they might hurt themselves or someone else. This responsibility is the same for the guest/host relationship in a hospitality business situation. Serving alcohol changes that relationship and enhances the level of responsibility. As business owners and managers, we have a **social responsibility** not only to our guests but also to society at large regarding the serving of alcohol.

LEGAL RESPONSIBILITIES

In addition to social responsibility and the guest/host relationship, there are legal requirements regarding alcohol service. Hospitality businesses in the United States are subject to a **duty of care** for guests and the public, which has evolved under the **common law** from the inns of England in the Middle Ages (Barth, Hayes & Ninemeier, 2007; Jeffries, 2010). **Dram shop legislation** refers to the legal burden on the provider of the alcoholic beverage. Alcohol is a drug and it is considered to be so reality-altering that inebriated persons are not held responsible for their own actions. The actions of an intoxicated person are the legal responsibility of the provider of those beverages with regard to injury to persons or property. In the instance of an injury that results from the actions of an intoxicated person, the server of the alcoholic beverages can be held responsible. The cocktail server, bartender, manager, owner of the establishment, and even the owner of the building will often be named in the suit.

Most companies take this responsibility very seriously, and they should. In addition to **in-house training**, many have opted for additional training by experts in responsible alcohol service. The TIPS program (http://www.tipsalcohol.com/) and ServSafe for Alcohol are the most recognized (http://www.servsafe.com/alcohol/training-and-certification).

In general, these programs include certification for employees who have passed an exam of some sort. Using a recognized program, like the ones mentioned, can mean substantial savings in terms of **liability insurance**, as the insurer recognizes that the business has taken steps to train employees to be aware of the consequences and legal ramifications of irresponsible alcohol service.

MANAGING A CASH BUSINESS

A business that involves cash is full of opportunities for employees to make costly mistakes, or to be less than honest. Checks and balances must always be in place, and managers must be aware and proactive whenever possible. There are techniques for controlling costs, which range from computer regulated shots that cannot be activated unless a sale is rung into an interfaced **POS (point of sale) terminal** to subjecting the proper use of measured portions (**shot glasses** or **measured pourers**) to management vigilance. From a marketing standpoint, guests in certain types of establishments may be averse to some of the more mechanized controls.

Secret shopper services are sometimes utilized to uncover or validate instances of inappropriate cash handling. These third parties write reports that can be used to modify employee behaviors that are damaging the profitability of the business (http://www.coylehospitality.com/mystery-shopping-services/restaurant-consulting/).

Technology offers many solutions to the problems presented in a cash business. The newest technologies include a DVR-based application that allows managers to view actual marked transactions that have been recorded on cameras in the bar (http://www.ezuniverse.com/).

THEFT

Regular **inventory reconciliation** is a commonly used technique for controlling costs. The drawback of using this method is that it is reactive rather than proactive, which is to say that it can only detect a problem after it has occurred. Security systems and surveillance equipment can also be used to reduce theft via pilferage or over pouring. It is important that these systems work together, and work well in combination with the management team's vigilance. There can be no substitute for awareness and constant training of all members of the staff. Theft is inviting because of the nature of the inventory. Who wouldn't want a nice bottle of champagne in their refrigerator for a special occasion, especially a bottle that did not cost anything? The unauthorized

© Kondor83/Shutterstock.com

A beverage business can lose profits due to bartenders pouring too much liquor in a drink.

taking of inventory constitutes theft. This is referred to as pilferage if the item is stolen for consumption by an employee (for instance, a bartender enjoying an energy drink meant for guests only). Managers must also be aware that there are more ways for employees to steal. Over pouring (using more than the recipe amount of the alcohol for a beverage) constitutes a loss for the business and is also considered to be theft. Tipped employees can be encouraged to add more to a beverage in return for a bigger gratuity. Left unchecked, tipped employees can even give drinks away.

A competent manager will also be aware that employees who are completely honest can cost a business profit through sloppiness (waste) and poor training (poor knowledge of recipes and standards). Again, training and vigilance are vital to the success of a bar and beverage operation.

LICENSING

In the United States, alcohol sales are regulated by individual states, which often allow municipalities to issue licenses and determine laws so long as those laws are compatible with any existing state regulations. In most states, background checks are completed regarding those applying for such a license to determine that those persons are of acceptable character (Egerton-Thomas, 1994). The number and locations of licenses are often stipulated per municipality. In many municipalities there is a certain distance that any establishment must be from churches and schools. Quite often, liquor licenses are very expensive and can be revoked for a number of violations. Once revoked, the license sometimes

cannot be replaced and the business will suffer. Serving minors or already intoxicated persons is often cause for suspension or revocation of the licensed privileges, but paying your bills late or failing to keep adequate records regarding sales and purchases of alcoholic beverages can also result in revocation. The rights and privileges associated with holding a license must be protected at all times by the owners, managers, and staff of an establishment serving alcoholic beverages.

Opportunities to **BYO** (bring your own) beverages do exist in many venues. **Corkage fees** can be charged by an operation that holds a license to sell alcoholic beverages, should a guest prefer to bring their own selection of beverage into the establishment. Of course in a BYO situation, the legal responsibilities vary from municipality to municipality.

Licensing regulations and requirements may vary from state to state in the United States; therefore the prudent beverage manager will always have a copy of those regulations on premise for reference and will be familiar with them.

CAREER OPPORTUNITIES

From attractions management to travel and tour operations, every chapter in this book is connected to bar and beverage operations in some way. Attractions such as Disney World and beach destination resorts quite often offer alcoholic, or some type of nonalcoholic, beverage service for their guests. Full-service hotels have lounges, restaurants, banquet and meeting facilities, room service, and mini bar operations. Restaurants and private clubs also have available alcoholic beverages for their guests, as do some non-commercial food service operations. Corporate dining rooms and catering operations usually include beverage service as do the vendors in airports and stadiums. It is hard to imagine a successful casino or cruise line that is not able to provide alcoholic beverages. Various methods of transportation from airlines to trains and even charter buses and limousines often offer alcoholic beverages.

DURING SCHOOL

For many students and indeed for many hospitality students, bar and beverage operations are a great way to earn money while you're still in school. Work

Baristas work in coffee or juice bars, which have grown in popularity recently.

schedules can often be made flexible to accommodate class schedules and gratuities can help to defray the cost of tuition, or add to spending money. Bar backs, bartenders, mini bar attendants, and cocktail servers as well as baristas are the entry-level line positions usually available. These positions require some knowledge about serving different types of beverages. Bartenders and bar backs are usually found behind a "front bar" in view of guests and which often has seating for guests. There are also service bars where only employees of the establishment can order drinks for the guests in the restaurant, lounge, or room service. Bartenders mix the drinks and are sometimes referred to as mixologists. Bar backs support the bartenders by leaving the bar to restock supplies; this way the bartenders can always be available to guests. Cocktail servers are out **"on the floor"** in a lounge environment; they order drinks from the bartender for their guests at the table. **Mini bar** attendants restock the in-room refrigerators, which have beverages and snacks in higher end hotels. These attendants are responsible to report the guest usage so that the guest can be properly charged. Baristas are found in a coffee bar or juice bar. Both types of nonalcoholic beverages have grown in popularity and availability in the past ten years. Companies such as Starbucks (http://www.starbucks.com/) and Jamba Juice (http://www.jambajuice.com/) lead these parts of the industry.

Customer service skills honed in this type of establishment in conjunction with the knowledge of the beverages served are useful skills to fall back on for the rest of your life. Particularly for hospitality students, this is a challenging beginning to a rewarding career.

AFTER GRADUATION

Entry-level supervisory positions in the area of beverage management can be found in virtually all of the types of operations in hospitality. In a large hotel or casino, there might be several layers of management after that initial position. In smaller operations a beverage career can successfully morph into a food and beverage career for a more mature, full-service manager, who will have more comprehensive management responsibilities. High-end wines are usually sold in full-service restaurants that employ wine consultants (**sommeliers**) who are experts. These sommeliers work for the establishment, ordering the wine and managing the wine list, and are tipped for their advice to the guests in addition to being salaried employees. Sommeliers are highly specialized employees who usually hold a credential which identifies them as experts. (http://www.mastersommeliers.org/)

Beverage management is a long-term career for a select few. The demands of the usually late night hours are more conducive to younger, single managers.

There are several **core competencies** that are critical for success in beverage management. Cleanliness, friendliness, awareness of potential problems, and knowledge of products and services are all important. Having a great eye for detail and great interpersonal communication skills are a must in this part of the industry as they are in all other segments of hospitality.

PROFITABILITY

COST CONTROL

"A beverage list (covering beer, wine, and distilled spirits) must be given the same careful thought and attention to detail and market trends that is involved in the planning of a food menu." (Lipinski and Lipinski, 1996, p. 288) Balancing the size of the inventory with the needs of the guests can be a difficult task. Increasing inventory (either levels or variety) means that more of the operation's funds are tied up in the storeroom and not immediately earning money. This is referred to as the inventory carrying cost or inventory turnover. Preventing loss and theft requires constant vigilance, control systems, and proper pricing techniques.

Tap beer has a very low cost compared to its selling price.

Katsigris and Porter in their book, *Pouring for Profit*, identify several necessary steps to controlling costs and maximizing profit in beverage management. Budgeting for profit, pricing for profit, establishing product controls, and establishing cash controls are all vital parts of the control process which require an in-depth understanding of the operation at hand, the market, the product, and security (1983, pp. 305–331).

PRICING TRENDS

"The well-known fact that the price of two martinis in the average bar will buy a whole bottle of gin or vodka at the liquor store, if you wish to drink at home, is indicative of what the bar business is all about" (Egerton-Thomas, 1994, p. 7). The price of a drink is determined by the cost of the drink. This means that the recipe for the drink and the cost of each individual ingredient must be considered. Mixers, such as juices and sodas, cost significantly less than does alcohol, so the cost of the bottle divided by the portion of the bottle used will determine the bulk of the cost for most drinks. The price is then based on the profit margin that a facility requires to cover its overhead costs in combination with the profit that the owners desire. This must also be balanced with the demands of the market.

Beer, particularly **draught (on tap) beer**, can cost less than $.25 for a 16 oz. portion (pint), and sell for $1.50–$5.00 depending on the establishment. Wine is often marked up 2 ½ times at the low end (house brands) to ½ times for a high-end wine. Recently there has been a trend towards limiting the markup for wines to a more acceptable level given that the public is more aware of the pricing of wines at retail than ever before.

SUMMARY

This chapter is just a brief overview of bar and beverage operations management. Many hospitality programs offer one or more courses in this exciting area of the hospitality industry. It is hoped that this introduction will inspire you to learn more, both while you are a student and afterward.

Bar and beverage operations management is an exciting and sometimes glamorous area to specialize in while working in the hospitality industry. Due to the nature of the products (often alcohol), managing this type of hospitality operation can be more challenging than others in many ways. Management positions for those knowledgeable in beverage management are available in virtually every type of hospitality operation.

RESOURCES

Internet Sites

Responsible Alcohol Training Sites

ServSafe Alcohol offered by the Educational Foundation of the National Restaurant Foundation http://www.nraef.org/servsafe/alcohol/book/

TIPS (Training for Intervention ProcedureS) http://www.gettips.com/index.shtml

Nonalcoholic Beverages

Jamba Juice http://jambajuice.com/

Starbucks http://www.starbucks.com/default.asp?cookie%5Ftest=1

Credentials

Master Sommelier Program https://www.master-sommeliers.org/apply;jsessionid=EC30F11F427E E2ACC42AAB6A79FFABB1

REFERENCES

Allan, T. (2015). Beer's flavor frenzy. *Market Watch*, 34(1), 76–79.

Barth, S., Hayes, D. and Ninemeier, J. (2007). *Restaurant Law Basics*. John Wiley & Sons, Inc.

Dias-Blue, A. (2004). *The Complete Book of Spirits: A guide to their history, production, and enjoyment*. Harper-Collins

Dowling, M. (2014). Bringing craft bars to smaller markets. *Cheers, 25*(7), 13.

Dunn, A., & Wickham, M. (2015). Craft brewery tourism best-practices: A research agenda. *Annals of Tourism Research, 56*, 140–142. http://doi.org/10.1016/j.annals.2015.10.009

Egerton-Thomas, C. (1994). *How to Manage a Successful Bar*, John Wiley and Sons, Inc.

Grossman, H., Revised by Harriet Lembeck. (1983). *Grossman's Guide to Wines, Beers, and Spirits, Seventh Edition, Revised*, John Wiley and Sons, Inc.

Harrison, T. (2015). I love the nightlife. *Travel Weekly Australia, 2015 Suppl*, 14–15.

Jeffries, J. (2010). *Understanding Hospitality Law. Fifth Edition*. Educational Institute of the American Hotel & Lodging Association

Katsigris, C. and Porter, M. (1983). *Pouring for Profit: A Guide to Bar and Beverage Management*. John Wiley & Sons.

Lipinski, B. and Lipinski, K. (1996). *Professional Beverage Management*, John Wiley and Sons, Inc.

Simonson, R. (2015). L.A.'s craft cocktail boom. *Saveur*, (177), 16–23.

Tales of the Cocktail's 2015 spirited awards winners . (n.d.).

Terrero, R. (2013). Rooftop bars. *Luxury Travel Advisor*, 24–26.

Tirola, D. (2013). *Hey Bartender!* U.S.A.: Showtime.

REVIEW QUESTIONS

1. Why is it important that alcohol is considered to be a drug?

2. What are some steps that a responsible company can take to ensure that alcohol is being served responsibly?

3. What are the benefits to being socially responsible regarding the service and sale of alcoholic beverages?

4. What is the most effective sales tool for beverages?

5. Given so many "harsh realities" to balance the glamour of the beverage business, why do you suppose that it remains a popular career path for hospitality graduates?

6. Why do you suppose nonalcoholic beverage establishments were included in this chapter?

7. What are some current trends that may give us a clue as to the future of this segment of the industry?

8. How can a beverage manager stay abreast of changes in the industry that can affect their business?

CHAPTER 26

© Pekka Akin/Shutterstock.com

PRIVATE CLUB OPERATIONS

AUTHORS

Denis P. Rudd, EdD, CHA, FMP, CTP, Robert Morris University
Richard J. Mills Jr., PhD, Robert Morris University

LEARNING OBJECTIVES

- Understand the components of the club management industry.
- Identify the function that private clubs play in the hospitality industry
- Explain the significance and economic impact made by clubs.
- Identify future employment opportunities in the club industry.

CHAPTER OUTLINE

Introduction
Fiscal Impact
Modern Environment
Varieties of Clubs
Club Personnel
Legal Form of Business
Management Styles
Summary

KEY TERMS

Athletic clubs	Full membership
City clubs	Golf clubs
Club	Member
CMAA	Military clubs
Country club	Professional clubs
Dining clubs	Proprietary clubs
Equity clubs	Service
Fraternal clubs	Social clubs

Social membership

Yacht clubs

University clubs

INTRODUCTION

A **club** is defined as a group of persons organized or united for social, literary, athletic, political, or other purposes. Clubs, historically, occurred in all ancient states throughout civilization. Once people started living together in larger groups, there was a need for people with common interests to be able to associate despite having no ties of kinship. While the roots of the ancient club can be traced back thousands of years to Egypt, Greece, and Rome, the beginning of the modern club surfaced in London during the 1700's with the introduction, growth, and development of the London coffee houses. These clubs were actually special rooms in taverns that operated on an invitation-only basis for their members. One of the most famous clubs of the time was the Bread Street Club. Members met at a tavern and individuals such as William Shakespeare and other literary notables of the Elizabethan time frequented these establishments. The Royal and Ancient Golf Club of St. Andrews, Scotland, founded in 1758 and said to be the birthplace of golf, is the forerunner of the modern country club. During Queen Victoria's reign, clubs were only for members of the upper class; but that changed. The notion of clubbing, mentioned as early as the 1600's in the *Diary of Samuel Pepys*, developed in England when groups who regularly met in taverns began to assume a more permanent character.

By the middle of the 19th century, the middle-class was able to join clubs. Clubs were developed for the working man, allowing them to escape from their tiring days, their wives, children, and from the gin palaces and public houses. The working men's club movement was a way to keep the middle class man sober. Many of these clubs provided amusement and refreshments as well as newspapers and books and were aimed to morally and socially improve the working man and to educate them.

In America the earliest known social club was the Fish House in Philadelphia. This club emphasized drinking and socializing, but by the mid 1700's, clubs had been established in Annapolis, Boston, Charleston, New Orleans, Philadelphia, and New York. Many of these American clubs were based on British antecedents. During the 1800's one of the most famous clubs formed was the first women's club called Sorosis. This club was for actresses, artisans, supporters of the union's causes, and those interested in the arts. In most cases these women's clubs focused on social services and promoted women who were in the business and professional fields.

Nowadays, people join clubs to engage in social discourses and to surround themselves with others who have similar interests. Growing steadily each year are the ever-increasing markets for private clubs. Catering to a multitude of clientele, clubs have existed for many millennia and include various interest groups, recreational activities, and organizations. With over 14,000 private clubs in the United States alone, clubs have created an atmosphere conducive to friendliness and comfort.

FISCAL IMPACT

The **Club Managers Association of America (CMAA)**, the premier industry professional association for 7,000 managers of approximately 3,000 membership clubs, recently released its *2014 Economic Impact Report* in conjunction with Club Benchmarking. The CMAA actively promotes and advances cooperation among individuals directly engaged in the club management profession, as well as other associations in the hospitality industry. In addition, CMAA encourages the education and professional advancement of its members, and assists club officers and managers through their management to secure the utmost in efficient and successful operations.

A student chapter of CMAA can be offered at any school that offers an undergraduate or graduate program in hospitality. As chapter members, students participate in professional development programs, site-visitation at local clubs, hands-on club operations and demonstrations and leadership development programs. The CMAA provides its student chapters with an internship directory, which provides more than two hundred internships at private clubs around the world.

Currently, a typical club pays over $150,000 in property taxes, provides over $367 million for charities with approximately 83% of this money moved into community charities, and reports an excess of $12 million in student scholarships. The economic impact of the club industry is highly local in nature, with the vast majority of club members and employees living in close proximity to their club. According to CMAA benchmarks, the majority of cash flow resulting in purchases, employment, taxes, charitable giving, and other economic activities are centered in the community in which the club operates. As such, clubs are significant producers of dense, highly local, economic activity. Some other interesting facts reported by the CMAA include:

- Member-managed clubs generate annual gross revenues of over $21 billion per year.
- Clubs employ 363,000 employees, and club payrolls equal $9.5 billion.
- Clubs serve between 1.8 and 2.1 million members.
- Clubs hosted an estimated 17,000 charitable golf tournaments in 2014, raising an estimated $150 million for those charities.
- The total income for clubs in 2014 was $21 billion.
- Clubs spend $2.8 billion on goods and an additional $2.2 billion on services in their local communities.
- Clubs as a whole pay $2.5 billion in total taxes, $1.7 billion of which are local and state taxes.

MODERN ENVIRONMENT

The competitive landscape has increased significantly over the past several years, placing never-before-experienced pressure on membership at private clubs. Specifically, industry experts have drawn a general consensus identifying the changing golf course marketplace and population demographics as key culprits.

Going back to the 1920's, about 80% of the golf courses were private. Public golf was almost unheard of, and up until the 1990's, most of the existing public courses were not comparable to private courses. Today, public facilities have grown in quality commensurate with their numeric growth. Steve Graves, president of Creative Golf Marketing, a membership-marketing firm, comments that private clubs today are in direct competition with up-scale daily fee courses. "These clubs are not your typical municipal courses that we all grew up around," suggested

You no longer have to belong to a club if you want to golf.

Graves, "These courses are being built and designed by the best in the industry and offer equal and many times better golf courses than a typical private club. [Therefore] the up-scale daily fee courses present an adequate golf experience without the high monthly cost associated with being a member of a private club."

Additionally, the influence of technology, ease of travel, and the transient lifestyle produced by the corporate career ladder has created a different societal need, and hence, a change in the population demographics. Because of this shift, national trends demonstrate that clubs are resorting to the "path of least resistance" by drastically reducing initiation fees or completely waiving initiation fees in order to compete with public clubs. The harder path, and ultimately more fruitful, is to set member retention, recruitment, and satisfaction as the club's highest priorities. Today, members have options with their leisure time and money and a key realization for the club manager is that this is a "consumer oriented world." Gregg Patterson, General Manager of the Beach Club of Santa Monica, CA, states, "All clubs need to find out what their members want and go after it aggressively. Every member has similar wants: goods, services, programs, facility and a sense of community but the expression of those wants changes with time." Therefore, it is of critical import for the club manager to stay abreast of the consumers' need and want continuum.

There are several options available to private clubs to ensure success. A club manager may take a more formal route such as hiring a membership director focused specifically on retention and recruitment, utilizing third-party firms in the consultation arena, or drawing upon survey information cultivated in-house or from broader industry outlets. This information can be used to tweak or remodel the product to fit the niche that is unique to each club situation.

VARIETIES OF CLUBS

Although all clubs share a common bond, the fee/due paying member, the private club industry has evolved into a vast landscape of variety. Listed and described below are some of the most common clubs in existence today.

COUNTRY CLUBS

Around 80% of all private clubs are **country clubs** and they often provide elaborate social amenities along with their outdoor recreational facilities. Activities in a typical country club usually center on the golf course; yet, many clubs also provide members with outdoor facilities for swimming, tennis, horseback riding, and other interests. Members might hold weddings, reunions, or other social events there. Recently many upscale housing projects have encouraged the building and growth of country clubs to attract neighboring communities and new residents. There are two types of memberships at country clubs: **full membership** which entitles the club member to the full use of the facilities the club offers, and **social membership** which permits the member to use specific facilities, such as the restaurant, lounge, bar, tennis courts, etc. Social membership sometimes requires that club members use

Country club members may hold weddings, reunions, or other social events at their club.

the club's facilities at certain times or days. Equinox Country Club in Manchester, Vermont and the California Country Club in Whittier, California are two examples of country clubs. In the past, country clubs were seen as the last bastions of the upper class elite. In some cases, this is still true. However, in most instances the stuffy cigar smoke and the Mayflower context are no longer used to determine whether an individual should be qualified for membership.

YACHT CLUBS

Yacht clubs are 4% of the total clubs. These clubs are designated for establishments near or on the water, and generally promote and regulate boating and yachting. The Montauk and Rochester Yacht Clubs are examples of this type of organization. Most yacht clubs own and operate a marina for their members, which may include the operation of a clubhouse with dining and recreation facilities. According to Terrie Berry of Defy Media, the five best yacht clubs in America are Buffalo Yacht Club (Buffalo, NY), Atlanta Yacht Club (Acworth, GA), Cambridge Yacht Club (Cambridge, MD), Centerboard Yacht Club (South Portland, ME), and William H. Seward Yacht Club (Anchorage, AK) (see http://www.mademan.com/mm/5-best-yacht-clubs-america.html#ixzz3wrY45Jus).

MILITARY CLUBS

Military clubs cater to the enlisted man, the non-commissioned officer (NCO), and the officer. Military bases in the United States and overseas provide these clubs for the welfare and the benefit of the soldiers. They provide extended amenities for their club members, such as guest quarters, recreational activities, food and beverage operations, and entertainment. In the past the clubs were run by military personnel, but recent changes in resource allocation have required the military to contract civilian firms to provide services. These facilities are located around the world and include the Bamberg Officer's Club in Bamberg, Germany, and the Fort Benning Officer's Club in Fort Benning, Georgia.

PROFESSIONAL CLUBS

Professional clubs are for people in the same profession for social and business interaction. The Engineer's Club of St. Louis is a professional club that appeals to engineers from the St. Louis area. Luxury and retail clubs inform and guide those interested in retail operations.

SOCIAL CLUBS

Social clubs similar to the Everglades Club in Palm Beach, Florida concentrate on serving the social needs of members who are normally from similar social-economic backgrounds. They are a modern combination of several types of clubs and reflect today's more eclectic and varied society. These clubs are centered around the activities available to the club members in the city or area in which the club is located. Some have a traditional clubhouse, bar, or restaurant where members gather; others do not.

CITY CLUBS

City clubs, as the name implies, are usually located in urban communities and range from luncheon-only clubs that serve segments of the business population to fully integrated dining and athletic clubs. City clubs make up about 11% of all clubs. Unlike most private clubs, city clubs may rent out guest rooms, organize themselves around a specialized profession, or associate with a particular college or university. City clubs fall into the following categories: professional, social, athletic, dining, fraternal, and university. Examples of city clubs include the City Club of New York, which was founded in 1892 by Edmond Kelly as a men's club to promote effective and honest government in New York City, and the Duquesne Club, which ranks number one among America's ten thousand private clubs according to a national survey conducted by the Club Managers Association of America.

ATHLETIC CLUBS

Athletic clubs, such as the Palm Beach Bath and Tennis Club and the Toronto Cricket and Skating Club, provide an outlet for working out, athletic activities, dining, and meeting. The New York Athletic Club (NYAC) was founded in 1868 in order to bring structure to the nascent world of amateur sport. In its journey through the ensuing decades, the NYAC has evolved to become an athletic powerhouse, globally renowned in sports such as wrestling, fencing, judo,

Athletic clubs offer exercise, athletic activities, dining, and other services to members.

water polo, rowing, and track and field. Concurrently, the NYAC has become a part of the cultural fabric of New York City, hosting banquets, receptions, and weddings, and welcoming leaders in the world of business, politics, and the arts to its magnificent dining room and 187 overnight guest rooms.

Through it all, the NYAC remains steadfastly committed to its roots, supporting athletes at the highest levels of Olympic competition while providing world class facilities at its two locations—the Manhattan City House and Travers Island in Westchester County—for those of its members who wish simply to remain fit and healthy.

The New York Athletic Club is an innovative organization, firmly adhered to its history but with its eyes set on its future. For this reason, its winged foot emblem is recognized throughout the world as being synonymous with excellence.

DINING CLUBS

Dining clubs are usually located in large office buildings, offering their members top-quality food service in urban surroundings. Examples include the Toronto Hunt Club and the Union Club of British Columbia.

FRATERNAL CLUBS

Fraternal clubs, like the Elks Club and the Veterans of Foreign Wars, provide organizations with a central location for meetings, dining, and social activities.

GOLF CLUB

According to the United States Golf Association, "a '**golf club**' is an organization of at least ten individual members that operates under bylaws with committees (including a Handicap Committee) to supervise golf activities, provide peer review, and maintain the integrity of the USGA Handicap System" (see http://www.usga.org). There are three types of golf clubs that exist. First, a golf club may be an organization located at a single specific course that uses the USGA rating systems, and where most of the events are played. Second, it may be an organization where the members are connected through business, fraternities, ethnic groups, or socially. Finally, it may be an organization where members have no previous affiliation before creating or joining the club.

UNIVERSITY CLUBS

University clubs are reserved for the activities of faculty, alumni, and guests. The Stanford Faculty Club of Stanford, the Harvard, Yale, Princeton Club of Pittsburgh, and the University of Toronto Faculty Club are perfect examples. The primary purpose of the Stanford Faculty Club is to provide Stanford University faculty, administrative staff, and other club members with a welcoming venue to promote social interaction, commingling, fellowship, congeniality, and the interchange of ideas and information.

CLUB PERSONNEL

As club types, country clubs are the largest employers, followed by golf clubs and city clubs. Taken together, the total employment in country clubs is four times the number employed in golf clubs, and almost 10 times the number of those employed by city clubs. The ratio of full-time and part-time non-seasonal employees is almost exactly the same for both golf clubs and country clubs. Approximately 43 percent of all employees in these clubs are full-time and non-seasonal. This contrasts sharply with city clubs, where 74 percent of the employees are full-time non-seasonal employees. Similar ratios were found among full-time and part-time seasonal employees in both golf and country clubs. However, among city clubs, only one-third of the seasonal employees are part-time.

LEGAL FORM OF BUSINESS

Club ownership includes two categories: equity clubs and proprietary clubs. **Equity clubs** are non-profit clubs and are the oldest form of club management; yet, they are still the most common form of ownership today. These clubs are owned and organized by the members for their own enjoyment. The board of directors then establishes the policies and budget, and does the hiring and firing of executives, such as the club manager. Any profits that are generated from the dues or club operations must be reinvested in the club's services and facilities and cannot be returned to the members.

Proprietary clubs are operated for profit and are owned by a corporation, company, business, or individual. These clubs became popular in the 1970's and 80's and provided an expansion of club membership and stringent admission requirements. Club members purchase a membership from the club's owner(s) and have limited input and control over the activities or management of the daily operations of the club. In some cases, contract organizations run the facility for the owner. The club manager reports to this organization or the owner of the facility. Depending on the type, interest, and development of all clubs, the category of ownership may vary.

MANAGEMENT STYLES

As a student, one of the most challenging experiences in life will be to choose a career. If you're looking for a career that is creative and combines business skills, human resource management, marketing, and public relations, welcome to the world of club management. It is one of the fastest-growing industries and hospitality fields and will provide you with outstanding career opportunities in the future. Club management is similar to that of hospitality management because it offers similar facilities. The largest difference is that the club, unlike a hotel or restaurant, is actually looked at as being owned by the members. The member pays a fee each year, which can vary drastically depending on the nature of the club. In turn, the members feel that they are the owners of the facility. Having one boss may be difficult, but imagine having thousands! This sometimes can put the manager in a difficult situation.

The manager of a club is actually governed by a constitution and the by-laws of the club. The board of directors and club president are elected by their peers to insure the goals and mission of the club are carried out effectively, and they create the constitution and by-laws that govern members' policies and standards. Club management structure is similar to that of company structure. There is a president, vice president, treasurer, secretary, and different committees. The manager of a club, usually referred to as the Chief Operating Officer or the General Manager, has to answer to and abide by the rules set forth by the governing body, and is responsible for all areas of club operation. While the board of directors and president may be responsible for the policy setting and implementation, it is the club manager's job to hire personnel to run the day-to-day operations of the club.

SUMMARY

Clubs provide a unique managing experience that combines many elements of the hospitality and tourism industries. Club managers must be versatile and open to the changing needs of the club members and the world around them. The most important job of a club manager is to provide club members with a positive experience every time they attend a function at the club. If managers fail to do this, attendance and membership will drop off and the club will cease to exist. Service is the key to a club manager's success and service is the core of the business. Club managers must remember that they "serve the world."

RESOURCES

Internet Sites

Algonquin Club of Boston: http://algonquinclub.memfirst.net/Club/Scripts/Home/home.asp

American Club in Singapore: http://www.amclub.org.sg/

American Society of Golf Course Architects: http://www.golfdesign.org/

Ariel Sands Beach Club: http://www.arielsands.com/

Army Navy Country Club: http://ancc.org/

Association of College and University Clubs: http://www.collegeanduniversityclubs.org/

Atlanta Athletic Club: http://www.atlantaathleticclub.org/

Ballantyne Country Club: http://www.crescent-resources.com/communit/charlott/ballanty/default.asp

Bear Creek Golf Club: http://www.bearcreekgc.com/Club/Scripts/Home/home.asp

Belmont Country Club: http://www.belmontcc.org/Club/Scripts/Splash/splash.asp

Boca Raton Resort & Club: http://www.bocaresort.com/

California Yacht Club: http://calyachtclub.com/cms/index2.htm

Capitol Hill Club: http://www.capitolhillclub.com/

Cedar Rapids Country Club: http://www.thecrcc.com/

Club Managers Association of America: www.cmaa.org

Club Services: http://www.clubservices.com

ClubCorp: http://www.clubcorp.com

Country Club of Lansing: http://www.cclansing.org/

Country Club of St. Albans: http://www.stalbans.com/

Golf Course Builders Association of America: http://www.gcbaa.org/

Golf Course Superintendents Association of America: http://www.gcsaa.org/

International Association of Golf Administrators: http://www.iaga.org/

International Club Network: http://www.privaccess.com/

International Health, Racquet, & Sportsclub Association: http://csdemo12.citysoft.com/IHRSA/viewPage.cfm?pageId=2

International Military Community Executives Association: http://www.imcea.com/

Ladies Professional Golf Association: http://www.lpga.com/

Lighthouse Point Yacht and Racquet Club: http://www.lpyrc.com/

National Association of Club Athletic Directors: http://www.nacad.org/

National Club Association: http://www.natlclub.org/

Professional Golfers Association of America: http://www.pga.com/

Sanctuary Golf Club: http://www.sanctuary-sanibel.com/

The ACE Club: http://www.theaceclubonline.com/

The Virtual Clubhouse/Club Management Magazine: http://www.club-mgmt.com

United States Golf Association: http:/www.usga.org

REFERENCES

Barnhart, C. L., ed. *The American College Dictionary*. New York: Random House 1990.

Barrows, C. W. & Walsh, J. 2002. Bridging the gap between hospitality management

programmes and the private club industry. *International Journal of Contemporary Hospitality Management*. 14(3); 120–127.

Brown, Mark M., Lu Donnelly, and David G. Wilkins. *The History of the Duquesne Club*. Pittsburgh: Art and Library Committee, 1989.

CMAA Benchmarking Club Industry 2014 Economic Impact Report, Club Managers Association of America http://www.cmaa.org, 2015.

Club Management Forum Virginia: Club Managers Association of America, 2000. http://www.cmaa.org/conf/conf2000/time.htm (Jan. 2, 2001).

Crossley, John C. and Lynn M. Jamieson. *Introduction to Commercial and Entrepreneurial Recreation*. Illinois: Sagamore Publishing, 1997.

Economic Impact Survey 2006. Club Managers Association of America. http://www.cmaa.org/EconImpactSurvey/2006EconImpactSurvey.doc. Retrieved June 29, 2005.

Membership issues: Opinions on what works in today's private club industry. http://www.boardroommagazine.com/fa59.cfm. Retrieved July 1, 2005.

Perdue, Joe, ed. *Contemporary Club Management*. Virginia: Club Managers Association of America, 1997

Perdue, J., Ninemeier, J. D., & Woods, R. H. 2002. Comparison of present and future competencies required for club managers. *International Journal of Contemporary Hospitality Management*. 14(3); 142–146.

Perfect storm: What does it mean for private clubs. http://www.boardroommagazine.com/fa58.cfm. Retrieved July 1, 2005.

Singerling, James, Robert Wood, Jack Nimemeier, and Joe Perdue. Success factors in private clubs. *Cornell Hotel and Restaurant Administration Quarterly* 38.5 (Oct. 1997).

The CMAA Student Advantage: A Commitment To Your Future. Virginia: Club Managers Association of America, 1999. http://www.cmaa.org/student/adv_bro/index.htm (Jan. 4, 2001).

Walker, John R. *Introduction to Hospitality* 3rd ed. New Jersey: Prentice-Hall, 2001.

Name: _____ Date: _____

REVIEW QUESTIONS

1. What types of facilities are likely to be found at a country club?

2. What types of services are likely to be offered at a city club?

3. Describe the types of military clubs and the purposes they serve.

4. Define an equity club.

5. Define a proprietary club.

6. Sketch an organizational chart for a private club that shows which positions report to whom.

7. What is CMAA? Visit their website at www.cmaa.org.

ASSIGNMENT 1

Visit Club Managers Association of America's Web site, ClubNet (www.cmaa.org). This Web site offers links to home pages for numerous private clubs throughout the United States. Visit as many of these home pages as possible to gain an understanding of the variety of private clubs available as well as the quality of facilities that are provided for members and their guests.

ClubNet also describes the numerous professional development opportunities available for club managers through CMAA. Peruse this section of ClubNet to better understand how professional development and learning is a life-long pursuit.

As you look ahead and plan your career, how will you pursue professional development and continuous educational opportunities?

ASSIGNMENT 2

According to an article in *Club Management* by Chris White (December 2000), the growth of the spa industry can provide opportunities for the private club sector. The spa industry has grown across the United States due to a number of reasons delineated by White (pg. 94):

- Baby Boomers' desire to slow the effects of aging
- The high costs of conventional, remedial healthcare as compared to preventive healthcare
- The increasing concern for the quality of the lengthening average life span
- Increasing amounts of personal disposable income

The variety of types of spas is also expanding. Spas no longer have to be the destination, resort, or cruise line spas also known as vacation spas. Day spas, which tend to cater to local clientele and offer hair salons, skin care, body treatments, and massage, are a growing segment. White emphasized in this article that the day spa market may provide enormous opportunities for private clubs particularly involving massage, body treatments, and possibly skin care.

What is your opinion of these expanded services for private clubs? What other types of amenities might be added that would be popular with private club members? How could these services be effectively marketed to the membership? What are potential disadvantages of offering "day spa" types of services?

ASSIGNMENT 3

Many clubs are increasingly experiencing quite varied demographics among their membership resulting in contrasting membership expectations and demands. For example, while clubs may still have a population of older members who have perhaps been with the club for many decades, younger members, often with children, are also a growing segment. While the older members may still enjoy dressing-up for an evening of fine dining, this may not be realistic or pleasurable for a family with three young children. How does a club cater to differing member preferences? The solution of operating different facilities to cater to the preferences of all members may work for some clubs but would be too costly and unrealistic for many operations.

If you were the new general manager of a club with these dilemmas (varied member preferences/limited budget, and the membership resistant to increases in dues), what would you suggest? Think of going before the club's board with at least three options to possibly increase member usage of the food and beverage facilities. What will you propose?

© Khoroshunova Olga/Shutterstock.com

CHAPTER *27*

SPORTS AND RECREATION MANAGEMENT

AUTHORS

Neil D. Marrin, MsEd, James Madison University

LEARNING OBJECTIVES

- Identify the different industry segments in recreation and sport management.
- Explain the various job opportunities to be found in each industry segment.
- Define the target populations each industry serves.
- Describe the skills needed to succeed in each industry segment.

CHAPTER OUTLINE

Overview of Sport and Recreation

Types of Recreation Careers

    Parks and Recreation Agencies

    Non-Profit Community Recreation

    Campus Recreation

    Morale, Welfare, and Recreation: Military Recreation

    Other Segments of the Recreation Profession

Types of Sport Management Careers

    Intercollegiate Athletics

    Professional Sports Franchises

    Sports Marketing

    Youth Sports

Summary

Campus recreation

Commercial recreation

Community non-profit
recreation

Correctional recreation

Intercollegiate athletics

Morale, welfare, and recreation

Municipal parks and recreation

National Park Service

Therapeutic recreation

OVERVIEW OF SPORT AND RECREATION

> "A life is not important except in the impact it has on other lives"
>
> **–Jackie Robinson, Baseball Legend.**

For those seeking the chance to impact the lives of others, a career path in recreation and sport management is a tremendous way to accomplish that. The fields of sport and recreation management share many of the characteristics of the hospitality industry. Students considering a career in either sport or recreation must generally possess strong interpersonal skills, a passion for working with people, and a solid understanding of what constitutes good customer service. In addition, they must understand the functions and structure of business and possess a creative mindset. Recreation and sport continue to be growing industries with job opportunities in the field of recreation alone projected to increase by ten percent by the year 2024.[1]

Opportunities in recreation are offered by a number of different providers, which allow young professionals to work with various and diverse populations. These agencies include parks and recreation departments (e.g., local city, town, and village departments), campus recreation departments (which serve college students on campuses throughout the country), non-profit recreation agencies (e.g., YMCA and Boys and Girls Clubs), and commercial recreation organizations (e.g., Walt Disney World and Busch Gardens). In addition, students pursuing study in the field of therapeutic recreation can work in hospitals, rehabilitation centers, and other medically related facilities. Depending on the specific provider, a professional in the field of recreation could be working with children, teens, college aged students, adults, and/or senior citizens. In a therapeutic recreation setting, professionals would be working with people of all ages who have permanent or temporary disabilities. Overall the Department of Labor reports that there over 370,000 people working in jobs designated as recreation positions so there are many opportunities for students considering pursuing jobs in those professions.[2]

The field of sport also possesses a variety of opportunities for those entering the workplace. Positions can be found with professional sport teams (major and minor league), sports marketing agencies, colleges and universities (intercollegiate sports), as well as youth sport organizations. Depending on the organization type, professionals could be working in the areas of player development, marketing, facility management, governance, sales, and community outreach.

TYPES OF RECREATION CAREERS

PARKS AND RECREATION AGENCIES

Parks and recreation organizations are usually governmentally run agencies (municipal agencies) and can take many forms and sizes. Of those agencies the smallest are generally the local village or town parks and recreation departments that serve your local community. The larger agencies may be a part of a big city, or as large as a state park system or even the **National Park Service** (a division of the U.S. Department of the Interior).

Those pursuing a career in parks and recreation can be involved in youth programming (day camps, after-school programs, youth sport programs), event planning, cultural programming (concerts, theater programs, fine art classes), senior citizen programming, aquatics, tennis, or golf. In addition, there are opportunities to work in horticulture, field maintenance, and landscape design. The specific opportunities available depend on the size of the agency and

National Parks, such as Arches National Park in Utah, are managed by the government.

its mission. Generally smaller agencies, like village and town recreation departments, are more focused on recreation services, while larger organizations, like the National Park Service, will be more focused on parks and the preservation of green space. The National Park Service employs over 20,000 employees in fields ranging from administration to botany, and from museum services to human resources.[3] Municipal parks and recreation agencies are primarily funded through tax dollars, but also subsidize their costs through fees and grants.

NON-PROFIT COMMUNITY RECREATION

The field of **non-profit community recreation** is often more focused on serving specific populations with a more tightly defined mission. Commonly, professionals in this field work in the areas of recreational programming, running after-school programs for children, day care programs, teen programs, and day camps. This segment of the recreation industry is represented by organizations such as the Boys and Girls Clubs or the YMCA (more popularly known as the "Y"). Many of these organizations are independently operated by a local board of directors and are formed as a result of a "grass roots" effort. They are represented nationally by the parent organization and are considered an affiliate association or member agency of that national organization. The Boys and Girls Clubs serve nearly four million children and teens nationally using over 50,000 professional staff and hundreds of thousands of volunteers,[4] while the YMCA, through its more than 2,600 local associations, serves twenty-one million people, half of whom are children.[5] Very often these non-profit agencies have a mission that focuses on larger

social issues. The mission of the Boys and Girls Clubs of America is "to enable all young people, especially those who need us most, to reach their full potential as productive, caring, responsible citizens,"[6] while the motto of the YMCA is "youth development, healthy living and social responsibility."[7]

Funding for non-profit community recreation agencies generally comes from donations, membership fees, and grants. Most of these organizations will provide scholarships or sliding fee scales (payments adjusted to a family's income) so children can participate regardless of their family's financial situation and ability to pay. Professionals who want to pursue a higher level career in the non-profit sector need to develop strong skills in fundraising (development) and potentially pursue a master's degree in non-profit management.

CAMPUS RECREATION

Campus recreation is a growing field providing professionals with the opportunity to work with a college-aged population. Professionals in this area often work in group fitness, personal training, outdoor adventure, intramural sports, and club sports. There are many outstanding campus recreation facilities in the nation (and internationally) that offer aquatics facilities, fitness centers, climbing walls, and gymnasiums. NIRSA, the National Intramural and Recreation Sports Association, the professional organization that represents this industry, claims over 4,500 professional members representing over 700 colleges and universities and serving nearly 8.1 million participants.[8] Funding for campus recreation programs primarily comes from student activity fees

Arts and crafts is a common activity in community recreation.

The University of Central Florida CFE Arena provides a venue for sports and entertainment.

and program fees. As with many career tracks in recreation, the sense of reward and satisfaction can be great. A study sponsored by NIRSA in 2010 indicated that, of those who responded to their survey, 93 percent were satisfied with their work.[9]

MORALE, WELFARE, AND RECREATION: MILITARY RECREATION

Morale, welfare, and recreation (MWR) is recreation carried out in a military setting, specifically in United States military organizations like the United States Army and Navy. The mission of MWR is to serve our military men, women, and their families. Locations can be domestic or international depending on base locations and, as such, careers in military recreation may offer wonderful opportunities for relocation and travel. Family and youth recreation programming may be similar to the types of programs one sees in community recreation, but often they serve an additional purpose. Very often military families are living in an unfamiliar location and, based on their duty assignment, could be far away from family and friends. In some cases, a member of the nuclear family, a spouse or parent, may be deployed elsewhere while serving their country. In these cases military recreation (MWR) serves an even greater purpose for these families. It can create a sense of community and it can help to create stability in a life that could be very transitional. Although community recreation may have a similar purpose, that function in a military recreation setting can be much more pronounced. In the words of Michael Huffstetler, a MWR professional, MWR "can offer you growth in experience and knowledge, recognition, an opportunity to do something unique and rewarding, a way to serve those who serve you, and an opportunity to travel and possibly see the world."[10]

OTHER SEGMENTS OF THE RECREATION PROFESSION

Therapeutic recreation is field that is generally practiced in rehabilitation centers, nursing homes, and hospitals. Therapeutic recreation utilizes recreation activities directed to reach a specific outcome that relates to rehabilitation and well-being.[11] Students thinking about pursuing a career in this field should consider majoring in therapeutic recreation and should consider seeking certification in the field. Certification for therapeutic recreation professionals is the CTRS, the Certified Therapeutic Recreation Specialist certification.

Another area of recreation is **correctional recreation**, recreation services that are carried out in prisons with inmate populations. Although the recreation activities in this environment may serve the same purpose as recreation activities in the general community, sometimes they have a greater focus on the social rehabilitation of the participant. **Commercial (for profit) recreation** may offer a higher level of a recreation experience, but one that is more tied to the profit driven mission. Typical examples of commercial recreation organizations include amusement parks (See the *Attractions* section of this text for more information about these industries), commercial fitness centers, and outdoor adventure companies. The primary source of revenue for these organizations is admission fees and user fees.

SPORT MANAGEMENT

Now that we have examined careers in recreation, we will survey the opportunities that exist in the field of sport management.

INTERCOLLEGIATE ATHLETICS

Students who enjoy athletics may wish to consider a career in **intercollegiate athletics**, working in any number of colleges and universities across the country. Professionals can serve as athletic directors (the senior administrative role in collegiate athletics), in coaching positions, or in support roles such as academic advising or physical training. These positions are well suited for the person who wants to work with college-aged students and enjoys the competitive athletic environment. More than 460,000 student-athletes participate in collegiate sports throughout NCAA (National Collegiate Athletic Association) institutions,[12] creating vast opportunities for those seeking to enter the field of intercollegiate athletics as a profession.

There are many opportunities for work in major and minor league sports.

PROFESSIONAL SPORTS FRANCHISES

Opportunities exist in the world of professional sports on both the major and minor league levels. Students pursuing these careers will work for baseball teams, basketball teams, football teams, and a host of teams that represent various sports. Other areas of professional sports include MMA (Mixed Martial Arts), X-Games, and NASCAR racing. Very often there are good opportunities for hospitality students in these organizations, working in stadium food and beverage concessions, catering departments, community outreach, marketing, ticket sales, and client services. Careers in professional sport can be gratifying and rewarding. When describing the world of minor league sports, baseball executive, Todd "Parney" Parnell, Vice President and Chief Operating Officer for the Richmond Flying Squirrels, states, "We are not in the baseball business, not in the entertainment business, we are in the memory making business." Career prospects in professional or semi-professional sports exist not only nationally but internationally as well.

SPORTS MARKETING

Sports marketing positions are often found within professional sports organizations, such as major and minor league teams and, on the collegiate level, in colleges and universities as part of a dedicated marketing team. In addition, small and large independent marketing agencies exist with the sole focus of the sport field, serving as consultants to the industry. Sports marketing professionals are responsible for developing the posters, promotional events, and advertisements you see and experience in college athletics or professional sports. In some organizations they are responsible for securing sponsorships for events or game takeaways. Students wishing to pursue a career in sports marketing must possess strong creative and analytical skills, the ability to clearly communicate their ideas, and a passion for sports.[13]

YOUTH SPORTS

For those who enjoy both sports and working with young people, the youth sport industry provides opportunities to combine those passions. This type of work is considered sports programming. Although many youth sport programs on the local level work solely with volunteer staff, the national organizations are staffed with full-time professionals. Youth sports are represented nationally by organizations like the Little League and U.S. Youth Soccer. As with many sport and recreation careers, a career in youth sports requires strong interpersonal and organizational skills.

SUMMARY

The fields of recreation and sport management offer extensive prospects for young professionals who possess a passion for working with people. The growth of the industry as a whole and the variety jobs within the industry are vast. In addition, those pursuing a career in recreation and sport will have the opportunity to work with a diversity of people from children to college students, adults to seniors, sports fans to enthusiasts of art and music. Careers in the field of

A career in youth sports requires strong interpersonal and organizational skills.

recreation and sport management can be very professionally and personally satisfying. After all, you're getting paid to make people's lives more fun.

RESOURCES

Internet Sites

National Recreation and Park Association: http://www.nrpa.org/

National Intramural Recreation Sports Association: http://www.nirsa.org/

YMCA of the USA: http://www.ymca.net/

National Council for Therapeutic Recreation Certification: http://nctrc.org/about-certification/ctrs-the-qualified-provider/

The National Collegiate Athletic Association (NCAA): http://www.ncaa.com/

ENDNOTES

1. Bureau of Labor Statistics, U.S. Department of Labor, *Occupational Outlook Handbook*, 2016–17 Edition, Recreation Workers

2. Ibid.

3. http://www.nps.gov/aboutus/workwithus.htm

4. http://www.bgca.org/Documents/2014-Annual-Report_FINAL_LO-REZ.pdf

5. http://www.ymca.net/news-releases/20080804-membership-reaches-21-million.html

6. http://www.bgca.org/whoweare/pages/mission.aspx

7. http://www.bgca.org/whoweare/pages/mission.aspx

8. http://nirsa.net/nirsa/about/

9. Job Satisfaction for Campus Recreation Professionals within NIRSA Institutions, Stier, Schneider, Kampf and Gaskins, *Recreational Sport Journal*, 2012, 34, 78–94, NIRSA Foundation

10. Huffstetler, M. (2015). *The Morale, Welfare and Recreation Experience*, Parks and Recreation, NRPA.org, November 2015.

11. Stavola Daly, F., & Kunstler, R. (2006). *Introduction to Recreation and Leisure.* Champaign, IL: Human Kinetics.

12. http://www.ncaa.org/about/resources/leadership-development-programs-and-resources/career-sports-forum

13. Career and Professional Development. (n.d.). Retrieved January 10, 2016, from http://career.opcd.wfu.edu/explore-careers/sports-marketing/#1

REFERENCES

Boys & Girls Clubs of America works hard every day to make a difference in the lives of youth in communities all over the world. (n.d.). Retrieved January 10, 2016, from http://www.bgca.org/whoweare/pages/mission.aspx

Career and Professional Development. (n.d.). Retrieved January 10, 2016, from http://career.opcd.wfu.edu/explore-careers/sports-marketing/#1

Career in Sports Forum. (2013, November 21). Retrieved January 10, 2016, from http://www.ncaa.org/about/resources/leadership-development-programs-and-resources/career-sports-forum

Huffstetler, M. (2015, November 1). The Morale, Welfare and Recreation Experience. *Parks and Recreation*

More People Turn to the YMCA Than Ever Before. (n.d.). Retrieved January 10, 2016, from http://www.ymca.net/news-releases/20080804-membership-reaches-21-million.html

Occupational Outlook Handbook 2016-17 Edition, Recreation Workers. (2016). Retrieved December 1, 2016, from http://www.bls.gov/

NIRSA. (n.d.). Retrieved January 10, 2016, from http://nirsa.net/nirsa/about/

Stavola Daly, F., & Kunstler, R. (2006). *Introduction to Recreation and Leisure.* Champaign, IL: Human Kinetics.

United States. National Park Service. (2015, December 31). Work with Us (U.S. National Park Service). Retrieved January 10, 2016, from http://www.nps.gov/aboutus/workwithus.htm

Career and Professional Development. (n.d.). Retrieved January 10, 2016, from http://career.opcd.wfu.edu/explore-careers/sports-marketing/#1

Name: _____ Date: _____

1. Describe how the mission of a non-profit community recreation agency differs from that of a commercial recreation organization.

2. In order to be successful in Sports Marketing a professional should possess what important skills?

3. In what way(s) does Military Recreation (MWR) differ in its service model from parks and recreation agencies?

4. What types of potential opportunities exist for hospitality majors in the world of professional sports?

5. How are municipal recreation and parks agencies, like the local town parks department, usually funded?

6. Looking at your own college campus, discuss what options for recreation are available to you as a student.

© Ikunl/Shutterstock.com

CHAPTER *28*

SPAS AND FITNESS CENTERS

AUTHOR	*Brad Engeldinger, Sierra College*
LEARNING OBJECTIVES	• Identify the similarities and differences between spa and fitness centers.
	• Examine various types of spa and fitness centers.
	• Explore future trends and opportunities in spa and fitness centers.
CHAPTER OUTLINE	Introduction to Spas and Fitness Centers
	Spas and Fitness Centers Defined
	Similarities and Differences
	Evolution of Spas
	Modern Spas
	Evolution of Fitness Centers
	Types of Spas
	Types of Fitness Centers
	Future Trends and Opportunities
	Future Trends in Spas
	Future Trends in Fitness Centers
	Summary

KEY TERMS

Aerobic centers

Amenity

Aromatherapy

Athletic clubs

Ayurvedic spas

Baths of Caracalla

Country club

Destination spas

Fitness center

Gymnasium

Hot springs

Medical spas

Mindfulness

Pilates

Resort spas

Spa

Thermal spas

Wellness tourism

Yoga

Food service is a dominant segment of the hospitality industry that represents a significant proportion of the economy.

INTRODUCTION TO SPAS AND FITNESS CENTERS

SPAS AND FITNESS CENTERS DEFINED

Have you ever wondered what sets spas and fitness centers apart from one another? Can you define what a spa is? How about a fitness center? Spas and fitness centers are two terms that are often used interchangeably, yet have distinct differences that set them apart from one another. Generally speaking, a spa is a business developed to enhance the guest's overall well-being through a variety of professional services that encourage the renewal of mind, body, and spirit; the true definition of the term spa recognizes healthcare services, therapeutic treatment, cultural arts, shared events, leisure, relaxation, and renewal. The American Society of Medical Hydrology and Climatology defines a spa as a place where mineral-containing waters flow from the ground naturally, or to which they are pumped or conducted, and are therefore used for therapeutic purposes. The International Spa Association (ISPA) identifies itself through the spa experience defined as time to relax, reflect, revitalize, and rejoice. Simply stated, **spas** are resorts that offer a multitude of health and personal care treatments with an emphasis on hot spring mineral-filled water baths. On the other hand, a **fitness center** (e.g., health club, fitness club, health spa, gym) is a facility that consists of exercise equipment for the purpose of physical exertion to acquire desired results to ultimately improve overall health and fitness levels of its members.

SIMILARITIES AND DIFFERENCES

Spas and fitness centers have similarities and differences that serve to distinguish themselves based on their unique product and service offerings, which are commonly referred to in the hospitality industry as **amenities**. They are similar in that they offer health-enhancing treatments, stress reduction, perspiration, and restoration to the body, mind, and spirit through various methods of stimulation and relaxation. They differ in the specific services that they offer. For example, on the one hand, most fitness centers have a main workout area that consists of exercise machines and free weights such as dumbbells and barbells and mirrors (to check posture and form), cardiovascular exercise equipment such as stair steppers, rowing machines, elliptical trainers, exercise bicycles, and treadmills accompanied by audiovisual display equipment either integrated into the equipment, displayed on the walls, and/or mounted from the ceiling in effort to keep exercise entertaining during workouts. On the other hand, spas offer services centered on the inclusion of natural element such as water and flow, air and breath, earth and mineral, fire and heat, light and energy, and tension and electricity. Spas also offer relaxation and restoration services such as beauty and salon treatments, hot baths containing mineral water, hot stone therapy (Ganban'yoku), mud baths (Fangotherapy), indoor/outdoor spas, body scanning chiropractic analysis, intense pulsed light (IPL), non-ablative skin rejuvenation, self-tracking technology—for sleep, diet, and calorie monitoring—behavior change analysis—mindfulness, biofeedback, and hypnotherapy—cognitive modeling, neurological mapping, brain chemical optimization, emotional cleansing, farm-to-table and slow-food meals, and aromatherapy.

Like fitness centers, spas also offer physical activities, but they are different in that they are primarily offered outdoors on the physical property such as climbing, trail running, skiing, mountain biking, horseback riding, and kayaking.

EVOLUTION OF SPAS

The waters can be traced back to early civilizations. The popularity of spas has accompanied cultures that have experienced increases in leisure time. Social bathing was an important cultural process practiced by ancient Mesopotamians, Egyptians, Minoans, Greeks, and Romans. The Roman Empire is credited

© Chameleonsaye/Shutterstock.com

Spas are centers for healing and nourishing the body, mind, and spirit.

with offering the first public bathing facility for all of its citizens called the **Baths of Caracalla** established by the Emperor Lucius Caracalla.

MODERN SPAS

During the 19th century, America offered its first spa in Saratoga Springs, New York and it quickly evolved into one of the most popular tourist destinations by the mid-1800s. The spa trend gained popularity during the last half of the nineteenth century with the implementation of natural hot and cold springs in many American resorts spanning from the Mississippi River all the way to the West Coast that were said to feature individualized bath tubs, vapor mists, and pool aquatic endeavors. More recently, at the turn of the century, medical spas of the early 2000s have become desirable due to a public shift in healthcare attitudes with non-traditional medicines gaining acceptance. Now spas are centers for healing and nourishing of the mind, body, and spirit. People visit in pursuit of fitness, stress management, peace of mind, pampering, pleasure, health, and wellness. Today's spas offer a unique balance of ancient traditions and modern medicinal wonders.

EVOLUTION OF FITNESS CENTERS

The ancient Greeks created the first gyms, which were originally intended to be used as training centers for Olympic athletes. Over time, the Olympics fell out of favor among the population and gyms disappeared for centuries. Prior to the mid-1900s, humans did not intentionally seek out forms of exercise to keep themselves fit; during the Medieval and Renaissance periods, for example, people got more

than enough exercise form completing daily tasks, chores, and agricultural work, eliminating the need for exercise facilities. By the 19th century, schools began to build gymnasiums throughout the developed world. Non-profit organizations were founded in America during this period, which offered after-school exercise activities for grade-school-aged boys. The YMCA, for example, built many gyms for physical exercise, social activities, sports, and games. During the 1930s, boxing gyms began to appear in the American Northeast with the intent of training boxers to become prize fighters.

The rise of the commercial fitness center (1960–2000) was driven by cultural changes that spanned a significant part of several generations. A new outlook on physical habits and leisure attitudes sparked a demand for fitness centers to become societal fixtures. There was a considerable change in the 1970s, when both men and women joined fitness centers to realize favorable images of health, beauty, professional success, and sexuality with an emphasis on athleticism and muscle tone. Fitness centers emerged as social centers where people went to see and meet members of the opposite or same sex. A Gallup poll indicated that only 24% of Americans exercised regularly in the 1970s, which increased to 69% by 1987, and by 1995 there were almost 16,000 clubs; that number increased to 20,000 by 2002, with memberships skyrocketing from 1.7 million in 1972 to 42.7 million by 2006 in the United States alone.

TYPES OF SPAS

There is a vast array of spas that vary in size, services offered, quality of products, amenities offered, location, client demographics, customer expectations, and business model (e.g., both independent and corporate ownership) that factor into the spa classification equation. Below is a list of spa classifications:

Hot Springs—geo-thermally warmed waters bubbling up from the earth's core, delivering minerals that are said to improve skin and relieve pain and other medical ailments.

Day Spas—offer a selection of treatments and therapies while providing salon services with the purpose of improving health, beauty, and relaxation by providing amenities such as jacuzzis, saunas, steam

Day spas offer a selection of services such as manicures.

rooms, hydrotherapy circuits, fitness centers, and swimming pools. Day spas cater to people who do not want to stay overnight and the quality of practitioners and level of services is not up to the same standards as resorts.

Resort Spas (or Hotel Spas)—are day spas located in hotels that offer spa treatments, fitness classes, and cuisine. They offer a combination of relaxation and active amenities such as golf and tennis. The quality of the accommodations, treatments, and cuisine are top class, especially at luxury hotels.

Destination Spas—provide comprehensive health programs that consist of spa treatments, holistic fitness activities, holistic exercise classes, wellness lectures, and healthy cuisine. They provide various healing programs that include consultations with specialists, accommodations, meals, treatments, educational classes by experts, and all a la carte treatments. Destination spas offer personalized programs based on customized goals and provide tailor-made dietary healthy meal plans, exercise, relaxation, and pampering that focus on specific purposes such as detoxification, weight loss, and stress relief. The average length of stay is two to seven days.

Medical Spas—are a hybrid between a medical clinic and a day spa. Medical spas are comfortable environments for patients to undergo medical procedures while ensuring a high degree of relaxation, security, and privacy. Treatments often focus on two areas: aesthetic enhancement and wellness. Treatments such as microdermabrasion, chemical peels, injectables such as Botox and fillers, and laser treatments such as photofacials require a doctor's supervision and other medical professionals such as physiotherapists, osteopaths, and aestheticians. They are more clinical than day spas, yet they provide a much higher degree of comfort and privacy than hospitals.

Ayurvedic Spas—from the Sanskrit meaning "the knowledge for long life," Ayurveda medicine is an ancient Hindu healing system. This concept improves one's health and well-being by creating a balance between mind, body, and spirit through lifestyle assessments. Treatments are based on herbal preparations, diet, purification, and yoga.

Thermal Spas—built around hot springs that are formed from heated water from the earth's crust, which stimulates blood flow and body metabolism while bringing improved nourishment to vital organs and muscles, aiding digestion, and removing unwanted toxins from the body. The minerals from the water can also relieve pain from injuries and ailments as well as improve the skin. These spas are typically located outdoors in remote locations.

TYPES OF FITNESS CENTERS

Like spas, fitness centers differ in size, services offered, quality of amenities, location, clientele demographics, customer expectations, and business models. The terms fitness center, gym, and athletic club are often used interchangeably as there is an overlap in the services that they provide; yet there are several distinct differences that set them apart from one another, which are explained in the list below:

Fitness Centers—are health, recreation, and social facilities geared towards exercise, sports, and other physical activities. Most fitness centers accommodate various types of workout facilities into a single location. For instance, most fitness centers offer their members a free-weight area, weight machines, cardiovascular equipment, exercise classes, yoga, a swimming pool, Jacuzzis, saunas, tanning beds, child care centers, sports retail stores, juice bars, snack bars, Pilates, sports fields, and racquetball courts. The multitude of offerings is meant to attract multiple target audiences. Fitness centers range in size, space, amenities, and activities offered. They create

Athletic clubs provide a place to play a variety of sports.

an atmosphere of comfort that leads to opportunities for socializing.

Gyms—(short for gymnasium) like fitness centers offer various activities, amenities, and events that come in many forms. Gyms focus solely on weight lifting, strength training, cardiovascular equipment, and various exercise classes with experienced, certified personal trainers and staff.

Athletic Clubs—provide a place for individuals to participate in virtually all of the amenities of fitness centers and gyms along with the ability to compete in sport. Common sports activities include basketball, racquetball, squash, pickle ball, and tennis. Athletic clubs are typically the most expensive type of fitness center to join.

Aerobic Centers—typically feature activities designed to focus on cardiovascular health and wellbeing. They feature a wide variety of classes associated with cardiovascular health, muscle toning, and flexibility.

Country Clubs—offer a variety of amenities and services similar to fitness centers along with an eighteen-hole golf course and a dining commons. Most country clubs require that their members pay yearly dues to maintain membership along with additional fees for many amenities that the club has to offer such as green fees for golfing. There is a certain level of pride and prestige associated with being a member of an exclusive members-only country club.

FUTURE TRENDS AND OPPORTUNITIES

What will the future bring? Though no one can predict the future, we can hypothesize outcomes based on past and present behaviors. What current trends, ideas, and actions will likely shape the outlook of this industry? *Technological advancements, innovative products, unique services, and state-of-the-art facilities* are four key components that future professionals will need to educate themselves on to effectively navigate the challenges and opportunities that lie ahead as society evolves. It will be critical for you to develop an awareness of current challenges and opportunities while understanding the skills professionals will need to cultivate to effectively manage spas and fitness centers in the years to come.

FUTURE TRENDS IN SPAS

Mindfulness—applications on smart phones, yoga classes, and meditation. Mental hygiene, which is the hygiene of emotion to reboot the brain to make people less anxious, happier, focused, and creative.

Healthy Hotel Rooms—stay well rooms, rejuvenate while on vacation through food, spa, massage, gym, cardiovascular training, sleep programs, interactions with nature, and organic, gluten-free, farm-to-table, slow-food dining options.

Wellness Tourism—where guests travel around the world visiting various spas for exploration, pleasure, and overall relaxation. The Global Spa and Wellness Summit (GSWS) categorizes wellness tourism as a $439 billion market in the United States with a 9% growth annually through the year 2020.

Non-Surgical Cosmetic Procedures—such as barbary fig oil made from cactus fruit used as an anti-aging skin treatment, IV drip bars, testosterone gels, and bio-identical hormones for women are projected to be in demand.

Aromatherapy—using mist sprayers consisting of exotic fragrances that nurture the body, mind, and spirit. These include orange blossom, lavender, and eucalyptus along with essential oils such as coca, sage, juniper, and mint aromas.

Destinations Spas—include offerings such as weight loss boot camps, botanical Vinyasa Yoga meditation, massage, and diet services, and urban wellness retreats. These locations are projected to double by the year 2050 as many properties will morph into hybrid spa resorts or destination spas.

FUTURE TRENDS IN FITNESS CENTERS

While the future is not certain, some leading industry affiliates have voiced their predictions for the next 20 years. Their forecasts include:

Expansion—growth in small and mid-sized clubs will yield larger operations; more small facilities will open with independent clubs of 10,000 square feet or less.

Competition Will Heat Up—especially for smaller independent clubs competing with the expansion of major chains.

Location—will become more important in smaller communities by taking fitness closer to where customers live through a practice called community outreach.

Niche Markets—will develop on both ends of the age spectrum, which will include both old and young individuals.

Entertainment Options—will be improved with virtual/interactive exercise products as the demand for exercise entertainment is growing.

Life-long Learning—fitness professionals should be prepared to serve better-informed members over the next twenty years.

New Ways to Profit—will be implemented by creating additional revenue streams though products and services.

Specialization—will set fitness centers apart by differentiating themselves from other facilities.

High-quality, Soft-skill Communications and Relationship-oriented Staff—will be mandatory.

Insurance Companies will Incentivize Fitness. Equipment Innovations—will expand. Both spas and fitness centers will continue to monitor new technology that can fit within their respective businesses.

SUMMARY

Spa and fitness centers have been a sought after means of restoration, recovery, and renewal since early civilizations emerged and they will continue to grow, develop, and expand long into the future. Spas and fitness centers are similar in that they feature various health-improving services, yet they differ in the activities that they provide with spas offering more relaxation and fitness centers emphasizing activities of exertion. There are various types of both spas and fitness centers that offer unique services and amenities that set themselves apart from one another to create varietal niches within the market segment. Both of these industries are changing at a rapid rate due to technological advancements that will require future professionals to be skilled in technology, creative and innovative in the products and services they offer, and constantly improving the ways in which they serve their customers. There will be a need to proactively exceed guest expectations from a clientele that is growing both domestically and internationally through ever-changing wants and needs. Future leaders must be able to analyze and identify current trends to comprehend future consumer behavior by conducting research and implementing technology while improving customer service and business practices.

RESOURCES

Internet Sites

American Demographics: www.demographics.com

American Society of Medical Hydrology and Climatology: www.asmh-direct.net

Global Spa and Wellness Summit: www.globalspaandwellnesssummit.org

Hospitality Trends: www.htrends.org

International Society of Hospitality Consultants: www.ishc.com

International Spa Association: www.experienceispa.com

Sales and Marketing Management: www.
claritas.com

Smith Travel Research: www.str-olnine.com

Travel Industry Association: www.tia.org

Travel and Research Association: www.ttra.com

Trends Research Institute: www.
trendsresearch.com

U.S. Bureau of the Census: www.census.gov

World Tourism Organization: www.wto.org

REFERENCES

Buchman, D. (2001). *The Complete Book of Water Healing* (2nd ed.). McGraw-Hill Publishing Co.

Buck, J. (2001). "The evolution of health clubs." *Club Industry.*

Crebbin-Bailey, J., Harcup, J., & Harrington, J. (2005). *The Spa Book: The Official Guide to Spa Therapy.* Cengage Learning Publishing Co.

DeVierville, J.P. (2003). "Spa industry, culture, and evolution." Retrieved November 3rd, 2015 from http://www.massagetherapy.com

Ellis, S. (2014). "Top 10 global spa and wellness trends forecast." Spafinder Wellness, Inc.

Luke, A. (2015). "The rise of the gym through history." Retrieved November 7th, 2015 from http://www.diet-blog.com

Register, J. (2015). "Spa evolution, a brief history." International Spa Association.

Samuria, S. (2015). "Guide to different types of spas." Retrieved October 31st, 2015 from http://www.healingholidays.com

Stern, M. (2008). "The fitness movement and the fitness center industry, 1960-2000." Retrieved October 29th, 2015 from Business and Economic History On-Line http://www.thebhc.org

The Spa Association (2014). "The spa association trends report." Retrieved October 31st, 2015 from http://www.thespaassociation.com

Thompson, W. (2015). "Worldwide survey of fitness trends for 2015." *American College of Sports Medicine Health and Fitness Journal* (Vol. 18, No. 6).

REVIEW QUESTIONS

28

1. Discuss the primary differences between spas and fitness centers.

2. Explain the similarities among spas and fitness centers.

3. What impact did the Baths of Caracalla have on both spas and fitness centers in modern times?

4. List and explain two spa classifications that you think will be most successful in the future. Justify your position.

5. List and explain two fitness center classifications that you think will experience challenges in the years to come. Justify your position.

6. Create, list, and explain three hypothetical service offerings that you think will be in demand in spas by the year 2020.

7. Create, list, and explain three hypothetical service offerings that you think will be in demand in fitness centers by the year 2020.

© Arkorn/Shutterstock.com

CHAPTER *29*

SPORTS AND ENTERTAINMENT CENTERS

AUTHOR
LEARNING OBJECTIVES

Molly J. Dahm, Lamar University

- Describe the historical origins of sports and entertainment services.
- Identify the advantages of downtown entertainment districts.
- Discuss the development of festival marketplaces and urban entertainment districts.
- Explain the strategic link between urban entertainment centers and sports/events centers.
- Discuss venue management and the services provided by key venue management companies.
- Identify key mega events and their link to sports and entertainment complexes.
- Establish the link between mega events and economic development.

CHAPTER OUTLINE

Introduction
Origins of Sports and Entertainment Services
Festival Marketplaces and Entertainment Centers
Urban Entertainment Centers and Districts
Venue Management
Mega Event Services and Management
The Future and Careers
Summary

KEY TERMS

Festival marketplace
Location-based entertainment
Mega developments
Mega event

Tourist bubble
Urban entertainment center
Venue management

INTRODUCTION

Many of you will choose to work in the hospitality industry because you want to be around people while they are having fun. You want to be where the excitement is. What could be more exciting than managing the Field House or the Golf Club at the world-famous Chelsea Piers in New York City? Supervising concessions or novelty sales at Oriole Park at Camden Yards, home of the Baltimore Orioles? Directing activities at the Verizon Center in Washington, D.C., home of the Washington Wizards? Or helping to feed athletes at the 2016 Rio de Janeiro Summer Olympics and Paralympics? All of these opportunities are available when you venture into a career in sports and entertainment centers, or venue management.

In major and second tier cities around the world, sports and entertainment complexes offer a focal point for urban development and/or revitalization. Thus, you may find yourself working for a public entity like the New Jersey Sports and Exposition Authority (NJSEA) at the Meadowlands in East Rutherford, New Jersey, or for a private entity like SMG (formerly known as Spectator Management Group) which manages services at locations such as the Long Beach Convention and Entertainment Center in Long Beach, California and Reliant Park and NRG Park and Astrodome in Houston, Texas. Opportunities are not limited to the United States. For instance, the Crown Perth Complex (formerly Burswood), on the outskirts of Perth, Western Australia, features a casino, hotels, restaurants, a sporting events dome and convention center, and a theatre. The O2 arena in London, England (see http://www.theo2.co.uk/) is considered a premier music venue that also includes exhibition space, restaurants, movie theatres, and diverse cultural experiences.

ORIGINS OF SPORTS AND ENTERTAINMENT SERVICES

People have long traveled to central locations to attend sporting events and enjoy accompanying entertainment. The birth of sport venues and what has come to be termed mega event entertainment began with the Greek Olympic Games in the fifth century B.C..[1] Other historical examples include gladiatorial events at the Roman Coliseum, jousting tournaments in Medieval Europe, and the initiation of team football, baseball, and soccer competitions in the late 19th century. Beyond the sporting events themselves, visitors seek peripheral entertainment, lodging, and dining services, often creating a multi-day trip based on product and service offerings at the destination. Today, events such as the Super Bowl, the Olympics, and the World Cup are international in scope, generate millions of dollars in revenue, take place over extended periods of time, demand extensive collaborative planning and management expertise, and provide the impetus for infrastructure development and the employment of thousands of people.

The development of sports and entertainment complexes in the United States follows the ebb and flow of efforts to maintain a vital and vibrant downtown district in cities. In the mid-twentieth century urban residents, responding to increased housing and transportation options outside the city versus reduced property values and higher crime rates in central urban environments, fled downtown areas and settled in the suburbs. By the 1970s, the suburban population located in metropolitan statistical areas far exceeded the population in cities, creating what is referred to as the "doughnut effect."[2] Eventually, retail businesses followed their primary customers and relocated to more densely populated suburban areas.

Subsequent efforts to revive downtown areas attempted to capitalize on remaining identifiable advantages, namely unique cultural experiences in historical urban neighborhoods, ready access to centralized transportation via the pre-existing hub-and-spoke model, expansive public parking spaces,

The Olympics is a worldwide event that is complicated to organize.

creative municipal and private funding incentives, existing large sports venues such as stadiums and arenas, and the steady growth of the events and meetings market as well as the continued presence of downtown business workers.[3]

FESTIVAL MARKETPLACES AND ENTERTAINMENT CENTERS

By the 1980s, developer James W. Rouse (The Rouse Company) integrated many of these favorable urban aspects into what became known as the **festival marketplace**. Rouse successfully integrated downtown cultural districts and convention facilities with entertainment facilities, taking advantage of natural urban boundaries such as waterfronts and bridges to create a designed space that was safe and easily accessible to pedestrian traffic. One of Rouse's earliest efforts was Faneuil Hall in Boston (see http://www.faneuilhallmarketplace.com/), where a wealth of stores and restaurants surrounded the historical waterfront marketplace and attracted both local and non-resident visitors. These marketplaces featured unique specialty stores, a wide variety of food and entertainment options, and historical and architectural sites of interest, and were readily accessible to downtown lodging accommodations as well as public transportation. Importantly, the marketplaces also attracted a broader, more affluent demographic.

Festival marketplaces remain successful in many cities throughout the United States. Faneuil Hall attracts 20 million visitors annually.[4] Other well-known marketplaces include Pier 39 in San Francisco, California (see http://www.pier39.com), St. Louis Union Station (see http://www.stlouisunionstation.com), and Harborplace in Baltimore, Maryland (see http://www.harborplace.com). Underground Atlanta in Atlanta, Georgia (see http://www.underground-atlanta.com/) is a five-block historic site that originally served as the supply depot for the Confederate Army during the Civil War. In 1970, Underground Atlanta opened as an entertainment district that featured dining areas, specialty shops, and bars. It closed down in 1980 as the city metrorail system was constructed, during which time city leaders were successful in having the district registered as a National Historic Place. Renovated at a cost of $142 million through a joint venture between the City of Atlanta and private industry, the site reopened in 1989 with an expressed

Faneuil Hall attracts 20 million visitors annually.

© Jorge Salcedo/Shutterstock.com

mission of preserving and revitalizing the center of Atlanta as the focal point of community life. Underground Atlanta offers a complete family experience, with specialty and gift shops, unique features and entertainment, special events, and fine restaurants. In addition, visitors can easily move from Underground to nearby attractions such as Centennial Olympic Park, CNN Center, the Georgia Aquarium, the World of Coca Cola, and the Georgia Dome.

As festival marketplaces grew in popularity, so too did other forms of entertainment centers. **Location-based entertainment** sites (LBEs) are entertainment sites commonly anchored by a multi-screen cinema. Beyond the movie theatre, LBEs typically feature themed restaurants, stores, museums, and sports arenas.[5] When adults rather than children or families are identified as target markets, these centers may be referred to as UECs, **urban entertainment centers**. Factors contributing to the growth of these centers included increased leisure time and disposable income among consumers, a growing market seeking family entertainment, and aggressive financing incentives from both public and private institutions. In many instances, these entertainment centers have supplanted the arcane shopping center or mall in the minds of consumers by adding elements of fun and variety to the shopping experience. The Verizon Center in Washington, D.C. (see http://verizoncenter.monumentalnetwork.com/) is an example of an LBE site that has made the obvious link to sports entertainment. The complex houses a 30-screen theatre, theme restaurants, museums, and a Disney store. The arena hosts three national sports teams: the Washington Wizards and Mystics (men's and women's basketball) and National Hockey League's Washington Capitals.

URBAN ENTERTAINMENT CENTERS AND DISTRICTS

In the 1990s, partnerships between retail and large-scale entertainment companies such as Sony, Paramount, and Disney created adult-oriented **urban entertainment destinations or centers** known as UECs.[6] The added expertise of successful theme park entertainment companies like Disney provided new and creative ways of integrating local attractions, shows, shopping, dining, lodging, and meeting/event space. UECs draw primarily upon downtown tourist traffic but also serve local residents. One of the first successful ventures was the collaborative effort between Disney and New York City interests that resulted in the revamped family-oriented entertainment destination, Times Square. This world-famous destination currently attracts 50 million visitors a year and is ranked as the third top travel destination in the world.[7] Another well-known example of a UEC is Dave & Buster's, which currently operates 83 venues in the United States and Canada.

It was a simple strategic step to link the urban entertainment center with other pre-existing facilities and services and thereby market the multi-purpose appeal of downtown districts. Hence, city planners and private developers worked together to link stadiums, arenas, convention centers, and other public facilities into a comprehensive and accessible destination location for sports and entertainment seekers. "Without exception, all cities turned to sports facilities to anchor development."[8] With these added venues, developers and municipal authorities could entice corporate investment interests with naming rights for stadiums and arenas as well as attract higher income fans. Many argued the economic advantages of bringing professional sports franchises to the city,[9] although economic downsides to the ventures were duly noted.[10]

Urban entertainment centers have thus expanded to become urban entertainment districts or **mega-developments**, expansive destinations that appeal to and serve many different customers. Judd (1999) referred to this safe, stylish, planned entertainment environment as a "**tourist bubble**." Various forms of public transportation provide tourists ready and affordable access to a host of entertainment options. And the relative proximity to a full range of downtown lodging accommodations makes such destinations ideal for meeting and event attendees. Urban entertainment districts offer a dense collection of services directly accessible to convention and conference centers, thereby providing the means and capacity to host thousands of tourists at one time.

Chelsea Piers Sports and Entertainment Complex in New York City (see http://venues.chelseapiers.com/index.com) is a 28-acre "waterfront sports village" located in Manhattan on the Hudson River. The complex, developed from the piers that originally served the great cruise ships of the early 20th century, offers a wide variety of sports venues including The Golf Club; The Sports Center Health Club and Spa; a state-of-the-art training center called the Blue Streak; the year-round ice skating Sky Rink; a Bowling Center; a Maritime Center; film, television, and photographic Silver Studios; and the Chelsea Piers Fieldhouse, which includes a gymnastics training center, a 28-foot rock climbing wall, basketball courts and batting cages, two indoor turf fields, a kids' gym, and special sports facilities to accommodate multiple competitive sports teams and leagues.

Times Square is a world-famous revamped family-oriented entertainment destination.

Chelsea Piers is a "waterfront sports village" on the Hudson River.

With added dining concepts and event and exhibition space, Chelsea Piers Sports and Entertainment Complex epitomizes the success of the urban entertainment vision.

An international example of a UEC is the Crown Perth Complex (formerly Burswood) (see https://www.crownperth.com.au/) located on the Swan River near Perth, Western Australia. Recently rebranded by Crown Limited (2012), one of Australia's largest gaming and entertainment management companies, the complex includes a casino, nightclubs, bars, and restaurants, two luxury hotel properties, a convention center, theatre, and the Crown Perth Dome (sports/event arena). Although not directly located in a downtown area, the complex is convenient to the Burswood Train Station so that visitors have quick and easy access to downtown Perth.

VENUE MANAGEMENT

When urban entertainment centers expanded in size, area, market, and purpose, they frequently attracted companies that already specialized in providing managed services to leisure and recreation sites such as stadiums and arenas or to convention and conference centers. In these companies, operations management for such venues was grouped in a division called Attractions or Leisure Services and primarily focused on providing food and beverage services. While there were similarities between managing services in a national park or racetrack and a stadium, there were some distinct differences. The result for many companies was to revise their organizational structure to separate off-site attractions management such as parks and campgrounds from meeting, event, and entertainment management. By contrast, ARAMARK's Sports and Entertainment Division currently accommodates the full range of facilities, from convention centers and stadiums to amphitheaters, racetracks, and parks and resorts.

As mega entertainment districts grew in scope, companies such as SMG, ARAMARK, and Delaware North expanded their managed service offerings to market their expertise under the guise of **venue management**. For these companies, there were also real economic advantages to managing a complex of venues versus individual properties. For example, there are many "dark days" in stadiums, arenas, and meeting sites. Events may take place on Thursday through Sunday, with no activity on the other days of the week. It is difficult to maintain a fully qualified staff in this type of environment, much less to secure adequate numbers of part-time staff to appropriately serve crowds numbering in the tens of thousands. Operational efficiencies can be more easily achieved when resources such as personnel can be utilized across multiple venues.

In the past, management services primarily included oversight of facilities and/or delivery of foods and beverages/concessions. Recent growth has provided opportunities to expand managed services to include housekeeping and maintenance, uniform and laundry, operations planning, programming and design, cash management and budgeting, security, parking, landscaping and property maintenance, and additional retail services. Property owners and investors as well as municipal authorities respond positively to contracting with companies like SMG to provide complete or partial managed services. SMG, Delaware North, and ARAMARK as well as other venue management companies have even expanded into gaming (casinos and racetracks), lodging and resorts, and convention and meeting services. In addition, venue management often takes the form of special event management. Venues may accommodate unique, one-time events, ranging from customized weddings to film openings to religious revivals to the Olympics. Ensuring quality services for such unique experiences is a challenge that these management companies welcome. In addition, management companies offer owners and developers further benefits such as sustainable practices programs that can be adapted and implemented in specific venues.

SMG (see http://www.smgworld.com), a venue management company based out of Pennsylvania, was founded in 1977. SMG's very first client was the Louisiana Superdome in New Orleans. At the Superdome, SMG provided food and beverage services through what would eventually become their food-services division, SAVOR. Since that time, SMG has expanded its client list as well as its services. Separate company divisions operate in the United States, Europe, Asia, Mexico, and Latin America; and management services serve convention centers, stadiums, arenas, theatres, and special use sites such as the Aquarium of the Pacific in Long Beach, California. SMG also manages the Long Beach Convention and Entertainment Center, a waterfront multi-purpose complex that houses two theatres, extensive meeting

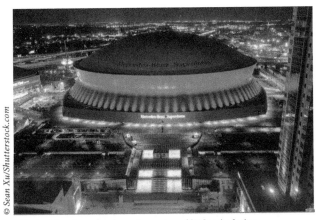
The Louisiana Superdome uses the services of SMG at the facility.

space/exhibit halls, and a sports arena. As with other UECs, it provides direct pedestrian access to downtown shopping, dining, and lodging.

Delaware North Companies (see http://www.delawarenorth.com/) is a family-run venue management company that offers a host of managed service options including real estate management, event management, and security services. The company operates in the United States, Canada, the United Kingdom, and Australia/New Zealand. Delaware North's operating divisions provide management expertise in food services, retail, resorts and hotels, special events catering, sports venues, parks and attractions, airports, and gaming. In fact, the Jacobs family (founders of Delaware North) are the owners of the National Hockey League Boston Bruins. The company provides management services at TD Garden Sports and Entertainment Arena (see http://www.tdgarden.com/), home to the Boston Celtics, Boston Blazers, and, of course, the Boston Bruins. The company also provides food services at MetLife Stadium in New Jersey, home to two NFL teams, the New York Giants and the New York Jets.

Evidence of the challenges of planning, developing, and completing sports and entertainment ventures can be found in the story of the Xanadu Meadowlands/American Dream project in New Jersey. Direction of this project falls under the New Jersey Sports and Exposition Authority (NJSEA). This massive complex includes MetLife Stadium, the IZOD Center (former home to the New Jersey Nets), Meadowlands Racetrack, the Timex Performance Center, and the original Giants Stadium. Railway lines directly access Hoboken and New York's Penn Station. Financial problems have plagued the project since its inception in 2002. However, in 2010, the NJSEA

signed a deal with Triple Five, operators of the Mall of America, to take over much of the project. A secondary agreement struck with DreamWorks has shed positive light on the current status of the project.[11] While the Complex successfully hosted one recent mega event, Super Bowl XLVIII (2014), original plans to bid for the 2018/2022 FIFA World Cup have been shelved. Estimated costs for the entire project currently exceed $5 billion. The success of the venture will depend on the collaboration and commitment of both private and public interests.

MEGA EVENT SERVICES AND MANAGEMENT

We cannot leave the subject of sports and entertainment centers without addressing **mega event** services. Urban entertainment districts as well as sporting facilities—or planned development of these complexes—are often selling points for cities that bid to host one of the premier mega sporting events. Among the most important are the Olympic Games (particularly the Summer Games), the FIFA World Cup, major league baseball's World Series, and football's Super Bowl. Cities, venue management companies, and host governments work closely with international and national organizations to successfully host these events, coordinating myriad services over an extended period of time. Strategic planning for these events usually starts at least five years in advance of the event itself.

As previously noted, ARAMARK Corporation is one of the leading venue management service companies. A particular area of expertise for ARAMARK is the provision of services during the Olympic

The FIFA World Cup is a mega event.

Games (see http://www.aramarkentertainment. com/). ARAMARK has been integrally involved in providing food and other services to athletes, officials, and media at Olympic Games venues since 1968, including the 2010 Vancouver Winter Olympics and the 2012 London Summer Olympics, and the 2016 Rio de Janeiro Summer Olympics. The company estimated the number of meals served within the London Olympic village at 70,000 per day.[12] During the Beijing Olympics in 2008, ARAMARK served three and a half million meals to over 28,000 people using approximately 7,000 employees.[13] ARAMARK proudly promotes its "Olympic Heritage," the ability to plan and implement services on such a scale. The company has developed mega event expertise over the almost 50 years it has been serving Olympics customers.

The 2014 FIFA World Cup in Brazil was considered a major tourism success by organizing authorities, who reported 1.35 million overall tourism arrivals during the two-month event period ("Successo!"). Venue management services for this event were provided at twelve different stadiums across the country, not to speak of the peripheral entertainment services required. The projected overall economic impact of the Brazil 2014 FIFA World Cup is estimated to be $130.7 billion. New jobs generated by the World Cup and the 2016 Summer Olympics are estimated at 3.6 million.[14] Organizers of such mega events look not only at the direct impact of tourist spending but also at infrastructure improvements and additions as well as worldwide market exposure that should have positive economic effects for years beyond the event itself.[15]

THE FUTURE AND CAREERS

The current revival and development of downtown entertainment districts and the continued passion that America and other countries has for sporting events of all kinds have served to brighten the future for sports and entertainment complexes. Certainly, the herculean efforts to complete the Meadowlands entertainment complex and its associated venues attest to the interests of civic authorities, venue management services, and consumers to provide a centralized, accessible, and safe environment in which customers of all types can be entertained. As previously noted, such projects take advantage of pre-existing infrastructure such as transportation

systems and parking, cultural attractions, and financial incentives. Revitalization and/or development efforts represent a significant long-term investment in metropolitan growth.[16]

Career opportunities in the sports and entertainment managed services industry are numerous and varied. The more traditional routes of working in this industry involve working for one of the major venue management companies such as ARAMARK or SMG. Entry points for employment would include food services in the form of concessions or catering services, sales and marketing, lodging services, maintenance, or human resources. You might also access this industry by working for one of the civic authorities in positions such as box office sales, event booking, or facilities management. Retail management provides another avenue of career growth. And finally, you may wish to work with an organization such as the Olympic Federation or FIFA in any number of event planning or operational capacities. Whichever path you choose, you will definitely find yourself in a fun, exciting, and challenging career.

SUMMARY

For thousands of years, sporting events and other forms of festivals and mass entertainment have served to draw people to urban centers. Such events—and the corresponding needs of patrons—have served to cement the importance of allocating public funds towards the maintenance of downtown neighborhoods as well as providing a crucial stimulus to further urban development. Mega events such as the Summer and Winter Olympics and the National Football League's Super Bowl are international in scope, drawing millions of tourists from all over the world, often—as in the case of FIFA's World Cup—for extended periods of time. Improved infrastructure and the creation of new jobs are just two of the benefits of hosting such an event. Others include the preservation and promotion of unique cultural environments and practices, expanded access to facilities for local residents, and long-term public-private project collaboration. More recently, urban entertainment centers (UECs), readily accessible to public transportation and downtown lodging accommodations, have significantly increased the appeal of many cities targeting the lucrative meeting and events market.

Increasingly, public-private partnerships involve venue management companies such as ARAMARK and Delaware North. The managed services of these companies have grown well beyond the food and beverage/concessions services that were the focus of early contracts to include services ranging from programming and design, security, and operations planning to special event management. The expertise offered by venue management companies plays an integral role in the success of these ventures. Employment opportunities with these companies or with the civic entities that provide the venues are plentiful, exciting, and available worldwide.

RESOURCES

Internet Sites

http://www.theo2.co.uk/

http://www.faneuilhallmarketplace.com/

http://www.pier39.com/

http://www.stlouisunionstation.com/

http://www.harborplace.com/

http://verizoncenter.monumentalnetwork.com/

http://www.underground-atlanta.com/

http://venues.chelseapiers.com/index.com

https://www.crownperth.com.au/

http://smgworld.com/

http://www.delawarenorth.com/

http://www.tdgarden.com/

http://www.aramark.com/

http://www.aramarkentertainment.com/

http://www.london2012.com/

http://www.rio2016.org.br/en/the-games/olympic/event)

Question Sources

http://aegworldwide.com/facilities/facilities

http://www.olympic.org/pyeongchang-2018-winter-olympics

REFERENCES

Anonymous. (1998, September). Entertainment centers. *E.S.P.* Retrieved from http://www.specialtyretail.net/issues/sept98/entertainmentpg2.htm

Appleton, K. (2014, November). These are the most visited tourist attractions in the world. *Time*. Time, Inc. Retrieved from http://time.com/3581918/most-visited-tourist-attractions/

Baade, R.A., & Sanderson, A.R. (1997). The employment effect of teams and sports facilities. In Roger G. Noll and Andrew Zimbalist (Eds.), *Sports, jobs, and taxes: The economic impact of sports teams and stadiums* (pp 92–118). Washington: The Brookings Institution Press.

Baedeker, R. (2010). America's top 10 tourist attractions. *Forbes Traveler.com*. Retrieved from http://travel.yahoo.com/p-interests-25465855

Bender, J.S. (2003). *An examination of the use of urban entertainment centers as a catalyst for downtown revitalization.* Unpublished master's thesis. Virginia Polytechnic Institute and State University, VA.

Coates, D., & Humphreys, B. (2003). Professional sports facilities, franchises and urban economic development. *Public Finance and Management, 3*(3), 335–357.

Deng, Y., & Poon, S.W. (2014). Positioning mega-event flagships – from Performing Arts Center of Expo 2010 to Mercedes-Benz Arena. *Architectural Engineering and Design Management, 10*(3–4), 233–250.

DreamWorks Announces Indoor Theme Park in New Jersey (2012, June 12). Retrieved from http://www.businessinsider.com/dreamworks-announces-indoor-theme-park-in-new-jersey-2012-7#ixzz2QTbGh2qUIt

Global Hospitality Insights: Top Thoughts for 2012. (2012) EYGM, Limited. Retrieved from http://www.ey.com/publication/vwluassets/top-thoughts-for-2012/$file/top-thoughts-for-2012.pdf

Harris, W. (2014, June 20). FIFA World Cup financial impact to Brazil economy. Retrieved from http://www.businessofsoccer.com/2014/06/20/fifa-world-cup-financial-impact-to-brazil-economy/

Judd, D. (1999). Constructing the tourist bubble. In D. Judd & S. Fainstein (Eds.), *The tourist city* (pp. 35–53). New Haven: Yale University Press.

Lentz, B.F., & Laband, D.N. (2008). *The impact of college athletics on employment in the restaurant and accommodation industries.* North American Association of Sports Economists (Working Paper No. 08–03). Retrieved from http://college.holycross.edu/RePEc/spe/LentzLaband_CollegeAthletics.pdf

Markerink, H.J., & Santini, A. (2004). The development of stadiums as center of large entertainment areas: The Amsterdam arena case. *SYMPHONYA Emerging Issues in Management, 2.* Retrieved from http://www.unimib.it/go/Home/Italiano/Symphonya-Emerging-Issues-in-Management/2004-Issue-2-Sport-Management-and-Global-Markets

Matheson, V. (2006). Mega-Events: The effect of the world's biggest sporting events on local, regional, and national economies. (Unpublished manuscript). College of the Holy Cross, Worcester, MA.

Mickle, T. (2008, August 12). Aramark serves record number of Olympic meals. Retrieved from http://www.sportsbusinessdaily.com/beijinggames/entries/2008/aramark-serves-record-number-of-olympic-meals

Turner, R.S., & Rosentraub, M.S. (2002). Tourism, sports, and the centrality of cities. *Journal of Urban Affairs, 24*(5), 487–492.

VonBergen, J.M. (2012, July 23). Philadelphia-based Aramark caters to Olympic athletes. Retrieved from http://articles.philly.com/2012-07-23/business /32789135_1_olympic-village-aramark-executive-olympic-athletes.

ENDNOTES

1. (Markerink & Santini, 2004).

2. (Bender, 2003).

3. (Bender, 2003; Turner & Rosentraub, 2002).

4. (Baedeker, 2010).

5. (Entertainment Centers, 1998).

6. (Bender, 2003).

7. (Appleton, 2014).

8. (Turner & Rosentraub, 2002, p. 489).

9. (Coates & Humphreys, 2003; Lentz & Laband, 2008).

10. (Baade & Sanderson, 1997; Matheson, 2006).

11. ("DreamWorks Announces Indoor Theme Park In New Jersey", July 12, 2012).

12. (VonBergen, 2012).

13. (Mickle, 2008).

14. (Harris, June 20, 2014).

15. (Deng & Poon, 2014; "Global Hospitality Insights: Top Thoughts for 2012").

16. (Deng & Poon, 2014).

Name: _____ Date: _____

1. What are some examples of historical forerunners of sports and entertainment events?

2. Explain how the economic conditions of urban areas affected the development of sports and entertainment centers.

3. How is a festival marketplace different from an urban entertainment district?

4. If you were presenting a proposal to a development company about the advantages of creating an urban entertainment district, what advantages would you identify?

5. Explain how sports centers became associated with urban entertainment centers. Give an example.

6. Visit a sports and entertainment complex website. Describe the location and the range of services offered. Identify nearby attractions and accommodations.

7. Based on this chapter, explain what type of environment and facilities are included in a "tourist bubble."

8. What are some managed services offered by a venue management company? Give an example of one company that provides these services.

9. Visit the website of AEG Worldwide to identify examples of sustainability practices that have been implemented on their managed properties (http://www.aegworldwide.com/about/companyovervicw/aeg1earth). What are some of these practices? Find and discuss another management company that promotes sustainable initiatives.

10. What is an example of a mega event? What makes a mega event unique?

11. Visit the website for the 2016 Rio de Janeiro Summer Olympics and Paralympics (http://www.rio2016.org.br/en/the-games/olympic/event) or the 2018 PyeongChang Winter Olympics (http://www.olympic.org/pyeongchang-2018-winter-olympics). Check out some of the quick facts and figures on the home page. What do you find most interesting? Identify and list the venue sites. What managed services should be offered at these sites?

CHAPTER *30*

© Krivosheev Vitaly/Shutterstock.com

GOLF MANAGEMENT

AUTHOR	*Don Farr, Florida State University*
LEARNING OBJECTIVES	• Understand the history of the game and the business of golf.
	• Recognize the economic impact golf has on the U.S. economy.
	• Identify recent trends within the golf industry.
	• Differentiate the various types of golf facilities and their functions in society.
	• Understand golf's role within the environmental, societal, and economic landscape.
CHAPTER OUTLINE	Brief History of the Game of Golf
	The Game of Golf
	The Business of Golf
	Careers in Golf
	Trends
	Summary
KEY TERMS	Club Managers Association of America PGA professional
	Golf formats Sustainability
	USGA handicap

BRIEF HISTORY OF THE GAME OF GOLF

Folklore tells us that the game of golf originated during the 15th century when shepherds passed time by propelling small rocks into rabbit holes, perfecting their new talent among naturally bunkered landscapes, using their crook designed for herding sheep as a club. In truth, the origins of golf can be traced back to 100 BC to the Roman game of paganica, a game where participants hit a leather ball stuffed with wool or feathers.[1] Over the years as the Roman Empire expanded throughout Europe the game moved with it. France, Belgium, and the Netherlands also stake claim to inventing the game, but they are likely recipients of the Roman expansion. Regardless, the game of golf grew.[2] It grew to the point that in 1457 the Scottish government and King James II enacted a law prohibiting its soldiers from participating in golf because it took away from its soldiers' archery practice.

In 1552 Archbishop Hamilton gave the right to citizens of St. Andrews, Scotland to play golf on the Old Course.[3] From that point on golf expanded throughout Scotland. Wealthy travelers brought the game with them to France, Switzerland, Spain, and as far away as South Africa. Golf was first brought over to the U.S. by Scottish immigrants in 1780, who built a course near Charleston, South Carolina. That course provided entertainment to local men before its collapse a few years after its creation. It was nearly 100 years later before North America hosted another golf course when the Montreal Golf Club was established in 1873, five years prior to the development of the New St. Andrews Club in Yonkers, New York. In the late 1890's and early 1900's golf course development expanded from Boston to Belleair, Florida, with a few golf courses as far west as Chicago and even California.

Today there are nearly 25 million golfers, averaging 19 rounds of golf a year, who play on the 15,500 golf courses scattered throughout the U.S.[5] However, the number of golfers has been stagnant over the past several years and the number of golf course closings have exceeding new development every year for nearly a decade. Some say golf is at a crossroads in the U.S. A combination of over development, economic crises, and a new generation of people who value time and experiences more than the prestige that membership in a golf club has historically offered, has made it more challenging for golf course operators to retain and attract new golfers. Additionally, the recent emphasis on social and environmental sustainability has put new golf course development on alert.

THE GAME OF GOLF

Golf is a game that is played on diverse landscapes, under different playing conditions, and in unique geographical settings. Unlike many games, the backdrop on which golf is played always differs; no two golf courses are the same. In fact, depending on weather conditions, the time of year, or even the time of day, the playing circumstances fluctuate every time a golfer plays the same golf course. During the morning round a slight breeze may be blowing in from the west with temperatures cool until the afternoon sun warms up the atmosphere. Later in the round the winds may shift and the temperatures may rise, both affecting the flight of a golf ball. Beach courses offer different views and playing conditions than mountain courses. In fact, barometric pressure, humidity, and even altitude can affect the flight of a golf ball in various ways, all adding to the challenge and inimitability of the game.

Golf is a game where you can compete against yourself, or, using a certified **USGA (U.S. Golf Association)** handicap, compete equally against other players of various skill levels. A plethora of **golf formats** (See Table 30.1) can be used depending on the purpose of

No two rounds of golf are ever the same.

© FloridaStock/Shutterstock.com

Table 30.1 Common Golf Formats

Individual Stroke Play "Gross"	An individual counts the total number of strokes played over the course of a round.
Individual Stroke Play "Net"	An individual counts the total number of strokes played over the course of a round and subtracts his or her USGA handicap from the total.
Match Play	A player or a team earns a point for each hole they win against an opponent.
Better "Best" Ball	A team of two or more golfers each play their own ball for a hole. Only the better or "best" score is chosen as the team's score for that hole.
Scramble	Every golfer on a team hits a tee shot. The best tee shot is selected and all golfers on the team hit their second shots from the location of the selected drive. This format is continued until the ball is holed.
Alternate Shot	Usually played with two-person teams, only one player hits the tee shot, the other player hits the second shot, and they continue alternating shots until the ball is holed.

the round. Business associates may engage in a game of golf to entertain a client in hopes of closing an important corporate deal, couples may play with friends for the purpose of social interaction, while professionals compete for prize monies. Most golf courses have 18 holes, although there are several 9-hole and executive golf courses that are much shorter and cater to senior citizens and beginning golfers. The distances with which a golf course is set up can be changed depending on a player's age, playing ability, or preference. Golf courses generally range in distance from 5000 yards for seniors and beginners to 7500 yards for golf professionals. The typical golf course has four sets of tees; on average about 5,000 yards for women, 5500 yards for seniors, 6300 yards for men, and 7100 for accomplished amateurs and golf professionals. Most golf courses consist of 18 holes made up of par 3's, par 4's, and par 5's. The standard total par for an 18-hole course is 72, but it can vary from 69 to 73 depending on the specific facility.

Before a person attempts to learn the game they should take a series of golf lessons from a **PGA (Professional Golfers' Association) of America golf professional**. The initial lesson generally starts with some tips on golf etiquette. Safety, which includes where to stand while others swinging a club, maintaining the golf course by raking bunkers, fixing ball marks, and replacing divots, and common courtesy such as being silent and not moving while others are playing a shot are all part of etiquette. Other etiquette tips are included in *The Official Rules of Golf* which is divided into three sections: etiquette, definitions, and the rules of play. The rule book consists

of 34 rules and is published in a joint venture by the United States Golf Association (USGA) and the Royal and Ancient Golf Club of St. Andrews. Major rules changes occur every four years, but verbiage can be altered every year as needed, to eliminate possible duplication or grammatical confusion.

The actual playing surface of a golf course generally consists of four areas, the teeing ground, the fairway, the putting green, and the rough. The teeing ground is the area where each hole begins and is the only place on the golf course where the player is actually permitted to use a "tee" to prop up the ball. The fairway is the closely mown area between the teeing ground and the eventual target, the putting green. The putting green is an area where the flagstick is located and, because of this, has the shortest and best maintained grass on the course. If any of your golf shots go astray it is likely that your ball

Before attempting to play golf, a person should take lessons.

will end up in the tall grass bordering the fairways called the rough. The rough is the least maintained turf and is frequently difficult to hit out of. In addition to the rough, many courses also have sand bunkers, water hazards, and trees that should be avoided if at all possible.

The ultimate goal of the game is to play the course in as few shots as possible. The average male golfer scores in the high 90's for 18 holes, whereas the best amateurs in the world and golf professionals often shoot in the 60's on good days. Golf is one of the few sports where you can play against yourself, play against par, play against a superior opponent using your USGA handicaps as an equalizer, or play socially with friends. Watching the rules of golf explained on television, or even listening to the men and women discussing rules situations at the local club, can seem daunting to the beginning golfer. However, in its simplest form, you hit the golf ball, find it, and hit it again until it is holed and continue that process until the round is completed.

THE BUSINESS OF GOLF

When many people think of the golf business they think about the mammoth golf companies such as Callaway or Titleist. However, retail sales is only a small part of the total economic impact golf has on the community. Other revenue sources generated by golf include: golf fees, television contracts, sponsorship, tournament revenues, food and beverage, and travel. In fact, the retail side of the golf industry only accounts for about 6.7% of the total golf industry in the United States. Of all the industry segments that directly affect our economy, the operations of the 15,350 golf facilities make up the largest amount of revenues at $28 billion.[6] In total, the latest economic indicators identify the direct contribution attributed to golf at nearly $70 billion with an indirect impact of $176 billion annually.[7] Furthermore, golf supports two million jobs and $55.6 billion in annual wages.[8] Golf is played by approximately 25 million Americans who play 455 million rounds per year.[9] In addition to the for-profit revenues generated by the different revenue sources, according to Steve Mona, the CEO of the World Golf Foundation, golf generated $3.9 billion for charities through the participation of 12 million golfers in 143,000 golf events.[10]

Retail companies like Callaway only make up a small portion of the total economic impact of golf.

© 360b/Shutterstock.com

The nearly $4 billion in charitable contributions was more than that of the NBA, MLB, NHL, and NFL combined.

Not included in these numbers is the countless business transactions that occur on golf courses. Golf, above any other sport, is the perfect setting for talking business. You get to spend about 4 hours or more riding in the same golf car as your client, with only a small portion of your time hitting balls. You can have a friendly match regardless of the difference in playing abilities because of the USGA handicap system, and golf is a game where character is tested. You can learn a lot about the client's ability to control his temper during adversity, how they handle pressure situations, and see their respect for fellow competitors and the golf course. Many business executives suggest all college students would benefit from taking a college course in the business of golf.

CAREERS IN GOLF

Because golf touches so many sectors of business, the jobs created by the golf industry are limitless. The following section will focus on the managerial opportunities at most golf facilities.

The general manager is usually the senior manager at most clubs and is responsible for the entire operation including membership, golf, food and beverage, and the facility's financials. His direct reports include the director of golf or head golf professional, the golf course superintendent, food and beverage manager, chief financial officer, and all other executive

Table 30.2	Golf Industry Jobs		
General Manager	PGA Professional	Course Superintendent	Director of Golf
Merchandiser	Developer	Architect	Golf Coach
Tournament Coordinator	Educator	Corporate Executive	Journalist
Rules Official	Revenue Manager	Revenue Manager	Tour Player

committee managers. Traditionally, most general managers are elevated through the ranks in the food and beverage department, but many managers hired now are PGA of America golf professionals. GMs usually have a minimum of a four-year undergraduate business degree and have often earned an MBA, have ten or more years of industry experience, and are members of the **Club Manager's Association of America (CMAA)**. At private clubs GMs do not make policy, that is the responsibility of the board of directors, but they are charged with the implementation of the policy.

The director of golf is responsible for the entire golf operation, including tournaments, merchandising, outside service operations, golf instruction, and daily play management. In addition to these traditional golf duties, the director of golf also must work directly with the general manager on setting the golf operation budget and controlling labor costs for her department. He/she must also work regularly with the golf course superintendent to monitor possible course issues that may need addressing. Most directors of golf are PGA of America golf professionals. Golf professionals have two options for earning their PGA accreditation: they can work as apprentices at

golf facilities managed by PGA golf professionals for a minimum of three years or they can graduate from one of the 19 PGA of America accredited universities. Both programs generally take a minimum of 4.5 years to complete before earning membership in the PGA of America. There are currently 23,630 PGA of America members and 4,225 apprentices.[11] Of the 28,000+ members, about 1,000 are females, showing both a need and an opportunity for the membership to become more diverse.

The golf course superintendent is the behind-the-scenes department head whose success or failure greatly affects everyone affiliated with the golf course. He/she is responsible for supervising the golf course maintenance associates, preparing and adhering to the maintenance budget, and, most importantly, assuring the health and playability of the turf grass. Like most managers in the golf industry, the superintendent's job performance relies greatly on the decisions made by his superiors; unlike most, their job performance is also at the mercy of nature. Combating drought conditions, extreme heat, excessive rain, damaging wind, turf grass disease, insect infestation, and seasonal flooding are all a part of golf course superintendent's day. Many golf course

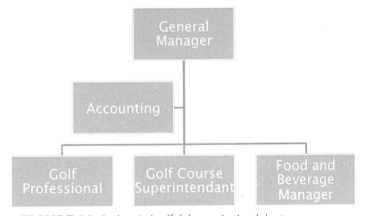

FIGURE 30.1 A typical golf club organizational chart.

FIGURE 30.2 A typical golf course organizational chart.

superintendents have a bachelor's degree in Agronomy or Turf Grass Management, a chemical application license, and commercial driver's license, and are certified by the Golf Course Superintendents Association of America (GCSAA). They must also have an extensive knowledge of irrigation systems, fertilizer applications, heavy equipment, and be able to manage their department in a sustainable manner.

The fourth element of the management team is the food and beverage (F&B) manager. The F&B manager must hire, train, and motivate their team of associates. He/she is responsible for compliance with all local, state, and federal liquor and food safety laws. He/she must provide a diverse menu that meets the needs of his/her customers while achieving the profit goals of the company. At many facilities he/she must be able to manage several different food venues, including fine dining, casual dining, weddings, banquets, bar food, halfway house, and even beverage cart foods and drink. The F&B manager must operate and control his/her department. He/she must understand food costs and other pertinent financial indicators, and he/she should be proficient in the use of computer spreadsheets, word processors, and database management.

The golf operation, like all hospitality industries, relies on their team of managers to work together to achieve the goals and objectives of the company. They must communicate with one another often because their jobs are so intertwined. The golf professional relies on the golf course superintendent for a playable golf course, allowing him/her to sell more tee times, which means more dollars to the club. The food and beverage manager relies on these additional rounds of golf, because each round produces ancillary F&B revenue for the facility. The golf course superintendent relies on these additional revenues to provide funds for special course projects, wages, and new equipment. The golf facility leaders are truly a team; when one succeeds all team members benefit, when one falls short of expectations, they all come together to find solutions.

TRENDS

A trend that has continued, initiated by the start of golf's decline in 2007, is the contracting of large management firms with the expertise and financial resources needed to prosper in a down economy. As the industry struggles to recover, more stressed

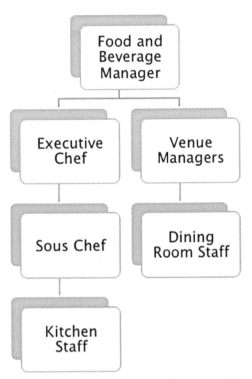

FIGURE 30.3 A typical golf club food and beverage service organizational chart.

public, resort, municipal, and private clubs will forgo the traditional route of managing their own facilities and hire these experts to lead them into the next decade.

The management companies listed in Table 30.3 own or operate 1200 golf facilities collectively, nearly doubling their ownership stake from four years ago as they look to add to their portfolios in the upcoming years.[12]

Another trend salient to golf is the economic, social, and environmental **sustainability** of the development and operation of golf facilities, especially overseas. Golf provides a landscape that can be argued is both conducive to the thriving of animal and fauna life and harmful to their natural habitat. Many golf courses have protected wet area sanctuaries that provide a haven for reptiles, insects, and small mammals to habitate safely to the environment. Additionally, golf facilities have developed successful water reclamation projects that could help municipalities better understand the practices involved in regenerating water run-off within the city. On the down side, golf still has a stigma for utilizing far too many harmful chemicals and fertilizers to maintain the pristine turf conditions showcased by the lush fairways of

Augusta National Golf Club, host of the Masters Golf tournament.

In addition to environmental challenges associated with golf course operations, social issues seem to be equally as prevalent and possibly more damaging. Throughout the development of the industry, the opportunity to purchase inexpensive land is at the forefront of many projects. Golf courses are often purchasing land in poor parts of town, promising a renaissance of the area. This gentrification often involves the displacement of low-income families, many of whom have to move several miles away from their homes because they can no longer afford the rent. Other social issues can include: the lack of representation from all stakeholders, exploitation of females and minors, and corruption.

SUMMARY

Golf is a game that has been described by some as "the greatest game on earth" and by others as a "good walk spoiled." What is not debatable is the hundreds of billions of dollars that are directly and indirectly added to our economy, the nearly $4 billion raised for charities, and the two million jobs created, simply to support the wants and needs of those who enjoy the game of golf. As the golf business is expected to grow for the next several years, it will be important for managers in all industries to understand the impact golf has on the lives of millions of people across the world while continuing to learn sustainable practices in order to reduce the harm done to the environment and unrepresented stakeholders.

RESOURCES

Internet Sites

American Society of Golf Course Architects: www.asgca.org

American Junior Golf Association: www.ajga.org

BBC: http://www.bbc.com/news/world-asia-china-34600544

Club Managers Association of America: www.cmaa.org

Executive Women's Golf Association: www.ewga.com

Golf Course Superintendents Association of America: www.gcsaa.org

International Golf Federation: http://www.igfgolf.org

Ladies Professional Golfers Association: www.lpga.com

National Alliance of Accessible Golf: www.accessgolf.org

National Amputee Golf Association: www.nagag-olf.org

National Golf Course Owners Association: www.ngcoa.org

National Golf Foundation: www.ngf.org

PGA Tour: www.pgatour.com

Professional Golfers' Association of America: www.pga.com

United States Golf Association: www.usga.org

Troon Golf http://www.troongolf.com/index.php

ENDNOTES

1. International Golf Federation, History of Golf, http://www.igfgolf.org/about-golf/history/

2. Pinner, J. (1988). *The History of Golf*. New York, NY: WH Smith Publishing Company.

3. International Golf Federation

4. Pinner, J. (1988). *The History of Golf*. New York, NY: WH Smith Publishing Company.

5. NGF, Industry Overview 2015

6. NGF, Golf Industry Overview 2012

7. Ibid

8. Forbes, Sport/Money, April 4 2015, The State of the Golf Industry in 2015, Darren Heitner,

9. Ibid

10. Ibid

11. PGA of America at http://www.pgalinks.com

12. Golf Inc. at http://www.golfincmagazine.com/management-companies

REVIEW QUESTIONS 30

1. Name one characteristic that differentiates golf from most other sports.

2. What is the standard "par" for a typical 18 hole golf course?

3. Identify one common golf format and briefly explain the distinguishing factors of the format you have selected.

4. Identify the various pecuniary impact factors the game of golf contributes to the economy in the United States.

5. How many charitable dollars can be attributed to fund raising efforts associated with the game of golf?

6. What is the largest golf management company in the world?

7. What area of the golf course is the flagstick located on?Identify turnover and discuss the difference between voluntary and involuntary turnover.

8. List some of the environmental benefits associated with the management of properly operated golf courses.

© EQRoy/Shutterstock.com

CHAPTER *31*

SPORTS, MEDICINE, AND TOURISM SPECIALTY AREAS

AUTHOR

Chris Brown, Kennesaw State University

LEARNING OBJECTIVES

- Understand and explain the travel and tourism industry.
- Explain the relationships between sport and tourism.
- Distinguish between the three types (i.e., active, event, and nostalgia) of sport tourism.
- Explain the relationship between medicine and tourism.
- Understand and define specialty or "niche" areas of tourism.

CHAPTER OUTLINE

Tourism
    Introduction
    Tourism Defined
Sport Tourism
    Introduction
    Sport Tourism Defined
    Active Sport Tourism
    Event Sport Tourism
    Nostalgia Sport Tourism
Medical Tourism
    Introduction
    Medical Tourism Defined
    Overview of Medical Tourism

**CHAPTER OUTLINE
(Continued)**

Specialty Areas
   Introduction
   Adventure Tourism
   Eco-tourism
   Food/Culinary Tourism
Summary

KEY TERMS

Active sport tourism	Hard adventure tourism
Adventure tourism	Medical tourism
Eco-tourism	Niche tourism
Economic impacts	Nostalgia sport tourism
Event sport tourism	Soft adventure tourism
Food/culinary tourism	Travel and tourism

TOURISM

INTRODUCTION

Tourism has become one of the world's fastest growing industries, and it has developed into a global economic force few could have anticipated. The massive scope of the travel and tourism industry serves the needs of many (i.e., leisure and business travelers, niche travel markets) through a variety of services and products. The services and products connected to the tourism industry vary and comprise a network that includes, but is not limited to, transportation, accommodation, food service, and tour operators.

Tourism has grown exponentially because of new travel interests and greater opportunities available. Countries are beginning to understand that tourism can provide a positive **economic impact**. More specifically, many travel destinations have invested in infrastructure that has made their localities easier, safer, and more attractive to visit. In addition, tourism suppliers are using the Internet and other sources to sell their products and services directly to the consumer, which has opened up new and exciting travel opportunities. As tourism continues to be one of the fastest growing economic sectors in the United States and globally, both in terms of economic impact and employment opportunities, it is important to understand its influence.

TOURISM DEFINED

As stated, the tourism industry is growing rapidly. To improve the global understanding of tourism, the World Tourism Organization (UNWTO), which is the United Nations agency accountable for the advancement of responsible, sustainable, and universally accessible tourism, developed a uniform definition. According to the WTO (1994), "**tourism** comprises the activities of persons traveling to and staying in places outside of their usual environment for not more than one consecutive year for leisure, business and other purposes" (p. 9).

Based on the information presented, it is easy to see why tourism will continue to be one of the fastest growing industries in the United States and globally. As the tourism industry has grown, so has the specialty or "niche" areas within tourism. Specifically,

sport and medical tourism have received increased participation and interest from tourists in the last 20 years. In this chapter, sport and medical tourism will be discussed in further detail, as well as some popular specialty or **niche tourism** areas. The intent is to provide future hospitality and tourism professionals with an overview and general understanding of the various forms of tourism, as well as the interdependent relationship between tourism and its various sectors.

SPORT TOURISM

INTRODUCTION

Sport tourism is one of the many sectors within the worldwide travel and tourism industry.[1] More specifically, sport tourism has been recognized as one of the fastest growing sectors within the global tourism industry. According to the National Association of Sport Commissions (NASC), in 2014, there were 25.65 million sports visitors in the United States, spending approximately $8.96 billion.[2] However, sport-related travel is not new to the 21st century. Baron Pierre de Coubertaine, the father of the Modern Olympic Games, gave support for the development of sport tourism. The Greeks traveled to take part in the ancient Olympic Games from as early as 900 BC, and the Romans regularly staged popular sport competitions that drew large crowds of spectators from various locations.[3]

Worldwide, there is an increasing recognition of the natural relationship between sport and tourism. De Knop (2004) suggested that the relationship between sport and tourism in our modern world is interdependent. It is not simply that sport influences tourism; tourism also influences sport. That interdependent relationship that De Knop refers to occurs with such sporting events as the Olympics, the FIFA World Cup, and the Super Bowl

Government policy has also been influenced by sport tourism. Globally, numerous governments have introduced initiatives to encourage tourism related to sport in their countries. For example, Canada created the Canada Sport Tourism Alliance (www.canadiansporttourism.com), whose mission is to market Canada internationally as a preferred sport tourism destination and to enhance the overall profile of sport

The Atlanta Sports Council helped attract and support major sporting events to the city.

tourism within the country. In addition, the CTSA measures the economic impact of sporting events in Canada. According to CTSA (2014), sport tourism is a $5.2 billion Canadian dollar a year industry.

At the state and local levels, there has also been an increasing awareness of the potential benefits of sport tourism. For example, in Atlanta, GA, within the Metro Atlanta Chamber, there is a division specifically created to bring sporting events to the city, called the Atlanta Sports Council (www.metroatlantachamber.com/business/sports/atlanta-sports-council). One of the main goals of the Atlanta Sports Council (ASC) is to address advance-planning issues associated with hosting major sporting events, as well as to be an advocate for Atlanta's professional and collegiate sports teams and annual events.[4] The Atlanta Sports Council has played a role in helping to attract and support more than 50 major sporting events to the city of Atlanta, including Super Bowl XXVIII and XXXIV, the Centennial Olympic Games, two NCAA Women's Final Four, and four NCAA Men's Final Four.[5]

SPORT TOURISM DEFINED

Over the years, various definitions of sport tourism have been put forward. Most current definitions of sport tourism distinguish between two types of behavior: active, in which a person travels to take part in a sport, or passive, in which a person travels to watch a sport.[6] For the purposes of this chapter, a more comprehensive definition will be used. Gibson (1998b, p. 49) stated that sport tourism is "leisure based travel that takes individuals temporarily outside of their home communities to participate in physical activities (active sport tourism), to watch physical activities (event sport tourism), or to venerate attractions associated with physical activities (nostalgia sport tourism)."

ACTIVE SPORT TOURISM

Active sport tourism can simply be defined as a trip in which the tourist travels to take part in a competitive or noncompetitive sport or physical activity. Gibson (1998a) suggested that active sport tourism refers to participation in sports away from the home community. Golf, skiing, and mountain biking are some of the most popular forms of active sport tourism. Resorts and other sectors within the hospitality industry have become increasingly aware of the need to provide state-of-the-art facilities for the active sport tourist. It is suggested that "championship golf courses, challenging, well-groomed alpine ski runs, high quality tennis courts, a wide range of water sports, and modern fitness facilities lure the discerning active sport tourist."[7]

EVENT SPORT TOURISM

Event sport tourism can be described as a trip in which the tourist travels to watch a sporting event. Traditionally, event sport tourism is concerned with the development and marketing of sporting events to obtain economic and community benefits. In examining event sport tourism, there are generally two levels: the major events that draw international attention, and the small-scale sport event.[8] The Olympics and the FIFA World Cup are examples of sporting events that have become major tourist attractions.

Fenway Park is a popular spot for nostalgia sports tourists to visit.

But many sporting events take place on a much smaller scale and are considered spectator-centered events. For example, professional, collegiate, and amateur sports can be considered smaller spectator-centered events.

NOSTALGIA SPORT TOURISM

Nostalgia sport tourism can be described as a trip in which the tourist visits a sport-themed attraction such as the NFL or MLB Hall of Fame. However, for the majority of nostalgia sports tourists, sport is not the prime purpose of their trip. Redmond (1991) identified nostalgia sport tourism as a type of sport tourism where tourists travel to visit sport halls of fame, take sport-themed vacations, attend fantasy sport camps, or tour famous sport stadiums, like Fenway Park or Wrigley Field.

MEDICAL TOURISM

INTRODUCTION

Medical tourism is also referred to as "health tourism" or "medical travel," and, similar to sport tourism, medical tourism is not a new phenomenon. In the past decade, the attempt to achieve better healthcare while on vacation, through relaxation, exercise, or visits to spas, has been taken to a new level with the emergence of medical tourism.[9] In the United States, medical tourism generally refers to people traveling to less-developed countries for medical care. The fundamental premise of medical tourism is that the same care, or even better quality of care, may be available in other countries, and obtained at a more affordable cost than in the home country.[10] According to Gaines and Nguyen (2015), medical tourism is a worldwide, multibillion-dollar phenomenon that is expected to grow substantially in the next 5–10 years. Also, studies show that global healthcare tourism generates approximately $35 billion in economic activity annually and is growing at a faster rate than overall travel and tourism.[11] However, research suggests that data on medical tourism should be taken with a grain of salt. Hudson and Li (2012) concluded that research on medical tourism to date has been largely conceptual in nature, with major gaps in data analysis.

The concept of medical tourism dates back thousands of years. Most ancient civilizations recognized the therapeutic effects of mineral thermal springs and sacred temple baths.[12] In ancient Greece, for example, Greek worshipers traveled from all over the Mediterranean to visit the Asclepia Temples, created for Asclepius, known as the healing god, to seek cures for their ailments.

MEDICAL TOURISM DEFINED

There are various definitions and conceptualizations provided in the literature about medical tourism. Some definitions simply suggest that medical tourism is traveling with the express purpose of obtaining healthcare services abroad. Some definitions include a tourism component. Konrad (2009) stated that medical tourism can vary in scope in terms of tourist services offered, suggesting that medical treatments are sometimes packaged with complementary sightseeing tours and other vacation-oriented services. While there are various definitions used to define medical tourism, for this chapter, Connell provided one of the most suitable descriptions of medical tourism. Connell (2006, p. 1094) defined **medical tourism** as "a niche that has emerged from the rapid growth of what has become an industry, where people travel often long distances to overseas countries to obtain medical, dental and surgical care while simultaneously being holidaymakers."

OVERVIEW OF MEDICAL TOURISM

The medical tourism model has focused on individuals who leave their home country to pursue healthcare at a destination that may provide less costly care and a vacation-like experience.[13] To support the "vacation-like experience," Hopkins, Labonte,

A medical tourism trip might include a mud bath.

SPECIALTY AREAS

INTRODUCTION

A tourism specialty area, or "niche tourism," refers to how a specific tourism product can be designed to meet the needs of a particular market segment. Niche tourism focuses on the consumer market segments, interests, and travel desires that make the destination more attractive and marketable.[15] With the tremendous growth of tourism worldwide, tourists have become more sophisticated travelers and are in search of more meaningful experiences. Destinations and tourism providers are continually searching for ways to differentiate themselves with specific niche tourism products.

There are numerous types of specialty or "niche tourism" sectors. In this chapter; the focus will be on three specific forms of niche tourism: 1) adventure tourism, 2) eco-tourism, and 3) food/culinary tourism.

Runnels, and Packer (2010) suggested that many medical tourists are motivated by the inclusion of travel and accommodations as part of their treatment. Since research has suggested that travel and "vacations" are beginning to describe medical tourism, a number of countries are seeking to develop medical tourism opportunities for international patients. According to Patients Beyond Borders (2014), popular medical travel destinations include: Costa Rica, Ecuador, India, Israel, Malaysia, Mexico, Singapore, South Korea, Taiwan, Thailand, Turkey, and the United States. These countries are looking to compete in the ever-expanding medical tourism market by advertising a wide variety of medical services that are offered in comfortable, modern, resort-style facilities. In addition, many international medical facilities are exploring partnerships with hotels and other hospital entities to promote entire medical tourism packages to interested patients.[14]

In many ways, the growth of medical tourism can be attributed to the Internet. Medical tourism websites and travel agencies typically offer package deals, with travel, accommodation, and recovery from surgery that is advertised like an all-inclusive vacation. Cortez (2008) supported the connection between medical tourism and the Internet by suggesting that the industry is facilitated by a growing number of Internet-based brokerages, linking patients to facilities, allowing consumers to schedule services, contact their surgeons, book airfare and accommodation, and arrange for tourist excursions.

ADVENTURE TOURISM

Adventure tourism is a rapidly growing type of niche tourism where tourists seek a more non-traditional vacation, oftentimes involving more challenges than the typical vacation. Adventure tourism is seen as a form of tourism that has an element of risk and danger, and provides the traveler with a sense of

White water rafting is a popular form of adventure tourism.

challenge and exhilaration.[16] Adventure tourism relies on natural and environmental features, such as mountains, rivers, or forests.

While there are various definitions used to define adventure tourism, all the definitions have a similar theme, suggesting that adventure tourism involves travel to remote areas, possibly hostile, where the tourist is provided a challenging and intense experience. For this chapter, the adventure tourism definition provided by the Adventure Travel Trade Association (ATTA) (see www.adventuretravel.biz) will be used. The ATTA defines **adventure tourism** as "a trip travelling outside a person's normal environment for more than 24 hours and not more than one (consecutive) year that includes at least two of the following three elements: physical activity, natural environment, and cultural immersion."[17] In addition, the ATTA states there are approximately 34 types of activities considered as different forms of adventure tourism, including but not limited to mountain biking, scuba diving, skiing, rock climbing, and white water rafting.

TYPES OF ADVENTURE

Research has suggested that there are different types and levels of adventure tourism, categorizing them as either "soft" or "hard" adventure.

Soft Adventure

Hill (1995) defined **soft adventure tourism** as activities with perceived risk but low levels of real risk; it is usually suitable for family involvement and provides an introduction to new and unique experiences. Soft adventure travel activities could include camping, canoeing, and wildlife viewing.[18]

Hard Adventure

Hill (1995) defined **hard adventure tourism** as activities with high levels of risk requiring advanced skills. "Participants usually join together because of an intense interest in some activity outside the confines of commercial outfitting."[19] Examples might include climbing Yosemite's El Capitan, or rafting Cataract Canyon.[20]

Millington, Locke, and Locke (2001) specified that the main difference between hard and soft adventure tourism was that hard adventure requires previous experience and proficiency in the activity prior to the experience, while soft adventure does not necessarily involve the need for prior experience.

ECO-TOURISM

One of the fastest growing travel markets within the tourism industry, specifically within the niche tourism segment, is eco-tourism. By design, eco-tourism intends to provide a low-impact adventure in a natural setting. A primary focus of eco-tourism is on experiencing natural areas in a manner that fosters environmental and cultural understanding, appreciation, and conservation.

One of the most widely used definitions of eco-tourism comes from the International Eco-tourism Society (TIES) (see www.ecotourism.org). The International Eco-tourism Society is an important organization within the tourism industry. TIES defines **eco-tourism** as "responsible travel to natural areas that conserves the environment, sustains the well-being of the local people, and involves interpretation and education."[21]

According to Crossley, Jamieson, and Brayley (2012), and the International Eco-tourism Society (2015b), eco-tourists, compared to other tourists, have a specific demographic profile. Eco-tourists are more likely than other tourists to travel internationally, and to be between the ages of 35 and 54, more highly educated than the average traveler, and affluent. Eco-tourists want to experience a natural environment and learn about the area's history and culture, and they typically stay longer at a destination. Eco-tourism opportunities include but are not limited to hik-

Hiking is an eco-tourism activity.

ing, snorkeling, cultural events, wildlife watching, and photography.

FOOD/CULINARY TOURISM

As a specialty or niche tourism area, food/culinary tourism has grown exponentially in recent years. For example, experiencing wonderful dining experiences while traveling has become part of the itineraries of many tourists while visiting cities and countries. Furthermore, with the growing global interest in nutrition, cuisine, and gastronomy, an increasing number of destinations are attempting to use their cuisine and culinary tradition as a tourism advantage and attraction for potential tourists.[22]

As with many tourism niche areas, there are a variety of definitions within the literature. Kalkstein-Silkes, Cai, and Lehto (2008, p. 66) define food/culinary tourism "as experiencing food and food related elements at a destination." Hall and Mitchell (2001) provide a more comprehensive definition, stating that food/culinary tourism is "visitation to primary and secondary food producers, food festivals, restaurants and special locations for which food tasting and/or experiencing the attributes of specialist food production region are the primary motivating factor for travel" (p. 308). For this chapter, the World Food Travel Association (2015) definition will be used, which states that "**food tourism** is the pursuit and enjoyment of unique and memorable food and drink experiences, both far and near."[23]

While tourists have always dined while traveling, food/culinary tourism as a specific and systematic business trend did not emerge in the tourism industry until the beginning of the millennium.[24] Since the emergence of food/culinary tourism, many organizations promoting food/culinary tourism have been established. Most notable is the World Food Travel Association (see www.worldfoodtravel.org/).

Historically, the two countries most associated with food/culinary tourism are Italy and France. Both have highly developed and respected cuisines.[25] However, other countries have also established themselves as food/culinary tourism destinations, specifically Canada, Australia, Great Britain, and the United States. An ever expanding form of food/culinary tourism is walking tours. By combining culinary interests with walking tours, sampling tours have become a popular tourist activity in cities like New Orleans, Seattle, New York, and Boston. A group can sample food and drink from several restaurants or vendors, oftentimes just blocks apart from each other. These tours generally have a specific theme or focus. Some tours focus on beer or wine, or locally sourced foods or even chocolate. For example, the New Orleans Culinary History Tours (see www.noculinarytours.com) offers daily walking tours that include several historical restaurants.

In addition to walking tours, food and wine festivals and beverage tours are becoming very popular forms of food/culinary tourism. For example, thousands of food and wine festivals are held annually, including the five-day Taste of Chicago and the Food Networks' South Beach Wine & Food Festival. The Distilled Spirits Council of the United States has developed the American Whiskey Trail with distillers in Virginia, Kentucky, and Tennessee. In addition, there is the Kentucky Bourbon Trail, created by the Kentucky Distillers Association.

SUMMARY

This chapter provides a brief overview of the sports, medicine, and specialty or "niche" sectors within the tourism industry. Sports, medical, and specialty areas of tourism continue to be exciting and ever-expanding sectors within the industry. For example, sport is becoming a multi-billion dollar a year industry and has become a significant part of everyday lives for millions of people. In addition, Patients Beyond Borders (2014) suggested that the population is aging and becoming more affluent at rates that exceed the availability of quality healthcare, suggesting that the global and national markets for medical tourism are likely to remain vibrant.

As tourism continues to grow exponentially over the next several years, it is important for managers in all areas of the industry to understand the impact travel and tourism has on the lives of all people involved within the industry. Sports, medicine, and tourism specialty areas provide an exciting and sometimes glamorous area to work in within the tourism industry. Due to the growing and international nature of the industry, managing and working in this business can be exciting and demanding at the same time.

RESOURCES

Internet Sites

Adventure Travel Trade Association: www.adventuretravel.biz

American Hospitality Academy: www.american-hospitalityacademy.com

American Resort Development Association - ARDA: www.arda.org

Creative Sports/Travel: www.creativetravelgroup.com

Esoteric Sports Tours: www.esotericsports.com

Fodor's: www.fodors.com

Food Tourism: www.tastetrekkers.com

Great Atlantic Sport Travel: www.greatatlanticsports.com

Great Outdoor Recreation: www.gorp.com

Green Travel Network: http://away.com

Legacy Global Sports: www.legacyglobalsports.com

Lonely Planet: www.lonelyplanet.com

Medical Tourism: www.medicaltourism.com

Medical Tourism Association: www.medicaltourismassociation.com

Medical Tourism Travel: www.medretreat.com

National Association of Sport Commissions: www.sportscommissions.org

National Camp Association Inc.: www.summercamp.org

National Geographic: www.nationalgeographic.com

National Golf Foundation: www.ngf.org

National Ski Area Association—NSAA: www.nsaa.org

National Park Service: www.nps.gov

Outdoor Recreation in America: www.funoutdoors.com

Recreation.gov: www.recreation.gov

Resort and Commercial Recreation Association—RCRA: www.rcra.org

Snow Sports Industries America: www.snowsports.org

Sports Travel and Tours: www.sportstravelandtours.com

The International Ecotourism Society—TIES: www.ecotourism.org

Total Sport Travel: www.totalsportstravel.com

Travel and Tourism Research AssociationTTRA: www.ttra.com

Travel Industry Association of America - TIA: www.tia.org

Travel Mole: www.travelmole.com

Travel News Daily: www.travelnewsdaily.com

World Food Travel Association:
www.worldfoodtravel.org

World Tourism Organization—WTO:
www2.unwto.org

ENDNOTES

1. (Gibson & Fairley, 2014).

2. (NASC, 2015).

3. (Coakley, 2009).

4. (ASC, 2015).

5. Ibid.

6. (Standeven & DeKnop, 1999).

7. (Gibson, 1998a, p.109).

8. (Gibson & Fairly, 2014).

9. (Connell, 2006).

10. (Medical Tourism Association, 2015).

11. (Milsa, 2015).

12. (Health-Tourism, 2015).

13. (Fottler, Malvey, Asi, Kirchner, & Warren, 2014).

14. (Hume & DeMicco, 2007).

15. (Francioni-Kraftchick, Byrd, Canziani, & Gladwell, 2014).

16. (Patterson & Pan, 2007).

17. (Adventure Travel Trade Association et al., 2015, p. 5).

18. (Schneider & Vogt, 2012).

19. (Hill, 1995, p. 59).

20. (Hill, 1995).

21. (TIES, 2015a, p. 1).

22. (Okumus, Kock, Scantleberry, & Okumus, 2013).

23. (Hall & Mitchell, 2001, p.1)

24. (Long, 2007).

25. Ibid.

REFERENCES

Adventure Tourism Trade Association. (2015, March). *The Adventure Tourism Development Index, 2015 Report*. Retrieved from http://www.adventureindex.travel/docs/atdi_2015.pdf

Canadian Sport Tourism Alliance. (2014). *About CSTA*. Retrieved from http://canadiansporttourism. com/about-csta/about-csta.html

Coakley, J.J. (2009). *Sport in Society: Issues and Controversies* (10th ed.). Boston, MA: McGraw-Hill.

Connell, J. (2006). Medical tourism: Sea, sun, sand and... surgery. *Tourism, Management, 27*, 1093–1100.

Cortez, N. (2008). Patients without borders: The emerging global market for patients and the evolution of modern health care. *Indiana Law Journal, 83*, 72–132.

Crossley, J. C., Jamieson, L. M., & Brayley, R. E. (2012). *Introduction to Commercial Recreation and Tourism: An Entrepreneurial Approach (6th ed.)*. Urbana, IL: Sagamore Publishing.

De Knop, P. (2004). Total Quality, a new issue in sport tourism policy. *Journal of Sport Tourism, 9(4)*, 303–314.

Fottler, M. D., Malvey, D., Asi, Y., Kirchner, S., & Warren, N. (2014). Can inbound and domestic medical tourism improve your bottom line? Identifying the potential of a U.S. tourism market. *Journal of Healthcare Management, 59(1)*, 50–63.

Francioni-Kraftchick, J., Byrd, E. T., Canziani, B., & Gladwell, N. J. (2014). Understanding beer tourist motivation. *Tourism Management Perspectives, 12*, 41–47.

Gaines, J., & Nguyen, D. B. (2015, July). *Medical Tourism*. Retrieved from http://wwwnc.cdc.gov/travel/yellowbook/2016/the-pre-travel-consultation/medical-tourism

Gibson, H. J. (1998a). The wide world of sport tourism. *Journal of Parks & Recreation, 33(9)*, 108–114.

Gibson, H. J. (1998b). Sport tourism: A critical analysis of research. *Sport Management Review, 1*, 45–79.

Gibson, H., & Fairley, S. (2014). Sport tourism. In P. M. Pedersen, & L. Thibault (Eds.), *Contemporary Sport Management* (pp. 264–285). Champaign, IL: Human Kinetics.

Hall, C. M., & Mitchell, R. (2001). Wine and food tourism. In Douglas, N., Douglas, N. and Derrett R. (Eds.), *Special Interest Tourism: Context and Cases* (pp. 307–329). New York, NY: John Wiley & Sons.

Health-Tourism. (2015). *The History of Medical Tourism*. Retrieved from https://www.health-tourism. com/medical-tourism/history/

Hill, B. J. (1995). A guide to adventure travel. *Parks and Recreation, 30(9)*, 56–65.

Hopkins, L., Labonte, R., Runnels, V., & Packer, C. (2010). Medical tourism today: What is the state of existing knowledge? *Journal of Public Health Policy, 31(2)*, 185–198.

Hudson, S. & Li, X. (2012). Domestic medical tourism: A neglected dimension of medical Tourism research. *Journal of Hospitality Marketing & Management, 21*, 227–246.

Hume, L. F., & DeMicco, F. J. (2007). Bringing hotels to healthcare: A Rx for success. *Journal Of Quality Assurance in Hospitality & Tourism, 8(1)*, 75–84.

Kalkstein-Silkes, C., Cai, L.A., & Lehto, X. Y. (2008). Conceptualizing festival-based culinary tourism in rural destinations. In Hall, C.M. & Sharples, L. (Eds.), *Food and Wine Festivals and Events Around the World: Development, Management and Markets*(pp. 65–77). Oxford: Butterworth-Heinemann.

Konrad, W. (2009, March 20). *Going abroad to find affordable health care.* Retrieved from http://www.nytimes.com/2009/03/21/health/21patient.html?_r=0

Long, L. M. (2007). Culinary Tourism. In G. Allen & K. Albala (Eds.), *The Business of Food: Encyclopedia of the Food and Drink Industries* (pp. 111–114). Westport, CT: Greenwood Press.

Milsa, R. (2015, September 24). Can medical tourism save Puerto Rico's healthcare? *Caribbean Business*, pp.14–19.

Medical Tourism Association. (2015). *Medical Tourism FAQ's.* Retrieved from http://www.medicaltourismassociation.com/en/medical-tourism-faq-s.html

Metro Atlanta Chamber (2015). *Atlanta Sport Council.* Retrieved from http://www.metroatlantachamber.com/business/sports/atlanta-sports-council

Millington, K., Locke, T., & Locke, A. (2001). Occasional studies: Adventure travel. *Travel and Tourist Analyst, 4,* 65–97.

National Association of Sports Commissions. (2015, October). *Report on the Sport Tourism Industry.* Retrieved from http://www.sportscommissions.org/Portals/sportscommissions/Documents/About/STI_report_Oct_15.pdf

Okumus, F., Kock, G., Scantlebury, M., & Okumus, B. (2013). Using local cuisines when promoting small Caribbean island destinations. *Journal of Travel and Tourism Marketing, 30*(4), 410–429.

Patients Beyond Borders. (2014). *Medical Tourism Statistics and Facts.* Retrieved from http://www.patientsbeyondborders.com/medical-tourism-statistics-facts

Patterson, I., & Pan, R. (2007). The motivations of baby boomers to participate in adventure tourism and the implication for adventure tour providers. *Annals of Leisure Research, 10*(1), 26–53.

Redmond, G. (1991). Changing styles of sport tourism: Industry/consumer interactions in Canada, the USA, and Europe. In M.T. Sinclair & M.J. Stabler (Eds.), *The Tourism Industry: An international analysis* (pp. 107–120). Wallingford, UK: CAB International.

Schneider, P., & Voght, C. (2012). Applying the 3M model of personality and motivation to adventure travelers. *Journal of Travel Research, 51,* 704–716.

Standeven, J., & De Knop, P. (1999). *Sport Tourism.* Champaign, IL: Human Kinetics.

The International Ecotourism Society. (2015a). *What is Ecotourism?* Retrieved from https://www.ecotourism.org/what-is-ecotourism

The International Ecotourism Society. (2015b). *Who are eco-tourists?* Retrieved from http://www.ecotourism.org/book/who-are-eco-tourists

World Food Travel Association. (2015). *What is food tourism?* Retrieved from http://worldfoodtravel.org/what-is-food-tourism/

World Tourism Organization. (1994). *Recommendations on tourism statistics.* Madrid, Spain: Author.

Name: _____ Date: _____

 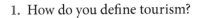

1. How do you define tourism?

2. How do you define sport tourism?

3. What are the three unique types of sport tourism? Define and provide an example of each.

4. Why has there been a global increase in medical tourism within the last 10 years, and what role has the Internet played?

5. Why are many countries using medical tourism as an economic driver for their economies?

6. What is the difference between "soft" and "hard" adventure tourism?

7. What are some examples of eco-tourism? Why do eco-tourists prefer a "low-impact adventure in a natural setting"?

8. Provide some example on why and how food/culinary tourism has grown so rapidly within the past few years.

9. Historically, what two countries are most associated with food/culinary tourism? Why?

10. In your opinion, why have "walking tours" become a popular form of food/culinary tourism?

© windmoon/Shutterstock.com

CHAPTER *32*

EVENT MANAGEMENT

AUTHOR

Inna Soifer, The University of Memphis

LEARNING OBJECTIVES

- Define a special event.
- Describe different phases of special event production.
- Discuss trends in the special events industry.
- Explain what skills and abilities are required for an event planner.
- Discuss the value of industry certifications.

CHAPTER OUTLINE

Introduction to the Special Events Industry

Types of Special Events

    Social Events

    Corporate Events

    Fairs/Festivals

    Galas/Fundraisers

    Mega-Events

Special Event Production

    Development Phase

    Pre-Production Phase

    Production Phase

    Post-Production Phase

Trends in the Special Events Industry

    Technology

    Engagement

    Sustainability

KEY TERMS

Banquet event order (BEO)	Meeting
Corporate event	Mega-event
Event planner	Professional association
Event production phases	Request for proposal (RFP)
Fair	Show flow
Festival	Social event
Fundraiser	Special event
Gala	Time line

INTRODUCTION TO THE SPECIAL EVENTS INDUSTRY

Not that long ago, the task of event planning was assigned to an administrative assistant or a human resources specialist in the case of a corporate event, or a creative family member or a friend in the case of a wedding or a family reunion. As events became more complex and their attendees developed into savvy participants, so grew the need to hire professional event planners. The U.S. Department of Labor has recognized the field of meeting, convention, and event planning as one of the fastest growing careers, with a 10 percent growth projection from 2014 to 2024.[1]

Is there a difference between a "meeting" and an "event"? Although these terms are often used interchangeably, they are not the same. The Accepted Practices Exchange (APEX) Industry Glossary defines the word **meeting** as "an event where the primary activity of the participants is to attend educational sessions, participate in discussions, social functions, or attend other organized events, with no exhibit component."[2] An **event** is defined as "an organized occasion such as a meeting, convention, exhibition, special event, gala dinner, etc., which is often composed of several different yet related functions."[3] Generally speaking, meetings are held for business and educational purposes, whereas events have more of an entertainment and creative component.

The Glossary defines **special event** as "a one-time event staged for the purpose of celebration; a unique activity."[4] As an example, consider a wedding. It's organized for a special occasion (two people are getting married), it's unique (even if they divorce and remarry again, their second wedding will most likely be different), and it's celebratory by nature, bringing excitement to the invitees and arousing their expectations.

According to the Glossary, an **event planner**, or an event organizer, is "a person whose job it is to oversee and arrange every aspect of an event."[5]

TYPES OF SPECIAL EVENTS

Before discussing a special event production, it is important to differentiate between varieties of events.

A wedding is a social event.

Each type has its own characteristics, advantages, challenges, and methods. Some event planners specialize in certain types of events, while others do not.

The following classification is based on the one suggested by the *Special Events Magazine*,[6] with some revisions:

SOCIAL EVENTS

Social events are private events used to celebrate special occasions such as weddings, birthdays, anniversaries, family reunions, graduations, and religious ceremonies. A "Sweet Sixteen" party, a baby shower, a baptism or Bar Mitzvah celebration, a bachelorette party, and a 50th "Golden" wedding anniversary are all examples of *social events*.

CORPORATE EVENTS

These events are funded by businesses to launch a product, build customer relationships, increase employee satisfaction, host an award ceremony, or celebrate a holiday or a company's special occasion gathering. A "Dealer of the Year" award ceremony, a company Christmas party, a 20th anniversary celebration are all examples of **corporate events**.

FAIRS/FESTIVALS

A **fair** is an "event principally devoted to the exhibition of agricultural products or industrial products. Fairs may also provide entertainment activities."[7] An example of a fair would be a county or state fair organized to showcase agricultural products and livestock and to offer a variety of entertainment activities for local residents and tourists.

The Tentertainment music festival has been held in Tenterden, England since 2008.

The *Oxford English Dictionary* defines **festival** as "1. A day or period of celebration, typically a religious commemoration. 1.1. An annual celebration or anniversary. 1.2. An organized series of concerts, plays, or movies, typically one held annually in the same place."[8] An example of a religious festival would be the Cornerstone Festival held annually in Illinois or the Greater Chicago Jewish Festival. Examples of secular festivals would be music, theater, or film festivals such as Coachella Valley Music and Arts Festival, the Notre Dame Shakespeare Festival, and the Sundance Film Festival.

GALAS/FUNDRAISERS

A **gala** is defined as a "primary social function of an event, usually in the evening, including entertainment or speeches after a formal meal."[9] A **fundraiser** is an event organized with a purpose of raising money for a non-profit organization and/or to increase awareness of a cause.

The Boston Marathon that supports different charities and the "Dream Home Giveaway" that raises money for St. Jude Children's Research Hospital, one of the world's premier pediatric cancer research centers, are examples of fundraisers. Another example would be the Met Gala, formally known as the Costume Institute Gala, which is an annual fundraiser to benefit the Metropolitan Museum Costume Institute in New York City.

MEGA-EVENTS

As defined by the United Nations Department of Economic and Social Affairs (UNDESA), a **mega-event** is a "large-scale, internationally sponsored, public entrepreneurship activity engaging a long-term multi-sector organization within the host city and nation with the double goal of supporting overall local and regional development and advancing universal values and principles to meet global challenges."[10] World Expos, the Olympic Games, the Super Bowl, the FIFA World Cup, and the NBA Finals are all examples of mega-events.

SPECIAL EVENT PRODUCTION

There is an "invisible army" of audio-video specialists, caterers, graphic designers, florists, decorators, photographers, musicians, and other professionals behind a special event production. An event planner is often compared to a conductor who is responsible for guiding the orchestra, making sure each performer is doing his or her job properly, setting the tempo, and communicating the overall vision to each member of the team.

All activities related to a special event production are classified by The International Special Events Society (ISES) into four **event production phases**.[11] The diagram in Figure 32.1 shows the phases and the amount of time an event planner spends working on each phase.

Here is a brief description of each phase, including some tasks and the order in which they must be performed (adapted from the CSEP Content Outline 2014 by ISES):

DEVELOPMENT PHASE

During initial meetings with the major stakeholders, that is, "all individuals who are invested in a project or event such as sponsors, attendees, vendors, media and others,"[12] the event's purpose, goals, and objectives have to be determined. With this main goal in mind, the event planner develops the event concept, creates a marketing plan, ensures that the event will comply with legislation and legal obligations, develops sustainability strategies, and prepares an initial budget.

During this phase, site requirements have to be determined and different options evaluated. A special event can take place indoors (hotel, restaurant, banquet hall, museum, arena, club) or outdoors

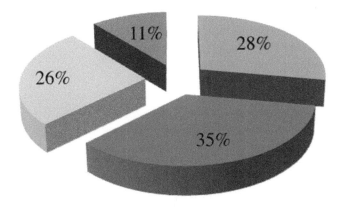

Development Phase
Pre-Production Phase
Production Phase
Post-Production Phase

FIGURE 32.1 Four phases of an event production. Data obtained from the Certified Special Events Professional (CSEP) Content Outline 2014 developed by the International Special Events Society (ISES).

(beach, park, tent). When possible sites are identified, the event planner issues a **request for proposals (RFP)** that contains the event description, dates, number of guests, required meeting space, food and beverage, audio/video, and other requirements and requests a bid from potential venues.

PRE-PRODUCTION PHASE

During this phase, the event planner develops **time lines** that "include each task to be accomplished and is the core of the program plan."[13] After conducting site inspections, the event planner selects an appropriate site and reviews a **Banquet event order (BEO)**, "detailed instructions for a particular event prepared by a facility; also known as a resume sheet or function sheet; includes detailed instructions related to room setups, food and beverage."[14] During the pre-production phase, all event element requirements have to be coordinated. They include, but are not limited to, site services, entertainment, food and beverage, technical production, rentals, décor, collateral material, staffing, and contingency plans. Event success is impossible without careful planning of all its aspects.

PRODUCTION PHASE

In this phase, it's all about event execution. The event planner conducts pre-event inspection and executes load-in and event space setup, manages staff and volunteers, and works with vendors. The event planner implements a **show flow**, a chart that describes

general logistics of the event with time breakdown and responsible parties. After the event, load-out and post-event inspection have to be conducted.

POST-PRODUCTION PHASE

After the event is over, the job is still not finished. During this phase, the event planner determines event success by utilizing event evaluation criteria, analyzes the entire event management process by conducting post-con meetings, audits the finances and prepares a final budget, archives information, and thanks those who made the event a success.

TRENDS IN THE SPECIAL EVENTS INDUSTRY

TECHNOLOGY

Technology has changed the world, and the world of special events is no exception. In fact, event planners are usually early adopters of new technology because it helps them exceed guests' expectations that have risen to new heights. It also allows them to handle heavy workloads during each phase of a special event production.

In the past decade, event planners have acquired new tools designed to streamline the planning process, from project management software to team communication platforms. Social Tables, a web-based event planning platform, enables the creation of a room layout; manages a guest list and table and meal assignments; and executes an on-site check-in. By using the Eventbrite platform, an event planner is able to create a webpage, sell tickets, promote the event via different social media, and host it. Slack, a messaging app, allows the facilitation of team communication, the discussion of ideas, file sharing, and creation of the data archive related to the event.

New technologies also help event planners at the event production phase. For example, a mobile app can be designed for a special event that allows attendees to find the event's information, register and connect with other participants, do check-in, get bonus points and other perks on-site, and provide feedback. The goal of creating such an app is to simplify and enhance event guests' experience. During the event, digital signage, social walls that display content from social media generated from a specific hashtag, beacons, and other technologies created for events can be utilized to make the event visually appealing and engaging.

At the post-production phase, event technologies help to gather attendees' feedback, analyze the data, and evaluate the return on investment (ROI) of the event. In the near future, event industry professionals will continue to adopt new technology and digital communications to increase engagement and to effectively plan and manage special events.

ENGAGEMENT

Audience engagement is crucial to event success because it's directly related to the level of satisfaction and subsequent repeat attendance. Event planners try to keep attendees engaged before, during, and after the event to create a stimulating environment in which people stay involved, connect to each other, and share their ideas and highlights from the event. Needless to say, technology plays a big role in creating such an environment.

Event planners utilize social media before the events to boost online discussion by creating an event group; providing a unique hashtag; and posting updates, behind-the-scenes photos, and videos.

During the event, event planners utilize live interaction technology that "requires the attendee to interact with an aspect of the event, whether it's learning, networking, or entertainment."[15] For example, live polling and live Q&A tools encourage the audience to respond to questions and submit their own, with the results shown in real time. Gamification is the "use of interactive game components (e.g. trivia, scavenger hunts, quizzes, leaderboards, or build-in rewards) for participation"[16] and is a fun way to promote engagement during events. Drones are effectively used for large events such as concerts, sporting events, and festivals to "add a unique perspective to filmed content and aerial photography, for virtual and unique tours of venues/events and to enable remote audience to experience the live event."[17]

Event planners will continue to explore new ways to make their events more exciting and memorable by allowing the attendees to be active participants and co-creators of the special occasion.

SUSTAINABILITY

According to the Convention Industry Council (CIC), "a green meeting or event incorporates environmental considerations to minimize its negative impact on the environment."[18] Commitment to environmental sustainability as part of their corporate social responsibility (CSR) creates demand from companies to work with the planners that employ green, that is, environmentally responsible, event practices. For example, some companies would only have their events at a Leadership in Energy & Environmental Design (LEED) certified hotel.

CIC's Accepted Practices Exchange initiative, in partnership with the American Society for Testing and Materials (ASTM) International, "has created the industry's first and only comprehensive

Event planners can develop apps for special events to simplify and enhance a guest's experience.

standards for environmentally sustainable meetings."[19] There are nine specifications covering the following areas of event planning: destination selection, accommodations, food and beverage, audiovisual, onsite offices, communication and marketing materials, transportation, exhibits, and venues.[20]

Below are just some of the best practices that help to lessen the environmental impact of a special event, as suggested by the CIC's Green Meetings Report:

- Consider venues willing to offer a recycling program that includes paper, metal, glass, and plastic products;
- Include in the contract that the caterer/vendor will use reusable cutlery, dishware, linens, and decorations, as well as locally produced seasonal and/or organic food and beverages when possible;
- Reduce paper usage as much as possible by using the web and e-mail to promote the event, offering electronic registration, and providing the event itinerary and proceedings online (including speaker notes and handouts);
- Reuse nametags made of recycled content and provide "reuse" collection bins for them.[21]

The growing threat of climate change will create a greater need for event planners to aggressively implement sustainable event practices in the near future.

CAREERS IN THE SPECIAL EVENTS INDUSTRY

STARTING OUT IN THE INDUSTRY

Event planning is often regarded as one of the most rewarding and fun careers one can pursue. In fact, the Meeting, Convention and Event Planner occupation made the #57 spot on the 100 Best Jobs and #12 spot on the Best Business Jobs in the *U.S. News and World Report* ranking.[22] Event planners often say that, despite the long hours and hectic work environment, the industry provides them with excellent opportunities for professional and personal growth, travelling, meeting new people, and being in charge of exciting events. This industry is also very competitive and makes newcomers wonder where to begin when trying to break into the profession.

The event industry offers numerous opportunities for newcomers to explore the field and get some entry-level experience. Volunteering at festivals, nonprofit, community, and other local events is a great way to start building one's event résumé. Becoming a member of a steering committee for some event is recommended to not only get some planning experience and gain decision-making skills, but also to develop business and personal contacts to further one's career. Another possibility is to get hired seasonally or ad hoc by an event planner or a destination management company. Finally, professional associations have several annual events and form planning committees to organize them. Students of Hospitality Management programs should use internships and job shadowing opportunities to apply the skills and knowledge gained in the classroom to the professional environment. Working as an intern for a professional event planner, an audiovisual company, a catering company, or an event agency is an opportunity to learn different aspects of event planning and get relevant work experience.

REQUIRED SKILLS AND ABILITIES

According to the U.S. Department of Labor, an event planner should possess the following important qualities:

- *Communication skills*, specifically excellent oral and written comprehension, are required to communicate ideas to clients, vendors/suppliers, and subordinates;
- *Composure* is essential due to the fast-paced and high-stress nature of the work;
- *Interpersonal skills*, such as establishing and maintaining positive relationships with clients and suppliers, are crucial for developing long-term partnerships;
- *Negotiation skills*, that is, the ability to reconcile differences and persuade others to change their mind or behavior, is crucial when discussing contract terms;
- *Organizational skills* such as time management, attention to details, and the ability to multitask, prioritize, and meet deadlines are essential to ensure event success;

- *Problem-solving skills* are required to be able to recognize potential problems and offer creative solutions.[23]

Good communication skills are essential for event planners to do their job well.

Event planners must attain technology proficiency, from spreadsheets and project management software to the event technologies discussed earlier.

POTENTIAL EMPLOYERS IN THE FIELD

According to the Bureau of Labor Statistics, the industry employed 100,000 meeting, convention, and event planners with a median pay of $46,490 per year in 2014.[24]

All event planning positions can be broken down into several categories:

- *Association/Non-profit event planner*—a person who is employed by an association or not-for-profit company to plan and oversee their events;
- *Corporate event planner*—a person who is employed by a corporation to plan and oversee their events;
- *Event planner working for an event agency*—a person who is employed by an event management company that provides event planning services to multiple clients;
- *Independent event planner*—a person who is a sole proprietor and provides event planning services to multiple clients.

PROFESSIONAL ASSOCIATIONS

The one piece of advice given to the newcomers to the special events industry is to join a **professional association**, "a body of persons engaged in the same profession, formed usually to control entry into the profession, maintain standards, and represent the

profession in discussions with other bodies."[25] There are several benefits of joining a professional association: enhancing one's professional development through access to up-to-date information published in the trade magazines and newsletters, obtaining countless networking opportunities, attending trade shows and other industry events, and supplementing one's résumé with a professional membership.

Another step is to join the board of directors of a local chapter of a national professional association, if available. Board members deal with strategic planning, budgeting, marketing, membership, and other areas that are crucial for one's career advancement. This gives one the opportunity to join different committees that plan the association and local chapter's events and develop skills such as event design and planning, fundraising, and working with volunteers.

INTERNATIONAL SPECIAL EVENTS SOCIETY

As stated on their website, "The International Special Events Society (ISES) is the premier society for Creative Event Professionals. Membership in ISES also allows you to build relationships with other professionals worldwide within the creative events industry."

Student memberships are available for those who are enrolled as a part or full-time students in a two or four-year college/university program. In accordance with the ISES's statement, "Student members are encouraged to get involved with the chapter by volunteering ten hours to their chapter per year, helping with chapter meetings and event registration, mailings, and other chapter business such as coordinating chapter community service and special projects" (see http://www.ises.com).

INTERNATIONAL FESTIVALS & EVENTS ASSOCIATION

According to their website, the International Festivals & Events Association (IFEA) is "The Premiere Association Supporting and Enabling Festival & Event Professionals Worldwide." The IFEA student initiative was formed with the goal "to begin building the largest network of future professionals interested in our industry, individually and through academic institutional chapters, with the goal of bringing them together with their peers and the leading industry professionals and events around the world." Students are encouraged to launch an IFEA Student Chapter at their own institution. Student scholarships are also available through the IFEA Foundation Legacy Scholarships (see http://www.ifea.com).

MEETING PROFESSIONALS INTERNATIONAL

According to their "About Us" statement, Meeting Professionals International (MPI) is "the largest and most vibrant global meeting and event industry association." Though it's not solely dedicated to the special events industry, this association provides several professional development opportunities for event planners such as certificate programs, streaming education sessions, and monthly webinars. Student memberships are available as well as the student club program. Grants and scholarships are offered through the MPI Foundation (see http://www.mpi-web.org).

AMERICAN ASSOCIATION OF CERTIFIED WEDDING PLANNERS

As stated on their website, the American Association of Certified Wedding Planners (AACWP) "is a professional organization for trained or certified wedding planners." The association provides in-depth training on wedding planning which is often considered a unique facet of the special events industry. Student memberships are available (see http://aacwp.org).

INDUSTRY CERTIFICATIONS

As reported by the U.S. Department of Labor, "Many employers prefer applicants who have a bachelor's degree and some work experience in hotels or planning. Although some colleges offer degree programs in meeting and event management, other common fields of study include hospitality and tourism management."[26]

Additional educational opportunities are available through different professional associations that offer industry certifications. These credentials are an important step in one's career path. The professional certifications below provide a competitive advantage when applying for a job or soliciting business as a special events planner or a vendor:

- *Certified Special Events Professional (CSEP)* designation is offered by the International Special Events Society (ISES).
- *Certified Festival and Event Executive (CFEE)* designation is offered by the International Festivals & Events Association (IFEA).
- *Certified Meeting Professional (CMP)* designation is offered by the Meeting Professionals International (MPI).
- *Certified Wedding Planner (CWP)* designation is offered by the American Association of Certified Wedding Planners (AACWP).

SUMMARY

The special events industry is a growing field that provides numerous opportunities for professional development. All special events can be classified by their type, including social events, corporate events, fairs and festivals, galas and fundraisers, and mega-events. An event planner might or might not specialize in certain type of events. The special event production process includes the following steps: development phase, pre-production phase, production phase, and post-production phase. There are three major trends that shape the future of the special events industry: technology, engagement, and sustainability. Event planners can be employed by associations and non-profit organizations, corporations, event agencies, or work as independent contractors. The special events industry has several professional associations that provide their members with certifications and educational and networking opportunities. The International Special Events Society (ISES), the International Festivals & Events Association (IFEA), and the Meeting Professionals International (MPI) are the most established professional associations in the field.

RESOURCES

Professional Associations Websites

American Association of Certified Wedding Planners: http://aacwp.org

International Special Events Society: http://www.ises.com

International Festivals & Events Association: http://www.ifea.com

Meeting Professionals International: http://www.mpiweb.org

Event Planning Blogs

A Practical Wedding: http://apracticalwedding.com

BizhBash: http://www.bizbash.com

Event MB: http://www.eventmanagerblog.com

Event Planning Blueprint: http://eventplanningblueprint.com/blog

Eventjuice: http://eventjuice.co.uk/blog

ENDNOTES

1. (U.S. Department of Labor, 2015).

2. (Meeting, 2011).

3. (Event, 2011).

4. (Special event, 2011).

5. (Event organizer, 2011).

6. (Special Events Magazine, n.d.).

7. (Fair, 2011).

8. (Festival, n.d.).

9. (Gala, 2011).

10. (United Nations Department of Economic and Social Affairs (UNDESA), 2012).

11. (International Special Events Society (ISES), 2014).

12. (Meetings Professionals International (MPI), 2006, p.586),

13. (Time lines, 2011).

14. (MPI, 2006, p. 564).

15. (Solaris, 2015).

16. (Cross, 2015).

17. Ibid.

18. (Convention Industry Council (CIC), n.d.).

19. Ibid.

20. (ASTM, 2012).

21. Ibid.

22. (U.S. News, 2015).

23. (U.S. Department of Labor, 2015).

24. Ibid.

25. (Professional association, 2015).

26. (U.S. Department of Labor, 2015).

REFERENCES

American Society for Testing and Materials (ASTM) International. (2012). *ASTM Standards for Green Meetings*. Retrieved from http://www.astm.org/BOOKSTORE/COMPS/GREENMTGS

Convention Industry Council. (2004, March 17). *Convention Industry Council's Green Meetings Report*. Retrieved from http://www.conventionindustry.org/Files/CIC_Green_Meetings_Report.pdf

Convention Industry Council. (n.d.). *APEX/ASTM Environmentally Sustainable Meeting Standards*. Retrieved from http://www.conventionindustry.org/StandardsPractices/APEXASTM.aspx

Convention Industry Council. (n.d.). *Green Meetings*. Retrieved from http://www.conventionindustry.org/StandardsPractices/GreenMeetings.aspx

Cross, B. (2015, July 8). Types of technology and features. In *Engaging Events* (p.77–87). Retrieved from http://books.eventmanagerblog.com/engaging-events/page/77

Event organizer. In *APEX Industry Glossary* (2011 ed.) [The glossary of the meetings, conventions and exhibitions industry]. Retrieved from http://www.conventionindustry.org/StandardsPractices/APEX/glossary.aspx

Event. (2011). In *APEX Industry Glossary* (2011 ed.) [The glossary of the meetings, conventions and exhibitions industry]. Retrieved from http://www.conventionindustry.org/StandardsPractices/APEX/glossary.aspx

Fair. In *APEX Industry Glossary* (2011 ed.) [The glossary of the meetings, conventions and exhibitions industry]. Retrieved from http://www.conventionindustry.org/StandardsPractices/APEX/glossary.aspx

Festival. (n.d.). In *Oxford online dictionary*. Retrieved from http://www.oxforddictionaries.com/us/definition/american_english/festival

Gala. In *APEX Industry Glossary* (2011 ed.) [The glossary of the meetings, conventions and exhibitions industry]. Retrieved from http://www.conventionindustry.org/StandardsPractices/APEX/glossary.aspx

International Special Events Society (ISES). (2014). *The Certified Special Events Professional (CSEP) Content Outline*. Retrieved from http://www.ises.com/docs/certified-special-events-professional/2014-csep-content-outline.pdf?sfvrsn=4

Meeting. (2011). In *APEX Industry Glossary* (2011 ed.) [The glossary of the meetings, conventions and exhibitions industry]. Retrieved from http://www.conventionindustry.org/StandardsPractices/APEX/glossary.aspx

Meetings Professionals International. (2006). *MPI's Planning Guide: A Source for Meeting and Conventions* (2nd ed.). Dallas, TX: MPI Foundation.

Professional association. (n.d.). In *Collins online dictionary*. Retrieved from http://www.collinsdictionary.com/dictionary/english/professional-association

Solaris, J. (2015, July 8). Live interaction technology: an overview. *In Engaging Events* (p. 12). Retrieved from http://books.eventmanagerblog.com/engaging-events/page/12

Special event. (2011). In *APEX Industry Glossary* (2011 ed.) [The glossary of the meetings, conventions and exhibitions industry]. Retrieved from http://www.conventionindustry.org/StandardsPractices/APEX/glossary.aspx

Special Events Magazine. (n.d.). *Event types*. Retrieved from http://specialevents.com/event-types

Time lines. In *APEX Industry Glossary* (2011 ed.) [The glossary of the meetings, conventions and exhibitions industry]. Retrieved from http://www.conventionindustry.org/StandardsPractices/APEX/glossary.aspx

U.S. Department of Labor, Bureau of Labor Statistics. (2015, December 17). *Occupational Outlook Handbook: Meeting, Convention, and Event Planners* (2016–17 ed.). Retrieved from http://www.bls.gov/ooh/business-and-financial/meeting-convention-and-event-planners.htm

U.S. News & World Report. (2015). Best business jobs. Retrieved from http://money.usnews.com/careers/best-jobs/meeting-convention-and-event-planner

U.S. News & World Report. (2015). The 100 best jobs. Retrieved from http://money.usnews.com/careers/best-jobs/meeting-convention-and-event-planner

United Nations Department of Economic and Social Affairs (UNDESA). (2012). *Shanghai Manual: A Guide for Sustainable Urban Development in the 21st Century.* Retrieved from https://sustainabledevelopment.un.org/content/documents/shanghaimanual.pdf

Name: _____ Date: _____

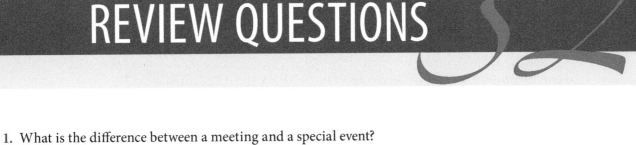

1. What is the difference between a meeting and a special event?

2. What is the purpose of a fundraising event?

3. What are the four phases of special event production?

4. How do you reduce the environmental impact of a special event?

5. Why is it important for an event planner to pay attention to details?

6. Are there any local chapters of the professional associations for the special events industry in the area where you live?

7. What are the advantages of earning the Certified Special Events Professional (CSEP) designation?

© kan_khampanya/Shutterstock.com

CHAPTER *33*

MEETINGS AND CONVENTIONS MANAGEMENT

AUTHORS
LEARNING OBJECTIVES

Elizabeth Aube-VanPatten, Johnson & Wales University

- Determine the purpose of the conventions and meeting management sector and its role in the organizational structure.
- Identify key conventions and meeting management stakeholders.
- Explain the roles of the conventions and meeting management organizer, attendee, and exhibitor.
- Identify the knowledge and skills needed to be a success in the conventions and meeting management industry.

CHAPTER OUTLINE

KEY TERMS

- Attendee
- Conference
- Convention
- Convention exhibit
- Decorator/official services contractor
- Exhibitor
- Horizontal convention
- Industry tradeshow
- Meeting
- Public/consumer show
- Show management team
- Tradeshow
- Venue
- Vertical convention

Conventions and meetings are a large part of the global economy.

INTRODUCTION

Often times referred to as the "invisible industry," conventions and meetings play a very large role in the global economy. The conventions and meeting management sector of the hospitality industry began as a catalyst for growth and expansion during much of the 20th century. Conventions and exhibition-based events were originally created specifically for the purpose of displaying and selling goods to end users in a particular market segment. For example, individuals within the auto industry gather several times a year to have an opportunity to view the latest model releases and sign contracts with dealerships and car companies, all in the convenience of a major city.

There are three key components when classifying a convention: Is it time sensitive? Is there a temporary marketing environment? Do the buyers come to the sellers? If you answered "yes" to the above questions, then a **convention** or **tradeshow** is most likely taking place. There are more than 13,000 conventions/tradeshows that take place in North America alone each year, and an estimated 25,000 to 30,000 conventions are held annually throughout the world.

In fact, hotels were actually the first venues to host conventions and meetings, and as the need grew, hotels responded by building large ballrooms and meeting rooms within their facilities. According to the site SmartMeetings.com, there are over 18 new convention/meeting properties that were christened in 2015. They include over 5,300 new sq. ft. of event space in Portland, Oregon at Hotel Eastlund; the Westin Denver International Airport, boasting more than 36,000 sq. ft. of event space and 10,000 sq. ft of

pre-function event space; and the Hunt Valley Inn, a Grand Wyndham property located in Baltimore, providing over 500 acres of recreational space, two golf courses, five restaurants, and more than 30,000 sq. ft. of pristine event space.[1]

CONVENTIONS IN THE U.S. ECONOMY

There are three unique catalysts that encouraged companies throughout the U.S. to engage in conventions in the latter half of the 20th century (Figure 33.1). The first was the introduction of purpose-built exhibition space like McCormick Place in Chicago, and dozens others like it around the country. The introduction in 1960 of the jet-powered aircraft cut transcontinental travel time in half for many individuals. In addition, the expansion of the U.S. economy and launch of new industries such as information technology and telecommunications afforded companies throughout the U.S. the opportunity to introduce new products and services, and also build their corporate image.

TYPES OF CONVENTIONS AND MEETINGS

There are three segments of the conventions and meetings industry: convention exhibits (exhibits, expos, marketplaces), industry conventions, and public/consumer shows. The **convention exhibit** is most often a part of a larger industry conference or meeting, where networking is key, sponsors have high visibility, and companies have the opportunity to interact with each other and build business relationships.

Industry tradeshows differ greatly from a convention exhibit, as the major focus has shifted from networking to business with buyers. Industry tradeshows are often only open to the trades which they are showcasing, but may have times where public hours exist.

The last segment of the conventions and meeting industry is what you may be most familiar with, **public/consumer shows**. These shows are marketed heavily and are always open to the public, and admission could be free or for a small fee. Public/consumer

| Purpose Built Exhibition Halls | Expansion of U.S. economy | Jet–Powered Aircraft |

FIGURE 33.1 Catalysts for the growth of the conventions/meeting industry in the late 20th century.

shows are great fillers for sales managers of slower convention center business months and often generate a great deal of sales for the vendors.

In addition to the three different segments of the conventions and meetings industry, one must also be familiar with the terms "horizontal" and "vertical" convention. A **horizontal convention** features all products from a specific industry; for example, the Great American Dessert Show held annually in Las Vegas. This particular convention showcases all types of desserts that are found in many restaurants throughout the United States. A **vertical convention** highlights a specific product type from a specific industry, for example, a cupcake only convention.

GOALS FOR CONVENTIONS AND MEETINGS

The value for the convention and meetings industry is that it costs about half as much to close a sale at a convention, as opposed to cold calling. Vendor success can be concretely measured immediately following the convention through booth sales and

Vendor success at conventions can be concretely measured through booth sales and convention attendance.

convention attendance. The conventions and meetings industry also requires extensive relationship building and the dynamic face-to-face client interaction creates opportunities for real-time sales.

STAKEHOLDERS

In order to ensure the success of any convention or meeting, there are several key stakeholders that ensure the success of the event for all parties involved. Over the next few paragraphs, you will be introduced to key terminology used within the conventions and meetings industry, as well as "who" is responsible for each segment in the planning process.

SHOW MANAGEMENT TEAM

The **show management team** consists of the planners who bring the show to fruition. Many times, the show management team consists of employees of a large professional association tasked with planning a convention. However, in recent years, the convention and meetings industry has shown an increase in individuals planning and executing shows as entrepreneurs organizing a convention for profit. This particular instance of growth in the conventions and meetings segment of the hospitality industry shows the strength in the numbers of events throughout the world. The show management team's key responsibilities include logistics planning, vendor coordination, and all marketing and creativity. More importantly, the show management team is responsible for ensuring that all stakeholder expectations are met and exceeded throughout the planning and execution of the convention/meeting.

When the planning process begins for a convention, the show management team must make several important decisions, including destination and site selection; whether the convention will be on a local, regional, or national scale; the length of the convention; and the event's time of year.

EXHIBITOR

The **exhibitor** at a convention/meeting is the show management team's most important customer as they are considered to be the longest "user" of the event. Exhibitors are inside the venue during move-in and move-out to ensure proper booth set-up, the exhibitors are at the convention/meeting during show hours to produce business for their company, and the exhibitors are also there during break-down and move-out of the event.

OFFICIAL SERVICES CONTRACTOR/ DECORATOR

The official services contractor, more commonly known as the "**decorator**" for the convention/ meeting, is often subcontracted out by the show management team and is considered to be a partner with the planning and execution of the event. The official services contractor provides a basic booth set-up per the show management contract for the convention/ meeting, but can also provide an additional list of services through which an exhibitor can choose to upgrade their booth on the show floor. Companies and organizations choose to exhibit at conventions/ meetings for several reasons including posturing (competition), increasing revenues, imagine, and identifying the competition.

VENUE

The **venue**, or place where the convention/meeting will be held and its employees, are another key stakeholder in the logistical planning process. The venue has several important responsibilities to not only the show management team, but also all those attending as exhibitors and attendees of the convention/meeting. These responsibilities include the overall management, safety and security of the facility, providing food and beverage, and parking and lavatory facilities (all of which are usually charged as a fee to the show management team).

ATTENDEES

The last stakeholder within the convention/meetings industry may or may not be the most obvious to you: it's the attendee! The attendee is considered to be the end-user of the event, and is therefore a customer of the show management team. The attendee may or may not pay a fee to enter a show floor or attend workshops/seminars. The attendee evaluates the event much like anyone else attending a concert, or even a wedding. Attendees evaluate their experiences pre-convention, during the convention, and post-convention, and determine if it would be of value to attend future dates. Attendees often choose to attend conventions/meetings throughout the world based on program, events, and location. Hotels, pricing, and times of the year play just as important a part in the decision making process to attend the event as show management does to plan the event. In addition, attendees may find added value in attending certain conventions/meetings if there are certain accreditations, certifications, keynote speakers, and networking opportunities available for them.

PRIMARY SOURCES OF REVENUE FOR CONVENTIONS AND MEETINGS

Since you have had the opportunity to understand the roles of the key stakeholders of conventions/ meetings, it's also important to look at the primary

Many factors need to be considered when choosing a meeting venue.

FIGURE 33.2 Revenue streams for venues.

sources of revenue for the conventions and meetings industry. Let's first take a look at the venue, the stakeholder that has the opportunity to make the most amount of revenue by hosting the convention/meeting throughout its facilities. The venue can generate lines of revenue through rental of space, including exhibit halls, meeting rooms, and ballrooms. Many major convention centers throughout the United States have over 150,000 sq. feet of rental space available for conventions/meetings. Venues also make a considerable amount of revenue through the selling of food and beverages throughout the convention/meeting, and if the venue has a parking facility, that can also be a revenue generating line (Figure 33.2).

When looking at the official services contractor, or decorators, of the convention/meeting, the most profit throughout the United States is derived from the moving of freight from one show to another. Exhibitors must pay the official services contractor to transport their equipment from the warehouse, to the facility, and back again. By providing this service, the official services contractor can make a considerable profit. Other lines of revenue that the official services contractor can generate include booth construction; labor services; rentals of furnishings,

floral, and carpet; and even the graphic production of signage used around the venue.

The exhibitor has only one opportunity to produce a line of revenue from the event—selling their products/services—even though they are the longest user of the convention/meeting. If the exhibitor does not produce sales during the convention/meeting, they may not return to that venue the following year and won't produce sales to continue business growth and development opportunities.

Much like exhibitors, the show management team has one significant line of revenue if the goal of the event is to make a profit; the cost of registration that exhibitors will pay to sell their products at the event, and the cost the attendee will pay to attend the event. In order to produce a line of revenue, the show management team must pay special attention to all budgetary lines and charges against them in the pre-planning process, so that they can cover expenses and make enough profit to pay their employees. If the goal of the show management team is to break-even for the particular convention/meeting, as with most major associations, the show management team must appropriately charge exhibitors and attendees in order to satisfy expenses.

CAREERS WITHIN THE CONVENTIONS AND MEETINGS SECTOR

There are various careers associated with the Convention and Meetings industry, including:

- Show Manager
- Exhibit Designer
- Exhibit Director
- Tradeshow Booth Coordinator
- Sales Representative
- Graphic Artist
- Logistics Director
- Exhibit Sales
- Convention Services

As noted in Figure 33.3 shown below, as with any sector of the hospitality industry, sales and service to the various stakeholders remains at the center of importance.

KEYS TO SUCCESS IN THE CONVENTIONS/MEETING INDUSTRY

- Networking
- Professional Development (check out industry certifications)
- Positive Attitude
- Personal Attention to Sales & Service
- Communication Style
- Education

WHERE CONVENTION/MEETINGS INDUSTRY PEOPLE CONNECT AND NETWORK

- Corporate Executive Marketing Association
- Event Service Professionals Association
- Exhibition Services & Contractors Association
- International Association Exhibition and Events
- International Association Venue Managers
- Meeting Professionals International
- Professional Convention Management Association

SOCIAL MEDIA MARKETING IN CONVENTIONS/MEETINGS

Social media marketing is continuing its climb of importance within the convention/meeting industry around the globe. Social media marketing is becoming more sophisticated on a day-to-day basis with ever changing technology, enabling show management and convention/meeting marketers to effectively

FIGURE 33.3 Careers in the conventions/meetings industry.

communicate with each stakeholder prior to arriving at the facility. This cycle of technological advances and corresponding increased social media marketing sophistication is going to move faster and grow stronger as time goes on. Staying current with these increases in marketing sophistication and applying them appropriately will have to become a permanent part of the exhibition industry's marketing practices. For more information on enhancing the social media presence at a meeting visit the recent article, "How to Use Twitter to Guarantee a Great Meeting."

SUMMARY

Conventions and meetings are but some of the many events that have evolved as a basic function of humanity. The art of buying and selling has stood the test of time. This chapter was organized to give an introduction into the often-misunderstood world of the convention/meetings sector of the hospitality industry.

RESOURCES

Internet Sources

www.pcma.org (Professional Convention Management Association)

www.iaee.org (International Association of Exhibitions and Events)

www.conventionindustry.org (Convention Industry Council)

ENDNOTES

1. SmartMeetings.com, 2015.

REFERENCES

18 New Meeting Properties Christened in 2015 | Smart Meetings. (2015,
December 28). Retrieved December 31, 2015, from http://www.smartmeetings.com/
news/82521/18-new-meeting-properties-christened-2015

Aube-VanPatten, E. (2015, September 11). JWU. Retrieved January 5, 2016, from https://online.jwu.
edu/blog/hospitality/How-to-Use-Twitter-to-Guarantee-a-Great-Meeting

REVIEW QUESTIONS

1. Why do companies exhibit at a tradeshow?

2. Why is a show attendee considered to be the "end-user" of the event according to the author?

3. What are some career opportunities in conventions and meeting management?

4. What are the main lines of revenue for a facility?

5. What are the three segments of the conventions and meeting industry?

6. Who are the major stakeholders in the conventions and meetings industry as noted by the author? Explain what each stakeholder is responsible for in the planning process.

CHAPTER *34*

CASINOS

AUTHOR

Chris Roberts, DePaul University

LEARNING OBJECTIVES

- Describe the different areas of the casino.
- Understand the business nature of gambling.
- Explain the possible careers in the gaming industry.
- Identify gambling that occurs outside of a casino.

CHAPTER OUTLINE

Introduction

Organization of the Casino

    Front of the House

    Back of the House

Management and Casino Careers

Gambling Outside of the Casino

    Sports Betting

    Internet Gambling

The Future of Gaming

Summary

KEY TERMS

Casino	Pit
Casino floor	Slot machines
Gambling	Table games

INTRODUCTION

Gambling has been an ingredient of American life since before the foundation of the country. The Revolutionary War of 1776 was funded, in part, by the proceeds of a national lottery. However, the public acceptance of **gambling** has come and gone in waves over the years. In the early 21st century, public acceptance of gaming is high, with 48 states currently having some form of legalized gaming. Casinos operate in 28 of the 50 states. Only Hawaii and Utah do not have any form of legalized gaming.

About 33% of Americans do not gamble, 46% gamble at casinos, and 21% gamble only at non-casino locations such as dog tracks, horse races, bingo parlors, etc., or play the lottery. Of those Americans who do gamble, about 10% are heavy gamblers who wager about 60% of all casino revenues. Most gamblers are considered light bettors (50%–60%). People who visit casinos once or twice a week are considered frequent gamblers (17%). It is from that smallest pool of heavy gamblers that most personal gambling problems and addictions emerge.

The global casino gaming market generates about $159 billion per year in revenue. Macau is the world's largest gaming destination, generating about $44 billion. The casinos in Las Vegas generate about $9.6 billion per year from its 41 million visitors and this makes the Nevada destination the second largest in the world. The more than 1,500 American casinos combined have gross annual revenues of about $65 billion. It is estimated that Americans illegally bet another $6 billion annually on the Internet, with those revenues leaving the U.S. to go wherever the off-shore web casino is based. In a typical year, about 55 million people visit U.S. casinos. Commercial casinos (more than 500 casinos) account for about 36% of the gross revenue; Indian casinos (486 casinos in 28 states operated by 230 tribes) produce another 26%; lotteries (42 states and Washington, DC) typically produce 26%; and pari-mutuel betting at racetrack casinos (41) accounts for the remaining 4%.

ORGANIZATION OF THE CASINO

The typical casino is organized in a functional manner. The various departments are usually table games and slots in the casino area, the hotel, food and beverage outlets, entertainment, and shopping. Managers of each area are organized in a similar fashion. Careers are built within this structure, with most employees starting at entry-level and working their way upward. The casino itself forms the heart and soul of the enterprise. It includes the front of the house, called the **casino floor**, where customers actually gamble at the table games or play the slot machines. It also includes the back of the house, where the accounting operations, security, and computer control systems are housed.

FRONT OF THE HOUSE

The casino floor is carefully designed to attract customers. The floor plan of the games takes into account the desired ease of movement, which can either slow customers down so they may linger and gamble, or speed them up to facilitate quick passage. A theme is often selected that is woven throughout the entire area. Color, sound, lighting, and even scents are chosen to maximize customer responses. Often the result is bold, bright, and noisy, but this is intentional. The bright lights and sounds attract attention, as does the general theme. However, while these strong attributes are used to entice the customer into the play area, softer hues, tones, and muted sounds are used further into the casino. This helps to keep the customer comfortable and continuing to gamble. If this change is not made, customers can easily become overwhelmed by the excessive noise and lighting, at which point they may leave the playing area.

The **table games** are arranged in what is called a **pit**. A pit will generally have as few as two and as many as eight tables. The tables are arranged in a circle. Customers are kept to the outside of the circle.

The casino floor is bright and noisy to attract attention.

© Vlada Photo/Shutterstock.com

This outside area is called the playing area. Dealers, supervisors, and other support staff such as security are the only people permitted inside this circle of tables. This is primarily for security reasons, so that the casino can effectively manage the cash as well as the integrity of the games.

The table games are generally located well inside the casino. **Slot machines** are placed near the entries to attract players. Gamblers must walk past them when desiring to play at the table games. The slot machines act as tempting devices to all customers passing by them.

A large cashier's office will be typically located either in the rear or along the side of the casino floor area. This office is referred to as the "cage" because of the iron bars placed along the front side of the office to separate customers from cashier employees. These bars are important security features to help protect the large sums of cash inside the cage. The primary function of the cage is to act as an intermediary between customers and employees inside the casino playing area and the accounting office in the back of the house. Employees in the cage will exchange cash and house chips for customers, establish credit for qualified players, manage debt collection activities, and provide the table games with sufficient cash reserves to operate.

Many casinos will also provide small cashier kiosks scattered about inside the casino play area. These kiosks are for customer convenience, and can provide limited service transactions such as exchanging cash for chips.

BACK OF THE HOUSE

The back of the casino houses the support departments, including accounting, security, human resources, marketing, and the general administrative offices. Accounting and security play key roles in the daily operation of the casino.

ACCOUNTING

The accounting department manages the immense cash holdings that flow through the casino. Virtually all transactions within the casino are made with cash. Cash is exchanged for casino chips at the cashier cage and at table games. Cash is used to gamble in slot machines. A dedicated collection box is provided for each gaming machine or table. This "drop box" is carefully labeled to record the shift and the device from which it came.

The drop boxes are collected from the casino floor by special teams of three people made up of staff from security and either the slots department or the table games department. The boxes are delivered to the counting room that is located in the back of the house. This special room is carefully monitored and protected. The cash from each device is counted and recorded, so that the productivity of each game can be monitored.

Counting room employees verify the count, double-checking the work of others. These employees wear special clothing designed to prevent the accidental or intentional loss of cash. Access to this room is extremely limited, even to other managers!

This department is also responsible for the standard accounting activities of any business such as payroll, accounts payable, accounts receivable, and collections. These functions are performed for the casino and any other support departments such as gift shops, restaurants, and hotels, if they are owned and operated by the casino.

SURVEILLANCE AND SECURITY

These two departments have the responsibility for the surveillance of the gaming areas, as well as the general safety and security of the casino property. They are separate departments to increase the protection of the business. Surveillance protects the games, and uses the latest in high-resolution video cameras and computer technology to monitor all gaming activities. Each table game has a camera mounted directly over the playing area so that all transactions can be observed. Cameras also carefully monitor each section of slot machines. With the advent of digital cameras, these images can be readily stored in computer format on disk drives. This reduces the bulky storage and retrieval problems associated with videotape. It also greatly reduces the surveillance cost.

Specially trained employees monitor the video images on a 24-hour basis. Often, these employees are ex-cheaters who have been recruited to watch other gamblers who may be cheating. These employees are required to sit in darkened rooms staring at video screens for eight-hour shifts. It takes a unique personality to do well at this job.

Before the advent of high-resolution video cameras, casinos had built "catwalks" into the ceilings over the gambling area. One-way mirrors were built into the ceiling so that personnel walking above the ceiling over these catwalks could observe players as they gambled. The mirrors were often incorporated into the casino design, making them less noticeable to patrons. However, the advent of the high-tech computers and digital cameras has made catwalks unnecessary in the modern casino. However, uniformed security personnel still periodically patrol the playing areas. Their presence can be a comfort to customers, and a clear warning to criminals. In addition, surveillance personnel sometimes dress in plain clothing and mingle unobtrusively with gamblers. This aids in the identification of problems before they escalate into disruptive events.

The security department is responsible for the safety and welfare of customers and employees throughout the entire facility. They focus on the physical assets of the casino rather than the games. Security patrols often walk the perimeter of the casino and throughout the hotel, restaurants, and shops to observe customer and employee behavior firsthand. Cameras are also used to monitor these areas. Their uniformed presence is frequently enough incentive to discourage crime.

OTHER BUSINESS SUPPORT DEPARTMENTS

As with any other line of business, casinos require the use of human resources, marketing, and general administrative departments. The casino is labor-intensive, so the human resources staff plays a major role in the hiring and training of the workers necessary to operate the casino. Given the large increase in the number of casinos around the country and, thus, in competition for the gambler, casino marketing departments have strengthened their efforts to attract and keep customers. Managing the entire operation requires a top management team to coordinate and oversee everything. The general office staff typically includes the casino manager, assistant

casino managers to supervise the evening and late night operations, and support staff to process paperwork and answer telephones.

MANAGEMENT AND CASINO CAREERS

Lifelong careers can be built in the casino industry. There are many entry-level positions in the restaurants, hotels, and shops. However, to create a career in the gaming industry, the vast majority of people begin as dealers and work their way up through the ranks. The casino career ladder leads into management positions, such as pit boss, shift supervisor, and casino manager. It has been a long-standing tradition within the casino industry that to move up the career ladder, an employee must start as a dealer so that they truly learn the integral elements of the world of casinos. However, this attitude is slowly changing. The need for professional managers with subject matter expertise, such as marketing and human resources, is becoming better understood.

To become a dealer, a potential employee must attend a dealer school and become qualified to deal prior to applying for a dealer position with a casino. This is a standard industry requirement. The casinos do not train their own employees to become basic dealers. Even employees who work in a different part of the organization must attend an external dealer school if they want to become a dealer. Once certified, the casinos then spend their time training the dealers in the particular approaches they use.

Employees can become members of the slots department without dealer certification. Positions in this department include the slot hostess, slot cashier, and slot machine maintenance. The slot hostess and slot cashier positions are entry-level positions that require only a small amount of training. The hostess greets slot machine players, offers them beverages, and helps to keep the playing area clean and tidy. The slot cashier walks about the slots playing area so that customers can conveniently exchange dollar bills for coins. The maintenance staff is responsible for the repair and upkeep of the slot machines. They handle both the routine maintenance as well as respond to customers who have an immediate problem with a machine while gambling.

While these positions are on the casino floor, these workers cannot become dealers without earning the outside certification provided by dealer schools. Employees of the slots department are often considered the lowest ranking employees within the casino.

Dealers also have their internal ranking order. Blackjack, or 21, is considered the simplest table game. Therefore, new dealers are assigned to this game. When dealers have more experience, they may then be moved to more complex games, such as roulette, and the variations of poker, such as Caribbean Stud and Pai Gow. The game that requires the most skill is craps because of the complexity of bets and payouts as well as the pressures of managing a crowd of excited players. Craps dealers have much more status within the dealer ranks. Because of the sophisticated image and high-stakes betting developed for baccarat that attracts premium players, only the most polished and experienced dealers are assigned to this game. These dealers are often considered at the top of the dealer status ranks.

Once a dealer becomes highly experienced, he or she may be promoted to become a pit boss. The pit boss manages a group of dealers. The next step is shift supervisor. Since the casinos often do not close their doors, three shifts each day are usually necessary to staff the playing areas. Therefore, shifts of workers are needed for each job level. A shift supervisor oversees all gaming operations that happen on that particular shift.

Blackjack is considered the simplest table game, so new dealers are assigned to it.

Coordinating and managing all casino operations is the responsibility of the casino manager. The shift supervisors report to this position. In the past, the casino manager had the authority and responsibility for the entire operation, including the hotel and food service. In more recent times, that has changed. Today, the casino manager is primarily responsible for the gaming areas of the business. Other top-level managers are responsible for the hotel, restaurants, shops, and entertainment departments. While at some casinos these other department managers report to the casino manager, more and more, these area managers all report to a central administration that has a chief operating officer (COO) who oversees the entire operation.

GAMBLING OUTSIDE OF THE CASINO

SPORTS BETTING

Betting on the outcome of athletic competitions has consistently been popular in the U.S. due to the highly competitive nature of the American culture. This includes horse and dog racing, as well as football, basketball, and baseball at both the college and professional sport levels. Unfortunately for most bettors, betting on sporting events is only legal in four states: Delaware, Montana, Nevada, and Oregon. Other states have discussed this issue, but none have permitted it to date. Delaware is the most recent, with their state Supreme Court clearing the way of constitutional issues in May 2009.[1]

Casinos in other states do attempt to cater to customers interested in betting on sporting events. They often provide a dedicated area within the casino that provides gamblers with information on the sporting events and the odds on the outcomes, as well as other features of the games. While these other casinos cannot accept sport bets, they can provide their customers with links to booking agents (bookies) in the other states that can accept the wagers.

INTERNET GAMBLING

Internet casinos have emerged over the past decade as the Internet has grown in use. American casino firms would like to take advantage of this technological development inside the U.S. but may not. Under existing U.S. law, gambling on the Internet is illegal. Therefore, firms that offer Internet gaming may not be based in the United States. A number of U.S. casino companies experimented with Internet-based gaming in other nations where it was legal, but have mostly withdrawn those operations as they were not as profitable as anticipated.

The federal law extends to the player. It is technically illegal for anyone in the U.S. to place a wager on the web. However, practicalities make it extremely difficult and costly to apprehend the individual gambler. While the technology exists to trace an illegal bet back to the computer where it was entered, it is very difficult for the law to prove who was sitting at the keyboard placing the bet. It could be a minor who cannot legally bet or be responsible for debts incurred. It may not necessarily be the owner of the computer terminal.

Prosecuting the individual gambler does nothing to stop the availability of web-based gambling opportunities. Many of the firms that offer Internet gaming are located offshore in different Caribbean nations. For example, Antigua has established a very gaming-friendly environment. While they do generally investigate the firms wishing to offer this service, they do not have a formal gaming commission that regulates the operation of the games themselves.

This situation makes it difficult for customers to know that the game they are playing is fair. In U.S. land-based casinos, state regulatory agencies monitor the games and help ensure they operated fairly. Online players have no such assurances, as there is little or no regulatory oversight.

Further, online players cannot be certain the Internet casino will honor their winnings. Credit cards are the most common form of establishing credit with an online casino (although the U.S. government has worked with the major American credit card issuers to stop the use of credit cards for bets by having them refuse to accept the transactions). Using this credit card method, it is very easy for the casino to receive the money for the bets placed. However, these casino firms do not often automatically return winnings back to the credit card. Instead, they establish policies that they will send large winnings directly to players. The player must then trust that the Internet casino will follow through on that promise.

If the winnings are not returned, the gambler has little or no legal recourse—especially if they reside in the United States, as the initial betting transaction is viewed as illegal. Furthermore, it may be difficult for the player to determine where the web-based casino is located if they wish to contact them directly or if they wish to pursue legal action. This situation makes gambling on the Internet very risky for players.

THE FUTURE OF GAMING

The future forecast for gaming is one of continued institutionalization. The gaming industry will suffer the usual ebb and flow cycles that all industries experience. For example, during the economic downturn of 2008–2009, the gaming industry suffered just as all other industries did. Casino employees experienced layoffs and reduced incomes as travelers curtailed their vacation plans to casino destinations. However, as the world economy improved, so did the health of the gaming industry.

The international dimension of modern commerce—especially the travel industry—over the long term will ensure a steady supply of customers. Further, governments have come to rely upon the tax revenues of lotteries and casinos as well as the increases in local employment. Rather than face the daunting prospect of lost revenues and unemployment, states will continue to support the casino industry. For example, in 2011, the Commonwealth of Massachusetts legalized three casino licenses. Firms were asked to submit site and design proposals by January 2014. Once bids were selected, construction was to follow in 2014 and 2015. As of early 2016, one of those casinos is open and operating. The other two are expected to begin operations soon. Any similar proposed gaming regulation or issuance of a casino license would be crafted with care, as it will directly impact state coffers.

Undoubtedly, there will be some areas of withdrawal from the gaming industry. As scandals emerge, there will be a call for a reduction or distancing from gaming. State lotteries may be adjusted or eliminated, and casinos may be more tightly controlled. Riverboat casinos may be banned from certain ports or states. The concept of NIMBY (not in my back yard) will certainly continue as an argument.

Several communities such as Reno depend on the gaming industry.

However, with entire communities supporting gaming, it is unlikely there would ever be a complete withdrawal. Las Vegas, Reno, and Atlantic City have limited other commerce of significance to sustain themselves without the gaming industry. If there is any general reduction in gaming across the country, these specialized communities will continue to operate. Gaming may, at the very least, become a geographic niche service as it was from the 1930s through the 1970s.

Gambling in virtual casinos on the Internet will not disappear. Governments cannot completely control the operation or the content of the web. New online casinos are appearing on the web on a regular basis. Therefore, gambling in virtual casinos will continue to be widely available, regardless of land-based casinos and any government regulation.

In conclusion, this recent surge in gambling popularity will not end in full prohibition as earlier waves of gaming have. It may dissipate to low levels of interest and use by society, but it will never completely disappear. Social acceptance may oscillate, but with softer peaks and valleys. There are simply too many jobs, dollars, and customers involved.

SUMMARY

Casinos are established as a significant sector of the U.S. economy. Annual wagers placed are estimated in the $900 billion range, resulting in gross revenues at about $96 billion. A comparison with gross revenue of the top five Fortune 500 companies is revealing. Exxon/Mobil typically reports annual gross income of about $340 billion, Wal-Mart at about $315 billion, General Motors at about $192 billion, Chevron Oil at about $190 billion, and Ford Motor Company at about $180 billion. Thus, casino firms collectively contribute a significant portion of the total business volume conducted within the U.S.

Corporations are now permitted to hold casino licenses and have bought out most of the individual owners of casinos. This has led to an infusion of capital through the issuance of stock to investors and a professionalization of the management of these businesses. Cooperative partnerships have been built between casinos and state regulating agencies to ensure both a safe, fair, and enjoyable playing environment for gamblers, and to oversee the accurate reporting of sales and tax revenues. While gaming continues to grow via Internet casinos, the land-based operations are maintaining their attractiveness to patrons. Casinos have become an integral aspect of our national identity and a widely accepted form of entertainment. The negative social impacts of casinos are understood, and for the most part, society has adapted to those issues because the positive impacts, especially the increase in tax revenues, have been viewed as worth the costs. Thus, the casino industry is well established in our way of life in the U.S., and is likely to continue to offer its products and services as a routine aspect of the hospitality and tourism industries.

ENDNOTES

1. NBCSports, 2009.

REFERENCES

American Gaming Association. (2016). *AGA Research. American Gaming Association.* Retrieved January 11, 2016 from https://www.americangaming.org/about

Christiansen Capital Advisors. (2008). 2006 Gross Gambling Revenues by Industry and Change from 2005. *U.S. International Gaming & Wagering Business (IGWB)*, February 5, 2008.

Elder, R. W. (1990). Opening the Mirage: The Human-Resources Challenge. *Cornell HRA Quarterly*, 31 (2), pp. 2–31.

Ettis, M. (1997). Personal comments given during a private casino tour to a student group at the Mohegan Sun Casino, Ledyard, CT.

Fereris, R. (2014). *These states raked in $34 in casino revenue.* USA Today, April 27, 2014. Retrieved from http://www.usatoday.com/story/money/business/2014/04/27/top-gambling-states/8168681/

Focus on the Family Issue Analysts. (2013). *Gambling.* Retrieved from http://www.focusonthefamily.com/socialissues/socialissues/gambling.aspx

Foxwoods Pays $58 Million in July. (September 10, 1998). *Daily Hampshire Gazette*, p. B1.

Gambling Addiction–Gambling Addiction Statistics. (2010). ClearLead, Inc. Retrieved July 26, 2010 from http://www.clearleadinc.com/site/gambling-addiction.html

Grinols, E. L. (2004). *Gambling in America: Costs and Benefits.* New York: Cambridge University Press.

Hashimoto, K. (1998). Cripple Creek, Colorado. In K. Hashimoto, S. F. Kline, and G. Fenich (eds.), *Casino Management: Past-Present-Future*, p. 11. Dubuque, IA: Kendall Hunt.

Heneghan, D. (March 20, 1994). Casinos Generate More Than $1b in State Economy. *Atlantic Free Press*, p. A1.

Las Vegas Convention and Visitors Authority. (2016). *Las Vegas Stats & Facts.* Retrieved January 11, 2016 from http://www.lvcva.com/stats-and-facts/

Michael Evans Group. (1996). *A Study of the Economic Impact of the Gaming Industry through 2005.* Reno: I.G.T.

NASPL. (2016). *Lottery Sales and Transfers.* North American Association of State & Provincial Lotteries (NASPL). Retrieved January 11, 2016 from http://www.naspl.org/index.cfm?fuseaction=content&menuid=17&pageid=1025&PageCategory=3

National Gambling Impact Study Commission Final Report. (June 1999). Retrieved August 21, 2008 from http://govinfo.library.unt.edu/ngisc/reports/3.pdf

National Indian Gaming Commission. (2015). *Indian Gaming and the NIGC.* Retrieved January 11, 2016 from http://www.nigc.gov/images/uploads/Fact%20Sheet%20August%202015.pdf

NBC Sports. (2009). *Delaware Supreme Court Gives OK to Sports Betting.* Retrieved July 26, 2010 from http://nbcsports.msnbc.com/id/30982541/

Reilly Opposes Casino Gambling. (March 17, 1999). *Associated Press* (Boston).

Roberts, C. and Fladmoe-Lindquist, K. (1999). Hypercompetition and Mega-Casinos. Unpublished manuscript, University of Massachusetts, Department of Hotel, Restaurant and Travel Administration.

Rose, I. N. (1996). The Rise and Fall of the Third Wave: Gambling Will Be Outlawed in Forty Years. In K. Hashimoto, S. F. Kline, and G. Fenich (eds.), *Casino Management for the 90's*, pp. 491–501. Dubuque, IA: Kendall Hunt.

Sylvester, K. (1992). Casinomania. In K. Hashimoto, S. F. Kline, and G. Fenich (eds.), *Casino Management: Past-Present-Future*, pp. 428–432. Dubuque, IA: Kendall Hunt.

Volberg, R. A., Gerstein, D. R., and Christiansen, E. M. (2001). Assessing Self-Reported Expenditures on Gambling. *Managerial and Decision Economics*, 22 (1–3), p. 82.

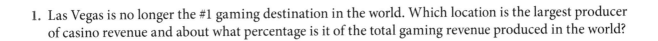

REVIEW QUESTIONS

1. Las Vegas is no longer the #1 gaming destination in the world. Which location is the largest producer of casino revenue and about what percentage is it of the total gaming revenue produced in the world?

2. The front of the house in a casino has two major departments. Name them and briefly describe them.

3. Acting as a bridge between the front and back of the house accounting operations is the "cage." Explain what the "cage" is and how it interacts with customers.

4. Casinos have security and surveillance departments to protect the games, the guests, and the business in general. Describe each of these two departments, highlighting what each does that is different from the another.

5. Sports betting is very popular around the world. Explain how casinos offer sports betting to their patrons.

6. Gambling on the Internet is growing each year, yet there are extra risks that customers take because of international borders and laws within various countries. Explain these added risks.

© Racheal Grazias/Shutterstock.com

CHAPTER *35*

ATTRACTIONS MANAGEMENT

AUTHOR	*Reginald Foucar-Szocki, James Madison University*
LEARNING OBJECTIVES	• Define an attraction.
	• Explain how attractions benefit local economies.
	• List the ways attractions are classified.
	• Describe the characteristics for each classification of attractions.
	• Classify examples of attractions according to their product offering or benefits they provide.
	• Apply your knowledge of why people travel might travel to certain attractions.
CHAPTER OUTLINE	What Are Attractions?
	Attractions Promote Travel to Destinations
	Attractions Help Satisfy Needs
	Attractions Are Economic Engines
	How Are Attractions Classified?
	Status
	Origin
	Life Span or Time-Oriented
	Ownership and Purpose
	Attractions: Product Attributes
	Topography
	Culture and Heritage Attractions
	Planned Play Environments
	Events

© Kendall Hunt Publishing Co.

CHAPTER OUTLINE
(Continued)

Industrial Attractions

Infrastructure

Summary

KEY TERMS

Amusement parks

Attractions

Cultural attractions

Economic benefits

Events

Gaming

Grand Tour

Heritage tourism

Historical attractions

Industrial attractions

Life span

Man-made attractions

Museums

Natural attractions

Non-profit entity

Primary attractions

Profit-seeking entity

Religious attractions

Secondary attraction

Shopping

Status of attraction

Theme parks

Topography

WHAT ARE ATTRACTIONS?

ATTRACTIONS PROMOTE TRAVEL TO DESTINATIONS

Go to Google.com, type *tourist attractions* in the search box, select the *image* function, and click search. Look over the various pictures presented to you in the next few pages, and you are likely to see pictures of Disney World and other theme parks such as Six Flags, natural environments such as Bryce Canyon and San Diego ocean beaches, cultural landmarks in the form of the Eiffel Tower or the Egyptian Pyramids, adventure experiences on the Blackfoot River in Montana, and Southern California hot-air balloon excursions. Venturing further into the web pages, you will see pictures of assorted museums, mountains and lakes, themed megaresorts, and hotels such as The Venetian or the MGM Grand in Las Vegas, and even a few proverbial "biggest ball of twine" roadside stops. Consider for a moment the diversity of the items that appeared on your computer screen. What do they all have in common? They are places, activities, and experiences sought out by leisure travelers. Some are wildly popular, whereas others may be just interesting stops along their way to the final destination. They are, in the vernacular of the hospitality industry, "attractions." **Attractions** *are the places we visit and the things we do while we are traveling for leisure.*

ATTRACTIONS HELP SATISFY NEEDS

Attractions are the lifeblood of tourism. Families take vacations to theme parks, or to the shores of Southern California to enjoy the ocean, to the mountains of Vermont and New Hampshire for recreational skiing, and to Washington, DC, to visit the capital's monuments and museums. Attractions are an integral part of the need satisfaction that fuels the desire to travel. Whether the need is belongingness (family vacation to Disney), physiological (rest and recuperating at the shore), or self-actualizing (visiting cultural and historical sites of Washington, DC), it is an attraction that the traveler will seek out to help fulfill that need. In short, attractions assist in satisfying the needs that motivate travel.

ATTRACTIONS ARE ECONOMIC ENGINES

Attractions provide economic benefit to the region in which they are located. The money spent for the theme park admission may only be a small percentage of the leisure traveler's expenditure; but then, consider all the other amounts the traveler will spend on lodging, food and beverage, souvenirs, rental cars and other forms of transportation, guided tours, and ancillary activities, as well as shopping in local stores and malls. These expenditures provide **economic benefits**, such as employment for the local residents, who in turn will use their wages to generate additional economic activity. Without the attraction, these jobs might not exist. In addition to providing employment, attractions also support local governments when they generate income, sales, and excise taxes. A visitor to Maui can visit Haleakalā (ha-lee-ah-ka-la), an extinct volcano that rises through the clouds, over 10,000 feet above sea level. Although the volcano is part of the U.S. national park system, local tourism entrepreneurs have flourished around the attraction. There are bike rental stores and tour packages starting on the mountain just outside the park limits.[1] In addition, there are also guided excursions 3,000 feet down into the crater itself, either on foot or by horseback, as well as helicopter and airplane tours, balloon rides, and ATV excursions all centered on the volcano.[2]

All these activities are available through local businesses and generate economic benefits to the providers and their employees, as well as to the community. The fees and taxes they generate circulate through the local economy. Without an attraction such as

Vacationers often visit attractions such as the monuments and museums in Washington, DC.

© Timothy Michael Morgan/Shutterstock.com

Haleakalā, none of these tourism business opportunities would exist, nor would the economic benefits that they generate.[3]

HOW ARE ATTRACTIONS CLASSIFIED?

The most common methods of classifying attractions are **status** (importance or interest to the traveler), origin, life span, ownership, profit orientation, and product attributes.[4]

STATUS

Attractions are often broadly characterized as either *primary* or *secondary* attractions. A **primary attraction** is essentially the main reason a visitor travels to the destination and spends several days. As a result, primary attractions are usually supported by extensive ancillary facilities: lodging, food and beverage, transportation, extensive retail, and other hospitality services. An excellent example of a primary attraction is Disney World in Orlando, Florida. Visitors, especially families, make the trip and stay for several days. They purchase multiday passes to the Disney theme parks and may stay in one of the many Disney-owned properties, eat at Disney food outlets, use the Disney transportation system, and shop for their needs at Disney retail outlets. Because Disney World has tremendous drawing power, significant non-Disney-owned hospitality facilities have developed around the theme park and have contributed to the growth of the Orlando area in Florida.

In contrast, a **secondary attraction** is of lesser importance to the traveler and might be considered simply something nice to do while on the way to or in the area of the primary attraction. Again, using the Orlando area as an example, there are many secondary attractions like Gatorland, which markets itself as "a unique and natural alternative to the larger theme parks of today."[5]

ORIGIN

Attractions may be classified according to whether they are *natural* or *man-made*. **Natural attractions** are those that occur in nature without human intervention. They include mountains, coastlines, lakes,

islands, forests, deserts, rainforests, and other landforms and seascapes. **Man-made** attractions owe their very existence to the intervention of humans. Examples of pure man-made attractions are theme parks, shopping centers, sports and entertainment facilities, festivals, casinos, and museums. Often, human intervention combines with nature to create a mixed origin attraction such as the Hoover Dam constructed on the Colorado River, which created Lake Mead. The surrounding area, referred to as the Lake Mead National Recreation Area, is a premier inland water recreation area managed by the National Park Service, and encompasses over 1.5 million acres of land, with 700 miles of shoreline. A top-ten national park destination, Lake Mead has brought millions of tourists and generated billions of dollars over the past decade for the local economy.[6] Some natural attractions are made more accessible by man-made attractions that are constructed on or about the natural formation, such as the rainforest cable tours available in Costa Rica and other parts of the world. In these locations, various forms of cable transportation and other viewing facilities have been constructed to permit visitors access to the natural attraction that would otherwise be relatively inaccessible to the visitor. The excitement of traveling along the cable itself has become one of the "things to do" for visitors to the area.[7]

LIFE SPAN OR TIME-ORIENTED

Attractions can be classified according to their **life span** or whether they are *relatively* permanent or temporary. Natural attractions such as lakes, mountains,

Often attractions are the result of human intervention with nature, such as the creation of Lake Mead due to Hoover Dam.

© Blulz60/Shutterstock.com

and other landforms and seascapes are permanent attractions. However, permanent attractions can also be man-made, such as an amusement park, a zoo, or a historical monument. Although these attractions can be demolished and moved, they are relatively permanent in comparison to temporary attractions, which are short lived or can be easily relocated. Examples of temporary attractions are concerts, state fairs, conferences, trade shows, parades, award shows, and certain sporting events like the Super Bowl, NCAA Football Championship, Final Four and festivals. Permanent attractions are sometimes referred to as *site* attractions, whereas temporary attractions are referred to as *event* attractions.

OWNERSHIP AND PURPOSE

Approximately 85% of all recreational land in the United States is under *public ownership*, managed by the federal and state governments for the benefit of the public at large. The National Park Service, part of the Department of the Interior, manages the majority of federal lands under the auspices of the national park system, which includes parks, monuments, and preserves. The world's first national park—Yellowstone—was created in 1872, at which time Congress set aside more than one million acres as a public park for the benefit and enjoyment of the people.[8] This American invention marked the beginning of a worldwide movement that has subsequently spread to more than 100 countries and 1,200 national parks and conservation preserves. Today, there are more than 409 units in the national park system, encompassing more than 84 million acres.[9] These units are variously designated as national parks, monuments, preserves, lakeshores, seashores, wild and scenic rivers, trails, historic sites, military parks, battlefields, historical parks, recreation areas, memorials, and parkways. All represent some nationally significant aspect of the American natural or cultural heritage.

The federal and state governments own and manage a significant portion of natural attractions, but *private ownership* accounts for the overwhelming number of man-made attractions. Major corporations such as Disney, Universal, and Six Flags own and operate theme and amusement parks; MGM Mirage operates megagaming resorts in Las Vegas, Nevada; and Simon Malls provide shopping opportunities throughout the United States in operating over 325 centers as it attempts to fend off Amazon and other online shopping entities.[10]

Closely aligned with ownership is the purpose for which attractions are operated, either as *non-profit* or *profit-seeking* entities. Generally, **non-profit entities** that own man-made attractions, such as museums, or natural attractions, such as nature preserves, do not have tourism as their primary goal. Rather, their interest is that of preservation of the natural environment or a historical, cultural, or religious consequence. **Profit-seeking entities**, on the other hand, are seeking to provide a return on investment to the private owners. There is a delicate balance for both types of owners. Profit-seeking entities cannot engage in unrestrained use and development without fear of public backlash resulting from spoiling the environment or encouraging unrestrained commercial development of the surrounding area. In addition, it would not be in the long-term interest of the private owners to exhaust or physically depreciate the attraction through overuse, thereby shortening its useful life. For non-profits, the balance is between their preservation goals and generating sufficient revenues to maintain the attraction, while at the same time permitting public access at an acceptable level. The National Park Service faces this very same dilemma. How do they provide the widest array of access to the public, while at the same time avoiding the overcrowding that would destroy the natural beauty of the environment, which is the very reason visitors come to the parks?

ATTRACTIONS: PRODUCT ATTRIBUTES

We can also categorize attractions based on what the attraction has to offer to the tourist as leisure activity. Common classifications include topography, culture and heritage, planned play environments, and events and entertainment.

TOPOGRAPHY

The **topography** of an area is significant as an attraction and has an added benefit to the tourist in that scenery is free. Topography attractions consist of three areas of interest (*landforms, wildlife,* and *ecology)* and provide a unique and natural alternative to the larger theme parks of today. Landforms such as beaches, mountain vistas, and deserts can all be visually appreciated for free, and in many instances be utilized for little or no dollar costs to the traveler. Often, because climate is closely aligned with topography, these attractions experience heavy seasonal demand. The beaches of Florida are in "high season" when the northern states are in their winter season, whereas, despite their ability to make snow, the ski slopes of the West and New England are largely dependent on a snowy winter for a successful ski season. The challenge for these seasonal attractions is to manage the heavy demand during peak season and to create additional off-season activities to create demand during slow times.[11] Each year, thousands of individuals travel to California's Sequoia National Park[12] to take in the majesty of giant sequoia trees, or to the California Redwood Coast[13] to view the giant redwoods.[14]

In addition to scenic beauty, topography is closely tied to recreational activities, as well as wildlife viewing and ecological activities. In recent years, concern for the environment has created a heightened awareness of the effects of tourism on the natural environment.[15] Efforts to control access and the types of tourism activities centered on natural attractions have been implemented by federal and state governments in the United States as well as by their counterparts around the world.[16] At the same time, this heightened awareness has created environmentally friendly or ecotourism opportunities centered on natural attractions. A prime example of this is the whale-watching excursions that permit visitors to Maui, Hawaii, to see and hear the humpback whales during the annual migrations in December and January.

CULTURE AND HERITAGE ATTRACTIONS

Since the early days of mankind, travel has been closely linked to culture and **heritage**. The preservation for future generations of artifacts and sites, in particular those associated with a people's origins, religion, war, and art, as well as science and myth, are commonplace among the world's cultures. **Cultural attractions** are very popular among travelers. In fact, most U.S. adult travelers attend a cultural activity or performing arts event and/or museums during a trip.[17]

Museums

Visitors are attracted to **museums** out of both curiosity and for education. The **Grand Tour**, a root of modern tourism, was a long, arduous, albeit cultural journey through Paris, Venice, Florence, and Rome, and a capstone educational experience for the elite of the 17th, 18th, and early 19th centuries. Today, a visitor can approximate the experience by visiting the plethora of museums around the world, such as the Metropolitan Museum of Art[19] or the Museum of Natural History,[19] both in New York City, wherein many great works reside. In addition to exhibits, awaiting the visitor of museum attractions are programs and events, which include lectures, performances, workshops, and films. Many have been designed for children, the tourists of tomorrow.[20]

Religious Attractions

Rivaling museums in their numbers and diversity are **religious attractions**, primarily consisting of cathedrals and churches, temples, and mosques. There are also geographic areas that consist of entire cities and the surrounding locales of religious significance, such as the Holy Land in Jerusalem, where many of the principal religious sites for Christianity, Judaism, and Islam converge; or the city of Mecca in Saudi Arabia, where millions of Muslims from around world make an annual pilgrimage.[21] Modern tourism has its roots in religion. During the Middle Ages, individuals made pilgrimages to visit religious sites, and many of the same are still visited by tourists

Visitors are attracted to museums such as the Met to see great works of art.

today. Much like travelers today, these pilgrims came from every strata of society.

Historical Attractions

Often quoted, George Santayana's statement, "Those who cannot learn from history are doomed to repeat it," is at the heart of **historical attractions**. They are the efforts to preserve the events of the past that demand remembrance. Primarily consisting of monuments and structures such as the Pyramids of Egypt, the Statue of Liberty, Tiananmen Square, or the Great Wall of China, they also encompass area attractions of historical significance, such as battlefields. A recent survey reveals that 41% of travelers say they visited a designated historic site such as a building, landmark, home, or monument during their trip. Three in 10 visited a designated historic community or town.[22] All too often, war provides tourism opportunities. American Civil War sites such as Gettysburg, Pennsylvania, are extremely popular, and many Civil War attractions involve battlefield reenactments (events), which heighten the visitors' understanding and appreciation of the event's historical significance, as well as increasing visitor involvement.[23] In addition to battlefield attractions, there are numerous memorials in Washington, DC, such as the Vietnam Veterans Memorial,[24] whose principal exhibit is The Wall, containing the names of the 57,939 men and women who gave their lives in the war, visited by about 5 million people yearly, as well as the World War I, National World War II, and Korean War Memorial.[25] Lest you start to believe that historical attractions are just about war, numerous attractions celebrate historic ideas that changed the world, and in particular America, many of which are found at the National Mall in Washington, DC. There a tourist can visit the Thomas Jefferson Memorial, the Lincoln Memorial, the Washington Monument, the Franklin Delano Roosevelt Memorial, and the recently completed Martin Luther King Memorial.[26] The King Memorial site is a four-acre plot on the northeast corner of the Tidal Basin, and creates a visual "line of leadership" from the Lincoln Memorial, where Martin Luther King, Jr., gave his famous "I Have a Dream" speech, to the Jefferson Memorial.[27] Like museums, many of these monuments also include programming and special events to enhance the experience of the visitor.

PLANNED PLAY ENVIRONMENTS

Planned play environments provide recreation and entertainment and are a significant sector of the tourism market. The ancient Greeks and Romans traveled for both theater and sport.

Sporting Facilities

Sports, recreation, and travel go together. The array of sporting and recreational attractions available to the traveler is almost endless. Fishing, hunting, cycling, mountain climbing, hang gliding, horseback riding, boating, surfing, snorkeling, and scuba diving are but a few, and for each there is a sporting attraction where one can engage in one's desired recreational activity to one's heart's content. Would you like to go fishing? Then try steelhead fishing in Northern British Columbia, Canada. Need a bit more excitement? Try your hand (wings) at Lookout Mountain Flight Park in Georgia,[28] where you can purchase a complete hang gliding instruction package that will have "most students flying the mountains in less than one week." The point is that no matter what your interest, there is either a natural or man-made attraction drawing you to a destination where you can recreate it.

Among the most popular sporting and recreational activities are skiing and golf. About 7% of the United States population are snow sport enthusiasts, making the ski industry a multibillion-dollar business. Twenty-five percent of all ski excursions are multiday visits more than 500 miles from home.[29] In the United States, the ski resorts of the Rocky Mountain West are the prime ski attractions, accounting for approximately 25% of all lift tickets sold in the United States.[30]

If ski and snow sports are a bit too adventuresome, consider golf. There are over 24 million golfers in the United States. Reportedly, a golf facility is the only significant sports activity that will influence a meeting planner's choice of destination.[31] In a recent year, one in eight U.S. travelers played golf while on a trip of 100 miles or more away from home.[32] Sixteen percent of travelers who played golf said that golf was the most important reason for taking the trip.[33] Golf is a time to be among friends and a time to compete, to relax, and to do business, as well as to just enjoy the beauty of the natural surroundings.[34]

Theme and Amusement Parks

Theme and amusement parks are likely the most often recognizable attractions to the general public. **Theme parks** offer escape and replicate both real, as well as "unreal," places that may or may not exist beyond the gates. **Amusement parks** on the other hand have rides, games, and exhibitions. Today, the distinction has been blurred, as both tend to contain elements of each in their offering. For more details about the economic impact of this phase of attractions please visit IIAPA, the International Association of Amusement Parks at http://www.iaapa.org/

Shopping

Shopping is one of the most popular trip activities for U.S. adult travelers.[36] This should be no surprise for anyone who has visited Disney World in Orlando, Florida. As you stroll along Main Street in the Magic Kingdom and the other streets of the park, you are flanked on both sides by retail opportunities. It may be that part of the genius of Walt Disney was his disguising a retail mall within a theme park. Approximately 87 million people, or 60% of adult travelers in 2010, included shopping as an activity on a trip.[37] In a reverse of the Disney strategy, the West Edmonton Mall in Alberta, Canada, contains the Galaxyland Amusement park (the world's largest indoor theme park), the World Waterpark (the world's largest indoor water park), the Ice Palace (a National Hockey League size ice arena), an exact replica of the Santa Maria (which is available for weddings and special functions), an 18-hole, par 46 miniature golf course, and the 354-room Fantasyland Hotel.[38] The West Edmonton Shopping Mall is listed in the Guinness Book of World Records as the "largest shopping center in the world." The mall's web page refers to the center as an "entertainment and shopping center, Alberta's *number one* tourist *attraction*."[39]

Lest you think that the West Edmonton Mall is an anomaly, consider the Mall of America, located in Minnesota, which, in addition to 520 stores, contains The Park at MOA™, which has 30 rides, including the Timberlane roller coaster, the Underwater Adventures® Aquarium, LEGO® Imagination Center, Dinosaur Walk Museum, A.C.E.S. Flight Simulation, and the NASCAR Silicon Motor Speedway. On the MOA website, you can plan your entire visit, including air, hotel, and auto packages. The MOA even hosts meetings at its Executive Meeting and Events Center.[40]

EVENTS

Events are temporary attractions. Relative to permanent site attractions, they are generally easier and less expensive to develop, although that may not always be the case, such as with the Olympics and other large-scale events, including the Super Bowl. Events include such activities as fairs and festivals, live entertainment offerings as in the performing arts, sports exhibitions, parades, pageants, and other celebratory gatherings such as New Year's Eve and "First Night" celebrations. In many instances events give birth to site attractions. The sporting facilities specially constructed for the Olympics live on as site attractions for future sport exhibitions.

Sporting events, both professional and intercollegiate, are significant attractions for travelers. Over 75 million U.S. adults attended an organized sports

VIGNETTE
THE TALLEST FASTEST ROLLER COASTER IN THE U.S.A.

The 456-foot Kingda Ka ride at Six Flags Great Adventure Park, a one-hour drive from Philadelphia, will reach 128 mph on its 50.6-second journey. The 18 riders on Kingda Ka's 4 cars will feel weightless at some points, as they are propelled to 128 mph in just 3.5 seconds before being shot vertically to 456 feet. After reaching the top, they will plunge straight back down while turning in a 270-degree spiral before climbing a 129-foot-high hill and returning to the starting point. A chest harness with two locking devices will be used to secure passengers. If fast isn't enough, you can see the tallest, longest, and biggest drops list at http://www.ultimaterollercoaster.com/coasters/records/

The Mall of America offers much more than shopping to its visitors.

event as either a spectator or as a participant while on a trip of 50 miles or more, one-way, in the past five years.[41] NASCAR stock racing gained enormous popularity within the last decade, and was dubbed one of the fastest-growing sporting events until the recent economic downturn.[42] NASCAR races are broadcast in over 150 countries. With 75 million fans, it holds many of the top 50 attended sporting events in the United States.[43]

The performing arts have always been events that attract travelers. They include theater, dance, and music of all forms. Some destinations such as Branson, Missouri, and Monterey, California, are well associated with music festivals that serve as primary tourist attractions for the area. New York City's Broadway theater district is just one of the performing arts attractions the city offers to visitors. A legendary musical performance event was the 1969 Woodstock Festival and Concert, which, though planned for 50,000 people, is believed to have been attended by over 500,000 individuals.[44]

The modern-day epitome of an "event" is the Super Bowl, which occurs annually at the end of January each year. The first Super Bowl was between the Green Bay Packers and the Kansas City Chiefs. Tickets cost only $12, and the game had less than 50% attendance. Today, ticket costs are measured in the thousands of dollars and are difficult to come by, as the game is sold out. On average, 100 to 120 million Americans are tuned in to the Super Bowl at any given moment. Cities compete to host the game in a selection bidding process similar to ones used by the Olympics and soccer's World Cup. Entertainment

has become a major component of the event. A number of popular singers and musicians have performed during the pregame ceremonies, the halftime show, or even just sang the national anthem of the United States. Among the notables have been Bruno Mars, Black Eyed Peas, Beyoncé, Katy Perry, Madonna, The Who, The Rolling Stones, and of course the infamous "wardrobe malfunction" by Janet Jackson and Justin Timberlake in 2005.[45]

INDUSTRIAL ATTRACTIONS

Industrial attractions consist of operating concerns, manufacturing and agricultural, whose processes and products are of interest to visitors. For example, many manufacturing concerns provide tours of their facilities. Ethel M in Las Vegas conducts free interactive tours where the visitor can watch them make chocolate confections. You can tour the kitchen, walk through the enrobing and molding rooms, then, finally, try a free sample. Of course your tour ends in their retail outlet.[46] The Boeing Everett factory tours are conducted to showcase The Boeing Company and the Everett product line: the 747, 767, 777, and 787 aircraft. Visitors can see airplanes in various stages of flight test and manufacture. The facility also contains conference space for 250 people, special event space for groups of up to 700 people, as well as a 240-seat theater, a 125-seat restaurant, and retail space. There is also an aviation education program for children.[47] Virtually every state has one or more factory tours that would qualify as industrial attractions. Some charge a fee, but most are free. You can get a comprehensive listing, by state, of available factory tours on the web at Factory Tours USA.[48]

Wine tourism is defined as visitation to vineyards, wineries, wine festivals, and wine shows for which grape wine tasting and/or experiencing the attributes of a grape region are the prime motivating factors for visitors.[49] Wine tourism is experiencing steady growth, edged along by the growing public interest in wines. The 2004 movie *Sideways* spurred the creation of wine tours, mirroring the journey of the film's two main characters through the Santa Barbara, California, wine country.[50] (Note how the movie is a convergence between culture and tourism.) Napa and Sonoma in California, both major wine-producing areas in the United States, have flourishing wine tourism industries centering on vineyards and wine tasting attractions. The Chappellet Vineyard is just one of many vineyards that provide tours and tastings to visitors.[51]

INFRASTRUCTURE

Although the infrastructure of a destination would not be considered an attraction, any discussion of attractions would be incomplete without some reference to infrastructure. For attractions to be viable tourism components, they must be supported by roads, airports, and other transportation facilities; municipal services such as water, police, and fire protection; and medical, power, and communication resources. In addition, there must be hospitality services to serve the travelers' needs while away from home. Hospitality services consist of lodging, food, and beverage services. Integral among all the infrastructure components, and in particular with hospitality services, are people available to work in the various supporting functions. For an attraction to be successful, the local employment base must be trained in the technical skills of each area of service. Yet, technical skills are not enough, because the hospitality industry is a people industry. The workforce as well as the community at large must also have a "hospitable" mind-set; that is, they must truly care about delivering a quality experience and being warm and friendly toward visitors. They must understand that their self-interest, and that of the visitor, is inextricably intertwined in a unique partnership that creates both a high-quality experience for the visitor, and a higher standard of living for them.

SUMMARY

For attractions to be viable tourism components, they must be supported by the area's *infrastructure*: roads, airports, and other transportation facilities; municipal services such as water, police, and fire protection; medical, power, and communication; and resources as well as *hospitality* services, lodging, food, and beverage facilities. In addition, the people of the area must have hospitality service skills and be open and amenable to the tourism industry and genuinely friendly to the visitor. According to the International Association of Amusement Parks of America (IAAPA), direct spending by resident and international travelers in the U.S. averaged $2.5 billion a day, $105.8 million an hour, $1.8 million a minute, and $29,398 a second, showing the economic engine of our industry.

RESOURCES

Internet Sites

50 Amazing places to go in 2016: http://travel-blog.viator.com/top-50-travel-destinations/

American Gaming Association: www.americangaming.org

American Museum of Natural History: www.amnh.org

Best attractions by state: http://www.businessinsider.com/best-tourist-attraction-in-every-state-2013-12

Civil War Traveler: www.civilwar-va.com/

Disney Theme Parks: www. disneyparks.disney.go.com/

Google: www.google.com

Factory Tours USA: www.factorytoursusa.com

Gatorland: www.gatorland.com

Mall of America: www.mallofamerica.com

Martin Luther King, Jr. Memorial: www.nps.gov/mlkm/index.htm

National Park Service: www.nps.gov

Maui Mountain Cruisers: www.mauimountaincruisers.com/

NASCAR: www.nascar.com

National Football League: www.nfl.com/

Olympic Movement: www.olympic.org/

Pacific Whale Foundation: www.pacificwhale.org

Top 25 Destitutions in the work from Trip Advisor: http://www.tripadvisor.com/TravelersChoice-Destinations

Travel Industry Association of America: www.tia.org

The Holy See: www.vatican.va/

Universal Theme Parks: www.universalorlando.com/

Some articles to look at

Bagnall, G. (2015). Performance and performativity at heritage sites. *Museum and society,* 1(2), 87-103.

Brown, J., & Scricco, A. (2015). Around the World in 80 Minutes: A Network Model of Walt Disney World's Epcot Park. (April 14, 2015). Furman Engaged!. Paper 54.

http://scholarexchange.furman.edu/furmanengaged/2015/all/54

Smith, L., Karosic, L., & Smith, E. (2015). Greening US National Parks: Expanding traditional roles to address climate change. *The Professional Geographer,* 67(4), 1-9.

ENDNOTES

1. United States. National Park Service. (2015, December 29). Haleakal National Park (U.S. National Park Service). Retrieved January 10, 2016, from http://www.nps.gov/hale/index.htm.

2. MAUI BIKE TRIPS. (n.d.). Retrieved January 10, 2016, from http://www.bikemaui.com

3. United States. National Park Service. (2015, December 29). Haleakalal National Park (U.S. National Park Service). Retrieved January 10, 2016, from http://www.nps.gov/hale.

4. Swarbrooke, J. (2002). *The development and management of visitor attractions* (2nd Ed.). Oxford: Butterworth-Heinemann.

5. (n.d.). Retrieved January 10, 2016, from http://www.mauimountaincruisers.com

6. (n.d.) Retrieved January 10, 2016, from http://www.nps.gov/lake/index.htm.

7. Hacienda Baru National Wildlife Refuge, (n.d.). Retrieved January 10, 2016, from http://www.haciendabaru.com/tours.htm.

8. United States, National Park Service. (n.d.). Retrieved January 10, 2016, from http://www.nps.gov/yell/index.htm.

9. United States. National Park Service. (2015, December 29). Frequently Asked Questions (U.S. National Park Service). Retrieved January 10, 2016, from http://www.nps.gov/aboutus/faqs.htm.

10. (n.d.). Retrieved January 10, 2016, http://www.mgmmirage.com.

11. Xiang, Zheng, Bing, Pan, and Fesenmaier, Daniel R. (2013). Search Engine Marketing For Tourist Destinations. 2011. *Journal of Travel Research*, 50 (4), pp. 365–377.

12. (n.d.). Retrieved January 10, 2016, from http://www.nps.gov/seki.

13. United States. National Park Service (n.d.). Retrieved January 10, 2016, from http://www.redwoods.info.

14. United States. National Park Service (n.d.). Retrieved January 10, 2016, from http://www.grandcanyonskywalk.com.

15. Newsome, David, Moore, Susan A., and Dowling, Ross K. (2012). *Natural Area Tourism: Ecology, Impacts and Management*, Vol. 58. Channel View Books.

16. Weaver, D. and Lawton, L. (2002). *Tourism Management*. Milton, Australia: John Wiley and Sons.

17. (n.d.). Retrieved January 10, 2016, from http://www.tia.org/pressmedia/domestic_a_to_z.html#c.

18. (n.d.). Retrieved January 10, 2016, from http://www.metmuseum.org/home.asp.

19. (n.d.). Retrieved January 10, 2016, from http://www.amnh.org.

20. (n.d.). Retrieved January 10, 2016, from http://www.metmuseum.org/home.asp.

21. (n.d.). Retrieved January 10, 2016, from http://www.vatican.va.

22. (n.d.). Retrieved January 10, 2016, from http://www.tia.org/pressmedia/domestic_a_to_z.html#s.

23. (n.d.). Retrieved January 10, 2016, from http://www.CivilWarTraveler.com.

24. (n.d.). Retrieved January 10, 2016, from http:///www.nps.gov/vive.

25. (n.d.). Retrieved January 10, 2016, at http://www.nps.gov/kwvm.

26. (n.d.). Retrieved January 10, 2016, fromhttp://www.nps.gov/nama.

27. (n.d.). Retrieved January 10, 2016, fromhttp://www.mlkmemorial.org/site/c.hkIUL9MVJxE/b.1190591/k.B083/About_the_Memorial.htm.

28. (n.d.). Retrieved January 10, 2016, from http://www.hanglide.com.

29. (n.d.). Retrieved January 10, 2016, from http://en.wikipedia.org/wiki/Comparison_of_North_American_ski_resorts.

30. Moore, G. (2015, May 10). Rocky Mountain skier count drops. *Idaho Mountain Express.*

31. (n.d.). Retrieved January 10, 2016, from http://www.golfdigest.com/story/number-of-golfers-steady-more.

32. (n.d.). Retrieved January 10, 2016, from http://www.tia.org/pressmedia/domestic_a_to_z.html#g.

33. (n.d.). Retrieved January 10, 2016, from http://www.usga.com/questions/faqs/usga_history.html.

34. (n.d.). Retrieved January 10, 2016, from http://golf.visitscotland.com

35. (n.d.). Retrieved January 10, 2016, from http://www.ultimaterollercoaster.com/coasters/records/.

36. Cook, R. A., Yale, L., and Marqua, J. J. (2002). Tourism: *The Business of Travel*. Upper Saddle River, NJ: Pearson Prentice Hall.

37. (n.d.). Retrieved January 10, 2016, http://www.tia.org/pressmedia/domestic_a_to_z.html#s.

38. (n.d.). Retrieved January 10, 2016, http://www.westedmall.com/about/wemtrivia.asp.

39. (n.d.). Retrieved January 10, 2016, from http://www.westedmall.com/about/.default.asp

40. Mall of America at http://www.mallofamerica.com/home.aspx

41. (n.d.). Retrieved January 10, 2016, from http://www.specialtytravel.com/stories/stories.cgi?id=1686

42. (n.d.). Retrieved January 10, 2016, from http://www.nydailynews.com/sports/more-sports/daytona-500-nascar-kicks-2012-season-sunday-super-bowl-stock-car-racing-article-1.1028459

43. (n.d.). Retrieved January 10, 2016, http://www.topendsports.com/world/lists/crowd-largest.htm

44. (n.d.). Retrieved January 10, 2016, from http://en.wikipedia.org/wiki/Woodstock_festival

45. (n.d.). Retrieved January 10, 2016, from http://en.wikipedia.org/wiki/Super_bowl

46. (n.d.). Retrieved January 10, 2016, from https://www.ethelm.com/category/about our chocolates.do

47. (n.d.). Retrieved January 10, 2016, from http://www.boeing.com/companyoffices/aboutus/tours/index.html.

48. Factorytourusa.com. (n.d.). Retrieved January 10, 2016, from http://factorytourusa.com/index.asp.

49. Hall, C., & Sharples, L. (2012). *Wine Tourism Around the World* (pp. 297-300). Hoboken: Taylor and Francis.

50. (n.d.). Retrieved January 10, 2016, from https://www.santabarbara.com/winecountry/tours/

51. (n.d.). Retrieved January 10, 2016, from http://www.chappellet.com/visit-our-winery

REVIEW QUESTIONS

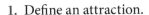

1. Define an attraction.

2. Explain how attractions benefit the community in which they are located. Provide an example.

3. For each of the following methods of classifying attractions, indicate the characteristics of each classification and provide an example for each type.

   a. Status

   b. Origin

   c. Life span

   d. Ownership

4. What are the methods for classifying attractions by product attributes? Provide an example for each.

5. What is the relationship between an attraction, infrastructure, and hospitality services in the surrounding area?

6. Revisit questions #3 and #4 and provide examples not found in the chapter for each.

7. Using *Google.com*, search the Internet for an attraction (as per the chapter introduction) and select one of the search results. Classify your choice, using as many of the classification techniques described in the chapter as possible. Support your answer with a brief explanation for each.

CHAPTER *36*

© PhotoRoman/Shutterstock.com

CRUISE SHIPS

AUTHOR

Chris DeSessa, Johnson and Wales University

LEARNING OBJECTIVES

- Categorize the types of cruises.
- Know the key players in the cruise industry.
- Compare the advantages and disadvantages of cruising.
- Determine the factors that affect the price of a cruise.
- Identify the major cruising areas.

CHAPTER OUTLINE

Introduction to the Cruise Industry

What Is Not Included in the Price of a Cruise?

History

The Ship Itself

    Cabins

Types of Cruise Lines

    The Major Cruise Lines

Career Opportunities

Activities

Cruising Areas

The Future of Cruising

Summary

KEY TERMS

Berth

Bow

Bridge

Cabin

Cruise Lines International Association (CLIA)

Deck plan

Flag of convenience

KEY TERMS
(Continued)

Galley

Gross registered tonnage
  (GRT)

Purser

Space ratio

Stabilizers

Stern

Tender

INTRODUCTION TO THE CRUISE INDUSTRY

The cruise industry is one of the fastest growing segments of the travel industry. More than 24 million people took a cruise vacation in 2015. The cruise industry's growth is also reflected in its expanding guest capacity. By the end of the year, there will be over 50 ships measuring over 100,000 tons in service with more new ships coming into service. 30 new ships of various sizes are scheduled for delivery between 2016 and 2020.

For many, a cruise vacation represents a vacation that allows one to do as little or as much as one wants. The number of Americans taking cruises continues to grow every year. More huge ships are being built, so the competition between cruise lines is very competitive. There are many reasons for the popularity of cruises. Historically, cruise ships were for people to sit in a deck chair and eat 24 hours a day. Now, you can book a fitness cruise with spa treatments, healthy dietary cuisine, and exercise programs for everyone. Cruise lines continue to build more new ships with more shopping, health clubs, casinos, and restaurants. In addition, cruise companies have expanded their choice of itineraries to include more exotic ports of call, and have introduced more innovative onboard facilities such as cyber-cafes, multiple themed restaurants, and state of the art meeting facilities to attract a more diverse clientele.

The size of cruise ships can be broken down into the following: large resort cruises (1,750–6,000 passengers), midsize cruises (750–1,750 passengers), small cruises (250–750 passengers), and boutique cruises (12–250 passengers). Some are small boats that sleep four or six people, which can travel up rivers to see places one cannot get to by any other means of transportation. There is a cruise for every budget, age group, eating habit, and activity level. It is easy to see why a cruise is the choice for many vacationers.

For many, a cruise represents both value and peace of mind. Unlike a land-based vacation, a cruise eliminates the hassles of paying for meals and entertainment and deciding where to eat. A cruise allows passengers to pack and unpack once. There

There is a cruise option for every budget, age group, eating habit, and activity level.

is security in knowing that everything is taken care of, and no money for necessities is needed once you are on the boat. On board, the problem of carrying money is eliminated, because on board one is part of the "cashless society," which allows the passenger to sign for extra expenses. You can relax and enjoy yourself. In addition, because there are a lot of people on the boat, you can meet new friends, have drinks, party, and know that you are steps away from your bed when it is over.

The price of the cruise includes one's accommodations, all meals and in-between snacks, entertainment, lectures, social functions, movies, and the use of a ship's facilities, including entry into the casino and fitness centers. Sometimes, the price also includes the price of flights to the ship and transfers (transportation between airport or hotel and the cruise port).

WHAT IS NOT INCLUDED IN THE PRICE OF A CRUISE?

Some people have the misconception that everything is included in the price of a cruise. Therefore, it is important to clarify in advance what is not included. With a little common sense, most of these are obvious. Alcoholic beverages and gambling debts are not included. In addition, the following are not included in the price of a cruise: shopping, liquor, photos, health spas, Internet cafes, tipping (on some ships), phone calls, seasickness inoculations, and shore excursions.

HISTORY

The concept of cruising has changed dramatically over the years. Not so long ago cruising was for the very rich or very poor. Cruise ships were divided into classes. Many of our ancestors came to America via cruise ship. Of course, the very rich could cross the oceans in elegance, cruising in first class accommodations on such famous ships as *The S.S. France*, *Queen Mary*, and the ships of the White Star Line.

Many of the early cruises were for transportation. Before airplanes, cruise ships were the main method of crossing from one continent to another. While the cruise could be luxurious, it was still basically walking around the deck, sitting in lounge chairs, and eating. Up until the 1960s, recreational cruising was considered a vacation option for senior citizens. That all changed with the creation of the hit television series, *The Love Boat*. TV viewers then saw cruising as a getaway to exotic ports such as Acapulco, where romance filled the air, and passengers were pampered with dinners with the captain and adventures with fellow passengers. The series portrayed passengers as young or young at heart, and adventuresome. Certainly, a more exciting image was created.

Another important event that changed the image of cruising was when Carnival Cruise Lines introduced the idea of a cruise ship as a destination in itself with its introduction of "The Fun Ships." The cruise ship itself was the focal point of activities, with myriad scheduled fun activities from morning until night. The ships contained everything that a small city would have, minus the crime. People could go rock climbing or skeet shooting. They could get a massage or facial at the spa or work out at a state of the art health club. Modern day cruise ships have mini golf courses, basketball courts, rock climbing walls, nightclubs, merry-go-rounds, skating rinks, and surfing. Sometimes, clients can take a tour of the **galley** (kitchen) or the **bridge** (area where the captain and crew navigate the ship). Or, as before, they could sit in a lounge chair and soak up the sun with occasional dips in the pool.

THE SHIP ITSELF

Ships come in various sizes. The modern cruise ship can be the height of a 10-story building and cover the space of three football fields. Currently the world's largest ship, Royal Caribbean International's *Oasis of the Seas*, and her sister ship, *Allure of the Seas*, can hold up to 6,296 guests. Some clients prefer large ships because of the many amenities. Others prefer the intimacy of a smaller ship. The size of a cruise ship is registered in **gross registered tonnage (GRT)**. Some large ships cannot pull into ports so passengers must be ferried to shore. A **tender** is a smaller boat that will ferry passengers from the larger ship to shore. Some of the tenders can hold more than 400 passengers.

Cruise passengers do not want to wait in long lines for service, so clients enjoy ships with plenty of room. The spaciousness of the cruise ship is measured by dividing the tonnage by the number of passengers. This is referred to as the **space ratio** and represents a rough approximation of how much space there is on a ship.

The left side of the ship facing forward is the port while the right side is the starboard. The front of the ship is referred to as the **bow** of the ship. The rear of the ship is referred to as the **stern**.

CABINS

Throughout your trip you will rest and relax in your **cabin**, sometimes called a stateroom. The cost of a cruise also depends on the location, size, and special amenities of your cabin. A **deck plan** is a chart that displays the location of cabins and public rooms (Figure 36.1). With larger ships, you have a choice of levels of floors, depending on how close to the activities one wants to be. On modern ships, all passenger cabins are above the water line. Only the crew's quarters are below the water line.

Often passengers prefer large ships because of the many amenities.

© CAN BALCIOGLU/Shutterstock.com

CARNIVAL BREEZE.

CARNIVAL VISTA.

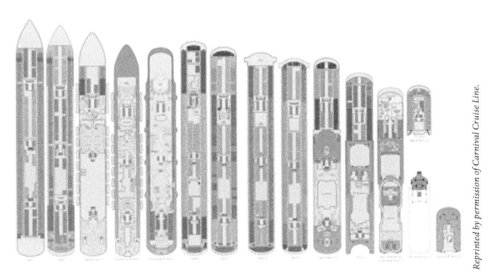

FIGURE 36.1 & 36.2   Deck Plans and Ship Profile

Cabins that have a porthole or window are referred to as outside or exterior cabins. These are more expensive than interior cabins. Some cabins have a porch or veranda to enjoy the scenery. Inside or interior cabins do not have a porthole or window. Inside cabins do have access to natural light.

Other considerations that may affect the choice of a cabin may be proximity to elevators, stairs, and public areas, and the propensity for seasickness. Like any hotel, when an elevator or stairs is next door, it is very noisy all day and all night, as people constantly are on the move.

Each deck on a ship is identified by a name or letter. A deck plan displays the location of decks and cabins. Normally, there is a cutaway view, which is a side view of the ship displaying the levels of the decks on the ship. Then there will be another map displaying the location of cabins and public spaces on each deck. Normally, the higher the deck, the more expensive the cabin. Also, cabins in the middle of the ship (amidship) are more expensive. These are more preferable to passengers who are prone to seasickness, since there is less ship movement in the middle of a ship. Modern day cruise ships have wing-like projections called **stabilizers** that are used in rough seas.

Beds on a cruise ship are referred to as **berths**. One can decide between king, queen, and twin. Many cabins have bunk bed type accommodations, which are referred to as upper/lower berths, which are perfect for accommodating children on a cruise.

TYPES OF CRUISE LINES

The **Cruise Lines International Association (CLIA)** is the world's premier cruise marketing and training association, comprising 60+ member cruise lines. From ocean to specialty cruise ships, CLIA member lines represent more than 90 percent of global cruise capacity. CLIA's goal is promoting the desirability, diversity, and high value of the cruise vacation experience. CLIA divides the cruise lines into three types: contemporary, luxury, and premium, depending upon quality, service, amenities, and itineraries.

Contemporary brands are geared to a mass market. Many of the contemporary brand cruise lines visit the same ports. Some distinctions between luxury and premium brands may have to do with the quality of food, level of service, and number of passengers on a ship. Another important factor for comparison would be the cruise itinerary. Premium cruise brands may visit more exotic ports. By comparing the passenger to crew ratio between two ships, one may get a rough estimate of the level of service.

River cruising has become another important niche in the cruise industry. River cruise ships are smaller than ocean-going cruise ships, typically holding 90 to 240 passengers. Due to their smaller size and low draft, river cruise ships can go where ocean cruise ships cannot. Examples of these would be sailing the Rhine and Danube Rivers in Europe and the Amazon River in South America.

Table 36.1 The Major Cruise Lines		
Name of Cruise Line	**No. of Ships**	**Brief Profile**
Carnival Cruises	24	Largest, most popular cruise line.
Celebrity Cruises	11	Most elegant ships and spas.
Costa Cruises	15	"Cruising Italian Style."
Cunard Cruises	3	Ocean liners—regularly scheduled transatlantic sailings.
Holland America	15	Preserves many traditions of the past—good cooking demonstrations.
Norwegian Cruise Line	13	Free style cruising. Hawaii cruising.
Princess Cruises	17	Best known name. The "Love Boats."
Royal Caribbean International	21	Has the world's largest two cruise ships.
MISC	12	For the most part, its ships traverse the Mediterranean (winter and summer)

THE MAJOR CRUISE LINES

All of the larger cruise lines listed in Table 36.1 offer a well-packaged cruise that includes a variety of itineraries, plenty of food, a variety of activities, and large-scale Broadway production shows. The lines differ in the facilities, space, food, and service. Each cruise line has its own niche.

CAREER OPPORTUNITIES

When one thinks of working for a cruise line there are two options: working on the ship or on land. The number of jobs is expected to grow due to the increased popularity of cruising, and the number of newer and larger ships that are being built. When one thinks about positions on a ship, one must realize that a modern cruise ship is a restaurant, hotel, resort, and activities center. Many of the positions offered at those land-based establishments are offered on a cruise ship.

All the cruise ships except one are registered in other countries such as Panama and Liberia. This is referred to as a **flag of convenience**. When flying a "flag of convenience" of another country, the cruise line does not have to follow United States standards in regard to taxes and minimum wage requirements. Traditionally, cruise lines tend to hire residents from less-developed countries for positions such as waiters, cabin stewards, and bartenders, because residents from those countries are willing to work for less pay than Americans. Things changed in 2005, when Norwegian Caribbean Line's ship, *The Pride of America*, was the first ocean-going passenger vessel in nearly 50 years to sail under the American flag. As such, NCL was required to hire an all-American crew. NCL fully touts its NCL American brand.

Hospitality students with a degree can aspire to some of the better positions on a cruise ship. The top position in the rooms department is the hotel manager. The chief **purser** is responsible for personnel services and accounting. The cruise director is responsible for ensuring that guests are enjoying themselves. He or she is in charge of arranging activities and procuring entertainment for the ship. The chief steward is in charge of guest accommodations. These positions are similar to those in land-based operations.

The top position in the restaurant side of the cruise ship is the executive chef. The food and beverage director and the maître d' report to him. Many cruise lines promote from within, so an employee may start as a children's activities director and work his or her way up to cruise director. Many workers sign contracts for six months.

Each cruise line has policies concerning crewmembers fraternizing with guests. Some lines will allow its officers to mingle with the guests in selected areas. The crew does have its own deck, which consists of cabins and shared space for activities. Oftentimes the crew shares living accommodations. Working on a ship might seem glamorous, but it does involve many hours of work per day. Members of the crew may get some time off when the ship is in port. At that time they may attend to their personal needs or take some time off at the beach. There are advantages to working on a ship. First of all, one gets to meet people from all parts of the world. Since the crew's accommodations and meals are taken care of, one does not have to spend a great deal of money while on the ship, so one has the opportunity to save money. The downside is that the crew is away from their family and friends for long periods of time.

Since life aboard a cruise ship may not be for everyone, it may be a good idea for a college-age student to seek summer employment on a cruise ship. Some larger cruise lines may hire youth activity directors for the summer. Other small cruise lines may hire one to act as both a steward and a waiter. Some cruise lines may have opportunities for internships during college.

On shore, one can work at the company's headquarters in the areas of marketing and sales, reservations, and finance and accounting. There are also limited numbers of positions working as a sales representative in major cities across the country. This position would entail visiting travel agents and groups, highlighting the features and benefits of your product.

ACTIVITIES

A passenger can do as little or as much as he or she wants on a cruise. Most ships have gyms, theatres, movie theatres, libraries, pools, basketball and

© Tony Moran/Shutterstock.com

A cruise offers many activities to choose from, including attending Broadway-type productions.

volleyball courts, jogging tracks, and art and photo galleries. These are all included in the price of a cruise.

The role of a cruise director is to ensure that clients have the opportunity to have a good time. Many activities are geared toward clients meeting each other: a typical cruise may have a singles party, grandmothers' bragging party, dance lessons, trivia contests, passenger talent shows, scavenger hunts, and poolside games. Other activities are geared toward teens or younger children.

Typically, a passenger will have an opportunity to attend a Broadway-type production before or after dinner. Another option could be to attend a first run movie in the ship's movie theatre.

The cruise lines have also introduced innovative onboard amenities and facilities, including cell phone access, Internet cafes, and wireless fidelity (Wi-Fi) zones, rock climbing walls, surfing pools, bowling alleys, multi-room villas, multiple themed restaurants, expansive spas, and health and fitness facilities that easily rival land-based options.

Oftentimes, a cruise line will deliver an activity sheet to a passenger's cabin at night so that the client is aware of activities for the next day.

When a cruise ship is planning to enter a port, the cruise director may give a port talk on sights to see or places to shop. Cruise lines also offer shore excursions which are half-day or full-day trips that can be bought on the cruise ship and are recommended by the cruise line. Sometimes these excursions can be previewed and bought ahead of time.

CRUISING AREAS

There are also more destinations to travel to and more ports to depart from. There are over 30,000 different cruises to choose from each year, and about 2,000 cruise destinations in the world. Cruises can range from a 3-day getaway cruise from Miami to the Bahamas, or an Around the World 180-day cruise. The Caribbean (and Bahamas) continues to be the number one destination for cruises. Other leading cruising areas are Europe, Alaska and Mexico, and the West Coast.

Most Caribbean 7-day cruises depart from Miami and usually visit three ports, a private island (where clients can enjoy water sports and beach-side activities), and 2–3 days at sea. One has the option of visiting the Eastern Caribbean, Western Caribbean (which is geared toward beach lovers), or the Southern Caribbean. A good choice for a first-time Caribbean cruiser who is more concerned with the itinerary than the ship could be a port-intensive cruise departing from San Juan, Puerto Rico, and visiting six islands. The ship is already in the Caribbean so it is easy to visit so many islands.

Cruises to Europe have become popular because a client only has to unpack once. Clients also like the fact that they go back each night to the familiar surroundings of their cabin and cruise ship. Alaska cruises became very popular following 9/11, because passengers felt safer cruising in U.S. waters.

Clients also have the option of taking "theme cruises." Some popular themes for cruises might be: sports, music, food, wine tasting, and murder mystery. Other options include adventure cruises or expeditions to such places as the Galapagos Islands and the South Pole. Lately river cruises have become popular. It is also possible to take a world cruise to various destinations, sometimes with the option of starting the journey on one ship and completing it on another.

THE FUTURE OF CRUISING

Cruising is constantly evolving. Future ships will have multi-hull designs with double skins to save energy. Wind energy will be used more effectively, and the new ships will be able to recycle waste and water. Exclusive communities at sea will continue to grow. Those willing to pay extra can enjoy private lounges, concierge levels, and private sunbathing. The future will bring new concepts in cruising. There will be a wider choice of ships, itineraries, amenities, and special interest trips. Cruising will continue to be a popular vacation option. Since only about 10% of the American people have taken a cruise, with about a 90% satisfaction rate, the number of people taking a cruise will continue to grow.

SUMMARY

Cruising continues to be one of the fastest growing segments of the travel industry. Each year more and bigger ships are being built to attract new and returning clients. New itineraries are being added to attract a more diverse clientele.

There are many reasons for the popularity of cruising. Some of these reasons include flexible and alternative dining options. The floating resorts offer myriad activities. A client can do nothing at all or take part in activities that appeal to a wide range of tastes. Each year cruise lines are offering new and more exciting activities that include zip lines, ice skating, bumper cars, merry go rounds, and surf flow riders.

Cruising also offers many career opportunities. Students with a college degree can opt to become officers or part of the cruise staff. Land-based career opportunities include working as sales representatives or working in the home offices of the cruise lines.

Cruising is constantly evolving. The cruise industry's success has been partly due to its ability to penetrate different market segments. New cruise destinations are constantly announced as countries recognize the value of bringing tourists to their destinations. Cruise lines are constantly attempting to upgrade their offerings. The future of cruising continues to look bright.

RESOURCES

Internet Sites

Carnival Cruises: www.carnivalcruiselines.com

Cruise Opinion: www.cruiseopinion.com

CLIA: www.cruising.org

Holland America: www.HollandAmerica.com

Norweigan Cruise Line: www.NCL.com

Royal Caribbean International: www.royalcaribbean.com

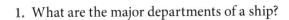

REVIEW QUESTIONS 36

1. What are the major departments of a ship?

2. What are the different career opportunities in the cruise industry?

3. What are the major trends in the cruise industry?

4. Please list the names of at least five cruise lines.

5. Where are the major cruise areas of the world?

6. What is the name of the organization that promotes the cruise industry?

7. What is included in the price of a cruise?

© Kzenon/Shutterstock.com

CHAPTER *37*

SENIOR SERVICES MANAGEMENT

AUTHOR
LEARNING OBJECTIVES

Bart Bartlett, The Pennsylvania State University

- Define and describe senior living, including the types and levels of care and the amenities and services associated with each level.
- Explain how and why the demand for senior living is predicted to grow.
- Understand and appreciate the unique advantages and challenges of working with the older adult population.
- Identify the variety and breadth of career opportunities for hospitality graduates in senior living.
- Recognize how managing communities with a hospitality perspective improves quality of life for older adults.

CHAPTER OUTLINE

Activities of Daily Living
(ADLs) and Instrumental
Activities of Daily Living
(IADLs)

Assisted living

Continuing care retirement
community (CCRC)

Demand for senior living

Hospitality perspective in
senior living

Independent living

Life plan community

Nursing care

Silver Tsunami

INTRODUCTION TO SENIOR LIVING

Senior living is among the fastest growing markets in the hospitality industry and offers a wide variety of employment and career opportunities for hospitality graduates. Over the next twenty years, the aging of the baby boom generation (people born post WWII; 1946–1964) will create unprecedented demand for accommodations and services, from 55-and-over communities to skilled nursing facilities and everything in between. And, while the sheer numbers of this generation will require more quantity of services, "boomers'" history suggests they will demand a broader range and higher quality of services as well, creating ever greater opportunity. Benefits of working in senior living include not just the vast business and financial opportunities in meeting these needs, but also satisfying careers and the "intrinsic paycheck" of working with and providing needed service for the older adult community. This chapter invites you to *Discover Senior Living*!

THE DEMOGRAPHIC IMPERATIVE: SILVER TSUNAMI

The average age of the population is increasing, and both the number of people and the proportion of the population over 65 are increasing dramatically. According to the Pew Research Center, 10,000 Americans are turning 65 every day, and will continue to do so for the next 19 years. While just 14% of Americans are currently 65 and older, that proportion will grow to 18% by 2030. Labeled the "**Silver Tsunami**," this increase in the senior population will create unprecedented demand for senior housing and services. And this demand creates extraordinary business and career opportunities for hospitality students.

TYPES OF ACCOMMODATIONS AND SERVICES PROVIDED FOR SENIORS

Senior living incorporates three levels of accommodations and services, designed to meet the changing needs of seniors at different stages in the aging process. Levels of care include independent living, assisted living or personal care, and nursing care.

INDEPENDENT LIVING

Independent living alternatives for seniors include freestanding homes, cluster homes, townhouses, garden apartments, or high rises. These are often part of "55 and over communities" committed to an active lifestyle. These communities typically provide grounds and indoor maintenance, and often offer some sort of common space community center with activities, aquatic and exercise facilities, and recreation programming. But, standalone independent living communities do not provide food and beverage services or any sort of healthcare.

ASSISTED LIVING AND NURSING

Typically, older adults will continue to live independently so long as they are able to manage the **Activities of Daily Living** and **the Instrumental Activities of Daily Living** (ADLs and IADLs – see Figure 37.1). If they are not able to live independently, there are a variety of alternatives. For those who prefer to "age in place" and stay in their home as long as possible, or cannot afford another option, some older adults and their families will choose home-care or at-home assisted living. Home-care can provide a range of services and assistance with ADLs/IADLs. If home care is not possible or not preferred, moving to an **assisted living** or personal care facility offers residents three meals a day and twenty-four hour

Senior living is among the fastest growing markets in the hospitality industry.

Many older adults prefer to live at home and are able to do that with the help of assisted living.

assistance as needed with the ADLs/IADLs. Still higher levels of care are available in **nursing** facilities, which may offer skilled nursing, rehabilitation, or long-term care. Memory care units, for adults with dementia, may be found in both assisted living and nursing facilities.

CONTINUING CARE RETIREMENT COMMUNITIES

As an alternative to seniors changing facilities and locations as their needs change, and the associated stress for them and their families, **Continuing Care Retirement Communities** (CCRCs) incorporate all three levels of care and comprehensive services in one setting or campus. (Recently, CCRCs are also being called "**Life Plan Communities**.") A CCRC offers a unique living arrangement with the opportunity to age in place and facilities and amenities designed to meet residents' changing needs as they age. New residents live independently in apartments or cottages. If the residents are no longer able to live independently, assisted living accommodations and services are available as part of the same community. Nursing care is also available as needed. This structure allows residents to age in place in one location even as their needs change. And, if spouses or partners age differently and one moves to a higher level of care while the other remains independent, they are readily able to visit and spend time together while living on the same campus. CCRCs have traditionally offered a life-care contract, which functions like insurance, with needed services guaranteed to be available at a fixed price. A more recent trend, particularly among for-profit operators, is toward an a la carte and pay as you go model. Both payment models provide all three levels of care, but provide potential residents with alternatives to match their financial circumstances and risk tolerance.

In addition to health related care, and often more important in the decision process for prospective residents, other services provided in a CCRC are much like an all inclusive resort or cruise ship, including food and beverage services, housekeeping, maintenance, grounds keeping, recreation and activities, exercise rooms and equipment, aquatics, spas, entertainment, transportation, and even a bar or lounge.

For residents, the type of living arrangement they choose will be influenced by their personal circumstances; the level of care that they need, their family situation, their financial status, and their personal preferences will all influence their options and choices. Irrespective of how the residents come to be

Activities of Daily Living		Instrumental Activities of Daily Living
• Bathing	• Housekeeping	• Managing money
• Dressing	• Managing medications	• Telephoning
• Toileting		• Grocery shopping
• Transferring (walking)		• Personal shopping
• Eating		• Using transportation

FIGURE 37.1 ADLs and IADLs

in a senior community or senior living facility, the job and career opportunities in providing services for this population are numerous and diverse.

TYPES OF OWNERSHIP AND MISSION

Senior living communities and facilities operate under a wide variety of ownership and operational models. Unlike most other hospitality segments, senior living communities can operate for-profit or not-for- profit. Also unique to senior living, communities can have a religious affiliation (faith based) or be secular. Like hotels and restaurants, however, senior communities can be affiliated with a multi-unit corporation or operate independently. And, as with other onsite venues, food service can be self-operated or under contract. Communities have been developed to target those seeking an urban or a rural setting, alumni in college towns, and gay and lesbian seniors. None of these models is necessarily better than another. Rather, each configuration has advantages and disadvantages, and each will be a better financial and psycho-social match for different types of residents, a better perceived opportunity for potential investors, and a better match for any individual as a potential manager.

CAREER OPPORTUNITIES IN SENIOR LIVING FOR HOSPITALITY GRADUATES

For hospitality students and graduates, senior living offers exciting and challenging management careers with multiple opportunities in each level of care or senior living venue. Standalone independent living communities offer positions in sales and marketing, facilities management, and recreation programming. Assisted living and nursing facilities offer these positions, and add multiple opportunities in foodservice management and environmental services. In both settings, as managers gain experience and broaden their exposure more opportunities become available.

In a CCRC, the operating departments are very similar to those in a hotel or resort hotel. As such, jobs are available in traditional hospitality operational departments (food and beverage, rooms division), environmental services (housekeeping, maintenance, engineering), recreation and activities, and in the staff and support functions of finance, accounting, revenue management, marketing and sales, and human resources. As with hotels, entry-level opportunities are available in all of these functional areas with the opportunity to move into department head and ultimately general manager or executive director roles. Unlike traditional hotel and restaurant jobs, however, CCRCs offer a more structured work schedule, predictable hours, and greater prospects for work-life balance. Incorporating healthcare into the product service mix creates additional challenges, but also offers an additional area of potential expertise. An individual does not need to be a healthcare licensed or certified professional to direct a senior living community, but individuals who build expertise in healthcare in addition to their expertise in hospitality create even more opportunities and security for their careers.

Continued growth in demand for senior living accommodations of all types will not only lead to increasing numbers of operations level positions, this growth also creates previously unseen opportunities in development and consulting. And, as multi-unit senior living corporations and management companies become more prevalent, corporate level positions in finance, marketing, information technology, and human resources also become options.

POTENTIAL CHALLENGES IN WORKING WITH SENIORS

Working in senior living does have unique features. First, the clientele are exclusively older adults whose life experiences and values may be different than those of the younger generation, and whose physical ability is more limited. New managers may find these differences enriching, or challenging. Second, the clientele are "residents." Unlike the transient interactions we experience with hotels and restaurant guests, the senior living staff serve the same residents day after day and build personal relationships with them. While this can also be enriching, this personal attachment can make it difficult to deal with the inevitability of end-of-life issues and the death of residents. Hospitality students are advised to self select in terms of whether working with older adults is right for them and whether the career potential and relationship benefits outweigh the potential challenges.

BENEFITS OF A HOSPITALITY PERSPECTIVE

Operating senior living communities from a hospitality and customer service perspective can dramatically enhance the quality of life for residents. The traditional perspective on seniors and senior living was based on a "medical model" with the focus on healthcare. Alternatively, a "hospitality model" focuses on service and quality of life.

In CCRCs, residents live the majority of their time at the community in independent living, and their focus is on the quality of their experience, from accommodations to food service to recreation and daily activities. Hospitality graduates' expertise in these areas allows them to create a resort-like life style and environment, delivering high quality and resident-focused accommodations, amenities, food service, and activities.

Even in standalone assisted living and nursing care facilities, the desire for quality customer service does not end at a particular age or with a particular change in health status. Hospitality management principles and practices provide a market oriented focus on identifying and meeting resident needs and wants, promote delivery of quality service, food quality and variety and amenities matched to the desires and abilities of residents. Communities and facilities with this perspective are not only more pleasant places to live and work, but current resident satisfaction is critical to attracting future residents and maintaining occupancy. Again, the hospitality orientation provides an advantage.

WHY HOSPITALITY STUDENTS SHOULD LEARN ABOUT SENIOR LIVING

Hospitality students are attracted to careers that they see as exciting and dynamic. At the time of graduation many hospitality students are most interested in what are perceived to be glamorous management positions in hotels and restaurants. After working in the field for several years, however, when managers' focus shifts to marriage or family, they sometimes find the work schedule and stress of these career paths conflicts with work life balance. Faced with this challenge, many hospitality graduates have transitioned from career paths in hotel and restaurant management to careers in senior living. This segment of the industry also offers exciting and dynamic management roles and rapid growth opportunities, but provides more structured work schedules and opportunities to be engaged in outside of work as well. Some students may choose senior living directly out of school, while others may decide to apply their skills in this field later on. Either way, they benefit from learning and knowing about this exciting market segment.

SUMMARY

As more of the Silver Tsumani population reaches retirement age, the demand for senior living options will continue to grow. In meeting this demand, the growth of senior living communities and other senior services creates countless career opportunities. Hospitality management graduates are uniquely positioned to capitalize on these opportunities; their lodging and food and beverage expertise is directly applicable in senior living and their service

A hospitality model of senior care focuses on service and quality of life.

orientation and hospitality perspective give them a distinct advantage. Hospitality graduates are just beginning to recognize their potential to excel in this exciting field, and the benefits for those delivering and those receiving hospitality focused senior services are only beginning to be realized.

RESOURCES

Internet Sites

AgeWave: http://www.agewave.com

American Seniors Housing Association (ASHA): http://www.seniorshousing.org/

A Place for Mom: http://www.aplaceformom.com/

Assisted Living Federation of America (ALFA): http://www.alfa.org/alfa/default.asp

ARAMARK Senior Living: http://www.aramark.com/Industries/SeniorLiving/

Flik Lifestyles: http://www.fliklifestyles.com

LeadingAge: http://www.leadingage.org/

Senior Housing Jobs: http://www.seniorhousing-jobs.com/

Sodexo Senior Living: http://sodexousa.com/usen/quality_life_services/on_site_services/seniors/senior_living.aspx

REFERENCES

CCR Task Force, J. E. Zarem, Editor (2010). Today's Continuing Care Retirement Community.

https://www.leadingage.org/uploadedFiles/Content/Consumers/Paying_for_Aging_Services/CCRC-characteristics_7_2011.pdf

Gerace, A. (2012). Could Hospitality-Style, Multi-Purpose Senior Living Attract Younger Retirees? http://seniorhousingnews.com/2012/04/17/could-hospitality-style-

multi-purpose-senior-living-attract-younger-retirees/

Koerner, G. & Berg, R. (2012). Top Ten Tips to Inject Hospitality Design into Your Senior

Living Community. http://www.alfa.org/News/2419/Top-Ten-Tips-to-Inject-Hospitality-

Design-into-Your-Senior-Living-Community

Maag, S. (2012). CCRCs Today: The Real Deal About Retirement Communities. http://www.leadingage.org/how_to_respond_to_media_inquiries.aspx

McCain, J. (2000). 'The Best Is Yet To Come' Managed Care for Affluent Elderly?

http://www.managedcaremag.com/archives/0012/0012.ccrc.html

Pew Research Center (2010). Baby Boomers Retire. Retrieved May 3, 2013 from

http://www.pewresearch.org/daily number/baby-boomers-retire/

WEB SITE - LEARNING AND DISCUSSION EXERCISE

Use a search engine to find a CCRC in your area. Look for the following in the site:

Is it for profit or not for profit? Religiously affiliated? Part of a larger group of communities?

What amenities are offered? What is the pricing structure? Is this a place you would want your grandparents or parents to live when they are ready? Why or why not?

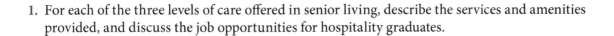

REVIEW QUESTIONS

1. For each of the three levels of care offered in senior living, describe the services and amenities provided, and discuss the job opportunities for hospitality graduates.

2. What advantages and disadvantages do you think there are for senior living organizations that operate for profit versus not for profit, and those that operate independently versus those that are affiliated with a larger organization or corporation?

3. How do you think the differences from Question 2 will affect resident service and satisfaction?

4. Explain how a hospitality perspective affects the design and delivery of senior living services.

5. Explain how a hospitality perspective affects senior living residents.

6. Discuss the advantages and disadvantages of jobs and careers in senior living.

7. Would you want a career in senior living management? Why or why not?

© canadastock/Shutterstock.com

CHAPTER *38*

HEALTHCARE SERVICE EXCELLENCE

AUTHOR	*Stowe Shoemaker, University of Nevada, Las Vegas*
LEARNING OBJECTIVES	• Understand why the healthcare industry is looking to those with hospitality degrees to help them be successful.
	• Explain how and why the healthcare industry and the hospitality industry are similar.
	• Illustrate how a framework that has been used successfully in hospitality can be applied in healthcare.
CHAPTER OUTLINE	Introduction
	Why the Healthcare Industry is looking for Hospitality Majors
	How and Why the Healthcare Industry and the Hospitality Industry are Similar
	Types of Services
	Customer Experiences
	Customer/Patient Satisfaction
	The Service Encounter
	How a Framework that has been Used Successfully in Hospitality can be Applied in Healthcare
	What Does All This Mean for You, the Student?
	Summary
KEY TERMS	Empathy Loved family member
	Experience mapping Patient-centered
	HCAHPS Service blueprinting

KEY TERMS
(Continued)

Service encounter

SERVQUAL

Sympathy

The Loyalty Circle©

INTRODUCTION

The previous chapters in this book have focused on the exciting opportunities available in the hospitality industry. This chapter is slightly different. Instead of focusing on career opportunities within the hospitality industry, this chapter focuses on career opportunities for those with a hospitality degree who do not want to work in a hotel, restaurant, integrated resort (e.g., MGM Resorts), cruise line, or private club. Specifically, this chapter will focus on career opportunities in the healthcare field.

WHY THE HEALTHCARE INDUSTRY IS LOOKING FOR HOSPITALITY MAJORS

In 2001 the Institute of Medicine[1] identified six crucial components used to provide quality healthcare. This report stated that healthcare should be: 1) safe, 2) effective, 3) timely, 4) efficient, 5) equitable, and 6) patient-centered. (http://www.ihi.org/resources/pages/improvementstories/acrossthechasmsixaims forchangingthehealthcaresystem.aspx).

Of the six, healthcare providers found the **"patient-centered"** component to be the biggest challenge given their historical focus on the first five goals. Suddenly, healthcare providers had to be like other service providers and understand the attitudes, opinions, and expectations of their patients in order to design processes that would meet these expectations.

The need for patient-centered care became critically important when in 2006 the Hospital Consumer Assessment of Healthcare Providers and Systems (**HCAHPS**) was launched. This is basically the survey that measures patient satisfaction. (http://www.hcahpsonline.org/surveyinstrument.aspx).

In 2007, Medicare required hospitals to collect and report these HCAHPS scores to the Centers for Medicare and Medicaid Services (CMS). These scores are now part of formulas for reimbursement, and a hospital's performance score on the HCAPHS survey determines the incentive payment they receive. Specifically, patient satisfaction scores determine 30% of the incentive payments, while improved clinical outcomes will determine the remaining 70%.[1] This formula essentially changed the model from procedure-based purchasing (i.e., a hospital gets paid $X for procedure Y) to value-based purchasing.

Here is how this works. CMS—the organization that pays hospitals for the services it renders to Medicare patients—withholds the money it owes hospitals and puts this money into a fund that is used to pay those hospitals that do well on their HCAPHS. Therefore, if you do well on HCAPHS you get paid the full amount owed to you. Hospitals that do not do well on these HCAPHS do not receive any extra money. In 2013, this fund was $850 million. Each of 3,500 hospitals nationwide was paid approximately $243,000 less than they should have been paid. Clearly the incentive is to have high HCAPHS scores.

Hospitals across the country are now spending much money, time, and resources to invest into improving the quality of the patient experience to increase their HCAHPS score, and thus to receive a larger amount of money. Although healthcare providers certainly understand the need to be "patient-centered," the question they face is how to do this.

The concept of "patient-centered" has been replaced by **"loved family member"** because research with

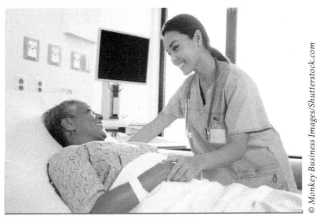

Patients feel most satisfied when they are treated like "loved family members".

---

[1] The Institute of Medicine (IOM) is a division of the National Academies of Sciences, Engineering, and Medicine. The Academies are private, non-profit institutions that provide independent, objective analysis and advice to the nation and conduct other activities to solve complex problems and inform public policy decisions related to science, technology, and medicine. The Academies operate under an 1863 Congressional charter to the National Academy of Sciences, signed by President Lincoln.—See more at: http://iom.nationalacademies.org/About-IOM.aspx

patients at two different hospitals (one in Texas and one in Nevada) revealed that patients feel most satisfied when they are treated liked "loved family members," not as numbers, customers, or even as patients.

One way to be patient-centered is to clearly understand the entirety of the medical experience from the patients' perspective. This includes not only the perspective of the experience within the facility, but from where patients gather information and from whom they seek advice regarding services prior to their experience on the premises. Once an understanding of this perspective is achieved, management can then develop strategies to control, meet, and occasionally exceed patient expectations. In the services marketing arena, understanding the process of the customer experience is referred to as **service blueprinting**. In healthcare, the term is coined, "**experience mapping**."[2] Regardless of the term, blueprinting/mapping involves a multitude of steps that can lead to great experience and corresponding great satisfaction.

In healthcare settings, hospitality is seen as an important attribute of patient satisfaction. For instance, the more at ease the patient feels, the sooner s/he will recover.[3] However, a frequent complaint is that patients feel depersonalized[4]—that they receive impersonal care, thus reducing their satisfaction.[5]

HOW AND WHY THE HEALTHCARE INDUSTRY AND THE HOSPITALITY INDUSTRY ARE SIMILAR

Traditionally, the concepts of customer satisfaction and experiences have not been closely tied to healthcare. The concern for healthcare providers has generally been about getting patients well—a noble purpose, but one that has often overlooked patient satisfaction or the experience s/he received.

Hospitality and healthcare share certain characteristics, which is why some of what has been learned in hospitality can be applied to healthcare. In order to further understand the similarities between hospitality and healthcare, it is necessary to better understand types of service, experiences, customer satisfaction, patient satisfaction, and the service encounter.

TYPES OF SERVICES

There are three types of services that customers usually receive:[6] 1) "neutral" or "routine" services or "mundane" services consisting of familiar experiences (e.g., dry cleaning, hair cuts, or lawn care; 2) "positive" services, such as those associated with travel and entertainment; and 3) "negative" services, where consumers deal with events most people hope they will never have to deal with (e.g., serious illnesses, leaky roofs, or collision repairs).

Services provided by hospitals belong to the third type—"negative" services. Patients/care givers visiting hospitals are typically under considerable stress due to the disease, its treatment, and major adjustments in many areas of their lives.[7] Therefore, making patients and their caregivers feel more like family members can help people to cope with the difficult situation, thus enhancing patient satisfaction.

CUSTOMER EXPERIENCES

Customer experiences and customer satisfaction have been the fundamental driving force of the hospitality sector for many years. Research has continuously shown that customer satisfaction and customer experiences are two of the major antecedents of long-term loyalty, positive word of mouth, and customer engagement with the organization. Experiences are composed of two crucial elements: the physical performance offered by an organization and the emotional responses that consumers have toward those performances.[8] An experience transpires when an organization provides services in a manner that elicits a memorable event for the consumer. Like the provision of goods and services, experiences must be deliverable, they must work properly, and they must, at a minimum, meet the consumer's expectations in order to be perceived as positive (Pine and Gilmore, 1998)

CUSTOMER/PATIENT SATISFACTION

Patient satisfaction has been defined as "the congruency between expectations of care and perceptions of the care received."[9] Patient satisfaction is important because previous studies have demonstrated that higher satisfaction with care is desirable due to its

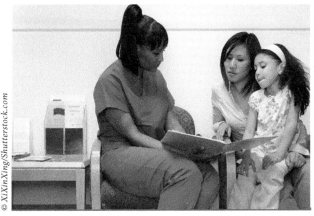
A visit to a doctor involves seeing several people in addition to the doctor.

© XiXinXing/Shutterstock.com

ability to influence patients' decisions to seek care, change medical plans or providers, and adhere to treatment regimens.[10]

THE SERVICE ENCOUNTER

The interaction between a customer and a service provider is called a **service encounter**.[11] Service encounters can vary from simple interactions with a salesman to complex discussions with professional service providers such as lawyers or doctors. For example, a visit to a doctor involves a series of mini encounters: a patient enters the office, talks to receptionist to check-in, meets a nurse then a doctor, and pays for the services at the check-out. It is the quality of each of these encounters that determines consumers' overall satisfaction.[12]

The classic **SERVQUAL** model developed by Parasuraman, Zeithaml, and Berry (1988) assesses the quality of the service encounter across five dimensions (Tangibles, Reliability, Responsiveness, Assurance, and Empathy). Empathy refers to caring and individualized attention and this dimension is highly salient in patient satisfaction. Hoffman (1984) states that **empathy** can be defined as being cognitively aware of another person's internal states and/or putting oneself in the place of another and experiencing his or her feelings. Wispé (1986) also defines the related concept of sympathy as "the heightened awareness of the suffering of another person as something to be alleviated". Consequently, showing empathy at each customer touch point is a prerequisite for patient satisfaction. In the context of cancer centers, the most effective way to show empathy is to treat patients and their caregivers as loved family members.

HOW A FRAMEWORK THAT HAS BEEN USED SUCCESSFULLY IN HOSPITALITY CAN BE APPLIED IN HEALTHCARE

Given the similarities between healthcare and hospitality, it is useful to look at the models the hospitality industry has used to drive customer satisfaction. Creative minds in the hospitality industry have long incorporated the idea of **The Loyalty Circle©** to help create high satisfaction scores and great customer experiences. The original The Loyalty Circle© has been adapted for healthcare and is shown in Figure 38.1.

Notice that in the center of The Loyalty Circle© is the term "loved family member." On the outer edges are the three main components of The Loyalty Circle©: Process, Value, and Communication. It is important to know that each of these three functions must be executed equally well. In fact, equality is the key to the Loyalty Circle. If a healthcare organization is great at creating value but not at effectively communicating with the loved family member, customer satisfaction suffers and people will find other hospitals.

On one side of The Loyalty Circle© is the Process, which is "how the service works." It involves all activities from both the patients' perspective and the healthcare providers' perspective. Ideally, there should be no gaps between what the patients want and what they receive from the healthcare organization. For the patients, the process includes everything that happens from the time they begin buying the service (e.g., deciding which healthcare provider to visit) to the time that they leave the facility. All interactions with all employees are part of this process. For the healthcare providers, the process includes all interactions between the employees and the patients, the design of the service operations, the hiring and training of service personnel, and the collection of information to understand patients' needs, wants, and expectations.

The Process part of The Loyalty Circle© can be illustrated by looking at the scheduling of patients' visits. Data collected at a major medical center in Texas revealed that scheduling was a major concern of respondents. Hospitals had established electronic

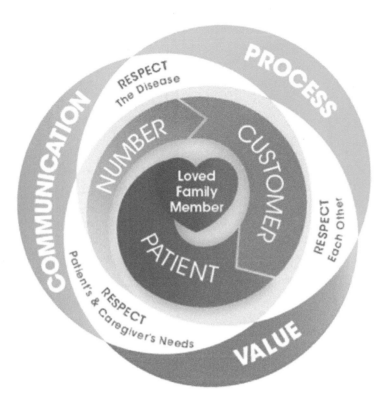

FIGURE 38.1 The Healthcare Loyalty Circle.

scheduling methods, assuming that Internet access and knowledge were true for all patients. This was not the case. Customers indicated difficulties getting their first appointments, namely due to limited access or lack of familiarity with the Internet. Since scheduling is one of the first points of contact with the hospital (like reservations and check-in are at a hotel), this can become a critical point of failure. If it is not done well, patients may go to other hospitals; or, if patients stay, they may leave feeling frustrated and upset.

A second component of The Loyalty Circle© is Value. Value creation is subdivided into two parts: value added and value recovery. Valued-added strategies help make patients feel like loved family members by providing more than just the core product, which is—helping patients recover. Valued-added strategies increase the long-term value of the relationship with the healthcare provider by offering greater benefits to patients than can be found at competing firms that charge a comparable price. There are six types of "value added" strategies: financial (e.g., the hospital is part of the insurance network thus saving the patient money); temporal (e.g., rather than having the patient visit all the different doctors they must see during one visit, the patient stays in one

room and all the doctors come to them, thus saving time); functional (e.g., the Mayo Clinic applies "evidence management" to illustrate to the patient that the service is working the way it was designed to work); experiential, or "enhancing the experience" (e.g., providing iPads and headsets so patients can entertain themselves while waiting); emotional (the practice of giving more recognition and/or more empathy); and social (e.g., Cancer Treatment Centers of America has created a group called "Cancer Fighters" that matches new patients with more experienced patients so that more experienced patients can offer help and hope).

Value-recovery strategies are designed to rectify a lapse in service delivery. In order to achieve success in value recovery, healthcare providers must empower employees to recognize patient frustrations, take complaints seriously, and take measures to prevent mistakes from recurring. Interviewed patients from the Texas hospital said they experienced a great sense of frustration because no one at the hospital would answer the phone or respond to messages. In addition, some expressed frustration about being continuously transferred without being able to reach one person directly.

The final component of The Loyalty Circle© is Communication. This side of the circle incorporates all forms of communication and the methods for communicating with stakeholders. When communicating with guests, it is critical that external communications do not over promise what the service can deliver. It is also important that the communiqué reflect the needs of the customer. The Texas hospital study, for example, revealed that a major cause of frustration among patients is that wait times are often miscommunicated by hospital staff. Many respondents reported that employees gave them incorrect wait time information or that incorrect wait times were listed on white boards in waiting areas. Others said they were given confusing information about discharge times. When doctors told patients they could "go home now," this meant immediate checkout for patients but signaled the beginning of the checkout process to the hospital—one that could potentially last for hours—resulting in patient frustration and low satisfaction scores for the hospital.

A smile projects confidence, enthusiasm, and a positive attitude.

© Monkey Business Images/Shutterstock.com

WHAT DOES ALL THIS MEAN FOR YOU, THE STUDENT?

The fact that hospital reimbursement is going to be tied to patient satisfaction scores guarantees that hospitals will do all that they can to make patients feel like loved family members by practicing all components of The Loyalty Circle©. The problem, as discussed earlier in the chapter, is that the majority of the senior executives in healthcare do not come from a hospitality background. Therefore, they do not understand how to build a service culture—one of the key components of making patients feel like loved family members. An example of this is hiring procedures. Instead of hiring for attitude and training the necessary skills as we do in hospitality, healthcare executives often do the opposite; they hire for skills and train for attitude. Clearly, there are many jobs in hospitals that require highly skilled workers, just as there are in hospitality (e.g., how would like to dine in a restaurant that was run by an unskilled chef?). But, there are also many jobs were attitude is more critical than the skillset the potential employee brings to the job. When a hospital executive asked a hospitality executive how he trained all those new employees to smile, the hospitality executive explained, "We didn't train them to smile, we hired them because

they smiled during the interview. That smile meant they were comfortable, confident, enthusiastic and positive: the kinds of things that attest to having a good attitude; and the kinds of things we also want employees to be. We then spend much time training them on the skills they need to best take care of the customer."

Throughout your undergraduate degree in hospitality, you will learn many things that will enable you to apply The Loyalty Circle© principles to jobs in healthcare. For instance, you will learn how to understand customers' needs and then how to design service operations to meet these needs. This is the Process side of The Loyalty Circle©. You will learn how to hire the right type of employee and how to train them properly to deliver an experience that meets or exceeds customers' expectations. This is the Value side of The Loyalty Circle©. Finally, you will learn how to listen to your customers and communicate with them in ways that make them loyal to you and your organization. This is the Communication side of The Loyalty Circle©. All this knowledge will make you invaluable to healthcare organizations as they try to improve their HCAHPS scores.

SUMMARY

This chapter has introduced the concept of the integration of hospitality and healthcare. This integration has occurred because of three major events: 1) the Institute of Medicine's decree in 2001 that one of the six components of quality healthcare be "patient-centered care," 2) the launch of Hospital Consumer Assessment of Healthcare Providers and Systems (HCAHPS), and 3), the requirement that

HCAHPS be reported to CMS for use in reimbursement. As mentioned, item number 3 basically stated that CMS is moving from procedure-based payment to value-based payment.

The chapter also discussed the similarities between hospitality and healthcare, specifically the need to understand the antecedents of great customer experiences and overall satisfaction.

Finally, the chapter introduced the concept of The Loyalty Circle©. In hospitality this framework is used to understand how to create long-term customer loyalty. In healthcare, it is used to make patients feel like loved family members. The key components of The Loyalty Circle© are process, value, and communication. As discussed in the chapter, each component must be executed equally well or customers will not remain loyal and patients will not feel like loved family members. Having great processes will not matter if communication is inadequate.

The opportunities in the healthcare field for students who study hospitality is unlimited and growing.

ENDNOTES

1. HCAHPS, 2012.

2. McKeever, 2004.

3. Hepple, Kipps, & Thomson, 1990.

4. Ibid.

5. Vahey, Aiken, Sloane, Clarke, & Vargas, 2004.

6. Morgan & Rao, 2006.

7. Wiggers, Donovan, Redman, & Sanson-Fisher, 1990.

8. Arora et al., 2009; Shaw & Ivens, 2002.

9. Beck et al., 2010, p. 101; Oliver, 1980.

10. Beck et al., 2010; Rosenthal & Shannon, 1997.

11. Bitner, Booms, & Tetreault, 1990.

12. Shostack, 1987.

REFERENCES:

Arora, N. K., Street Jr., R. L., Epstein, R. M., & Butow, P. N. (2009). Facilitating patient-centered cancer communication: A road map. *Patient Education and Counseling, 77*(3), 319–321. doi:10.1016/j.pec.2009.11.00.

Beck, S.L, Towsley, G.L., Berry, P.H., Lindau, K., Field, R.B., & Jensen, S. (2010). Core aspects of satisfaction with pain management: Cancer patients' perspectives. *Journal of Pain and Symptom Management 39*(1), 100–115.

Bitner, M. J., Booms, B. H., & Tetreault, M. S. (1990). The service encounter: Diagnosing favorable and unfavorable incidents. *Journal of marketing, 54*(1).

Hospital Consumer Assessment of Healthcare Providers and Systems (HCAHPS). "HCAHPS Hospital 2012 Survey Instrumentals." HCAHPS. Last modified 2016. http://www.hcahpsonline.org/surveyinstrument.aspx.

Hepple, J., Kipps, M., & Thomson, J. (1990). The concept of hospitality and an evaluation of its applicability to the experience of hospital patients. *International Journal of Hospitality Management, 9*(4), 305–318.

Hoffman, M. L. (1984). Interaction of affect and cognition in empathy. *Emotions, Cognition, and Behavior*, 103–131.

Oliver, R.L. (1980). A cognitive model of the antecedents and consequences of satisfaction decisions. *Journal of Marketing Research, 17* (3), 460–467.

Pine, I.,B.J., & Gilmore, J. H. (1998). Welcome to the Experience Economy. *Harvard Business Review, 76*(4), 97-105. Retrieved from http://ezproxy.library.unlv.edu/login?url=http://search.ebscohost.com/login.aspx?direct=true&db=bsh&AN=780230&site=ehost-live

McKeever, J. (2004). Mapping the Patient Experience. *Marketing Health Services, 24*(4), 14–19.

Morgan, I., & Rao, J. (2006). Growing negative services. *MIT Sloan Management Review, 47*(3), 69.

Parasuraman, A., Zeithaml, V. A., & Berry, L. L. (1988). *Servqual. Journal of Retailing, 64*(1), 12–37.

Rosenthal, G.E., & Shannon, S.E. (1997). The use of patient perceptions in the evaluation of health-care delivery systems. *Medical Care. 35*(11), NS58–NS68.

Shaw, C., & Ivens, J. (2002) *Building great customer experiences.* New York, NY: Palgrave Macmillan.

Shoemaker, S., & Shaw, M. (2008). *Marketing essentials in hospitality and tourism: Foundations and practices.* Upper Saddle River, NJ: Pearson Prentice Hall.

Shostack, G. L. (1987). Service positioning through structural change. *The Journal of Marketing,* 34–43.

Vahey, D.C., Aiken, L.H., Sloane, D.M., Clarke, S.P., Vargas, D. (2004) Nurse burnout and patient satisfaction. *Medical Care, 42*(2 Suppl):II57–66.

Wiggers, J. H., Donovan, K. O., Redman, S., & Sanson-Fisher, R. W. (1990). Cancer patient satisfaction with care. *Cancer, 66*(3), 610–616.

Wispé, L. (1986). The distinction between sympathy and empathy: To call forth a concept, a word is needed. *Journal of Personality and Social Psychology, 50*(2), 314.

Zeithaml, V. A., Bitner, M. J., & Gremler, D. D. (2006). *Services marketing: Integrating customer focus across the firm.* New York: McGraw-Hill Education.

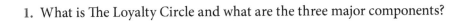

REVIEW QUESTIONS

1. What is The Loyalty Circle and what are the three major components?

2. Why is The Loyalty Circle an important framework in hospitality and healthcare?

3. What are the three types of services customers usually receive?

4. What does SERVQUAL stand for and why is it important?

5. What are HCAHPS and why are they important?

6. Define each of the following terms and describe why, if at all, they are important.

   a. Loved family member

   b. Experience mapping

   c. Service blueprinting

   d. Service encounter

   e. Patient experience

© Songquan Deng/Shutterstock.com

CHAPTER 39

MANAGEMENT CONSULTING

AUTHOR

Cydna Bougae, Ph.D., New York University

LEARNING OBJECTIVES

- Learn the role of a management consultant.
- Learn the practices and processes in management consulting.
- Learn the types of management consulting firms.
- Identify the skills, knowledge, and behaviors needed as a consultant.
- Recognize the personal characteristics to become an effective consultant.
- Learn about the career of a management consultant.

CHAPTER OUTLINE

Introduction
The Role of the Management Consultant
    Internal Consultants
    External Consultants
The Practice of Management Consulting
    Consulting Activities
    Phases of the Management Consulting Process
Types of Management Consulting Firms
    General Management Consulting Firms
    Consulting in Large Accounting Firms
    Specialist or Niche Management Consulting Firms

CHAPTER OUTLINE (CONTINUED)

The Competencies of a Management Consultant
  Technical Skills
  Interpersonal Skills
  Consulting Skills
A Career as a Management Consultant
  Personal Characteristics
  The Consultant's Day-to-Day Duties and Responsibilities
Summary

KEY TERMS

Business judgment

Case solving

Certified management consultant

Consultant competency framework

Consulting

Consulting career

Consulting skills

External consultant

General consulting firms

Internal consultant

Interpersonal skills

Management consultant

Specialist consulting firms

Structured thinking

Technical skills

INTRODUCTION

Management consulting is both an industry and a practice. The consulting industry has consistently grown over the past few decades and is projected to be one of the fastest growing industries worldwide. Businesses have found that hiring consultants is beneficial because the consultants are experienced, well trained, and keep current with the latest technologies, regulations, and management and production techniques. They are also cost effective, because they can be hired temporarily and they leave when the job is done.

The practice of management consulting includes a broad range of activities and is dependent on the consultant's area of expertise. For the hospitality industry, hospitality **consulting** is the counsel and expertise given by consulting professionals to hotel operators, restaurant owners, club management, golf course owners, and other segments in the hospitality industry. A consultant is someone who improves the client's condition by providing strategic advisory services with the goal to produce positive change within an organization. Consultants in the hospitality industry generally earn a degree in hospitality management. Many have an advanced degree. Hospitality managers and executives retain consultants to assist with specific tasks, ranging from conducting a hotel feasibility study to implementing IT systems to designing kitchen space.

This chapter will provide an overview of management consulting as a profession. This will include

discussing the role and practice of management consulting, the types of consulting firms, the skill requirements to be a successful consultant, and making a career as a consultant.

THE ROLE OF THE MANAGEMENT CONSULTANT

There are close to a million management consultants worldwide. A **management consultant** is someone who provides value to an organization through the application of specialized expertise, behavior, skill, or other resources to improve the performance of an organization in return for mutually agreed upon compensation. This is achieved through rendering objective advice and/or the implementation of business solutions addressing an organizational issue or problem.

INTERNAL CONSULTANTS

Consultants can be internal to an organization and work full time for the organization or they can be an external consultant. The **internal consultant** may be an individual acting as a personal advisor to an individual, a group, department, or whole organization. These individuals may be an employee of the organization, perhaps in a corporate office, or they can be contracted to work solely for the organization. Most restaurant and lodging chains have these in-house, internal personnel. They provide operations assistance to the organization. For example, they may be involved in developing a feasibility study for a new location, designing or decorating new facilities, renovating a property, negotiating a real estate purchase, developing and launching a new menu, or training staff.

EXTERNAL CONSULTANTS

The **external consultant** is hired to work on a project for a period ranging from a couple of weeks to many months depending on the nature of the consulting project. External consultants may be part of a large consulting organization serving clients in numerous industries over many locations or they may be solo practitioners.

Hospitality consulting is the counsel and expertise given by consulting professionals to those working in the hospitality industry.

© Andrey Popov/Shutterstock.com

THE PRACTICE OF MANAGEMENT CONSULTING

The basic activities of the consultant, whether internal or external, are to work on interventions that are based on results and outcomes and not just on activities and tasks. Management consulting includes a broad range of activities. One way to categorize the activities is in terms of the consultant's area of expertise. This could include corporate strategy, operations management, competitive analysis, marketing, technology, culinary, human resources, design, or corporate development.

CONSULTING ACTIVITIES

Within their area of expertise, the purpose of the consultant's work includes any of the following consulting purposes: providing information to a client, solving operational problems, making a diagnosis or redefinition of a problem, making recommendations based on the diagnosis, assisting with implementation of recommended solutions, building consensus for corrective action, facilitating client learning, improving organizational effectiveness and productivity, assisting with organizational change, developing a new product or service, or implementing corporate initiatives, projects, or strategies.

PHASES OF THE MANAGEMENT CONSULTING PROCESS

The consultant will engage the client in the consulting process through five phases. The following are the consulting phases:

1. *Entry and Contract:* meet with the client and explore the problem or determine the consulting purpose.
2. *Discovery and Dialog:* the consultant asks questions to assess the client's problem to determine what data will be collected, methods that will be used to collect the data, and how long it should take.
3. *Feedback and Decision to Act:* the collected data is analyzed and feedback about the data is given to the client to set goals for the project and to determine action steps.
4. *Engage and Implement:* the project is planned and the action steps are implemented.
5. *Evaluate:* determine if the goals of the project were achieved and whether the project will continue or end.

TYPES OF MANAGEMENT CONSULTING FIRMS

Hospitality companies will choose consulting firms that they feel can help them resolve their particular business issues. They must first determine their needs and assess the capabilities of the various management consulting firms. Individuals who would like to work as a consultant in the hospitality industry would also consider the same issues. Management consulting firms can be classified according to their size; consulting specialization; their business model; the kind of services they offer or their practice areas; their location; the clients, industries, and sectors they support; and their influence in an industry.

GENERAL MANAGEMENT CONSULTING FIRMS

Consulting firms can be generalist firms or boutique or niche firms. Generalist firms work on diverse projects while niche firms are more specialized. Generalist or **general consulting firms** provide general management consulting services to many different industries. They can provide a broad range of services to their clients and can tailor their services to the specific needs of the client. They provide solutions to

Consultants do everything from providing information to a client to facilitating client learning.

challenging strategic and operational problems. These practice areas might include business technology, corporate finance, marketing and sales, operations, organizations, risk, strategy, human capital, innovation, mergers and acquisitions, equity investments, and transformation plans. These general management consulting firms include McKinsey, Bain & Company, the Boston Consulting Group, Booz & Company, and Accenture. For example, Accenture is a global management consulting firm and has a hospitality services team. They have worked with Marriott for many years by providing the finance and accounting services and helped to reduce costs and improve controls throughout the organization.

CONSULTING IN LARGE ACCOUNTING FIRMS

Another management consulting group of firms which have a presence in the hospitality industry are the consulting divisions in large accounting firms. These firms provide services related to strategy and operations, technology, human capital, asset management, finance, and real estate and have a focus in hotel development. These accounting firms with a consulting divisions include PricewaterhouseCoopers, Ernst & Young, and Deloitte Consulting.

SPECIALIST OR NICHE MANAGEMENT CONSULTING FIRMS

The **specialist consulting firms** operate in a variety of different markets in a similar manner to the generalist management consulting firms. These niche firms concentrate on and service a particular market segment such as the hospitality industry. Within these consulting firms they may focus on a particular hospitality segment such as hotels, restaurants and food service, golf courses, or clubs.

PFK Consulting USA, a CBRE Company, is one such niche firm that is active throughout the hospitality industry marketplace. They perform financial and market studies and valuations involving hotels, resorts, golf courses, and a variety of mixed use developments and other hospitality oriented land uses. Having worldwide experience and a network of consultants, they have been successful in assisting numerous domestic and international hotel chains with their strategic planning. This includes selection of specific real estate sites, assessment of costs associated with regional development, product development, acquisition strategies, and market analysis.

THE COMPETENCIES OF A MANAGEMENT CONSULTANT

The consultant's role is to study problems, collect, review, analyze, and synthesize information and recommend solutions to the client based on their findings to improve organizational performance and implement change. There is not a formal training for becoming a management consultant. There is no general licensing like in other careers and no standard way that the consulting industry is regulated. The most well-known consulting designation is the **certified management consultant** (CMC) which is administered by a national management consulting institute, The International Council of Management Consulting Institutes (ICMCI). The CMC designation is relevant for all practicing consultants, including those in large and medium sized firms, boutique or niche firms, internal consultants and independent consultants.

Successful management consultants possess and demonstrate certain competencies in their work. A **consultant competency framework** defines those competencies. Competencies are the behaviors, skills, and knowledge than a management consultant is expected to understand, apply, and demonstrate. Understanding the competency framework is important for those who wish to have a career as a consultant or for practicing consultants to guide their professional development.

There are three broad skills or competencies necessary for the management consultant to be effective. These are technical skills, interpersonal skills, and consulting skills.

TECHNICAL SKILLS

Technical skill is the application of knowledge specific to a discipline. This includes understanding the client's business and having a functional specialization or expertise in that business. The foundation for being a successful consultant is having an expertise, something in which the consultant is an expert. An example in the hospitality industry would be understanding hotel operations and having expertise in the sales and marketing of a hotel, having a knowledge of golf course management and expertise in golf course design, or understanding restaurant operations and having the culinary expertise to develop new menu items.

INTERPERSONAL SKILLS

Management consulting requires **interpersonal skills**, that is, the ability to work with and connect with people and maintain a relationship. This is necessary for effective consultation. Written communication is very important. A career in consulting is going to involve extensive amounts of writing, including presentations, documents, memos, and emails to clients and partners. This skill needs to be done efficiently and quickly. Oral communication is the ability to respond to questions or challenges and is used during conversations and interactions with the client and other professionals. Consultants must also maintain and promote the image of their consulting firm through social interactions with employees and other professionals.

CONSULTING SKILLS

Consulting skills encompasses the collection of behaviors needed to become a skillful consultant. These include business judgment, structured thinking, problem solving, organizing and planning, and influencing. **Business judgment** is the capacity for good judgment and the ability to understand strategic issues. This skill is important for **case solving**, a key

Management consulting requires the ability to work with and connect with people and maintain a relationship.

management consulting discipline. It is the ability to understand and identify underlying issues and choose the right strategies in order to solve the issues.

Structured thinking is the ability to think in a clear and organized way to define, analyze, and solve problems. Math skills are used in structured thinking. It is the ability to look at a situation, identify and analyze the problem, and propose solutions in a structured way. This includes the ability to effectively gather data and information, analyze financial and statistical data, check and analyze information, select courses of action, use resources, and suggest viable solutions.

The management consultant must arrange their work as well as the work and resources of others in order to accomplish the tasks necessary in their day-to-day work. Being organized and having a planned approach to a project is necessary to successfully fulfill their duties and responsibilities.

Since a consultant's key functions are to advise and recommend and does not include making the decision or implementing the change, the ability to influence others is vital. It is a skill to be able to persuade others to do something or adopt a point of view in order to produce the desired results and take action. An effective management consultant will demonstrate they can impact other people and are able to persuade others to act on their recommendations.

A CAREER AS A MANAGEMENT CONSULTANT

Consulting is primarily a relationship business. No matter how technical the project, the success of the work of the consultant will always hinge on the quality of the relationship with the client. As such, it is important that the management consultant have certain characteristics necessary in order to succeed as a management consultant.

PERSONAL CHARACTERISTICS

For management consultants to excel, they need to be self-motivated and disciplined. The typical management consultant works with minimal supervision so the consultant must have the ability to start and complete tasks and assignments without guidance.

© Pressmaster/Shutterstock.com

Consulting projects are challenging assignments and require long hours. It requires a drive and the energy to get things done and the ability to persevere when things get tough. It also requires a tolerance for stress and uncertainty. There may be pressure and opposition to outcomes and recommendations prescribed by the management consultant. During these times tenacity is the key. It is the ability to pick one's self up after a defeat and carry on.

Many consulting projects require the consultant to work with a team of other consultants or employees. Being a team player is important. For the team to produce excellent results, members must collaborate and update each other on what they are working on. They decide as a team how to approach a problem or complete a project. The team members must consider the needs of others, be considerate, and be aware of the impact and implications of decisions important to others.

Since teamwork is important in consulting, a consultant must also exhibit leadership behavior by providing focus to their teams. This means setting objectives and goals. Giving this focus is important to achieving the results of a particular project or task. It also means understanding the strengths and weaknesses of others on the team in order to achieve a positive outcome.

THE MANAGEMENT CONSULTANT'S DAY-TO-DAY DUTIES AND RESPONSIBILITIES

On a daily basis, consultants work on and manage their projects. They must communicate and manage all of the stakeholders involved in their projects and prepare and meet the work deadlines. Their days are varied and may involve meeting with their team, conducting research, meeting with the client, checking and analyzing information and data, preparing presentations and proposals, facilitating a focus group, developing communication plans, or developing a program.

The work of a consultant is complex and project-based and many require long hours in order to meet deadlines. Many management consultants may work in their client's offices to get the information they need and get a feel for the company and the culture. They may also work at home or at their own company's office.

A consulting job varies in length depending on the client demands and type of project. Certain projects may be based in one site alone or across several locations. As a result, consulting may require travel. When a client is in a different city, state, or country, the consultant may be required to be away from home for days and perhaps weeks at a time.

SUMMARY

The consulting industry has consistently grown over the past few decades and is projected to be one of the fastest growing industries worldwide. This provides career opportunities for individuals as they graduate from college or for professionals who wish to make a career change. The management consultant can work as an internal consultant or as an external consultant. If the consultant is external they can work for a general management consulting firms or specialty or niche firms. For those who might be interested in a career in consulting, they should understand the skills and personal characteristics that are important in order to have a successful career as a management consultant. Their work is complex and project-based and varies depending on the client, the client's location, and the type of project.

INTERNET RESOURCES

International Council of Management Consulting Institutes: www.imusa.org

McKinsey & Company: www.mckinsey.com

Bain & Company: www.bain.com

Boston Consulting Group: www.bcg.com

Accenture: www.accenture.com

Deloitte Consulting: www.deloitte.com

PKF Consulting USA: www.pkfhotelconsulting.com

REFERENCES

Barrington, G. (2012). *Consulting Start-Up and Management.* Los Angeles; Sage Publications.

Biggs, D. (2010). *Management Consulting.* United Kingdom: Cengage Learning.

Block, P. (2000). *Flawless Consulting* 2nd Ed.
San Francisco: Wiley.

Greiner, L. & Poulfelt, F. (2005). *Management Consulting Today and Tomorrow.* New York: Routledge.

How to Land a Management Consulting Job, www.consultingfact.com

The Management Consulting Competency Framework at http://www.imcusa.org/?page=CONSULTINGCOMPETENCY-

Walsh, K. (2002). Service-delivery strategies, three approaches to consulting for hospitality. *Cornell Hotel and Restaurant Administration Quarterly,* December, 2002, pp. 37–45.

Weiss, A. (2009). *Million Dollar Consulting,* 4th Ed. New York: McGraw Hill.

Name: _____ Date: _____

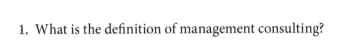

1. What is the definition of management consulting?

2. What is the role of the management consultant?

3. What are some activities in which a hospitality management consultant could engage?

4. What are internal and external management consultants?

5. Describe the five phases of the consulting process.

6. What are the three types of management consulting firms?

7. Describe the three skills needed to be a management consultant.

8. Identify the behaviors needed to become a skillful consultant.

9. What are some of the activities that a consultant might engage in on an average day?

10. Identify the personal characteristics needed to be a successful management consultant.

CHAPTER *40*

© mariakraynova/Shutterstock.com

REAL ESTATE

AUTHORS

Bernard N. Fried, Hotelschool The Hague, The Netherlands
Christiaan J.C. Vos, Hotelschool The Hague, The Netherlands

LEARNING OBJECTIVES

- Understand an important and dynamic sector of the hospitality industry—the real estate area.
- Understand the importance of real estate.
- Understand the variety of career choices that are available for students who wish to focus on hospitality real estate.
- Identify the skills, background, and experience required to effectively engage in the real estate field.
- Distinguish which hospitality programs offer specific classes in real estate at the present time.

CHAPTER OUTLINE

Typical Hospitality Real Estate Positions
  Company Real Estate Representatives
  Appraisers
  Real Estate Sales
  Vacation-Ownership Sales
  Business Opportunity Sales
  Site Analysts
  Separation of Ownership and Management
  Asset Management
  Capital Management
  Job Opportunities in Asset and Capital Management
  Financial Positions

KEY TERMS

Appraiser
Asset manager
Broker
Business opportunity
  brokerage
Capital partner

Hospitality Valuation Services
  (HVS)
Real estate representative
Site analyst
Vacation-ownership firm

TYPICAL HOSPITALITY REAL ESTATE POSITIONS

Hospitality real estate offers a number of interesting and worthwhile career opportunities. Several hospitality firms employ real estate specialists, including market analysts, location analysts, and lease negotiators. However, you do not have to be employed by a hospitality company to work in this field. For instance, you could be an independent appraiser, or work for a lender, private investor, or real estate brokerage firm.

Several career options in real estate relate directly or indirectly to the hospitality industry. Persons wishing to work in this area may find employment with real estate departments in multi-unit hospitality corporations, appraisal firms, real estate brokerages, vacation-ownership firms, business brokerages, site selection firms, asset management firms, capital management firms, and lending institutions. The skills needed to perform well in hospitality real estate are very diverse and depend upon the specific area of emphasis that a person chooses. The skills are identified and discussed later in this chapter, but first, the wide variety of positions that are available in hospitality real estate will be considered.

COMPANY REAL ESTATE REPRESENTATIVES

Many large multi-unit hospitality corporations employ a real estate director and one or more **real estate representatives**. These persons are usually responsible for the following activities:

1. Performing location analyses (i.e., evaluating real estate sites to determine whether the company should construct new businesses in these locations).

2. Evaluating existing business locations from the perspective of acquiring and managing the business that is situated there.

3. Working with a hospitality company's franchisees (if the firm franchises its business) to assist with the site selection decisions, provide design advice, or help coordinate the activities of the company's internal resources with the franchisees.

4. Working with a variety of external agents (e.g., negotiating lease or purchase agreements with brokers and/or owners).

5. Interfacing with the company's legal, construction, operations, and financial personnel.

Although the Internet has allowed company real estate representatives to perform more efficiently from the corporate office, these representatives nevertheless typically travel a great deal. It is not unusual for them to be on the road four days a week. Such extended travel, however, is necessary in order to evaluate a site properly. Real estate, by its very nature, is a highly localized business opportunity, even for very large national or international firms. If insufficient time is spent researching a location, the company may make a rash decision. Because location is a critical factor influencing a hospitality property's success, it is very important to make solid, well-informed site selection decisions.

APPRAISERS

Real estate **appraisers** are employed to render estimates of value. They are trained to value real estate (i.e., land and buildings); furniture, fixtures, and equipment (FFE); collectibles and artifacts; and going-concern businesses.

Commercial lenders, investors, sellers, insurance companies, contractors, attorneys, accountants, pension funds, and other entities having a financial stake in a project engage appraisers. For example, before a commercial lender, such as a bank or savings and loan, can lend money, it must have the collateral (i.e., assets) appraised by an independent appraiser it selects. A hospitality firm that needs to borrow money to build a new property must pay the cost of the appraisal needed to satisfy this regulatory requirement.

Some appraisers specialize exclusively in the hospitality industry. The major one, **Hospitality Valuation Services (HVS)**, was founded in 1980. Currently, HVS has 18 offices in the United States, including New York, San Francisco, Miami, Dallas, Chicago, Las Vegas, and Denver, as well as offices in Mexico City, Toronto, London, Milan, Hong Kong, Beijing, Singapore, Jakarta, Buenos Aires, Dubai, New Delhi, and the Bahamas. Although its array of client services has expanded in recent years, HVS's major focus is the appraisal of lodging properties.

It is unusual, however, for individual appraisers to specialize in hospitality, because there may be insufficient work available to make it a full-time job. Generally speaking, appraisers tend to specialize in a particular category and not in a particular industry. For instance, a business valuation specialist who appraises restaurants will also typically appraise related businesses, such as taverns, liquor stores, bakeries, and food marts.

In other cases, appraisers may be part of a larger consulting practice. The firm *Ernst & Young* is representative of these types of appraisers, and has consultants who are specifically designated to serve the hospitality industry through its Construction and Real Estate Advisory Services Group. Besides their appraisal work, these firms also conduct a wide variety of other assignments designed to assist their client companies.

In addition to appraisal assignments, appraisers usually counsel clients. For example, a motel owner may hire an appraiser to estimate the most likely sales price for the property. He or she may also ask the appraiser to suggest things the owner could do to make the motel more attractive to potential buyers. In this role, the appraiser is required to draw upon his/her considerable expertise in the real estate field to make sound recommendations to the property owner.

Last, over and above an appraising or counseling role, some appraisers also get involved with real estate sales, property management (such as overseeing a shopping center complex), and loan brokerage (such as helping clients search for and secure the most favorable debt financing available). It is important to note, however, that in all aspects of appraisal work, it is essential for appraisers to render objective, unbiased advice, and to avoid any situations that might be possible conflicts of interest between themselves and their clients. To do otherwise would severely impair their reputations.

REAL ESTATE SALES

Although property owners are free to sell their properties without help from other professionals, most prefer using a third party to represent their interests. The same is true for potential buyers. Thus, **brokers** play a valuable role by serving as an intermediary in a real estate sales transaction.

Several brokerages specialize in the sale of lodging properties. For example, there are consortiums of brokerages in the United States that account for a majority of all lodging properties sold nationwide.

A brokerage office may also specialize in the sale of restaurants, taverns, liquor stores, and other similar hospitality businesses. In large cities, it is not unusual to find offices that deal exclusively with the sale and purchase of restaurants or with tavern operations.

Persons working in a sales office generally are in business for themselves; that is, they are independent contractors. Their livelihood depends on the amount of property sold, in that their main (and most often, only) source of income is sales commissions generated when deals are concluded. Some sales associates represent sellers and some represent buyers. Few represent both parties in a transaction, because doing so may be a conflict of interest.

Although sales commissions are their primary source of income, some sales associates prefer to operate as independent consultants. In the typical sales transaction, the seller pays the commission, which is then divided among the relevant sales offices that helped consummate the deal. However, some salespersons work strictly for hourly fees and are paid regardless of the outcome of a transaction. In effect, they sell their time and are compensated accordingly.

A day in the life of the typical real estate sales associate finds him or her showing property to potential buyers, shopping and analyzing other properties in the market, gathering pertinent data, suggesting appropriate sales and purchase strategies, recommending alternative financing arrangements, estimating the most likely sales prices, organizing and

© Dragon Images/Shutterstock.com

One part of a real estate associate's job is to show property to potential buyers.

completing deal-related paperwork, negotiating contract terms and conditions, and shepherding the deal to ensure that it stays on track and is finalized.

The role of a real estate sales associate is evolving due to the impact of technology and growth of the Internet. The Internet is making it possible for companies to circumvent intermediaries and "go direct" to potential buyers and sellers on a worldwide basis. Although many aspects of being a real estate sales associate will not be affected by these developments, students who are interested in this area should carefully explore the impact of these trends on the future of working in a real estate sales position.

VACATION-OWNERSHIP SALES

A **vacation-ownership firm** is in business to sell long-term vacation packages to guests. They sell "slices of time," in that they normally sell a guest the right to use a vacation apartment, hotel room, or condominium for a specified time period per year (usually 2 weeks) for several years (usually 7 to 20 years) at a specific property in a specific location. Alternatively, they can also purchase "points" from a vacation-ownership firm that allow them to take future vacations in various locations in exchange for using a specified number of the "points" that they own each year.

Guests who prepay for these vacations usually have the option of swapping their time at one location for comparable time at other vacation locations that are part of a time-share exchange network. Normally the guest pays a small fee for this exchange privilege.

In most cases, the prepaid vacation is an economical alternative to paying for vacations every year. Usually the guest needs to pay only a relatively modest maintenance fee each year in order to defray the cost of routine repairs, necessary remodeling, and so forth. In addition, the guest will pay local property taxes on a proportionate basis—normally, these annual tax payments are also fairly modest amounts.

At one time, these "time-share operations" had a seedy reputation. Most of them were high-pressure sales operations that generated numerous consumer complaints. However, while a few of these boiler-room operations probably still exist, the industry is now generally considered to be quite legitimate. This is due primarily to the involvement of major lodging firms in the field, such as Disney, Hilton, Marriott, Wyndham, Four Seasons, and Starwood. Their participation has legitimized the industry. In addition, other large firms, such as Bluegreen, Welk Resorts, Raintree, and Royal Resorts, have specialized in providing high-quality time-share properties for guests. Today, this sector represents a growth area in the hospitality field. It offers excellent opportunities for hospitality students who are interested in the variety of careers available in vacation-ownership sales. For those uninterested in sales, there are many positions in vacation-ownership operations, such as housekeeping, maintenance and engineering, and property management.

BUSINESS OPPORTUNITY SALES

A business opportunity is an ongoing business located in leased real estate facilities. The owner typically sells the furniture, fixtures, and equipment (FFE); leasehold improvements (i.e., interior finishing of the leased premises); the business's name and reputation; and perhaps some other types of assets, such as inventory or a valuable liquor license. The business opportunity purchase usually includes everything except the real estate.

A **business opportunity brokerage** is very similar to the typical real estate brokerage. Although business brokers do not normally sell real estate, they do sell businesses that must be transferred to buyers. In effect, the work performed by business sales associates parallels almost exactly that performed by most real estate sales associates. However, like the role of the real estate sales associate, this intermediary role will likely continue to evolve due to the development of new technology and the growth of the Internet, so students should be mindful of the potential impact of these trends on future careers in this area.

SITE ANALYSTS

Some research firms, real estate brokerages, and business brokerages provide location analysis for persons or firms unable or unwilling to do the work themselves. These **site analyst** companies typically maintain computerized databases that can be adapted to suit any need or answer any question. Their reports help clients make sound real estate and business decisions.

Some hospitality firms prefer to contract out this type of work to independent firms, because it is more economical than maintaining their own real estate divisions. This concept is known as outsourcing. However, even those large hospitality companies that have real estate divisions are apt to use an outside firm on occasion, because it is not always feasible for them to study every potential site, especially if a site is in a market where the firm does not have any existing properties under management.

SEPARATION OF OWNERSHIP AND MANAGEMENT

An important development in hospitality real estate is the separation of ownership and management. This separation enhanced further specialization of all the parties involved in setting up a successful hospitality investment. For a successful hospitality investment, you need highly specialized hospitality staff and a good property. But this property might as well be owned by a company other than the operating company. For instance, the Hilton-operated iconic Waldorf Astoria in New York City is owned by a Chinese company, the Anbang Insurance Group. In 2014 it was sold for $1.95 billion and leased back to Hilton worldwide for an indefinite period of time.

This was a large deal, but not exceptional. The separation of ownership and management has several advantages for both the operator and the owner. Think of how many hotels Hilton Worldwide could operate investing the $1.95 billion that was first locked in the building, yielding less than it could yield being invested in operating hotels. In general, teaming up with a landlord that has efficient access to the needed capital for a hospitality investment has boosted the growth of many hotel operators.

The separation of ownership and management opened up the hospitality real estate market for any real estate investor, as any owner can hire a company to operate his property. The owner of the property need not have the skills necessary for running a great hospitality business. Owners of property bring other skills, like asset management and strategic capital allocation. A good example of a real estate investor that invests worldwide in hotels, without operating any of them itself, is Host Hotels & Resorts. Their properties are operated by a wide range of premium brands like Marriott, Hilton, Accor, etc.

ASSET MANAGEMENT

The key driver for the separation of ownership and management is the further professionalization of asset management. Previously, it was a profession mainly focused on buying, developing, and maintaining properties; nowadays it is a value-adding profession that actively manages hospitality properties. An **asset manager** will continuously assess the assets under management. Questions like "should we hold or sell the property?", or "can we redevelop or reposition this property to create value?" are an asset manager's daily business. Running feasibility studies and making marketing plans for the repositioning of existing real estate are good examples of the tasks of an asset manager. The asset manager works in close contact with the general manager of the hotels to continuously unlock value. That's what makes this real estate career opportunity such an interesting position for those who are interested in hospitality and real estate.

CAPITAL MANAGEMENT

The hospitality industry is a capital-intensive industry. Therefore, next to state of the art asset management, as described in the previous paragraph, an efficient allocation of capital can add substantial value to the investment. The **capital partner** in a

Capital management professionals excel at working with finances.

hospitality investment is able to source the most efficient financing needed for an investment opportunity. Leveraging equity with cheap debt, while managing the financial risks involved, the capital partner's function adds financial value to hospitality real estate investments. Although directly related to real estate and hospitality, this function is more finance oriented and will suit anyone who works well with numbers and with hospitality. The capital partner is the third highly specialized professional, next to the asset manager and the hotel operator, who adds substantial value to a hospitality investment.

JOB OPPORTUNITIES IN ASSET AND CAPITAL MANAGEMENT

If you choose to specialize and seek a job as asset manager or capital manager, you will find a lot of opportunities. Locally, multiple asset management firms and capital management firms are active in the market, although, due to the high specialization needed, these firms are not widespread. The larger ones, like the global player CBRE Hotels, are continuously hiring motivated and skilled specialists. But you could also look at opportunities at the larger hospitality corporations that have in-house specialized departments for asset and capital management. A good example is the French company Accor, operating nearly 4,000 hotels on 5 continents. Next to their hospitality business unit, called HotelServices, Accor runs a second business unit for owning and investing in hospitality real estate, called HotelInvest. HotelInvest has turned into a highly specialized asset and capital management business unit.

FINANCIAL POSITIONS

The capital partner knows his way to the many lending institutions, debt and equity providers, that are active in hospitality finance. In close cooperation they provide the discretionary capital that allows new properties to be conceived and developed, or existing properties to be refinanced. The major players include the following organizations:

1. Life insurance companies that specialize in financing lodging properties.
2. Pension funds that invest in lodging properties or lend to them.
3. Capital management companies.
4. Family offices.
5. Banks and savings and loans that make real estate and business loans to qualified hospitality operators.
6. Government agencies (such as the Small Business Administration) that make direct loans or guarantee loans made by a third party.
7. Leasing companies that will construct a property and/or provide all necessary equipment and lease these assets to a manager/operator (especially in the gaming or restaurant sector of the hospitality industry) on a rent-to-use or a rent-to-own plan.

Lenders must qualify potential borrowers. Before recommending a loan, the lender must ensure that there is a high probability that the money will be repaid in a timely manner. Lenders must perform "due diligence," which means that they must evaluate a borrower's credit worthiness, character, reputation, capacity to repay, business skill, and collateral. These evaluations require that a skilled financial professional is involved in the decision to extend credit to a borrower.

Lenders who are heavily involved in hospitality finance may employ real estate experts on their own staffs to perform these functions. For example, DePfa Bank AG (Deutsche Pfandbriefbank) is a German-based institution that has a specialized hotel financing team based out of New York City—DePfa Real Estate Financial Services USA. This team has financed first class hotels all over Europe and the United States, including properties such as the Plaza

Hotel in New York City and the Adam's Mark Hotel in Dallas. In other cases, a lending institution may outsource these tasks to appraisers or consulting firms on an as-needed basis. Whichever approach is taken, it creates an opportunity for you to build a hospitality real estate career in a financial position.

DESIRABLE BACKGROUND FOR HOSPITALITY REAL ESTATE POSITIONS

If these career opportunities seem exciting, you should begin to prepare for them now. It is never too early to select the right college courses and the work experiences that are most likely to give you an edge when applying for this type of work.

These positions are very academically oriented, in that a great deal of research, writing, and computer skills are needed to be successful in a hospitality real estate position. You should take college courses designed to develop and enhance these skills.

You should also take a basic real estate course, real estate investments course, and real estate appraisal course. These classes will give you the best perspective of the industry, as well as highlight the various career opportunities that may exist in your local area. The next section of this chapter discusses which hospitality programs presently offer such courses.

Accounting and finance courses are also necessary. At the very least, you should take the basic accounting and financial principles classes. Generally, however, additional finance courses are necessary to acquire the techniques needed to prepare the types of research projects you will encounter.

Further, you must be very adept with word processing, database, and spreadsheet software packages. In addition to working with your own computer files, you must be able to use the computerized databases most offices subscribe to. For instance, a real estate sales office usually subscribes to a computerized multiple listing service (MLS). Sales offices also typically use services that provide demographic data and updated lists of lenders and their current loan terms and conditions. The number of service firms offering these data has expanded significantly in recent years in order to meet the industry's ever-increasing demand for information. Also, geographic mapping software is now available, offering detail that can be used to examine a potential site on-screen before ever leaving the office for a site inspection.

This type of advanced computer literacy is also needed to efficiently access information available on the Internet. In recent years, there has been an explosion of real estate information that can be downloaded from Internet sources. This information could include such things as local market data and reports, national economic trends and conditions, financing availability and terms, and federal and state guidelines for site development activity. Thus, a broker, appraiser, or real estate director can now obtain a great deal of pertinent information without ever leaving the office. However, because real estate is inherently a localized business opportunity, there is no substitute for on-site visits by a trained real estate professional.

Many real estate positions require licensing or certification, or both. For instance, if you want to be an appraiser, you will likely need a state license as well as certification from a nationally recognized appraisal association, such as the Appraisal Institute (AI). AI's designations (either the MAI or SRA) require that you possess a college degree, appraisal experience, and have passed a comprehensive exam in order to demonstrate your knowledge of the appraisal field. Further, you must be an AI member in good standing, of high moral character, who has also passed an ethics exam administered by AI.

Finally, you should acquire a reasonable amount of operations experience before tackling one of these staff positions. If you want to work in a hospitality company's real estate division, you should have a basic understanding of how the company's food, lodging, or gambling units are operated and managed. This operating experience provides the perspective needed when wrestling with decisions that can make or break your employer's bottom line.

YOUR FUTURE IN HOSPITALITY REAL ESTATE

Currently, eleven leading programs offer at least one real estate course (Cornell, Michigan State, UNLV, Penn State, DePaul, University of Central Florida,

San Diego State, Georgia State, ESSEC Business School (Paris), les Roches (Switzerland), and Florida International University) as a part of their hospitality programs. Further, Cornell, Michigan State, DePaul, San Diego State, les Roches, ESSEC Business School, and Georgia State appear to be the only seven of these eleven hospitality programs that also offer a specialization, or concentration, in this area. Students who are serious about a career in hospitality real estate may want to carefully consider their choice of a program and select one that offers a real estate curriculum, either in the hospitality program itself, or in a related business program at the university.

This chapter introduced you to the opportunities that are available for hospitality students who have an interest in real estate. Real estate will continue to be a vitally important aspect of most sectors of the hospitality industry, and those students who decide to pursue a career in this area will find it to be a rewarding and challenging career option. They would be well advised to take full advantage of the quantitative courses that are available in the hospitality school in which they are already enrolled. Alternatively, they may choose to attend one of the hospitality programs that offer either specific real estate courses or a concentration in this unique and exciting area.

SUMMARY

Many opportunities are available for real estate hospitality careers. A typical position is an appraiser. Some real estate appraisers appraise real estate and some specialize in the hospitality industry. Other positions include being a lender or dealing in the private sector. Vacation ownership is another expanding area. In the past, time-shares had a seedy reputation, but that has changed with the involvement of major lodging companies that have legitimized the industry. Another growing area is asset management, where ownership and management are separated. An asset manager will continually evaluate the asset they manage. Some tasks are running feasibility studies and preparing marketing plans for repositioning the real estate. To prepare for the opportunities, you should select college courses that develop your writing, research, and computer skills. Furthermore, you should take basic real estate, investment, appraisal, accounting, and finance courses.

This chapter introduced you to the opportunities that are available to hospitality students with an interest in real estate that can provide you with a rewarding career.

RESOURCES

Internet Sites

Hospitality Valuation Services: www.hvsinternational.com

Ernst & Young: www.ey.com/global/content.nsf/ International/Industries_-_REHC

Fairfield Resorts Vacation Ownership: www.fairfieldresorts.com

Real Estate Terms and Definitions: www.realestateabc.com/glossary

Appraisal Institute: www.appraisalinstitute.org

AccorHotels Group:

http://www.accorhotels-group.com/en/group/ accorhotels-strategic-vision.html

Host Hotels & Resorts: http://www.hosthotels. com/home.asp

CBRE Hotels: http://www.cbrehotels.com/EN/ Pages/Home.aspx

Name: _____ Date: _____

1. List the typical hospitality related real estate positions that are available to you.

2. What are the functions of a real estate director and real estate representatives who work for large, multi-unit hospitality corporations?

3. Discuss the importance of real estate representatives making well-informed site selection decisions when working with hospitality companies.

4. What functions are performed by real estate appraisers? Who would typically hire an appraiser? How do most appraisers handle areas of specialization?

5. Discuss what is involved in becoming a certified real estate appraiser.

6. Explain the concept of "independent contractor" as applied to persons working in real estate sales. How are these people usually compensated?

7. List what is typically included in a business opportunity purchase. What is the function of the business opportunity brokerage?

8. What types of businesses may be involved in conducting a site analysis?

9. What is a vacation-ownership firm? How has the vacation-ownership industry been legitimized?

10. List the types of organizations that are most active in hospitality finance and are major lenders in this industry.

11. Describe the type of skills and experience that would be beneficial for someone seeking a career in hospitality real estate.

12. What are the typical day-to-day jobs an asset manager will do for his or her clients?

13. Why is it important for an asset manager to work in close contact with the general manager of a hotel?

© Wuttichok Panichiwarapun/Shutterstock.com

CHAPTER *41*

TEACHING, RESEARCH, AND SERVICE

AUTHORS	*Linda J. Shea, University of Massachusetts, Amherst* *Chris Roberts, DePaul University*
LEARNING OBJECTIVES	• Recognize the growing need for educators in hospitality and tourism. • Understand educators' qualifications, responsibilities, and characteristics. • Understand the differences in types of schools offering educational opportunities in hospitality and tourism. • Recognize compensation ranges and lifestyle characteristics for faculty. • Identify appropriate professional associations for hospitality and tourism educators.

CHAPTER OUTLINE	Growth in the Industry
	Growth in H&T Education
	Hospitality and Tourism Educators' Qualifications and Responsibilities
	    Careers in Secondary and Vocational Schools
	    Culinary Schools
	    Two-Year Colleges
	    Four-Year Colleges and Universities
	International Opportunities
	Characteristics of Educators
	Compensation
	It's More than Money
	Professional Associations for Educators
	Summary

© Kendall Hunt Publishing Co.

There's only one career more exciting, challenging, and rewarding than working in the hospitality and tourism industry, and that is *teaching* in hospitality and tourism educational programs. With the growth in the industry and in educational programs to support them, the opportunities for careers in hospitality and tourism education abound. Whether the job is in a culinary school in Switzerland, a research university in the United States, or anywhere in between, the possibilities for a fulfilling career as an educator are limitless.

In this chapter, the need for hospitality and tourism educators will be presented. The types of educational institutions, the responsibilities of educators, as well as the skills, experience, academic preparation, and compensation will be reviewed. Finally, professional associations for hospitality and tourism educators will be provided.

GROWTH IN THE INDUSTRY

The demand for hospitality and tourism educators is derived directly from the demand for people working in the hospitality and tourism industry, all of whom have to be educated and trained in some fashion. Tourism is the largest industry in the world and the third largest industry in the United States generating $7.6 trillion to the world economy (global GDP) and accounts for 1 in 11 jobs, or about 277 million worldwide. The segments of lodging accommodation and foodservice comprise almost 10% of all employment nationally.[1] According to the Bureau of Labor Statistics (BLS) of the U.S. Department of Labor, the hospitality industry increased nearly 17% in wage and salary employment between 2004 and 2014.[2] Some sectors of the industry are predicted to experience even greater growth rates. For example, the expected growth of the convention and event sector between 2013 and 2025 is 44%.[3]

Employment in the restaurant industry is also expected to increase in the future. More specifically, according to the National Restaurant Association,[4] restaurant sales have reached $709 billion in sales with an estimated 14 million employees for the restaurant industry, representing 10% of the U.S. workforce. In addition, employment in the restaurant industry is expected to increase by 8%, reaching 15.7 million by 2025.[5] Restaurant sales constitute 4% of the U.S. GDP.

Employment in the restaurant industry is expected to increase in the future.

The United States travel and tourism (T&T) industry is also expected to once again increase its contribution to the gross domestic product in 2014, generating $458 billion, and is expected to rise 3% in 2015 to $471 billion. It is expected to increase at a rate of 3.5% up to the year 2015. The T&T industry is expected to increase to $628.5 billion by 2023.[6] Travel and tourism forecasts over the next ten years also look extremely favorable with predicted growth rates of 3.7% annually (3.6% for 2016), outperforming all other sectors of the economy. By 2025 it is anticipated that travel and tourism will contribute US$11.3 trillion in GDP to the world economy (2014 prices and exchange rates) and will support 355 million jobs globally. This translates to approximately 10.5% of the world economy in terms of both GDP and employment.

All of this projected growth in various sectors of the industry points to a substantive need to prepare individuals for careers in hospitality and tourism. It is no surprise that formal programs in schools, colleges, and universities around the world are experiencing growth to meet the needs of the industry.

(Read more at: http://www.wttc.org/research/economic-research/economic-impact-analysis/ Copyright @ WTTC 2016.)

GROWTH IN H&T EDUCATION

While career-oriented vocational and culinary schools have been a part of the educational system in the U.S. and abroad since the early 1900s, growth in the late 1900s and 21st century has been in the four-year baccalaureate granting institutions, offering degrees in hospitality and tourism management. In the early 1970s, there were only about 40 such hospitality management programs. According to the *Guide to College Programs in Hospitality, Tourism, & Culinary Arts* (2016), this number has grown to nearly 300 in recent years.

Among the U.S. schools in hospitality and tourism education, there are about 300 of each type of institution: two-year, four-year institutions, and culinary programs, with two-thirds of them in the U.S and about one third outside of the U.S., spread throughout the world.

The numbers of schools in each category are identified based on the *Guide to College Programs in Hospitality, Tourism, & Culinary Arts* and the Collegesource Online database. While all schools may not be represented, it is apparent that there are close to 900 schools of various types in the hospitality and tourism arena.

HOSPITALITY AND TOURISM EDUCATORS' QUALIFICATIONS AND RESPONSIBILITIES

Educators of all subjects require different sets of skills, experience, and academic preparation, and hospitality and tourism educators are no exception. Differences in the duties, the number of courses taught, the type of academic research, and the salaries are related to the type of institutions in which they work. In this section, a review of these key factors in secondary or vocational, culinary, two-year, and four-year colleges are presented.

CAREERS IN SECONDARY AND VOCATIONAL SCHOOLS

Students taking hospitality courses at the high school or vocational level are preparing for entry-level positions in foodservice and lodging operations. The educator's primary responsibility is to teach daily and follow a secondary school schedule, with hours extending from morning to mid-afternoon on a nine-month appointment. Careers in secondary and vocational schools typically require a bachelor's degree and a teaching certificate. Those teaching are expected to demonstrate their own skills as they train the students.

© goodluz/Shutterstock.com

Culinary schools focus on developing skills and training for entry-level positions in food and beverage operations.

CULINARY SCHOOLS

As implied by the name, culinary schools focus on teaching culinary related skills. They are engaged in activities that prepare students for careers in restaurants, banquets and catering, and institutional food service in settings such as hospitals, schools, and corporate facilities. Courses on beverage management, food purchasing, preparation, presentation and service, as well as food safety are taught. Instructors are usually required to have a substantial number of years of experience in the field, and many have baccalaureate degrees or hold certificates from culinary schools themselves. Culinary schools focus on developing skills and training for entry-level positions in food and beverage operations, with an emphasis on back of house functions. Many of the international (non-U.S.-based) hospitality programs are in the culinary school category.

TWO-YEAR COLLEGES

Students in two-year programs are typically in community colleges where they earn an associate degree. The curriculum is broader than a vocational or culinary program and includes some general education courses. The focus is on entry-level positions in foodservice or lodging operations, clubs, or catering companies. Upon completion of the program, some students transfer to baccalaureate degree-granting four-year institutions to earn a Bachelor of Science in Hospitality and Tourism Management. Faculty teaching in two-year associate degree programs are often required to hold a master's level degree, and to have a few years of experience in at least one sector of the industry. They typically will teach three to four courses per semester or manage several laboratory classes. Other duties may include sponsoring a student club, student advising, and serving on college committees.

FOUR-YEAR COLLEGES AND UNIVERSITIES

The job of faculty in four-year colleges and universities is to prepare students for management positions in the industry. Students earn a bachelor's degree and assume positions in hotels, restaurants, resorts, or clubs. Faculty members teaching in these institutions are usually required to have a Ph.D. (doctorate of philosophy) from an accredited hospitality or business program. Some faculty members hold other terminal degrees, such as an Ed.D. (doctorate of education) or J.D. (juris doctorate). The duties are typically three-fold and reflect a mission that includes teaching, research, and service components. Research universities often offer graduate degrees, a Master of Science, and/or Ph.D. Faculty members in these positions are expected to advance the discipline of hospitality and tourism management through scholarly research published in academic journals. In departments offering graduate degrees, scholarly activity would also include serving on thesis or dissertation committees and serving on editorial review boards of academic journals. Teaching loads in these universities are likely two courses or fewer per semester, with research publication requirements and service duties. Service duties demonstrating good citizenship include such contributions as serving on committees at the departmental, school/college or university level, graduate student advising, and student club sponsorship.

INTERNATIONAL OPPORTUNITIES

While the majority of hospitality and tourism institutions outside of the U.S. are culinary or two-year certificate or associate degree programs, there are some four-year and graduate programs offered as well. European schools tend to be two-year, and Asian and Australian schools tend to be four-year. It is quite common for international programs to link with U.S. programs to offer exchange, internship, and summer abroad opportunities. Faculty and students alike enjoy and benefit from these collaborations.

CHARACTERISTICS OF EDUCATORS

Regardless of the type of school setting, there are several skills all hospitality and tourism educators should hold. They should be good communicators: both writing and speaking. They should be educated in and have some degree of experience in the content areas in which they teach. They have a responsibility to keep abreast of the discipline and any changes occurring within. They should have respect and admiration for students who want to learn from them. Finally, they should have a strong love of learning themselves and an ability to think creatively.

COMPENSATION

There is a wide range of salaries for hospitality and tourism educators. An instructor level educator may earn $50,000 base salary per nine-month contract, whereas a distinguished professor may earn additional compensation up to $250,000 or more. Differences in salary levels are related to professional rank: instructor (non-tenure track), assistant professor, associate professor, full professor, and distinguished or chaired professor. Furthermore, many faculty members earn additional compensation by taking on administrative duties, by teaching additional courses (for instance, summer or online courses), or from consulting work outside of their respective institutions. Differences can also be accounted for between two-year and four-year institutions, public versus private, U.S. versus international, and gender. Average salary figures for faculty in different ranks in non-U.S.-based programs, U.S.-based two-year programs, as well as four-year U.S. private and public institutions for 2008 and 2012 are presented in Table 41.2.[7]

Faculty rank is the strongest indicator of salary level, despite institutional differences. Overall, salaries are higher at four-year institutions than at two-year, at U.S.-based institutions over non-U.S.-based, and at private over public institutions.

About 50% of two-year and four-year college faculty participate in, or are interested in pursuing, administrative positions. Some hold positions such as graduate program director, chief advisor, internship

Table 41.1	Faculty Salaries (US$)					
Non-U.S. (All)			**U.S. Two-Year (All)**			
	2008	**2016**		**2008**	**2016**	
Assistant Professor (*part-time)	51,892	54,200	Assistant Professor	52,888	64,980	
Associate Professor	51,364	62,000	Associate Professor	61,334	81,333	
Full Professor	86,813	98,653	Full Professor	79,083	86,219	
U.S. Public Four-Year			**U.S. Private Four-Year**			
	2008	**2012**		**2008**	**2012**	
Assistant Professor	65,796	74,660	Assistant Professor	61,967	81,255	
Associate Professor	84,234	105,199	Associate Professor	74,822	97,112	
Full Professor	119,893	125,964	Full Professor	100,729	149,009	

coordinator, associate chair, department head, or dean. Each of these positions may add year round obligations as well as additional compensation. Positions with administrative duties typically add between $7,000 and $20,000 to total earnings. Full professors at public institutions earn, on average, $20,000 annually from work performed outside of their home institutions.

Regarding gender in the Shea and Roberts study (2016), it is still a distinguishing factor in salaries at all ranks; however, the change from 2008 to 2016 represents significant improvement in equality. As shown in Table 41.1, there was about an $8,000 to $18,000 pay differential in 2008, depending on rank, but that was reduced to an average differential of between $3,000 and $6,000 by 2012. Differences are much more pronounced when comparing salaries of women at U.S. universities versus non-U.S. universities. The average differential between male and female professors is more than $35,000 among all ranks.[8]

IT'S MORE THAN MONEY

In addition to monetary compensation, careers in hospitality education offer many other benefits. Full-time positions often offer a standard array of health insurance and retirement benefits, and most positions allow an attractive lifestyle. Unless administrative duties are involved, faculty often work nine or ten months of the year with frequent one-week- to one-month-long holiday and break sequences. Working with young people in a campus environment is intellectually stimulating, interesting, and frequently entertaining. Compared to the fast-paced, long, nontraditional hours (late nights, early mornings, weekends, and holidays) and often stressful working conditions of those with careers in hospitality and tourism operations, educators enjoy an equally meaningful, slightly more relaxed, but dynamic lifestyle. Similar to careers in the industry, educators have opportunities for travel for the purposes of collaborating in teaching and research with colleagues around the world, attending academic conferences, and sponsoring student programs overseas or in other nontraditional venues.

PROFESSIONAL ASSOCIATIONS FOR EDUCATORS

Additional information can be found through some of the following professional associations for educators in the hospitality and tourism field.

American Society of Travel Agents
www.asta.org

American Hotel & Lodging Association
www.ahla.com

Council on Hotel, Restaurant, and Institutional Education (CHRIE)
www.chrie.org

Educational Institute of the American Hotel &
Lodging Association
www.ahla.com

International Society of Travel and Tourism Educators (ISTTE)
www.isste.org

International Hospitality Information
Technology Association
http://hita.camp7.org

Hospitality Financial and Technical Professionals
www.hftp.org

Hospitality Sales and Marketing
Association International
www.hsmai.org

Meeting Professionals International
www.mpiweb.org

National Restaurant Association
Educational Foundation
www.nraef.org

National Restaurant Association
www.restaurant.org

Professional Convention
Management Association
www.pcma.org

Travel and Tourism Research
Association (TTRA)
www.ttra.com

Travel Industry Association of America
www.ustravel.org

Tourism Cares
www.tourismcares.org

Membership in professional associations keeps faculty members in touch with industry professionals and other academics. Each association sponsors annual conferences where ideas are exchanged, and innovations in teaching, program development, and research are discussed. Workshops, panels and symposiums, and research presentations offer opportunities for educators to hone their skills in these areas. These ideas are then brought back to the classroom to benefit the students they serve.

SUMMARY

The benefits, lifestyle, and sheer joy of a career in hospitality and tourism education make it an attractive option for many interested in the industry. While four to six additional years of education beyond the bachelor's degree is required for four-year and graduate degree-granting colleges and universities, the benefits are worth the extra time and effort. The education industry offers a plethora of opportunities to which potential educators can match their various combinations of background experience, education, and interests. Having the appropriate academic degrees, a connection to the hospitality industry, effective communication skills, and a creative imagination all contribute to a successful career as an educator.

ENDNOTES

1. United States Department of Labor, 2015.

2. Ibid.

3. Ibid.

4. NRA, 2015.

5. Ibid.

6. WTTC, 2013.

7. Shea & Roberts, 2016, forthcoming.

8. Ibid.

REFERENCES

Bureau of Labor Statistics, U.S. Department of Labor. *Occupational Outlook Handbook, 2013–14 Edition), Career Guide to Industries.* Retrieved from http://www.bls.gov/careeroutlook/2015/article/projections-industry.htm.

Guide to College Programs in Hospitality, Tourism, & Culinary Arts Online Database. (2015). Richmond, VA: International CHRIE.

National Restaurant Association. (NRA). (2015). *2015 NRA Industry Impact.* Retrieved from http://www.restaurant.org/Industry-Impact/Employing-America/Economic-Engine

Riegel, C. and Dallas, M. (2006). *Hospitality and Tourism: Careers in the World's Largest Industry. Guide to College Programs in Hospitality, Tourism & Culinary Arts,* 9th ed. [CD-ROM]. Richmond, VA: International CHRIE.

Shea, L. J. and Roberts, C. (2016 forthcoming). Compensation Analysis: The 2016 I-CHRIE Salary Study. *Journal of Hospitality and Tourism Education.* Retrieved from https://www.doleta.gov/BRG/Indprof/Hospitality_profile.cfm

World Travel & Tourism Council (WTTC). (2015). *Travel & Tourism Economic Impact: United States.* Retrieved from http://www.wttc.org/research/economic-research/economic-impact-analysis/

REVIEW QUESTIONS

1. What hospitality and tourism industry growth factors influence the growth of hospitality education?

2. Discuss the differences in careers among the types of educational institutions.

3. Given the differences, qualifications needed, and emphases of various types of educational institutions, identify which type is most appealing to you and explain why.

4. If you were considering teaching in a country other than your own, where would it be and why?

5. How does compensation for hospitality and tourism educators differ between 2-year and 4-year schools and by rank?

6. How do you account for the inequity of compensation between men and women in academia?

7. Name two different professional associations for educators in hospitality, two in the tourism area specifically, and two in specialty areas of the discipline.

GENERAL GLOSSARY OF HOSPITALITY TERMS

Acoustical Engineers   Professionals who offer advice and planning for acoustic or sound issues and suggest materials to solve noise problems or enhance sound; usually are employed by the architects

ADR (Average Daily Rate)   This is computed by dividing room revenue by the number of rooms occupied

Aesthetics   The beauty of an establishment; can play a primary role in touching the emotions of people and can influence whether they come back or not

Airlines Reporting Corporation   A nonprofit organization representing U.S. airlines that facilitate funds transfer between suppliers and agents, and ensures that travel agencies have experienced management through licensing

Alternate Current (AC)   The form of electricity supplied by local electric utility companies to businesses unless there is an on-site power production plant

Ambience or Servicescape   The landscape within which service is experienced has been used to describe the physical aspects of the setting that contribute to the guests' overall physical "feel" of the experience

American Culinary Federation, Inc. (ACF)   The premier professional chefs' organization in North America, with more than 230 chapters nationwide and 20,000 members. ACF offers culinarians of all ages, skill levels, and specialties the opportunity to further their career, as well as enhance their life

Americans with Disabilities Act   Federal legislation that forbids discrimination against people with disabilities; expanded the list of included disabilities from earlier legislation

Amperes   Measures the rate of electrical flow through a device or appliance

Amusement Parks   Commercially operated enterprise that offers rides, games, and other forms of entertainment

Animation   Energy, liveliness, vigor, spirit, vivacity, exuberance, cheerfulness

Answer   The responding document filed by a defendant which responds to the allegations in the plaintiff's complaint

AP (As Purchased)   Before a menu item is prepared and any waste has been removed

Appraisers   A professional who is trained to value land and buildings, and is hired to render estimates of value

Apprenticeship   Apprenticeship is an on-the-job training program combined with technical classroom instruction. The American Culinary Federation Foundation (ACFF) operates both 2- and 3-year apprenticeship programs. Currently, there are nearly 2,000 apprentices learning in approximately 80 American Culinary Federation Foundation (ACFF)-sponsored culinary apprenticeship programs in the United States

Architects   Professionals that prepare and review plans for the overall facility construction; qualified architects will have an AIA (American Institute of Architects) appellation

Association   Membership organizations which are organized around a common interest and the group schedules meetings to explore and discuss their common interest

Attractions   Places we visit and the things we do while we are traveling or visiting

Base Fees   These are the basic management fees that contract management companies receive for operating a foodservice or lodging property. These fees are typically a percentage of gross revenues

Bed and Breakfast   Lodging facilities with 2–12 rooms, which are either current or former private residences converted by the owner to accommodate guests

Berth   A bed on a ship

Board Plan   This is a type of meal plan offered on college and university campuses. The board plan allows students to pre-purchase a certain number of meals in the dining halls

Boutique Hotel   Small uniquely designed hotels with 100 rooms; contemporary, design-led hotels, which offer unique levels of personalized service and high-tech facilities; niche emerged from society's growing interest in history, art, culture and design

Bow   The front of the ship

Brand   In a brand management form a mega-corporation owns multiple chain operations under the same parent umbrella structure. A mega-corporation that owns multiple chains under the same umbrella would prefer to treat each of the chains as a separate brand to emphasize the different images projected by the chains

Brand Heritage   An emerging topic within the marketing discipline that suggests that the consumer appeal of products and services offered by older companies may be enhanced by the historical characters of their brands

Branding   This term refers to the foodservice products offered in on-site foodservice locations. There are national brands like Quiznos or Pizza Hut, as well as regional brands, which are specific to a region of the country. On-site foodservice operators also have their own brands

Bridge   The navigational and control center of the ship

Broker   A professional who serves as an intermediary in a real estate sales transaction

Bylaws   Governing rules for an organization

BYO   An acronym used to communicate "**B**ring **y**our **o**wn" alcoholic beverage to a public establishment because it is not licensed to sell alcohol

Cabin   A room on a ship; also called a stateroom

Career Fair   An event where many recruiters come together on-campus or at a local convention center to meet and interview potential employees for employment opportunities

Casual Dining Restaurant   A foodservice establishment that offers food and beverages at moderate prices and offers a level of service below that of an upscale property

Catalyst   An event that brings on a change without being affected itself

Cause of Action   The legal theory under which the injured party believes that someone else should be held responsible for their injuries

Cellaring   The process of storing a wine which will age to a better, more drinkable and mellow wine

Chain   A company with multiple locations

Chain Operations   Chain-operated hotels, restaurants, and other similar businesses owned by the same company and offer similar goods and services, but are found in different geographic locations

Chef   A chef is a leader in charge of a kitchen and the term comes from the French for "chief" or "director." Today we use this term to describe the chief cook in the kitchen

City Clubs   Establishments that are in urban areas and cater to the businessman or woman; and they provide dining services and occasionally athletics

Civil Rights Act of 1964   Federal legislation that prohibits discrimination on the basis of race, sex, religion, color, and national origin; it has become the cornerstone piece of legislation protecting workers and their rights

Classic Full-Service Hotel Hotel properties that provide refined standards of accommodation and service; may be classified midscale, upscale or luxury according to the services and amenities offered, the pricing structure, and location; amenities cater to both the business traveler and the vacation or leisure traveler

CLIA Cruise Line International Association

Client This is the specific individual within the host organization that is responsible for monitoring the foodservice operator's performance

Club A group of persons organized for social, literary, athletic, political, recreational, or other purposes

CMAA Club Managers Association of America formed in 1920

Code of Hammurabi Laws established around 1750 BC by Hammurabi, the ruler of Babylonia; regulations for inn-keepers and tavern-keepers on issues related to pricing and licensing are included among others

Color In design, color can be used to communicate a strong message to the guests, and those messages can be controlled by proper use in layout and design

Commercial Kitchen Designers Professionals that provide planning and drawings for commercial kitchens as well as equipment specifications

Common Law A system where the courts can apply the "generally accepted rules and principles enunciated by courts in earlier similar cases"

Conceptual Skills The ability to see the company or department as a whole and understand how the different parts work together

Conferences Gatherings that are large business or educational meetings and do not have a trade show; can last from one day to several; held at one venue

Consolidators Businesses that purchase large blocks of airline seats or cruise berths at a substan-

tial discount and resell them to travel agents or the public at a lower than normal fare

Consultant An individual who has a specific area of expertise and is compensated for providing advice or other services to a client

Consulting Careers Individuals who work as consultants for many of their working years; the consulting industry is anticipated to continue to outpace the growth of the U.S. economy by a wide margin

Consulting Firms Business organizations that provide consulting services; may be classified according to a number of characteristics, such as their size, level of specialization, industries served, geographical location, or types of clients they serve

Consulting Qualifications A person needs years of experience within a specific industry segment and a talent for identifying problems and finding creative solutions to be successful in a consulting career

Consulting Skills The specific skill set needed by a consultant will vary according to the nature of services provided, the industries served, and the size of the firm; most consultants will need to possess technical skills, communication skills, interpersonal skills, administrative skills, as well as marketing and selling skills

Consumer Behavior The study of how consumers (individuals and groups) behave; used often to increase the effectiveness of marketing to specific target populations

Contract Services Management The term used to describe the segment of the hospitality industry dedicated to operating foodservice locations and lodging properties that are owned by another individual or corporation. Owners contract with organizations in this segment to manage their properties

Contractors Professionals that are licensed by the state; typically oversee the entire building project; may be hired by bid or recommendation

Control Comparing the performance of employees in a workforce against the objectives and goals that have been set by the company

Convention and Visitors Bureau (CVB) Local area tourism and marketing organizations that specialize in bringing conventions, meetings, conferences and visitations to a city, county, or region

Conventions A special type of meeting held in a specific location often comprised of meetings and presentations as well as a trade show or exhibition

Core Competencies Those skills that are necessary for success

Corkage A fee charged to bring your own beverage selection if it is not available at the establishment. This is ostensibly used to cover the cost of the beverage service or the profit that would be gained from a sale and/or the ownership of the license

Cost Control The management concept of controlling costs through effective management practices

Country Clubs Hospitality establishments that provide elaborate social events, and offer dining, pool, tennis, and golf

Culinology® An approach to food that blends the culinary arts and food technology. One type of culinologists® are research chefs developing recipes and products for food manufacturers, restaurants, food suppliers, or on-site operators

Cultural Tourism Travel directed toward experiencing the arts, the heritage, the special character of people and places

Curb Appeal The attractiveness of the physical operations; the facility's visual appeal

Deck Plan Diagram that shows the locations and public spaces on a cruise ship

Defamation An untrue statement about another that is published or communicated to a third party who understood it, which resulted in damages

Defendant The person against whom a lawsuit has been filed

Destination Marketing Organization (DMO) A company that promotes the long-term development and marketing of a tourist destination by focusing on convention sales and tourism amenities in order to increase the amount of visitors to that specific destination

Discounting The method of reducing an item from the regular price

Discovery The process of taking depositions and requesting documents to learn about the other party's case

Distribution Services The vast network of peripheral companies that help hospitality enterprises get their products and services from creation to consumption

Dram Shop Laws Makes a business that sells alcoholic drinks or a host who serves liquor to a drinker who is obviously intoxicated or close to it, strictly liable to anyone injured by the drunken patron or guest

Duty of Care A legal obligation requiring a particular standard of conduct

E-Commerce A form of web retailing that features the buying and selling of goods and services on the Internet; characterized by a global reach and twenty-four hour availability

E-Hospitality An innovative service known as "total solutions" where distributing, servicing, and supporting hospitality products to all size organizations in the industry in order to offer more amenities and support services to potential guests

Economic Growth The increase over time in the capacity of an economy to produce goods and services and (ideally) to improve the well-being of its citizens

Economic Impact The change in the economy brought about by a specific event or industry segment; examines the economic prosperity of a specific geographic area, such as a town or city; may influence the building up or infrastructure of an area, for example, the conference and convention industry's economic impact on a city

Electrical Engineers Professionals that are usually employed by the architects and design all of the electrical systems

Electronic Travel Agencies Providing extensive information and online ticketing via the Internet

Employment Brand The image of the business as viewed through the eyes of prospective employees.

It can also be defined as the image of the applicant as viewed through the eyes of the business

Empowering   Where a contemporary leader has created the organizational work environment in which staff members are trained in necessary skills, enabling them to handle most customer service encounters; management must support the decisions made by the staff members

Energy Management   The management and control of heat, air conditioning, water usage, electric usage, and gas usage

Engineering Systems   The physical plant operating systems, comprised of the water and wastewater systems, refrigeration systems, heating, ventilation, and air-conditioning systems, electrical systems, and safety and security systems; knowledge of these various systems helps the manager adequately explain what needs to be accomplished by the facilities management team

Entrepreneur   A term often used to define a person's risk taking behavior that results in the creation of new opportunities for individuals and organizations

Environmentally Friendly   Integrating strategies into the design that reduce consumption of raw materials as well as favorably influence the establishment's practices

EP (Edible Portion)   After a menu item has been prepared and all waste has been discarded

Equity Clubs   Those facilities owned by their membership, are nonprofit; oldest form of clubs

Ethics   A set of principles that managers apply when interacting with people and their organizations; fair and equal treatment, truth, lack of bias, consistency, and respect of others

Etiquette   Socially understood rules of conduct

Evaluation   Employee evaluations take place after an employee has been selected, trained, and been on the job for a period of time; provides official feedback; used as backup documentation necessary if an employee is terminated based on performance

Event   A type of meeting or a function within a meeting; see APEX glossary

Featherie   A golf ball made in the 17th century consisting of a hand sewn leather pouch and stuffed with goose or chicken feathers; the pouch would be boiled and as it cooled, the hide would shrink, and the feathers expanded to result in a compact ball

Festivals   Gatherings that highlight local heritage; often men and women with specific skills or trades (artists, musicians, or craftsmen) help preserve many cultures through celebration, demonstration, and education

Flag of Convenience   When a ship is registered in a foreign country for purposes of reducing operating costs and avoiding government regulations

Flow   An important factor in making a decision about how a hospitality facility should be planned and maintained; different layouts can influence guest perception positively or negatively and affect whether or not they return for future business

Food Cost   The cost to produce a food item for sale; this includes actual cost of the food, labor costs, and energy costs

Foreign Independent Tour (FIT)   A travel package that normally includes airfare, lodging, and some recreational activities, but is not necessarily just in foreign countries. The traveler is independent when it comes to travel and must get from destination to destination on their own by driving a rental car or catching trains and busses

Franchise   A form of business organization in which a firm that has a successful product or service (the franchisor) enters into a contractual relationship with other businesses (franchisees), operates under the franchisor's trade name, and uses the franchisors methods and expertise in exchange for a fee

Full Care Centers/Nursing Homes   Residency centers for seniors who need the most care. These facilities offer the full array of support including medical, pharmacy, and personal services

Full Membership   Entitles a member to full use of the club and all amenities during any hour of operation

Function   An important factor in layout and design that addresses how a facility will be operated and maintained; can also affect guest perception of the facility and whether or not they come back

Furniture, Fixtures, and Equipment (FF&E) A major portion of hospitality capital expenditures

Galley A kitchen on a cruise ship

Gaming/Gambling Casino style activities offered on a cruise ship or at a resort

Globalization The concept that companies are conducting business transactions with both consumers and suppliers who are located around the world. Historically, businesses were limited to a smaller local marketplace, but the Internet and expedited shipping services have created a worldwide marketplace for conducting business

Golf Club Head The lower end of the golf club that strikes the ball

Golf Club Shaft The upper part of the golf club that is a long, tapered tube, usually made of graphite or carbon steel, that connects the club head to the golfer's hands

Golf Management Companies Companies that have the expertise and resources needed to operate and manage golf courses

Global Destination Systems Powerful database systems, such as Apollo, Sabre, and Amadeus, which list and offer ticketing for millions of air, hotel, and rental car services and provide worldwide attraction information

Grand Tour A kind of education for wealthy noblemen. It was a period of European travel that could last from a few months to 8 years

Green Hospitality Where hospitality industry operators have implemented green initiatives in response to demands from the government, environmental groups, and the general public; common goals are twofold: 1) enhancing broader appeal to improve business, while 2) having an increasingly positive impact on the environment

Gross Registered Tonnage A measurement of a ship's enclosed space

Guest Room Maintenance An activity applied to guest rooms of a lodging establishment, a form of problem prevention conducted to ensure guest comfort

Health Inspectors Professionals that are employed by the state and interpret state codes; they inspect existing facilities and must review and approve plans for new or remodeled food preparation areas, service areas, and restrooms

Heating, Ventilation, and Air Conditioning (HVAC) This system is an infrastructure of pipes, ducts, pumps, thermostats, valves, and pressure sensors that should provide suitable temperature and humidity levels for guests, staff, and management

Heritage Tourism The practice of people traveling outside of their home community to visit historic sites; to participate in local festivals; and to enjoy local arts and crafts, sightseeing, and recreation

Hospitality Consultant An individual or business organization that serves only hospitality industry clients and provides specialized consulting services by focusing on a specific industry segment or sub-segment and/or one or more functional areas

Hospitality Managers Professionals that may represent the owner of the facilities; within layout and design he/she will coordinate the design team and keep them on track with the concept and budget; often is the final decision maker

Hospitia Guest places or lodging venues for travelers along an extensive network of roads throughout the Mediterranean region; built by Romans during the classical period of the Roman Empire

Hotel Ratings System The system or process by which hotels are evaluated, usually by independent auditors

Human Resource Management The process of how organizations treat their people in order to accomplish the goals and objectives of the firm; the department within the organization that handles the paperwork regarding selection, termination, legal mandates, benefits, training, and compensation

Hybrid Restaurant A restaurant unit that combines two different styles of establishments to make a new concept; provides more options for the consumer within one location

Incentive Fees These are additional fees given by owners to contract management companies to encourage them to manage the lodging or foodservice property in a way that increases the property's overall profit

Incentive Travel A vacation package offered to employees as a bonus to motivate them to achieve a certain goal

Incentive Travel Houses These agencies develop customized programs for corporations who offer incentives to induce high employee productivity by providing deluxe travel rewards

Independent A single unit operation without any franchise or chain affiliation

Independent Operation Operations that have one or up to a few units that have distinct characteristics from other units; differences often occur in how the operations look and feel

Industrial Attractions Consist of operating concerns, manufacturing, and agricultural, whose processes and products are of interest to visitors

Industry Association An association or organization that represents the needs of members of a certain profession

In-House Training That training which is provided by the company, usually by the management team as a normal part of the training process of a new employee

Intangibility Not perceived by touch, cannot be visualized. Service would be an example of an intangible in the hospitality industry

Interior Designers Professionals that design interior spaces involving materials, finishes, colors, space planning, and layout; can be employed by the architects or have their own firm

Interior Plantscapers Professionals that advise the proper selection and positioning of plants as well as their maintenance; generally are hired by recommendation

International Special Events Society (ISES) A professional organization that seeks to promote, educate, and advance the industry of special events and its network of professionals as well as related industries

Internship A paid or unpaid temporary employment experience designed to acquaint the student with business operations by providing them an opportunity to shadow managers in various positions within a foodservice or lodging facility

Interpersonal Skills The ability to understand people and work well with them on an individual basis and in groups

Interview A formal meeting between two or more individuals

Interviewee Person being interviewed

Interviewer Person conducting the interview

Inventory Reconciliation A physical count of inventory that is matched to the sales figures in order to determine discrepancies that can point to problems with the control systems

Job Analysis An HR tool that focuses on what work needs to be accomplished within a specific job

Job Descriptions A written document that identifies the tasks, responsibilities, and duties under which jobs are performed

Job Design The task of determining how the job should be performed; examines how the job is organized and how it can be planned to provide both productivity to the organization and the most job satisfaction to the employee

Job Enlargement The process of broadening the job by adding tasks

Job Enrichment The process of adding responsibilities to the job

Job Rotation Allowing an employee to work different jobs within the same operation; requires cross-training

Job Simplification The process of determining the smallest components of the job and assessing how they fit into the whole job

Job Specifications A list of the knowledge, skills, and abilities necessary to perform a specific job successfully

Labor Cost   The cost of labor in running your operation; this includes wages and benefit costs

Labor-Intensive   The business or industry that employs a large number of employees to provide customers with a product or service

Labor-Intensive Business   Many of the services provided by the industry require high levels of personal service and attention to detail. This is a key element of the hospitality industry

Leadership   The influencing of others to channel their activities toward reaching the goals of the business

Liability Insurance   Most businesses carry liability insurance in case of accident. If you have auto insurance, this is a type of liability insurance coverage. Some businesses are self-insured, which means that they have to absorb the costs of legal judgments or settlements

Life Cycle Costing   The process of judging the selecting and analysis of capital projects, including the consideration of all aspects of the initial costs, operating costs, fixed costs, and tax implication

Life Span   An attraction classification according to their lifespan or time-related criteria based upon their duration

Limited-Service   Lodging facilities that provide a limited number of services to the guests

Long-Term Stay   Lodging facilities where all guest rooms include a kitchenette and provide clean, comfortable, inexpensive rooms that meet the basic needs of the guests

Luxury Hotel   Properties with an emphasis on service often providing extraordinary experiences that exceed customer expectations and create lifelong memories; a small hotel segment, yet these hotels enjoy high profile status within brands and customers

Man-Made Attractions   Owe their very existence to the intervention of humans

Management   The process of getting tasks accomplished through people

Management Consultant   An individual or business organization that are considered generalists; they provide a broad range of services to their clients and tailor their services to the specific needs of each client

Management Contract   A contractual arrangement between a property owner (who is often an independent investor) and a hotel company to operate the facilities to the specifications of that hotel company's brand name

Meeting Professionals International (MPI)   The leading international organization of professional meeting planners

Meetings   A gathering that brings people together for a common purpose such as conducting business, engaging in social ritual, educating people, and fundraising

Member   Regardless of type of club, each is made up of members, who have applied for and been accepted into membership

Member Benefits   Products, services, or perks available to an individual as part of an organizational membership

Merit Pay   The management approach that connects employee performance to pay raises; it identifies employees, who are performing at, or above, expected levels and provides them with increased wages

Military Clubs   Cater to enlisted men and women and the noncommissioned officer; provides a social outlet, often has golf

Mini Bar   In room units (usually refrigerators) that contain snacks and beverages for the guest's convenience at a charge. These are found in full-service hotels

Mission Statement   A statement of purpose that defines an organization. A mission statement is usually one to two sentences long and outlines the values and identity of the organization

Moment of Truth   Actual person-to-person interactions between the customer and the person delivering the service experience

Moral Development Theory   Lawrence Kohlberg's conception of the three components for morality and leadership: preconventional, conventional, and postconventional

Museum   Typically a nonprofit, permanent institution in the service of society and of its development and open to the public, that acquires, conserves, researches, communicates, and exhibits for purposes of study, and education enjoyment, the tangible and intangible evidence of people and their environment

Myth   A false belief

Natural Attractions   Those that occur in nature without human intervention

NCA   National Club Association

Negligence   The cause of action that arises when a duty owed to someone on the property is breached, resulting in injury or damages to the individual

Networking   The process of connecting with people of like interests who may be of help to you and you a help to them

Noncommercial/Institutional Foodservice   Foodservice operations where the service of food is not the primary function of the operation where food is being served

Nonprofit Organization   An economic institution that operates like a business but does not seek financial gain

Occupancy Percentage   The ratio relating the number of rooms sold to the number of rooms available

Official Rules of Golf   A specific set of rules developed by the USGA that govern the game of golf; provides the universally accepted rules of the game of golf

On-Site Foodservice   Noncommercial foodservice usually thought of as institutional that serves the dining needs in areas such as health care, schools and universities, corporate and manufacturing operations, military, children and adult communities, and correctional facilities

On-Site Foodservice Management   This is the term used to describe the contract foodservice segment of the hospitality industry

On the Floor   An expression to indicate the sales floor or where food and beverages are sold. Usually refers to the area where guests can sit at the tables

Operator   The individual or organization that manages the day-to-day operations of the lodging property or foodservice location

Operator Loan and Equity Contributions   This is a way for contract management companies to contribute to reducing the debt incurred by the owners. It is also a method of gaining some ownership (equity) in the property. Operators may offer loans to the owners to help offset start-up costs or cover initial cash flow losses. Operators may also offer funding or equity in the property. These equity contributions are typically 5 to 15% of the total equity investment

Operator System Reimbursable Expenses   These are the funds paid to the operator by the owner for property management systems, marketing programs, management information systems, foodservice management systems, etc.

Organization's Culture   A system of shared meaning held by members that distinguishes the organization from other organizations

Organizing   The efforts involved with determining what activities are to be done and how employees are grouped together to accomplish specific tasks

Origin   Classifies if the attraction is natural or man-made

Outside Sales Agents   Individual who is affiliated with the travel agency, acting as an independent contractor, not employee, who sells travel products and shares commissions with their affiliated agency

Owner   The individuals or corporations that legally own the lodging property or foodservice location

Peripheral Careers   The employment opportunities that help hospitality enterprises get their products and services from creation to consumption

Perishability   A product with a determined shelf life. Food would be an example of a perishable product in the hospitality industry

PGA Professional   A professional who has successfully completed specific education and experience criteria as defined by the Professional Golf Association (PGA) including passing a PGA Playing Ability test

Plaintiff   The alleged aggrieved person who commences the lawsuit

Planned Play Environments   These provide recreation and entertainment sporting facilities, such as ski and golf resorts; commercial attractions that include themes and amusements

Planning   The establishment of goals and objectives and deciding how to accomplish these goals

PMS   The computerized systems used by hotels to manage its rooms revenue, room rates, reservations and room assignments, guest histories, and accounting information, as well as other guest service and management information functions

Portfolios   A collection of holdings, consisting of different hotel brands, assembled by the major hotel companies

Portion Control   The designation of specific portion size as a means of controlling costs

POS (Point of Sale)   A network of electronic cash registers and pre-check terminals that interface with a remote central processing unit

POS Terminal   A location at which goods and services are purchased. Often referred to as a cash register, this type is connected to a computer system that manages the revenue

Preferred Providers   Agencies sign contracts with specific suppliers to try and sell their services first and in return receive a large sales commission

Preventive Maintenance (PM)   Includes the routine duties of the facility maintenance personnel who possess advanced skills, such as conducting inspections, minor repairs, or adjustments

Price Points   The set pricing for categories of the beverages, which, when compared to the costs the establishment, determine the cost percentages, hence the profit margins for those categories

Profitability   What is left over from a sales transaction after all of the costs are deducted is the profit. Profitability is the measure of how a business performs financially

Progressive Discipline Policy   An employment policy where an employee's performance is scrutinized, warnings are given, and an opportunity for retraining is provided before termination might take place; it allows employees to receive increasingly more stringent discipline for infractions

Property   A specific hotel site or individual location

Property Operation and Maintenance (POM)   The line item of the income statement where the actions of the facility manager are reported

Proprietary Clubs   Those owned by a corporation, company, business, or individual; they are for profit businesses

Purchasing   The job of procuring general and specialized equipment, materials, and business services for use by an establishment

Purser   The person on a ship responsible for the handling of money on board

Quick-Service Restaurant (QSR)   Considered to be informal dining establishments that specialize in delivering food quickly

Real Estate Representative   A person who works for the hospitality firm that specializes in real estate transactions, including site location and analysis

Recreational Amenities   Amenities such as golf, tennis, scuba diving, spa, fishing, and hiking activities that are provided to the guest at a resort

Receptive Operator   A company may meet and greet groups at airports, make arrangements for lodging, and shuttle them to the lodging at one particular destination and offer foreign language interpreters

Recruiting   The process of communicating job opportunities to larger populations of people in an attempt to acquire qualified job candidates

Refrigerant   A fluid with a low boiling point that starts as a liquid, absorbs heat, and becomes a gas, and then is placed under pressure to become a liquid again

Relocation   The act of moving from one place to another for employment advancement

Request for Proposals (RFPs)   A document used to solicit bids from service providers and to determine price and availability of goods and services; can be used to outline the planner's needs for the meeting/convention, including dates, meeting and exhibit space, lodging, food and beverages, telecommunications, audiovisual requirements, transportation, and any other necessities

Resort Hotel   Hotels that range in size from a few to thousands of rooms and are self-contained environments, appealing to business and leisure guests seeking relaxation, lodging, recreation activities, and meeting facilities on site

Resort Spa   Located on resort property, offering many spa treatments that are often available to both resort and outside guests

Restaurant   An establishment where meals are served to customers

Restaurant Ratings System   The system or process by which restaurants are evaluated, usually by independent auditors

Résumé   A written document that lists a person's personal and professional qualifications for a position

Routine Maintenance   Includes the general everyday duties of the facility staff, which requires relatively minimal skills or training, such as emptying trash cans or picking up litter

Royal and Ancient Golf Club of St. Andrew's   One of the oldest and most esteemed golf courses in the world; located in St. Andrews, Scotland; many championship tournaments are played there and it is considered to be the home of golf

Sales Commission   A percentage of the sales price paid by the supplier to the agent upon the purchase of a travel product or service

Seasonality   The time frame of the year when a property is at its peak business demand, often includes several months; a property may have more than one peak season

Secondary Attraction   Of lesser importance to the traveler and might be considered simply a stop along the way to get to the primary attraction

Segment   Different price and quality levels that progress upward from the economy segment to the luxury segment

Segmentation   Allows companies to reach travelers who are most likely to book reservations based on their past behavior

Selection   The act of choosing the best job candidate to hire for a position to achieve the best fit for the organization

Self-Operators   These are organizations that manage their own foodservice locations, even though foodservice is not their area of expertise

Service   A type of product that is intangible, goods that are inseparable from the provider, variable in quality, and perishable. The reason why private clubs exist; members receive high-end, personalized service at their club

Service Experience   Sum total of the experience that the customer has with the service provider on a given occasion

Service Product   Entire bundle of tangibles and intangibles in a transaction that has a significant service component

Shot   A measure of alcohol to be used in a recipe. Standards of measure may differ from establishment to establishment, but 1 oz., 1¼ oz., or 2 oz. are often used. In order to control costs and ensure consistency a shot glass, or jigger, can be used for a measured pour

Silk Road   Encompassed of a variety of ancient routes between Europe and points in Asia; used by merchants and traders to transport goods

Single-Unit Operation   The independent operator; can be used when referring to managing one unit; that unit can be part of any industry in the economic sector of the world

Social Media   Internet applications that help consumers share opinions, insights, experiences, and perspectives

Social Membership   Entitles a member to limited use of a country club, typically dining, pool, and tennis, but not golf; reduced initiation fee and dues structure

Social Networking   Interacting with people who can impact your career options or advancement

Social Responsibility   Alcohol so alters one's perception of reality that it is not responsible to allow an intoxicated person to be put into a position where they could harm themselves or someone else. The sale or service of alcohol creates a social responsibility to both the guest and society at large to act in a manner to protect everyone from harm

Sommelier   A wine expert employed by a beverage serving establishment to help the guests select the best wine for their meal

Space Ratio   An approximation of how much space is on a cruise ship; divide the GRT by the number of passengers

Spirits   Common distilled beverages (spirits) are vodka, gin, whisky, tequila, etc.

Sponsor   A person, group, or corporation that provides funds for an event or activity

Stabilizers   Winglike projections on a cruise ship that are used to reduce and eliminate roll (side-to-side movement)

Staffing   Supplying the human requirements necessary to service guests

Statute of Limitations   The minimum timeframe during which a plaintiff must file their lawsuit in order to proceed with the litigation

Student Organizations   These are groups of students that come together in their free time to organize activities to support their common vocational interests

Style   A particular, distinctive mode or form of construction or execution in work

Supplier   A person, group, or corporation that provides something that is required, needed, or desired

Support Staff   Professionals who work in hospitality and tourism but not in an operations management position

Sustainability   The capacity to maintain, support, or endure; an ecological term that describes how biological systems remain productive through diversity over an extended period of time

Sustainable Design   Integrating strategies into the design for reducing consumption; involving design practices that are environmentally friendly

Team Building   Views employees as members of work groups, rather than as individuals

Technical Skills   The skills involving knowledge of and the ability to perform a particular job or task

Tender   A boat that ferries passengers from the ship to the port when the cruise ship is too big to dock at the pier

Term   This is the length of the contract between the operator and owner

The Training Cycle   A systematic process used by human resources departments to determine what training knowledge or skills is needed for an individual to successfully perform their job; used to assess the needs of both newly hired individuals and tenured employees

Theme Parks   Offer escape; as a result of modern technology they replicate both real as well as "unreal" places that may or may not exist beyond the gates

Ticketing Fee   An additional charge above the base cost of the ticket that is charged by a TMC to cover their ticketing costs

Top-Down Approach   Is a method of attempting to sell the most expensive item first and then offering a less expensive item next if there is continued sales resistance

Topography   Can be broadly subdivided into three areas of interest: landforms, wildlife, and ecology

Torts   A large classification of different types of civil wrongs that result in injury or damages to either people or property

Tour Escort   A person who travels with a group and acts as guide and business manager, using the skills of a teacher, entertainer, accountant, doctor, and psychologist

Tour Operators   Organize markets and operate packages of travel services with a variety of themes, ranging from adventure to sightseeing, for groups or individuals

Trade Show   A large gathering of suppliers who display, demonstrate, or exhibit their new or existing products in a common marketplace

Travel Agent   Individuals within a travel management company that match and ticket the travel desires of leisure and business travelers with the most appropriate suppliers of tourist services

Travel Management Company   A contemporary term for travel agencies that provide consulting, ticketing, and management of travel products for the leisure and business traveler

Turnover   The situation created when an employee leaves (voluntarily or involuntarily) and must be replaced

Units   A term used in the hotel industry that is more commonly referred to as a hotel room

Universal Design   The term used to convey the idea that products (furnishings, hardware, etc.) and architectural changes could be made to make life easier for all people whether or not they have a disability

Upscale Restaurant   A foodservice establishment that offers the best in food, beverages, and level of service

Up-Selling   A selling technique used to convince customers to purchase one of your more expensive items first

USGA Handicap   A scoring procedure used in the game of golf; it allows for golfers with different skill levels to compete equally

Vacation-Ownership Firm   A business focused on selling long-term vacation packages to guests; these "slices of time" may be hotel rooms or condominium units located at a specific property, or they may be sold as "points" that are used for future vacations

Vacation Ownership/Timeshare Resorts/Condo Hotels   In the most basic form it is the right to accommodations and use of recreational facilities at a vacation development for a specified time period for a defined number of years or into perpetuity, as defined in the purchase agreement or redeemable through purchased vacation club points

Venue   The facility where an event is hosted

Virtual Meeting   A business discussion that is carried out through an Internet broadcast, e-mail, or similar mode

Vision   Leadership quality for creating the future. An essential quality for leadership; a successful vision is leader initiated, shared, and supported by followers

Volume Purchasing   Purchasing in bulk volume in order to save money as most suppliers will offer a discount for volume purchasing

Yacht Club   Establishments near or on the water, activities center around sailing and boating, with dining also available

Yield Management   A combination of occupancy percentage and the average daily rate

INDEX

F